Lecture Notes in Computer Science 7439

Commenced Publication in 1973
Founding and Former Series Editors:
Gerhard Goos, Juris Hartmanis, and Jan van Leeuwen

Yang Xiang   Ivan Stojmenovic
Bernady O. Apduhan   Guojun Wang
Koji Nakano   Albert Zomaya (Eds.)

Algorithms and Architectures for Parallel Processing

12th International Conference, ICA3PP 2012
Fukuoka, Japan, September 4-7, 2012
Proceedings, Part I

 Springer

Volume Editors

Yang Xiang
Deakin University, Burwood, VIC, Australia
E-mail: yang@deakin.edu.au

Ivan Stojmenovic
University of Ottawa, SEECS, Ottawa, ON, Canada
E-mail: stojmenovic@gmail.com

Bernady O. Apduhan
Kyushu Sangyo University, Fukuoka, Japan
E-mail: bob@is.kyusan-u.ac.jp

Guojun Wang
Central South University, Changsha, Hunan Province, P.R. China
E-mail: csgjwang@csu.edu.cn

Koji Nakano
Hiroshima University, Higashi-Hiroshima, Japan
E-mail: nakano@cs.hiroshima-u.ac.jp

Albert Zomaya
University of Sydney, NSW, Australia
E-mail: albert.zomaya@sydney.edu.au

ISSN 0302-9743   e-ISSN 1611-3349
ISBN 978-3-642-33077-3   e-ISBN 978-3-642-33078-0
DOI 10.1007/978-3-642-33078-0
Springer Heidelberg Dordrecht London New York

Library of Congress Control Number: 2012945393

CR Subject Classification (1998): F.2, H.4, D.2, I.2, F.1, G.2, H.3, C.2

LNCS Sublibrary: SL 1 – Theoretical Computer Science and General Issues

Typesetting: Camera-ready by author, data conversion by Scientific Publishing Services, Chennai, India

Printed on acid-free paper

Springer is part of Springer Science+Business Media (www.springer.com)

Message from the ICA3PP 2012 General Chairs

We are privileged and delighted to welcome you to the proceedings of the 12th International Conference on Algorithms and Architectures for Parallel Processing (ICA3PP 2012).

Following the traditions of the previous successful ICA3PP conferences held in Hangzhou, Brisbane, Singapore, Melbourne, Hong Kong, Beijing, Cyprus, Taipei, Busan, and Melbourne, this year ICA3PP 2012 was held in Fukuoka, Japan. The objective of ICA3PP 2012 was to bring together researchers and practitioners from academia, industry, and government to advance the theories and technologies in parallel and distributed computing. ICA3PP 2012 focused on two broad areas of parallel and distributed computing, i.e., architectures, algorithms and networks, and systems and applications. The ICA3PP 2012 conference was organized by Kyushu Sangyo University, Japan, and Deakin University, Australia.

We sincerely thank the many people who helped organize ICA3PP 2012. We would like to thank the Program Chairs, Ivan Stojmenovic, University of Ottawa, Canada, Bernady O. Apduhan, Kyushu Sangyo University, Japan, and Guojun Wang, Central South University, China, for their leadership in providing the excellent technical program. We are also grateful to the members of our Program Committee and other reviewers who helped us in producing this year's exciting program.

September 2012

Koji Nakano
Albert Zomaya
Yang Xiang

Message from the ICA3PP 2012 Program Chairs

A warm welcome to the proceedings of the 12th International Conference on Algorithms and Architectures for Parallel Processing (ICA3PP 2012) held in Fukuoka, Japan.

ICA3PP 2012 was the 12th in this series of conferences started in 1995 that are devoted to algorithms and architectures for parallel processing. ICA3PP is now recognized as the main regular event in the world covering the many dimensions of parallel algorithms and architectures, encompassing fundamental theoretical approaches, practical experimental results, and commercial components and systems. As applications of computing systems have permeated in every aspect of daily life, the power of computing systems has become increasingly critical. ICA3PP 2012 provided a widely known forum for researchers and practitioners from countries around the world to exchange ideas on improving the computation power of computing systems.

In response to the ICA3PP 2012 call for papers, we received 156 submissions from 27 countries. These papers were evaluated on the basis of their originality, significance, correctness, relevance, and technical quality. Each paper was reviewed by at least three members of the Program Committee. Based on these evaluations, of the papers submitted, 39 regular papers and 26 short papers were selected for presentation at the conference, representing 25% of acceptance for regular papers and 16.7% of acceptance for short papers.

We would like to thank the Program Committee members and additional reviewers from all around the world for their efforts in reviewing the large number of papers. We appreciate all the associated Workshop Chairs for their dedication and professionalism. We would like to extend our sincere thanks to the ICA3PP Steering Committee Chairs, Wanlei Zhou, Yi Pan, and Andrzej Goscinski, and the General Chairs, Koji Nakano, Hiroshima University, Japan, Albert Zomaya, The University of Sydney, Australia, and Yang Xiang, Deakin University, Australia. They provided us with invaluable guidance throughout the process of paper selection and program organization. We also thank Yu Wang for his help in completing the final proceedings.

Last but not least, we would also like to take this opportunity to thank all the authors for their submissions to ICA3PP 2012.

September 2012

Ivan Stojmenovic
Bernady O. Apduhan
Guojun Wang

Organization

ICA3PP 2012 Committees

Honorary General Chair

Iwao Yamamoto — Kyushu Sangyo University, Japan

General Chairs

Koji Nakano	Hiroshima University, Japan
Albert Zomaya	The University of Sydney, Australia
Yang Xiang	Deakin University, Australia

Program Chairs

Ivan Stojmenovic	University of Ottawa, Canada
Bernady O. Apduhan	Kyushu Sangyo University, Japan
Guojun Wang	Central South University, China

International Advisory Committee

Tadashi Dohi	Hiroshima University, Japan (Chair)
Takashi Naka	Kyushu Sangyo University, Japan
Toshinori Sueyoshi	Kumamoto University, Japan

Steering Committee

Wanlei Zhou	Deakin University, Australia
Yi Pan	Georgia State University, USA
Andrzej Goscinski	Deakin University, Australia

Workshop Chairs

Xu Huang	University of Canberra, Australia
Bin Xiao	Hong Kong Polytechnic University, Hong Kong

Publicity Chairs

Kejie Lu   University of Puerto Rico at Mayaguez,
                                      Puerto Rico
Wen Tao Zhu   Chinese Academy of Sciences, China
Muhammad Khurram Khan   King Saud University, Saudi Arabia
Toshinori Sato   Fukuoka University, Japan

Demo/Exhibition Chair

Jun Zhang   Deakin University, Australia

Local Arrangements Committee

Kai Cheng   Kyushu Sangyo University, Japan
Kazuaki Goshi   Kyushu Sangyo University, Japan
Masaki Hayashi   Kyushu Sangyo University, Japan
Toshihiro Shimokawa   Kyushu Sangyo University, Japan
Toshihiro Uchibayashi   Kyushu Sangyo University, Japan
Yoshihiro Yasutake   Kyushu Sangyo University, Japan

Program Committee

Bechini Alessio   University of Pisa, Italy
Giuseppe Amato   ISTI-CNR, Italy
Srinivas Aluru   Iowa State University, USA
Hideharu Amano   Keio University, Japan
Henrique Andrade   Goldman Sachs, USA
Cosimo Anglano   Università del Piemonte Orientale, Italy
Dorian Arnold   University of New Mexico, USA
Purushotham Bangalore   University of Alabama, USA
Novella Bartolini   University of Rome La Sapienza, Italy
Ladjel Bellatreche   ENSMA, France
Jorge Bernal Bernabe   University of Murcia, Spain
Ateet Bhalla   NRI Institute of Information Science and
                                      Technology, India
Arndt Bode   Technische Universität München, Germany
George Bosilca   University of Tennessee, USA
Luc Bougé   ENS Cachan, France
Rajkumar Buyya   The University of Melbourne, Australia
Surendra Byna   Lawrence Berkeley National Lab, USA
Massimo Cafaro   University of Salento, Italy
Andre Carvalho   Universidade de Sao Paulo, Brazil
Tania Cerquitelli   Politecnico di Torino, Italy
Ruay-Shiung Chang   National Dong Hwa University, Taiwan

Soo-Kyun Kim	PaiChai University, Korea
Harald Kosch	University of Passau, Germany
Joel Koshy	Yahoo!, USA
Morihiro Kuga	Kumamoto University, Japan
Pramod Kumar	Institute for Infocomm Research, Singapore
Edmund Lai	Massey University, New Zealand
Marco Lapegna	University of Naples Federico II, Italy
Rob Latham	Argonne National Laboratory, USA
Changhoon Lee	Hanshin University, Korea
Che-Rung Lee	National Tsing Hua University, Taiwan
Laurent Lefevre	"Laurent Lefevre, INRIA, University of Lyon", France
Keqin Li	State University of New York at New Paltz, USA
Keqin Li	SAP Research, France
Keqiu Li	Dalian University of Technology, China
Yingshu Li	Georgia State University, USA
Kai Lin	Dalian University of Technology, China
Wei Lu	Keene University, USA
Paul Lu	University of Alberta, Canada
Kamesh Madduri	Penn State University, USA
Amit Majumdar	San Diego Supercomputer Center, USA
Shiwen Mao	Auburn University, USA
Tomas Margalef	Universitat Autonoma de Barcelona, Spain
Juan M. Marin	University of Murcia, Spain
Alejandro Masrur	University of Technology, Munich, Germany
Susumu Matsumae	Saga University, Japan
Jogesh Muppala	Hong Kong University of Science and Technology, Hong Kong
Koji Nakano	University of Hiroshima, Japan
Amiya Nayak	University of Ottawa, Canada
Esmond Ng	Lawrence Berkeley National Lab, USA
Michael O'Grady	University College Dublin, Ireland
Hirotaka Ono	Kyushu University, Japan
Marion Oswald	Hungarian Academy of Sciences, Hungary
Tansel Ozyer	TOBB University of Economics and Technology, Turkey
Deng Pan	Florida International University, USA
Karampelas Panagiotis	Hellenic American University, Greece
Apostolos Papadopoulos	Aristotle University of Thessaloniki, Greece
Eric Pardede	La Trobe University, Australia
Dana Petcu	West University of Timisoara, Romania
Kevin Pedretti	Sandia National Laboratories, USA
Kalyan Perumalla	Oak Ridge National Lab, USA
Fabrizio Petrini	IBM Research, USA

Ronald Petrlic	University of Paderborn, Germany
Sushil Prasad	University of Georgia, USA
Enrique Quintana	Universidad Jaume I, Spain
Rajeev Raje	Indiana University-Purdue University Indianapolis, USA
Thomas Rauber	University of Bayreuth, Germany
Cal Ribbens	Virginia Polytechnic Institute and State University, USA
Morris Riedel	Jülich Supercomputing Centre, USA
Etienne Rivière	University of Neuchatel, Switzerland
Pedro Pereira Rodrigues	University of Porto, Portugal
Marcel C. Rosu	IBM, USA
Giovanni Maria Sacco	Università di Torino, Italy
Françoise Sailhan	CNAM, France
Subhash Saini	NASA, USA
Kenji Saito	Keio University, Japan
Rafael Santos	National Institute for Space Research, Brazil
Erich Schikuta	University of Vienna, Austria
Martin Schulz	Lawrence Livermore National Laboratory, USA
Edwin Sha	University of Texas at Dallas, USA
Rahul Shah	Louisiana State University, USA
Giandomenico Spezzano	ICAR-CNR, Italy
Alexandros Stamatakis	Heidelberg Institute for Theoretical Studies, Germany
Peter Strazdins	The Australian National University, Australia
Ching-Lung Su	National Yunlin University of Science and Technology, Taiwan
C.D. Sudheer	Sri Sathya Sai Institute of Higher Learning, India
Anthony Sulistio	High Performance Computing Center Stuttgart (HLRS), Germany
Wei Sun	NEC Coporation, Japan
Mineo Takai	University of California, USA
Kosuke Takano	Kanagawa Institute of Technology, Japan
Yasuhiko Takenaga	The University of Electro-Communications, Japan
Uwe Tangen	Ruhr-Universität Bochum, Germany
Ramesh Thirumale	Boeing, USA
Hiroyuki Tomiyama	Ritsumeikan University, Japan
Paolo Trunfio	University of Calabria, Italy
Tomoaki Tsumura	Nagoya Institute of Technology, Japan
Vidhyashankar Venkataraman	Yahoo!, USA
Luis Javier García Villalba	Universidad Complutense de Madrid (UCM), Spain
Natalija Vlajic	York University, Canada

Chao Wang   Suzhou Institute For Advanced Study of USTC,
                                    China
Chen Wang   CSIRO ICT Centre, Australia
Xiaofang Wang   Villanova University, USA
Gaocai Wang   Guangxi University, China
Martine Wedlake   IBM, USA
Qishi Wu   University of Memphis, USA
Fatos Xhafa   Polytechnic University of Catalonia, Spain
Feiyu Xiong   Drexel University, USA
Jiang Xu   Hong Kong University of Science and
                                    Technology, Hong Kong
Jason Xue   Hong Kong City University, Hong Kong
Toshihiro Yamauchi   Okayama University, Japan
Chao-Tung Yang   Tunghai University, Taiwan
Laurence T. Yang   St. Francis Xavier University, Canada
Bo Yang   University of Electronic Science and
                                    Technology of China, China
Zhiwen Yu   Northwestern Polytechnical University, China
Sherali Zeadally   University of the District of Columbia, USA
Yong Zhao   University of Electronic Science and
                                    Technology of China, China
Xingquan(Hill) Zhu   Florida Atlantic University, USA
Sotirios G. Ziavras   NJIT, USA
Roger Zimmermann   National University of Singapore, Singapore

Table of Contents – Part I

ICA3PP 2012 Regular Papers

Table of Contents – Part II

ICA3PP 2012 Short Papers

CDCN 2012 Workshop Papers

Accelerating the Dynamic Programming for the Optimal Polygon Triangulation on the GPU

Kazufumi Nishida, Koji Nakano, and Yasuaki Ito

Department of Information Engineering, Hiroshima University,
Kagamiyama 1-4-1, Higashi Hiroshima 739-8527, Japan
{nishida,nakano,yasuaki}@cs.hiroshima-u.ac.jp

Abstract. Modern GPUs (Graphics Processing Units) can be used for general purpose parallel computation. Users can develop parallel programs running on GPUs using programming architecture called CUDA (Compute Unified Device Architecture). The optimal polygon triangulation problem for a convex polygon is an optimization problem to find a triangulation with minimum total weight. It is known that this problem can be solved using the dynamic programming technique in $O(n^3)$ time using a work space of size $O(n^2)$. The main contribution of this paper is to present an efficient parallel implementation of this $O(n^3)$-time algorithm on the GPU. In our implementation, we have used two new ideas to accelerate the dynamic programming. The first idea (granularity adjustment) is to partition the dynamic programming algorithm into many sequential kernel calls of CUDA, and to select the best size and number of blocks and threads for each kernel call. The second idea (sliding and mirroring arrangements) is to arrange the temporary data for coalesced access of the global memory in the GPU to minimize the memory access overhead. Our implementation using these two ideas solves the optimal polygon triangulation problem for a convex 16384-gon in 69.1 seconds on the NVIDIA GeForce GTX 580, while a conventional CPU implementation runs in 17105.5 seconds. Thus, our GPU implementation attains a speedup factor of 247.5.

Keywords: Dynamic programming, parallel algorithms, coalesced memory access, GPGPU, CUDA.

1 Introduction

The GPU (Graphical Processing Unit), is a specialized circuit designed to accelerate computation for building and manipulating images [4,5,7,12,14]. Latest GPUs are designed for general purpose computing and can perform computation in applications traditionally handled by the CPU. Hence, GPUs have recently attracted the attention of many application developers [4,9]. NVIDIA provides a parallel computing architecture called *CUDA* (Compute Unified Device Architecture) [10], the computing engine for NVIDIA GPUs. CUDA gives developers

Y. Xiang et al. (Eds.): ICA3PP 2012, Part I, LNCS 7439, pp. 1–15, 2012.
© Springer-Verlag Berlin Heidelberg 2012

access to the virtual instruction set and memory of the parallel computational elements in NVIDIA GPUs. In many cases, GPUs are more efficient than multicore processors [8], since they have hundreds of processor cores running in parallel.

Dynamic programming is an important algorithmic technique to find an optimal solution of a problem over an exponential number of solution candidates [2]. A naive solution for such problem needs exponential time. The key idea behind dynamic programming is to:

- partition a problem into subproblems,
- solve the subproblems independently, and
- combine the solution of the subproblems

to reach an overall solution. Dynamic programming enables us to solve such problems in polynomial time. For example, the longest common subsequence problem, which requires finding the longest common subsequence of given two sequences, can be solved by the dynamic programming approach [1]. Since a sequence have an exponential number of subsequences, a straightforward algorithm takes an exponential time to find the longest common subsequence. However, it is known that this problem can be solved in $O(nm)$ time by the dynamic programming approach, where n and m are the lengths of two sequences. Many important problems including the edit distance problem, the matrix chain product problem, and the optimal polygon triangulation problem can be solved by the dynamic programming approach [2].

The main contribution of this paper is to implement the dynamic programming approach to solve *the optimal polygon triangulation problem* [2] on the GPU. Suppose that a convex n-gon is given and we want to triangulate it, that is, to split it into $n-2$ triangles by $n-3$ non-crossing chords. Figure 1 illustrates an example of a triangulation of an 8-gon. In the figure, the triangulation has 6 triangles separated by 5 non-crossing chords. We assume that each of the $\frac{n(n-3)}{2}$ chords is assigned a weight. The goal of the optimal polygon triangulation is to select $n-3$ non-crossing chords that triangulate a given convex n-gon such that the total weight of selected chords is minimized. This problem is applied to matrix chain multiplication that is an optimization problem. Matrix chain multiplication is a special case of optimal polygon triangulation problem, i.e., instances of matrix chain multiplication can be computed as optimal polygon triangulation problem [2]. A naive approach, which evaluates the total weights of all possible $\frac{(2n-4)!}{(n-1)!(n-2)!}$ triangulations, takes an exponential time. On the other hand, it is known that the dynamic programming technique can be applied to solve the optimal polygon triangulation in $O(n^3)$ time [2,3,6] using work space of size $O(n^2)$. As far as we know, there is no previously published algorithm running faster than $O(n^3)$ time.

In our implementation, we have used two new ideas to accelerate the dynamic programming algorithm. The first idea is to partition the dynamic programming algorithm into a lot of sequential kernel calls of CUDA, and to select the best method and the numbers of blocks and threads for each kernel calls (*granularity adjustment*). The dynamic programming algorithm for an n-gon has $n-1$

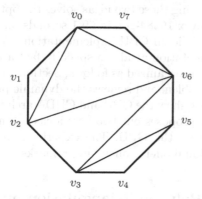

Fig. 1. An example of a triangulation of a convex 8-gon

stages, each of which involves the computation of multiple temporary data. Earlier stages of the algorithm are *fine grain* in the sense that we need to compute the values of a lot of temporary data but the computation of each temporary data is light. On the other hand, later stages of the algorithm are *coarse grain* in the sense that few temporary data are computed but the computation is heavy. Thus, in earlier stages, a single thread is assigned to the computation of each temporary data and its value is computed sequentially by the thread (*OneThreadPerEntry*). In middle stages, a block with multiple threads is allocated to the computation for each temporary data and the value of the temporary data is computed by threads of a block in parallel (*OneBlockPerEntry*). Multiple blocks are allocated to compute each temporary data in later stages (*BlocksPerEntry*). Also, the size of each block (i.e. the number of threads), and the number of used blocks affects the performance of algorithms on the GPU. We have tested all of the three methods for various sizes of each block and the number of blocks for every stage, and determined the best way, one of the three methods and the size and the number of blocks for computing the temporary data in each stage.

The second idea is to arrange temporary data in a 2-dimensional array of the global memory using two types of arrangements: *sliding arrangement* and *mirroring arrangement*. The temporary data used in the dynamic programming algorithm are stored in a 2-dimensional array in the global memory of the GPU. The bandwidth of the global memory is maximized when threads repeatedly performs coalesced access to it. In other words, if threads accessed to continuous locations of the global memory, these access requests can be completed in minimum clock cycles. On the other hand, if threads accessed to distant locations in the same time, these access requests need a lot of clock cycles. We use the sliding arrangement for OneThreadPerEntry and the mirroring arrangement for OneBlockPerEntry and BlocksPerEntry. Using these two arrangements, the coalesced access is performed for the temporary data.

Our implementation using these two ideas solves the optimal polygon triangulation problem for a convex 16384-gon in 69.1 seconds on the NVIDIA GeForce GTX 580, while a conventional CPU implementation runs in 17105.5 seconds. Thus, our GPU implementation attains a speedup factor of 247.5.

The rest of this paper is organized as follows; Section 2 introduces the optimal polygon triangulation problem and reviews the dynamic programming approach solving it. In Section 3, we show the GPU and CUDA architectures to understand our new idea. Section 4 proposes our two new ideas to implement the dynamic programming approach on the GPU. The experimental results are shown in Section 5. Finally, Section 6 offers concluding remarks.

2   The Optimal Polygon Triangulation and the Dynamic Programming Approach

The main purpose of this section is to define the optimal polygon triangulation problem and to review an algorithm solving this problem by the dynamic programming approach [2].

Let $v_0, v_1, \ldots, v_{n-1}$ be vertices of a convex n-gon. Clearly, the convex n-gon can be divided into $n - 2$ triangles by a set of $n - 3$ non-crossing chords. We call a set of such $n - 3$ non-crossing chords *a triangulation*. Figure 1 shows an example of a triangulation of a convex 8-gon. The convex 8-gon is separated into 6 triangles by 5 non-crossing chords. Suppose that a weight $w_{i,j}$ of every chord $v_i v_j$ in a convex n-gon is given. The goal of *the optimal polygon triangulation problem* is to find an optimal triangulation that minimizes the total weights of selected chords for the triangulation. More formally, we can define the problem as follows. Let T be a set of all triangulations of a convex n-gon and $t \in T$ be a triangulation, that is, a set of $n - 3$ non-crossing chords. The optimal polygon triangulation problem requires finding the total weight of a minimum weight triangulation as follows:

$$\min\{ \sum_{v_i v_j \in t} w_{i,j} \mid t \in T\}.$$

We will show that the optimal polygon triangulation can be solved by the dynamic programming approach. For this purpose, we define *the parse tree* of a triangulation. Figure 2 illustrates the parse tree of a triangulation. Let l_i ($1 \le i \le n-1$) be edge $v_{i-1} v_i$ of a convex n-gon. Also, let r denote edge $v_0 v_{n-1}$. The parse tree is a binary tree of a triangulation, which has the root r and $n - 1$ leaves $l_1, l_2, \ldots, l_{n-1}$. It also has $n - 3$ internal nodes (excluding the root r), each of which corresponds to a chord of the triangulation. Edges are drawn from the root toward the leaves as illustrated in Figure 2. Since each triangle has three nodes, the resulting graph is a full binary tree with $n - 1$ leaves, in which every internal node has exactly two children. Conversely, for any full binary tree with $n - 1$ leaves, we can draw a unique triangulation. It is well known that the number of full binary trees with $n+1$ leaves is the Catalan number $\frac{(2n)!}{(n+1)!n!}$ [13]. Thus,

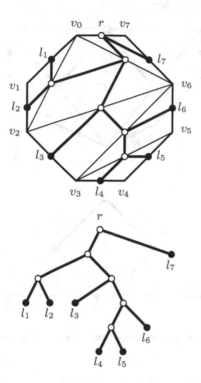

Fig. 2. The parse tree of a triangulation

the number of possible triangulations of convex n-gon is $\frac{(2n-4)!}{(n-1)!(n-2)!}$. Hence, a naive approach, which evaluates the total weights of all possible triangulations, takes an exponential time.

We are now in position to show an algorithm using the dynamic programming approach for the optimal polygon triangulation problem. Suppose that an n-gon is chopped off by a chord $v_{i-1}v_j$ ($0 \leq i < j \leq n-1$) and we obtain a $(j-i)$-gon with vertices $v_{i-1}, v_i, \ldots, v_j$ as illustrated in Figure 3. Clearly, this $(j-i)$-gon consists of leaves $l_i, l_{i+1}, \ldots, l_j$ and a chord $v_{i-1}v_j$. Let $m_{i,j}$ be the minimum weight of the $(j-i)$-gon. The $(j-i)$-gon can be partitioned into the $(k-i)$-gon, the $(j-k)$-gon, and the triangle $v_{i-1}v_kv_j$ as illustrated in Figure 3. The values of k can be an integer from i to $j-1$. Thus, we can recursively define $m_{i,j}$ as follows:

$$m_{i,j} = 0 \quad \text{if } j - i \leq 1,$$
$$m_{i,j} = \min_{i \leq k \leq j-1} (m_{i,k} + m_{k+1,j} + w_{i-1,k} + w_{k,j}) \quad \text{otherwise.}$$

The figure also shows its parse tree. The reader should have no difficulty to confirm the correctness of the recursive formula and the minimum weight of the n-gon is equal to $m_{1,n-1}$.

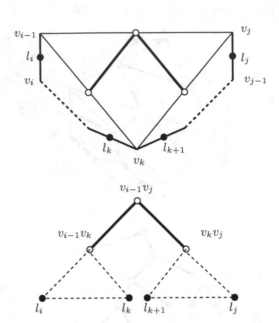

Fig. 3. A $(j-i)$-gon is partitioned into a $(k-i)$-gon and a $(j-k)$-gon

Let $M_{i,j} = m_{i,j} + w_{i-1,j}$ and $w_{0,n-1} = 0$. We can recursively define $M_{i,j}$ as follows:

$$M_{i,j} = 0 \quad \text{if } j - i \leq 1,$$
$$M_{i,j} = \min_{i \leq k \leq j-1} (M_{i,k} + M_{k+1,j}) + w_{i-1,j} \quad \text{otherwise.}$$

It should be clear that $M_{1,n-1} = m_{1,n-1} + w_{0,n-1} = m_{1,n-1}$ is the minimum weight of the n-gon.

Using the recursive formula for $M_{i,j}$, all the values of $M_{i,j}$ can be computed in $n-1$ stages by the dynamic programming algorithm as follows:

Stage 0 $M_{1,1} = M_{2,2} = \cdots = M_{n-1,n-1} = 0.$
Stage 1 $M_{i,i+1} = w_{i-1,i+1}$ for all i $(1 \leq i \leq n-2)$
Stage 2 $M_{i,i+2} = \min_{i \leq k \leq i+1}(M_{i,k} + M_{k+1,i+2}) + w_{i-1,i+2}$ for all i $(1 \leq i \leq n-3)$

$$\vdots$$

Stage p $M_{i,i+p} = \min_{i \leq k \leq i+p-1}(M_{i,k} + M_{k+1,i+p}) + w_{i-1,i+p}$ for all i $(1 \leq i \leq n-p-1)$

$$\vdots$$

Stage $n-3$ $M_{i,n+i-3} = \min_{i \leq k \leq n+i-4}(M_{i,k} + M_{k+1,n+i-3}) + w_{i-1,n+i-3}$ for all i $(1 \leq i \leq 2)$
Stage $n-2$ $M_{1,n-1} = \min_{1 \leq k \leq n-2}(M_{1,k} + M_{k+1,n-1}) + w_{0,n-1}$

Figure 4 shows examples of $w_{i,j}$ and $M_{i,j}$ for a convex 8-gon. It should be clear that each stage computes the values of table $M_{i,j}$ in a particular diagonal position. Let us analyze the computation performed in each Stage p ($2 \le p \le n - 2$).

- $(n - p - 1)$ $M_{i,j}$'s, $M_{1,p+1}, M_{2,p+2}, \ldots, M_{n-p-1,n-1}$ are computed, and
- the computation of each $M_{i,j}$'s involves the computation of the minimum over p values, each of which is the sum of two $M_{i,j}$'s.

Thus, Stage p takes $(n - p - 1) \cdot O(p) = O(n^2 - p^2)$ time. Therefore, this algorithm runs in $\sum_{2 \le p \le n-2} O(n^2 - p^2) = O(n^3)$ time.

From this analysis, we can see that earlier stages of the algorithm is *fine grain* in the sense that we need to compute the values of a lot of $M_{i,j}$'s but the computation of each $M_{i,j}$ is light. On the other hand, later stages of the algorithm is *coarse grain* in the sense that few $M_{i,j}$'s are computed but its computation is heavy.

3   GPU and CUDA Architectures

CUDA uses two types of memories in the NVIDIA GPUs: *the global memory* and *the shared memory* [10]. The global memory is implemented as an off-chip DRAM of the GPU, and has large capacity, say, 1.5-6 Gbytes, but its access latency is very long. The shared memory is an extremely fast on-chip memory with lower capacity, say, 16-48 Kbytes. The efficient usage of the global memory and the shared memory is a key for CUDA developers to accelerate applications using GPUs. In particular, we need to consider *the coalescing* of the global memory access and *the bank conflict* of the shared memory access [11,7,8]. To maximize the bandwidth between the GPU and the DRAM chips, the consecutive addresses of the global memory must be accessed in the same time. Thus, threads should perform coalesced access when they access to the global memory. Figure 5 illustrates the CUDA hardware architecture.

CUDA parallel programming model has a hierarchy of thread groups called *grid*, *block* and *thread*. A single grid is organized by multiple blocks, each of which has equal number of threads. The blocks are allocated to streaming processors such that all threads in a block are executed by the same streaming processor in parallel. All threads can access to the global memory. However, as we can see in Figure 5, threads in a block can access to the shared memory of the streaming processor to which the block is allocated. Since blocks are arranged to multiple streaming processors, threads in different blocks cannot share data in shared memories.

CUDA C extends C language by allowing the programmer to define C functions, called *kernels*. By invoking a kernel, all blocks in the grid are allocated in streaming processors, and threads in each block are executed by processor cores in a single streaming processor. The kernel calls terminates, when threads in all blocks finish the computation. Since all threads in a single block are executed by a single streaming processor, the barrier synchronization of them can be done by calling CUDA C `syncthreds()` function. However, there is no direct way to synchronize threads in different blocks. One of the indirect methods of inter-block

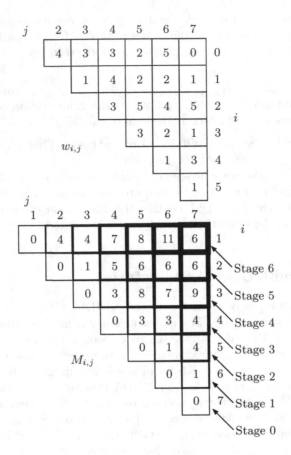

Fig. 4. Examples of $w_{i,j}$ and $M_{i,j}$

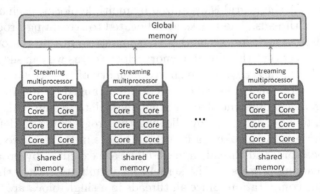

Fig. 5. CUDA hardware architecture

barrier synchronization is to partition the computation into kernels. Since continuous kernel calls can be executed such that a kernel is called after all blocks of the previous kernel terminates, execution of blocks is synchronized at the end of kernel calls. Thus, we arrange a single kernel call to each of $n - 1$ stages of the dynamic programming algorithm for the optimal polygon triangulation problem.

As we have mentioned, the coalesced access to the global memory is a key issue to accelerate the computation. As illustrated in Figure 6, when threads access to continuous locations in a row of a two-dimensional array (*horizontal access*), the continuous locations in address space of the global memory are accessed in the same time (*coalesced access*). However, if threads access to continuous locations in a column (*vertical access*), the distant locations are accessed in the same time (*stride access*). From the structure of the global memory, the coalesced access maximizes the bandwidth of memory access. On the other hand, the stride access needs a lot of clock cycles. Thus, we should avoid the stride access (or the vertical access) and perform the coalesced access (or the horizontal access) whenever possible.

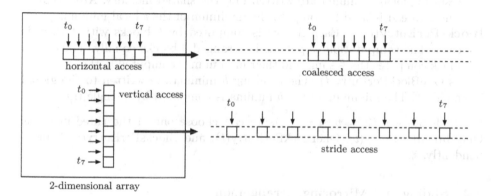

Fig. 6. Coalesced and stride access

4 Our Implementation of the Dynamic Programming Approach for the Optimal Polygon Triangulation

The main purpose of this section is to show our implementation of dynamic programming for the optimal polygon triangulation in the GPU. We focus on our new ideas, granularity adjustment and sliding and mirroring arrangements for accelerating the dynamic programming algorithm.

4.1 Granularity Adjustment Technique

Recall that each Stage p $(2 \leq p \leq n - 2)$ consists of the computation of $(n - p - 1)$ $M_{i,j}$'s each of which involves the computation of the minimum of p values. We consider three methods, *OneThreadPerEntry*, *OneBlockPerEntry*, and *BlocksPerEntry* to perform the computation of each of the $n - 2$ stages. In OneThreadPerEntry, each $M_{i,i+p}$ is computed sequentially by one thread. In OneBlockPerEntry, each $M_{i,i+p}$ is computed by one block with multiple threads in parallel. In BlocksPerEntry, each $M_{i,i+p}$ is computed by multiple blocks in parallel.

Let t be the number of threads in each block and b be the number of blocks. In our implementation of the three methods, t and b can be the parameters that can be changed to get the best performance. The details of the implementation of the three methods are spelled out as follows:

OneThreadPerEntry(t): Each $M_{i,i+p}$ is computed by a single thread sequentially. Thus, we use $(n-p-1)$ threads totally. Since each block has t threads, $\frac{n-p-1}{t}$ blocks are used.

OneBlockPerEntry(t): Each $M_{i,i+p}$ is computed by a block with t threads. The computation of $M_{i,i+p}$ involves the p sums $M_{i,k} + M_{i+p,k+1}$ ($i \leq k \leq i + p - 1$). The t threads compute p sums in parallel such that each thread computes $\frac{p}{t}$ sums and their local minimum of the $\frac{p}{t}$ sums is computed. The resulting local t minima are written into the shared memory. After that, a single thread is used to compute the minimum of the t local minima.

BlocksPerEntry(b, t): Each $M_{i,i+p}$ is computed by b blocks with t threads each. The computation of p sums is arranged b blocks equally. Thus, each block computes the $\frac{p}{b}$ sums and their minimum is computed in the same way as OneBlockPerEntry(t). The resulting b minima are written to the global memory. The minimum of the b minima is computed by a single thread.

For each Stage p ($2 \leq p \leq n - 2$), we can choose one of the three methods OneThreadPerEntry(t), OneBlockPerEntry(t), and BlocksPerEntry(b, t), independently.

4.2   Sliding and Mirroring Arrangement

Recall that, each Stage p ($2 \leq p \leq n-2$) of the dynamic programming algorithm involves the computation

$$M_{i,i+p} = \min_{i \leq k \leq i+p-1} (M_{i,k} + M_{k+1,i+p}) + w_{i-1,i+p}.$$

Let us first observe *the naive arrangement* which allocates each $M_{i,j}$ to the (i, j) element of the 2-dimensional array, that is, the element in the i-th row and the j-th column. As illustrated in Figure 7, to compute $M_{i,i+p}$ in Stage p

- p temporary data $M_{i,i}, M_{i,i+1}, \ldots, M_{i,i+p-1}$ in the same row and
- p temporary data $M_{i+1,i+p}, M_{i+2,i+p}, \ldots, M_{i+p,i+p}$ in the same column

are accessed. Hence, the naive arrangement involves the vertical access (or the stride access), which decelerates the computing time.

For the coalesced access of the global memory, we present two arrangements of $M_{i,j}$s in a 2-dimensional array, *the sliding arrangement* and *the mirroring arrangement* as follows:

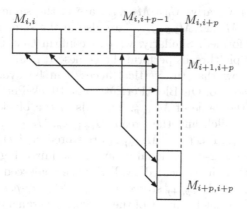

Fig. 7. The computation of $M_{i,i+p}$

Sliding Arrangement: Each $M_{i,j}$ ($0 \le i \le j \le n-1$) is allocated to $(i - j + n, j)$ element of the 2-dimensional array of size $n \times n$.

Mirroring Arrangement Each $M_{i,j}$ ($0 \le i \le j \le n-1$) is allocated to (i, j) element and (j, i) element.

The reader should refer to Figure 8 for illustrating the sliding and mirroring arrangements. We will use sliding arrangement for OneThreadPerEntry and the mirroring arrangement for OneBlockPerEntry and BlocksPerEntry.

We will show that the vertical access can be avoided if we use the sliding arrangement for OneThreadPerEntry. Suppose that each thread i computes the value of $M_{i,i+p}$. First, each thread i reads $M_{i,i}$ in parallel and then read $M_{i+1,i+p}$ in parallel. Thus, $M_{0,0}, M_{1,1}, \ldots$ are read in parallel and then $M_{1,1+p}, M_{2,2+p}, \ldots$

					$M_{0,5}$
				$M_{0,4}$	$M_{1,5}$
			$M_{0,3}$	$M_{1,4}$	$M_{2,5}$
		$M_{0,2}$	$M_{1,3}$	$M_{2,4}$	$M_{3,5}$
	$M_{0,1}$	$M_{1,2}$	$M_{2,3}$	$M_{3,4}$	$M_{4,5}$
$M_{0,0}$	$M_{1,1}$	$M_{2,2}$	$M_{3,3}$	$M_{4,4}$	$M_{5,5}$

Sliding arrangement

$M_{0,0}$	$M_{0,1}$	$M_{0,2}$	$M_{0,3}$	$M_{0,4}$	$M_{0,5}$
$M_{0,1}$	$M_{1,1}$	$M_{1,2}$	$M_{1,3}$	$M_{1,4}$	$M_{1,5}$
$M_{0,2}$	$M_{1,2}$	$M_{2,2}$	$M_{2,3}$	$M_{2,4}$	$M_{2,5}$
$M_{0,3}$	$M_{1,3}$	$M_{2,3}$	$M_{3,3}$	$M_{3,4}$	$M_{3,5}$
$M_{0,4}$	$M_{1,4}$	$M_{2,4}$	$M_{3,4}$	$M_{4,4}$	$M_{4,5}$
$M_{0,5}$	$M_{1,5}$	$M_{2,5}$	$M_{3,5}$	$M_{4,5}$	$M_{5,5}$

Mirroring arrangement

Fig. 8. Sliding and Mirroring arrangements

are read in parallel. Clearly, $M_{0,0}, M_{1,1}, \ldots$ are in the same row of the sliding arrangement. Also, $M_{1,1+p}, M_{2,2+p}, \ldots$ are also in the same row. Thus, the coalesced read is performed. Similarly, we can confirm that the remaining read operations by multiple threads perform the coalesced read.

Next, we will show that the vertical access can be avoided if we use the mirroring arrangement for OneBlockPerEntry and BlocksPerEntry. Suppose that a block computes the value of $M_{i,i+p}$. Threads in the block read $M_{i,i}, M_{i,i+1}$, $\ldots$, $M_{i,i+p-1}$ in parallel, and then read $M_{i+1,i+p}, M_{i+2,i+p}, \ldots, M_{i+p,i+p}$ in parallel. Clearly, $M_{i,i}, M_{i,i+1}, \ldots, M_{i,i+p-1}$ are stored in $(i, i), (i, i+1), \ldots, (i, i+p-1)$ elements in the 2-dimensional array of the mirroring arrangement, and thus, threads perform the coalesced read. For the coalesced read, threads read $M_{i+1,i+p}, M_{i+2,i+p}, \ldots, M_{i+p,i+p}$ stored in $(i+p, i+1), (i+p, i+2), \ldots, (i+p, i+p)$ elements in the 2-dimensional array of the mirroring arrangement. Clearly, these elements are in the same row and the threads perform the coalesced read.

4.3 Our Algorithm for the Optimal Polygon Triangulation

Our algorithm for the optimal polygon triangulation is designed as follows: For each Stage p $(2 \leq p \leq n-2)$, we execute three methods OneThreadPerEntry(t), OneBlockPerEntry(t), and BlocksPerEntry(b,t) for various values of t and b, and find the fastest method and parameters. As we are going to show later, OneThreadPerEntry is the fastest in earlier stages. In middle stages, OneBlockPerEntry is fastest. Finally, BlocksPerEntry is the best in later stages. Thus, we first use the sliding arrangement in earlier stages computed by OneThreadPerEntry. We then convert the 2-dimensional array with the sliding arrangement into the mirroring arrangement. After that, we execute OneBlockPerEntry and then BlocksPerEntry in the remaining stages. Note that the computing time of our algorithm depends only on the number of vertices, i.e., it is independent from the weights of edges. Therefore, given the number of vertices, we can find and determine the fastest method and parameters.

5 Experimental Results

We have implemented our dynamic programming algorithm for the optimal polygon triangulation using CUDA C. We have used NVIDIA GeForce GTX 580 with 512 processing cores (16 Streaming Multiprocessors which has 32 processing cores) running in 1.544GHz and 3GB memory. For the purpose of estimating the speedup of our GPU implementation, we have also implemented a conventional software approach of dynamic programming for the optimal polygon triangulation using GNU C. We have used Intel Core i7 870 running in 2.93GHz and 8GB memory to run the sequential algorithm for dynamic programming.

Table 1 shows the computing time in seconds for a 16384-gon. Table 1 (a) shows the computing time of OneThreadPerEntry(t) for $t = 32, 64, 128, 256, 512, 1024$. The computing time is evaluated for the naive arrangement and the sliding arrangement. For example, if we execute OneThreadPerEntry(64) for all stages on the naive arrangement, the computing time is 854.8 seconds. OneThreadPer-Entry(64) runs in 431.8 seconds on the sliding arrangement and thus, the sliding arrangement can attain a speedup of factor 1.98.

Table 1 (b) shows the computing time of OneBlockPerEntry(t) for $t =$ 32, 64, 128, 256, 512, 1024. Suppose that we select t that minimizes the computing time. OneBlockPerEntry(128) takes 604.7 seconds for the naive arrangement and OneBlockPerEntry(128) runs in 73.5 seconds for the mirroring arrangement. Thus, the mirroring arrangement can attain a speedup of factor 8.23.

Table 1 (c) shows the computing time of BlocksPerEntry(b, t) for $b = 2, 4, 8$ and $t =$ 32, 64, 128, 256, 512, 1024. Again, let us select b and t that minimize the computing time. BlocksPerEntry(2,128) takes 610.9 seconds for the naive arrangement and BlocksPerEntry(2,128) runs in 97.8 seconds for the mirroring arrangement. Thus, the mirroring arrangement can attain a speedup of factor 6.25.

Table 1. The computing time (seconds) for a 16384-gon using each of the three methods

(a) The computing time of OneThreadPerEntry(t)

t	32	64	128	256	512	1024
naive arrangement	596.8	854.8	863.3	889.2	1202.0	1614.2
sliding arrangement	312.8	431.8	442.2	541.0	668.3	1023.2

(b) The computing time of OneBlockPerEntry(t)

t	32	64	128	256	512	1024
naive arrangement	631.8	606.8	604.7	612.3	678.7	1286.5
mirroring arrangement	169.5	98.5	73.5	80.4	225.0	824.8

(c) The computing time of BlocksPerEntry(b, t)

t		32	64	128	256	512	1024
	$b = 2$	650.2	614.6	610.9	627.3	828.8	2007.8
naive arrangement	$b = 4$	650.5	617.5	624.9	673.1	1174.9	3585.0
	$b = 8$	655.6	630.5	670.0	815.1	1917.8	6779.5
	$b = 2$	176.3	110.8	97.8	129.1	422.6	1611.7
mirroring arrangement	$b = 4$	188.5	136.2	148.2	229.8	820.3	3188.6
	$b = 8$	216.0	189.9	250.5	433.6	1613.7	6337.9

Figure 9 shows the running time of each stage using the three methods. For each of the three methods and for each of the 16382 stages, we select best values of the number t of threads in each block and the number b of blocks. Also, the sliding arrangement is used for OneThreadPerEntry and the mirroring arrangement is used for OneBlockPerEntry and BlocksPerEntry. Recall that we can use different methods with different parameters can be used for each stage independently. Thus, to attain the minimum computing time we should use

- OneThreadPerEntry for Stages 0-49,
- OneBlockPerEntry for Stages 50-16350, and
- BlocksPerEntry for Stages 16351-16382.

Note that if we use three methods for each stage in this way, we need to convert the sliding arrangement into the mirroring arrangement. This conversion takes only 0.21 mseconds. Including the conversion time, the best total computing time of our implementation for the optimal polygon triangulation problem is 69.1 seconds. The sequential implementation used Intel Core i7 870 runs in 17105.5 seconds. Thus, our best GPU implementation attains a speedup factor of 247.5. Recall that the computing time does not depend on edge weights shown in the above section. Therefore, for another 16384-gon whose weights are different, we can obtain almost the same speedup factor as that of the above experiment.

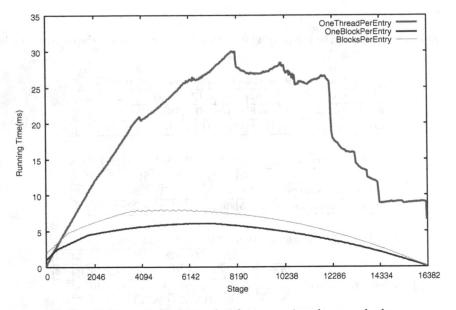

Fig. 9. The running time of each stage using three methods

6   Concluding Remarks

In this paper, we have proposed an implementation of the dynamic programming algorithm for an optimal polygon triangulation on the GPU. Our implementation selects the best methods, parameters, and data arrangement for each stage to obtain the best performance. The experimental results show that our implementation solves the optimal polygon triangulation problem for a convex 16384-gon in 69.1 seconds on the NVIDIA GeForce GTX 580, while a conventional CPU implementation runs in 17105.5 seconds. Thus, our GPU implementation attains a speedup factor of 247.5.

References

1. Bergroth, L., Hakonen, H., Raita, T.: A survey of longest common subsequence algorithms. In: Proc. of International Symposium on String Processing and Information Retrieval (2000)
2. Cormen, T.H., Leiserson, C.E., Rivest, R.L.: Introduction to Algorithms, 1st edn. MIT Press (1990)
3. Gilbert, P.D.: New results on planar Triangulations. M.Sc. thesis. Report R-850 (July 1979)
4. Hwu, W.W.: GPU Computing Gems Emerald Edition. Morgan Kaufmann (2011)
5. Ito, Y., Ogawa, K., Nakano, K.: Fast ellipse detection algorithm using Hough transform on the GPU. In: Proc. of International Conference on Networking and Computing, pp. 313–319 (December 2011)
6. Klincsek, G.T.: Minimal triangulations of polygonal domains. Annals of Discrete Mathematics 9, 121–123 (1980)
7. Man, D., Uda, K., Ito, Y., Nakano, K.: A GPU implementation of computing Euclidean distance map with efficient memory access. In: Proc. of International Conference on Networking and Computing, pp. 68–76 (December 2011)
8. Man, D., Uda, K., Ueyama, H., Ito, Y., Nakano, K.: Implementations of a parallel algorithm for computing Euclidean distance map in multicore processors and GPUs. International Journal of Networking and Computing 1(2), 260–276 (2011)
9. Nishida, K., Ito, Y., Nakano, K.: Accelerating the dynamic programming for the matrix chain product on the GPU. In: Proc. of International Conference on Networking and Computing, pp. 320–326 (December 2011)
10. NVIDIA Corp., NVIDIA CUDA C Programming Guide Version 4.1 (2011)
11. NVIDIA Corp., CUDA C Best Practice Guide Version 4.1 (2012)
12. Ogawa, K., Ito, Y., Nakano, K.: Efficient Canny edge detection using a GPU. In: International Workshop on Advances in Networking and Computing, pp. 279–280 (November 2010)
13. Pólya, G.: On picture-writing. Amer. Math. Monthly 63, 689–697 (1956)
14. Uchida, A., Ito, Y., Nakano, K.: Fast and accurate template matching using pixel rearrangement on the GPU. In: Proc. of International Conference on Networking and Computing, pp. 153–159 (December 2011)

Security Computing for the Resiliency of Protecting from Internal Attacks in Distributed Wireless Sensor Networks

Xu Huang, Dharmendra Sharma, and Muhammad Ahmed

Faculty of Information Sciences and Engineering, University of Canberra, Australia
{Xu.Huang,Dharmendra.Sharma,Muhammad.Ahmed}@canberra.edu.au

Abstract. Wireless sensor network (WSNs) have been making up of a mass of spatially distributed autonomous sensors to monitor physical or environmental conditions. However, security threats to WSNs become increasingly diversified, prevention based due to their open nature. An adversary can easily eavesdrop and replay or inject fabricated messages. Different cryptographic methods can be used to defend against some of such attacks but very limited. For example, node compromise, another major problem of WSNs security, raised a serious challenge for WSNs as it allows an adversary to enter inside the security perimeter of the network. This paper is focusing on investigating internal attacks of distributed wireless sensor networks with multi-hop and single sinker, where we show our novel algorithm, with our new concept of *controllable resiliency* of WSNs, to ensure the targeted WSN always running at the designed resiliency level. The final experimental and simulation results showed that that the proposed algorithm does work well at the designed level.

Keywords: security computing, resiliency, distributed wireless sensor networks, internal attacks, sensor optimum deployment.

1 Introduction

In our today's life, it is noted that wireless sensor networks (WSNs) and their applications are becoming popular, which is because that a large number of low cost, low power, rapid deployment, self-organization capability and cooperative data processing, wireless sensor networks (WSNs) have a great advantage for various applications in our real life [1], such as battlefield surveillance, habitat monitoring, intelligent agriculture, home automation, etc.

The properties of WSNs inevitably face the fact that a sensor node is extremely restricted by resources, including energy, memory, computing, bandwidth, and communication. Normally the base station is a more powerful node, which can be linked to a central station via satellite or internet communication to form a network. There are many deployments for wireless sensor networks depending on various applications such as environmental monitoring e.g. volcano detection [2,3], distributed control systems [4], agricultural and farm management [5], detection of radioactive sources [6], and computing platform for tomorrows' internet [7]. Generally a typical

Y. Xiang et al. (Eds.): ICA3PP 2012, Part I, LNCS 7439, pp. 16–29, 2012.

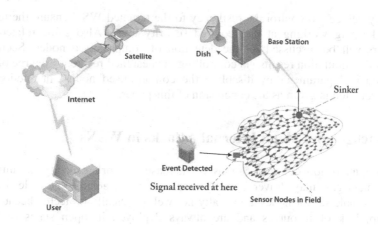

Fig. 1. A Typical WSN architecture

WSN is composed of a large number of distributed sensor nodes responsible for sensing data and a sink node responsible for collecting and processing data as shown in Fig.1.

However, it is obviously to observe that WSNs normally have a open nature of the wireless medium therefore an adversary can easily eavesdrop the information from the targeted sensors, which is called a "passive attack", or actively do something such as manipulate or inject fabricated messages, which is the case called an "active attack." It is well known that for the protection from some WSNs attacks, various cryptographic methods can be used but sometimes are not very efficient and effective [8-10]. Moreover, because of WSN deployments are in open states and possibly in hostile environments, attackers can easily lunch "denial-of-service" (DoS) attacks, cause physical damage to the sensors or even capture them to extract sensitive data including identities, encryption keys, address, other privacy information, etc. Recently internal attacks attracted great attentions to the people who have been working in the fields as they allowed adversaries to enter inside the security perimeter of the network. For example, a node is so-called compromised, the attack can produce internal attacks such as Sybil attacks, node replication or black-grey-worm-sink holes. As mentioned above that cryptography to secure routing functionalities is inappropriate against such aforementioned internal attacks, because the attacks can introduce false topological, neighborhood, control, and routing information within the existed networks. The attack also may just simply drop message as a black hole. So far, there is little research literature in investigating and analyzing against those internal attacks. In our current paper, we are focusing on investigating those internal attacks for wireless sensor networks, by which, in our current paper, we can show our novel algorithm, with our new definition of *resiliency degree,* the targeted WSN can be controllable in terms of security and resiliency by some proper operations.

This paper comprises of five sections. A brief description of the background about related algorithms is given in Section II. Section III describes our new algorithm to detect internal attack and compromised nodes, which consists of three major parts, namely (a) identifying the compromised nodes in a targeted WSN; (b) detecting the location of compromised node with the known beacons (c) following defined "resiliency degree" to control the resiliency to the targeted WSN ensure the targeted network keeping working at the required security level. Also some related other parameters will be discussed for the detection of compromised nodes. Section IV describes the simulation results via controlling the designed resiliency degree of WSN by the required parameter by disabling the compromised nodes. In Section V, a briefly discussion is given as the conclusion of this paper.

2   Background about Internal Attacks in WSNs

WSNs use multi-hop communications to increase network capacity, in multi-hop routing, messages may traverse many hops before reaching their destinations. However, simple sensor nodes are usually not well physically protected because they are cheap, lack of resources and are always deployed in open states or hostile environments where they can be easily captured and compromised. An adversary can extract sensitive information and control the compromised nodes to make use of those nodes service for the attackers. Therefore, when a node is compromised, an adversary gains access to the network and can produce malicious activities. The attacks are involved in corrupting network data or even destroying the whole network.

Karlof and Wagner discussed attacks at the network layer in their paper [11] and mentioned altered or replayed routing information and selective forwarding, node replication, Sybil attacks or black-grey-sink holes, and HELLO flooding. Some papers discussed various attacks in term of network's resiliency, such as [12], to show how to keep WSN routing protocols as stateless as possible to avoid the proliferation of specific attacks and provide for a degree of random behavior to prevent the adversary from determining which the best nodes to compromise are. They defined three items, namely (a) average delivery ratio, (b) average degree of nodes, and (c) average path length to describe the networks resiliency.

Unlike traditional routing, where intermediate nodes just forward input packets, in network coding intermediate nodes actively mix or code input packets and forward the resulting coded packets. The nature of packet mixing also subjects network coding systems to a severe security threat, knows as a pollution attack, where attackers inject corrupted packets into the network. Since intermediate nodes forward packets coded from their received packets, as long as least one of the input packets is corrupted, all output packets forwarded by the node will be corrupted. This will further affect other nodes and result in the epidemic propagation of the attack in the network. In [13] it was addressed pollution attacks against network coding systems in wireless mesh networks. They proposed a lightweight scheme that uses time-based authentication in combination with random liner transformations to defend against pollution attacks.

A few other papers also addressed pollution attacks in internal flow coding systems use special crafted digital signatures [14-15] or hash functions [16-17]. Recently some papers discuss the preventing the internal attacks by related protocols [19, 20].

In the Sybil attack, a malicious device illegitimately takes multiple identities. The malicious nodes can fill up the buffers of their neighbors with non-existing neighbors and create a messy topology.

It is noted that resiliency of WSNs are related to the security of WSNs [21], where a definition of network resiliency was discussed based on the comparisons with other similar terminologies such as robustness etc. In this paper we follow the definition of [21], i.e. *resiliency is the ability of a network to continue to operate in presence of k compromised nodes* to present our definition of "resiliency degree" and an algorithm to control the compromised nodes in the targeted WSN. Here, we automatically take the assumption that the attacks are from internal when we highlighted the nodes become "compromised nodes."

It is well know that in the traditional situations most of existing mechanisms for the security in wireless sensor networks are based essentially on cryptographic primitives. In cryptographic approaches, the source uses cryptographic techniques to create and send additional verification information that allows nodes to verify the validity of coded packets. Then the polluted packets can then be filtered out by intermediate nodes with those validities. The most described schemes rely on techniques such as homomorphic hash functions or homomorphic digital signatures. These schemes have high computational overhead, as any verification requires a large number of modular exponentiations. In addition, they require the verification information, such as hashes or signatures to be transmitted separately and reliably to all nodes in advance, which is normally difficult to achieve efficiently in wireless networks.

In terms of the attack model, synoptically speaking there are two types of international attacks, namely (a) exceptional message attack, by which the attacks will tamper the message content or generate fake messages and (b) abnormal behavior attacks, by which the transmission will be abnormally changed such as dropping the messages, forwarding the message to a particular receivers, broadcasting redundant or meaningless messages to increasing the traffic load in the network, etc. As we are focusing on the controllable resiliency based on the internal attackers we shall focus on the case abnormal attributes and some of cases (a) can be extended to what we discussed in this paper.

3   Proposed Security Computing for Protecting WSNs

The system under our consideration consists of an area of interest where region wise detection requirements are provided by the end user. We model the area of interest as a grid Ω of $N_x \times N_y$ points. The ratio of the detection to miss requirements at every point on the grid are ordered in two $N_x N_y \times 1$ vector of the ratio of the probability, p_d/ p_m. Moreover, the sensing model and the number of sensors available serve as inputs to our sensor deployment algorithm. Given these inputs, the objective of this work is to determine the optimal sensor placement that would maximize the highest ratio of the signal/noise (S/N). Or it is even simpler case that we are looking for the parameter related to S/N for fixed deployment sensors network, by which we can control the sensor states.

It is important to note that we assumed a simple detection model where a target is declared to be detected if at least a single sensor in the network is able to detect it.

We first investigate the simplest case, one sensor, called detecting node. Then the case will be extended to more than one detecting notes.

There are two common sensing models found in literature, binary detection model and the exponential detection model. Both models share the assumption that the detection capability of a sensor depends on the distance between the sensor and the phenomena, or target to be detected.

Following [18] notations we have the case that for the binary detection model, the probability of detection p_d (t,s) is given as:

$$p_d(t,s) = \begin{cases} 1 & \text{if } d(t,s) \le r_d \\ 0 & \text{if } d(t,s) > r_d \end{cases} \tag{1}$$

where r_d is the detection radius and $d(t,s)$ is the distance between the target's position "t" and the sensor location "s" on a plane. If the distance between the sensor and target is greater than r_d, then the target is not detectable by that sensor. But if the target is within the detection radius, it will be always detected. This is a simple model, which is not close to realistic. The exponential model is a more realistic model, where the probability of detection corresponds to

$$p_d(t,s) = \begin{cases} e^{-\alpha d(t,s)} & \text{if } d(t,s) \le r_d \\ 0 & \text{if } d(t,s) > r_d \end{cases} \tag{2}$$

In above equation, α is a decay parameter that is related to the quality of a sensor or the surrounding environment. In the exponential model of equation (2), even if a target is within the detection radius, there is a probability that it will not be detected, which means it will be missed. Because this model is closer to the realistic case, we shall use this model in our paper.

The process of linking individual sensors' detection characteristic to the overall probability of detection requirements on the grid is mathematically quantified using miss probabilities, $p_{miss} = 1 - p_d$, where p_d is the probability of detection. The probability of a target being detected by any sensor on the grid is the complement of the target being missed by all the sensors on the grid. The overall miss probability $M(x, y)$ corresponds to the probability that a target at point (x, y) will be missed by all sensors, which is

$$M(x,y) = \prod_{(i,j) \in \Omega} p_{miss}((x,y),(i,j))^{u(i,j)} \tag{3}$$

where $u(i,j)$ represents the presence or absence of a sensor at the location (i, j) on the grid, and corresponds to

$$u(i,j) = \begin{cases} 1, & \text{if there is a sensor at } (i,j) \\ 0, & \text{if there is no sensor at } (i,j) \end{cases} \tag{4}$$

Taking the natural logarithm of the both sides in equation (3), we have

$$m(x,y) = \sum_{(i,j) \in \Omega} u(i,j) \ln p_{miss}((x,y),(i,j)) \tag{5}$$

where $m(x, y)$ is so-called the overall logarithmic miss probability at the point (x, y). Thus, we have the function $b(x, y)$ as

$$b(x, y) = \begin{cases} \ln p_{miss}((x, y), (0,0)), & d((x, y), (0,0)) \leq r_d \\ 0, & d((x, y), (0,0)) > r_d \end{cases} \tag{6}$$

The overall logarithmic miss probabilities for all points on the grid can be arranged in a vector $\mathbf{m}$ of dimension $N_x N_y \times 1$ that corresponds to equation (7) as shown below:

$$\mathbf{m} = [m(x, y), \forall(x, y) \in \Omega]^T$$

$$\mathbf{u} = [u(i, j), \forall(i, j) \in \Omega]^T$$

and

$$\mathbf{m} = \mathbf{Bu} \tag{7}$$

The $((i-1)N_y + j)$-th element of $\mathbf{u}$ indicates the number of sensors deployed at point (i, j) on the grid. The matrix $\mathbf{B}$ is of dimension $N_x N_y \times N_x N_y$, and it contains

$$\{b(x - i, y - j), \forall(x, y) \in \Omega, (i, j) \in \Omega\}$$

$b(x - i, y - j)$ corresponds to the (r, c)-th entry of $\mathbf{B}$, where $r = (x - 1)N_y + y$ and $c = (i - 1)N_y + j$.

Essentially, $b(x - i, y - j)$ quantifies the effect of placing a sensor at the point (i, j) on the logarithmic miss probability at the point (x, y) on the grid.

In fact, in the real life, the signal transmitted will suffer from the noise, which caused by the complex environment, including the sensor node noise, wireless noise, and transition noise, etc., which forces us to take care of the signal to noise ratio rather than just talking about signal that cannot existed by its own in the real wireless sensor networks.

The following description is focusing on how could the compromised nodes can be detected by their so-called abnormal attributes over the network, such as irregular change of hop count that implicates sinkhole attacks; the signal power is impractically increasing which may indicate wormhole attacks; abnormally dropping rate traffic behaviors related the related nodes most likely to be compromised, etc.

We propose each sensor node can establish pair wise keys with its one-hop neighbors. When the nodes are deployed, each node is pre-distributed an initial key, K_I. A node, Q_i with $Q_i \in \Omega$, can use K_I and one way hash function H_f to generate its master key, K_M:

$$K_M = H_f(ID_i)K_I \tag{8}$$

Here, we highlight the identification of Q_i is ID_i in the above equation. Then node Q_i broadcasts an advertisement message $(ID_i, Nonce_i)$ which contains a nonce, and waits for other neighbor Q_j (here $i \neq j$) to respond with its identity. So the process will be as follows:

$$Q_i \Rightarrow * : ID_i, Nonce_i$$

$$Q_j \Rightarrow Q_i : ID_j. MAC\ (K_j, ID_j \mid Nonce_i)$$

Therefore, at the same time, Q_j can also generate the key K_j. Then both nodes Q_i and Q_j can generate the pair-wise key $K_{i,j} = H_f K_j(ID_i)$. So each node can use these nodes' ID to calculate its one hop-neighbors' key, i.e. $\forall Q_i \in N_1$, where N_1 is the space of one-hop for a fixed node in the targeted WSN. If there is any stranger node, such as the adversaries' node, it will be distinguished by those pair-wise keys. But there is the case needs to be noted as shown in Fig.2 that there may be some multi-hop neighbors such as node x_k and node x_p in Fig.2. Among those no-one-hop nodes may have some compromised nodes if we can identify the one-hop nodes which are compromised nodes.

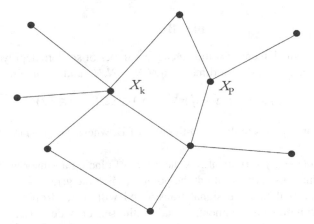

Fig. 2. Pseudo one-hop neighbor x_k and x_p in a WSN

Considering this case we need to check those nodes who are sitting in the group belong to more than one hop neighbor. There are many ways to do this for example in [22] there is a filter used via so called "minimum acceptable trust value." In order to reduce the computing costs, we believe that the second order parameter will be good enough to prevent form compromised nodes, where $\forall Q_i \notin N_1$, as it will be ultimately checked by abnormal attributes. It is noted that a target node can only send data packets over the sensor channel. The neighboring sensor nodes, which are within the sensing radius of the target node as shown in equation (2), will then receive the stimulus over the sensor channel. That receives and detects over the sensor channel has to forward its sensing results to one or more sink nodes over the wireless channel. Inside a sensor node the coordination between the sensor protocol stack and the wireless protocol stack is done by the sensor application and transport layers. Any networking processing mechanism can be implemented in the sensor application layer.

Assume that the $S_i/N_i = R_i$ for a reference node $Q_i \in N-N_1$, when $N \subset N_{\text{multi-hop}}$ and $N_1 \subset N$. we have the following parameters:

$$\bar{\mu}_j = \frac{1}{n_1} \sum_{i=1}^{n_1} R_i \tag{9}$$

$$\bar{\sigma}_j = \sqrt{\frac{1}{n_1 - 1} \sum_{i=1}^{n_1} (R_i - \bar{\mu}_j)^2} . \tag{10}$$

Then we have

$$CK_j = \left| \frac{R_i - \bar{\mu}_j}{\sigma_j} \right| \tag{11}$$

It is noted that CK_j is smaller than the designed threshold, it would be taken as normal case otherwise it would be assume the checked node $Q_i \notin N_1$ and $Q_i \in N$.

The following section is focusing on checking so-called abnormal attributes over the network, such as irregular change of hop count; the signal power is impractically increasing; abnormally dropping rate, etc. In order to make the processing simple we just take one major parameter to be checked the others are the same way to be carried on. We are focus on the transmission attribute, including forward rate and dropping rate.

Now let's defined the transmission rate, T_i as the i-th node in the targeted WSN to express its transmission attribute:

$$T_i = \frac{T_i^{out}}{T_i^{In}} \tag{12}$$

where up script "out" and "In" denoted the signal sending to next one-hop node and received from pervious node. It is noted that equation does not loss the generality for example, in the case that multi-one hop nodes to be sent, the transmission will follow the designed particular protocol, where is beyond the scope of the current paper. The checking threshold will take the consideration for the designed protocol. So we can let the signal "out" and "In" situation absorbed by the particular protocol.   Then we can simply apply the equations (9) to (11) subject to R_i replaced by T_i. For example, it is noted that if T_i is out of the mean value the value obtained by equation (10), it will be taken by compromised node if there is no pervious knowledge about the WSN. Also if we have the information about the WSN empirical data we may use the Chi-square curve to check the fitting.

Algorithm for checking abnormal attributes

1. Input: p^{req}_d (detection requirement), K (number of available sensors), α (decay parameter), r_d (detection radius), $d(t, s)$ (the distance between the target's position) and **B**.

2. Output: **u** (deployment vector) and taking input signal rate

3. for $k = K$ -1:-1:0 do

4. evaluate G_k

5. end for

6. initialization: $k = 0$, **u** =0

7. while $k \cdot K$ do

8. find set of grid points with unsatisfied detection requirements $\{i: p^k_d(i) \cdot p^{req}_d(i)\}$

9. Set $x_{k-1}(i) = 0$

10. Calculate the control vector $\mathbf{u}_k = -\mathbf{G}_k\mathbf{x}_k$

11. Find the S/N and index j_{max}, where $j_{max} = \max_{index} (\mathbf{u}_k)$.

12. Update the deployment vector (i.e. $\mathbf{u}(j_{max}) = 1$)

13. Calculate $\mathbf{m}_k = \mathbf{Bu}$

14. for $i = N$ -1:-1:0 do

15. Obtain the output signal rate

16. Taking T_i by equation (12)

17. Calculate equation (9)

18. Calculate equation (10)

19. Calculate equation (11)

20. Input the designed value *Threshold*

21. If $CK_j <$ *Threshold* go 22

    Otherwise go 14

22. Increment number of sensors in the grid: $k = k + 1$

23. End while

Now we are focusing on the contributions to our controllable resiliency of WSN. Following the definition of resiliency *is the ability of a network to continue to operate in presence of k compromised nodes* [21] we assume the threshold for the targeted WSN is 30% of the total nodes became compromised nodes. We may describe those sick nodes become a group denoted as S_q, where q is the q-th sick group. The operation for resilient WSN is

$$\forall Q_i \in \sum_q S_q \geq 0.3 N \qquad (13)$$

With this condition, there is an operation needed to disable or isolated those compromised nodes by their locations in the targeted WSN.

Following our previous paper [23], we know that a WSN, such as CC2431 includes hardware 'Location Engine' that can calculate the nodes position given the RSSI (Radio Signal Strength Indication) and position data of reference nodes. The main inputs to the location engine are the; (x,y) location and RSSI of reference nodes, and the parameters A and n used internally to convert RSSI values into ranges. The output of the engine is the calculated (x,y) position. The engine presumably uses a multiliteration technique optimized for minimum resource use and speed.   The precision for the (x,y) location coordinates is 0.25meters. The precision of A is 0.5dB, while n uses an index into a lookup table that limits its precision. The range of valid RSSI to the location engine is 40 to 81 (in -dBm), so RSSI values higher than -40dBm must be set to -40dBm. This means that the minimum measurable range is around 1 meter (assuming an RSSI of -40dBm at 1 meter). The RSSI as a function of distance can be checked in our experimental work that is shown by Fig.3. As described in [23] that another factor that affects received signal strength is antenna polarization, which is one of focuses of this paper. Small simple antenna's produce linearly polarized radiation. For the linear polarized case, the electrical magnetic (EM) field remains in the same plane as the axis of the antenna. When the antenna produces an electric filed that remains in a plane parallel with respect to earth the polarization is said to be horizontal. Likewise when the electric field remains in a plane normal to earth the polarization is vertical. To receive maximum power the receiving antenna axis must be in the same plane as the transmitting antenna.

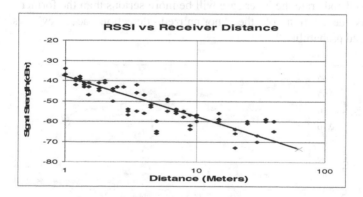

Fig. 3. A chart of RSSI as a function of distance

4   Simulation and Discussion

For this section, we consider a homogenous WSN with 1024 sensors uniformly distributed in the network area, which is in the network region b by b squared field located in the two dimensional Euclidean plan. In order to investigate the interference effects to the WSNs, we take two cases, namely, 32×32 (low density case) and 16×16 (high density case) squared fields. All sensors have the same capabilities and communicate through bidirectional links. Also we made all the sensors in the proximity burdened with similar workloads and expected them to have similarly under normal conditions. All the sensors can be in either "enabled" and "disabled" states controlled by the base station. The transmission algorithm is following the "minimize delay". The simulations were running 50 times with the final averaging the data as shown in Fig.4,

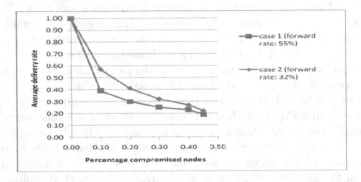

Fig. 4. Chart of "the "normalized average delivery rate" vs. "percentage compromised nodes."which is the "normalized average delivery rate" vs. "percentage compromised nodes."

It is noted that the "case 1" in the Fig.4 is the chart about the average forward rate ≅55% and the "case 2" is the case average forward rate ≅ 32%. At the same compromised node rate the latter case will be more serious than the former.

Fig.5 is description of the "normalized detection accuracy" vs. "sensor compromised probability."

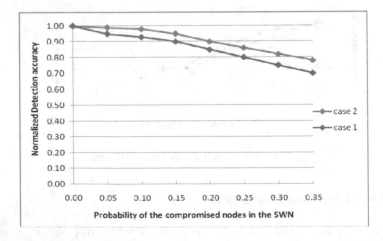

Fig. 5. normalized detection accuracy against the propability of the compromised nodes

There are two charts the "case 1" is the sensors deployed in the smaller area (16×16) and the same sensors were distributed in the larger area (32×32) is the case of "case 2". Due to the crowd sensors will impact each other by the interferences so the detection accuracy are impacted.

Fig.6 shows the situations about "normalized resiliency ration" vs. "the simulation period time."

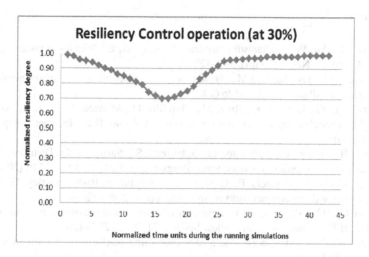

Fig. 6. Normalized resiliency degree against the normalized time units

From above description, we may give the normalized resiliency degree, which defined by

$$\frac{\text{total compromised nodes}}{\text{total sensor nodes}}$$

In our simulations, if it decreased by 30% the operation is taken to identify the compromised nodes and disable them with their locations. In our experiments we have divided the whole areas by 6 regions each region we design three beacons (locations known) by which with RSSI to get the locations for compromised nodes and then disable them when the "operation is running." From the Fig.6 we can see that the resiliency is under a reasonable level to be controllable.

5   Conclusion

In this paper we have been focusing on protecting from internal attacks via controllable resiliency in a WSN, in particularly it was carefully to investigate the case that those compromised nodes in a WSN, which appear to be legitimate nodes but service for attacker. We first discussed the method to identify those compromised nodes by their abnormal attributes. Then, follow our previous paper we used RSSI to find the locations for the conformed compromised nodes. We also defined resiliency degree for a WSN based on the definition of paper. With the designed resiliency degree for the WSN, there is a operation can be taken and keeping the resiliency degree for in the targeted WSN, therefore, the WSN will be recovered from the risk state to a normal operation state as shown by Fig.6. The whole security computing for the distributed WSN created a new way to ensure the distributed network security.

References

1. Akyildiz, I.F., Su, W., Sankarasubramaniam, Y., Cayirci, E.: Wireless sensor networks: a survey. Computer Networs 38(4), 393–422 (2002)
2. Chung-Kuo, C., Overhage, J.M., Huang, J.: An application of sensor networks for syndromic surveillance, pp. 191–196 (2005)
3. Werner-Allen, G., Lorincz, K., Ruiz, M., Marcillo, O., Johnson, J., Lees, J., Welsh, M.: Deploying a wireless sensor network on an active volcano. IEEE Internet Computing 10, 18–25 (2006)
4. Sinopoli, B., Sharp, C., Schenato, L., Schaffert, S., Sastry, S.S.: Distributed control applications within sensor networks. Proceedings of the IEEE 91, 1235–1246 (2003)
5. Sikka, P., Corke, P., Valencia, P., Crossman, C., Swain, D., Bishop-Hurley, G.: Wireless ad hoc sensor and actuator networks on the farm, pp. 492–499 (2006)
6. Stephens Jr., D.L., Peurrung, A.J.: Detection of moving radioactive sources using sensor networks. IEEE Transactions on Nuclear Science 51, 2273–2278 (2004)
7. Feng, Z.: Wireless sensor networks: a new computing platform for tomorrow's Internet, vol. 1 p. I-27 (2004)
8. Huang, X., Wijesekera, S., Sharma, D.: Fuzzy Dynamic Switching in Quantum Key Distribution for Wi-Fi Networks. In: Proceeding 6th International Conference on Fuzzy Systems and Knowledge Discovery, Tianjin, China, August 14-16, pp. 302–306 (2009)
9. Huang, X., Shah, P.G., Sharma, D.: Multi-Agent System Protecting from Attacking with Elliptic Curve Cryptography. In: The 2nd International Symposium on Intelligent Decision Technologies, Baltimore, July 28-30 (2010) (accepted to be published)
10. Huang, X., Sharma, D.: Fuzzy Controller for a Dynamic Window in Elliptic Curve Cryptography Wireless Networks for Scalar Multipication. In: The 16th Asia-Pacific Conference on Communications, APCC 2010, Langham Hotel, Auckland, New Zealand, October 31-November 3, pp. 509–514 (2010) ISBN: 978-1-4244-8127-9
11. Karlof, C., Wagner, D.: Secure routing inn wireless sensor networks: attacks and countermeasures. Ad Hoc Networks 1(2-3), 293–315 (2003)
12. Ochir, O.E., Minier, M., Valois, F., Kountouris, A.: Resiliency of Wireless Sensor Networks: Definitions and Analyses. In: 17th International Conference on Telecommunications, pp. 828–835 (2010)
13. Dong, J., Curtmola, R., Rotaru, C.N.: Parctical Defenses Against Pollution Attacks in Intra-Flow Network Coding for Wireless Mesh Networks. In: WiSec 2009, zurich, Switzerland, March 16-18, pp. 111–122 (2009)
14. Charles, D., Jain, K., Lauter, K.: Signatures for network coding. In: 40th Annual Conference on Information Sciences and Systems (2006)
15. Yu, Z., Wei, Y., Ramkumar, B., Guan, Y.: An efficient signature-based scheme for securing network coding against pollutions attacks. In: Proc. of INFOCOM OS, Phoenix, AZ (April 2008)

16. Krohn, M., Freedman, M., Mazierres, D.: On-the-fly verification of rateless erasure codes for efficient content distribution. In: Proc. IEEE Symposium on Security and Privacy, May 9-12, pp. 226–240 (2004)
17. Gkantsdis, C., Rodriguez, P.: Cooperative security for network coding file distribution. In: Proc. of INFOCOM (2006)
18. Ababnah, A., Naatarajan, B.: Optimal control based strategy for sensor deployment. IEEE Tran. On Systems, Man, and cybernetics, Part A: Systems and Humans 41(1) (Janaury 2011)
19. Sobeih, A., Hou, J.C., Kung, L.-C., Li, N., Zhang, H., Chen, W.P., Tyan, H.-Y., Yat-Sen, S., Lim, H.: J-Sim: A simulation and emulation environment for wireless sensor networks. IEEE Wireless Communications, 104–119 (August 2006)
20. Huang, X., Ahmed, M., Sharma, D.: A Novel Algorithm for Protecting from Internal Attacks of Wireless Sensor Networks. In: 2011 Ninth IEEE/IFIP International Conference on Embedded and Ubiquitous Computing, Melbourne, October 24-26 (2011)
21. Erdene-Ochir, O., Mibier, M., Valois, F., Kountouris, A.: Resiliency of wireless sensor networks: definitions and analyses. In: 17th International Conference on Telecommunications, pp. 828–835 (2010)
22. Liu, F., Cheng, X., Chen, D.: Insider attacker detection in wireless sensor networks. In: IEEE INFOCOM 2007, pp. 1973–1945 (2007)
23. Liu, F., Cheng, X., Chen, D.: Insider attacker detection in wireless sensor networks. In: IEEE INFOCOM 2007, pp. 1973–1945 (2007)

Parallel Algorithm for Nonlinear Network Optimization Problems and Real-Time Applications

Shin-Yeu Lin and Xian-Chang Guo

Department of Electrical Engineering, Chang Gung University, Tao-Yuan, Taiwan
shinylin@mail.cgu.edu.tw, shenchon008@yahoo.com.tw

Abstract. In this paper, we propose a parallel algorithm to solve a class of nonlinear network optimization problems. The proposed parallel algorithm is a combination of the successive quadratic programming and the dual method, which can achieve complete decomposition and make parallel computation possible. The proposed algorithm can be applied to solve nonlinear network optimization problems in the smart grid.

We have tested the proposed parallel algorithm in solving numerous cases of power flow problems on the IEEE 30-bus system. The test results demonstrate that the proposed parallel algorithm can obtain accurate solution. Additionally, neglecting the data communication time, the proposed parallel algorithm is, ideally, 13.1 times faster than the centralized Newton Raphson's method in solving the power flow problems of the IEEE 30-bus system.

Keywords: Parallel computation, nonlinear network optimization, smart grid, power flow, successive quadratic programming, dual method.

1 Introduction

Nonlinear network optimization problems over the network that was equipped with processor at each node and two way communication optical fibers in between edges are studied in this paper. In general, existing nonlinear programming methods can be used to solve the considered nonlinear network optimization problem, however, centrally. To exploit the considered network's computing power and data exchange capability for real-time applications, parallel algorithms should be developed and implemented in the considered network. A typical example for such a network is the future power system, *smart grid* [1-4]. Smart grid possesses *processing units* in each *bus* of the power system and every pair of buses connected by transmission line is linked by optical fiber. In other words, the smart grid can be viewed as a *super computer*, which is capable of performing the real-time computation. Fundamental issues in power system such as power flow, state estimation and optimal power flow [5-8] can be formulated as nonlinear network optimization problems. In conventional power system, the power flow problem was solved in the central control center. However, such a type of centralized solution processes is not suitable for smart grid [9]. Therefore, the purpose of this paper is proposing a parallel algorithm to solve nonlinear network optimization problems in smart grid with applications to the power flow problem.

Y. Xiang et al. (Eds.): ICA3PP 2012, Part I, LNCS 7439, pp. 30–40, 2012.

We organize our paper in the following manner. In Section 2, we will describe the structure of the smart grid and present the considered class of nonlinear network optimization problems. In Section 3, we will present the proposed parallel algorithm. In Section 4, we will formulate the power flow problem into the form of the considered nonlinear network optimization problem. In Section 5, we will present the numerical simulations of applying the proposed parallel algorithm to power flow problems. In Section 6, we will draw a conclusion.

2   Statement of Nonlinear Network Optimization Problems

We assume that the structure of the smart grid is as presented in Fig. 1, where each bus of the power system is denoted by a bar, and each bus is equipped with a processor denoted by a black square; solid lines represent the transmission lines between buses, and dashed lines represent the fiber links.

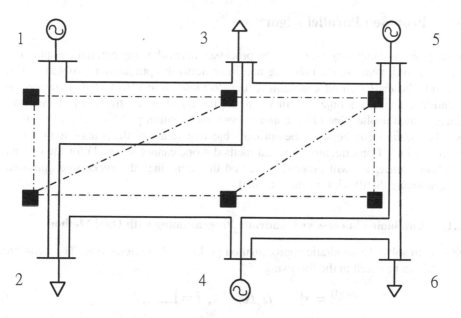

Fig. 1. An example smart grid and the associated processor network

Based on this structure, we can use a graph $G = (\mathcal{N}, L)$ to represent the smart grid, where $\mathcal{N}$ represents the set of all buses, and L represents the set of all communication links. The considered nonlinear network optimization problem can be stated in the following.

$$\begin{aligned} \min \quad & f(x) \\ \text{subject to} \quad & g_i(x_i, x_{J_i}) = 0, \quad i = 1, 2, \ldots N \end{aligned} \tag{1}$$

Where N denotes the total number of buses, i.e. $N = |\mathcal{N}|$ and $|(\bullet)|$ denotes the cardinality of the set $(\bullet)$; x_i represents the state variables associated with bus i; the *objective function* $f(x)$ is *nonlinear*; J_i represents the index set of the busses connecting with bus i such that $J_i = \{j \mid e(i, j) \in L\}$, and $e(i, j)$ represents a line connecting buses i and j; $x_{J_i} (= [x_{j_1}^T, x_{j_2}^T, \cdots, x_{j_{|J_i|}}^T]^T)$ represents the state vector of all busses in J_i, where $j_k, k = 1, \cdots, |J_i|$ represent the index of the bus in J_i; $g_i(x_i, x_{J_i}) = 0$ represents the *nonlinear equality constraint*. The nonlinear equality constraints show the *coupling* between neighboring buses, which concludes that (1) is a coupling nonlinear network optimization problem provided that the network is connected.

3   Proposed Parallel Algorithm

To exploit the computing power of the processor network using parallel computation, we need to decompose the coupling nonlinear network optimization problem (1). In general, the *dual method* can achieve the *decomposition* effect [10]. However, as mentioned above, the objective function and the equality constraints of (1) are non-linear, which implies that (1) is a *non-convex* optimization problem. Therefore, there will be a *duality gap* between the optimal objective values of the *primal* and the *dual* problems [10]. Consequently, the dual method alone cannot solve (1) for the optimal solution. Hence, we will propose a method that combines the *successive quadratic programming* (SQP) with the dual method.

3.1   Combining Successive Quadratic Programming with Dual Method

SQP is to solve the quadratic approximation problem of (1) iteratively. The iterations of SQP can be stated in the following.

$$x_i^{(k+1)} = x_i^{(k)} + \alpha_k \Delta x_i^{(k)} \quad , \quad i = 1, \ldots, N \tag{2}$$

Where k represents the iteration index, α_k represents the step-size, and $\Delta x_i(k)$ is the solution of the following *quadratic programming problem* (QPP), which is the quadratic approximation of (1):

$$\min \quad \sum_{i=1}^{N} \frac{1}{2} \Delta x_i^T \nabla^2 f_i(x^{(k)}) \Delta x_i + \nabla f_i(x^{(k)})^T \Delta x_i + \eta \Delta x_i^T \Delta x_i \tag{3}$$

subject to $\quad g_i(x_i^{(k)}, x_{J_i}^{(k)}) + \nabla_{x_i} g_i^T(x_i^{(k)}, x_{J_i}^{(k)}) \Delta x_i + \nabla_{x_{J_i}} g_i^T(x_i^{(k)}, x_{J_i}^{(k)}) \Delta x_{J_i} = 0$

Where $\nabla^2 f_i(x^{(k)})$ and $\nabla f_i(x^{(k)})$ are the diagonal submatrix of $\nabla^2 f(x^{(k)})$ and the subvector of $\nabla f(x^{(k)})$ corresponding to x_i, respectively; η is a positive constant that is large enough to make the objective function of (3) *strictly convex*; therefore, the objective function of (3) is a quadratic approximation of the objective function of (1); the equality constraint in (3) is the *linearization* of the nonlinear equality constraint in (1). Consequently, (3) is a *convex programming* problem. Therefore, we can use a dual method to solve it to achieve the *complete decomposition* effect.

The dual method is solving the dual problem of (3), which is stated in (4), instead of solving (3) directly.

$$\max_{\lambda} \quad \phi(\lambda) \tag{4}$$

Where the *dual function* $\phi(\lambda)$ is defined as

$$\phi(\lambda) = \min_{\Delta x_i, i=1,\ldots N} \sum_{i=1}^{N} \left[\frac{1}{2}\Delta x_i^T \nabla^2 f_i(x^{(k)})\Delta x_i + \nabla f_i(x^{(k)})^T \Delta x_i + \eta \Delta x_i^T \Delta x \right]$$
$$+ \sum_{i=1}^{N} \lambda_i^T \left[g_i(x_i^{(k)}, x_{J_i}^{(k)}) + \nabla_{x_i} g_i^T(x_i^{(k)}, x_{J_i}^{(k)})\Delta x_i + \nabla_{x_{J_i}} g_i^T(x_i^{(k)}, x_{J_i}^{(k)})\Delta x_{J_i} \right] \tag{5}$$

in which $\lambda_i, i = 1, \cdots, N$ denotes the Lagrange multiplier vector, and the dimension of λ_i is the same as g_i, and the λ in (4) equals $(\lambda_1^T, \lambda_2^T, \cdots, \lambda_N^T)^T$.

The iterations of the dual method can be stated in the following [10]:

$$\lambda_i^{(\ell+1)} = \lambda_i^{(\ell)} + \beta_l \Delta \lambda_i^{(\ell)}, \quad i = 1, \ldots, N \tag{6}$$

Where l denotes the iteration index, β_l denotes the step-size, and

$$\Delta \lambda_i^{(\ell)} = \nabla_{\lambda_i} \phi(\lambda^{(\ell)})$$
$$= g_i(x_i^{(k)}, x_{J_i}^{(k)}) + \nabla_{x_i} g_i^T(x_i^{(k)}, x_{J_i}^{(k)})\Delta x_i(\lambda^{(\ell)}) + \nabla_{x_{J_i}} g_i^T(x_i^{(k)}, x_{J_i}^{(k)})\Delta x_{J_i}(\lambda^{(\ell)}) \tag{7}$$

in which $\Delta x_i(\lambda^{(l)})$ and $\Delta x_{J_i}(\lambda^{(l)})$, $i = 1, \cdots, N$ represent the optimal solution of the *unconstrained minimization problem* on the right-hand side of (5) when $\lambda = \lambda^{(l)}$.

To compute $\Delta \lambda_i^{(l)}$, $i = 1, \cdots, N$ from (7), we need to obtain $\Delta x_i(\lambda^{(l)})$ and $\Delta x_{J_i}(\lambda^{(l)})$, $i = 1, \cdots, N$ first. To do so, we begin with rewriting the right-hand side of (5) into (8).

$$\min_{\Delta x_i, i=1,\dots,N} \sum_{i=1}^{N} \{\Delta x_i^T \left(\frac{1}{2}\nabla^2 f_i\left(x_i^{(k)}\right)+\eta I\right)\Delta x_i + \nabla f_i\left(x_i^{(k)}\right)^T \Delta x_i + \lambda_i^T g_i\left(x_i^{(k)}, x_{J_i}^{(k)}\right)$$
$$+\lambda_i^T\left[\nabla_{x_i} g_i^T\left(x_i^{(k)}, x_{J_i}^{(k)}\right)\Delta x_i\right]+\sum_{j\in J_i}\lambda_j \nabla_{x_i} g_j^T\left(x_j^{(k)}, x_{J_j}^{(k)}\right)\Delta x_i\} \tag{8}$$

Since (8) is a *separable* optimization problem, Δx_i, $i=1,\cdots,N$ can be obtained from solving the following N independent subproblems and achieve the decomposition:

For $i=1,\dots.,N$

$$\min_{\Delta x_i} \Delta x_i^T \left(\frac{1}{2}\nabla^2 f_i(x_i^{(k)})+\eta I\right)\Delta x_i + \nabla f_i\left(x_i^{(k)}\right)^T \Delta x_i + \lambda_i^T g_i(x_i^{(k)}, x_{J_i}^{(k)}) \tag{9}$$
$$+\lambda_i^T\left[\nabla_{x_i} g_i^T(x_i^{(k)}, x_{J_i}^{(k)})\Delta x_i\right]+\sum_{j\in J_i}\lambda_j\nabla_{x_i} g_j^T(x_j^{(k)}, x_{J_j}^{(k)})\Delta x_i$$

Notably, subproblem i shown in (9) to be solved in processor i is an unconstrained optimization problem with quadratic objective function, which can be solved *analytically*.

3.2   Complete Decomposition Effect of Proposed Parallel Algorithm

The complete decomposition achieved by the dual method using (6), (7) and (9) to solve the dual problem (4) for the given $x^{(k)}$ can be summarized in the following. The $\Delta\lambda_i^{(l)}$ required in (6) is calculated from (7). But the terms $\Delta x_i(\lambda^{(l)})$ and $\Delta x_{J_i}(\lambda^{(l)})$ required to compute (7) will be available once (9) is solved. Each subproblem in (9) can be solved analytically in the corresponding bus as long as the neighboring buses $j\in J_i$ send the data of λ_j and $\nabla_{x_i} g_j^T(x_j^{(k)}, x_{J_j}^{(k)})$. Once $\Delta x_i(\lambda^{(l)})$ is obtained at bus i for every i, then buses $j\in J_i$ will send the data of $\Delta x_j(\lambda^{(l)})$ to bus i, these $\Delta x_j(\lambda^{(l)})$ from all $j\in J_i$ form $\Delta x_{J_i}(\lambda^{(l)})$, which can then be used to compute (7) to obtain $\Delta\lambda_i^{(l)}$ and update $\lambda_i^{(\ell+1)}$ by (6) to proceed with next iteration. From the above description, we see that as long as the neighboring buses can send the required data, then each bus can carry out the required computations independently and in parallel.

Once the dual method converges, $\Delta x_i^{(k)}$ is obtained at bus i. The SQP will update $x_i^{(k)}$ by (2) using the obtained $\Delta x_i^{(k)}$ and proceed with next iteration. Therefore, the combination of the SQP and the dual method has achieved the complete decomposition.

3.3   Computational Efficiency of Proposed Parallel Algorithm

Though it looks cumbersome that we have to execute a complete dual method for each SQP iteration, the dual method requires only simple arithmetic operations in performing (6), (7) and (9). Notably, (9) can be solved analytically. This implies that we may need a lot of dual-method iterations, however the computing time for each iteration of the dual method is very short. Above all, all the required computations in (2), (6), (7) and (9) are carried out in the N buses independently and in parallel.

3.4   Convergence of Proposed Parallel Algorithm

Convergence of the *centralized* SQP method for solving (1) with step-size α_k determined by the Armijo's rule had been shown in [11-13]. Similarly, the convergence of the *centralized* dual method with step-size β_l determined by the Armijo's rule had also been shown in [11-13]. Since the parallel algorithm does not use a central processor to calculate a centralized Armijo-type step-size, we will use a small enough step-size, which is taken to be the smallest Armijo-type step-size determined among all iterations. For *typical* application systems, these smallest step-sizes for α_k and β_l can be empirically obtained from numerous simulations.

3.5   Algorithmic Steps at Each Bus of Proposed Parallel Algorithm

The algorithmic steps of the parallel algorithm for each bus, say bus i can be stated below.

Step 0: Initially guess $x_i^{(0)}$; set $k = 0$.

Step 1: Initially guess $\lambda_i^{(0)}$; set $l = 0$.

Step 2: Send the value of $\lambda_i^{(l)}$ to all buses j, $j \in J_i$.

Step 3: If the values of $\lambda_j^{(l)}$ from all buses j, $j \in J_i$ are received, solve (9) analytically for $\Delta x_i(\lambda^{(l)})$.

Step 4: Send the values of $\Delta x_i(\lambda^{(l)})$ to all buses j, $j \in J_i$.

Step 5: If the value of $\Delta x_j(\lambda^{(l)})$ from all buses j, $j \in J_i$ are received, compute $\Delta \lambda_i^{(l)}$ by (7).

Step 6: Update $\lambda_i^{(l+1)} = \lambda_i^{(l)} + \beta \Delta \lambda_i^{(l)}$.

Step 7: Check whether $\| \Delta\lambda_i^{(l)} \| < \varepsilon$, where ε is a small positive real number

$(\varepsilon \approx 10^{-8})$.

Step 8: If not, return to Step 2; if yes, send the convergence signal to the root node.

(Note: the root node will send the convergence signal of the dual method to all busses once receiving the convergence signal from all busses.)

Step 9: If the signal of the convergence of the dual method sent from the root node is received, update $x_i^{(k+1)} = x_i^{(k)} + \alpha\Delta x_i^{(k)}$; otherwise, wait to receive the signal.

Step 10: Check whether $\| \Delta x_i^{(k)}(\lambda^{(l)}) \| < \varepsilon$.

Step 11: If not, return to Step 1; if yes, send the convergence signal to the root node.

Step 12: If the signal of the convergence of the SQP method sent from the root node is received, stop and output the solution; otherwise, wait to receive the signal.

(Note: the root node will send the convergence signal of the SQP method to all busses once receiving the convergence signal from all busses.)

4   Power Flow Problem of Smart Grid

4.1   Preliminaries

The power flow problem in power system is to solve a set of nonlinear power flow balance equations stated in (11) [5-7]:

$$P_{Gi} - P_{Di} - \sum_{j \in J_i} \left[G_{ij}(E_i E_j + F_i F_j) + B_{ij}(F_i E_j - E_i F_j) \right] = 0, \quad i = 1, ..., N$$

$$Q_{Gi} - Q_{Di} - \sum_{j \in J_i} \left[G_{ij}(E_i E_j - F_i F_j) - B_{ij}(F_i E_j + E_i F_j) \right] = 0, \quad i = 1, ..., N \tag{10}$$

Where $P_{G_i}, P_{D_i}, Q_{G_i}$ and Q_{D_i} represent the real power generation, real power demand, reactive power generation and reactive power demand of bus i, respectively; E_i and F_i are the real and imaginary parts of bus i's complex voltage, respectively; G_{ij} and B_{ij} are conductance and subseptance of transmission line from bus i to bus j. In general, there are three types of busses in a power system: *PQ, PV* and *slack bus*. PQ bus has fixed P_{D_i}, Q_{D_i}, P_{G_i} and Q_{G_i}. PV bus has the capability of *regulating* the voltage magnitude, therefore, the P_{G_i} and Q_{G_i} of PV bus can be adjusted to maintain the *desired* voltage magnitude. The slack bus is a bus to pick up all the *slacks* in power system, therefore, the *largest generation bus* in the system is usually taken as the slack bus; this bus's voltage magnitude and phase angle are usually assumed to be given, and its P_{G_i} and Q_{G_i} can be adjusted to maintain the power flow balance of the whole system. For the sake of simplicity in explanation, we assume all the generation buses are PQ buses, while the modifications for taking care of the PV buses can be found in [14].

We can reformulate the power flow balance equations (11) into the following optimization problem:

$$\min \quad \sum_{i=1}^{N} z_{Pi}^2 + z_{Qi}^2$$

$$\text{subject to} \quad P_{Gi} - P_{Di} - \sum_{j \in J_i} \left[G_{ij}(E_i E_j + F_i F_j) + B_{ij}(F_i E_j - E_i F_j) \right] = z_{pi}, \quad i = 1, ..., N \quad (11)$$

$$Q_{Gi} - Q_{Di} - \sum_{j \in J_i} \left[G_{ij}(E_i E_j - F_i F_j) - B_{ij}(F_i E_j + E_i F_j) \right] = z_{qi}, \quad i = 1, ..., N$$

Where z_{pi} and z_{qi} are *slack variables* for the real power and reactive power flow balance equations at bus i. It can be easily proved that if the solution of (11) exists, (11) and (12) are equivalent.

Clearly, (12) has exactly the same form as the nonlinear network optimization problem (1). Therefore, we can use the proposed parallel algorithm to solve (12) in the smart grid.

5 Numerical Simulations

To test the proposed parallel algorithm in solving the power flow problem, we use the standard IEEE 30-bus power system [15] presented in Fig. 2 as the test system. Due to the unavailability of 30 PCs, the simulations are carried out in single *Core 2 Quad* with 2.00 *GB RAM* PC.

We have run twenty cases of power flow problems on the IEEE 30-bus system, and different cases have different power generations and load demands. For each case, we first solve the power flow problem (11) using the conventional *centralized Newton-Raphson's method*, then solve the equivalent optimization problem (16) by the proposed parallel algorithm.

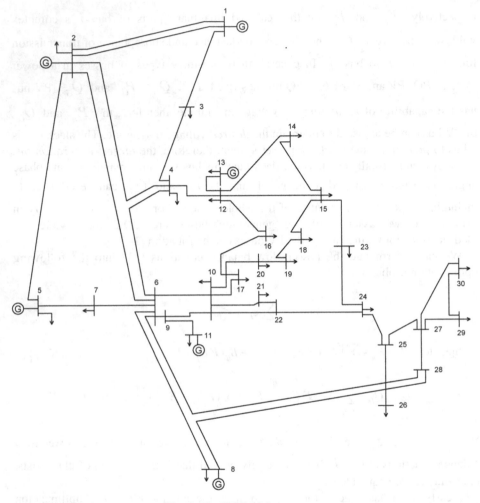

Fig. 2. The IEEE 30-bus system

We use $E_i = 1.0$ p.u. and $F_i = 0.0$ p.u. for every i, $i = 1, \ldots, N$, as the initial guesses of all cases solved by both methods, where p.u. denote the per unit value in power systems [5-7]. Notably, $N = 30$ for the IEEE 30-bus power system. The parameters used in the proposed parallel algorithm are $\alpha_k = 1.0$ for every k, $\beta_l = 0.05$ for every l, $\varepsilon = 10^{-5}$ and $\eta = 20$. Using the solutions obtained by the Newton Raphson's method as the standard solutions, we define

$$\mu_E = \frac{1}{N} \sum_{i=1}^{N} |E_i^{DP} - E_i^{NR}| \quad \text{and} \quad \mu_F = \frac{1}{N} \sum_{i=1}^{N} |F_i^{DP} - F_i^{NR}| \quad \text{as the average}$$

absolute errors of the real and imaginary parts of the complex bus voltage obtained by the proposed parallel algorithm, respectively, where (E_i^{DP}, F_i^{DP}) and (E_i^{NR}, F_i^{NR}) represent the solutions of (E_i, F_i) for $i = 1, \cdots, N$ obtained by the proposed parallel algorithm and Newton Raphson's method, respectively. We also define

$$\sigma_E = \frac{1}{N} \sum_{i=1}^{N} (|E_i^{DP} - E_i^{NR}| - \mu_E)^2 \quad \text{and} \quad \sigma_F = \frac{1}{N} \sum_{i=1}^{N} (|F_i^{DP} - F_i^{NR}| - \mu_F)^2 \quad \text{as}$$

the corresponding variance.

Table 1 presents the average absolute errors and the corresponding variance of the twenty cases. We found that the solutions obtained by the proposed parallel algorithm are exactly the same as the standard solutions up to the third digit after the decimal point. For example, the μ_E for case 1 is 0.00023. Additionally, the variance is also very small. For example, the σ_E for case 1 is 0.00013, which implies that the variations of absolute errors of E_i and F_i of all buses are very small. This demonstrates the accuracy of the proposed parallel algorithm.

Table 1. The average absolute errors and the corresponding variance of the proposed parallel algorithm for solving power flow problems

Case	1	2	3	4	5	6	7	8	9	10	11	12	13	14	15	16	17	18	19	20
$\mu_E \times 10^4$	2.3	2.7	1.9	3.4	2.5	2.6	2.4	2.2	2.7	3.4	2.5	2.1	2.7	2.7	2.4	2.5	2.5	3.2	2.5	2.3
$\sigma_E \times 10^4$	1.3	2.1	1.3	2.3	1.2	1.7	1.6	1.4	1.4	0.2	1.3	1.5	1.3	1.8	1.4	1.9	1.4	1.9	1.4	1.4
$\mu_F \times 10^4$	1.2	1.2	0.9	1.0	0.8	0.9	0.9	0.8	0.9	0.9	0.8	0.9	0.9	0.8	1.0	1.0	1.1	0.8	0.9	1.0
$\sigma_F \times 10^4$	0.8	0.8	0.5	0.6	0.7	0.7	0.6	0.7	0.6	0.6	0.5	0.6	0.6	0.5	0.9	0.8	0.7	0.8	0.7	0.5

The average CPU times consumed by the Newton Raphson's method and the proposed parallel algorithm are 2.16 seconds and 4.95 seconds, respectively. Assuming the communication time for data exchange in the smart grid is negligible, then the proposed parallel algorithm executed in the smart grid will be approximately 13.1 times, which is calculated by $\dfrac{2.16}{(4.95/30)}$, faster than the centralized Newton Raphson's method for solving the power flow of the IEEE 30-bus system in the ideal condition.

6   Conclusions

In this paper, we have presented a parallel algorithm for solving a class of nonlinear network optimization problems in the smart grid with application to the power flow problem. We have demonstrated the accuracy of the proposed algorithm in solving numerous cases of the power flow problem on the IEEE 30-bus system and revealed a speed up factor as high as 13.1 times in the ideal condition in comparison with the centralized Newton Raphson's method.

Acknowledgment. This research work is supported by National Science Council in Taiwan under grant NSC 100-2221-E-182-035.

References

1. Liu, W.-H.E.: Analysis and information integration for smart grid applications. IEEE Power and Energy Society General Meeting (2010)
2. Wei, C.: A conceptual framework for smart grid. In: Asia Pacific Power and Energy Engineering Conference (2010)
3. Rosenfield, M.G.: The smart grid and key research technical challenges. In: Symposium on VLSI Technologies (2010)
4. He, H.: Toward a smart grid: integration of computational intelligence into power grid. In: The 2010 International Joint Conference on Neural Networks (2010)
5. Grainger Jr., J., Stevenson, W.: Power system analysis. McGraw-Hill Inc., New York (1994)
6. Debs, A.S.: Modern power systems control and operation. Kluwer Academic Publishers (1988)
7. Anderson, P.M., Fouad, A.A.: Power system control and stability, 2nd edn. Wiley-IEEE Press (2002)
8. Erisman, A.M., Neves, K.W., Dwarakanath, M.H.: Electric power problems: the mathematical challenge. SIAM (1980)
9. http://gcep.stanford.edu/pdfs/iq9bO_11bOrRuH_veOA2jA/Wollenberg
10. Luenberger, D.G.: Linear and nonlinear programming, 2nd edn. Kluwer Academic Publishers (2003)
11. Lin, C.-H., Lin, S.-Y.: A new dual-type method used in solving optimal power flow problems. IEEE Trans. Power Syst. 12, 1667–1675 (1997)
12. Lin, S.-Y., Ho, Y.C., Lin, C.-H.: An ordinal optimization theory based algorithm for solving the optimal power flow problem with discrete control variables. IEEE Trans. Power Syst. 19(1), 276–286 (2004)
13. Lin, C.-H., Lin, S.-Y.: Distributed optimal power flow problem with discrete control variables of large distributed power systems. IEEE Trans. Power Syst. 23(3), 1383–1392 (2008)
14. Guo, X.-C.: Power flow and state estimation problems in smart grid. Master Thesis, Dept. of EE. Chang Gung Univ, Tao-Yuan, Taiwan, ROC (2011)
15. Abou EL Ela, A.A.: Optimal power flow using differential evolution. Electr. Eng. 91, 69–78 (2009)

Optimization of a Short-Range Proximity Effect Correction Algorithm in E-Beam Lithography Using GPGPUs

Max Schneider, Nikola Belic, Christoph Sambale,
Ulrich Hofmann, and Dietmar Fey

Friedrich-Alexander-University Erlangen-Nuremberg,
Martensstr. 3, 91058 Erlangen, Germany
GenISys GmbH, Eschenstr. 66, 82024 Taufkirchen, Germany
{max.schneider,dietmar.fey}@uni-erlangen.de,
{belic,sambale,hofmann}@genisys-gmbh.com

Abstract. The e-beam lithography is used to provide high resolution circuit patterning for circuit fabrication processes. However, due to electron scattering in resist and substrate it occurs an undesired exposure of regions which are adjacent to the actual exposed regions. These proximity effects represent an essential limitation to the attainable lithographic resolution. Since these effects can be described mathematically, different approaches were investigated to simulate and correct them. The developed algorithms provide the required precision for printing of circuit patterns, but on the other side demand a tremendous computational power. Modern GPGPUs consist of hundreds of processing cores and provide the same computational power as a small cluster. Therefore, the required computational power of correction algorithms may be achieved using GPGPUs. In this paper, we evaluate the achievable performance for a short-range proximity effect correction algorithm using GPGPUs.

Keywords: E-beam lithography, Proximity effect correction, PEC, short-range proximity effect, GPGPUs.

1 Introduction

E-beam lithography is an advanced high resolution technique for writing circuit patterns onto substrates using electron beams. However, electron scattering effects (forward scatter, back-scatter) and process effects (e.g. process blur, beam blur or etch effects) limit the lithographic quality. For example, beam blur results from coulomb interactions between electrons within the emitted electron ray and leads in case of low voltage e-beam processes to a less accurate deposition into the resist [16]. Mask making e-beam lithography systems used in industry have a beam blur of approximatelly 40 nm in diameter [7], whereas systems used in R&D and prototyping can have a beam blur as low as 3 nm. As the trend in manufacturing processes goes to smaller and smaller critical dimensions (CD), these short-range blur effects become the limiting factor in making

Y. Xiang et al. (Eds.): ICA3PP 2012, Part I, LNCS 7439, pp. 41–55, 2012.

the devices. The printed patterns will show strong CD non-linearities, and may even exhibit bridging of circuit patterns. Furthermore, back-scattering events due to electron-nucleus interactions in substrate leads to unwanted resist exposure in areas surrounding the written circuit features. Process and scattering effects combined severely degrade the resolution of written patterns. Therefore, correctional steps are required, such that in resist an energy dose distribution is achieved which corresponds to the desired pattern.

These effects, known as proximity effects, are mathematically describable and thus correctable. There exist many different approaches, which differ in attained quality and required computational power [13]. E.g., correcting blurring effects is complexer and demands more computational power than the operational steps required for compensation of long-range effects (back-scattering). Therefore, physical approaches reducing short-range effects due to beam blur were proposed [1]. However, since manufacturing processes advance to smaller CDs and higher integration densities, short-range effects gain more and more influence. Thus, they need to be corrected too. As the computational complexity of SR-PEC operational steps is even in present extremely challenging, it is necessary to harvest the available parallel processing ressources e.g. multi-core and cluster architectures to achieve acceptable runtimes [11][21].

Our experience with GPGPUs in previous works [19][18][20] have shown that harvesting the computational power of such accelerator devices may provide the means to achieve required processing power, which couldn't be attained through utilization of conventional CPUs alone. Therefore, using GPUs smaller cluster or even a standard PC may be enough for calculating the required exposure dose corrections within by industry imposed timing constraints. In an evaluation study with an industrial partner, the GenISys GmbH in Taufkirchen, Germany, that developes software for proximity effect correction we have investigated which computational speed-up is achievable for the implementation of the short-range proximity effect correction algorithm (SRPEC) by use of NVIDIA's Tesla C2050 GPUs. Depending on the pattern density and specific parameters of the e-beam process (forward scattering range, electron energy, beam blur) performance speed-ups up to approximately 23 times to the original CPU-solution, provided by GenISys GmbH, have been achieved.

This paper is structured as follows: In Section 2 the problem of the scattering effects is presented in more detail, explaining the necessity for proximity effect correction algorithms. Section 3 describes relevant work regarding attempts to reduce proximity effects using different physical methods or correcting them by computational approaches. We present also in literature found solutions using parallel processing. Section 4 describes shortly the manner in that the evaluated SRPEC algorithm processes the data to achieve the correction of proximity effects. Furthermore, we describe also the important implementation details of our GPGPU-algorithm using NVIDIAs CUDA programming framework. In Section 5 we discuss the achieved results of our implementation in comparison to the original implementation. Section 6 concludes this work.

2   Proximity Effect Correction in Detail

In the e-beam writer a tiny focused electron beam is used to scan serially across a surface covered with a resist which is sensitive to electrons. Exposed resist areas undergo molecular transformation, as existing bonds between polymers are destroyed by incident electrons or new bonds are created as those electrons are captured in resist molecules.

Due to Coulomb interactions between electrons within the e-beam current the exposure beam is broadening resulting in a blurring effect on resist surface. While the incident electrons penetrate the resist, and in cases of high energy used they reach also the substrate layer, they can experience small angle forward scattering and large angle back-scattering events. Forward scattering is an event which arises when an incident electron collide with an electron from the exposed matter (figure 1a). The incident electron is repelled by the other, changes minimal its trajectory, because the energy of the incident electron is larger as that of stationary electrons, and transfers a small part of its energy to the atom of the other electron [5]. With this additional energy the atom becomes exited or ionized, whereby in resist matter the molecular chain holding the atoms together may break, changing the solubility characteristic of the resist. If the atom changes its state to ionized then one of its electrons leaves the atom and become a free electron with a small energy level, compared to that of the incident electrons. These so called secondary electrons are responsible for a major part of the resist exposure process. The second scattering effect - back-scattering - occurs when an incident electron collides with the nucleus of a substrate atom. This results in a large scattering angle and thus in a considerable change of original trajection direction, as can be seen in figure 1a. The back-scattered electrons retain most of their original energy, which can lead to an undesired exposure in resist if the electrons are back-scattered into the resist (figure 1b).

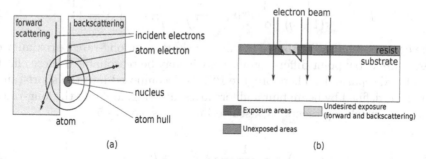

(a)

(b)

Fig. 1. Figure (a) shows a simplified representation of the cause for emergence of electron scattering effects. In figure (b) undesired exposure due to forward and back-scattering effects is demonstrated. The red areas are the actual exposed regions in resist. The yellow region shows undesired exposure, as incident electrons from neighbor areas are scattered into that region. To what level the area is exposed depends on the amount of intruding electrons and their energy.

Both described scattering events and the blurring due to Coulomb interactions are known as the proximity effects and are responsible for degradiation of achievable patterning resolution, e.g. due to undesired exposure in high density circuits patterns components may merge together, resulting in defective circuits. Thus, to achieve high resolution in circuit patterning using e-beam lithography process, correction steps for those effects are required. This is achieved using a digital image processing model of the e-beam process. The main target of this computational model is to determine the energy dose distribution in resist matter due to direct exposure and scatter events and to adjust this distribution in such a manner that the resulting exposure areas match the desired pattern features.

The energy dose distribution $E(x, y)$ in resist matter due to direct exposure and scatter events can be described mathematically by the convolution of the point spread function (PSF) f with the function I describing the exposed layout (eq. 1) [8].

$$E(x, y) = (f * I)(x, y) \tag{1}$$

Depending on the used variation in electron energy during the writing procedure, the layout function I can be represented either as a binary (no variation is applied) or a grayscale image (pattern writing is done using different energy dosage). The PSF itself is a radial symmetric function, which describes the energy deposited in resist when a single point is exposed. It is discretized by a grid of equal sized pixels, assuming that the exposure of each point within the pixel is the same as the exposure at the center of the pixel. The PSF is generally approximated by a sum of two Gaussian functions, which represent the forward and back-scattering, see eq. 2, with η as the ratio factor of forward-to-backward scattering events, r as the radial distance of the currently investigated point from the center of the actual exposed point, α representing the influence range of forward scattering and, β expressing the influence range of back-scattering effects [6].

$$f(r) = \frac{1}{\pi(1 + \eta)} \left[\frac{1}{\alpha^2} \exp\left(-\frac{r^2}{\alpha^2}\right) + \frac{\eta}{\beta^2} \exp\left(-\frac{r^2}{\beta^2}\right) \right] \tag{2}$$

As the energy amount distributed within the short- and long-range proximity of the exposure entry point differs significantly it may be reasonable if these effects are analyzed separately. Therefore, the PSF is decomposed into the short-range component, defined by beam blur and forward scattering, and into the long-range component, which represents back-scattering effects, eq. 3 - 5.

$$f(x, y) = \frac{1}{\pi(1 + \eta)} (s(x, y) + l(x, y)) \tag{3}$$

$$s(x, y) = \frac{1}{a^2} \exp\left(-\frac{r^2}{a^2}\right) \tag{4}$$

$$l(x, y) = \frac{\eta}{\beta^2} \exp\left(-\frac{r^2}{\beta^2}\right) \tag{5}$$

$$E(x,y) = (f \oplus I)(x,y)$$

$$= \frac{1}{\pi(1+\eta)} \left[(s+l) \oplus I\right](x,y) \tag{6}$$

$$= \frac{1}{\pi(1+\eta)} \left[(s \oplus I) + (l \oplus I)\right](x,y)$$

Due to the small range of short-range proximity effects (below 1 μm) a pixel resolution of 1 to 10 nm per pixel for the PSF and layout bitmaps is required to achieve the necessary precision of exposure dosage calculation. In case of the long-range component pixel sizes of about 1 μm are sufficient. Due to these differences in required precision the correction of scattering effects in short- and long-range is accomplished separately as described in equation 6.

3   Related Work

There are two major types of approaches to address proximity effects: the physical and the computational approaches. As the cause for these effects are the physical interactions between electrons in e-beam ray or between intruding electrons and resist or substrate matter the emphasis of the physical approaches lies in investigation of factors affecting these interactions and reducing these effects. However, the proposed approaches are contradictory in the achieved results. E.g., by using low voltage writing procedure [10] back-scattering effects could be reduced. However, pattern writing using low energy electron beams has also a not negligible drawback of broadening beam blur and amplified forward scattering effects in resist. On the other side, among others Rosenfield et al. investigated the resulting proximity effects at higher electron beam settings [17]. They have shown that process and forward scattering effects can be reduced using high voltage lithography systems. However, also this approach is not ideal, as the exposure range of back-scattered electrons increases. Nevertheless, since short-range effects due to beam blur and forward scattering have more impact on the achievable pattern fidelity established e-beam lithography systems, e.g. JEOL [3], Anaheim [11] etc., apply high acceleration voltage writing strategy.

As described, by adjusting the physical characteristics of the e-beam system alone the proximity effects cannot be completely eliminated. Thus, complementary studies for correction of process and scattering effects through computational models have been conducted. Specifying the target of the correctional steps following major correction methods emerged from these research studies.

Linear Methods

Due to back-scattering effects the CD linearity for written pattern features varies. E.g., in high density pattern areas a large number of back-scattering electrons arise lifting the background exposure dosage in the resist to higher levels as in low density or non-pattern areas. Therefore, during the development stage of lithography process the rates of resist dissolution of exposed areas are not identical and the pattern features develop to different widths. To correct this non-linearity of CD widths linear methods try to equalize the resist background exposure dosage in pattern and non-pattern areas to the same level [13]. E.g., GHOST scheme [13] achieves this by a compensating secondary pattern exposure. In the first step the original pattern is used as exposure target. In the second step, the reversed field of the original pattern is used as exposure target adjusting the exposure dosage of pattern and non-pattern areas through superimposing effects. However, since in the correction step a defocused e-beam ray is used, the achievable contrast (defined as normalized difference between maximum and minimum absorbed energy intensity in resist for a given feature) is degraded [4]. This means that the fidelity of developed feature edges is compromized.

Non-linear Equalization Methods

Using non-linear convolution of the PSF with a function representing the desired dose distribution within the resist non-linear equalization methods try to improve the contrast of pattern features. The PSF itself models process and scattering effects in resist and substrate using the characteristics of the particular matter and energy settings of the e-beam writer. One representative of the non-linear equalization approaches is the self-consistent dose correction method from M. Parikh [14]. Parikh proposed a pixel-based convolution method of the PSF and the pattern data, considering only the pattern and completely disregarding non-pattern areas. Thus, the achieved correction results were not exact [12]. In contrast to the convolution method H. Eisenmann et. al [6] proposed the deconvolution of the PSF and the pattern function in Fourier domain for proximity effect correction. But also this method doesn't achieve the required precision due to necessary filtering of high frequency oscilations resulting from inversed PSF function.

Non-linear Edge Equalization Methods

From non-linear equalization methods developed non-linear edge equalization methods accomplish proximity effect correction by correction of the exposure dosage at feature edges. They specify that, for all feature edges the following must apply:

- exposure dosage at the edge middle corresponds to minimum value required for dissolution in development stage
- exposure dosage for all points below the edge middle is smaller than the minimum value required for dissolution
- exposure dosage for all points above the edge middle is larger than the minimum value required for dissolution

Thus, applying to the whole resist area (also non-pattern) extended convolution method, described by M. Parikh [14], and considering the above requirements, edge equalization and thus better CD control is accomplished. One of the first published methods representing the edge equalization approach is the integral equation approximate solution method from Pavkovich [15]. However, in his work Pavkovich ignored the short-range effects as the feature sizes were considerable larger than from short-range effects resulting exposure blurring. However, as already stated the trend of manufacturing processes goes to smaller CDs and thus short-range effects must be considered, too.

As the feature sizes and the distances between pattern elements shrink pattern density increases resulting in higher computational requirements for PEC algorithms. To meet these requirements parallel architectures are utilized. To the best of our knowledge currently only PC-cluster systems and multi-threading (multi-core CPUs, DSPs) solutions are available [2][11]. E.g., S.-Y. Lee from the Department of Electrical Engineering at Auburn University used a MPI cluster of 10 to 24 Sun Ultra Sparc workstations to analyze the achievable performance. For that, his group developed proximity effect correction tool, named PYRA-MID. They attained a speed-up of approximately factor 15 using 20 worker for a large non-uniform (regarding the distribution of circuit features on the pattern) circuit pattern and a factor of 10 for a pattern with uniformly distributed feature elements [9]. Fujitsu Limited, Japan, and Semiconductor Leading Edge Technologies Inc., Japan, have published results achieved by utilization of a cluster system with 10 workstations based on Intel Pentium IV 1.8 GHz and 2.4 GHz for their approach for proximity effect correction. For an actual 70 nm design-rule SoC device data, the computation time of 7.8 hours on an UltraSPARC II 360 MHz processor with four cores, was reduced to only 10.3 minutes using their cluster system [11]. Therefore, this group suggests increasing the cluster size to achieve acceptable timings for larger pattern layouts [21].

4   Short-Range Proximity Effect Correction Algorithm

The difference between the short- and long range correction algorithm is the way the convolution is carried out. In case of the long range PEC a 2D pixel based convolution is used, as described in eq. 1, that covers the whole layout area. Due to high requirements regarding the pixel resolution in short-range algorithm the resulting timings for applying the convolution operation to the whole layout area would be too high for a practical application. Therefore, for the short range part a figure based convolution is performed, due to the fact that in general the number of figures is much lower than the number of pixels required to resolve the short range interactions. This approach is similar to the approximate solution method presented by Pavkovich [15]. Using polygon elements corresponding to the pattern features and a set of pre-computed lookup tables that deliver the convolution result per basic element, e.g. a trapezoid, a magnitude faster processing is achieved compared to the pixel-based approach.

Three steps are required to compute the necessary energy dose settings for the e-beam writer used for patterning of feature elements. At first a neighbor search is conducted for each figure within the influence range of short-range effects. Subsequently, the influence factors are computed, which describe to what degree the exposure distribution in neighboring figures contributes to the exposure of the current figure. The last step is an iterative procedure which is used to adjust the final exposure dosage of each feature in such a way that a uniform energy distribution in layout material is achieved.

4.1   Neighbor Search

To achieve the required correction for a feature element not all other figures present in a layout must be considered. Only figures within the short-range proximity of the currently examined element must be included in correction process. Thus, the first step of figure based correction method is a search of neighboring elements in proximity of each shape.

In figure 2 an exemplary feature layout is presented. The simplest way to determine the neighborhood relationship between existing polygons would be a overlap comparison of each figures bounding box[1]. For the SRPEC the original bounding boxes are expanded by three times the range of influence of short-range effects in order to obtain all SRPEC-relevant polygons. The factor three is an assurance criterium, by that also unanticipated forward scattering influences from polygons farther away are considered. If the boxes overlap then it is assumed that the corresponding figures are neighbors. Of course, in case of triangle or trapezoid elements it may be the case that although the extended bounding boxes overlap the figures itself are not neighbors.

To reduce the required time for finding the neighbors for each figure the number of comparisons have to be reduced to the necessary ones only. This is achieved by establishing an order within the polygon entries by sorting the entries using the lower left x-coordinate of the bounding boxes. In figure 2 this order is shown through the "Sort LLx"-values at the bottom of the figure. Then, we determine the search range within the sorted entries to find the necessary comparison elements. E.g., in figure 2 it can be seen that the search range for polygon with index 2 within the sorted polygon entries is set to polygons with indices 1, 2 - 4, 6 and 14 -15, even though polygons 14 and 15 reside not within short-range proximity. In next step the determined search range is used to establish the described relationships using the range of forward scattering events.

In our CUDA implementation we use CUDPP's radix sort implementation to establish the described order of polygon entries. Furthermore, an one-thread-for-each-polygon based approach is used to determine the required neighbor search range and the neighbor relations. Used polygon data is stored in a manner such that the load/store accesses to main memory in GPGPU are executed in coalescent way allowing best possible usage of available memory bandwidth. However, as the search ranges for each polygon may differ the coalescing access to polygon data may also be compromized. Therefore, we set the shared memory

---

[1] Bounding box corresponds to a rectangle figure with minimal dimension which surrounds entirely the feature element.

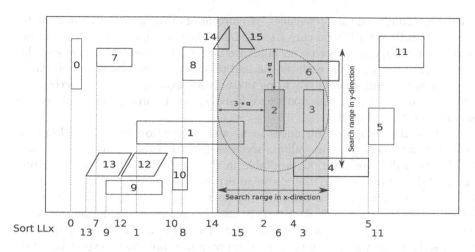

Fig. 2. Exemplary feature layout and neighborhood relations. "Sort LLx" shows by lower x-coordinates sorted polygon indices. The green elipse is the actual range of short-range proximity effects affecting polygon with index 2. The red rectangle is the used discretized search range for neighbor polygons within the influence range of short range effects.

/ L1 cache configuration of GPU architectures with compute capability 2.0 and above such that L1 cache is prefered (in case of Tesla C2050 it means, we use a 48 KByte L1 cache). By this, we achieve a high reusage rate of already accessed polygon data relieving the pressure on the main memory bandwidth.

4.2 Influence Calculation

After neighborhood relations are established it is necessary to compute each neighbors exposure influence degree due to scattering events. In general the exposure influence of other figures to another figure is computed through calculating the distance in x- and y-direction of neighboring polygon corner points to the currently processed figure and determine the exposure dosage described by the discretized two-dimensional PSF-look-up table using the distance values as coordinate values. In our algorithm the PSF is separated in short- and long-range component and stored in look-up tables. For our evaluation only the short-range PSF-tables are necessary.

In our CUDA implementation we use a thread block per figure approach. This means, each thread block running on a different multi-processor of a GPU computes the influence degree of all neighbors for one pattern feature. If there are lesser thread blocks than elements in layout, then some thread blocks compute the influence values for multiple elements. Within a thread block each thread is assigned to a neighbor. If more neighbor elements are present than threads exist in a thread block, then some threads compute the exposure influence degree on current figure for multiple neighbor elements. Furthermore, the PSF look-up tables are not stored in conventional memory space of the GPUs, but are accessed through texture references. If conventional memory space is used for these tables then GPU's on-chip L1 and L2 caches are shared between accesses to polygon data, e.g. corner point, influence factors etc., and table accesses. This may result in higher cache replacement and reload rates impairing the achievable memory access performance. By using textures for look-up tables the accesses to PSF data are routed through texture exclusive caches improving the replacement and reload rates of all data.

Because the computed distances in x- and y-direction used as look-up coordinates are floating point values, accesses to PSF tables may occur, which lies between discrete positions available in digital domain. In case single precision PSF values are used the native interpolation feature of texture accesses is automatically applied to compute the correct value at these floating point coordinates. However, our algorithm is based completely on double precision computations. Therefore, it cannot benefit from this feature. To compensate this disadvantage we have implemented an own interpolation method based on accesses to four nearest discrete coordinates and linear interpolation between these positions. Because texture caches are optimized for two-dimensional spatial locality, these additional memory accesses don't impaire the main memory bandwidth performance.

4.3   Equation Solver

After the last step we have for each layout feature a list of neighbors with their corresponding exposure influence factors on that feature. The next and also the last step is an iterative process where the following equation 7 has to be solved for each figure.

$$X = I_i * D_i + \sum_{j=0, j!=i}^{N} I_j * D_j \tag{7}$$

I_i is the exposure influence factor of the figure i on itself and I_j corresponds to the influence factor of neighbor element j on figure i. D_x is the electron dosage used to write the figure x. N is number of neighbors for current figure and may vary from figure to figure. X is the target dosage which is wanted for final resist exposure result in a written pattern. The aim of this step is to optimize the dose D_x for each figure x in such a way, that an uniform energy distribution is achieved in exposed layout. In each equation we set in the first iteration the energy dose value D_j of neighbor elements j to a specific value, assuming D_i in equation i as unknown and solve this equation for D_i. Then the values of all dose values D_x are updated to computed ones and next iteration is executed using these dose values. This procedure is repeated until no further alteration of dose values is attained.

In case of the equation solver we use also a thread block per figure approach like in the case of influence calculation. For computation of dose times influence values of available neighbors we use shared memory reduction kernel in each thread block. Therefore, to compute a complete iteration we don't have to restart our kernel for synchronization of memory accesses within different thread blocks. However, because each following iteration requires in last iteration computed dose values of neighboring figures we have to restart the kernel between iterations. This results in additional overhead for cache and register values reinitialization which impaires the achieved performance for this kernel. Using the same thread block count as multi-processors available in GPU hardware, a kernel wide global synchronization without restarting may be achieved. On the other side, as the multi-processor count is currently relatively small (14 multiprocessors in case of the Tesla C2050) it may result in even worser performance if the figure count is considerably larger as the processor count. Nevertheless, this issue is one important point in our future work.

5   Results

We have evaluated the achievable performance of our CUDA SRPEC algorithm using a 256×256 thread-grid on a NVIDIA's Tesla C2050 GPGPU card installed in a server system with two sockets each of those with an Intel Xeon X5650 Hexcore-CPU running at 2.66 GHz. We compared the required runtimes of the original SRPEC CPU implementation using in parallel up to 8 CPU cores versus our CUDA implementation using a combination of one CPU and the desribed GPU card. For evaluation we used a scope of different pattern layouts and e-beam settings.

Table 1. Evaluation pattern details

Design Description	Dimension (in μm^2)	Figure size (in μm^2)	Figure distance (in μm)	Figure count
CA pattern	1.37×1.14	0.04×0.04	0.01	appr. 360
RA pattern	199.95×99.95	0.05×0.05	0.05	1997001
RRA pattern	92.02×99.95	0.05×0.05	0.05	915400
OPC pattern	235.08×115.14	variable	variable	-

For manufacturing of memory devices typical patterns are rectangular contact hole arrays (RA). We used such a test-pattern with a size of $199.95 \times 99.95\ \mu m^2$, figure CDs of $0.05 \times 0.05\ \mu m^2$ and a constant pitch between contact holes of $0.05\ \mu m$ (small extract shown in figure 3a). A further evaluation pattern is by 10 degree rotated contact hole pattern with a dimension of $92.02 \times 99.95\ \mu m^2$, shown in figure 3b and abbrevated as RRA in table 1. In table 1, the given figure number for RRA pattern corresponds to the number of non-rotated rectangles in original RA pattern. As trapezoidal figures may be fractured by preprocessing steps before SRPEC algorithm to enable a simpler computational model the exact figure count for this pattern is not known, but it is either equal or larger to the given number. Also a typical pattern in current manufacturing processes is the OPC pattern (figure 3c). It consists mostly of long rectangular features with CDs between $0.04\ nm$ and $0.2\ nm$ and with a variable length. As the fracturing process is also applied to these features and due to the high density

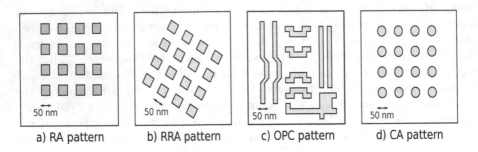

a) RA pattern   b) RRA pattern   c) OPC pattern   d) CA pattern

Fig. 3. For performance evaluation used patterns

Table 2. E-beam process settings

Design Description	alpha (in μm)	gamma (in μm)	nue
CA pattern	0.05	0.1	0.5
RA pattern	0.1	0.2	0.5
RRA pattern	0.1	0.2	0.5
OPC pattern	0.1	0.5	0.52

of this pattern no exact number can be given, but there are several thousands of described feature elements. One from R&D field comming pattern is the circle array layout (CA), shown in figure 3d. It is similar to the RA pattern, but instead of rectangles it consists of circle elements with a $0.04 \times 0.04 \ \mu m^2$ CD and 0.01 μm pitch between the cirles.

Used e-beam settings are given in the table 2. The parameter *gamma* is an extension to in equation 2 described PSF function model. It represents the so called mid-range effects (scattering effects arising in complex material) and is frequently used to achieve a better correction of proximity effects. Mid-range effects contributes also to additional exposure in short-range domain. Parameter *nue* represents the energy deposited in the resist due to mid-range scattering effects.

In table 3 the achieved correction runtimes for the described patterns and e-beam settings are presented. The shown timings for our GPU implementation are achieved using one CPU thread and one Tesla C2050 device. As can be seen except for the RA pattern for our CUDA implementation a large speed-up factor of up to 22.84 times (see table 4) compared to the original CPU implementation using one thread is attained. The achievable performance is dependent on from pattern features resulting computational complexity of required correction steps. In case of more complex polygons like circles in CA pattern or trapezoidal figures in OPC and RRA pattern more look-ups and complexer operations are required as in case of simple rectangles. Thus, these patterns benefit from the tremendous computational power provided by GPGPUs. In case of the RA pattern it can

Table 3. Achieved SRPEC runtimes (in minutes : seconds) for evaluated designs. Shown GPU implementation runtimes are attained using 1 CPU Thread and 1 Tesla C2050.

CPU count	CA		RA		RRA		OPC	
	only cpus	gpu	only cpus	gpu	only cpus	gpu	only cpus	gpu
1	4:57		3:52		26:30		12:00	
2	2:49		2:16		15:54		9:13	
4	1:26	0:13	1:47	2:04	8:54	1:40	5:46	0:45
6	1:01		1:26		6:01		4:10	
8	0:49		1:10		4:40		3:27	

be seen that not only the GPU does not provide a high speed-up but also the CPU implementation is not able to achieve a considerable performance upgrade. As the computational complexity of this pattern is low, the sequential accesses to the pattern database for storing the computed results limit the achievable performance. In case of CUDA SRPEC algorithm this leads to even higher performance degradation, because the required time for computation shrinks to a fraction of original timings and thus more sequential accesses to the database are necessary at the same time. Furthermore, due to an additional optimization in CPU code, which enables reusage of already computed results for all figures, a better speed-up is attainable using CPUs compared to GPUs. This optimization is not yet implemented in our CUDA code. Furthermore, GPU memory initialization and data transfers between system and GPU memory are required for GPU SRPEC algorithm. All these facts result in severely impaired GPU performance.

Table 4. Corresponding speed-ups to the runtimes shown in table 3. All speed-up factors are calculated in regard to the required computation runtime using 1 CPU.

CPU count	CA		RA		RRA		OPC	
	only cpus	gpu	only cpus	gpu	only cpus	gpu	only cpus	gpu
1	1.00		1.00		1.00		1.00	
2	1.75		1.70		1.67		1.30	
4	3.47	22.84	2.17	1.87	2.98	15.90	2.08	16.00
6	4.83		2.69		4.40		2.88	
8	6.11		3.30		5.68		3.48	

6 Conclusion and Future Work

We presented an evaluation study for achievable performance through utilization of GPGPU acceleration devices for the short-range proximity effect correction algorithm. By efficiently harvesting the available GPGPU ressores like texture or shared memory, running hundreds of threads in parallel a significant performance speed-up compared to conventional multi-core CPU-systems is yielded. Thus, in contrast to present approaches achieving runtime reduction through increasing of used cluster size, an even larger runtime reduction can be achieved if instead of additional PCs GPGPU devices are deployed. The shown speed-up factors suggest that even smaller cluster may attain the same or even higher performance level.

In future work, we would like to extend the current GPU implementation by additional algorithm steps used for correction of long- and mid-range proximity effects. This is necessary as the currently achieved speed-up for the whole PEC algorithm implemented in LayoutBEAMER is not significant enough (maximum speed-up is factor 5) to make the investment in GPGPU technology reasonable. Additionally, we want to investigate which speed-up is attainable in case multiple GPUs in the same system are used in cooperational manner for PEC processes.

References

1. Abe, T., Hattori, Y., Iijima, T., Anze, H., Shimizu, S.O.K.T., Matsuki, K., Tojo, H.I., Takigawa, T.: High-accuracy proximity effect correction for mask writing. Japanese Journal of Applied Physics 46(2), 826–833 (2007)
2. Boegli, V., Johnson, L., Kao, H., Veneklasen, L., Hofmann, U., Finkelstein, I., Stovall, S., Rishton, S.: Implementation of real-time proximity effect correction in a raster shaped beam tool. Papers from the 44th International Conference on Electron, Ion, and Photon Beam Technology and Nanofabrication, vol. 18, pp. 3138–3142 (November 2000)
3. Bojko, R.J., Li, J., He, L., Baehr-Jones, T., Hochberg, M., Aida, Y.: Electron beam lithography writing strategies for low loss, high confinement silicon optical waveguides. Journal of Vacuum Science & Technology B: Microelectronics and Nanometer Structures 29(6), 06F3091–06F3096 (2011)
4. Crandall, R., Hofmann, U., Lozes, R.L.: Contrast limitations in electron-beam lithography. Papers from the 43rd International Conference on Electron, Ion, and Photon Beam Technology and Nanofabrication, AVS, vol. 17, pp. 2945–2947 (November 1999)
5. Dal'zotto, B., Dugourd, H., Lerme, M., Méot, F.: Advances in proximity effect measurement and correction in electron beam lithography. Microelectronic Engineering 3(1-4), 105–112 (1985)
6. Eisenmann, H., Waas, T., Hartmann, H.: Proxecco - proximity effect correction by convolution. Journal of Vacuum Science & Technology B: Microelectronics and Nanometer Structures 11(6), 2741–2745 (1993)
7. Keil, K., Hauptmann, M., Kretz, J., Constancias, C., Pain, L., Bartha, J.-W.: Resolution and total blur: Correlation and focus dependencies in e-beam lithography. Journal of Vacuum Science & Technology B: Microelectronics and Nanometer Structures 27(6), 2722–2726 (2009)
8. Klimpel, T., Schulz, M., Zimmermann, R., Stock, H.-J., Zepka, A.: Model based hybrid proximity effect correction scheme combining dose modulation and shape adjustments. Journal of Vacuum Science & Technology B: Microelectronics and Nanometer Structures 29(6),06F315 – 06F315 (2011)
9. Lee, S.-Y., Anupongpaibool, N.: Optimization of distributed implementation of grayscale electron-beam proximity effect correction on a temporally heterogeneous cluster. In: Proceedings of the 19th IEEE International Parallel and Distributed Processing Symposium (IPDPS 2005) - Workshop 13, vol. 14. IEEE Computer Society (2005)

10. Marrian, C.R.K., Dobisz, E.A., Dagata, J.A.: Electron-beam lithography with the scanning tunneling microscope. Journal of Vacuum Science & Technology B 10(6), 2877–2881 (1992)
11. Ogino, K., Hoshino, H., Machida, Y., Osawa, M., Arimoto, H., Takahashi, K., Yamashita, H.: High-performance proximity effect correction for sub-70 nm design rule system on chip devices in 100 kv electron projection lithography. Journal of Vacuum Science & Technology B: Microelectronics and Nanometer Structures 21(6), 2663–2667 (2003)
12. Owen, G.: Methods for proximity effect correction in electron lithography. Journal of Vacuum Science & Technology B: Microelectronics and Nanometer Structures 8(6), 1889–1892 (1990)
13. Owen, G., Rissman, P.: Proximity effect correction for electron beam lithography by equalization of background dose. Journal of Applied Physics 54(6), 3573–3581 (1983)
14. Parikh, M.: Corrections to proximity effects in electron beam lithography. ii. implementation. Journal of Applied Physics 50(6), 4378–4382 (1979)
15. Pavkovich, J.M.: Proximity effect correction calculations by the integral equation approximate solution method. Journal of Vacuum Science & Technology B: Microelectronics and Nanometer Structures 4(1), 159–163 (1986)
16. Rio, D., Constancias, C., Saied, M., Icard, B., Pain, L.: Study on line edge roughness for electron beam acceleration voltages from 50 to 5 kV. Journal of Vacuum Science & Technology B: Microelectronics and Nanometer Structures 27(6), 2512–2517 (2009)
17. Rosenfield, M., Rishton, S., Kern, D., Seeger, D., Whiting, C.: A study of proximity effects at high electron-beam voltages for x-ray mask fabrication part 1: Additive mask processes. Microelectronic Engineering 13(1-4), 165–172 (1991)
18. Schäfer, A., Fey, D.: High performance stencil code algorithms for gpgpus. Procedia Computer Science 4(0), 2027–2036 (2011)
19. Schneider, M., Fey, D., Kapusi, D., Machleidt, T.: Performance comparison of designated preprocessing white light interferometry algorithms on emerging multi- and many-core architectures. Procedia Computer Science 4(0), 2037–2046 (2011)
20. Seidler, R., Schmidt, M., Schäfer, A., Fey, D.: Comparison of selected parallel path planning algorithms on gpgpus and multi-core. In: Proceedings of the Annual International Conference on Advances in Distributed and Parallel Computing, pp. A133–A139 (November 2010)
21. Yamashita, H., Yamamoto, J., Koba, F., Arimoto, H.: Proximity effect correction using blur map in electron projection lithography. In: Advanced Lithography Applications, vol. 23, pp. 3188–3192 (December 2005)

Exploiting Multi-grain Parallelism for Efficient Selective Sweep Detection

Nikolaos Alachiotis, Pavlos Pavlidis, and Alexandros Stamatakis

The Exelixis Lab, Scientific Computing Group
Heidelberg Institute for Theoretical Studies
Heidelberg, Germany
{Nikolaos.Alachiotis,Pavlos.Pavlidis,Alexandros.Stamatakis}@h-its.org

Abstract. Selective sweep detection localizes targets of recent and strong positive selection by analyzing single nucleotide polymorphisms (SNPs) in intra-species multiple sequence alignments. Substantial advances in wet-lab sequencing technologies currently allow for generating unprecedented amounts of molecular data. The increasing number of sequences and number of SNPs in such large multiple sequence alignments cause prohibiting long execution times for population genetics data analyses that rely on selective sweep theory. To alleviate this problem, we have recently implemented fine- and coarse-grain parallel versions of our open-source tool OmegaPlus for selective sweep detection that is based on the ω statistic. A performance issue with the coarse-grain parallelization is that individual coarse-grain tasks exhibit significant run-time differences, and hence cause load imbalance. Here, we introduce a significantly improved multi-grain parallelization scheme which outperforms both the fine-grain as well as the coarse-grain versions of OmegaPlus with respect to parallel efficiency. The multi-grain approach exploits both coarse-grain and fine-grain operations by using available threads/cores that have completed their coarse-grain tasks to accelerate the slowest task by means of fine-grain parallelism. A performance assessment on real-world and simulated datasets showed that the multi-grain version is up to 39% and 64.4% faster than the coarse-grain and the fine-grain versions, respectively, when the same number of threads is used.

1 Introduction

Charles Darwin attributed evolution to natural selection among species. Natural selection occurs when members of a population of species die and are replaced by offsprings that are better adapted to survive and reproduce in a given environment. The field of population genetics studies the genetic composition of populations as well as changes in this genetic composition that are, for instance, driven by natural selection or genetic drift. The input data for population genetic analyses is a multiple sequence alignment (MSA), essentially an $n \times m$ data matrix that contains n DNA sequences with a length of m nucleotide characters each (also denoted as columns or alignment sites). Recent advances in sequencing technology (e.g., Next-Generation Sequencers (NGS)) are currently generating a

Y. Xiang et al. (Eds.): ICA3PP 2012, Part I, LNCS 7439, pp. 56–68, 2012.
© Springer-Verlag Berlin Heidelberg 2012

spectacular amount of molecular sequence data because entire genomes can now be rapidly and accurately sequenced at low cost. Therefore, we urgently need to adapt, optimize, and parallelize state-of-the-art tools for population genetic data analysis such that they scale to large emerging genomic datasets and keep pace with the molecular data avalanche.

In population genetics, statistical tests that rely on selective sweep theory [1] are widely used to identify targets of recent and strong positive selection. This is achieved by analyzing single nucleotide polymorphisms (SNPs) in intra-species MSAs. A recently introduced method for detecting selective sweeps is the ω statistic [2], which has been implemented by Jensen et al. [3] and Pavlidis et al. [4]. We recently released OmegaPlus (http://www.exelixis-lab.org/software.html), a fast sequential open-source implementation of the ω statistic. OmegaPlus has lower memory requirements than competing codes and can analyze whole-genome MSAs on off-the-shelf multi-core desktop systems. The kernel function of OmegaPlus that dominates execution times consist of a dynamic programming algorithm for calculating sums of so-called linkage-disequilibrium (LD) values in sub-genomic regions (fractions of the genome). We also developed two parallel versions: OmegaPlus-F, which parallelizes the dynamic programming matrix computations at a fine-grain level, and OmegaPlus-C, which divides the alignment into sub-regions and assigns these individual and independent tasks to threads (coarse-grain parallelism).

The above, relatively straightforward parallelization schemes yielded acceptable, yet sub-optimal speedups because both approaches exhibit some drawbacks. Exploiting fine-grain parallelism in dynamic programming matrices, especially when these are relatively small, can exhibit unfavorable computation-to-synchronization ratios. This is the case in OmegaPlus-F, despite the fact that we used an efficient thread synchronization strategy based on busy waiting [5]. Thus, because of the relatively small amount of operations required per dynamic programming matrix cell, the fine-grain parallel version only scales well if the input MSA comprises hundreds to thousands of sequences. Unfortunately, the coarse-grain OmegaPlus-C version also faces a parallel scalability problem: the variability of the density of SNPs in the MSA can cause substantial load imbalance among threads. Despite the fact that all sub-genomic regions are of the same size, tasks that encompass regions with high SNP density require significantly longer execution times. Note that the time required to compute the ω statistic in a sub-genomic region (a task) increases quadratically with the number of SNPs in that region. Hence, the parallel performance of OmegaPlus-C is limited by the slowest thread/task, that is, the thread assigned to the sub-genomic region with the highest SNP density.

To alleviate this load imbalance issue, we developed a multi-grain parallelization strategy that combines the coarse- and fine-grain approaches. The underlying idea is to use fast threads that have completed their task to accelerate the ω statistic computations of slower threads in a fine-grain way. In other words, when a thread completes its coarse-grain task early, it is assigned to help the thread that is expected to finish last at that particular point in time. Multi-grain parallelization approaches have also been reported in evolutionary placement of short reads [6] as well as to compute the phylogenetic likelihood function on the Cell Broadband Engine [7].

The remainder of this paper is organized as follows: In Section 2, we describe the ω statistic that relies on linkage disequilibria, and we briefly outline the fine- and coarse-grain parallelization approaches in Section 3. Thereafter, we introduce the multi-grain approach and the implementation of the dynamic helper thread assignment mechanism (Section 4). A detailed performance evaluation of the multi-grain version of OmegaPlus is provided in Section 5. We conclude in Section 6 and address directions of future work.

2   The LD Pattern of Selective Sweeps

The LD is used to capture the non-random association of states at different MSA positions. Selective sweep theory [1] predicts a pattern of excessive LD in each of the two alignment regions that flank an evolutionarily advantageous *and* recently fixed mutation. This genomic pattern can be detected by using the ω statistic.

Assume a genomic window with S SNPs that is split into a left and a right sub-region with l and $S - l$ SNPs, respectively. The ω statistic is then computed as follows:

$$\omega = \frac{\left(\binom{l}{2} + \binom{S-l}{2}\right)^{-1}\left(\sum_{i,j\in L} r_{ij}^2 + \sum_{i,j\in R} r_{ij}^2\right)}{(l(S - l))^{-1}\sum_{i\in L, j\in R} r_{ij}^2}, \tag{1}$$

where r_{ij}^2 represents one common LD measure that simply is the squared correlation coefficient between sites i and j. The ω statistic quantifies to which extent average LD is increased on either side of the selective sweep (see numerator of Equation 1) but *not across* the selected site (see denominator of Equation 1). The area between the left and right sub-regions is considered as the center of the selective sweep.

In sub-genomic regions, that is, candidate regions of limited length (some thousand bases/sites long), the ω statistic can be computed at each interval between two SNPs. S refers to the total number of SNPs, and the goal is to detect that l which will maximize the ω statistic. When scanning whole-genome datasets, the analysis becomes more complicated. Evaluating the ω statistic at each interval between two SNPs can become computationally prohibitive since hundreds of thousands of SNPs may occur in an entire chromosome. Furthermore, S can not be defined as the overall amount of SNPs along the whole chromosome. This would also be biologically meaningless because a selective sweep usually only affects the polymorphic patterns in the neighborhood of a beneficial (advantageous) mutation.

To process whole-genome datasets, we assume a grid of equidistant locations L_i, $1 < i < k$; k is defined by the user, for which the ω statistic is computed. We also assume a user-defined sub-genomic region of size R_{MAX} that extends to either side of a beneficial mutation. Such a sub-genomic region represents the genomic area (neighborhood) in which polymorphic patterns may have been affected by the selective sweep. OmegaPlus evaluates the ω statistic for all possible sub-regions that are enclosed in R_{MAX} and reports the maximum ω value as well as the sub-region size that maximizes the ω statistic. Figure 1 illustrates two consecutive steps of the ω statistic calculation at a specific location. The user-defined R_{MAX} value determines the left and right borders (vertical thin lines). The ω statistic is computed for all possible sub-regions that lie within the left and right borders, and the maximum ω value is reported. The process is repeated for all locations for which the ω statistic needs to be computed.

step i

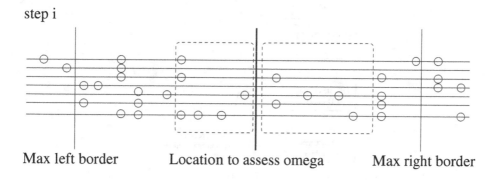

step i+1

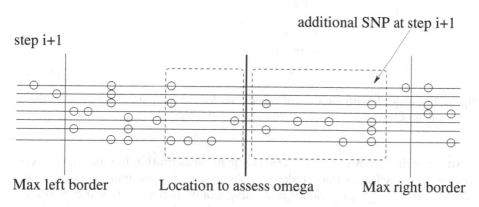

Fig. 1. The process of detecting the sub-regions that maximize the ω statistic for a given location/selective sweep. The goal is to evaluate the ω statistic at the alignment position denoted by the thick vertical line. The thin vertical lines to the left and right side of the thick line indicate the sub-region borders as defined by R_{MAX}. At step i, only the SNPs enclosed within the dashed-line areas contribute to the calculation of the ω statistic. At step $i + 1$, one more SNP that belongs to the right sub-region contributes to the ω statistic calculation. Calculations are repeated for all possible sub-regions within the left and right borders (vertical thin lines). The maximum ω value and the associated sub-region sizes are then reported.

An overview of the computational workflow of OmegaPlus on whole-genome datasets is provided in Figure 2. The Figure shows the basic steps for the calculation of an ω statistic value at a given position. The same procedure is repeated to compute ω statistic values at all positions that have been specified by the user. Initially, we check whether sub-genomic regions, as defined by R_{MAX}, overlap. If they overlap, the data is re-indexed to avoid recalculation of previously already computed values and thereby save operations. Thereafter, all required new LD values are computed as well as all sums of LDs in the region. Finally, all possible ω statistic values for the specific region are computed.

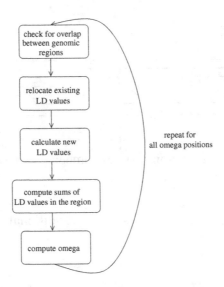

Fig. 2. The basic algorithmic steps of OmegaPlus for the computation of the ω statistic at a number of alignment positions requested by the user

An algorithmic advance of the ω statistic implementation in OmegaPlus over previous approaches is that it deploys a dynamic programming algorithm to calculate all $\sum_{i \in L, j \in R} r_{ij}^2$ values in a sub-genomic region G. Given S SNPs in G, a matrix M of size $S^2/2$ is computed as follows:

$$
M_{i,j} = \begin{cases} 0 & 1 \leq i \leq S, \ j = i \\ r_{ij} & 2 \leq i \leq S, \ j = i - 1 \\ M_{i,j+1} + M_{i-1,j} + & \\ M_{i-1,j+1} + r_{ij} & 3 \leq i < S, \ i - 1 > j \geq 0. \end{cases} \tag{2}
$$

Thereafter, all $\sum_{i \in L, j \in R} r_{ij}^2$, $\sum_{i,j \in L} r_{ij}^2$, and $\sum_{i,j \in R} r_{ij}^2$ values required by Equation 1 are retrieved from the matrix.

3   Fine- and Coarse-Grain Parallelizations

The fine-grain parallelization of Equation 2 is implemented by evenly distributing the independent r_{ij}^2 calculations (that dominate run-times for computing M) among all threads. Furthermore, the computation of all ω values at an alignment position (one ω value for every l in Equation 1) is also evenly distributed among threads. Figure 3 illustrates how the basic algorithmic steps of Figure 2 are executed by multiple threads using this fine-grain parallelization scheme. As already mentioned in Section 1, the computation of the r_{ij}^2 values is relatively fast for a small number of sequences compared to thread synchronization times. Furthermore, if the infinite site model [8] is assumed, the DNA input data can be transformed into a binary data representation. In this case, r_{ij}^2 computations become even faster because computing r_{ij}^2 on DNA data requires approximately 10 times (on average) more arithmetic operations than on binary data.

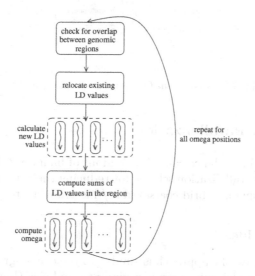

Fig. 3. Fine-grain OmegaPlus parallelization

Unlike the fine-grain approach, our coarse-grain scheme is not affected by an unfavorable computation-to-synchronization ratio since no thread synchronization is required. Each thread is assigned a different sub-genomic region (part of the input MSA) and carries out all ω statistic operations in that region. Note that we generate as many sub-genomic regions (tasks) as there are threads/cores available. Thus, threads need to synchronize only once to determine if they have all completed the analysis of their individual sub-genomic region/task. Figure 4 outlines this coarse-grain parallelization scheme. Since synchronization is only required to ensure that all tasks have been completed, the performance of the coarse-grain approach is limited by the run time of the slowest thread/task. The slowest thread is always the one that has been assigned to the sub-genomic region with the highest number of SNPs.

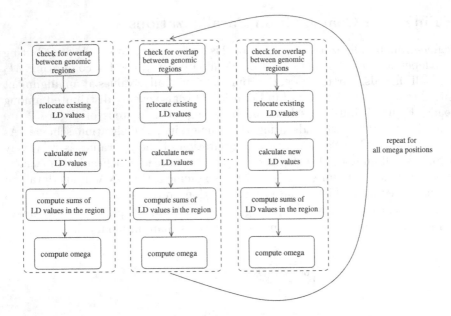

Fig. 4. Coarse-grain OmegaPlus parallelization

4   Multi-grain Parallelization

To alleviate the load imbalance caused by regions of high SNP density, we introduce a multi-grain parallelization scheme for reducing the runtime of the slowest threads/tasks by using a hybrid coarse-grain/fine-grain strategy.

4.1   Underlying Idea

During the first stages, the approach is similar to the coarse-grain scheme, since each thread is assigned a sub-genomic region of equal size (but potentially distinct density) and carries out the ω statistic operations independently and sequentially within that region. However, when a thread finishes processing its task/region in the coarse-grain approach, it starts executing a busy-wait until the last thread has completed its task. As already mentioned, the threads are only synchronized once via such a busy-wait barrier in the very end. In the multi-grain implementation, when a thread finishes processing its own task, it notifies the other threads that are still working on their tasks that it is available to help accelerate computations. At each point in time, only the slowest among all threads will obtain help from all other available threads that have completed their tasks. Henceforth, we use the term *temporary workers* to refer to the threads that are available to help others and the term *temporary master* to refer to the thread that is getting help from the *temporary workers*.

The *temporary master* is responsible to assign temporary thread IDs to the *temporary workers*, synchronize them, and release them again after a certain period of time. The *temporary master* can not use the *temporary workers* for an unlimited amount of time since another thread will become the slowest thread at some later point in time because of the speedup in computations attained by using the *temporary workers*. The current *temporary master* is entitled to announce the next *temporary master*. This approach is used to prevent slow threads to compete for *temporary workers* and also to avoid excessive occupation of the *temporary workers* by the same *temporary master*. Every *temporary master* occupies the workers for the calculation of the ω statistic at 25 positions. This number has been determined experimentally. Smaller numbers lead to increased synchronization overhead between threads while larger numbers lead to larger execution time differences between the slowest threads. While the *temporary master* is working with the *temporary workers* using fine-grain parallelism, the other threads (on remaining regions) are still operating in coarse-grain mode. When a *temporary master* renounces its privilege to use the *temporary workers* it returns to coarse-grain parallel mode. Figure 5 outlines the possible operational states of a thread during the analysis of a MSA using the multi-grain approach.

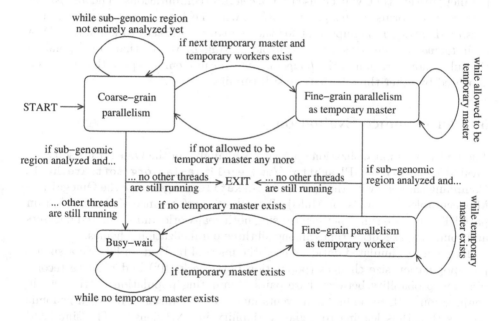

Fig. 5. Processing states of a thread according to the multi-grain parallel model in OmegaPlus

4.2 Implementation

The multi-grain parallelization and synchronization is implemented via integer arrays (*available* array, *turn* array, *progress* array). The *available* array shows which threads have completed their task and are ready to help others with computations. The *turn* array indicates which thread is allowed to occupy the *temporary workers* at each point in time. Finally, the *progress* array shows the progress each thread has made with the analysis of its sub-genomic region. Progress is measured as the number of calculated L_i values ($1 < i < k$, k is defined by the user, see Section 2) that lie in the sub-genomic region of the thread.

At a given point in time, the slowest thread is determined by searching for the highest number of—still uncalculated—L_i values in the *progress* array. The *temporary master* scans the *progress* array and announces which thread shall become the next *temporary master* by updating the *turn* array. After each L_i value computation by every unfinished thread, all threads check their corresponding entry in the *turn* array to find out whether it is their turn to utilize the *temporary workers*. The thread that is allowed to utilize the *temporary workers* acquires them by marking them as unavailable in the *available* array. Then, temporary thread IDs are assigned by the *temporary master* to all available workers in the *worker_ID* array. The *temporary master* also assigns a temporary thread ID to itself. The temporary thread ID assignment guarantees correct indexing and work distribution in fine-grain parallel computations of the M matrix. For the *temporary master*, the temporary ID also corresponds to the total number of parallel threads that will be used to accelerate computations. The *temporary master* also informs the *temporary workers* who the *temporary master* is via the *master_ID* array. It is important for the *temporary workers* to know the ID of their *temporary master* such as to avoid storing L_i values that correspond to the sub-genomic region of the *temporary master* in memory space that has been allocated by other threads that are still running.

5   Performance Evaluation

The multi-grain parallelization approach is available in the OmegaPlus software (available under GNU GPL at http://www.exelixis-lab.org/software.html). Compiling the code with the appropriate `Makefile` will generate the OmegaPlus-M executable (M stands for Multi). To evaluate performance of the multi-grain parallelization, we run experiments using both real-world and simulated datasets and compared execution times among all three parallelization schemes.

To generate simulated data, we used the ms tool by Hudson [9]. We assumed past population size changes (population bottleneck [10]) and positive recombination probability between base pairs. Simulating population bottlenecks in conjunction with recombination events increases the variance between genomic regions [11], thus leading to higher variability in SNP density. The simulated alignment was generated with the following command:

`ms 1000 1 -r 50000 1000 -eN 0.001 0.001 -eN 0.002 10 -s 10000`.

Flags `-eN 0.001 0.001` and `-eN 0.002 10` specify a population bottleneck. Backward in time (from present to past), the population has contracted to the 0.001 of its present-day size at time 0.001. Then, at time 0.002, the population size became 10 times larger than the present-day population size. Time is measured in $4N$ generations [9], where N is the effective population size. Regarding recombination (`-r 50000 1000`), we assume that there are 1,000 potential breakpoints where recombination may occur and the total rate of recombination is 50,000 (i.e. $4Nr = 50000$, where r is the recombination rate between two adjacent sites in the alignment and N the effective population size). Furthermore, we analyzed the X chromosome of 37 *Drosophila melanogaster* genomes sampled in Raleigh, North Carolina. The sequences (available from the Drosophila Population Genomics Project at `http://www.dpgp.org`) were converted from fastq to fasta format using a conversion script (also available at `http://www.dpgp.org`). We obtained a DNA alignment comprising 22,422,827 sites with 339,710 SNPs.

As test platform we used an AMD Opteron 6174 12-core Magny-Cours processor running at 2.2 GHz. Table 1 provides the total execution times required by OmegaPlus-F (fine-grain), OmegaPlus-C (coarse-grain), and OmegaPlus-M (multi-grain) using 2 up to 12 cores for analyzing an average-size alignment with 1,000 sequences and 100,000 alignment sites comprising 10,000 SNPs. All OmegaPlus runs calculated the ω statistic at 10,000 positions along the alignment assuming that the maximum size of the neighborhood of a beneficial mutation that a selective sweep might affect is 20,000 alignment sites. The sequential version of the code (OmegaPlus) required 317 seconds to process this alignment on one core of the test platform.

Table 1. Total execution times (in seconds) of OmegaPlus-F, OmegaPlus-C, and OmegaPlus-M to analyze an alignment of 1,000 sequences and 100,000 sites (10,000 SNPs). The last two rows show the performance improvement of the multi-grain version over the fine-grain (Multi vs Fine) and the coarse-grain (Multi vs Coarse) implementations, respectively.

Parallelization approach	Number of threads					
	2	4	6	8	10	12
Fine-grain	211.1	156,6	126,0	113.3	107.5	99.5
Coarse-grain	237.8	214,4	164,5	110,7	116.1	101.1
Multi-grain	197.8	135,0	100,3	87,2	77.1	63.8
Multi vs Fine (%)	6.3	13.7	20.3	23.0	28.2	35.9
Multi vs Coarse (%)	16.8	37.0	39.0	21.2	33.6	36.9

The last two rows of Table 1 show the performance improvement over the fine- and coarse-grain parallel implementations for different numbers of threads. On this simulated dataset, the multi-grain approach is between 6.3% (using two threads) and 35.9% (using 12 threads) faster than the fine-grain approach. In comparison to the coarse-grain parallelization, the multi-grain approach is between 16.8% (using two threads) and 39.0% (using 6 threads) faster.

The improvement differences (last two rows of Table 1) among runs with different number of threads are caused by changes in the size of the sub-genomic regions when coarse-grain parallelization is used. Since there are as many subgenomic regions as threads available, the number of threads affects the size of these regions and as a consequence the variability of SNP density among them. The improving parallel efficiency of OmegaPlus-M with increasing number of

threads when compared to OmegaPlus-F can be attributed to the effectiveness
of the initial coarse-grain parallel operations on binary data. As already mentioned, ω statistic computations on binary data require 10 times less operations
(on average) than on DNA data. Therefore, when the fine-grain parallel scheme
is used to analyze binary data, the synchronization-to-computation ratio is high
in comparison to a DNA data analysis. As a consequence, the coarse-grain parallelization is more efficient to analyze binary data than the fine-grain approach.

Table 2 shows the results of the runs on the real-world *Drosophila melanogaster*
MSA. Once again, we calculated the ω statistic at 10,000 positions along the
alignment, but this time using a maximum neighborhood size of 200,000 alignment sites. On a single core of our test platform, the sequential version required 1,599.8 seconds. Once again, OmegaPlus-M outperformed OmegaPlus-F
and OmegaPlus-C in all runs with different number of threads. OmegaPlus-M
yielded parallel performance improvements ranging between 22.4% and 64.4%
over OmegaPlus-F and between 1.0% and 17.7% over OmegaPlus-C.

Unlike the results on the simulated dataset, the performance continuously
improves on the real dataset as we use more threads. This is because the actual number of SNPs in the *Drosophila melanogaster* alignment is one order of
magnitude larger than the number of SNPs in the simulated dataset. Despite
the fact that the number of ω statistic positions per region is the same in both
MSAs, the ω statistic computations on the real-world dataset comprise approximately 45,000 to 60,000 SNPs in every region whereas only 2,500 to 6,000 are
present in the simulated dataset. A detailed analysis of the computational load
per region revealed that the size of the dynamic programming matrices when
the *Drosophila melanogaster* DNA MSA (average number of cells: 4,859,088)
is analyzed is twice the size of the respective matrices for the analysis of the
simulated binary dataset (average number of cells: 2,239,508). The load analysis also revealed that the overlap between neighborhoods around consecutive ω
statistic positions is higher for the simulated dataset. As a consequence, a significantly higher amount of operations is required per matrix for the *Drosophila
melanogaster* MSA thus reducing the synchronization-to-computation ratio in
the fine-grain scheme and allowing better scalability. Therefore, the more pro-
nounced performance advantages are obtained by deploying fine-grain computations in conjunction with coarse-grain computations in OmegaPlus-M as we
increase the number of threads.

The multi-grain approach aims at improving the parallel efficiency of the
coarse-grain approach. This is achieved by reducing the runtime of the slowest
threads/tasks by means of fine-grain parallelism. Figure 6 depicts the effect of the
multi-grain parallelization on the execution times of the individual threads/tasks
for the case of using 12 threads to analyze the real-world *Drosophila melanogaster*
MSA. The red and blue horizontal lines show the points in time when the slowest
threads in OmegaPlus-C and OmegaPlus-M terminate, respectively.

Table 2. Total execution times (in seconds) of OmegaPlus-F, OmegaPlus-C, and OmegaPlus-M to analyze a real-world dataset that comprises 37 sequences and 22,422,827 alignment sites (339,710 SNPs).

Parallelization approach	Number of threads					
	2	4	6	8	10	12
Fine-grain	1105.8	760.8	599.9	565.6	555.1	534,0
Coarse-grain	866.5	477.8	348.9	277.3	247.2	231.7
Multi-grain	857.1	437.3	312.1	248.0	210.8	190.6
Multi vs Fine (%)	22.4	42.5	47.9	56.1	62.1	64.4
Multi vs Coarse (%)	1.0	8.3	10.3	10.4	14.9	17.7

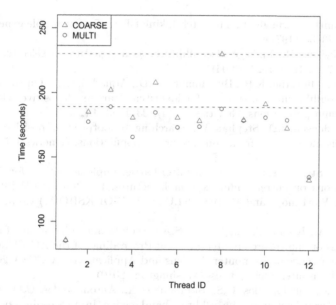

Fig. 6. Per-thread execution times (in seconds) of OmegaPlus-C and OmegaPlus-M when the *Drosophila melanogaster* MSA is analyzed

6 Conclusion and Future Work

We described, implemented, evaluated, and made available an efficient multi-grain parallelization scheme in the open-source OmegaPlus population genetics code. Fast threads that finish their own tasks early can subsequently help slower threads in accomplishing their tasks by deploying fine-grain parallelism. The multi-grain parallelization scheme, in conjunction with previous algorithmic and data structure optimizations in OmegaPlus, now allows for seamless computation of the ω statistic on large whole-genome datasets using off-the-shelf multi-core desktop and server systems.

In terms of future work, we intend to explore alternative strategies for scheduling/assigning fast threads to slower threads that can potentially further increase parallel efficiency. At present, we assign *all* available threads to help only one thread, that is, the thread that will most likely terminate last at each point in time. We expect that, a pre-analysis of MSA SNP density in combination with a detailed empirical investigation of thread behavior as a function of the assigned alignment region will allow for further optimizing *worker threads* to *master thread(s)* assignments. In addition, we plan to explore alternative hardware platforms such as reconfigurable devices and GPUs for offloading the compute-intensive parts of OmegaPlus.

References

1. Maynard Smith, J., Haigh, J.: The hitch-hiking effect of a favourable gene. Genet. Res. 23(1), 23–35 (1974)
2. Kim, Y., Nielsen, R.: Linkage disequilibrium as a signature of selective sweeps. Genetics 167(3), 1513–1524 (2004)
3. Jensen, J.D., Thornton, K.R., Bustamante, C.D., Aquadro, C.F.: On the utility of linkage disequilibrium as a statistic for identifying targets of positive selection in nonequilibrium populations. Genetics 176(4), 2371–2379 (2007)
4. Pavlidis, P., Jensen, J.D., Stephan, W.: Searching for footprints of positive selection in whole-genome snp data from nonequilibrium populations. Genetics 185(3), 907–922 (2010)
5. Berger, S.A., Stamatakis, A.: Assessment of barrier implementations for fine-grain parallel regions on current multi-core architectures. In: Proc. IEEE Int Cluster Computing Workshops and Posters (CLUSTER WORKSHOPS) Conf., pp. 1–8 (2010)
6. Stamatakis, A., Komornik, Z., Berger, S.A.: Evolutionary placement of short sequence reads on multi-core architectures. In: Proceedings of the ACS/IEEE International Conference on Computer Systems and Applications (AICCSA 2010), pp. 1–8. IEEE Computer Society Press, Washington (2010)
7. Blagojevic, F., Nikolopoulos, D.S., Stamatakis, A., Antonopoulos, C.D.: Dynamic multigrain parallelization on the cell broadband engine. In: Proceedings of the 12th ACM SIGPLAN Symposium on Principles and Practice of Parallel Programming. PPoPP 2007, pp. 90–100. ACM, New York (2007)
8. Kimura, M.: The number of heterozygous nucleotide sites maintained in a nite population due to steady ux of mutations. Genetics 61(4), 893–903 (1969)
9. Hudson, R.R.: Generating samples under a wright-fisher neutral model of genetic variation. Bioinformatics 18(2), 337–338 (2002)
10. Gillespie, J.H.: Population genetics: a concise guide. Johns Hopkins Univ. Pr. (2004)
11. Haddrill, P.R., Thornton, K.R., Charlesworth, B., Andolfatto, P.: Multilocus patterns of nucleotide variability and the demographic and selection history of drosophila melanogaster populations. Genome Res. 15(6), 790–799 (2005)

Vectorized Algorithms for Quadtree Construction and Descent

Eraldo P. Marinho and Alexandro Baldassin

Univ Estadual Paulista (UNESP), Departamento de Estatística, Matemática
Aplicada e Computação, IGCE, Rio Claro, Brazil
{emarinho,alex}@rc.unesp.br

Abstract. This paper presents vectorized methods of construction and
descent of quadtrees that can be easily adapted to message passing parallel computing. A time complexity analysis for the present approach
is also discussed. The proposed method of tree construction requires a
hash table to index nodes of a linear quadtree in the breadth-first order. The hash is performed in two steps: an internal hash to index child
nodes and an external hash to index nodes in the same level (depth).
The quadtree descent is performed by considering each level as a vector
segment of a linear quadtree, so that nodes of the same level can be
processed concurrently.

1 Introduction

A quadtree is a special kind of tree in which each internal node has four de-
scendants [1]. From the geometrical point of view, a quadtree is a data-structure
that indexes a surface (space) distribution of particles (*records*) in a hierarchy
of quadrants (octants).

Quadtrees are widely used in digital image processing and computer graphics
for modeling spatial segmentation of images and surfaces [2] and image compression [3]. Other applications of quadtrees include finite element mesh generation [4], motion estimator for video compression [5], DNA sequence alignment
problems [6,7], and nearest neighbor searching [8,9].

Due to the wide range of quadtree applications, it is of fundamental relevance
to find out efficient algorithms for quadtree methods. In particular, parallel algorithms for such methods are of special interest since they can provide a significant
performance improvement. Consider, for instance, image processing applications.
They are typically data intensive and can benefit the most from parallelism.

This work introduces vectorized algorithms for quadtree construction and descent. Vectorized quadtrees allow an optimized form of tree descent on parallel
computers. A vectorized tree is a linear tree whose nodes are conveniently indexed to allow any level (depth) to be processed as a single-indexed array of
nodes. The level-wise segmentation of a tree can easily be translated to a message passing computing within the single program stream, multiple data stream
(SPMD) paradigm, as showed in this work. A further contribution of this paper
is the semi-analytical time complexity analysis for the given algorithms, so that

Y. Xiang et al. (Eds.): ICA3PP 2012, Part I, LNCS 7439, pp. 69–82, 2012.

benchmarks were performed by simulating a message passing SPMD workload runing on a computer cluster with a variable number of nodes.

This paper is organized as follows. Section 2 provides the necessary background on quadtrees and also presents related works. Section 3 introduces the hash approach, while Section 4 describes the parallel algorithms for quadtree construction and descent. Section 5 presents a time complexity analysis for the proposed algorithms considering the message passing parallel model. Finally, Section 6 concludes the paper.

2   Background and Related Work

2.1   Quadtrees

The standard quadtree definition can be easily extended to a 2^D-tree to index D-dimensional spaces. However, for historical reasons, even in a multidimensional space we refer to a 2^D-tree as simply a *quadtree*.

Definition 1. *A quadtree is a tree data-structure with the following geometrical basis:*

- *a region including a discrete set of distinct points of a D-dimensional data space is assigned to a node;*
- *any node with more than one point is resolved into 2^D children, which represents, respectively, the 2^D subregions delimited by D-mutually orthogonal hyperplanes passing through an arbitrary point, called the* partition vertex.

From the definition above, the node of a quadtree has zero or 2^D children, where at least one is a non-empty node. Thus, the path along with the nodes are taken from the hierarchical divisions is terminated either with an empty or with a unitary node. Usually, children are labeled as $0, 1, 2, ..., 2^D - 1$, in the order by which they arise from the node division.

Each node can be interpreted as a semi-open region bounded by D orthogonal hyperplanes. Each region contains a selection (subset) of the original data points. We call this region a *hyperquadrant* or *node-region*. We assume that the list of points inside this region is assigned to the node, so that a node is also associated to the collection of points inside the corresponding hyperquadrant. The definition for partition vertex is arbitrary. Any position in the hyperquadrant can be a partition vertex. However, this arbitrary choice may allow all the node-assigned points to be transferred to one single hyperquadrant (child node). When this occurs, the node is called a *degenerated node*.

Definition 2. *A quadtree node is said to be* degenerated *if and only if the node has only one non-empty child.*

The following theorem assures us that no degeneracy occurs if the partition vertex is defined as the mean data position (center of mass) of the points assigned to the node.

Theorem 1. *Let a quadtree be constructed in such way that any internal node has its partition vertex defined as the mean data position (center of mass) of the collection of records assigned to the node. In this case, all the internal nodes of such a quadtree are non-degenerated ones.*

Proof. It is to be proved that any internal node has at least two non-empty children if the partition vertex is defined as the mean data position in the node. If a node is internal $(n > 1)$, there is at least one j-direction $(1 \leq j \leq d)$ for which the *maximum* and the *minimum* of the coordinates x^j are not identical $(\min\{x^j_{i_1}, \ldots, x^j_{i_n}\} < \max\{x^j_{i_1}, \ldots, x^j_{i_n}\})$, where the superscripts represent the coordinate direction and the subscripts represent the data-index. From the expectation definition, the j-coordinate of the mean data position $\bar{x}^j$ in the given node obeys the relation

$$\min\{x^j_{i_1}, \ldots, x^j_{i_n}\} \leq \bar{x}^j \leq \max\{x^j_{i_1}, \ldots, x^j_{i_n}\}.$$

Thus, as each record is uniquely determined in space by its D coordinates, there is at least one direction for which the list of records assigned to the node is split into two distinct sublists. For instance, one list for $\bar{x}^j \geq \min\{x^j_1, \ldots, x^j_n\}$ and the other one for $\bar{x}^j < \max\{x^j_1, \ldots, x^j_n\}$. It can be consequently interpreted as there existing at least two non-empty children among the 2^D possible ones. □

Corollary 1. *The one-dimensional case $(D = 1)$ of theorem 1 results in a strictly binary tree.*

Degenerated nodes can eventually be a serious problem if the data distribution has a high degree of clustering. In this case, the tree may reach several degrees of degeneracy, which may hazardously overflow the required storage memory.

A well known case of quadtrees from computational astrophysics literature is the original Barnes & Hut oct-tree approach [10], where the data space is a cubic box, and the partition vertex is defined as the cube centroid (see Fig. 1), which naturally allows node degeneracy since not all particles are necessarily distributed over more than one cubic cell. The BH-oct-tree was originally used on N-body simulations, and also is used on D-dimensional nearest neighbors search in smoothed particle hydrodynamics (SPH) [11,12,13,14].

2.2 Vectorized Quadtrees

In order to improve the vectorized quadtree construction and descent, we must first introduce the concept of a vectorized quadtree as a special case of linear quadtree.

Definition 3. *A vectorized quadtree, or simply $V2^D$-tree, is a special case of linear quadtree so that nodes in the same level (depth) can be constructed (processed) at once (concurrently) before any descent, and each level can be formally represented as a vector segment of the quadtree.*

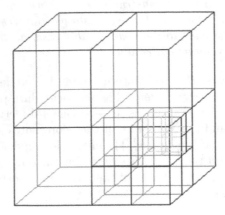

Fig. 1. The hierarchical octal division of the 3D space associated to the construction of the BH oct-tree

From the last definition two main conclusions can be drawn. The first conclusion is that no data dependency occurs among nodes in the same level, which is sufficient to allow a stackless (non-recursive) construction. The second conclusion is that a quadtree level l corresponds to a single-indexed array of nodes, with the indices in the range $[n_A^l, n_B^l]$, where n_A^l and n_B^l are, respectively, the first and the last indices (nodes) in the quadtree level l.

A vectorized quadtree is illustrated in Fig. 2. Definition 3 is necessary to construct a cursor-based quadtree with the nodes enumerated in the order as shown in Fig. 2. Some operations required along with the tree construction cannot be easily vectorized nor parallelized as, e.g., sorting the hash table on the external hash index as shown in Section 3. However, most operations performed on the hash table have no data dependency between table entries (e.g., the hash process).

2.3   Related Work

The body of work on sequential algorithms for quadtree manipulation is discussed by Samet in [15]. Parallel algorithms for quadtrees have been devised for different architectures, including mesh-connected computers [16], transputers [17], hypercubes [18,19], and shared memory abstract machines [20]. Most of the algorithms presented on those works use the linear quadtree representation first introduced by Gargantini [21].

The methods discussed in this paper rely on vectorized quadtrees, a technique similar to the one employed by Hernquist [22]. Different from previous works, the algorithms introduced here are based on a two-level hashtable. A unique spatial-key (d-tuple) is transformed into an internal-hash index from which is calculated the external-hash index to map nodes in the same level of the quadtree. Internal hash is also necessary to link nodes to their respective children. By this way,

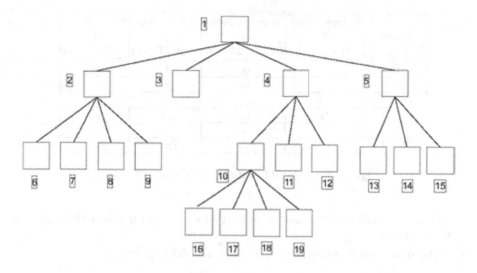

Fig. 2. A vectorized quadtree, where labels express the order of both construction and descent

the construction method requires a hash table to index nodes in the same level as one single array. Rather than the approaches shown in previous works in the literature [10,22,11], the internal hash is calculated as a function of the relative position of the points with respect to their mean position.

3 The Hash Approach

The process of partitioning the data space (node) into hyperquadrants (children) can also be interpreted as a kind of hash. In the hash approach, the sequence of space partition is mapped by a hash table until no more hyperquadrants remain to be partitioned.

Consider a discrete set (cluster) C_N of N records uniquely (no duplicates) distributed in the data space $\Gamma \subseteq \Re^D$. As Γ is virtually partitioned into 2^D hyperquadrants $(\Gamma_0, \Gamma_1, \ldots, \Gamma_{2^D-1})$, the cluster C_N is also divided into 2^D subclusters $(C_{N_0}, C_{N_1}, \ldots, C_{N_{2^D-1}})$. From Theorem 1, if the partition vertex is the center of mass of C_N, we have at least 2 non-empty subclusters. Either a cluster or a hyperquadrant can be assigned as a node in the quadtree. For instance, a more complete case of quadtree data-structure must store both the data properties and the hyperquadrant boundaries as in an R-tree.

A hash table $\mathcal{H}$ is used to map records of a data space according to the clusters (nodes) they belong to. Fig. 3 illustrates the adopted model for $\mathcal{H}$. The table requires four attributes to aid the tree construction:

- t: the external-hash index to point left-to-right to all nodes of the same level. This index is also used as a sort key;
- q: the internal-hash index used to hash entries (records) into quadrants;

Entry $(0,1,2,\ldots)$	External hash t $(0,1,2,\ldots)$	Internal hash q $(0,1\ldots2^d-1)$	IsLeaf-flag f $(true/false)$	Space index i $(1,2,\ldots,N)$
0	t_0	q_0	f_0	p_0
1	t_1	q_1	f_1	p_1
...	...	...	...	...
k	t_k	q_k	f_k	p_k
...	...	...	...	...
$N-1$	t_{N-1}	q_{N-1}	f_{N-1}	p_{N-1}

Fig. 3. The hash table data structure for a 2^d-tree

- $IsLeaf$: a predicate that marks an entry for deletion if this is the only one for a given t;
- i: the space index, which maps points in the data space.

The external-hash index t identifies which node a given record belongs to. For each contiguous sequence of entries with identical external-hash index is assigned an internal-hash index q, which is used to resolve nodes into 2^d children – this is a required procedure to construct the next level.

Each hyperquadrant with more than one point inside, $Num(\Gamma) > 1$, belongs to the same *partition-level* l, which is an abstraction of the collective partitioning of the remaining hyperquadrants into child-hyperquadrants. Also, for each partition-level l corresponds a unique $\mathcal{H}$, which expresses how the data is structured into clusters with the same external-hash index t. For each level is assigned a label, e.g., 0 at the root, 1 at the first partitioning etc. Of course the maximum number of possible partitions in level l is $2^{l\,d}$. When a record is identified as the unique point inside a hyperquadrant (table-partition) it is removed from the hash table, which is in turn equivalent to assign the single record a tree-leaf. Such a destructive approach implies that the process stops when the hash table becomes empty ($\mathcal{H} = \lambda$).

The quadtree construction is then performed top-down, in a breadth-first order. Parental link is defined by prefixedly calculating the internal-hash index q to group records from the same node into children. This internal index enters in the hashing-formula to calculate the hash index in the next tree-level if the remaining hash table is not empty.

There are several hashing functions that can be applied to partition data points into hyperquadrants. The best approach is to find a function that converts coordinates into indexes $0, 1, \ldots, 2^d - 1$. A notorious one is the inverse of the function used to map the Morton's space-filling curve. A variant of such a function is the following:

$$\phi(x^1, x^2 \ldots, x^d) = \sum_{j=1}^{d} 2^{j-1} \operatorname{ord}(x^j > x_o^j), \qquad (1)$$

where $(x_o^1, \ldots, x_o^d)$ is the partition vertex. The external hash can be improved straightforwardly using the hashing function given below:

$$h_l = \begin{cases} 0 & \text{if } l = 0, \\ 2^d\, h_{l-1} + q_l, & \text{if } l > 0. \end{cases} \tag{2}$$

The recursive formula given by Equation 2 is an external-hash function for a $V2^d$-tree at level l, where q_l is the internal hash index determined in previous level, if $l > 1$, or zero if $l = 0$.

Both hash indexes are semantically distinct: the external hash identifies nodes and the internal hash identifies children. A node is a segment in $\mathcal{H}$, lexically defined as the *token* formed by a sequence of repeated symbols:

$$node \to a^*, \forall a \in \aleph,$$

the alphabet $\aleph$ is the set of values appearing in the $\mathcal{H}.t$ column. A level in the quadtree corresponds consequently to a unique sentence, e.g., "0001123333...", if the table is prior sorted on the key t. The trivial token λ signals an empty table. In order to avoid integer overflow, the column $\mathcal{H}.t$, after sorting, is normalized to a sequence of consecutive integers $(0, 1, 2\ldots)$.

An instance of $\mathcal{H}$ is shown in Fig. 4. The figure shows a given configuration of $N = 17$ remaining data points ($\Gamma \subseteq \Re^2$), at some partition-level. The table is illustrated segmented by nodes (delimited by double horizontal line). The first node is the sequence of entries with $t = 0$. For each entry with $t = 0$ there is

Entry	t	q	$IsLeaf$	i
0	0	3	false	281
1	0	0	false	109
2	0	0	false	4095
3	1	1	true	0
4	2	2	false	12
5	2	1	false	6
6	3	3	false	987
7	3	3	false	112
8	3	0	false	11
9	3	0	false	99
10	4	2	false	911
11	4	1	false	734
12	4	0	false	23
13	5	1	true	1
14	6	2	true	1023
15	7	1	false	122
16	7	0	false	2

Fig. 4. An instance of the hash table shown in Figure 3

a value for q pointing to which child the entry will belong to in the next level. For instance, entry 0 will belong to the child labeled as 3, entries 1 and 2 both will belong to the child 0. Nodes with only one entry (entries 3, 13 and 14) are marked as leaf (*true* in the fourth column). The actual data-index is the sequence of integers in the last column. For example, the entry 0 points to the record 281 in the original base.

The hash table is initialized with default values. Both the external-hash index and the leaf-flag are initially null. The space index is set as the sequence of indexes 0, 1, 2, ..., $N - 1$, which corresponds to the initial data configuration $x_0, x_1, \ldots, x_{N-1}$, with any vector x being associated to their coordinates $x \equiv (x_0, x_1, \ldots, x_{d-1})$.

4   Algorithms

4.1   Tree Construction

In the previous section it was described the process of recursive division of the data space into 2^D hyperquadrants, until no more subregions having more than one data point is found. Such a space segmentation virtually corresponds to reordering the hash table by grouping together records belonging in the same node (hyperquadrant). Any node in a given level is uniquely determined by the external-hash index (t-column in the hash table). The construction algorithm will be described in the following paragraphs.

The partitioning process stops when the partition-level becomes empty, i.e., when there is no more hyperquadrant Γ in the level with $Num(\Gamma) > 1$. As the partition can also be abstracted as the hash table $\mathcal{H}$ itself, then $\mathcal{H}$ is also empty at the end of the spatial segmentation.

The vectorized quadtree is a cursor-based data structure, where the node has the following attributes:

- an integer single-indexed array $Child[2^D]$ to point to the 2^D child-nodes;
- a real single-indexed vector $x[d]$ to mark the D partition vertex coordinates, about which is performed the space partitioning – in the present method it is defined as the mean data-position;
- further problem-specific attributes such as *image-segment* etc.

The level-wise construction proceeds as described in the algorithm illustrated in Figure 5. *Level*, *Node*, *NextNode* are global integers. *Level* is used to label the partition-level, *Node* points node (hyperquadrant) to be created, and *NextNode* points to the next child to create in level *Level* + 1 as previously mentioned. $Child[\text{MAXNODES}][2^d]$ is an integer array in $\{0, 1, \ldots, 2^d - 1\}$, which points to the 2^d children.

The external-hash t can be interpreted as giving a lexical definition for nodes in the table. In fact, a node is identified by a token formed with identical symbols t in the table – this corresponds to perform the t-selection mentioned in Figure 5.

1: **Initial conditions**:

    $Level := 0$;
    $Node := 0$;
    $NextNode := 1$;
    Clear the entire column $\mathcal{H}.t$, $\mathcal{H}.t := 0$,
    Clear the collision counter: $Collision\,[q = 0, 1, 2, \ldots 2^d - 1] := 0$;

2: **While** $\mathcal{H} \neq \lambda$, **do**

3:     Segment $\mathcal{H}$ into selections $\mathcal{S}(t) \subseteq \mathcal{H}$ with the same t;
4:     **Foreach** selection $\mathcal{S}(t)$, **do in parallel**

5:         Set the partition vertex as the center of mass $\boldsymbol{x}_{\mathrm{m}}\,[Node]$ over $\mathcal{S}(t)$;

6:         **If** $Num(\mathcal{S}(t)) > 1$, **then**
7:             Update q-column in $\mathcal{S}(t)$: $\mathcal{S}(t).q := qHash(\mathcal{S}(t).i, \boldsymbol{x}_{\mathrm{m}}\,[Node])$;
8:             Count the collisions in $\mathcal{H}.q$: $Collision\,[\mathcal{H}.q\,[i]]$ ++;
9:             **For** $q = 0, 1, \ldots, 2^d$, **do**
10:                 **If** $Collision\,[q] \neq 0$, **then**
11:                     Make the child link: $Child\,[Node][q] := NextNode$;
12:                     Postfixly count the just predicted child: $NextNode$ ++;
13:                 **Endif**
14:             **Endfor**;
15:             Perform further computations on the hyperquadrant attributes;
16:         **Elif** $Num(\mathcal{S}(t)) = 1$, **then**
17:             Bind present *record* (point) to the newly created *leaf*;
18:             Mark for deletion the present entry (unitary $\mathcal{S}(t)$) from $\mathcal{H}$
19:         **Endif**;

20:         Postfixly count the just created node: $Node$ ++

21:     **Endfor**;

22:     Bookmark $Node$ as the level-end: $LevelEnd\,[Level$ ++$] := Node$;
23:     Remove from $\mathcal{H}$ all entries marked as leaves
24:     Update column $\mathcal{H}.t$: $\mathcal{H}.t := tHash(\mathcal{H}.t, \mathcal{H}.q)$;
25:     Sort $\mathcal{H}$ on key t

26: **Endwhile**

Fig. 5. The algorithm for a level-wise vectorized construction of a quadtree

4.2 Vectorized Tree Descent

The vectorized algorithm to perform a top-down breadth-first visitation is illustrated in Fig. 6. The predicate **IsAllowed**(*query, node*) (line 6) in conjunction with the inherited result of a single-indexed array *allowed*[] (lines 6 and 11) are

```
1:  Procedure TreeWalk (query: index type)
2:      Set all terms of allowed [] vector as True;
3:      Clear level offset: LevelBegin := 0;
4:      Foreach level, do
5:          ForInParallel node := LevelBegin, ..., LevelEnd[level] − 1, do
6:              allowed[node] := allowed[node] ∧ IsAllowed (query, node);
7:              If allowed[node], DoWhatever (query, node)
9:          Endfor
10:         For node := LevelBegin, ..., LevelEnd[level] − 1, do
11:             If Num[node] > 1 ∧ not(allowed[node]), then
12:                 For q := 0, 1, ..., 2^d − 1, do
13:                     r := Child[node][q];
14:                     allowed[r] := False
15:                 Endfor
16:             Endif
17:         Endfor
18:         LevelBegin := LevelEnd[level]
19:     Endfor
20: End TreeWalk
```

Fig. 6. A vectorized pseudocode to perform a prefixed tree descent

used to control the tree descent. The heritage is performed in lines 10–17 where disallowed nodes propagate their status to their children.

The **For**–block comprising lines 5–9 is the critical part of the descent method so that it is performed in parallel. On the other hand, the **For**–block comprising lines 10–17 can be considered a scalar block since it is limited to integer operations only, which are usually much faster than any communication done.

5   Complexity Analysis

It is assumed a message passing parallel computing using a homogeneous cluster of P machines communicating with each other by means of a single communication device, with bandwidth B. For simpler cluster architectures, the relative bandwidth drops down to B/P. In the SPMD paradigm, the parent process streams the segments of the original data-structure to the children in the form of messages. The total time spent on message passing can be roughly represented by

$$T_{\text{msg}} = \left(\frac{\sigma}{B} \lfloor n/P \rfloor P + \tau \right) (P - 1), \tag{3}$$

where σ is the length of a message element (node), τ is the time of communication overhead, which can be neglected in comparison to the message transfer time, and n is the current number of table entries.

The relevant operations invoked along with both the tree construction and tree descent are essentially floating-point operations taken either to calculate the internal hash via Eq. (1) or to perform floating comparisons on the tree descent.

The number of floating operations is essentially proportional to the segment size $\sigma \lfloor n/P \rfloor$. Thus, if α is the time to perform the floating operations per node, which depends on the number of records per t-selection in the hash table in the case of the quadtree construction, the CPU time is roughly $\alpha \lfloor n/P \rfloor$.

The best case top-down construction occurs for a complete quadtree, where all the leaves are in the lowest level. In this special case, the number of hash table entries is always N until the deepest level where all the leaf entries are pruned at once from the table.

For a complete quadtree, the tree height is

$$H(N, d) = \left\lceil \frac{\log N}{\log Q} \right\rceil, \tag{4}$$

where $Q = 2^d$. The tree height is the number of required parallelization workloads to construct the entire quadtree.

The number of nodes in level l is $n_l = Q^l$, so that the number of records per node is $N/Q^l = Q^{H-l}$. For the present SPMD algorithm, the level (hash table) must be partitioned into P segments, with each of the first $P-1$ having $\lfloor Q^l/P \rfloor$ nodes (t-selections) but with the remainder segment having $\lfloor Q^l/P \rfloor + Q \bmod P$ nodes. In this case, the total message time is given by

$$T_{\mathrm{msg}} = \beta \frac{N}{Q^l} \left\lfloor \frac{Q^l}{P} \right\rfloor P(P - 1). \tag{5}$$

As the possibly larger partition is the remainder one, the calculation time is given by

$$T_{\mathrm{calc}} = \alpha \frac{N}{Q^l} \left\{ \left\lfloor \frac{Q^l}{P} \right\rfloor + Q^l \bmod P \right\} \tag{6}$$

The total time required to construct a best case quadtree is then

$$T_{\mathrm{best}} = \alpha \sum_{l=0}^{H} \frac{N}{Q^l} \left\{ \alpha \left(\left\lfloor \frac{Q^l}{P} \right\rfloor + Q^l \bmod P \right) + \beta \left\lfloor \frac{Q^l}{P} \right\rfloor P(P - 1) \right\}. \tag{7}$$

Fig. 7 illustrates some results from a simulation of the previously discussed message-passing computing model for a best case quadtree, with different values for N and P, assuming $\alpha/\beta = 512$ and $d = 3$.

The worst case occurs when the tree has N levels. This is the case where the data distribution conspired in such a way that each level l has two nodes: one is a leaf and the other one is the subtree storing the remainder of the data to be indexed. In this case, only one processor can be allocated by level, so that no parallelization occurs.

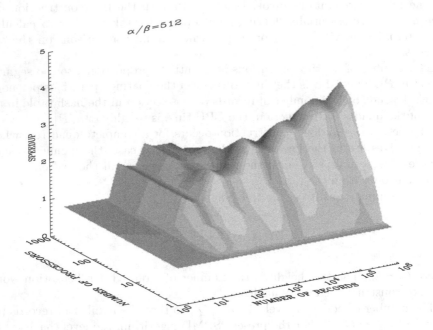

Fig. 7. Best-case speedup surface for $1 \leq N < 10^6$ points, $d = 3$ dimensions, $1 \leq P \leq 512$, and $\alpha/\beta = 512$.

By induction, the number of floating operations taken in level l is proportional to $N - l$ since l is exactly the number of points removed from the table as they became leaves. Hence, the total time for the worst case construction is

$$T_{\text{calc}} = \alpha \sum_{l=0}^{N-1} (N - l) = \frac{\alpha N(N + 1)}{2} = O(N^2). \tag{8}$$

6   Conclusion

It was presented and discussed a vectorized approach for both construction and descent of quadtrees. The tree construction algorithm uses a two-level hash table: an internal hash to resolve data points into hyperquadrants per node and an external hash to resolve nodes per level.

The vectorized tree walk algorithm was designed to be easily adapted to the SPMD and SIMD paradigms. For instance, some scalar-machine instructions like if-statements were avoided inside loops in detriment of a slight increase in complexity.

A semi-analytical time complexity analysis was conducted for both best and worst cases. The worst case is a hypothetical situation in which there is only a single internal node per level, which limits the number of allocated processors (cluster nodes) to one. The best case occurs to a complete (hyper)quadtree in which internal node has 2^d non-empty children.

Acknowledgements. This work was partially financed by FAPESP grants number 2010/52175-0 and number 2011/19373-6.

References

1. Finkel, R.A., Bentley, J.L.: Quad Trees: A data structure for retrieval on composite keys. Acta Inf. 4, 1–9 (1974)
2. Gaede, V., Günther, O.: Multidimensional access methods. ACM Computing Surveys 2(30), 170–231 (1998)
3. Poulakidas, A.S., Srinivasan, A., Eğecioğlu, Ö., Ibarra, O., Yang, T.: Image compression for fast wavelet-based subregion retrieval. Theoretical Computer Science 240(2), 447–469 (2000)
4. Fischer, A., Bar-Yoseph, P.Z.: Adaptive mesh generation based on multi-resolution quadtree representation. International Journal For Numerical Methods In Engineering 48, 1571–1582 (2000)
5. Schustere, G.M., Katsaggelos, A.K.: An optimal quadtree-based motion estimation and motion-compensated interpolation scheme for video compression. IEEE Transactions on Image Processing 7(11), 1505–1523 (1998)
6. Ichinose, N., Yada, T., Takagi, T.: Quadtree representation of DNA sequences. Genome Informatics 12, 510–511 (2001)
7. McNaughton, M., Lu, P., Schaeffer, J., Szafron, D.: Memory-efficient A* heuristics for multiple sequence alignment. In: Proceedings of the Eighteenth National Conference on Artificial Intelligence and Fourteenth Conference on Innovative Applications of Artificial Intelligence, July 28-August, pp. 737–743. AAAI Press, Edmonton (2002)
8. Callahan, P.B.: Optimal parallel all-nearest-neighbors using the well-separated pair decomposition. In: Proc. 34th Symp. Foundations of Computer Science, pp. 332–340. IEEE (1993)
9. Arya, S., Mount, D.M., Netanyahu, N.S., Silverman, R., Wu, A.Y.: An optimal algorithm for approximate nearest neighbor searching in fixed dimensions. J. ACM 45(6), 891–923 (1998)
10. Barnes, J., Hut, P.: A hierarchical O(N log N) force-calculation algorithm. Nature 324, 446–449 (1986)
11. Warren, M.S., Salmon, J.K.: A parallel hashed tree N-body algorithm. In: ACM Proceedings, Supercomputing 1993, November 15-19, pp. 12–21. ACM Press, Portland (1993)
12. Warren, M.S., Salmon, J.K.: A portable parallel particle program. Comput. Phys. Comm. (87), 266–290 (1995)
13. Marinho, E.P., Lépine, J.R.D.: SPH simulations of clumps formation by dissipative collision of molecular clouds. I. Non magnetic case. Astronomy and Astrophysics Supplement 142, 165–179 (2000)
14. Marinho, E.P., Andreazza, C.M., Lépine, J.R.D.: SPH simulations of clumps formation by dissipative collisions of molecular clouds. II. Magnetic case. Astronomy and Astrophysics 379, 1123–1137 (2001)
15. Samet, H.: The design and analysis of spatial data structures. Addison-Wesley Longman Publishing Co., Inc. (1990)

16. Hung, Y., Rosenfeld, A.: Parallel processing of linear quadtrees on a mesh-connected computer. J. Parallel Distrib. Comput. 7(1), 1–27 (1989)
17. Mason, D.: Linear quadtree algorithms for transputer array. IEEE Proceedings of Computers and Digital Techniques 137(1), 114–128 (1990)
18. Dehne, F., Ferreira, A.G., Rau-chaplin, A.: Parallel processing of pointer based quadtrees on hypercube multiprocessors. In: Proc. International Conference on Parallel Processing (1991)
19. Yang, S., Lee, R.: Efficient parallel nighbor finding algorithms for quadtrees on hypercube. Journal of Information Science and Engineering 9, 81–102 (1993)
20. Bhaskar, S.K., Rosenfeld, A., Wu, A.Y.: Parallel processing of regions represented by linear quadtrees. Computer Vision, Graphics, and Image Processing 42(3), 371–380 (1988)
21. Gargantini, I.: An effective way to represent quadtrees. Commun. ACM 25(12), 905–910 (1982)
22. Hernquist, L.: Vectorization of Tree Traversals. Journal of Computational Physics 87, 137–147 (1990)
23. N-body algorithm. In: ACM, editor, Proceedings, Supercomputing 1993, Portland, Oregon, November 15-19, pp. 12–21. ACM Press (1993)

A Multi-level Monitoring Framework for Stream-Based Coordination Programs

Vu Thien Nga Nguyen, Raimund Kirner, and Frank Penczek

School of Computer Science
University of Hertfordshire
Hatfield, United Kingdom
{v.t.nguyen,r.kirner,f.penczek}@herts.ac.uk

Abstract. Stream-based Coordination is a promising approach to execute programs on parallel hardware such as multi-core systems. It allows to reuse sequential code at component level and to extend such code with concurrency-handling at the coordination level. In this paper we identify the monitoring information required to enable the calculation of performance metrics, automatic load balancing, and bottleneck detection. The monitoring information is obtained by implicitly instrumenting multiple levels: the runtime system and the operating system.

We evaluate the monitoring overhead caused by different use cases on S-Net as it is a challenging monitoring benchmark with a flexible and fully asynchronous execution model, including dynamic mapping and scheduling policies. The evaluation shows that in most cases the monitoring causes a negligible overhead of less than five percent.

1 Introduction

The ongoing trend towards increasing numbers of execution units running in parallel raises challenges for the field of software engineering, for example, mastering concurrency issues to exploit a high fraction of parallel computations.

Stream-based coordination programs are networks of components connected by communication channels, called streams. They have been proposed as a paradigm to reduce the complexity of parallel programming, since the stream communication provides an intuitive form of implicit synchronisation. However, it is challenging in stream-based coordination to analyse and improve the performance without understanding of the program's internal behaviour. Thus, the availability of monitoring frameworks that provide specific insights into the internal temporal behaviour is important.

There exist numerous monitoring frameworks for performance debugging, with the commercial ones typically covering generic parallel programming approaches. However, stream-based coordination does provide special properties like implicit synchronisations through communication channels, for which dedicated monitoring support would be beneficial. Monitoring the temporal behaviour would also require to extract information about the operation of the underlying operating system, as the resource management of the operating system typically has a significant influence on the performance of the parallel program.

Y. Xiang et al. (Eds.): ICA3PP 2012, Part I, LNCS 7439, pp. 83–98, 2012.

In this paper we analyse the needs for monitoring of stream-based coordination programs in order to enable the calculation of performance metrics, automatic load balancing, and bottleneck detection. We evaluate these based on a concrete implementation on S-Net and LPEL.

The remainder of this paper is structured as follows. Section 2 introduces some concepts used in this paper. The conceptional monitoring framework for stream-based coordination programs is given in Section 3. The first contribution is given in Section 4 as an analysis of the monitoring information required for different monitoring use cases such as calculation of performance metrics, automatic load balancing, and bottleneck detection. In Section 5 we describe the implementation details of our monitoring framework, being embedded into the runtime system of the coordination language S-Net [8] and one of its execution layers LPEL [18]. As the second contribution we evaluate the overhead of the different monitoring use cases in Section 6. Related work on monitoring is discussed in Section 7. Section 8 concludes the paper.

2   Definitions

2.1   Stream-Based Coordination Programs

A stream-based coordination program [10,22] consists of a set of processing components connected by directed communication channels, called *streams*. These components communicate by sending and receiving messages through streams. All components within a program may be placed on a single machine, in which case stream communication is typically established through shared memory, or components may be distributed across several nodes in a cluster of machines.

2.2   Performance Metrics

We are interested in the performance of stream-processing systems in terms of throughput, latency, and jitter:

Throughput describes how much data (determined by either the data volume or the number of messages) is passed through a stream-based coordination program or a processing component per time unit.

Latency is the delay between the receipt of data by a stream-based coordination program or a processing component and the release of the processing results into the output channel(s).

For high-performance systems the average latency is important, while for real-time computing the maximum latency is significant.

Jitter describes the variability of the latency. For high-performance computing the jitter can be a useful metric to guide the dimensioning of internal implementation-specific mechanisms needed to store data. In real-time computing information on jitter is important for control applications to reason about the quality of control.

2.3   Timing Metrics

Execution time, is the time spent for performing computations.

Idling time, is the time spent for waiting, i.e. where no computations are carried out, for example because no data is available.

Response time, is the total time required for both waiting and performing computations. It equals to the sum of execution time and idling time.

3   Conceptions of the Monitoring Framework

Generally, a stream-based coordination program is specified by some sort of description language. It then is compiled into a program to be executed on a runtime system built on top of a host operating system. The runtime system maps processing components into executable tasks. Typically, there is a one-to-one mapping between components and tasks. In addition, the runtime system should support streams as communication channels. Data is expressed as messages which are transferred over streams. The operating system supplies a scheduler to assign tasks to computational resources. The scheduler also decides when to execute tasks on a computational resource.

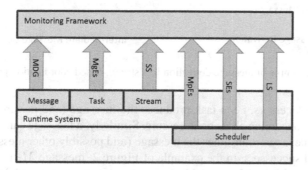

Fig. 1. Monitoring framework

In the following, we present the concept of our monitoring framework as shown in Figure 1. The framework collects the information from both levels: the runtime system and the operating system.

3.1   Monitoring the Runtime System

At the runtime system level, the monitoring framework observes the following information:

- **Message Derivation Graph (*MDG*).** This is a directed graph describing the m-to-n relation between the input messages and output messages of every task. Each node in the graph represents a message. A directed edge between two message is placed if during execution a task consumes one message and produces another. The source node is the consumed or input message; and the destination is the produced or output message. It is said that the output message is derived from the input message; or the input message derives to the output message. One node or message can have

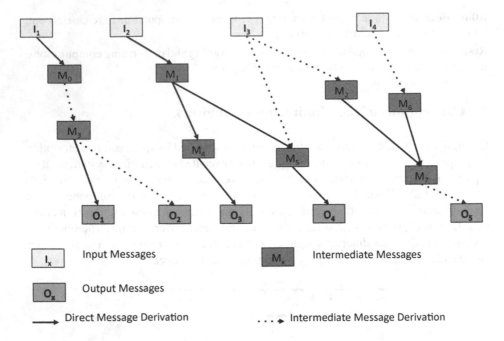

Fig. 2. An example of message derivation in a stream-based coordination program

multiple predecessors, i.e. a task produces the message (and possibly other messages) after consuming all its predecessors. Similarly, a message can have multiple successors, i.e. a task consumes the message (and possibly other messages) to produce several successors. In the example of Figure 2, message M_7 is derived from both messages M_2 and M_6, and M_1 derives two messages M_4 and M_5.

- **Message Event (MgE).** When a task consumes or produces a message, the monitoring framework records this as a message event, i.e. message-consumed or message-produced, respectively. The event information comprises the time it happens, the processing task, and the message involved.
- **Stream State (SS).** The monitoring framework observes every communication channel, i.e. stream, to memorise tasks reading from the stream (called the *task reader*), tasks writing to the stream (called the *task writer*), and the number of messages waiting on the stream (called the *fill level*). Together with the stream's maximum capacity, the fill level is used to determine if the stream is *full* or *empty*.

3.2 Monitoring the Operating System

On the operating system level, the monitoring framework focuses on scheduling activities including space scheduling and time scheduling. Within this paper we refer to space scheduling as mapping and to the time scheduling simply as scheduling. The monitoring framework observes the scheduler to capture all mapping events and scheduling events, and to monitor the resource load.

- **Mapping Event (*MpE*)**. A mapping event occurs when a task is assigned to a computational resource. For these events, the monitoring framework records the event time, the computational resource and the task.
- **Scheduling Event (*ScE*)**. A scheduling event occurs when a task changes its state. There are four basic states of a task: *task-created*, *task-destroyed*, *task-dispatched* and *task-blocked*. The information of these events comprises the task identification, the time when the task changes its state, and its new state. Scheduling events of a task can be used to calculate the task's execution time during a certain period, that is, the total of all intervals between a *task-created* or *task-dispatched* event and its next *task-destroyed* or *task-blocked*.
- **Resource Load (*RL*)**. The monitoring framework keeps track of the work load on each computational resource including execution time and idling time. Adding these two values provides the response time.

4 Benefits of the Monitoring Framework

As presented in Section 3, the monitoring framework provides six kinds of information: Message Derivation Graph (*MDG*), Message Event (*MgE*), Stream State (*SS*), Mapping Event (*MpE*), Scheduling Event (*ScE*) and Resource Load (*RL*). These kinds of information can be used for different purposes including monitoring and optimisation. In this section, we present three potential usages from different combinations of the information (Table 1).

Table 1. Monitoring information needed by different use cases

Information	Performance Metric Calculation	Automatic Load Balancing	Bottleneck Detection
MDG	✓		
MgE	✓		
SS			✓
MpE		✓	
ScE	✓	✓	✓
RL		✓	

4.1 Performance Metric Measurement

The performance of stream-based coordination programs is usually evaluated for individual processing components and for the overall program in terms of latency, throughput and jitter (see Section 2). As the jitter can be deduced from the different observed latencies, this section focuses on calculating other two metrics.

Latency of an Individual Processing Component for Processing a Specific Message.
Let C be a processing component, M be a processed message, and T be the corresponding task of C. The latency of C to process M is the execution time of T within the interval between two points: i) C consumes M (S in Figure 3), and ii) C produces M's last output message (E in Figure 3). The monitoring framework provides this information as follows. The MDG is used to find M's output messages, i.e. M's successors. Then appropriate $MgEs$ are used to determine the two interval points: the event time S

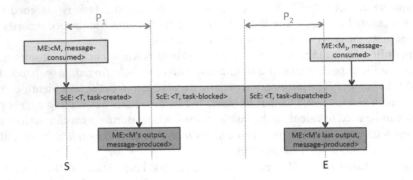

Fig. 3. Latency of an individual processing component

when M is consumed and the event time E when the last output message is produced. Finally, *ScEs* of T help to yield T's total execution time within the specified period. In the example in Figure 3, the latency is the sum of P_1 and P_2.

Throughput of an Individual Processing Component. It is calculated by dividing the total execution time of the corresponding task by the number of processed messages. As mentioned in Section 3.2, the total execution time is obtained from the task's *ScEs* and the number of processed message is gained from the *MgEs* during the task execution.

Latency of a Stream-based Coordination Program for Processing a Single Message. Let N be a stream-based coordination program and M be a processed message. We define the latency here is the time interval from M is consumed by N until all of M's output messages are produced. Again, the *MDG* helps to determine all M's output messages as leaves of the tree rooted by M. For example, O_3 and O_4 in Figure 2 are the output messages of I_2. Then *MgEs* help to determine when M is consumed and when its last output is produced.

Throughput of a Stream-based Coordination Program. It is computed based on the number of messages the program has consumed and the total response time of the program. The number of consumed messages can be deduced from *MpEs*. The total execution time is counted from the first task creation until the last task is destroyed. These events are extracted from the *ScEs*.

4.2   Automatic Load Balancing

Load balancing is a basic strategy to improve system performance by maximising resource utilisation. There are two types of algorithms for load balancing: static and dynamic. The static ones are applied before any input processing and require prior assumption about runtime behaviour such as response time of each task. The dynamic load balancing algorithms are different that they use the system-state and are applied at the runtime. For this reason, dynamic algorithms are a natural use case for our monitoring framework. In the following, we present two approaches of using the monitoring information to guide dynamic load balancing.

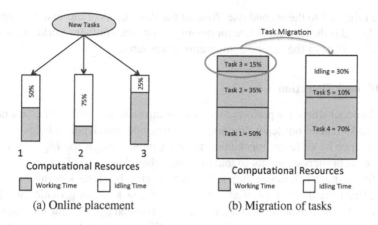

(a) Online placement   (b) Migration of tasks

Fig. 4. Deployment of automatic load balancing

The first approach is the online placement balancing technique (also called centralised load balancing in [24]) in which new tasks are dynamically assigned to computation resources depending on the system state (Figure 4a). Using the monitoring framework, the system state can be expressed by the *RL* in terms of execution time and idling time. This information is used to implement the mapping policy: a task is assigned to the computation resource with the least execution time, i.e. most idling time. In the example in Figure 4a the second computational resource will be chosen for the new task. This simple dynamic mapping aims to balance the working load while minimising the idling time of computational resources.

The second approach is a task migration technique which controls the load balance by moving tasks among computational resources (Figure 4b). Many algorithms have been designed using this approach [5,20,21,27,11]. Algorithms of this approach usually have four components: (1) *Information Policy*: specifies what information about the system-state is necessary and how to collect such information; (2) *Transfer Policy* determines whether a computational resource should to participate in a task migration; (3) *Location Policy* identifies the suitable destination for the task migration; and (4) *Selection Policy* decides which tasks are eligible to migrate.

In the following, we define a simple instance of this approach using the monitoring information to define these policy:

- *Information Policy*. The collected information includes *RL* and *ScEs*, and the method of collecting is using our monitoring framework.
- *Transfer Policy*. A computational resource R_s should participate in a task migration if its current load is 100%, i.e. the idling time is zero.
- *Location Policy*. A computation resource R_d should be a destination if its idling time is non-zero.
- *Section Policy*. If there exists a R_d and a R_s, a task T is chosen from R_s to migrate if T's current load is smaller than the idling time of R_d. T's current load is calculated by using *ScEs* (discussed in Section 3.2).

In the example in Figure 4b, the first computational resource is busy all the time while the second one has 30% idling time. Therefore, tasks from the first computational resource are migrated to the second one. Among the three tasks of the first computational resource, *Task 3* is the best candidate for the migration since only its workload is smaller than the idling time of the second computational resource.

4.3   Bottleneck Detection

Bottlenecks occur where the performance of a system is limited by a single task or a limited set of tasks (called bottleneck points). Detecting bottleneck points helps to improve the performance by different mechanisms: for example, assign the higher scheduling priority for the bottleneck points so that they are scheduled more often.

In the following, we demonstrate a technique to detect bottleneck points by using *SSs* and *ScEs*. Catching the *task-blocked* state, *ScEs* of a task A can provide the blocking frequency of A. The reason for A being blocked is provided by *SS* of the communication streams between A and other tasks. In particular, *SS* of a stream keeps track of alternations on the stream revealing the dynamic interrelation among the stream reader and stream writer. Consider task A and task B connected by a stream, A is blocked by B if A tries to read from the communication stream while it is empty; or A tries to write to the communication stream while it is full.

After obtaining the frequency of which a task blocks others, determining bottleneck points is straightforward. Tasks that cause high blocking frequencies to others tasks are considered bottleneck points.

5   Instantiation of the Monitoring Framework for S-Net

In the following we present a concrete instantiation of the monitoring framework, based on the S-Net runtime system and the LPEL micro kernel.

5.1   Stream-Processing with S-Net

S-Net is a stream-based coordination language [9]. S-Net connects different components called *boxes* via streams. These boxes are not implemented in S-Net, but a separate computational language, e.g. ISO C. Boxes communicate over the streams with typed messages. S-Net is meant to support the transition from sequential code to parallel code, as the concurrency handling is all managed by S-Net. S-Net programs are constructed hierarchically by combinators, such as parallel or serial composition, etc.; always maintaining the SISO property (single input and single output). The available combinators ensure that each stream has a single writer and a single reader.

The S-Net development framework consists of a compiler and a runtime system [8], which translate each box and combinator into a concurrently running computational unit. The streams are realised as uni-directional bounded FIFO buffers.

Instrumenting the S-Net Runtime System. Our goal is to obtain the monitoring information presented in Section 3 for the S-Net runtime system:

– **Message Derivation Graph.** To construct the message derivation graph, all messages must be distinguishable. The monitoring framework therefore attaches each

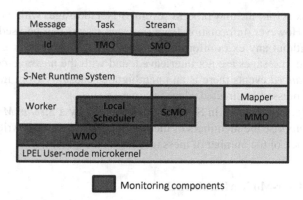

Monitoring components

Fig. 5. The implementation in S-Net and LPEL

message with a *unique identifier (ID)*. Each node in the *MDG* is defined by a message identifier. Edges of the graph are constructed from *MgEs*. This is explained in more detail below.

- **Message Event.** Each task in S-Net is assigned with a unique identifier and is also equipped with a *Task Monitor Object (TMO)* as shown in Figure 5. The TMO monitors the task execution to catch two kinds of message events: *message-consumed* and *message-produced*. Whenever any of these events happens, the TMO records the time and the message identifier.

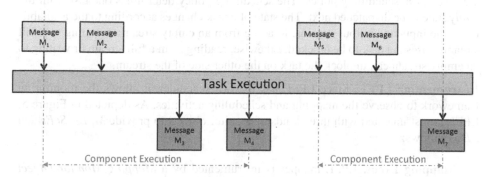

(a) Task execution with *MgEs* and *ScEs*

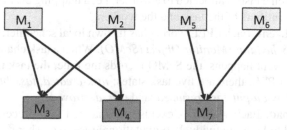

(b) The corresponding *MDG*

Fig. 6. Component executions within a task execution

An S-Net task at runtime may process several S-Net messages within one execution (Figure 6a). However, information from message events can be used to construct the *MDG* without any extra information. This is because the box executions for different input messages are not interleaved, and with the *message-consumed* and *message-produced* events there is an unambiguous causality from input to output messages, expressed as directed edges in Figure 6.

- **Stream State.** Each stream in S-Net is instrumented by a *Stream Monitor Object (SMO)* to memorise the identifiers of the task reader and the task writer. The SMO also keeps track of the number of messages inside the stream.

5.2   LPEL - A User-Mode Microkernel

The Light-Weight Parallel Execution Layer (LPEL) [18] is an execution layer designed for S-Net to give control over the mapping and scheduling on shared memory platforms. LPEL adopts a user-level threading scheme to provide the necessary threading and communication mechanisms in user-space. It builds upon the services provided by the underlying operating system or virtual hardware, such as kernel-level threading, context switching in user-space, and atomic instructions.

The S-Net boxes are mapped to tasks in LPEL. Each LPEL task is implemented as a user-level thread. Tasks are distributed onto LPEL workers, each of which represents a kernel-level thread. Task distribution happens upon task creation according to a task allocation strategy. Each worker manages its own set of assigned tasks and facilitates a worker-local scheduling policy. The scheduling policy determines one task with the *ready* state to be dispatched next. The state of a task changes according to the availability of the input and output streams. Reading from an empty stream or writing to a full stream causes the task to be blocked. Likewise, reading from a full stream or writing to an empty stream can unblock the task on the other side of the stream.

Instrumenting LPEL. Since LPEL has its own scheduler, it allows the monitoring framework to observe the mapping and scheduling activities. As depicted in Figure 5, LPEL is instrumented with three kinds of monitor objects to provide *MpEs*, *ScEs* and *RL* as follows:

- **Mapping Event.** LPEL mapper is instrumented by a *Mapping Monitor Object (MMO)* to capture mapping events. Each worker in LPEL is assigned a unique identifier. When a task is allocated to a worker, i.e. a mapping event happens, MMO records the identifiers of the task and the worker.
- **Scheduling Event.** Each LPEL worker has its own local scheduler, which is instrumented by a *Scheduling Monitor Object (ScMO)*. When a task changes its state, i.e. a scheduling event happens, the ScMO records the time, the task identifier and its new state. In LPEL, there are five task states: *task-created*, *task-blocked-by-input*, *task-blocked-by-output*, *task-resumed*, and *task-destroyed*.
- **Resource Load.** Each worker is exclusively mapped to a processor/core, which is considered to be an individual computational resource. Therefore, each worker is instrumented by a *Worker Monitor Object (WMO)*. The worker's WMO produces the execution time by accumulating execution time of all its tasks. A worker

becomes idling when it has no *ready* task. The WMO also observes these occurrences to form the worker's idling time.

5.3 Operation Modes

The implementation of the monitoring framework in LPEL and S-Net supports different monitoring flags to control the level of desired monitoring information.

- MAPPING_FLAG indicates mapping events are captured
- SCHEDULING_FLAG is set to catch scheduling events
- STREAM_FLAG indicates SMOs are active to observe stream states
- MESSAGE_FLAG is set to record message events
- LOAD_FLAG is set to collect the resource load
- ALL_FLAG claims that all other flags are set

If no flag is set, the application is executed as normal but without producing any monitoring information. Different flags can be combined for specific purposes.

6   Evaluation of the Monitoring Framework

The monitoring framework instruments LPEL and the S-Net runtime system by placing control hooks to collect monitoring information. This causes some overhead compared to the original S-Net and LPEL implementation even if no information is collected. Currently, all monitoring information is sent to the file system and stored in log files. The overhead is evaluated experimentally in terms of response time and size of log files. In the experiments we measure the overhead with different use cases by setting the following different flag combinations:

- **COM1**: no flag is set. This is used to measure the minimum overhead caused by monitoring controls without observing any events.
- **COM2**: the combination of MESSAGE_FLAG and SCHEDULING_FLAG is used for performance metric calculation (Section 4)
- **COM3**: MAPPING_FLAG, SCHEDULING_FLAG and LOAD_FLAG are set for automatic load balancing (Section 4)
- **COM4**: SCHEDULING_FLAG and STREAM_FLAG are combined to detect bottlenecks (Section 4)
- **COM5**: ALL_FLAGS is used to capture all events are captured, providing the maximum overhead

The monitoring overhead is caused by observing messages (TMO), streams (SMO), workers (WMO), the mapper (MMO), and the scheduler (ScMO). The overhead caused by observing messages and streams is proportional to the number of messages and streams, respectively. The overhead of MMO depends on the amount of mapping events while the overhead of ScMO and WMO depends on the number of scheduling events. These kinds of overhead are therefore affected by LPEL's scheduling policies. The experiment is performed on different applications with various values of these variables as shown in Table 2. These applications include:

Table 2. Application properties running on a 48-core machine

Application	#MpE	#ScE	#Message	#Stream
ANT	$278 \cdot 10^3$	$2.4 \cdot 10^6$	$1.15 \cdot 10^6$	$10 \cdot 10^3$
DES	$320 \cdot 10^3$	$4.7 \cdot 10^6$	$470 \cdot 10^3$	62
MC	$5 \cdot 10^6$	$33.8 \cdot 10^6$	$19.3 \cdot 10^6$	$5 \cdot 10^6$
RT	$1.8 \cdot 10^3$	$20 \cdot 10^3$	$23 \cdot 10^3$	100

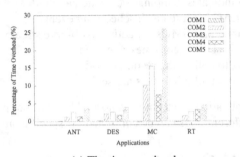

(a) The time overhead

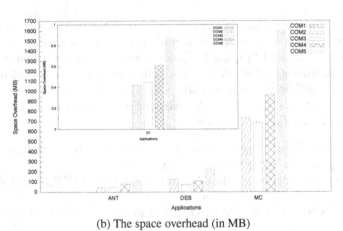

(b) The space overhead (in MB)

Fig. 7. The overhead of the monitoring framework in time and space

- **ANT** is a solver for combinatorial optimisation problems based on the behaviour of ants [4]. Several ants iteratively construct solutions to a given problem and leave a pheromone trail behind. Following ants use these trails as guide and base their decisions on it, refining previously found good solutions. In this experiment, the application computes a schedule for 1000 jobs using 45 parallel ants that repeat the solver step 1000 times.
- **DES** implements a DES encryptor [3]. The experiment encrypts 500kB of data.
- **MC** is an application to calculate option prices using the Monte Carlo method [2]. The experiment is performed with 1 million price paths.

- **RT** implements a distributed solver for ray-tracing [16]. In the experiment, the 100 scenes are dynamically allocated to one of the four solvers with automatic load balancing.

All applications are run on a 48-core machine comprising 4 sockets with 2 by 6 core AMD Opteron 6174 CPUs and a total of 256 GB main memory. The time and space overhead is shown in Figure 7. Generally, the time overhead depends on the number of monitored events. The minimum overhead (COM1) is negligible for most of the cases. There even appears a negative overhead for MC and RT. We attribute this negative overhead to scheduling anomalies similar to timing anomalies in processors [23].

The time overhead of different combinations of flags varies from application to application depending on the number of monitored objects (mapping events, scheduling events, messages and streams). In the current implementation, the monitoring information is sent to the file system and therefore the time overhead is also affected by the response time of the application. As the file I/O is performed asynchronously by the operating system, the time overhead is quite small for relatively long running application. Consequently, for most of the applications the time overhead is relatively small for all flag combinations. For the MC application the overhead is quite large because it has a very large number of monitored objects while the response time is small compared to the amount of data which outweighs any benefits of asynchronous I/O operations.

The space overhead is proportional to the amount of collected data, or the number of monitored objects. As shown in Figure 7b, MC with the highest number of monitored objects has the highest space overhead. Similarly, RT has the least space overhead as it has the smallest number of monitored objects.

7 Related Work

Analysing the performance of parallel code is a challenging task. The performance of a sequential program typically stays stable as long as the conditions of the executing environment stay stable as well, i.e. performance fluctuations are caused by external factors. For parallel code this is not necessarily the case as program-internal load distribution and scheduling techniques may influence the performance of the program as much as external factors such as competition for computing resources and the scheduler's arbitration policy. In the presented execution framework where tasks can execute fully asynchronously the resource mapping and scheduling strategies of the execution layer are as important factors in performance analysis as the sequential performance of individual tasks. It is tools measuring the impact of the former that we survey here. We limit our comparison to approaches that do not require explicit instrumentation of code, i.e. to approaches that are transparent for the application programmer. The main point of comparison shall be the induced overhead.

An early approach to tool-assisted and automated performance analysis of parallel and distributed programs is IPS and its successor IPS-2 [26,13]. IPS allows for fine-grained control over the detail level of captured runtime information ranging from low-level events such as task entry and exit, scheduler blocks and unblocks and message sending over process-level based events such as competition for shared resources to top-level observations such as the total response time of a program. The inflicted overhead lies at around 40% when capturing all information.

Paradyn [14] features a configuration language that allows for the specification of performance metrics and points for instrumentation, but does not require programmers' intervention as instrumentation is dynamically inserted into running executables. The system uses system-level daemons and user-level techniques to gather runtime information. The system self-monitors and adjusts observations based on a user-defined threshold for tolerable overhead. Shared-memory specific analysis techniques in Paradyn are discussed in [25]. No manual instrumentation is required as analysis is based (and depends) on querying software-implemented cache coherence protocols. The overhead of data-collection ranges from 3% - 11%. In recently developed frameworks of the same research group, agent-based dynamic instrumentation and flow-based analysis techniques incur overheads of 1% for I/O-bound workloads. Where large numbers of function calls are involved, the overhead increases to up to 35% [15].

The TAU parallel performance system [19] allows for automatic instrumentation of source code as well as it exposes an API to application programmers for tightly orchestrated observations. The framework provides an extensive collection of tools for performance data-collection, interpretation and visualisation. Although the overheads can be substantial, the system can automatically correct the measurements to represent the runtimes of unobserved runs of an application. Because of the similarities between S-Net and component-based software system it is worth noting that the TAU framework is used for dynamic instrumentation of components in CCA [12].

Several other extensive toolkits for performance analysis exist, as for example, Scalasca [7], Periscope [17] and HPCToolkit [1], which we can only mention but not treat in detail here. All of these tools support automatic instrumentation or sampling and include analysis tools for their collected data sets. These toolkits, as the ones mentioned above, are targeted on large-scale (HPC) programming but maintain a broad applicability. Because of this, these toolkits are complex instruments on its own and require some proficiency in using them. Also, although mainly focussed on debugging stream-based applications, we shall mention SPADE [6] here for it is by its nature related to S-Net. The issue of semantically debugging stream-based applications is not in the scope of this paper but we acknowledge its importance as an essential research area on which we will focus in future work within the S-Net project.

8   Conclusion

The support of monitoring is essential for achieving high system utilisation of parallel execution platforms. In this paper we presented a monitoring framework that is geared towards stream-based coordination programs to monitor data for the use cases of the calculation of performance metrics, automatic load balancing, and bottleneck detection. This monitoring framework extracts information from both, the runtime system of the stream-based coordination programs, as well as from the underlying operating system. The extracted information provides the trace of non-deterministic behaviours of the application at both levels.

The main contribution of this paper is summarised by the results given in Table 1 and Figure 7a. Table 1 shows for stream-based coordination programs what kind of monitoring data are needed for the different use cases including calculation of performance metrics, automatic load balancing, and bottleneck detection. This relation is specific for the chosen S-Net framework, but can be generalised also to other coordination programs as we described why each specific kind of information is needed.

The monitoring approach is fully transparent to the user and is purely software-based. The overhead of different monitoring scenarios is given in Figure 7a, which shows for most benchmarks a negligible overhead of less than 5%. Just for the MC benchmark the overhead is up to about 26%, which is explained by the fact that in this benchmark the concurrency is too fine grained to be efficiently exploited using S-Net.

Acknowledgements. The research leading to these results has received funding from the IST FP7 research project "Asynchronous and Dynamic Virtualization through performance ANalysis to support Concurrency Engineering (ADVANCE)" under contract no IST-2010-248828.

References

1. Adhianto, L., Banerjee, S., Fagan, M., Krentel, M., Marin, G., Mellor-Crummey, J., Tallent, N.R.: Hpctoolkit: tools for performance analysis of optimized parallel programs. Concurrency and Computation: Practice and Experience 22(6), 685–701 (2010)
2. Black, F., Scholes, M.: The Pricing of Options and Corporate Liabilities. The Journal of Political Economy 81(3), 637–654 (1973)
3. DES. Data Encryption Standard. In: FIPS PUB 46-3. Federal Information Processing Standards Publication (1977)
4. Dorigo, M., Stützle, T.: Ant Colony Optimization. Bradford Book (2004)
5. Eager, D.L., Lazowska, E.D., Zahorjan, J.: Adaptive load sharing in homogeneous distributed systems. IEEE Trans. Softw. Eng. 12(5), 662–675 (1986)
6. Gedik, B., Andrade, H., Frenkiel, A., De Pauw, W., Pfeifer, M., Allen, P., Cohen, N., Wu, K.-L.: Tools and strategies for debugging distributed stream processing applications. Softw. Pract. Exper. 39, 1347–1376 (2009)
7. Geimer, M., Wolf, F., Wylie, B.J.N., Ábrahám, E., Becker, D., Mohr, B.: The Scalasca performance toolset architecture. Concurrency and Computation: Practice and Experience 22(6), 702–719 (2010)
8. Grelck, C., Scholz, S., Shafarenko, A.: Asynchronous Stream Processing with S-Net. International Journal of Parallel Programming 38(1), 38–67 (2010)
9. Grelck, C., Scholz, S.-B., Shafarenko, A.: A Gentle Introduction to S-Net: Typed Stream Processing and Declarative Coordination of Asynchronous Components. Parallel Processing Letters 18(2), 221–237 (2008)
10. Kahn, G.: The semantics of a simple language for parallel programming. In: Rosenfeld, J.L. (ed.) Proc. IFIP Congress on Information Processing, Stockholm, Sweden (August 1974) ISBN: 0-7204-2803-3
11. Lai, A.-C., Shieh, C.-K., Kok, Y.-T.: Load balancing in distributed shared memory systems. In: IEEE International on Performance, Computing, and Communications Conference, IPCCC 1997, pp. 152–158 (February 1997)

12. Malony, A., Shende, S., Trebon, N., Ray, J., Armstrong, R., Rasmussen, C., Sottile, M.: Performance technology for parallel and distributed component software. Concurrency and Computation: Practice and Experience 17(2-4), 117–141 (2005)
13. Miller, B., Clark, M., Hollingsworth, J., Kierstead, S., Lim, S.-S., Torzewski, T.: Ips-2: the second generation of a parallel program measurement system. IEEE Transactions on Parallel and Distributed Systems 1(2), 206–217 (1990)
14. Miller, B.P., Callaghan, M.D., Cargille, J.M., Hollingsworth, J.K., Irvin, R.B., Karavanic, K.L., Kunchithapadam, K., Newhall, T.: The paradyn parallel performance measurement tool. Computer 28, 37–46 (1995)
15. Mirgorodskiy, A.V., Miller, B.P.: Diagnosing Distributed Systems with Self-propelled Instrumentation. In: Issarny, V., Schantz, R. (eds.) Middleware 2008. LNCS, vol. 5346, pp. 82–103. Springer, Heidelberg (2008)
16. Penczek, F., Herhut, S., Scholz, S.-B., Shafarenko, A., Yang, J., Chen, C.-Y., Bagherzadeh, N., Grelck, C.: Message Driven Programming with S-Net: Methodology and Performance. In: International Conference on Parallel Processing Workshops, pp. 405–412 (2010)
17. Petkov, V., Gerndt, M.: Integrating parallel application development with performance analysis in periscope. In: 2010 IEEE International Symposium on Parallel Distributed Processing, Workshops and Phd Forum (IPDPSW), pp. 1–8 (April 2010)
18. Prokesch, D.: A light-weight parallel execution layer for shared-memory stream processing. Master's thesis, Technische Universität Wien, Vienna, Austria (February 2010)
19. Shende, S.S., Malony, A.D.: The tau parallel performance system. Int. J. High Perform. Comput. Appl. 20(2), 287–311 (2006)
20. Shivaratri, N., Krueger, P.: Two adaptive location policies for global scheduling algorithms. In: Proceedings of 10th International Conference on Distributed Computing Systems, May-1 June, pp. 502–509 (1990)
21. Shivaratri, N., Krueger, P., Singhal, M.: Load distributing for locally distributed systems. Computer 25(12), 33–44 (1992)
22. Wadge, W.W., Ashcroft, E.A.: LUCID, the dataflow programming language. Academic Press Professional, Inc., San Diego (1985)
23. Wenzel, I., Kirner, R., Puschner, P., Rieder, B.: Principles of timing anomalies in superscalar processors. In: Proc. 5th International Conference of Quality Software, Melbourne, Australia (September 2005)
24. Wilkinson, B., Allen, M.: Parallel programming - techniques and applications using networked workstations and parallel computers, 2nd edn. Pearson Education (2005)
25. Xu, Z., Larus, J.R., Miller, B.P.: Shared-memory performance profiling. In: Proceedings of the Sixth ACM SIGPLAN Symposium on Principles and Practice of Parallel Programming, PPOPP 1997, pp. 240–251. ACM, New York (1997)
26. Yang, C.-Q., Miller, B.: Performance measurement for parallel and distributed programs: a structured and automatic approach. IEEE Transactions on Software Engineering 15(12), 1615–1629 (1989)
27. Zhang, Y., Kameda, H., Shimizu, K.: Adaptive bidding load balancing algorithms in heterogeneous distributed systems. In: Proceedings of the Second International Workshop on Modeling, Analysis, and Simulation of Computer and Telecommunication Systems, MASCOTS 1994, January-2 February, pp. 250–254 (1994)

An Optimal Parallel Prefix-Sums Algorithm on the Memory Machine Models for GPUs

Koji Nakano

Department of Information Engineering, Hiroshima University,
Kagamiyama 1-4-1, Higashi Hiroshima 739-8527, Japan
nakano@cs.hiroshima-u.ac.jp

Abstract. The main contribution of this paper is to show optimal algorithms computing the sum and the prefix-sums on two memory machine models, the Discrete Memory Machine (DMM) and the Unified Memory Machine (UMM). The DMM and the UMM are theoretical parallel computing models that capture the essence of the shared memory and the global memory of GPUs. These models have three parameters, the number p of threads, the width w of the memory, and the memory access latency l. We first show that the sum of n numbers can be computed in $O(\frac{n}{w} + \frac{nl}{p} + l \log n)$ time units on the DMM and the UMM. We then go on to show that $\Omega(\frac{n}{w} + \frac{nl}{p} + l \log n)$ time units are necessary to compute the sum. Finally, we show an optimal parallel algorithm that computes the prefix-sums of n numbers in $O(\frac{n}{w} + \frac{nl}{p} + l \log n)$ time units on the DMM and the UMM.

Keywords: Memory machine models, prefix-sums computation, parallel algorithm, GPU, CUDA.

1 Introduction

The research of parallel algorithms has a long history of more than 40 years. Sequential algorithms have been developed mostly on the Random Access Machine (RAM) [1]. In contrast, since there are a variety of connection methods and patterns between processors and memories, many parallel computing models have been presented and many parallel algorithmic techniques have been shown on them. The most well-studied parallel computing model is the Parallel Random Access Machine (PRAM) [5,7,19], which consists of processors and a shared memory. Each processor on the PRAM can access any address of the shared memory in a time unit. The PRAM is a good parallel computing model in the sense that parallelism of each problem can be revealed by the performance of parallel algorithms on the PRAM. However, since the PRAM requires a shared memory that can be accessed by all processors in the same time, it is not feasible.

The GPU (Graphical Processing Unit), is a specialized circuit designed to accelerate computation for building and manipulating images [10,11,13,20]. Latest GPUs are designed for general purpose computing and can perform computation

Y. Xiang et al. (Eds.): ICA3PP 2012, Part I, LNCS 7439, pp. 99–113, 2012.

in applications traditionally handled by the CPU. Hence, GPUs have recently attracted the attention of many application developers [10,16]. NVIDIA provides a parallel computing architecture called *CUDA* (Compute Unified Device Architecture) [18], the computing engine for NVIDIA GPUs. CUDA gives developers access to the virtual instruction set and memory of the parallel computational elements in NVIDIA GPUs. In many cases, GPUs are more efficient than multi-core processors [14], since they have hundreds of processor cores and very high memory bandwidth.

CUDA uses two types of memories in the NVIDIA GPUs: *the global memory* and *the shared memory* [18]. The global memory is implemented as an off-chip DRAM, and has large capacity, say, 1.5-6 Gbytes, but its access latency is very long. The shared memory is an extremely fast on-chip memory with lower capacity, say, 16-64 Kbytes. The efficient usage of the global memory and the shared memory is a key for CUDA developers to accelerate applications using GPUs. In particular, we need to consider *the coalescing* of the global memory access and *the bank conflict* of the shared memory access [13,14,17]. To maximize the bandwidth between the GPU and the DRAM chips, the consecutive addresses of the global memory must be accessed in the same time. Thus, threads of CUDA should perform coalesced access when they access to the global memory. The address space of the shared memory is mapped into several physical memory banks. If two or more threads access to the same memory banks in the same time, the access requests are processed sequentially. Hence to maximize the memory access performance, threads should access to distinct memory banks to avoid the bank conflicts of the memory access.

In our previous paper [15], we have introduced two models, *the Discrete Memory Machine (DMM)* and *the Unified Memory Machine (UMM)*, which reflect the essential features of the shared memory and the global memory of NVIDIA GPUs. The outline of the architectures of the DMM and the UMM are illustrated in Figure 1. In both architectures, *a sea of threads (Ts)* is connected to *the memory banks (MBs)* through *the memory management unit (MMU)*. Each thread is a Random Access Machine (RAM) [1], which can execute one of the fundamental operations in a time unit. We do not discuss the architecture of the sea of threads in this paper, but we can imagine that it consists of a set of multi-core processors which can execute many threads in parallel and/or in time-sharing manner. Threads are executed in SIMD [4] fashion, and the processors run on the same program and work on the different data.

MBs constitute a single address space of the memory. A single address space of the memory is mapped to the MBs in an interleaved way such that the word of data of address i is stored in the $(i \bmod w)$-th bank, where w is the number of MBs. The main difference of the two architectures is the connection of the address line between the MMU and the MBs, which can transfer an address value. In the DMM, the address lines connect the MBs and the MMU separately, while a single address line from the MMU is connected to the MBs in the UMM. Hence, in the UMM, the same address value is broadcast to every MB, and the same address of the MBs can be accessed in each time unit. On the other hand, different addresses of the MBs can be accessed in the DMM. Since the memory access of the UMM is more restricted than that of the DMM, the UMM is less powerful than the DMM.

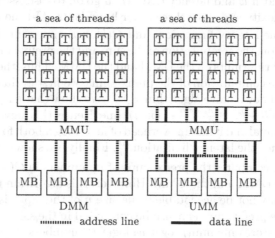

Fig. 1. The architectures of the DMM and the UMM

The performance of algorithms of the PRAM is usually evaluated using two parameters: the size n of the input and the number p of processors. For example, it is well known that the sum of n numbers can be computed in $O(\frac{n}{p} + \log n)$ time on the PRAM [5]. We will use four parameters, the size n of the input, the number p of threads, the width w and the latency l of the memory when we evaluate the performance of algorithms on the DMM and on the UMM. The width w is the number of memory banks and the latency l is the number of time units to complete the memory access. Hence, the performance of algorithms on the DMM and the UMM is evaluated as a function of n (the size of a problem), p (the number of threads), w (the width of a memory), and l (the latency of a memory). In NVIDIA GPUs, the width w of global and shared memory is 16 or 32. Also, the latency l of the global memory is several hundreds clock cycles. In CUDA, a grid can have at most 65535 blocks with at most 1024 threads each [18]. Thus, the number p of threads can be 65 million.

Suppose that an array a of n numbers is given. The prefix-sums of a is the array of size n such that the i-th ($0 \le i \le n-1$) element is $a[0]+a[1]+\cdots+a[i]$. Clearly, a sequential algorithm can compute the prefix sums by executing $a[i+1] \leftarrow a[i+1] + a[i]$ for all i ($0 \le i \le n-1$). The computation of the prefix-sums of an array is one of the most important algorithmic procedures. Many algorithms such as graph algorithms, geometric algorithms, image processing and matrix computation call prefix-sums algorithms as a subroutine. In particular, many parallel algorithms uses a parallel prefix-sums algorithm. For example, the prefix-sums computation is used to obtain the pre-order, the in-order, and the post-order of a rooted binary tree in parallel [5]. So, it is very important to develop efficient parallel algorithms for the prefix-sums.

The main contribution of this paper is to show an optimal prefix-sums algorithm on the DMM and the UMM. We first show that the sum of n numbers can be computed in $O(\frac{n}{w} + \frac{nl}{p} + l\log n)$ time units using p threads on the DMM and the UMM with width w and latency l. We then go on to discuss the lower bound of the time complexity and show three lower bounds, $\Omega(\frac{n}{w})$-time bandwidth limitation, $\Omega(\frac{nl}{p})$-time latency limitation, and $\Omega(l\log n)$-time reduction limitation. From this discussion, the computation of the sum and the prefix-sums takes at least $\Omega(\frac{n}{w} + \frac{nl}{p} + l\log n)$ time units on the DMM and the UMM. Thus, the sum algorithm is optimal. For the computation of the prefix-sums, we first evaluate the computing time of a well-known naive algorithm [8,19]. We show that a naive prefix-sums algorithm runs in $O(\frac{n\log n}{w} + \frac{nl\log n}{p} + l\log n)$ time. Hence, this naive prefix-sums algorithm is not optimal and it has an overhead of factor $\log n$ both for the bandwidth limitation $\frac{n}{w}$ and for the latency limitation $\frac{nl}{p}$. Finally, we show an optimal parallel algorithm that computes the prefix-sums of n numbers in $O(\frac{n}{w} + \frac{nl}{p} + l\log n)$ time units on the DMM and the UMM. However, this algorithm uses work space of size n and it may not be acceptable if the size n of the input is very large. We also show that the prefix-sums can also be computed in the same time units, even if work space can store only $\min(p\log p, wl\log(wl))$ numbers.

Several techniques for computing the prefix-sums on GPUs have been shown in [8]. They have presented a complicated data routing technique to avoid the bank conflict in the computation of the prefix-sums. However, their algorithm performs memory access to distant locations in parallel and it performs non-coalesced memory access. Hence it is not efficient for the UMM, that is, the global memory of GPUs. In [9] a work-efficient parallel algorithm for prefix-sums on the GPU has been presented. However, the algorithm uses work space of $n\log n$, and also the performance of the algorithm has not been evaluated.

This paper is organized as follows. Section 2 reviews the Discrete Memory Machine (DMM) and the Unified Memory Machine (UMM) introduced in our previous paper [15]. In Section 3, we evaluate the computing time of the contiguous memory access to the memory of the DMM and the UMM. The contiguous memory access is a key ingredient of parallel algorithm development on the DMM and the UMM. Using the contiguous access, we show that the sum of n numbers can be computed in $O(\frac{n}{w} + \frac{nl}{p} + l\log n)$ time units in Section 4. We then go on to discuss the lower bound of the time complexity and show three lower bounds, $\Omega(\frac{n}{w})$-time bandwidth limitation, $\Omega(\frac{nl}{p})$-time latency limitation, and $\Omega(l\log n)$-time reduction limitation in Section 5. Section 6 shows a naive prefix-sums algorithm, which runs in $O(\frac{n\log n}{w} + \frac{nl\log n}{p} + l\log n)$ time units. Finally, we show an optimal parallel prefix-sums algorithm running in $O(\frac{n}{w} + \frac{nl}{p} + l\log n)$ time units. Section 8 offers conclusion of this paper.

2   Parallel Memory Machines: DMM and UMM

The main purpose of this section is to review the Discrete Memory Machine (DMM) and the Unified Memory Machine (UMM). introduced in our previous paper [15].

We first define *the Discrete Memory Machine (DMM)* of width w and latency l. Let $m[i]$ $(i \geq 0)$ denote a memory cell of address i in the memory. Let $B[j] = \{m[j], m[j + w], m[j + 2w], m[j + 3w], \ldots\}$ $(0 \leq j \leq w - 1)$ denote *the j-th bank* of the memory. Clearly, a memory cell $m[i]$ is in the $(i \bmod w)$-th memory bank. We assume that memory cells in different banks can be accessed in a time unit, but no two memory cells in the same bank can be accessed in a time unit. Also, we assume that l time units are necessary to complete an access request and continuous requests are processed in a pipeline fashion through the MMU. Thus, it takes $k + l - 1$ time units to complete k access requests to a particular bank.

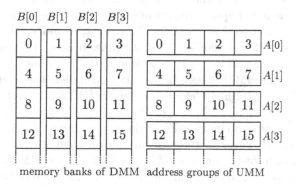

Fig. 2. Banks and address groups for $w = 4$

We assume that p threads are partitioned into $\frac{p}{w}$ groups of w threads called *warps*. More specifically, p threads are partitioned into $\frac{p}{w}$ warps $W(0), W(1),$ $\ldots, W(\frac{p}{w} - 1)$ such that $W(i) = \{T(i \cdot w), T(i \cdot w + 1), \ldots, T((i + 1) \cdot w - 1)\}$ $(0 \leq i \leq \frac{p}{w} - 1)$. Warps are dispatched for memory access in turn, and w threads in a warp try to access the memory in the same time. In other words, $W(0), W(1), \ldots, W(w - 1)$ are dispatched in a round-robin manner if at least one thread in a warp requests memory access. If no thread in a warp needs memory access, such warp is not dispatched for memory access. When $W(i)$ is dispatched, w thread in $W(i)$ sends memory access requests, one request per thread, to the memory. We also assume that a thread cannot send a new memory access request until the previous memory access request is completed. Hence, if a thread send a memory access request, it must wait l time units to send a new memory access request.

For the reader's benefit, let us evaluate the time for memory access using Figure 3 on the DMM for $p = 8$, $w = 4$, and $l = 3$. In the figure, $p = 8$ threads are partitioned into $\frac{p}{w} = 2$ warps $W(0) = \{T(0), T(1), T(2), T(3)\}$ and $W(1) = \{T(4), T(5), T(6), T(7)\}$. As illustrated in the figure, 4 threads in $W(0)$ try to access $m[0], m[1], m[6]$, and $m[10]$, and those in $W(1)$ try to access $m[8], m[9], m[14]$, and $m[15]$. The time for the memory access are evaluated under the assumption that memory access are processed by imaginary l pipeline stages with w registers each as illustrated in the figure. Each pipeline register in the first stage receives memory access request from threads in an dispatched warp. Each i-th ($0 \leq i \leq w - 1$) pipeline register receives the request to the i-th memory bank. In each time unit, a memory request in a pipeline register is moved to the next one. We assume that the memory access completes when the request reaches the last pipeline register.

Note that, the architecture of pipeline registers illustrated in Figure 3 are imaginary, and it is used only for evaluating the computing time. The actual architecture should involves a multistage interconnection network [6,12] or sorting network [2,3], to route memory access requests.

Let us evaluate the time for memory access on the DMM. First, access request for $m[0], m[1], m[6]$ are sent to the first stage. Since $m[6]$ and $m[10]$ are in the same bank $B[2]$, their memory requests cannot be sent to the first stage in the same time. Next, the $m[10]$ is sent to the first stage. After that, memory access requests for $m[8], m[9], m[14], m[15]$ are sent in the same time, because they are in different memory banks. Finally, after $l - 1 = 2$ time units, these memory requests are processed. Hence, the DMM takes 5 time units to complete the memory access.

We next define *the Unified Memory Machine* (*UMM*)) of width w as follows. Let $A[j] = \{m[j \cdot w], m[j \cdot w + 1], \ldots, m[(j + 1) \cdot w - 1]\}$ denote the j-th address group. We assume that memory cells in the same address group are processed in the same time. However, if they are in the different groups, one time unit is necessary for each of the groups. Also, similarly to the DMM, p threads are partitioned into warps and each warp access to the memory in turn.

Again, let us evaluate the time for memory access using Figure 3 on the UMM for $p = 8$, $w = 4$, and $l = 3$. The memory access requests by $W(0)$ are in three address groups. Thus, three time units are necessary to send them to the first stage. Next, two time units are necessary to send memory access requests by $W(1)$, because they are in two address groups. After that, it takes $l - 1 = 2$ time units to process the memory access requests. Hence, totally $3 + 2 + 2 = 7$ time units are necessary to complete all memory access.

3   Contiguous Memory Access

The main purpose of this section is to review the contiguous memory access on the DMM and the UMM shown in [15]. Suppose that an array a of size n ($\geq p$) is given. We use p threads to access to all of n memory cells in a such that each thread accesses to $\frac{n}{p}$ memory cells. Note that "accessing to" can be "reading from" or "writing in." Let $a[i]$ ($0 \leq i \leq n - 1$)denote the i-th memory cells in a. When $n \geq p$, the contiguous access can be performed as follows:

[**Contiguous memory access**]
for $t \leftarrow 0$ to $\frac{n}{p} - 1$ do
  for $i \leftarrow 0$ to $p - 1$ do in parallel
    $T(i)$ access to $a[p \cdot t + i]$

We will evaluate the computing time. For each t ($0 \leq t \leq \frac{n}{p} - 1$), p threads access to p memory cells $a[pt], a[pt + 1], \ldots, a[p(t + 1) - 1]$. This memory access

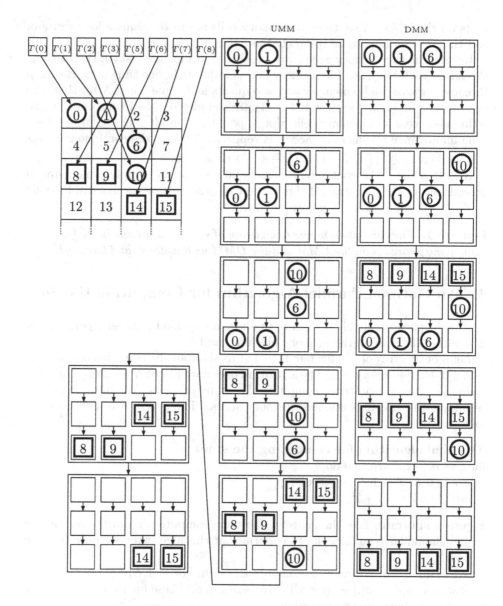

Fig. 3. An example of memory access

is performed by $\frac{p}{w}$ warps in turn. More specifically, first, w threads in $W(0)$ access to $a[pt], a[pt + 1], \ldots, a[pt + w - 1]$. After that, p threads in $W(1)$ access to $a[pt + w], a[pt + w + 1], \ldots, a[pt + 2w - 1]$, and the same operation is repeatedly performed. In general, p threads in $W(j)$ $(0 \leq j \leq \frac{p}{w} - 1)$ accesses to $a[pt + jw], a[pt + jw + 1], \ldots, a[pt + (j + 1)w - 1]$. Since w memory cells are accessed by a warp are in the different bank, the access can be completed in l time units on the DMM. Also, these w memory cells are in the same address group, and thus, the access can be completed in l time units on the UMM.

Recall that the memory access are processed in pipeline fashion such that w threads in each $W(j)$ send w memory access requests in one time unit. Hence, p threads $\frac{p}{w}$ warps send p memory access requests in $\frac{p}{w}$ time units. After that, the last memory access requests by $W(\frac{p}{w}-1)$ are completed in $l-1$ time units. Thus, p threads access to p memory cells $a[pt], a[pt+1], \ldots, a[p(t+1)-1]$ in $\frac{p}{w}+l-1$ time units. Since this memory access is repeated $\frac{n}{p}$ times, the contiguous access can be done in $\frac{n}{p} \cdot (\frac{p}{w}+l-1) = O(\frac{n}{w}+\frac{nl}{p})$ time units.

If $n < p$ then, the contiguous memory access can be simply done using n threads out of the p threads. If this is the case, the memory access can be done by $O(\frac{n}{w}+l)$ time units. Therefore, we have,

Lemma 1. *The contiguous access to an array of size n can be done in $O(\frac{n}{w}+\frac{nl}{p}+l)$ time using p threads on the UMM and the DMM with width w and latency l.*

4   An Optimal Parallel Algorithm for Computing the Sum

The main purpose of this section is to show an optimal parallel algorithm for computing the sum on the memory machine models.

Let a be an array of $n = 2^m$ numbers. Let us show an algorithm to compute the sum $a[0]+a[1]+\cdots+a[n-1]$. The algorithm uses a well-known parallel computing technique which repeatedly computes the sums of pairs. We implement this technique to perform contiguous memory access. The details are spelled out as follows:

[Optimal algorithm for computing the sum]
for $t \leftarrow m-1$ down to 0 do
  for $i \leftarrow 0$ to $2^t - 1$ do in parallel
    $a[i] \leftarrow a[i] + a[i + 2^t]$

Figure 4 illustrates how the sums of pairs are computed. From the figure, the reader should have no difficulty to confirm that this algorithm compute the sum correctly.

We assume that p threads to compute the sum. For each t ($0 \leq t \leq m-1$), 2^t operations "$a[i] \leftarrow a[i] + a[i + 2^t]$" are performed. These operation involve the following memory access operations:

- reading from $a[0], a[1], \ldots, a[2^t - 1]$,
- reading from $a[2^t], a[2^t + 1], \ldots, a[2 \cdot 2^t - 1]$, and
- writing in $a[0], a[1], \ldots, a[2^t - 1]$,

Since these memory access operations are contiguous, they can be done in $O(\frac{2^t}{w} + \frac{2^t l}{p} + l)$ time using p threads both on the DMM and on the UMM with width w and latency l from Lemma 1. Thus, the total computing time is

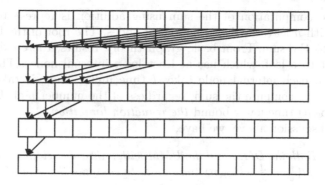

Fig. 4. Illustrating the summing algorithm for n numbers

$$\sum_{t=0}^{m-1} O(\frac{2^t}{w} + \frac{2^t l}{p} + l) = O(\frac{2^m}{w} + \frac{2^m l}{p} + lm)$$

$$= O(\frac{n}{w} + \frac{nl}{p} + l \log n)$$

and we have,

Lemma 2. *The sum of n numbers can be computed in $O(\frac{n}{w} + \frac{nl}{p} + l \log n)$ time units using p threads on the DMM and on the UMM with width w and latency l.*

5   The Lower Bound of the Computing Time and the Latency Hiding

Let us discuss the lower bound of the time necessary to compute the sum on the DMM and the UMM to show that our parallel summing algorithm for Lemma 2 is optimal. We will show three lower bounds, $\Omega(\frac{n}{w})$-time bandwidth limitation, $\Omega(\frac{nl}{p})$-time latency limitation, and $\Omega(l \log n)$-time reduction limitation.

Since the width of the memory is w, at most w numbers in the memory can be read in a time unit. Clearly, all of the n numbers must be read to compute the sum. Hence, $\Omega(\frac{n}{w})$ time units are necessary to compute the sum. We call the $\Omega(\frac{n}{w})$-time lower bound *the bandwidth limitation*.

Since the memory access takes latency l, a thread can send at most $\frac{t}{l}$ memory read requests in t time units. Thus, p threads can send at most $\frac{pt}{l}$ total memory requests in t time units. Since at least n numbers in the memory must be read to compute the sum, $\frac{pt}{l} \geq n$ must be satisfied. Thus, at least $t = \Omega(\frac{nl}{p})$ time units are necessary. We call the $\Omega(\frac{nl}{p})$-time lower bound *the latency limitation*.

Each thread can perform a binary operation such as addition in a time unit. If at least one of the two operands of a binary operation is stored in the shared memory, it takes at least l time units to obtain the resulting value. Clearly, addition operation must be performed $n - 1$ times to compute the sum of n

numbers. The computation of the sum using addition is represented using a binary tree with n leaves and $n - 1$ internal nodes. The root of the binary tree corresponds to the sum. From basic graph theory results, there exists a path from the root to a leaf, which has at least $\log n$ internal nodes. The addition corresponds to each internal node takes l time units. Thus, it takes at least $\Omega(l \log n)$ time to compute the sum, regardless of the number p of threads. We call the $\Omega(l \log n)$-time lower bound *the reduction limitation*.

From the discussion above, we have,

Theorem 1. *Both the DMM and the UMM with p threads, width w, and latency l takes at least $\Omega(\frac{n}{w} + \frac{nl}{p} + l \log n)$ time units to compute the sum of n numbers.*

From Theorem 1, the parallel algorithm for commuting the sum shown for Lemma 2 is optimal.

Let us discuss about three limitations. From a practical point of view, width w and latency l are constant values that cannot be changed by parallel computer users. These values are fixed when a parallel computer based on the memory machine models is manufactured. Also, the size n of the input are variable. Programmers can adjust the number p of threads to obtain the best performance. Thus, the value of the latency limitation $\frac{nl}{p}$ can be changed by programmers.

Let us compare the values of three limitations.

$wl \leq p$: From $\frac{n}{w} \geq \frac{nl}{p}$, the bandwidth limitation dominates the latency limitation.

$wl \leq \frac{n}{\log n}$: From $\frac{n}{w} \geq l \log n$, the bandwidth limitation dominates the reduction limitation.

$p \leq \frac{n}{\log n}$: From $\frac{nl}{p} \geq l \log n$, the latency limitation dominates the reduction limitation.

Thus, if both $wl \leq p$ and $wl \leq \frac{n}{\log n}$ are satisfied, the computing time is of the sum algorithm for Lemma 2 is $O(\frac{n}{w})$. Note that the memory machine models have wl imaginary registers. Since more than one memory requests by a thread can not be stored in imaginary pipeline registers, $wl \leq p$ must be satisfied to fill all the pipeline registers with memory access requests by p threads. Since the sum algorithm has $\log n$ stages and expected $\frac{n}{\log n}$ memory access requests are sent to the imaginary pipeline registers, $wl \leq \frac{n}{\log n}$ must also be satisfied to fill all the pipeline registers with $\frac{n}{\log n}$ memory access requests. From the discussion above, to hide the latency, the number p of threads must be at least the number wl of pipeline registers and the size n of input must be at least $wl \log(wl)$.

6 A Naive Prefix-Sums Algorithm

We assume that an array a with $n = 2^m$ numbers is given. Let us start with a well-known naive prefix-sums algorithm for array a [8,9], and show it is not optimal. The naive prefix-sums algorithm is written as follows:

[A naive prefix-sums algorithm]
for $t \leftarrow 0$ to $p - 1$ do
  for $i \leftarrow 2^t$ to $n - 1$ do in parallel
    $a[i] \leftarrow a[i] + a[i - 2^t]$

Figure 5 illustrates how the prefix-sums are computed.

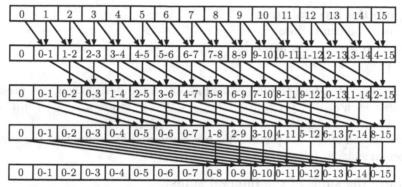

Fig. 5. Illustrating the naive prefix-sums algorithm for n numbers

We assume that p threads are available and evaluate the computing time of the naive prefix-sums algorithm. The following three memory access operations are performed for each t $(0 \leq t \leq p - 1)$: can be done by

- reading from $a[2^t], a[2^t + 1], \ldots, a[n - 2]$,
- reading from $a[2^t + 1], a[2^t + 2], \ldots, a[n - 1]$, and
- writing in $a[2^t + 1], a[2^t + 2], \ldots, a[n - 1]$.

Each of the three operations can be done by contiguous memory access for $n - 2^t$ memory cells. Hence, the computing time of each t is $O(\frac{n - 2^t}{w} + \frac{(n - 2^t)l}{p} + l)$ from Lemma 1. The total computing time is:

$$\sum_{t=0}^{p-1} O(\frac{n - 2^t}{w} + \frac{(n - 2^t)l}{p} + l) = O(\frac{n \log n}{w} + \frac{nl \log n}{p}),$$

Thus, we have,

Lemma 3. *The naive prefix-sums algorithm runs in* $O(\frac{n \log n}{w} + \frac{nl \log n}{p})$ *time units using p threads on the DMM and on the UMM with width w and latency l.*

Clearly, from Theorem 1, the naive algorithm is not optimal.

7   Our Optimal Prefix-Sums Algorithm

This section shows an optimal prefix-sums algorithm running in $O(\frac{n \log n}{w} + \frac{nl}{p} + l \log n)$ time units. We use $m - 1$ arrays $a_1, a_2, \ldots a_{m-1}$ as work space. Each a_t

$(1 \leq t \leq m - 1)$ can store $2^t - 1$ numbers. Thus, the total size of the $m - 1$ arrays is no more than $(2^1 - 1) + (2^2 - 1) + \cdots + (2^{m-1} - 1) = 2^m - m < n$. We assume that the input of n numbers are stored in array a_m of size n.

The algorithm has two stages. In the first stage, interval sums are stored in the $m - 1$ arrays. The second stage uses interval sums in the $m - 1$ arrays to compute the resulting prefix-sums. The details of the first stage is spelled out as follows.

[Compute the interval sums]
for $t \leftarrow m - 1$ down to 1 do
  for $i \leftarrow 0$ to $2^t - 1$ do in parallel
    $a_t[i] \leftarrow a_{t+1}[2 \cdot i] + a_{t+1}[2 \cdot i + 1]$

Figure 6 illustrated how the interval sums are computed. When this program terminates, each $a_t[i]$ $(1 \leq t \leq m - 1, 0 \leq i \leq 2^t - 2)$ stores $a_t[i \cdot \frac{n}{2^t}] + a_t[i \cdot \frac{n}{2^t} + 1] + \cdots + a_t[(i + 1) \cdot \frac{n}{2^t} - 1]$.

In the second stage, the prefix-sums are computed by computing the sums of the interval sums as follows:

[Compute the sums of the interval sums]
for $t \leftarrow 1$ to $m - 1$ do
  for $i \leftarrow 0$ to $2^t - 2$ do in parallel
    begin
      $a_{t+1}[2 \cdot i + 1] \leftarrow a_t[i]$
      $a_{t+1}[2 \cdot i + 2] \leftarrow a_{t+1}[2 \cdot i + 2] + a_t[i]$
    end
$a_m[n - 1] \leftarrow a_m[n - 2] + a_m[n - 1]$

Figure 7 shows how the prefix-sums are computed. In the figure, "$a_{t+1}[2 \cdot i + 1] \leftarrow a_t[i]$" and "$a_{t+1}[2 \cdot i + 2] \leftarrow a_{t+1}[2 \cdot i + 2] + a_t[i]$" correspond to "copy" and "add", respectively.

When this algorithm terminates, each $a_p[i]$ $(0 \leq i \leq 2^t-)$ stores the prefix sum $a_p[0] + a_p[1] + \cdots + a_p[i]$. We assume that p threads are available and evaluate the computing time. The first stage involves the following memory access operations for each t $(1 \leq t \leq m - 1)$:

- reading from $a_{t+1}[0], a_{t+1}[2], \ldots, a_{t+1}[2^t - 2]$,
- reading from $a_{t+1}[1], a_{t+1}[3], \ldots, a_{t+1}[2^t - 1]$, and
- writing in $a_t[0], a_t[1], \ldots, a_t[2^t - 1]$.

Since every two addresses is accessed, these four memory access operations are essentially contiguous access and they can be done in $O(\frac{2^t}{w} + \frac{2^t l}{p} + l)$ time units. Therefore, the total computing time of the first stage is

$$\sum_{t=1}^{p-1} O(\frac{2^t}{w} + \frac{2^t l}{p} + l) = O(\frac{n}{w} + \frac{nl}{p} + l \log n).$$

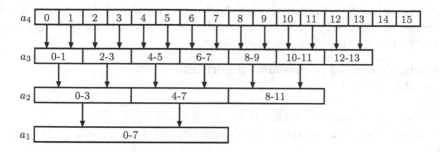

Fig. 6. Illustrating the computation of interval sums in $m - 1$ arrays

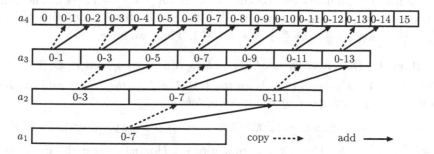

Fig. 7. Illustrating the computation of interval sums in $m - 1$ arrays

The second stage consists of the following memory access operations for each t ($1 \le t \le m - 1$):

- reading from $a_t[0], a_t[1], \ldots, a_t[2^t - 2]$,
- reading from $a_{t+1}[2], a_{t+1}[4], \ldots, a_{t+1}[2^{t+1} - 2]$,
- writing in $a_{t+1}[1], a_{t+1}[3], \ldots, a_{t+1}[2^{t+1} - 3]$, and
- writing in $a_{t+1}[2], a_{t+1}[4], \ldots, a_{t+1}[2^{t+1} - 2]$.

Similarly, these operations can be done in $O(\frac{2^t}{w} + \frac{2^t l}{p} + l)$ time units. Hence, the total computing time of the second stage is also $O(\frac{n}{w} + \frac{nl}{p} + l \log n)$. Thus, we have,

Theorem 2. *The prefix-sums of n numbers can be computed in $O(\frac{n}{w} + \frac{nl}{p} + l \log n)$ time units using p threads on the DMM and on the UMM with width w and latency l if work space of size n is available.*

From Theorem 1, the lower bound of the computing time of the prefix-sums is $\Omega(\frac{n}{w} + \frac{nl}{p} + l \log n)$.

Suppose that n is very large and work space of size n is not available. We will show that, if work space no smaller than $\min(p \log p, wl \log(wl))$ is available, the prefix-sums can also be computed in $O(\frac{n}{w} + \frac{nl}{p} + l \log n)$. Let k be an arbitrary number such that $p \le k \le n$. We partition the input a with n numbers into

$\frac{n}{k}$ groups with k ($\geq p$) numbers each. Each t-th group ($0 \leq t \leq \frac{n}{k} - 1$) has k numbers $a[tk], a[tk+1], \ldots, a[(t+1)k-1]$. The prefix-sums of every group is computed using p threads in turn as follows.

[Sequential-parallel prefix-sums algorithm]
for $t \leftarrow 0$ to $\frac{n}{k} - 1$ do
  begin
    if($t > 0$) $a[tk] \leftarrow a[tk] + a[tk-1]$
    Compute the prefix-sums of k numbers $a[tk], a[tk+1], \ldots, a[(t+1)k-1]$
  end

It should be clear that this algorithm computes the prefix-sums correctly. The prefix-sums of k numbers can be computed in $O(\frac{k}{w} + \frac{kl}{p} + l \log k)$. The computation of the prefix-sums is repeated $\frac{n}{k}$ times, the total computing time is $O(\frac{k}{w} + \frac{kl}{p} + l \log k) \cdot \frac{n}{k} = O(\frac{n}{w} + \frac{nl}{p} + \frac{nl \log k}{k})$. Thus, we have,

Corollary 1. *The prefix-sums of n numbers can be computed in $O(\frac{n}{w} + \frac{nl}{p} + \frac{nl \log k}{k})$ time units using p threads on the DMM and on the UMM with width w and latency l if work space of size k is available.*

If $k \geq p \log p$ then, $\frac{nl \log k}{k} \leq \frac{nl \log(p \log p)}{p \log p} < \frac{nl}{p}$. If $k \geq wl \log(wl)$ then $\frac{nl \log k}{k} \leq \frac{nl \log(wl \log(wl))}{wl \log(wl)} < \frac{n}{w}$. Thus, if $k \geq \min(p \log p, wl \log(wl))$ then the computing time is $O(\frac{n}{w} + \frac{nl}{p})$.

8   Conclusion

The main contribution of this paper is to show that an optimal parallel prefix-sums algorithm that runs in $O(\frac{n}{w} + \frac{nl}{p} + l \log n)$ time units. This algorithm uses work space of size $\min(n, p \log p, wl \log(wl))$.

We believe that two memory machine models, the DMM and the UMM are promising as platforms of development of algorithmic techniques for GPUs. We plan to develop efficient algorithms for graph-theoretic problems, geometric problems, and image processing problems on the DMM and the UMM

References

1. Aho, A.V., Ullman, J.D., Hopcroft, J.E.: Data Structures and Algorithms. Addison Wesley (1983)
2. Akl, S.G.: Parallel Sorting Algorithms. Academic Press (1985)
3. Batcher, K.E.: Sorting networks and their applications. In: Proc. AFIPS Spring Joint Comput. Conf., vol. 32, pp. 307–314 (1968)
4. Flynn, M.J.: Some computer organizations and their effectiveness. IEEE Transactions on Computers C-21, 948–960 (1872)
5. Gibbons, A., Rytter, W.: Efficient Parallel Algorithms. Cambridge University Press (1988)

6. Gottlieb, A., Grishman, R., Kruskal, C.P., McAuliffe, K.P., Rudolph, L., Snir, M.: The nyu ultracomputer–designing an MIMD shared memory parallel computer. IEEE Trans. on Computers C-32(2), 175–189 (1983)
7. Grama, A., Karypis, G., Kumar, V., Gupta, A.: Introduction to Parallel Computing. Addison Wesley (2003)
8. Harris, M., Sengupta, S., Owens, J.D.: Chapter 39. parallel prefix sum (scan) with CUDA. In: GPU Gems 3. Addison-Wesley (2007)
9. Hillis, W.D., Steele Jr., G.L.: Data parallel algorithms. Commun. ACM 29(12), 1170–1183 (1986), http://doi.acm.org/10.1145/7902.7903
10. Hwu, W.W.: GPU Computing Gems Emerald Edition. Morgan Kaufmann (2011)
11. Ito, Y., Ogawa, K., Nakano, K.: Fast ellipse detection algorithm using hough transform on the GPU. In: Proc. of International Conference on Networking and Computing, pp. 313–319 (December 2011)
12. Lawrie, D.H.: Access and alignment of data in an array processor. IEEE Trans. on Computers C-24(12), 1145–1155 (1975)
13. Man, D., Uda, K., Ito, Y., Nakano, K.: A GPU implementation of computing euclidean distance map with efficient memory access. In: Proc. of International Conference on Networking and Computing, pp. 68–76 (December 2011)
14. Man, D., Uda, K., Ueyama, H., Ito, Y., Nakano, K.: Implementations of a parallel algorithm for computing euclidean distance map in multicore processors and GPUs. International Journal of Networking and Computing 1, 260–276 (2011)
15. Nakano, K.: Simple memory machine models for GPUs. In: Proc. of International Parallel and Distributed Processing Symposium Workshops, pp. 788–797 (May 2012)
16. Nishida, K., Ito, Y., Nakano, K.: Accelerating the dynamic programming for the matrix chain product on the GPU. In: Proc. of International Conference on Networking and Computing, pp. 320–326 (December 2011)
17. NVIDIA Corporation: NVIDIA CUDA C best practice guide version 3.1 (2010)
18. NVIDIA Corporation: NVIDIA CUDA C programming guide version 4.0 (2011)
19. Quinn, M.J.: Parallel Computing: Theory and Practice. McGraw-Hill (1994)
20. Uchida, A., Ito, Y., Nakano, K.: Fast and accurate template matching using pixel rearrangement on the GPU. In: Proc. of International Conference on Networking and Computing, pp. 153–159 (December 2011)

A Multi-GPU Programming Library
for Real-Time Applications

Sebastian Schaetz[1] and Martin Uecker[2]

[1] BiomedNMR Forschungs GmbH at the
Max Planck Institute for biophysical Chemistry, Goettingen
sschaet@gwdg.de
[2] Department of Electrical Engineering and Computer Sciences
University of California, Berkeley
uecker@eecs.berkeley.edu

Abstract. We present MGPU, a C++ programming library targeted at single-node multi-GPU systems. Such systems combine disproportionate floating point performance with high data locality and are thus well suited to implement real-time algorithms. We describe the library design, programming interface and implementation details in light of this specific problem domain. The core concepts of this work are a novel kind of container abstraction and MPI-like communication methods for intra-system communication. We further demonstrate how MGPU is used as a framework for porting existing GPU libraries to multi-device architectures. Putting our library to the test, we accelerate an iterative non-linear image reconstruction algorithm for real-time magnetic resonance imaging using multiple GPUs. We achieve a speed-up of about 1.7 using 2 GPUs and reach a final speed-up of 2.1 with 4 GPUs. These promising results lead us to conclude that multi-GPU systems are a viable solution for real-time MRI reconstruction as well as signal-processing applications in general.

Keywords: GPGPU, multi-GPU, hardware-aware algorithm, real-time, signal-processing, MRI, iterative image reconstruction.

1 Introduction

Within the last five years general-purpose computation on graphics hardware has become increasingly attractive among industry and academia. The combination of convenient programming tools and libraries with the striking performance-to-dollar and performance-to-watt ratio makes graphics processing units the default solution to many data-parallel problems. Several such devices can be used in a cluster configuration with multiple nodes connected via a local area network. These systems lend themselves well to solve large high performance computing problems such as scientific simulations, as the cluster can be sized to fit the problem. Cluster implementations generally exhibit good weak scaling, i.e. they perform efficiently if the problem size increases with the number of processing units.

Y. Xiang et al. (Eds.): ICA3PP 2012, Part I, LNCS 7439, pp. 114–128, 2012.

Real-time signal-processing problems have different requirements. Their problem size is fixed and usually defined by physical constraints. In addition, calculation results must be available before an operational deadline expires. The processing delay of a real-time algorithm must be bounded as it runs in synchronism with the data acquisition process. If such real-time applications are very compute intensive and require the floating point performance of more than one GPU, single-node desktop systems with multiple compute devices are preferable over multi-node clusters. Single-node systems exhibit higher memory bandwidth and lower latency compared to clusters, resulting in better data locality. This matches the fixed problem size of real-time applications and the requirement for strong scaling. Despite these advantages, we are not aware of any programming tools or libraries that explicitly target desktop multi-GPU systems.

In this work we present a programming library for multi-GPU systems called MGPU that supports the development of strong scaling applications. We describe the core concepts, the interface, and important implementation details of the library. Performance is evaluated with a number of micro-benchmarks. We further document our efforts of speeding up an iterative non-linear image reconstruction algorithm for real-time magnetic resonance imaging (MRI) - a prime example for computationally demanding digital signal-processing algorithms.

2   MGPU

MGPU is a combination of a C++ template header library and a small static link library and depends on a number of Boost C++ libraries [8] including Test, Thread, Bind and Function. It is tested on both Linux and Windows platforms and can be built using a standard C++ compiler. MGPU is implemented as a layer on top of existing GPU computing frameworks and numerical libraries, designed for single-GPU systems, and combines them under a coherent interface. It is modelled after the C++ Standard Template Library.

The modular design of MGPU supports different frameworks such as CUDA and OpenCL. The current version of MGPU focuses on the CUDA backend as it exposes hardware features not yet supported by OpenCL. MGPU applications must be compiled for each specific target system. The build process detects various performance relevant architecture features such as the number of devices present and the capabilities of each device. This allows MGPU to enable optimized versions of functions such as peer-to-peer for inter-GPU communication which is much faster than transfers staged through the host.

Since MGPU is designed to support real-time signal-processing applications it forgoes advanced automated parallelization methods employed in modern high performance computing frameworks. Instead MGPU allows full control over the hardware at all times and carefully employs convenient abstractions such as well-known MPI-based communication functions and segmented containers. These segmented containers facilitate the implementation of hardware-aware algorithms, a prerequisite for good efficiency on distributed memory systems. In addition, MGPU does not limit access to lower level GPU computing frameworks, giving developers full access to performance relevant hardware features that might not yet be supported by MGPU.

2.1 Runtime Environment

MGPU contains a single-threaded and multi-threaded runtime environment to interact with all GPUs in the compute node. The multi-threaded runtime creates a thread for each GPU. The single-threaded version handles each GPU from within one thread by switching GPU contexts. The runtime is initialized by instantiating an **environment** object. The following code snippet shows how the number of devices can be selected at runtime.

```
environment e;                          // use all devices
environment e(dev_group::from_to(0, 2));  // use device 0 and 1
```

With the default constructor, all devices present in the system are used for computation. Specifying a `dev_group` limits the number of devices that are available for computation to a subset.

2.2 Memory Management

GPU based architectures are distributed memory systems: main memory is often arranged in a non-uniform manner and each compute device has a separate memory block. A basic abstraction the library employs is the device vector, a container that manages data on a single GPU. It represents the device equivalent of a vector in main memory such as `std::vector`. On instantiation, it allocates the requested amount of data on the device that is associated with the calling thread. Algorithms can interface with the container through iterators. The container allows access to a raw pointer `T*` as well as a device pointer `dev_ptr<T>`.

To manage data across multiple devices, MGPU offers an implementation of the segmented container concept. It is based on the work by Austern on segmented iterators [1]. An elementary implementation is the segmented vector that can be modelled as a vector of local vectors but is a large vector that is

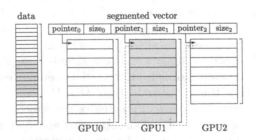

Fig. 1. Data stored across 3 GPUs using a segmented vector container: a vector of tuples for pointer and size represents each local device vector

split in segments and distributed across the local memory of all GPUs. Figure 1 illustrates this for 3 GPUs. The container segments data automatically, depending on the number of compute devices used by the runtime. The way data is split across GPUs can be controlled during construction of the segmented vector. Natural and block-wise splitting as well as cloning and 2D overlapped splitting are possible. The container implicitly holds information about the location of each memory segment. This location awareness of segmented vectors makes them the major building block for implementing algorithms that scale across multiple compute devices and exploit segmentation. MGPU communication methods, linear algebra functions as well as the fast Fourier transform are aware of the data segmentation through this hierarchical abstraction. By modifying the number of devices used by the runtime environment, an algorithm can be scaled up to multiple devices.

2.3 Data Transfer

Today's commercial off-the-shelf multi-GPU systems can contain up to 8 or more compute-devices. Figure 2 shows the block diagram of a state of the art Tyan FT72-B7015 computer equipped with 8 GPUs. The various memory transfer paths that are possible in such a system are highlighted. Host memory performance was measured using a NUMA version of the STEAM benchmark [4] and GPU memory throughput was measured using modified CUDA SDK examples.

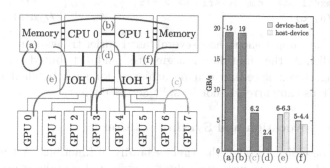

Fig. 2. Octo-GPU system showing various memory transfer paths and their throughput. Due to the non-uniform memory architecture, there is a difference between transfer paths (a) and (b). And since the I/O hubs (IOH) on this mainboard only support memory-mapped I/O (MMIO) between peers, GPUs connected to IOH 0 can not directly communicate with GPUs connected to IOH 1. Memory transfers between these GPUs have to be staged through main memory which accounts for the difference in (c) and (d).

Not only are there multiple possible memory transfer paths on such devices, with segmented containers there are also various modes to transfer data. MGPU implements a subset of the MPI standard communication routines. Figure 3 shows communication primitives involving segmented containers that the MGPU library implements.

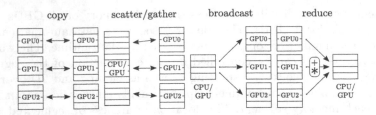

Fig. 3. Segmented data transfer primitives supported by MGPU: copying a segmented vector to another segmented vector, scattering and gathering a local vector from CPU or GPU to a segmented vector, broadcasting a local vector to a segmented vector and reducing a segmented vector to a local vector using an operation.

2.4   Libraries

MGPU also acts as a framework to use single-GPU libraries on multi-GPU systems and consolidates them under a coherent interface. Existing algorithms are extended to interoperate with segmented containers resulting in hierarchical implementations that are aware of the memory segmentation. Currently MGPU supports the CUDA FFT and the CUDA BLAS library. The interfaces are part of the modular backend architecture and can thus be ex. This will enable us to support APPML through the same interface in the future.

```
seg_dev_vector<complex<float> > d(x*y*batch, x*y);   // segment data
fft<complex<float>, complex<float> > f(x, y, batch); // fft handle
f.forward(d, d);                                     // distributed fft
```

The above code snippet shows how several fast Fourier transforms can be calculated in parallel. As the input data is segmented and distributed across multiple devices, a significant speed-up can be achieved for such batched transforms. Individual FFTs can currently not be split across devices.

2.5   Kernel Invocation and Synchronization

Kernels can be called through the `invoke` family of functions. A kernel can be launched on all devices or just on a subset. Segmented containers are forwarded as device ranges referencing only local memory. If the entire segmented vector must be known by the kernel for peer-to-peer access, a pass-through type is provided to directly forward the segmented vector. The following listing shows various options of this mechanism:

```
invoke_kernel(kernel_caller, par1, par2, dev_rank);
invoke_kernel_all(kernel_caller, par3, par4);
```

The first function call invokes a kernel caller in the device context of `dev_rank`. The second call launches the kernel for each device in the `environment`. The `kernel_caller` function is a stub provided by the user that configures the kernel call with the proper grid- and block-size or number of work-groups and work-group size and finally calls the kernel.

MGPU is by default asynchronous. Synchronizing separate operations and multiple compute-devices in a system is done through a family of barrier and fence functions provided by MGPU. Calling for example

```
barrier_fence();
```

blocks all devices until all devices finished pending operations. Synchronization functions are implemented using condition variables and GPU driver synchronization mechanisms for device-local operations and incur a respective overhead.

2.6   Evaluation

A number of micro-benchmarks help to measure the performance of core functions of MGPU and are used to assess the benefits of using a multi-GPU system in combination with our library. Type and size of the test input data is chosen explicitly with typical real-time applications in mind.

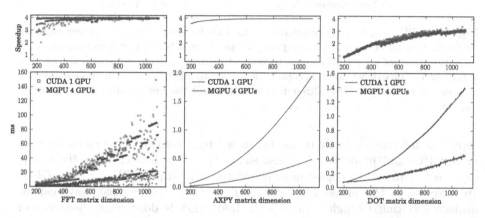

Fig. 4. Algorithm performance comparison of the fast Fourier transform, and basic linear algebra subprograms $a * X + Y$ as well as $A \cdot B$. Input data are 12 complex square matrices of single precision floating point values. The MGPU implementation internally calls CUDA functions.

The first benchmark compares the runtime of three common algorithms. Figure 4 shows that both FFT and $a * X + Y$ operations scale well, especially for larger matrix sizes. The variance in the FFT performance is caused by the CUFFT implementation. The measured time shows the combined performance of the forward and inverse Fourier transform. The $A \cdot B$ operation does not exhibit strong scaling and an efficiency of $\frac{3}{4}$ can be achieved only for larger data sets. This is due to the reduction step in the operation that can not distributed across devices efficiently and requires and additional inter-device reduction step for the final result.

Figure 5 illustrates the performance of MGPU host to device and device to host data transfer primitives. The strong copy test, where the amount of data is constant, shows that data can be copied faster to multiple GPUs. The weak

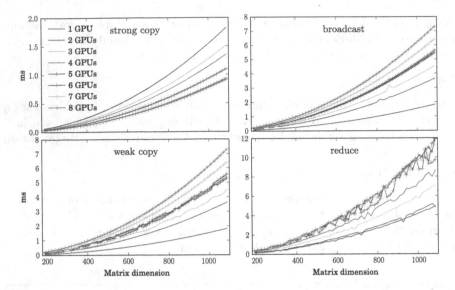

Fig. 5. MGPU data transfer primitives; data used for these test are squared complex single floating point matrices. Strong copy keeps the number of matrices constant with varying number of GPUs. Weak copy increases the number of matrices with the number of GPUs. The broadcast function copies one matrix to all GPUs and the reduce function merges one matrix per GPU through summation and the final result is transferred to host memory.

copy test behaves similarly to the broadcast test: transfer time increases with more GPUs and more data but also shows the same behaviour as the strong copy test: data can be copied more efficiently to multiple GPUs. If more GPUs are involved in the memory transfer, multiple PCI Express pathways can be utilized resulting in higher bandwidth. Reduction is done using peer-to-peer communication. 1 GPU of each PCIe domain performs a reduction through peer-to-peer data access and directly transfers the result to CPU memory. If GPUs attached to different I/O hubs are involved, peer-to-peer access is not possible between all devices and a final reduction has to be calculated by the host. For our test system this is the case if more than 4 GPUs participate. From 1 to 2 GPUs, there is negligible overhead but with increasing peer-to-peer transfer the parallel efficiency decreases.

After assessing the relative performance of individual operations using artificial benchmarks, an image reconstruction algorithm with existing single-GPU implementation is modified using MGPU to support multiple compute-devices.

3   MRI Image Reconstruction

Recently, iterative image reconstruction algorithms for MRI have made unprecedented temporal resolution at high image quality attainable. This is made possible by reducing the data necessary for image reconstruction to a minimum (see for example [20,5,17,21,14]). These new methods pave the way for new insights into human physiology and are a valuable new tool for scientists and radiologist to study dynamic processes such as the beating heart, joint movement and speech production.

Due to the algorithms' iterative nature, they are orders of magnitude more compute-intensive than traditional methods and reach the limits of modern high-performance computer systems. Fast image reconstruction, however, is key to facilitate adoption of these advantageous methods in a clinical setting. In such an environment, images should be reconstructed without a perceivable delay to not compromise clinical workflow and maintain patient throughput.

In the following, we document our efforts of porting an existing single-GPU implementation of the nonlinear inverse reconstruction algorithm [21,22] to a multi-GPU system using the MGPU library. Using this particular algorithm, it is possible to acquire real-time MRI movies up to a temporal resolution of 20ms [23]. This achievable frame-rate widens the gap between acquisition and reconstruction time and is the primary motivation to look into new ways of accelerating the reconstruction beyond the possibilities of the existing single-GPU implementation.

3.1   Reconstruction Problem and Algorithm

During data acquisition multiple radio frequency coils J positioned around the subject measure the MRI signal. Each coil possesses a unique spatial sensitivity map c_j. The signal equation for an image ρ is:

$$y_j(t) = \int_\Omega dx \rho(x) c_j(x) e^{-ik(t)x} \tag{1}$$

where k describes the trajectory in k space and y_j the signal received in coil j. The algorithm interprets this as an ill-conditioned nonlinear inverse problem $Fx = y$. The operator F maps the unknown image ρ to the acquired k space positions using the sensitivities c_j. On a discretized rectangular Cartesian grid, the operator F can be written as

$$F = P_k \, \text{DTFT} \, M_\Omega C W^{-1} \tag{2}$$

where P_k is a projection onto the measured sample positions, DTFT is the multidimensional discrete-time (here: space) Fourier transform and M_Ω is a mask that restricts the reconstructed image to the area Ω. The non-linear operator C multiplies image and coil sensitivities. W is a weighted discrete Fourier transform applied to the coil sensitivities, which represents an assumption about the smoothness of c_j that is included in the equation.

Equation $Fx = y$ is then solved using the iteratively regularized Gauss-Newton method [2]. In each iteration x_{n+1} is estimated from the current result x_n by solving the regularized equation

$$(\text{DF}_{x_n}^{\text{H}} \, \text{DF}_{x_n} + \alpha_n I)(x_{n+1} - x_n)$$
$$= \text{DF}_{x_n}^{\text{H}}(y - Fx_n) - \alpha_n(x_n - x_{\text{ref}}) \, . \tag{3}$$

with the conjugate gradient algorithm. The regularization parameter is α_n. After an initial interpolation of the data to the grid which is performed as a pre-processing step on the CPU, all further operations can be performed on the grid. The operation $\mathrm{DTFT}^{-1} P_k \mathrm{DTFT}$ embedded in the left-hand side of the equation can be understood as a convolution with the point spread function and is implemented by applying two Fourier transforms.

3.2   Single- and Multi-GPU Implementation

The data used in this work is acquired using a 3T MRI system (Tim Trio, Siemens Healthcare, Erlangen, Germany) that is capable of recording up to 32 data channels simultaneously. For real-time applications, spatial image resolution usually varies between $1.5 \times 1.5 \ mm^2$ and $2 \times 2 \ mm^2$ which yields a matrix size of 192 to 384 depending on the field of view. The grid size is then doubled to implement the non-periodic convolution with the point spread function and to achieve a high accuracy when initially interpolating the measured data onto the Cartesian grid. Computation is carried out in complex single precision floating point format. A principal component analysis preprocessing step is applied before reconstruction to compress the 32 channels to $8-12$ [12]. The multi-GPU target system for this application is a Tyan FT72-B7015 computer equipped with two Intel X5650 six-core processors, 96GB main memory and 8 GeForce GTX 580 compute-devices with 1.5GB memory each.

The algorithm consists of a number of Fourier transform calculations applied separately to each channel, point-wise matrix operations involving one fixed matrix and the separate channel matrices as well as scalar products of all data. The original implementation utilizes the parallel computation capabilities of a single GPU to individually speed up each operation. The CUDA FFT library batched-mode is used to calculate the Fourier transforms of all channel matrices. Custom CUDA kernels handle the point-wise operations and the CUDA BLAS library is used to calculate the scalar products. Single pixels are mapped to GPU threads, image and coil sensitivities are calculated at the same time.

Successive frames in a movie are calculated subsequently, as each x_n depends on the result of the previous frame x_ref. This temporal regularization makes it impossible to use a straight-forward pipeline-approach to parallelize the reconstruction of movies on a multi-GPU system. The MGPU implementation of the algorithm instead distributes the coil sensitivity maps c_j across all GPUs G and the image ρ is split into one ρ_g per GPU with $\rho = \sum^G \rho_g$. This summation amounts to a block-wise all-reduce operation, since all GPUs require ρ. An alternative decomposition is not feasible due to the FFT that operates on an entire matrix.

MGPU simplifies the process of extending the existing implementation to support multiple compute-devices. Existing containers can be replaced with segmented vectors. Only kernel interfaces have to be modified to accept local ranges instead of containers but kernel bodies can be reused and called through `invoke_kernel` functions. The FFT and BLAS library of MGPU exhibits a custom C++ interface and all calls to those libraries have to be changed. In addition, since MGPU operations are asynchronous, synchronization points have to be chosen carefully as to ensure completion of dependent operations.

Table 1 gives a breakdown of the three operators from equation 3 and one entry that includes all additional conjugate gradient operations.

Table 1. Algorithm operator breakdown showing the number of Fourier transforms, element-wise operations, channel summations, scalar products and communication steps in each operator

	FFT	AB	$\sum c_j$	$A \cdot B$	$\sum \rho_{n_g}$
F	2	4		1	
DF	2	5			
DF^{H}	2	4	1		1
CG		6		2	

While F is only required once per Newton step, DF and DF^{H} are applied in each conjugate gradient iteration with the consequence of continual inter-GPU data transfer. $\sum \rho_g$ is implemented using the peer-to-peer communication capabilities of the GeForce GTX 580 GPUs. This restricts the number of parallel GPUs used for image reconstruction to 4 on our particular system because direct peer-to-peer communication is only possible between those devices. The following listing shows the peer-to-peer communication kernel for 4 GPUs.

```
__global__ void kern_all_red_p2p_2d(cfloat * dst, cfloat* src0,
  cfloat* src1, cfloat* src2, cfloat* src3, int dim, int off)
{
    int i = off + blockIdx.x * dim + threadIdx.x;
    dst[i] = src3[i] + src2[i] + src1[i] + src0[i];
}
```

Each GPU runs this kernel at the same time. To speed up this operation further, the kernel only transfers a 2D section of ρ_g. This is possible because a mask M_Ω is applied immediately after the summation. A double-buffering solution is chosen to avoid local overwrites of data that is not yet transferred to neighbouring devices. Therefore, destination and local source pointers reference distributed memory blocks.

3.3   Results

The goal is an implementation of a non-linear iterative image reconstruction algorithm that is capable of calculating images without perceivable delay. While images can be measured at up to 50 Hz, clinically relevant protocols are envisioned to encompass frame rates of 5-30 Hz. The existing single-GPU implementation is capable of reconstructing about $3 - 4.5$ frames per second. This version however is not taken into account in this comparison because of MGPU-unrelated code optimization. Instead we benchmark the algorithm with varying

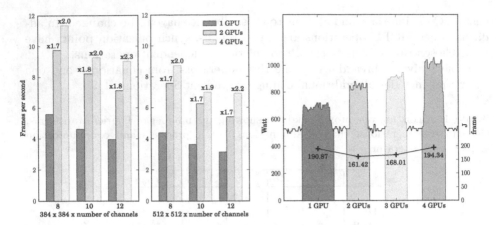

Fig. 6. Performance comparison with varying number of GPUs, channels, and size

Fig. 7. Overall power drain and energy
consumption per frame

number of GPUs since MGPU permits a seamless adjustment of the number of
GPUs used for reconstruction.

The number of channels the algorithms operates on can be reduced using
a principle component decomposition. Acceptable image quality is achievable
by compressing the 32 data channels to no less than eight. Figure 6 shows the
performance in frames per second as well as the speed-up for 2 different image
resolutions, varying number of GPUs and different numbers of channels. Setup
as well as pre- and post-processing steps are excluded from these measurements.
Peak performance of 11.4 frames per second is reached with the smaller matrix
size, 8 channels and 4 GPUs. Due to unequal data distribution, the frame-rate
is the same for 10 and 12 channels if 4 GPUs are used.

Figure 8 shows a breakdown of the runtime for the 2 main operators DF and
DF^H. For the DF curve, the gradient increases if more channels are calculated. If
the GPUs are given more work it can be distributed more efficiently. The performance of the Fourier transform greatly influences the performance of the overall
image reconstruction algorithm as it is the most time-consuming operation. Its

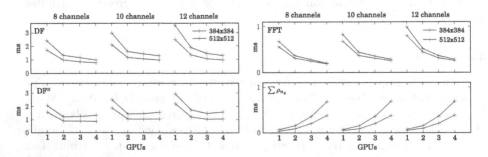

Fig. 8. DF and DF^H performance

Fig. 9. FFT and all-reduce performance

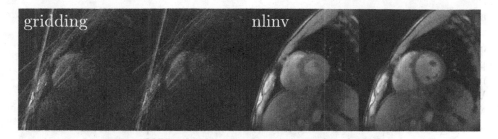

Fig. 10. Non-iterative (gridding) and non-linear inversion (nlinv) reconstruction of short-axis view of a healthy human heart at a temporal resolution of 33ms

scalability is a function of batch- and matrix size as shown in figure 9. The operator DF^H includes peer-to-peer communication which causes a performance decrease if more than 2 GPUs are used. This communication overhead increases and neutralizes a large portion of the speed-up in this operator. Execution time even increases for 4 GPUs. Figure 9 illustrates this interrelation. If only 1 GPU is used, the communication kernel effectively copies data on-device.

Alongside the runtime performance of this algorithm the energy consumption of this multi-GPU implementation is investigated. We monitor power-drain of our system using its integrated baseboard management controller. Figure 7 shows the power consumption for reconstructing an MRI video with 400 frames using a variable number of compute-devices. The figure also shows the energy consumed per frame, calculated by integrating power over time. While using 2 and 3 GPUs is most power efficient, using 4 GPUs does not consume significantly more energy compared to single GPU image reconstruction.

Figure 10 shows the difference between a non-iterative image reconstruction method and the non-linear inversion algorithm described in this work. While the extreme radial undersampling causes severe streaking artefacts, the iterative algorithm is capable of reconstruction high-quality images.

4   Related Work

Developers can choose between a number of tools and libraries such as CUDA, OpenCL and C++ AMP to develop code for single-GPU architectures. As to our knowledge, none exist that explicitly target single-node multi-GPU systems or provide facilities to describe algorithms regardless of the number of accelerators in the target system. There exist however a number of tools for GPU clusters such as the many GPUs package published by Barak et al. [3] in 2010. The framework allows parallel OpenMP, C++ and unmodified OpenCL applications to run on multiple GPUs in a cluster. Network latency is a limiting factor in their implementation that is targeted at massive parallel and high performance computing applications. SkePU [9] is a multi-backend (CUDA, OpenCL) library based on algorithmic skeletons [7] for solving data-parallel problems on GPU and multi-GPU systems. The library can utilize multiple GPUs and automatically distributes data across all devices, the authors report issues with a multi-GPU gaussian blur implementation because of inter-GPU communication staged through main memory. A MGPU implementation of this algorithm could be designed to take the disjoint memory areas into account and utilize peer-to-peer memory transfer. AGILE [16] is an open source library for magnetic resonance image reconstruction using graphics card hardware acceleration. While restricted to a single GPU, their library targets the same applications as MGPU. Another high-level GPGPU library is Thrust [11]: a selection of parallel algorithms closely following the C++ Standard Template Library. Thrust does not support data decomposition across multiple GPUs but can be used on multi-GPU systems through the use of the lower level CUDA API. ViennaCL [19] is a high level linear algebra library that supports both GPUs and multi-core CPUs through OpenCL. While the library provides mechanisms to use multiple devices for computation, data decomposition and synchronization is left to the user.

The viability and usefulness of GPU and multi-GPU systems for real-time applications has previously been shown. A medical signal-processing application running on a multi-GPU system is described by Jang et al. [13]. Their implementation of an iterative image reconstruction algorithm for computed tomography achieves a speed-up of about 2 when comparing single- and quad-GPU implementations. Verner et al. [24] present a hard real-time stream scheduling algorithm for GPU based systems and Chilingaryan et al. implement [6] a near real-time GPU-base reconstruction software for synchrotron experiments. Suitability of GPUs for MRI reconstruction is shown early on by Hansen et al [10]. Later Kim et al. [15] compare implementations of an iterative algorithm for 3D compressive sensing MRI reconstruction on various many-core architectures including Nvidia GPUs and the novel Intel MIC architecture. A comprehensive discussion of multi-core and multi-GPU implementation of a novel iterative 3D algorithm for MRI with clinically feasible reconstruction time is presented by Murphy et al. [18].

5   Conclusion

We presented MGPU, a C++ template-based multi-GPU programming library for real-time applications. We demonstrated the benefits of the segmented container concept and pointed out the developer-friendly implementation of the various data transfer routines. An evaluation of our library through various micro-benchmarks yields expected results. Batched fast Fourier transforms and element wise matrix operations scale well across multiple devices. We have further demonstrated that the concepts of MGPU and its generic structure are suitable to extend existing single-GPU libraries with multi-GPU interfaces. High data locality due to low latency and high bandwidth, compact form factor compared to GPU clusters, manageable power consumption, low cost and the convenient but efficient tools MGPU provides are the reasons why multi-GPU systems are suitable to solve data-parallel real-time problems. MGPU is certainly not limited to the problem domain described in this work and we can imagine that general high performance computing problems can benefit from the combination of multi-GPU hardware and the MGPU framework.

The modular architecture of MGPU renders the extension of the current device interface with OpenCL support possible, which we plan to implement as a next step. This will enable us to compare the performance of Nvidia and AMD systems. Beyond that we will incorporate even more single-GPU libraries in our library. In addition, we plan to investigate how MGPU concepts can apply to emerging multi-core architectures such as Intel MIC and AMD Fusion.

Encouraged by our micro-benchmark results we used MGPU to extend an existing numerical algorithm for MRI image reconstruction and submit evidence that indeed, multi-GPU systems are suitable for speeding up signal-processing and real-time applications. We measured a speed-up by 1.7 when using two compute-devices and a speed-up of more than 2 when using 4 GPUs. To overcome the problem of inter-GPU communication overhead when using 4 GPUs we plan to investigate alternative data decomposition schemes. Since the performance of the Fourier transform is the major determining factor of this algorithm we are also experimenting with different implementations that are capable of exploiting the sparsity of our data.

Although the reconstruction frame rate does not yet match the temporal resolution of data acquisition process, the multi-GPU implementation of the algorithm is fast enough so that simultaneous recording and reconstruction is feasible. Thus, results are immediately available for scientists and physicians to interpret. The existence of an on-line iterative algorithm will ease the adoption of real-time MRI in a clinical setting. We expect that the high temporal resolution that is made possible by these advanced iterative algorithms will give radiologists new insights and might ultimately result in a more accurate diagnosis for patients.

References

1. Austern, M.H.: Segmented Iterators and Hierarchical Algorithms. In: Jazayeri, M., Musser, D.R., Loos, R.G.K. (eds.) Dagstuhl Seminar 1998. LNCS, vol. 1766, p. 80. Springer, Heidelberg (2000)
2. Bakushinskiĭ, A., Kokurin, M.: Iterative Methods for Approximate Solution of Inverse Problems, vol. 577. Kluwer Academic Pub. (2004)
3. Barak, A., Ben-Nun, T., Levy, E., Shiloh, A.: A package for OpenCL based heterogeneous computing on clusters with many GPU devices. In: 2010 IEEE International Conference on Cluster Computing Workshops and Posters (Cluster Workshops), pp. 1–7. IEEE (2010)
4. Bergstrom, L.: Measuring NUMA effects with the Stream benchmark. CoRR abs/1103.3225 (2011)
5. Block, K., Uecker, M., Frahm, J.: Undersampled radial MRI with multiple coils. Iterative image reconstruction using a total variation constraint. Magnetic Resonance in Medicine 57, 1086–1098 (2007)
6. Chilingaryan, S., Mirone, A., Hammersley, A., Ferrero, C., Helfen, L., Kopmann, A., dos Santos Rolo, T., Vagovic, P.: A GPU-Based Architecture for Real-Time Data Assessment at Synchrotron Experiments. IEEE Transactions on Nuclear Science (99), 1–1 (2011)

7. Cole, M.: Algorithmic Skeletons: Structured Management of Parallel Computation. Pitman (1989)
8. Dawes, B., Abrahams, D., Rivera, R.: Boost C++ libraries, http://www.boost.org
9. Enmyren, J., Kessler, C.: SkePU: A Multi-Backend Skeleton Programming Library for Multi-GPU Systems. In: Proceedings of the Fourth International Workshop on High-Level Parallel Programming and Applications, pp. 5–14. ACM (2010)
10. Hansen, M., Atkinson, D., Sorensen, T.: Cartesian SENSE and k-t SENSE reconstruction using commodity graphics hardware. Magnetic Resonance in Medicine 59(3), 463–468 (2008)
11. Hoberock, J., Bell, N.: Thrust: C++ Template Library for CUDA (2009)
12. Huang, F., Vijayakumar, S., Li, Y., Hertel, S., Duensing, G.: A software channel compression technique for faster reconstruction with many channels. Magnetic Resonance Imaging 26, 133–141 (2007)
13. Jang, B., Kaeli, D., Do, S., Pien, H.: Multi GPU Implementation of Iterative Tomographic Reconstruction Algorithms. In: IEEE International Symposium on Biomedical Imaging: From Nano to Macro, ISBI 2009, pp. 185–188. IEEE (2009)
14. Jung, H., Sung, K., Nayak, K., Kim, E., Ye, J.: k-t focuss: A general compressed sensing framework for high resolution dynamic mri. Magnetic Resonance in Medicine 61(1), 103–116 (2009)
15. Kim, D., Trzasko, J., Smelyanskiy, M., Haider, C., Dubey, P., Manduca, A.: High-performance 3D compressive sensing MRI reconstruction using many-core architectures. Journal of Biomedical Imaging 2 (2011)
16. Knoll, F., Freiberger, M., Bredies, K., Stollberger, R.: AGILE: An open source library for image reconstruction using graphics card hardware acceleration. Proc. Intl. Soc. Mag. Reson. Med. 19, 2554 (2011)
17. Lustig, M., Donoho, D., Pauly, J.: Sparse MRI: The application of compressed sensing for rapid MR imaging. Magnetic Resonance in Medicine 58, 1182–1195 (2007)
18. Murphy, M., Alley, M., Demmel, J., Keutzer, K., Vasanawala, S., Lustig, M.: Fast ℓ_1-SPIRiT Compressed Sensing Parallel Imaging MRI: Scalable Parallel Implementation and Clinically Feasible Runtime. IEEE Transactions on Medical Imaging 1, 99 (2012)
19. Rupp, K., Rudolf, F., Weinbub, J.: ViennaCL - A High Level Linear Algebra Library for GPUs and Multi-Core CPUs. In: Proc. GPUScA, pp. 51–56 (2010)
20. Tsao, J., Boesiger, P., Pruessmann, K.: k-t blast and k-t sense: Dynamic mri with high frame rate exploiting spatiotemporal correlations. Magnetic Resonance in Medicine 50(5), 1031–1042 (2003)
21. Uecker, M., Hohage, T., Block, K., Frahm, J.: Image Reconstruction by Regularized Nonlinear Inversion - Joint Estimation of Coil Sensitivities and Image Content. Magnetic Resonance in Medicine 60(3), 674–682 (2008)
22. Uecker, M., Zhang, S., Frahm, J.: Nonlinear inverse reconstruction for real-time MRI of the human heart using undersampled radial FLASH. Magnetic Resonance in Medicine 63, 1456–1462 (2010)
23. Uecker, M., Zhang, S., Voit, D., Karaus, A., Merboldt, K.D., Frahm, J.: Real-time MRI at a resolution of 20 ms. NMR in Biomedicine 23, 986–994 (2010)
24. Verner, U., Schuster, A., Silberstein, M.: Processing Data Streams with Hard Real-time Constraints on Heterogeneous Systems. In: Proceedings of the International Conference on Supercomputing, pp. 120–129. ACM (2011)

Optimal Linear Programming Solutions
for Multiprocessor Scheduling
with Communication Delays

Sarad Venugopalan and Oliver Sinnen

The University of Auckland
sven251@aucklanduni.ac.nz, o.sinnen@auckland.ac.nz

Abstract. Task parallelism does not automatically scale with the use of parallel processors. Optimised scheduling of tasks is necessary to maximise the utilisation of each available processor. It is common to use heuristics to find solutions for task scheduling problem instances. However, there is no guarantee that the heuristic solution is close to the optimal solution. The outcome of this work is to provide optimal solutions for small and medium sized instances of the task scheduling problem. Two optimal scheduling formulations using Integer Linear Programming (ILP) are proposed for the Multiprocessor Scheduling Problem with Communication Delays: ILP-REVISEDBOOLEAN LOGIC and ILP-TRANSITIVITY CLAUSE. ILP-REVISEDBOOLEANLOGIC is designed to work efficiently when the number of processors available to be scheduled on is small. ILP-TRANSITIVITYCLAUSE is efficient when a larger number of processors are available to be scheduled on. Each formulation uses a different linearisation of the Integer Bilinear Programming formulation and is tested on CPLEX using known benchmark graphs for task scheduling.

Keywords: Multiprocessor, Task Scheduling Problem, Communication Delays, Linear Programming, Optimal.

1 Introduction

For the performance and efficiency of a parallel program, the scheduling of its (sub)tasks is crucial. Unfortunately, scheduling is a fundamental hard problem (an NP-hard optimisation problem[14]), as the time needed to solve it optimally grows exponentially with the number of tasks. Existing scheduling algorithms are therefore heuristics that try to produce good rather than optimal schedules, e.g.[9],[10],[6],[12],[18],[19],[20],[2],[7]. However, having optimal schedules can make a fundamental difference, e.g. for time critical systems or to enable the precise evaluation of scheduling heuristics. Optimal scheduling is central in minimising the task schedule length . An efficient parallelisation permits scheduling of a large number of tasks onto a large number of dedicated parallel processors to find solutions to generic and specialised problems. It is hence of enormous practical significance to be able to schedule small and medium sized task graphs optimally on parallel processors.

Y. Xiang et al. (Eds.): ICA3PP 2012, Part I, LNCS 7439, pp. 129–138, 2012.

Many heuristics have been proposed for scheduling. While heuristics often provide good results, there is no guarantee that the solutions are close to optimal, especially for task graphs with high communication costs[17][16]. Given the NP-hardness, finding an optimal solution requires an exhaustive search of the entire solution space. For scheduling, this solution space is spawned by all possible processor assignments combined with all possible task orderings. Clearly this search space grows exponentially with the number of tasks, thus it becomes impractical already for very small task graphs.

The objective is to develop a method that solves the scheduling problem optimally for small to medium sized problem instances using Integer Linear Programming. This will make the efficient parallelisation of more applications viable. To achieve this, two formulations for the Multiprocessor Scheduling Problem with Communication Delays are proposed: ILP-REVISEDBOOLEANLOGIC (ILP-RBL) and ILP-TRANSITIVITYCLAUSE (ILP-TC).

The rest of the paper is organised as follows. Section 2 describes the task scheduling model. Section 3 discusses the related work in solving the task scheduling problem optimally. Section 4 details the proposed formulations and compares their complexities in terms of number of constraints generated, with previous approaches. Section 5 compares the computational results of the proposed formulation with the packing formulation. Section 6 concludes the paper.

2   Task Scheduling Model

The tasks that are to be scheduled may or may not be dependent on each other and are represented as an acyclic directed graph. The nodes in the graph represent the tasks and the edges between the nodes, the communications. The node cost is the time required for the task to complete and the edge cost is the communication time between two tasks on different processors. We assume a connected network of processors with identical communication links. Further, there is no multitasking or parallelism within a task. Each processor may execute several tasks but no concurrent execution of tasks is permitted. The tasks are to be assigned in such a way as to minimise the makespan [3][11]. This model fits the definition of the Multiprocessor Scheduling Problem with Communication Delays (MSPCD) defined as follows: tasks (or jobs) have to be executed on several processors; we have to find where and when each task will be executed, such that the total completion time is minimal. The duration of each task is known as well as precedence relations among tasks, i.e., which tasks should be completed before some others can begin. In addition, if dependent tasks are executed on different processors, data transfer times (or communication delays) that are given in advance are also considered.

More formally, the tasks to be scheduled are represented by a directed acyclic graph (DAG) defined by a 4-tuple $G = (V, E, C, L)$ where $i \in V$ denotes the set of tasks; $(i, j) \in E$ represents the set of communications; $C = \{c_{ij} : i, j \in V\}$ denotes the set of edge communication costs; and $L = \{L_1, \ldots, L_n\}$ represents the set of task computation times (execution times length). The communication cost $c_{ij} \in C$ denotes the amount of data transferred between tasks i and j if they are executed on different processors. If both tasks are scheduled to the same processor the communication cost equals zero. The set E defines precedence relation between tasks. A task cannot be executed unless all of its predecessors have completed their execution and all relevant data is available. If tasks i and j are executed on different processors $h, k \in P, h \neq k$, they incur a communication cost penalty γ_{ij}^{hk} dependent on the distance d_{hk} between the processors and on the amount of exchanged data c_{ij} between tasks ($\gamma_{ij}^{hk} = \Gamma c_{ij} d_{hk}$, where Γ is a known constant). Let $\delta^-(j)$ be the set of precedents of task i, that is $\delta^-(j) = \{i \in V | (i, j) \in E\}$. For a fully connected processor network γ_{ij}^{hk} is equivalent to γ_{ij} since the distance d_{hk} is unity. i.e. $\gamma_{ij} = \Gamma c_{ij}$.

3 Related Work

Very few attempts have been made to solve the MSPCD optimally. There are two different approaches, one is based on an exhaustive search of the solution space and the other on an Integer Linear Programming formulation. For many problems, heuristics provide a best effort solution of the scheduling problem. It is possible to begin the search with a best guess and then refine it incrementally until it reaches the solution state. The A* algorithm is one such search algorithm used to solve the MSPCD[8][15]. A* is a best-first search technique[5][13] and also a popular Artificial Intelligence algorithm guided by a problem specific cost function $f(s)$ for each solution state s, which underestimates the final cost of any solution based on s. The main drawback of A* is that it keeps all the nodes in memory and it usually runs out of memory long before it runs out of time making it unusable for a medium and large sized problem instances.

We propose an optimal scheduling alternative for the solution of the MSPCD that makes use of Linear Programming [3]. It involves linearisation of the bilinear forms resulting from communication delays. The work in [3] discusses a classic formulation and a packing formulation of the MSPCD. Their results indicate that the packing formulation is about 5000 times faster than the classic formulation. In this paper we propose two significantly improved Linear Programming formulations of the MSPCD and compare them with the packing formulation in [3].

4 Proposed Formulations

The performance of the ILP formulations in [3] suffer from the need to linearise bilinear equations. Two formulations to solve the MSPCD are proposed here: ILP-RBL and ILP-TC. ILP-RBL uses a new technique to linearise the bilinear forms of the packing formulation in [3] resulting from communication delays by readjusting the Boolean logic. ILP-TC reworks the linearisation of the bilinear forms in the packing formulation using a transitivity clause in a manner that aids the elimination of over defined linear equations in ILP-RBL. The runtime complexity of each ILP formulation depends on the number of constraints generated and the number of variables per constraint. The packing formulation and its linearisations in [3] is briefly discussed and the proposed ILP formulations are compared with the packing formulation in terms of constraints generated and number of variables per constraint.

4.1 ILP-RevisedBooleanLogic

For each task $i \in V$ let $t_i \in \mathbf{R}$ be the start execution time and $p_i \in \mathbf{N}$ be the ID of the processor on which task i is to be executed. Let W be the total makespan and $|P|$ the number of processors available. Let x_{ik} be 1 if task i is assigned to processor k, and zero otherwise. In order to enforce non-overlapping constraints, define two sets of binary variables as in [3]:

$$\forall i,j \in V \quad \sigma_{ij} = \begin{cases} 1 & \text{task } i \text{ finishes before task } j \text{ starts} \\ 0 & \text{otherwise} \end{cases}$$

$$\forall i,j \in V \quad \epsilon_{ij} = \begin{cases} 1 & \text{the processor index of task } i \text{ is strictly less than task } j \\ 0 & \text{otherwise} \end{cases}$$

$$\begin{align}
& min & W & \tag{1} \\
& \forall i \in V & t_i + L_i \leq W & \tag{2} \\
& \forall i \neq j \in V & t_j - t_i - L_i - (\sigma_{ij} - 1)W_{max} \geq 0 & \tag{3} \\
& \forall i \neq j \in V & p_j - p_i - 1 - (\epsilon_{ij} - 1)|P| \geq 0 & \tag{4} \\
& \forall i \neq j \in V & \sigma_{ij} + \sigma_{ji} + \epsilon_{ij} + \epsilon_{ji} \geq 1 & \tag{5} \\
& \forall i \neq j \in V & \sigma_{ij} + \sigma_{ji} \leq 1 & \tag{6} \\
& \forall i \neq j \in V & \epsilon_{ij} + \epsilon_{ji} \leq 1 & \tag{7} \\
& \forall j \in V : i \epsilon \delta^-(j) & \sigma_{ij} = 1 & \tag{8} \\
& \forall j \in V : i \in \delta^-(j), \forall h,k \in P & t_i + L_i + \gamma_{ij}^{hk}(x_{ih} + x_{jk} - 1) \leq t_j & \tag{9} \\
& \forall j \in V : i \in \delta^-(j) & t_i + L_i \leq t_j & \tag{10} \\
& \forall i \in V & \sum_{k \epsilon P} k x_{ik} = p_i & \tag{11} \\
& \forall i \in V & \sum_{k \epsilon P} x_{ik} = 1 & \tag{12} \\
& & W \geq 0 & \tag{13} \\
& \forall i \in V & t_i \geq 0 & \tag{14} \\
& \forall i \in V & p_i \in \{1, \ldots, |P|\} & \tag{15} \\
& \forall i \in V, k \in P & x_{ik} \in \{0,1\} & \tag{16} \\
& \forall i,j \in V & \sigma_{ij}, \epsilon_{ij} \in \{0,1\} & \tag{17}
\end{align}$$

where W_{max} is an upper bound on the makespan W.

$$W_{max} = \sum_{i \in V} L_i + \sum_{i,j \in V} c_{ij} \tag{18}$$

The formulation is a min-max problem which involves minimising the maximum start execution times. This is achieved by minimising the makespan W and introducing constraint (2). Constraint (3) defines the time order on the tasks in terms of the σ variables, i.e. ensure $t_i + L_i \leq t_j$ if σ_{ij} defines an order. The CPU ID order on the tasks in terms of the ϵ variables in defined in (4). If the ϵ_{ij} variable is set, it implies $p_j > p_i$. By (5), at least one or both of the following conditions must be true: task i must finish before task j starts and the processor index of task i must be strictly less than that of task j. By (6) a task cannot both be before and after another task; similarly, by (7) a task cannot be placed both on a higher and lower CPU ID than another task. Constraints (8) enforce the task precedences defined by the edges of the graph; constraints (9) and (10) model the communication delays between task i on processor h and task j on processor k. Since x_{ih} and x_{jk} are both binary variables and to simulate a Boolean multiplication $x_{ih} \cdot x_{jk}$, we use $x_{ih} + x_{jk} - 1$ in constraint (9). To compensate for the subtraction by 1 in (9) for the case that x_{ih} and x_{jk} both are 0, (10) is introduced, which must always be true (for local as well as remote communication). It is also clear from constraint (9) that the processor network need not be fully connected and can take up any connection configuration. Constraints (11) link the assignment variable x with the CPU ID variables p and (12) ensures that any given task runs only on one processor.

The complexity of this ILP formulation, in terms of constraints and variables, is dominated by Eq. 9. For the entire graph, Eq. 9 generates $|P|(|P|-1)$ inequalities in terms of processor combinations for each edge of E and the number of variables per constraint is $O(1)$. Therefore the number of constraints formed by ILP-RBL is $O(|E||P|^2)$. In the worst case there are $|E| = |V|(|V|-1)/2$ edges, hence in terms on number of nodes ILP-RBL's complexity is $O(|V|^2|P|^2)$. However, for task graphs representing real applications, we usually have $O(|E|) = O(|V|)$.

4.2   ILP-Transitivity Clause

The focus of this ILP formulation is to eliminate the x variables from the formulation, as the ILP is over defined in terms of variables. If we can reformulate equation (9) without x, we can drop equations 11, 12 and 16. We replace the x variables in Eq. 9 with ϵ variables that enforce partial ordering of the processor indices with the help of an additional transitivity clause. Eq. 9 and 10 are replaced with Eq. 19 and 20. All other equations are retained.

$$\forall j \in V : i \in \delta^-(j) \quad t_i + L_i + \gamma_{ij}(\epsilon_{ij} + \epsilon_{ji}) \le t_j \qquad (19)$$
$$\forall i \ne j \ne k \in V \qquad \epsilon_{ij} + \epsilon_{jk} \ge \epsilon_{ik} \qquad (20)$$

For the entire graph, Eq. 19 produces $|E|$ constraints and Eq. 20 produces $|V|^3$ additional constraints but are independent of the number of processors unlike in Eq. 9. The number of variables in Eq. 19 is $O(1)$. So the complexity of this linearisation is $O(|V|^3)$, which can be better than $O(|E||P|^2)$ of the ILP-RBL formulation for graphs with many edges, i.e. E is large, and relatively higher number of processors in comparison with V.

4.3   Packing Formulation

The packing formulation in [3] introduces a binary variable z to aid the linearisation of the bilinear equation. Eq. 9 and Eq. 10 of ILP-RBL are replaced by

Eq. 21. Depending on the linearisation used either Eq. 22 or Eq. 23-24 is also used in the packing formulation. All other equations from 1 to 18 are retained. Equation 21 uses a linearisation variable z_{ij}^{hk}

$$\forall j \in V : i \in \delta^-(j) \qquad t_i + L_i + \sum_{h,k \in P} \gamma_{ij}^{hk} z_{ij}^{hk} \leq t_j \qquad (21)$$

where $\forall j \in V : i \in \delta^-(j), h, k \in P \ (z_{ij}^{hk} = x_{ih} x_{jk})$.

The packing formulation uses two linearisation approaches. The first linearisation uses Eq. 22

$$\forall j \in V, i \in \delta^-(j), h, k \in P \ (x_{ih} \geq z_{ij}^{hk} \wedge x_{jk} \geq z_{ij}^{hk} \wedge x_{ih} + x_{jk} - 1 \leq z_{ij}^{hk}) \ (22)$$

The second linearisation uses Eq. 23 and Eq. 24

$$\forall i \neq j \in V, k \in P \qquad \sum_{h \in P} z_{ij}^{hk} = x_{jk} \qquad (23)$$

$$\forall i \neq j \in V, k \in P \qquad z_{ij}^{hk} = z_{ji}^{kh} \qquad (24)$$

Both linearisation approaches require Eq. 21 to model communication between tasks running on different processors. Eq. 21 produces $|E|$ constraints and $O(|P|^2)$ variables in terms of the processor combinations over z_{ij}^{hk}. Eq. 22 produces $|E||P|^2$ constraints and $O(1)$ variables per constraint. Hence, the complexity of the first linearisation by Eq. 21 and Eq. 22 in terms of number of constraints is $O(|E||P|^2)$. Eq. 23 produces $O(|V|^2|P|)$ constraints and $O(|P|)$ variables per constraint. So, the complexity of the second linearisation by Eq. 21 and Eq. 23 in terms of number of constraints is $O(|E| + |V|^2|P|) = O(|V|^2|P|)$. However, through the linearisation of Eq. 21, there are always $|V|^2|P|^2$ z variables for both linearisations. Experimental results from [3] indicate that the first linearisation is beneficial for sparse graphs and the second linearisation is better for dense graphs. When the first linearisation is run over sparse graphs, the $|E|$ to $|P|^2$ ratio decreases as the sparsity of the graph increases making it faster.

Comparing the number of constraints complexity, ILP-RBL ($O(|E||P|^2)$) has the same complexity as the first linearisation. The constraint complexity comparison between ILP-RBL and the second linearisation ($O(|V|^2|P|)$) will depend on the number of edges and processors. ILP-TC ($O(|V|^3)$) will have a competitive number of constraints if $|P|$ is high. The major advantage of the two proposed formulations is that we have only $O(|V||P| + |V|^2)$ variables (x_{ik} and $\sigma_{ij}, \epsilon_{ij}$) for ILP-RBL and only $O(|V|^2)$ variables ($\sigma_{ij}, \epsilon_{ij}$) for ILP-TC to assign a value to.

5   Computational Results

In this section we compare the performance of the two new proposed ILP formulations with both linearisations of the packing formulation in [3]. The result table for the packing formulation displays the best solution time amongst its two linearisations and is compared with ILP-RBL or ILP-TC. The computations are carried out using CPLEX 11.0.0[1] on an Intel Core i3 processor 330M, 2.13 GHZ CPU and 2 GB RAM running with no parallel mode and on a single thread on Windows 7. 2 GB RAM was found to be a reasonable amount of physical memory for executing the ILP's used in this experiment. Extra RAM does not improve the speed of the program execution, but delays CPLEX running out of memory with large problems.

5.1   Experimental Setup

For comparability, all experiments are run for a fully connected processor network with identical bandwidth capacity. The input graphs for this comparison are taken from those proposed and used in [3,4]. The graph files with a name starting with ogra_ are suffixed with the number of tasks in that file followed by its edge density in terms of a percentage of the maximum possible number of edges (i.e. $|V|(|V| - 1)$). According to [3], they have a special graph structure that makes it hard to find the task ordering which yields the optimal solution when the number of mutually independent tasks are large. The graph file with a name starting with t_ were generated randomly and are suffixed with the number of tasks in that file followed by its edge density and the index used to distinguish graphs of the same characteristics. The experiments are run on small to medium sized instances of the graphs on 4 and 8 processors.

5.2   Result Table

The computational results for the graphs are given in Table 1, Table 2 and Table 3 over 4 processors and 8 processors. Not all problem instances were solved with all ILP formulations due to the excessive runtimes of the experiments, but the shown results are representative. The h:m:s notation is the standard Hours:Minutes:Seconds taken by the ILP formulation to find the solution. If the formulation is unable to find the optimal solution within 24 hours, the program is terminated and the gap (the difference between the lower bound and the best solution at that time (SL*)) is recorded. If the optimal schedule length is found, its value is displayed in the column corresponding to SL. Columns p and n record the number of processors and the number of tasks in the graph, respectively.

Table 1 compares the solution time for ILP-REVISEDBOOLEANLOGIC (ILP-RBL) with the best solution time for the Packing linearisations in [3] for a 4 processor configuration over 30 to 50 nodes with varying densities. For these instances the solution time was 20 times or upward faster than the best version of the packing linearisations over a fully connected processor network. As can be observed, the speedup was achieved across different densities (ranging from

Table 1. Solution Time Comparison of Packing with ILP-RBL

Graph	p	n	SL	Packing	Gap	ILP- RBL	Gap
t30_60_1	4	30	467	7m:32s	0%	16s	0%
t40_10_1	4	40	233	10h:31m:37s	0%	24m:45s	0%
t40_25_1	4	40	270	4h:54m	0%	1m:37s	0%
Ogra50_60	4	50		24h	26.33%,SL*=826	24h	3.02%,SL*=612

Table 2. Solution Time Comparison of Packing with ILP-TC

Graph	p	n	SL	Packing	Gap	ILP-TC	Gap
Ogra20_75	8	20	100	51m:28s	0%	2m:37s	0%
t20_90	8	20	242	2m:24s	0%	7s	0%
t30_30_2	8	30	262	24h	0.69%,SL*=287	4h:36m:18s	0%
t30_60_1	8	30	467	7h:22m:19s	0%	2h:6m:54s	0%

10% to 60%). Hence, the influence of the number of edges on ILP-RBL's relative performance was not as pronounced as could have been expected from the number of constraints complexity $O(|E||P|^2)$. For the second linearisation of the packing formulation the constraint complexity is $O(|V|^2|P|)$, so the ILP-RBL also benefited from the low number of processors. Despite this it seems that the strong improvement by ILP-RBL is explained with the lower number of variables, namely $O(|V||P| + |V|^2)$ variables for ILP-RBL compared with $O(|V|^2|P|^2)$ for the packing formulation.

Table 2 compares the solution time of ILP-TRANSITIVITYCLAUSE (ILP-TC) with the best solution time for the packing linearisations in [3]. The results in Table 2 are for ILP-TC on an 8 processor configuration over 20 to 30 nodes of varying density. We see that the solution time was 3 to 20 times faster than the best version of the packing formulation. The complexity of ILP-TC in terms of number of constraints is $O(|V|^3)$. This is independent of the number of processors unlike the packing formulation. Hence, ILP-TC benefits from the larger number of processors. But again, a large performance advantage is likely to come from the even further reduced number of variables, which is $O(|V|^2)$, thus does not depend on the number of processors.

Table 3. Solution Time Comparison of ILP-RBL with ILP-TC

Graph	p	n	SL	ILP-RBL	Gap	ILP-TC	Gap
t30_60_1	4	30	467	16s	0%	2h:39m:31s	0%
t40_25_1	4	40	270	1m:37s	0%	24h	34.72%
t30_90_1	8	30	562	4m:34s	0%	1m:19s	0%
t20_90	8	20	242	2m:23s	0%	7s	0%

Table 3 directly compares the two proposed ILP formulations. ILP-RBL, as expected, has a better solution time than ILP-TC when the number of processors is low. This is clear from the task graphs with 30 and 40 nodes on 4 processors, which have a better solution using ILP-RBL. ILP-TC was found to run faster on 20 and 30 nodes over 8 processors and high graph densities. This is in line with the expectation based on the complexities. We have seen that the complexity of ILP-RBL in terms of number of constraints is $O(|E||P|^2)$ and that of ILP-TC in terms of number of constraints is $O(|V|^3)$. Clearly, a higher density graph increases the solution time of ILP-RBL. A combination of the edge density and the number of processors serves as an indicator to decide between ILP-RBL and ILP-TC.

6   Conclusion

This paper proposed two Linear Programming formulations for the Multiprocessor Scheduling Problem with Communication Delays. The improvement was in reducing the number of variables and constraints by the effective linearisation of the bilinear equation arising out of communication delays in the MSPCD model. The first of the proposed formulation ILP-RBL reworked the logic for Boolean multiplication and eliminated variables used to achieve the same result as in the packing formulation. The second proposed formulation ILP-TC also eliminates variables used in the packing formulation by enforcing the partial ordering of the processor indices with the help of an additional transitivity clause. We performed an experimental evaluation comparing the two proposed ILP formulations with the best previously published results. The linearisation used in ILP-RBL resulted in the formulation running faster over a small number of processors and the linearisation in ILP-TC resulted in it running faster over a larger number of processors.

Acknowledgement. We gratefully acknowledge that this work is supported by the Marsden Fund Council from Government funding, Grant 9073-3624767, administered by the Royal Society of New Zealand.

References

1. ILOG CPLEX 11.0 User's Manual. ILOG S.A., Gentilly, France (2007)
2. Coffman Jr., E.G., Graham, R.L.: Optimal scheduling for two-processor systems. Acta Informat. 1, 200–213 (1972)
3. Davidović, T., Liberti, L., Maculan, N., Mladenovic, N.: Towards the optimal solution of the multiprocessor scheduling problem with communication delays, pp. 128–135 (2007)
4. Davidović, T., Crainic, T.G.: Benchmark-problem instances for static scheduling of task graphs with communication delays on homogeneous multiprocessor systems. Comput. Oper. Res. 33, 2155–2177 (2006)
5. Dechter, R., Pearl, J.: Generalized best-first search strategies and the optimality of A*. J. ACM 32(3), 505–536 (1985)
6. Hagras, T., Janecek, J.: A high performance, low complexity algorithm for compile-time task scheduling in heterogeneous systems. Parallel Computing 31(7), 653–670 (2005)
7. Hwang, J.-J., Chow, Y.-C., Anger, F.D., Lee, C.-Y.: Scheduling precedence graphs in systems with interprocessor communication times. SIAM J. Comput. 18(2), 244–257 (1989)
8. Kwok, Y.-K., Ahmad, I.: On multiprocessor task scheduling using efficient state space search approaches. Journal of Parallel and Distributed Computing 65(12), 1515–1532 (2005)
9. Löwe, W., Zimmermann, W.: Scheduling Iterative Programs onto LogP-Machine. In: Amestoy, P.R., Berger, P., Daydé, M., Duff, I.S., Frayssé, V., Giraud, L., Ruiz, D. (eds.) Euro-Par 1999. LNCS, vol. 1685, pp. 332–339. Springer, Heidelberg (1999)

10. Palmer, A., Sinnen, O.: Scheduling algorithm based on force directed clustering. In: Ninth International Conference on Parallel and Distributed Computing, Applications and Technologies, PDCAT 2008, pp. 311–318 (December 2008)
11. Price, C.C., Pooch, U.W.: Search techniques for a nonlinear multiprocessor scheduling problem. Naval Research Logistics Quarterly 29(2), 213–233 (1982)
12. Radulescu, A., van Gemund, A.J.C.: Low-cost task scheduling for distributed-memory machines. IEEE Transactions on Parallel and Distributed Systems 13(6), 648–658 (2002)
13. Russell, S.J., Norvig, P.: Artificial intelligence: a modern approach. Prentice Hall (2010)
14. Sarkar, V.: Partitioning and scheduling parallel programs for multiprocessors. MIT Press (1989)
15. Shahul, A.Z.S., Sinnen, O.: Scheduling task graphs optimally with A*. Journal of Supercomputing 51(3), 310–332 (2010)
16. Sinnen, O., Sousa, L.: Scheduling Task Graphs on Arbitrary Processor Architectures Considering Contention. In: Hertzberger, B., Hoekstra, A.G., Williams, R. (eds.) HPCN-Europe 2001. LNCS, vol. 2110, pp. 373–382. Springer, Heidelberg (2001)
17. Sinnen, O., Sousa, L.: Experimental evaluation of task scheduling accuracy: Implications for the scheduling model. IEICE Transactions on Information and Systems E86-D(9), 1620–1627 (2003)
18. Sinnen, O.: Task Scheduling for Parallel Systems (Wiley Series on Parallel and Distributed Computing). Wiley- Interscience (2007)
19. Yang, T., Gerasoulis, A.: List scheduling with and without communication delays. Parallel Computing 19(12), 1321–1344 (1993)
20. Zomaya, A.Y., Ward, C., Macey, B.: Genetic scheduling for parallel processor systems: comparative studies and performance issues. IEEE Transactions on Parallel and Distributed Systems 10(8), 795–812 (1999)

A Bitstream Relocation Technique to Improve Flexibility of Partial Reconfiguration

Yoshihiro Ichinomiya*, Motoki Amagasaki, Masahiro Iida,
Morihiro Kuga, and Toshinori Sueyoshi

Graduate School of Science and Technology, Kumamoto University,
2-39-1, Kurokami, Kumamoto 860-8555, Japan
ichinomiya@arch.cs.kumamoto-u.ac.jp,
{amagasaki,iida,kuga,sueyoshi}@cs.kumamoto-u.ac.jp

Abstract. The latest commercial field programmable gate array (FPGA) like a Virtex-6 can perform partial reconfiguration (PR). PR can take full advantage of FPGA's reconfigurability. However, PR bitstream (PRB) which created by authorized design flow cannot be relocated to other partially reconfigurable regions (PRRs). This indicates that the preparation of many PRBs are needed to perform a flexible partial reconfiguration. This paper presents a uniforming design technique for PRRs in order to relocate their PRB. Additionally, our design technique enables to implement large partial module by combining neighboring PRRs. To make relocatable, our technique only restricts the placement of reconfigurable resource and the route of interconnection. Therefore, our design can be achieved only using Xilinx EDA tools. Through verification, the correct operation of the relocated PRBs is confirmed.

Keywords: Partial Reconfiguration, Reconfigurable Computing, Bitstream Relocation.

1 Introduction

SRAM-based Field Programmable Gate Array (FPGA) is widely used in numerous applications. An FPGA is a reconfigurable LSI which can reconfigure its application by downloading circuit configuration data in the configuration memory. The configuration memory controls logic functions and their interconnections. The FPGA is often used for parallel computing because FPGA can be matched to the computational requirements of an application. Further, it allows the user to create any number of task-specific cores as long as they do not exceed the limit of usable FPGA resourses. The cores run like simultaneous parallel circuits inside one FPGA chip.

Some of the latest FPGAs support dynamic partial reconfiguration (DPR). For example, Xilinx supports it through the Virtex-4 with integrated software environment (ISE) 12.2 [1], while Altera supports it through the Stratix-V series

---

* Research Fellow of the Japan Society for the Promotion of Science.

Y. Xiang et al. (Eds.): ICA3PP 2012, Part I, LNCS 7439, pp. 139–152, 2012.

FPGA with Quartus II [2]. Partial reconfiguration (PR) can change a part of the implemented circuit without reconfiguring whole system. In other word, PR can switch system components with continuing the operation of the remaining components. This is performed by downloading the configuration data for partially reconfigurable regions (PRRs). The PR can extend the dynamic task allocation feature for parallel computing on reconfigurable system.

In the case of the Xilinx PR design flow[1], PRRs have to be designed before "Placement & Routing (PAR)" and bitstream generation. In addition, PR modules must be assigned to the PRR at the same design phase. The PR module refers to the functional module that is reconfigured by PR. The PR module is optimized to each PRR at the PAR phase. Thus, a created PR bitstream (PRB) is only usable for an associated PRR. In order to implement a same module on several PRRs, PRBs have to be created for each PRR from the same module. For example, "N × M" of PRBs must be prepared and stored in memory if 'M' modules will be implemented into 'N' PRRs. Hence, there is a trade-off between reconfigurability and memory size in such conventional DPR systems.

Moreover, the PRR size cannot be changed after system design. To implement both of small and large PR modules, PRRs should be designed large enough to implement the largest PR module. This induces a waste of reconfigurable resources if the differences between PRR size and PR modules size are large.

This paper presents a relocation design technique for PRRs to improve the flexibility of PR. Our design technique creates uniform PRRs in order to relocate same PRB on their PRRs. Therefore, the number of PRBs is reduced to the same number of PR modules. This means our technique can reduce the memory size for RPBs. In addition, our technique enables to combine multiple PRRs to implement large PR modules. This feature is an application of uniform PRRs. We present a design technique to resolve the issues for uniforming PRRs by applying design constraints for EDA tools. We target the Xilinx Virtex-6 FPGA in this work, and use Xilinx EDA tools to design uniform PRRs.

The remainder of this paper is organized as follows. Section 2 describes related research on techniques to improve the flexibility of PR. Technical problems of bitstream relocation and their solutions are given in Section 3. Section 4 describes the application of uniform PRRs to implement large PR module. Section 5 describes the verification system and its results. Finally, conclusions and future work are presented in Section 6.

2   Related Research

A large number of bitstream relocation techniques have been studied. These studies are categorized as manipulating bitstream or designing relocatable PRRs.

The former techniques modify bitstream contents for relocating. For example, they modify the frame address, the cyclic redundancy check (CRC) data, and the configuration data. Frame address is the start address of the PR [3]. Kalte [4] proposed the relocation filter for the Virtex-2pro FPGA, which called REPLICA2Pro. REPLICA2Pro is hardware module which implemented in FPGA. This module modifies the frame address and CRC value when downloading the bitstream from off-chip memory. Corbetta [5] proposed the relocation filters that are implemented both in software and hardware. The filters operate in the same way as REPLICA2Pro, but they can handle Virtex-2 Pro, Virtex-4, and Virtex-5. Sudarsanam [6] proposed the PRR-PRR relocation technique for Virtex-4. This technique generates the frame addresses for both source and destination PRRs. When performing relocation, the PRB is read from an active PRR (source PRR). Then, the frame address of read PRB is modified by their technique, and the modified PRB is written on the destination PRR. All of the above techniques, however, consider only how to manipulate a PRB, and not consider how to create a relocatable PRB.

Becker [7] introduced the techniques for a relocatable design and a relocation process for heterogeneous PRRs. They create compatible subsets of regions to design relocatable PRRs. In the case of the Virtex-4, all CLB, DSP, and BRAM columns have same routing structure. Further, their addressing for configuration memory is identical. To create compatible PRRs, the logic part of non-identical column is not used when creating relocatable PRB. In addition, the PRB data are partitioned based on the column type. When relocating the PRB to non-identical regions, these partitioned PRBs are combined and downloaded. At this time, both the configuration data and frame address are manipulated. Montminy et al. [8] and Koester et al. [9] proposed an interconnect module to maintain the interface between PR modules and static modules after PR. Montminy [8] introduced a interconnect PRR to keep the connection. When relocating the PR module, the interconnect PRR is simultaneously reconfigured. Koester et al. [9] presented an interconnect structure, which is embedded in PRRs. Authorized interconnection circuits, such as proxy logic, are not modified during PR. Therefore, if PRB is relocated from another region, the interconnection between PRR and static module will be disconnected. Koester's interconnect circuit is reconfigured simultaneously and maintain their interconnection after PRB relocation. Moreover, their technique is not restricted by Xilinx's PR design. The Montminy's technique uses only the Xilinx design constraint and EDA tools, but the area efficiency is reduced. Further, bitstream reduction is not considered. On the other hand, the Koester's technique can reduce memory and improve area efficiency, but it requires the design of a special interconnect circuit.

In this work, we focus on a design technique for PRR. Our technique enables to relocate the PRB by only modifying the frame-address and CRC by uniforming PRRs. In addition, this technique allows implementing large modules by combining uniform PRRs. Different from Koester's work [9], our design technique uses only commercial EDA tools and an interconnection circuit. Our technique is better for maintaining general versatility.

3   Designing Uniformed Reconfigurable Regions

3.1   Issues of PRB Relocation

Figure 1 shows an example of the partial reconfiguration system. PRR is isolated from static region in order to prevent reconfiguring a static region. A

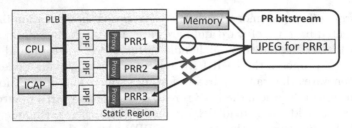

Fig. 1. General partial reconfiguration system

communication between PRR and static region is performed through an intermediate circuit which called "proxy logic." PRB is downloaded through external configuration port such as JTAG, or downloaded through internal configuration access port (ICAP). A PRB is unique to a PRR, thus, JPEG for PRR1 cannot be implemented on PRR2 and PRR3 in the case of figure 1.

The reason that a PRB cannot be relocated to another PRR is the difference between the PRR configuration and the PRB information. PRB controls logic functions and interconnections by controlling configuration memories. If the configurations of PRRs are different, a relocated bitstream may control incompatible hardware resource. For example, the bitstream controlling logic function may control interconnection if the bitstream is relocated to different PRR.

In order to relocate PRB, configurations of PRR have to be uniform among designed PRRs. The design points of uniforming are the followings:

- Amount of reconfigurable resources
- Relative layout of reconfigurable resource
- Relative placement of proxy logic
- Relative routing path between proxy logic and static region
- Rejection of the wire from PRR, which does not through proxy logic

Reconfigurable resources indicate all FPGA resources which are controlled by configuration memory. They are, for example, configurable logic block (CLB), switch matrix, interconnection of digital signal processor (DSP), embedded block RAM (BRAM), I/O block, and so on. CLB consists of look up table (LUT). Further, layout means the physical position in FPGA device, and placement means the assigned resource address resulted in implementation flow.

In the authorized design flow of Xilinx, PRRs are designed using PlanAhead which is an application of ISE suites. PlanAhead supports the design of PR system; floor-planning, creating design constraints, design rule check, and so on. For example, PlanAhead checks whether the amount of reconfigurable resource is enough to implement PR module. Further, it checks the nonexistence of prohibited resource like clock manager into the PRR.

However, PlanAhead does not consider the PRB relocation. PlanAhead put a priority on performance than reconfigurability during PAR process. The layout of reconfigurable resources and the placement of proxy logic are not considered in authorized design flow. Thus, we design the uniform PRR by adding design constraints to the authorized design flow.

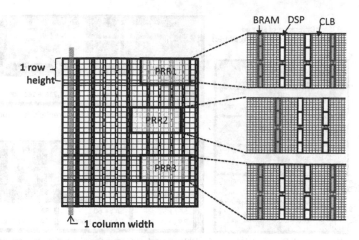

Fig. 2. Example of three distinct PRRs

3.2   Uniforming Included Reconfigurable Resource

Figure 2 shows the example of three distinct PRRs. They have identical size of rows and columns. However, PRR1 and PRR2 consist of different types of reconfigurable resources. Information of their PRBs will be different. For example, the size of PRBs are different because 1 row × 1 column of CLB consists of 36 frames of configuration data, but that of BRAM consists of 30 frames. Note that, a frame is the minimum unit of configuration memory addressing in Xilinx FPGA, and it consists of 2,592 bits in Virtex-6 FPGA[3]. In contrast to PRR2, PRR3 has same reconfigurable resources with PRR1. The relative addresses in PRR2 and PRR3 are identical when focusing on the inside of PRRs. Thus, their PRBs can be relocated by modifying the reconfiguration address if remained problems, which are shown in section 3.1, are resolved.

To relocate PRB, the included reconfigurable resources have to be identical like PRR1 and PRR3. The uniform PRR for vertical direction can be created by aligning column address and column width. The reconfigurable resources are vertically aligned through the FPGA device in Virtex-6. Thus, the Virtex-6 has nearly identical row architecture in all rows. By the way of exception, the I/O pins and the hardware macro related to I/O module, such as PCI Express, are not identical. Thus, I/O and I/O modules must not be included or not be used in uniform PRRs.

The uniform PRRs for horizontal direction is defined by simply selecting identical resources. However, the types of CLB have to be considered. The CLB has two types of architecture which are CLBLL and CLBLM. CLBLM can be used as distributed memory, but CLBLL cannot be used as memory. The type of CLB can be distinct by showing the detail of CLB on PlanAhead.

Figure 3 shows the examples of identical regions on Virtex-6 XC6VLX240T. Figure 3(a) shows the identical clock regions, (b) shows identical regions on the same row, and (c) shows identical regions in the same clock region. Here, (5-1) and (5-2) are located in same clock regions. The range of PRRs in figure3(b) and (c) are the largest range of uniform PRRs on the same row and same clock

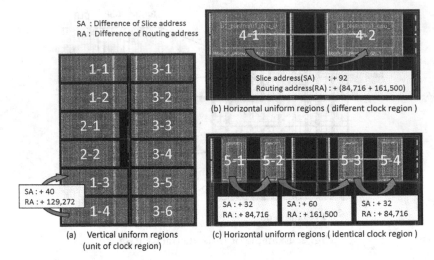

SA : Difference of Slice address
RA : Difference of Routing address

Slice address(SA)   : + 92
Routing address(RA) : + (84,716 + 161,500)

(b) Horizontal uniform regions (different clock region)

SA : + 40
RA : + 129,272

SA : + 32   SA : + 60   SA : + 32
RA : + 84,716   RA : + 161,500   RA : + 84,716

(a)   Vertical uniform regions   (c) Horizontal uniform regions (identical clock region)
(unit of clock region)

Fig. 3. Identical regions in Virtex-6 XC6VLX240T

Table 1. The X-range of identical PRRs

	Left border	Right border
(4-1)	CLBLM_X01	CLBLL_X38
(4-2)	CLBLM_X58	CLBLL_X95
(5-1)	CLBLM_X06	CLBLM_X17
(5-2)	CLBLM_X26	CLBLM_X37
(5-3)	CLBLM_X63	CLBLM_X74
(5-4)	CLBLM_X83	CLBLM_X94

regions. Table 1 shows the X-range of each identical region. They are represented by the CLB address. The PRRs which have same initial number can implement same PRB if remained problems are resolved.

Note that, the height of a PRR must be the unit of a row. The minimum PRR size is 1 row × 1 column. PRR size can be increased in units of the row and the column. Thus, the height of uniform PRR can become more than 2 rows. However, if the PRR is smaller than 1 row, the PRB may include configuration data of static region. These PRB cannot be relocated because they may reconfigure static region.

To reduce the circuit constraints, we assign a "blank module" on PRRs as a PR module during the uniforming design. This is because the subsequent uniforming design flow handles much number of design constraints. Blank module is the module which does not have any circuit and routing. Thus, the extra constraints are not appeared. This module can be assigned by the authorized PR design flow.

3.3   Uniforming Placment of Proxy Logic

To keep the interconnection between PR module and static module, the relative placement of the proxy logic must be uniform in all uniform PRRs. Figure 4

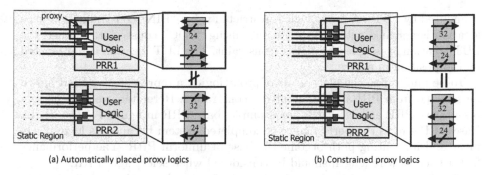

(a) Automatically placed proxy logics   (b) Constrained proxy logics

Fig. 4. Example of placement of proxy logic

```
# Location constraints for Reconfigurable Module Partition Pins
PIN "math_0/math_0/USER_LOGIC_I/rp_instance.ain(0)" LOC = SLICE_X18Y176;
PIN "math_0/math_0/USER_LOGIC_I/rp_instance.ain(1)" LOC = SLICE_X19Y178;
                              ⋮
PIN "math_0/math_0/USER_LOGIC_I/rp_instance.ain(0)" BEL = D6LUT;
PIN "math_0/math_0/USER_LOGIC_I/rp_instance.ain(1)" BEL = D6LUT;
                              ⋮
```

Fig. 5. Report of pr2ucf command

shows an schematic diagram of the placements of proxy logic. The order of input and output is different for each PRR as shown in figure 4(a). When relocating the bitstream from PRR1 to PRR2, the interconnection will be disconnected. To maintain the interconnection, relative placements of proxy logics have to be uniform like figure 4(b). The relative placements of ploxy logics are uniformed with that of PRR2 The design flow to uniform placement of proxy logic is following:

1. Proceeds a design flow until creating a routed NCD file
2. Extracts the placement constraint of proxy logic using "PR2UCF" command
3. Selects a representative PRR from PRRs for homogenization
4. Applies placement constraint to PRRs using the extracted constraints from the representative PRR
5. Operates PAR process to reflect the constraints

Firstly, the authorized PRR design flow is proceeded without any special constraints. This is performed to decide initial placements of proxy logics. Then, the placement data of proxy logics are extracted from the routed Native Circuit Description (NCD) file. "PR2UCF" command can extract the placement information of proxy logic from NCD file. The results are output to Xilinx User Constraint File (UCF) [10]. The execution command is following:

$$pr2ucf - bel - o\ \{output\_file\_name\}.ucf\ \{input\_file\_name\}.ncd$$

Figure 5 shows the output example of a "PR2UCF" command. The proxy logics are implemented by using the LUT. Thus, the placement of proxy logics is fixed by the units of Slice and LUT. The slice is the component of CLB and it is configured by LUTs. A proxy logic is restricted using "PIN" constraint. The slice location is assigned with coordinate data using "LOC" constraint. Further, the LUT location is assigned by "BEL" constraint. The LUT location is represented by the position in a slice.

To be uniforming the placements of proxy logics, a representative PRR has to be selected from PRRs before applying constraints. Hereafter, we call the representative PRR as base-PRR. For example, base-PRR in figure 4 is the PRR2. Base-PRR affects the performance of completed system because its logic placement and its routing path become the base of uniform PRR. The performance factor such as wire length should be considered when selecting a PRR.

Then, to uniform the relative placement of proxy logic, the coordinate data of slice are modified. When uniforming on vertical direction, multiples of 40 is added to or subtracted from the Y-coordinate of the base-PRR. For example, when the PRR(1-3) in figure 3 is uniformed with the PRR(1-4), 40 is added to the Y-coordinate of PRR(1-4). Here, PRR(1-4) is base-PRR, and hereafter we will represent it as base-PRR(1-4). On the other hand, the X-coordinate is modified when uniforming horizontal direction. In the case that PRR(5-2) is uniformed with PRR(5-1), 32 is added to the X-coordinate of the base-PRR(5-1). As above, multiples of 32 is added or subtracted to X-coordinate of the base-PRR. The coordination of the slice can be confirmed in PlanAhead.

Furthermore, the location of LUT must be uniform with that of the base-PRR. This is simply achieved by copying the constraints from base-PRR to other PRRs. Finally in this flow, placement and routing is re-operated to apply these constraints on NCD.

3.4   Uniforming Interconnect between Proxy Logic and Static Module

The proxy logic may be placed inside of the PRR. Thus, the wire information between the proxy logic and the static region is included in the PRB. The uniforming design flow of routing path is following:

1. Extracts the path information using a "FPGA editor" in ISE suite
2. Copies the path information from the base-PRR to the other PRRs
3. Modifies the absolute address of signal source excluding base-PRR
4. Disable the constraint description for proxy logics
5. Operate PAR process to apply constraints

Firstly, the path information is extracted from the NCD file using "Directed Routing Constraints (DRC)" program included in FPGA editor. This program can obtain the routing address of selected wire. To uniform the routing path of PRRs, all signals between proxy logics and static modules have to be analyzed.

Figure 6 shows the example result of DRC program. The path is constrained using "NET" and "ROUTE" constraint. NET indicates the target wire for constraining. ROUTE indicates the routing path information. This is described with the absolute address of the signal source, and the related addresses to the subsequent routing switches from the signal source. The coordinate value (x, y) which is

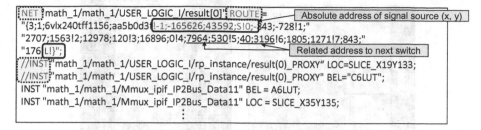

Fig. 6. Report of Directed Routing Constraints

clipped between "! − 1;" and "$S!0;$" indicates the absolute source address of a selected signal. The following coordinate values are relative address to the next routing switch. They are compartmented by '!x'. The number 'x' subsequent to '!' is the number of passed switches. Then, "$L!$}" means that the path arrives to the sink.

After the analysis of routing path, routing addresses are modified to be uniform. The related routing path can be uniformed by copying the related routing address from base-PRR to other PRRs. Then, the source addresses of signals have to be modified to connect the path and the proxy logic. The placements of proxy logics are already uniformed in section 3.3. Thus, the routing path can be connected to proxy logics by shifting the absolute address of signal source.

To be uniform routing path in vertical direction, multiples of 129,272 is added to or subtracted from Y-address to shift the signal source. For example, when PRR(1-3) and PRR(1-2) in figure 3 are uniformed with base-PRR(1-4), "129,272" and "4 × 129,272" are added to Y-address of base-PRR(1-4).

Further, to be uniform PRRs in horizontal direction, the X-address is added or subtracted. When uniforming in same clock region like figure 3(c), "84,716" is added or subtracted. For example, when the PRR(5-2) is uniformed with base-PRR(5-1), "84,716" is added to the X-address of PRR(5-1). This is same with the case that PRR(5-4) is uniformed with base-PRR(5-3). When uniforming beyond the center column, "161,500" is added or subtracted. For example, when PRR(5-3) is uniformed with base-PRR(5-2), "161,500" is added to the X-address of base-PRR(5-2). Furthermore, to uniform PRR(4-2) with base-PRR(4-1), "84,716 + 161,500" is added to the X-address of base-PRR(4-1). This is same with the case PRR(5-3) is uniformed with base-PRR(5-1). The absolute routing address is confirmed using FPGA editor.

Then, the placement constraints about proxy logics which were analyzed by DRC have to be disabled. Their constraints are overlapped here because they are already applied at section 3.3. Finally in this flow, placement and routing is re-operated to apply these constraints.

3.5 Excluding Crossing Wire

Although the uniforming technique is applied, the PRR mismatch may occur due to wire crossing. Figure 7 shows an example of wires crossing in the PRR. The wire shown in figure 7(a) crosses the PRR without passing the proxy logics.

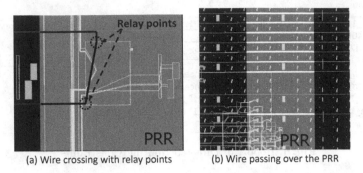

(a) Wire crossing with relay points   (b) Wire passing over the PRR

Fig. 7. Crossed wire problem

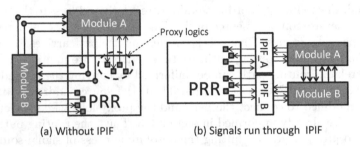

(a) Without IPIF   (b) Signals run through IPIF

Fig. 8. Abstraction of signal alignment

Further, it has a relay point into the PRR. This affects the information of PRB. If PRB is relocated from another PRR, the crossing wire will be disconnected. In contrast to figure 7(a), the wires that pass over the PRR like figure 7(b) do not affect the information of the PRB. To be uniform the PRRs, the crossing wires have to be eliminated.

The wire crossing is resolved by rewiring them using FPGA editor and ISE router. The crossed wire is released by using FPGA editor, and then, it is rewired using ISE. If ISE router cannot eliminate wire crossing, the crossed wire has to be manually rerouted using FPGA editor.

The wire crossing may often occur if static modules are placed around PRR. Thus, we isolate the PRR from static modules to reduce the wire crossing. Figure 8 shows the abstract image of PRR isolation. When the placements of the static modules are not considered, the related static modules are placed around PRR as shown in figure 8(a). In this case, the wire between Module_A and Module_B may run through the switches in PRR.

To isolate the PRR, all input and output signals are run through the interface module as shown in figure8(b). Here, we call it intellectual property interface (IPIF) module. Placement of IPIF is constrained using "AREA_GROUP" constraint to align the signal direction. If the IPIF is placed on the right side of the PRR, the static modules are more likely to be placed on the same side of IPIF. Thus, the probability of wire crossing is reduced by implementing IPIF. Figure 9 shows the example of PRR and IPIF placement. As shown in the figure, the signal directions between PRR and IPIF are aligned. Further, PRR is isolated from static modules.

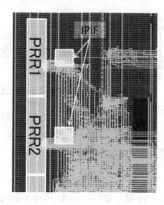

Fig. 9. Example of placement of IPIF and PRR

3.6   Modifying Configuration Bitstream

As a result of above design flow, the uniforming of PRRs is completed. Thus, their PRRs can relocate PRBs among them. However, the configuration commands of PRB have to be modified in order to download the configuration bitstream. The modification points of the PRB are "frame address" and "CRC parameter" [3].

The frame address is placed in the header of the PRB. It indicates the start address of the partial reconfiguration [3]. This address described after $(3000\ 2001)_{16}$ command, and the frame address has to be adapted to relocation target PRR. This information is obtained from created PRB files.

The CRC parameter is placed in the footer, and checks the validity of the bitstream. To download a PRB, we need to recalculate the CRC syndrome, or need to invalidate the CRC. To invalidate the CRC, we have to modify the access command to the CRC register. This is represented as $(3000\ 0001)_{16}$ in footer command, and the subsequent word is CRC value. The $(3000\ 0001)_{16}$ must be modified to $(3000\ 8001)_{16}$, and the subsequent word must be modified to $(0000\ 0007)_{16}$. $(3000\ 8001)_{16}$ is an access command to the command register (CMD), and $(0000\ 0007)_{16}$ is the CRC reset command.

4   PRR Conjunction

The uniform PRRs are able to be conjunction if they are adjacent and aligned vertically. Figure 10 shows an abstraction of the conjunction of adjacent PRRs. In figure 10, two uniform PRRs are designed. Their PRRs have identical configuration and don't have irregular circuit and wire such as crossed wires. Further, there are no circuit and no space between their PRRs. Thus, adjacent uniform PRR, like them, can be handled as large PRR.

However, the current ISE suite cannot handle the combined PRRs as a large PRR. Therefore, PRB for combined PRR has to be created from the start of design flow. The PRR in restarted flow must have a uniform configuration with combined PRR to migrate PRB. This means that the large PRR has twice size and twice proxy logics. The migrated PRB has large configuration, but some of proxy logics

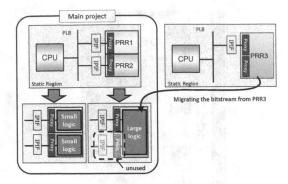

Fig. 10. Outline of the utilization of a relocatable PRR

Table 2. Development Environment

Development board	ML605 Evaluation Kit
FPGA device	Virtex-6 XC6VLX240T-FF1156
Development tools	Integrated software environment 12.3

may not be used. In spite of this, the migrated PRB has to keep the number and configuration of proxy logics to keep the interface with static modules. The signals for unused proxy logics have to be handled as pull-up or pull-down signals.

5   Verification of Bitstream Relocation

In this section, we show the design environment and verification. Table 2 shows the development environment and figure 11 shows the verification system based on the Xilinx reference design [11]. We added three PRRs to the reference design and applied the uniforming design technique to all PRRs to verify the PRB relocation. The sample circuits for relocation are the 16 bit multiplier and 32 bit adder. The default configuration of PRRs is a 16 bit multiplier.

To verify the PRB relocation, we prepare two PRBs. They are PRB for adder and PRB for multiplier. Figure 12 shows the placement of the uniform PRRs. In order to verify the PRB relocation, we take following verification procedures.

1. Downloading the full bitstream of the verification system
2. Reconfiguring one of PRRs using the PRB for adder
3. Inputting the operands from the CPU, and monitoring the output
4. Reconfiguring the same PRRs using the PRB for multiplier
5. Inputting the operands from the CPU, and monitoring the output
6. Repeating the steps 2~5 until completing all PRRs and PRBs combination

As a result of output monitoring, we confirmed that all combinations of uniform PRR and PRB could perform correct operation. Further, we performed the uniform PRR design for MIPS based softcore processor called Plasma[12]. The operation of the relocated plasma could perform correctly, too. Consequently, the PRR was correctly uniformed by our design flow.

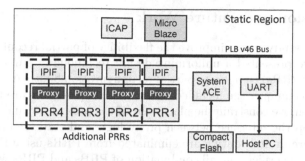

Fig. 11. The verification system

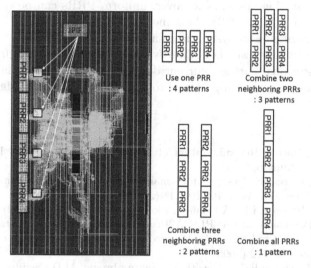

Fig. 12. Placement and the combinations of PRRs

The PRRs shown in figure 12 are aligned vertically. Therefore, they can be used as large PRRs like the right side of figure 12. Their operations are verified by the same procedure with previously mentioned one. As a result of confirmation, we confirmed their operations are correct.

Based on the results of the verification, we could confirm the correct operation of all relocated PRBs. The proposed technique only requires 4 uniform PRRs and 8 types PRBs to implement all PRBs shown in the figure 12. In contrast, the conventional DPR design requires PRBs in each PRR and in each combined PRR. This means that the system shown in figure 11 requires additional large PRRs and 2×10 kinds PRBs to achieve the same flexibility. In addition, the PRB size depends on PRR size. As a result, our technique could reduce the total PRB size to a half of the conventional technique in the case of this evaluation. Thus, our design technique can improve the flexibility of partial reconfiguration. Further, we can reduce the memory usage because our technique can reduce the number of PRBs. Moreover, our technique has a possibility to reduce the design time of the DPR system. This is because our technique can reduce the bitstream creation time.

6   Conclusion and Future Work

The aim of this study was to improve the flexibility of partial reconfiguration. To achieve this, we presented a uniforming design technique of partially reconfigurable regions (PRRs) to relocate partial reconfiguration bitstream (PRB). First of our design technique, the included reconfigurable resources are uniformed in each PRR. Then, we constrain the placement of the proxy logic and routing path in order to keep the interface between proxy logic and static modules. Finally, the irregular circuit and routing are eliminated from PRRs using FPGA editor. As a result of the verification, all combination of PRBs and PRRs were operated correctly after relocation. Thus, we can reduce the number of PRBs for dynamic partial reconfiguration system. Moreover, uniform PRRs can be combined and can be relocated a large PRB. This means that our technique improves the flexibility of reconfigurable system in small memory usage.

In the future works, we should verify and evaluate our design method on practical applications. Further, current design flows depend on manual design. Thus, we will develop the support tool to ease the uniforming design.

References

1. Xilinx Inc., Partial Reconfiguration of Xilinx FPGAs Using ISE Design Suite, WP374(v1.1) (July 6, 2011)
2. Altera Inc., Increasing Design Functionality with Partial and Dynamic Reconfiguration in 28-nm FPGAs, WP374(v1.1) (July 2010)
3. Xilinx Inc., Virtex-6 FPGA Configuration User Guide, UG360(v3.2) (2010)
4. Kalte, H., Porrmann, M.: REPLICA2Pro: Task relocation by bitstream manipulation in Virtex-II/Pro FPGAs. In: Proceedings of the 3rd Conference on Computing Frontiers, pp. 403–412 (2006)
5. Corbetta, S., Morandi, M., Novati, M., Santambrogio, M.D., Sciuto, D., Spoletini, P.: Internal and External Bitstream Relocation for Partial Dynamic Reconfiguration. IEEE Transactions on Very Large Scale Integration (VLSI) Systems 17(11) (November 2009)
6. Sudarsanam, A., Kallam, R., Dasu, A.: PRR-PRR Dynamic Relocation. IEEE Computer Architecture Letters 8(2) (July-December 2009)
7. Becker, T., Luk, W., Cheung, P.Y.K.: Enhancing Relocatability of Partial Bitstreams for Run-Time Reconfiguration. In: 15th Annual IEEE Symposium on Field-Programmable Custom Computing Machines 2007, pp. 35–44 (April 2007)
8. Montminy, D.P., Baldwin, R.O., Williams, P.D., Mullins, B.E.: Using Relocatable Bitstreams for Fault Tolerance. In: Second NASA/ESA Conference on Adaptive Hardware and System 2007, pp. 701–708 (August 2007)
9. Koester, M., Luk, W., Hagemeyer, J., Porrmann, M., Rückert, U.: Design Optimizations for Tiled Partially Reconfigurable Systems. IEEE Transactions on Very Large Scale Integration (VLSI) Systems 19(6), 1048–1061 (2011)
10. Xilinx Inc., Constraints Guide, UG625 (v12.3) (September 21, 2010)
11. Xilinx Inc., PlanAhead Software Tutorial Partial Reconfiguration of a Processor Peripheral, UG744 (v13.2) (July 6, 2011)
12. Plasma - most MIPS(TM) opcode: Overview: Open-Cores,
    http://opencores.org/project,plasma,overview

A Hybrid Heuristic-Genetic Algorithm
for Task Scheduling in Heterogeneous Multi-core System

Chuan Wang, Jianhua Gu, Yunlan Wang, and Tianhai Zhao

School of Computer, NPU HPC Center, Xi'an, China
wangnwpu@163.com,
{gujh,wangyl,zhaoth}@nwpu.edu.cn

Abstract. Task scheduling on heterogeneous multi-core systems is NP-complete problem. This paper proposes a novel hybrid static scheduling algorithm named Hybrid Successor Concerned Heuristic-Genetic Scheduling (HSCGS) algorithm. The algorithm is a combination of heuristic and genetic scheduling algorithm. In the first phase we propose a heuristic algorithm named Successor Concerned List Heuristic Scheduling (SCLS) to generate a high quality scheduling result. SCLS algorithm takes the impact of current task's scheduling to its successor into account. The second phase implements an Improved Genetic Algorithm (IGA) for scheduling, to optimize the scheduling results of SCLS iteratively. The comparison experiments are based on both random generated applications and some real world applications. The performance of HSCGS is compared with some famous task scheduling algorithms, such as HEFT and DLS. The results show that HSCGS is the best of them, and the advantages go up with the increase of the heterogeneous factor of inter-core link bandwidth.

Keywords: Heterogeneous multi-core, Task scheduling, Heuristic algorithm, Genetic algorithm, Hybrid Scheduing, Directed acyclic graph.

1 Introduction

By integrating a number of cores with different capability together, heterogeneous multi-core architecture provides better performance compared with homogeneous system [1]. In order to make good use of heterogeneous multi-core system, tasks of parallel applications should be scheduled appropriately. The quality of task schedule has great impact on application execution efficiency. Traditional task scheduling algorithms are mostly designed for homogeneous systems and are difficult to achieve desired results on heterogeneous systems. The development of heterogeneous multi-core system brings new challenges to task scheduling algorithm. Task scheduling problem on heterogeneous multi-core systems is NP-complete [2].

Task scheduling algorithms are generally divided into static scheduling and dynamic scheduling [3]. In static scheduling algorithm, all information needed for scheduling must be known in advance, including the execution time of each task, the characteristics of the cores, and the amount of data passed between tasks and so on.

Y. Xiang et al. (Eds.): ICA3PP 2012, Part I, LNCS 7439, pp. 153–170, 2012.

Static scheduling make decisions in compile time which does not increase the running cost of the application. Dynamic scheduling algorithms gather information needed for scheduling and make scheduling decisions at run time which can adapt to different circumstances.

Because of its key importance, task scheduling algorithm has been studied extensively, and a lot of static scheduling algorithms [2] have been proposed. These algorithms can be divided into three categories: heuristic algorithm, guided random search algorithm, hybrid of the previous two kinds of algorithms. List-based heuristic algorithm is a widely used heuristic algorithm, which can generate high quality task schedule in a short time, but it will not perform well in all cases. Genetic algorithm (GA) is the most widely used guided random search techniques. It aims to obtain near-optimal task schedules by imitating the process of biological evolution. Genetic Algorithm can usually get good scheduling results after sufficient number of generations, but its time complexity is much higher than heuristic algorithm [2]. Hybrid scheduling algorithms which combine heuristic algorithm and GA properly can overcome their shortcomings. Heuristic algorithm can offer high quality initial population for GA thereby decreasing the number of generations needed for getting good scheduling results.

In this paper, we propose a new hybrid static task scheduling algorithm, named Hybrid Successor Concerned Heuristic-Genetic Scheduling (HSCGS) algorithm. It is a two-phase algorithm for heterogeneous multi-core system. In the first phase, we propose a new list-based heuristic algorithm, named Successor Concerned List Scheduling (SCLS), to generate a high quality task schedule. Then, we propose an Improved Genetic Algorithm (IGA) in the second phase to optimize the task schedule generated by SCLS.

This paper is organized as follows: Section 2 describes task scheduling problem for heterogeneous system and related terminology; Section 3 introduces some task scheduling algorithms for heterogeneous systems; Section 4 gives a detailed description of the the HSCGS algorithm we proposed; Section 5 presents comparison experiments of HSCGS with H2GS, HEFT, CPOP and DLS, based on both random generated applications and some real world applications. In section 6, we present the conclusion of the whole paper and the plan of our future work.

2   Problem Description

Task scheduling on heterogeneous multi-core systems aims to minimize the schedule length(which is also called *makespan*), by assigning tasks to appropriate cores and arranging the execution order of tasks on each core without violating the precedence constraint between tasks. In general, static scheduling algorithms are based on the following assumptions:

1) The entire system is dedicated;
2) All cores in the computing system is fully-connected;
3) There is no link contention between cores;
4) Each task can run on any core in the system.

A parallel application is represented by a Directed Acyclic Graph (DAG), $G = (V, E)$, where V represents the set of v tasks with, E is the set of e edges between tasks. V_i is the amount of data that task n_i need to process. Each $edge(i, j) \in E$ represents a precedence constraint between task n_i and task n_j, such that the execution of n_j cannot start before n_i finishes its execution. Data is a $v * v$ matrix, $data_{i,j}$ is the amount of data transported from the task n_i to task n_j. A task with no parent is called an entry task, and a task with no children is called an exit task.

Q represents the set of q cores of the heterogeneous system, Q_i represents the capability of core p_i. W is a $v * q$ matrix, $w_{i,j}$ indicates the execution time of task n_i on core p_j.

$$w_{i,j} = V_i/Q_j \tag{1}$$

The average execution time of task n_i is $\overline{w}_i$ as defined in (2).

$$\overline{w}_i = \Sigma_{j=1}^q w_{i,j}/q \tag{2}$$

The bandwidth of links between cores is represented by a $q * q$ matrix B. Communication initialization time is represented by array L with size q. The communication cost between task n_i and n_j is $c_{i,j}$ as defined in (3) (n_i is allocated on core p_m, n_j is allocated on core p_n).

$$c_{i,j} = L_m + \frac{data_{i,j}}{B_{m,n}} \tag{3}$$

$\overline{c}_{i,j}$ represents the average time to transfer data from task n_i to n_j.

$$\overline{c}_{i,j} = \overline{L} + \frac{data_{i,j}}{\overline{B}} \tag{4}$$

$\overline{L}$ represents the average communication initialization time of all the cores, $\overline{B}$ represents the average bandwidth of all the links.

Then we define two important attributes for heuristic algorithm, $EST(n_i, p_j)$ (earliest start time of task n_i on core p_j) and $EFT(n_i, p_j)$ (earliest finish time of task n_i on core p_j).

$$EST(n_{entry}, p_j) = 0 \tag{5}$$

$$EST(n_i, p_j) = max\{ avail[j], max_{n_m \in pred(n_i)}\{AFT(n_m) + c_{m,j}\} \} \tag{6}$$

$$EFT(n_i, p_j) = w_{i,j} + EST(n_i, p_j) \tag{7}$$

n_{entry} is the entry task of the application, $avail[j]$ is the first available time at which core p_j is ready for task execution, $pred(n_i)$ is the set of parents of task n_i. When a task n_m is assigned to a core, its start time and finish time is certain, and represented by $AST(n_m)$ and $AFT(n_m)$ [2].

After all tasks are scheduled, the finish time of exit task $AFT(n_{exit})$ is the finish time of the total application, named makespan. If there are more than one exit tasks, the makespan is the maximum.

$$makespan = max\{ AFT(n_{exit})\} \tag{8}$$

The primary goal of task scheduling is minimizing the makespan of the application.

3   Related Work

The quality of task schedule has great impact on the performance of applications running on the heterogeneous multi-core system. Some scheduling algorithms that support heterogeneous multi-core systems have been proposed, such as Heterogeneous Earliest Finish Time (HEFT) [2], Critical Path on a Processor (CPOP) [2], Longest Dynamic Critical Path (LDCP) Algorithm [4], Dynamic Level Scheduling (DLS) [8] and Hybrid Heuristic–Genetic Scheduling (H2GS) [3].

In this section, we describe 3 static scheduling algorithms (HEFT, DLS and H2GS) for heterogeneous systems in detail.

3.1   Heterogeneous Earliest Finish Time Algorithm

The HEFT algorithm has two major phases: a task prioritizing phase for computing the priorities of all tasks and a core selection phase for scheduling the task with the highest priority to the "best" core, which minimizes the task's finish time [2].

The priority of task n_i is equal to its upward rank ($rank_u$) value as defined in (9).

$$rank_u(n_i) = \overline{w}_i + max_{n_j \in succ(n_i)}\{ \overline{c}_{i,j} + rank_u(n_j)\} \tag{9}$$

Upward rank is the length of the critical path from current task to the exit task, including the tasks' average running cost and average communication cost. $succ(n_i)$ is the set of immediate successors of task n_i. After the computation of each task's priority, all the tasks are pushed into a task queue in decreasing order of priorities. Tie-breaking is done randomly.

At each step of the core selection phase, the task with the highest priority is selected and assigned to the core that minimizes the EFT value using the insertion-based policy.

The time complexity of HEFT algorithm is $O(q * e)$ when there are q cores in the heterogeneous system and e edges in the application DAG. The experiment results in paper [2] indicate that HEFT is better than CPOP, DLS, MH [12] and LMT [13] with different DAG size and CCR value. HEFT only concerns the EFT of the header task in the priority queue in core selection phase, and this may not perform well in some cases (Fig. 2).

3.2 Dynamic Level Scheduling Algorithm

DLS algorithm uses dynamically-changing priorities to match tasks with processors. Scheduling decision is made based on Dynamic Level (DL) of each [task, core] pair. For task n_i, core p_j, the DL value is defined as (10) and (11).

$$DL(n_i , p_j) = rank_{ur}(n_i) - EST(n_i , p_j) \qquad (10)$$

$$rank_{ur}(n_i) = \overline{w}_i + max_{n_j \in succ(n_i)}\{rank_{ur}(n_j)\} \qquad (11)$$

At each step of the algorithm, DLS computes the DL value of every [task, core] pair if the task was not scheduled. The pair $[n_i , p_j]$ that has the largest DL value is selected for scheduling.

The time complexity of DL algorithm is $O(q * v^3)$, when there are q cores and v tasks. The experiment results in paper [8] indicate that DL algorithm is better than MH and LMT.

3.3 Hybrid Heuristic–Genetic Scheduling Algorithm

H2GS algorithm is a hybrid scheduling algorithm. Firstly, H2GS use a heuristic algorithm named LDCP [4] to generate a near-optimal scheduling result. Then, H2GS optimize the scheduling result generated by LDCP iteratively using Genetic Algorithm for Scheduling (GAS) [3].

GAS is a genetic algorithm for task scheduling. In GAS, a two-dimensional string chromosome is used to encode the task schedule. Customized genetic operators are developed specifically for the task scheduling problem to maintain population diversity and simultaneously enable an efficient stochastic search process [3]. GAS uses 1/makespan as the fitness value for selection mechanism. The fittest 10% of the chromosomes in the population are copied without change to the next generation. GAS algorithm runs for a predetermined number of generations which is set according to the characteristics and real-world context of the parallel application [3].When the GAS algorithm finished, H2GS select the scheduling result which has the largest fitness value as the final task schedule.

The experiment results in paper [3] shows that H2GS gets a better task scheduling result than HEFT and DLS, but it takes longer time to generate the result. GAS does not take care of the the regeneration phenomenon (generating similar chromosomes) which leads to premature convergence [15].

4 The HSCGS Algorithm

In this section, we describe the HSCGS algorithm in detail. HSCGS is a hybrid static task scheduling algorithm for heterogeneous multi-core system. In the first phase we propose a list heuristic algorithm, named Successor Concerned List Scheduling

(SCLS), to generate a near-optimal scheduling result in a short time. Then, we propose an Improved Genetic Algorithm (IGA) to optimize the scheduling result generated by SCLS algorithm.

4.1   Successor Concerned List Scheduling Algorithm

SCLS (Fig. 1) is a list heuristic scheduling algorithm that has two phases. Firstly, SCLS computes the priority of each task and pushes them in a task queue by decreasing order of their priorities. Then, pop the task with the highest priority and schedule it on the most appropriate core. SCLS cares about not only current task's upward rank but also the impact on its successors. SCLS schedules tasks in a more global perspective in order to minimize the makespan of the application.

Compute *priorities* for all task as equation (12);

Push all tasks into a *task queue* by decreasing order of *priorities;*

While there are unscheduled tasks in the *task queue* **do**

    Select the task n_i which has the highest *priority;*

    If n_i has unscheduled parents

        Select the parent n_j which has the highest *priority* as the *selected task;*

    Else

        Set n_i as the *selected task;*

    For each core in the system **do**

        Compute *appropriate* value as equation (13);

    Assign the *selected task* to the core with the minimum *appropriate* value;

End While

Fig. 1. The SCLS algorithm

Task Prioritizing Phase: In this phase, the priority of each task is set with a combination of normalized upward rank and numbers of successors. SCLS concerns not only upward rank of current task but also how many successors it has. For parallel applications, scheduling tasks with more successors early can improve efficiency apparently. SCLS computes the priority of task n_i as (12).

$$Priority(n_i) = \frac{rank_u(n_i)}{rank_u(n_{entry})} + \frac{succ_i}{v} \tag{12}$$

n_{entry} is the entry task of the application, $succ_i$ is the number of n_i's successors, v is the total number of tasks.

When all tasks' priorities are computed, push them into a task queue in decreasing order of their priorities.

Core Selection Phase: At each step of this phase, SCLS selects the task with the highest priority if it has no unscheduled parent, and assigns it to the core which minimizes the appropriate value. If the task has one or more unscheduled parents, SCLS selects the one with the highest priority and assign it to the core which minimizes the appropriate value. The appropriate value of a core p_m is computed as (13).

$$\text{Appropriate}(n_i, p_m) = \text{Min}(\text{EFT}(n_i, p_m) + \text{Max}_{n_j \in succ(n_i)}(\overline{c}_{m(i,j)})) \quad (13)$$

$$\overline{c}_{m(i,j)} = L_m + \frac{data_{i,j}}{\overline{B}_m} \quad (14)$$

$$\overline{B}_m = \Sigma_{i=1...q} B_{m,i} / q \quad (15)$$

n_i is the selected task that to be scheduled, $succ(n_i)$ is the set of successors of task n_i. $\overline{B}_m$ is the average bandwidth of links between core p_m and other cores. L_m is the communication **initialization time** on core p_m.

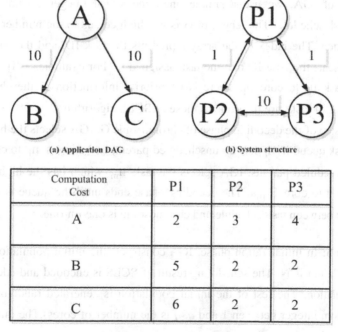

(a) Application DAG   (b) System structure

Computation Cost	P1	P2	P3
A	2	3	4
B	5	2	2
C	6	2	2

(c) Computation cost matrix

Fig. 2. An example of Core Selection

Fig. 2 shows a circumstance that the core selection strategy of SCLS is better than algorithms that only cares about the EFT value (such as HEFT). Fig.2 (a) is the application DAG, the value on the edge shows the size of data communications between tasks. Fig.2 (b) is the system structure and the value on the edge is the bandwidth of the link. Fig2(c) is the computation cost matrix. The HEFT scheduling result is {A—>P1, B—>p1, C—>P1}, and the makespan is 2+5+6=13. The SCLS scheduling result is {A—>P2, B—>p2, C—>P3}, and the makespan is max {3+2, 4+2} =6.

4.2   Improved Genetic Algorithm

This section proposes the Improved Genetic algorithm (IGA) and describes how to use it to optimize task scheduling result. IGA add a preprocessing process before the selection phase to avoid the regeneration phenomenon (generating similar chromosomes) which leads to premature convergence [15]. IGA uses a three-phase selection mechanism, in order to maintain the diversity of the population and optimize the population at the same time.

Schedule Encoding and Chromosome Decoding: The ways of coding and decoding have great influences on crossover and mutation operation. In order to decrease the complexity of IGA, we use a simple one-dimensional integer chromosome G to encode a task schedule. The length of G is v, which equals to the number of tasks of the application. The index of the array represents the task ID, and the value at each index represents the core ID that the task assigned to. For example, $G[i] = j$ means assigning task n_i to core p_j. There is no priority information in the chromosome. The priorities of tasks are the same as those of SCLS algorithm.

At each step of the decoding phase of chromosome G, IGA selects the head task n_i from the task queue if n_i has no unscheduled parent, and assigns n_i to core $P_{G[i]}$. If n_i has unscheduled parents, IGA selects the task n_m which has the highest priority and assigns it to core $P_{G[m]}$. The decoding phase ends until the queue is empty. The relationship between task schedule and chromosome is one-on-one.

Initialization: In initialization phase, IGA constructs the initial population. The size of the population is N. The scheduling result of SCLS is encoded and added into the initial population. The rest of the initial population is generated randomly (set $G[i]$ with a random integer between 1 and q, q is the number of cores).The minimum size of population is q.

Fitness Evaluation: The fitness value represents the quality of the chromosome. IGA evaluates fitness value as (16).

$$fitness = 1/makespan \tag{16}$$

Crossover and Mutation

1) Crossover: IGA uses a simple two-point swap crossover operator. Firstly, IGA selects two chromosomes from the chromosome pool randomly. Then randomly select two points and exchange the subsequences of each selected chromosome between the two points. Finally, add the new generated chromosomes to the chromosome pool. This process is performed with probability P_c.

2) Mutation: The mutation works on a single chromosome in the chromosome pool. The mutation operation selects a chromosome and a mutation point randomly, and then changes the value to a random integer from 1 to q. Then add the new generated chromosome to the chromosome pool. This process is performed with probability P_m.

Preprocessing: Some new chromosomes which are similar with existing ones will be generated in the process of IGA (called regeneration phenomenon). This may cause the search process traps in a local optimum [15]. IGA adds the preprocessing phase to avoid this. Fig. 3 shows the preprocessing algorithm. This process is performed with probability P_w, $P_w < (P_c + P_m)$.

Select two chromosomes *G1* and *G2* from the chromosome pool randomly;
Counter = 0;
v is the length of the chromosomes;
T is the threshold defined in advance;
For *i* = 0 to *v*-1 **do**
    If *G1[i]* = *G2[i]* **do**
          Counter = *Counter*+1;
    End If
End For
S = *Counter* / *v* ;
If *S* > *T* **do**
    Calculate the fitness of *G1* and *G2;*
    Remove the chromosome which has the smaller fitness value;
End If

Fig. 3. The preprocessing algorithm

Selection: In selection phase, IGA selects N chromosomes from the chromosome pool as the population of next iteration using a three-phase selection mechanism.

In the first stage, IGA compares the new chromosomes generated by crossover and mutation with their parents. If a new chromosome's fitness value is bigger than its parents', IGA moves it to the new population. Assuming there are N_1 chromosomes in the new population after this stage. In the second stage, IGA sets N_2 as $N - N_1$, and moves the fittest $N_2 * 20\%$ chromosomes to the new population. In the third stage, move $N_2 * 80\%$ chromosomes selected randomly to the new population.

After the selection phase, there are N chromosomes in the new population. Then the next iteration begins.

Termination: There are several termination strategies to stop the iteration. IGA runs for a predetermined number of generations which is set according to the characteristics and real-world context of the parallel application [15].

5   Experiment Results and Discussion

In this section, the performance of HSCGS is presented in comparison with H2GS, HEFT, CPOP, and DLS on our simulation framework. We consider two sets of benchmark application graphs as the workload for testing the algorithms: randomly generated DAGs and DAGs that represent some of the real world problems.

First, we present the performance metrics used for evaluating the quality of these scheduling algorithms. Then, we describe the mechanism for generating random application DAGs and the experimental parameters. At last, we present the experimental results.

5.1   Performance Metrics

The metrics we used includes Normalized Schedule Length (NSL) [16], Speedup [2] and Efficiency of the algorithms [3].

Normalized Schedule Length (NSL): The NSL of a task schedule is defined as the makespan to the lower bound of the schedule length. It is calculated as (17).

$$NSL = makespan/min_{j \in (1...p)}(\textstyle\sum_{n_i \in CP} w_{i,j}) \tag{17}$$

p is the number of cores. CP is the critical path of the application DAG. The lower bound of the schedule length is the total cost of tasks on the CP when they are assigned to the fastest core.

Speedup: The speedup of a task schedule is the ratio of the serial schedule length obtained by assigning all tasks to the fastest core, to the makespan of task schedule.

$$Speedup = min_{j \in (1...p)}(\textstyle\sum_{i=1}^{v} w_{i,j})/makespan \tag{18}$$

v is number of tasks in the DAG.

Efficiency: The efficiency of a task schedule is defined as the speedup to the number of cores.

$$\text{Efficiency} = \text{Speedup}/\,q \qquad (19)$$

We use the average value of these metrics over a set of DAGs to compare the quality of the scheduling algorithms.

5.2   Generating Random DAGs

We use a synthetic DAG generator to create random application DAGs. The synthetic DAG generator uses a set of input parameters to determine some characteristics of the random DAGs.

1) $N= \{20, 40, 60, 80, 100\}$, the total number of tasks in each DAG.
2) Mindata =2048, the minimum size of data processed by a task in Flop.
3) Maxdata=11268, the maximum size of data processed by a task in Flop.
4) Fat= $\{0.1, 0.2, 0.8\}$, width of the DAG, that is maximum number of tasks that can be executed concurrently. A small value will lead to a thin DAG with a low task parallelism, while a large value induces a fat DAG with a high degree of parallelism.
5) Density= $\{0.2, 0.8\}$, the numbers of dependencies between tasks of two consecutive DAG levels.
6) CCR= $\{0.2, 0.5, 1, 2, 5\}$, communication to computation cost ratio, the average communication cost divided by the average computation cost of the application DAG.

5.3   Experimental Parameters

The characteristics of the simulated heterogeneous computing system and parameters of the IGA algorithm we used in our experiment are as below.

1) Number of cores $q=\{2, 4, 8, 16, 32\}$
2) Heterogeneity factor of cores $P_h = \{2, 4, 8, 16\}$
3) Heterogeneity factor of links' bandwidth between cores $B_h = \{1, 5, 10, 15\}$
4) $P_c = 0.7$
5) $P_m = 0.5$
6) $P_w = 0.8$
7) Population size of IGA $\text{PopSize} = 2 * q$
8) Number of generations of IGA $\text{NG} = \{5, 10, 15, 20\}$

5.4   Performance Results and Discussion

The results are presented over two kinds of application DAGs: randomly generated DAGs and DAGs that represent Fast Fourier Transformation and Gauss elimination algorithm.

Results of Randomly Generated DAGs: We create 300 random DAGs over each value of DAG size (so, there are 1500 DAGs in total), and calculate the average NSL and speedup of task schedules generated by HSCGS, H2GS, HEFT, CPOP and DSL.

The results are presented by Fig. 4 and Fig. 5. The NSL based performance ranking is {H2GS, HSCGS, HEFT, DLS, CPOP}, and the average NSL value of H2GS is nearly equal with that of HSCGS. The average NSL value of HSCGS is better than HEFT by 7%, DLS by 10% and CPOP by 12%. The average speedup value of HSCGS is better than HEFT by 4.7%, DLS by 6% and CPOP by 10%.

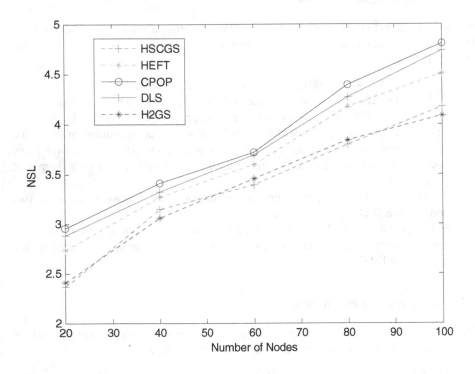

Fig. 4. Average NSL of random DAGs

Results of Fast Fourier Transformation: A fast Fourier transform (FFT) is an efficient algorithm to compute the discrete Fourier transform (DFT) and its inverse. The DAG of the FFT algorithm is characterized by the size of the input vector. If the vector size is M, the number of tasks is $(2 * M - 1)(M * \log_2 M)$. Fig. 6(b) shows the DAG of FFT with input vector size of 4.

In our experiment, the input vector size ranges from 2^1 to 2^5. Fig. 7 presents the average NSL of these four scheduling algorithms over different vector size. The NSL based performance ranking is {H2GS, HSCGS, HEFT, DLS, CPOP}. The average NSL of HSCGS is almost the same as that of H2GS. Fig. 8 presents the average Efficiency of these four scheduling algorithms over different number of cores (range from 2^1 to 2^5). The Efficiency based performance ranking is the same as that of NSL.

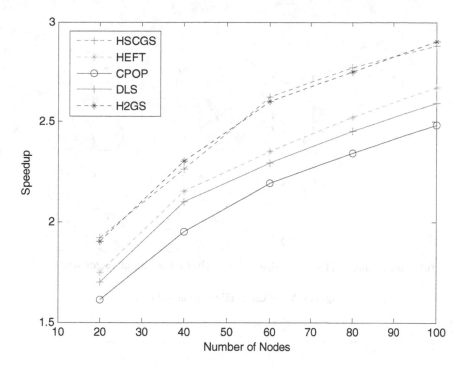

Fig. 5. Average Speedup of random DAGs

Results of Gauss Elimination Algorithm: In linear algebra, Gaussian elimination is an algorithm for solving systems of linear equations. It can also be used to find the rank of a matrix, to calculate the determinant of a matrix and the inverse of an invertible square matrix. The DAG of the Gauss elimination algorithm is characterized by the size of the input matrix. If the matrix size is $M * M$, the number of tasks is $(M^2 + M - 2)/2$. Figure 6(a) shows the DAG of Gauss elimination with input matrix size of 5.

The matrix size we used in the experiment ranges from 5 to 20, with an increment of 2 or 3. Fig. 9 presents the average NSL of these four scheduling algorithms over different matrix size. The NSL based performance ranking is {HSCGS, H2GS, HEFT, DLS, CPOP}. Fig. 10 presents the average Efficiency of these four scheduling algorithms over different number of cores (range from 2^1 to 2^5). The Efficiency based performance ranking is the same as that of NSL.

The extension of our experiment compares the average NSL of HSCGS, H2GS, HEFT, CPOP and DLS over different heterogeneity factor of links' bandwidth between cores($B_h = \{1, 5, 10, 15\}$). The result indicates that the superiority of HSCGS goes up, with the increase of B_h.

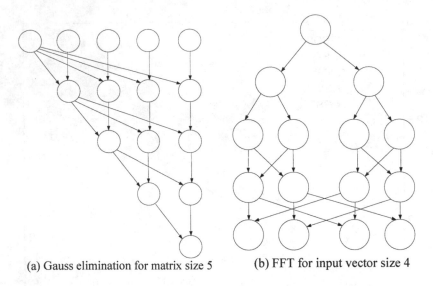

(a) Gauss elimination for matrix size 5   (b) FFT for input vector size 4

Fig. 6. DAG of Gauss elimination and FFT

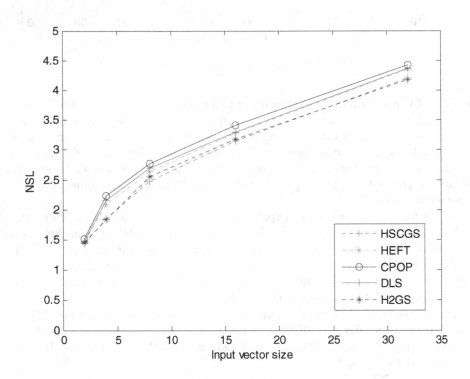

Fig. 7. Average NSL of FFT

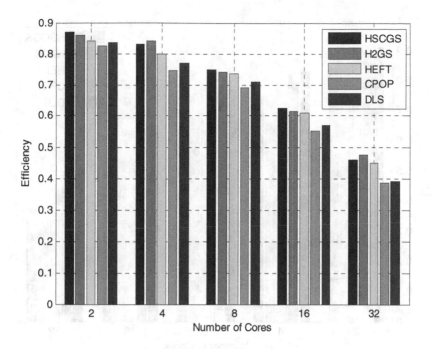

Fig. 8. Average Efficiency of FFT

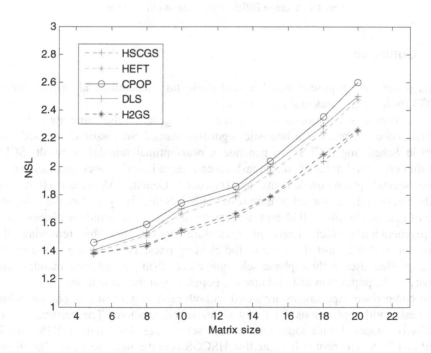

Fig. 9. Average NSL of Gauss elimination

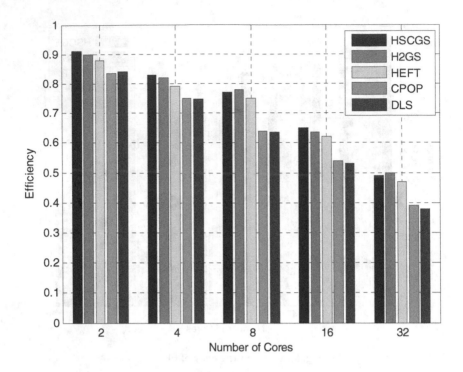

Fig. 10. Average Efficiency of Gauss elimination

6   Conclude

In this paper, we propose a novel hybrid static task scheduling algorithm named HSCGS for heterogeneous multi-core systems.

The algorithm is a combination of heuristic and genetic scheduling algorithm. In the first phase we propose a heuristic algorithm named Successor Concerned List Heuristic Scheduling (SCLS), to generate a near-optimal scheduling result. SCLS algorithm takes the impact of current task scheduling to its successors into account.

The second phase implements an Improved Genetic Algorithm (IGA) for scheduling, to optimize the scheduling result of SCLS iteratively. Before the selection phase of genetic algorithm, IGA adds a preprocessing phase to avoid the phenomenon of "regeneration" which leads to premature convergence by removing the chromosomes that almost the same as the existing ones. The selection phase of the IGA algorithm uses a three-phase selection mechanism, in order to maintain the diversity of the population and optimize the population at the same time.

The comparison experiments are based on both random generated applications and some real world applications (FFT and Gaussian elimination). The performance of HSCGS is compared with some famous task scheduling algorithms, H2GS, HEFT, CPOP and DLS. The results indicate that HSCGS is better than the other algorithms, and the advantages go up with the increase of the heterogeneous factor of inter-core links' bandwidth.

HSCGS is based on the assumption that all cores are fully-connected, but the heterogeneous distributed computing systems in the real world usually do not correspond with this assumption. So we plan to extend our algorithm on heterogeneous arbitrarily-connected systems and implement a task scheduling platform on top of StarPU [14].

Acknowledgements. This research is supported by the National High-tech R&D Program of China (863 Program) under Grand No.2009AA01Z142 and the Research Fund of Sugon.

References

1. Kumar, R., Tullsen, D., Jouppi, N., Ranganathan, P.: Heterogeneous Chip Multiprocessors. IEEE Computer, 32–38 (November 2005)
2. Topcuoglu, H., Hariri, S., Wu, M.Y.: Performance-Effective and Low-Complexity Task Scheduling for Heterogeneous Computing. IEEE Trans. Parallel and Distributed Systems 13(3), 260–274 (2002)
3. Daoud, M.I., Kharma, N.: A hybrid heuristic–genetic algorithm for task scheduling in heterogeneous processor networks. J. Parallel Distrib. Comput. 71, 1518–1531 (2011)
4. Daoud, M.I., Kharma, N.: A high performance algorithm for static task scheduling in heterogeneous distributed computing systems. J. Parallel Distrib. Comput. 68, 399–409 (2008)
5. Wen, Y., Xu, H., Yang, J.: A heuristic-based hybrid genetic-variable neighborhood search algorithm for task scheduling in heterogeneous multiprocessor system. Information Sciences 181, 567–581 (2011)
6. Eswari, R., Nickolas, S.: Path-based Heuristic Task Scheduling Algorithm for Heterogeneous Distributed Computing Systems. In: 2010 International Conference on Advances in Recent Technologies in Communication and Computing (2010)
7. Kwok, Y.K., Ahmad, I.: Static scheduling algorithms for allocating directed task graphs to multiprocessors. ACM Comput. Surveys 31(4), 406–471 (1999)
8. Sih, G.C., Lee, E.A.: A compile-time scheduling heuristic for interconnection constrained heterogeneous processor architectures. IEEE Trans. Parallel Distributed Systems 4(2), 175–187 (1993)
9. Kwok, Y.K., Ahmad, I.: Dynamic critical-path scheduling: an effective technique for allocating task graphs to multiprocessors. IEEE Trans. Parallel Distributed Systems 7(5), 506–521 (1996)
10. El-Rewini, H., Lewis, T.G.: Scheduling parallel program tasks onto arbitrary target machines. J. Parallel Distributed Comput. 9(2), 138–153 (1990)
11. Eiben, A.E., Michalewicz, Z., Schoenauer, M., Smith, J.E.: Parameter control in evolutionary algorithms. Stud. Comput. Intell. 54, 19–46 (2007)
12. Ilavarasan, E., Thambidurai, P., Mahilmannan, R.: Performance effective task scheduling algorithm for heterogeneous computing system. In: Proc. 4th International Symposium on Parallel and Distributed Computing, France, pp. 28–38 (2005)
13. Iverson, M., Ozguner, F., Follen, G.: Parallelizing existing applications in a distributed heterogeneous environment. In: Proc. 4th Heterogeneous Computing Workshop, Santa Barbara, CA, pp. 93–100 (1995)

14. Augonnet, C., Thibault, S., Namyst, R., Wacrenier, P.-A.: STARPU: a unified platform for task scheduling on heterogeneous multicore architectures. University of Bordeaux – LaBRI – INRIA Bordeaux Sud-Oues

15. Moghaddam, M.E., Bonyadi, M.R.: An Immune-based Genetic Algorithm with Reduced Search Space Coding for Multiprocessor Task Scheduling Problem. Int. J. Parallel Prog., doi:10.1007/s10766-011-0179-0

16. Bansal, S., Kumar, P., Singh, K.: An improved duplication strategy for scheduling precedence constrained graphs inmultiprocessor systems. IEEE Trans. Parallel Distrib. Syst. 14, 533–544 (2003)

17. Chung, Y.C., Ranka, S.: Application and performance analysis of a compile-time optimization approach for list scheduling algorithms on distributed-memory multiprocessors. In: Proc. Supercomputing 1992, Minneapolis, MN, pp. 512–521 (1992)

18. Wu, M., Dajski, D.: Hypertool: A programming aid for message passing systems. IEEE Trans. Parallel Distrib. Syst. 1, 330–343 (1990)

Efficient Task Assignment on Heterogeneous Multicore Systems Considering Communication Overhead

Li Wang[1], Jing Liu[1], Jingtong Hu[3], Qingfeng Zhuge[2],
Duo Liu[2], and Edwin H.-M. Sha[2,3]

[1] College of Information Science and Engineering
Hunan University, Changsha, China
[2] College of Computer Science
Chongqing University, Chongqing, China
[3] Dept. of Computer Science
University of Texas at Dallas, Richardson, Texas 75080, USA
{ericliwang,ljing.suxin,qfzhuge,coredliu}@gmail.com,
{jthu,edsha}@utdallas.edu

Abstract. This paper addresses task assignment problem on heterogeneous multicore systems with time constraint considering communication overhead. Processing cores in a heterogeneous system considered in this paper are grouped into clusters according to core types. Therefore, clusters have different computation capabilities. Communication links among various clusters have different communication capacities as well. The goal of heterogeneous task assignment problem is to minimize the total system cost for allocating a set of given tasks with data dependencies to a group of heterogeneous clusters while the time constraint is satisfied. The system cost considered in this paper is related to both execution load and communication load on various clusters and communication links. The general heterogeneous assignment problem is NP-complete. In this paper, we present the ILP formulation for solving the heterogeneous assignment problem. We also propose a heuristic, the Ratio Greedy Assign algorithm (RGA), to solve the problem efficiently for directed acyclic graphs (DAG). According to our experimental results, the Ratio Greedy Assign algorithm generates near-optimal results efficiently for all the benchmarks, while the ILP method cannot find a solution with acceptable computation time for large-sized benchmarks, such as 10-4lattice filter. Compared with a method that assigns all the tasks to a cluster of homogeneous cores, the RGA algorithm reduces the total system cost by 35.1% on average with four heterogeneous clusters. It reduces the cost by 24.6% on average with three heterogeneous cluster.

Keywords: Task assignment, Multicore system, ILP, Greedy algorithm.

1 Introduction

Due to physical limits, it is more and more difficult to keep increasing the CPU performance by solely increasing the CPU clock rates. Instead, multicore

Y. Xiang et al. (Eds.): ICA3PP 2012, Part I, LNCS 7439, pp. 171–185, 2012.

processors are becoming the mainstream for high-performance computer systems. In order to meet various performance requirements with stringent cost limitation, it is very popular to equip different types of cores on a single chip for multicore systems such as IBM's Cell Processor [1] and latest Tegra 3 processor from NVIDIA [2]. In heterogeneous processors, cores of the same type are normally grouped together as a cluster. Applications are divided into small tasks and assigned to different clusters of cores. The system performance can be tremendously improved using multicore processors. However, large costs such as power consumption can also be incurred along with performance improvement considering that different task assignment can affect the system cost greatly. Therefore, the problem of finding a task assignment that incurs the minimal system cost under time constraint becomes a critical problem for maximizing the benefit of heterogeneous multicore systems. The total system cost considered in this paper include both execution and communication costs.

A heterogeneous multicore computing system usually consists of a number of heterogeneous clusters of cores connected to communication links. Each cluster has a limited computation capability depending on the configuration of the cores in cluster. Thus, the execution time of a task varies on different clusters. Also, the communication links among clusters have various communication capacities and propagation delays. The execution of multiple tasks in an application incurs an execution cost from their assigned clusters, and also incurs a communication cost from communication links. Usually, the communication cost between a pair of cores belonging to different clusters is much higher than that between two cores in the same cluster.

There have been plenty of research efforts on task assignment problem. Some mainly focus on minimizing the total system cost [3], minimizing the application completion time [4], and maximizing the system reliability [5]. Many techniques are introduced by previous works to solve the task assignment problem to obtain optimal and near optimal solutions. Graph theoretic [6] and integer linear programming [7] can obtain optimal solutions. However, these methods normally take exponential time to complete. Heuristic algorithms, like genetic algorithm [8], branch and bound technique [9], and greedy algorithm can obtain near optimal solutions. Among these research works, some consider that the communication cost or communication time between two tasks is merely decided by tasks; some consider that the communication cost or communication time between two tasks is only related to the clusters. Only a few papers [10,11] consider that the communication cost depends on both tasks and clusters. However, they also only consider the communication cost regardless of the communication time.

In this paper, we consider task assignment problem on heterogeneous multicore system considering communication load with time constraint. The communication time and cost considered in this paper are mainly decided by two factors. The first one is the communication capability such as communication bandwidth. The second one is the amount of data transferred among tasks. In this paper, we study the heterogeneous task assignment problem when the task graph is a DAG.

The main contributions of this paper include:

- We present an ILP formulation for solving the heterogeneous task assignment problem optimally.
- We propose an efficient heuristic, the Ratio Greedy Assign algorithm, for the heterogeneous task assignment problem when the task graph is a DAG.
- To authors' best knowledge, this is the first work that associates both tasks and clusters when considering the communication time and cost.

The experimental results show that the task assignments generated by ILP method reduce the total system cost by 26.2% on average on a simulated architecture with three heterogeneous clusters, and reduce the total system cost by 33.0% on average with four clusters, compared with the Homogeneous Assign method which assigns all the tasks to one cluster to satisfy the time constraint. However, the ILP method cannot find a solution with an acceptable time for large-sized benchmarks, such as 10-4lattice filter. On the other hand, our Ratio Greedy Assign algorithm generates near-optimal solutions effectively for all the benchmarks. The Ratio Greedy Assign algorithm reduces the total system cost by 24.6% on average on an architecture with three clusters and 35.1% on average with four clusters, compared with the Homogeneous Assign method.

The remainder of this paper is organized as follows. We present heterogeneous cluster model, task model and problem definition in Section 2. A motivational example is presented to illustrate the motivation of this paper in Section 3. In Section 4, we design integer linear programming (ILP) model for solving the heterogeneous task assignment problem optimally. In Section 5, we propose an efficient heuristic for the cases that the task graphs are DAGs. Experimental results are shown in Section 6. Section 7 concludes the paper.

2 Models

In this section, we first describe the heterogeneous cluster model. Then, we introduce Communication Data Flow Graph (CDFG) model for tasks to be assigned to heterogeneous clusters. Last, the Heterogeneous Task Assignment with Communication (HTAC) problem is defined.

2.1 Heterogeneous Cluster Model

In a heterogeneous multicore system, cores of the same type are usually grouped together as a cluster. Applications are divided into small tasks and assigned to clusters of cores. The architectural model considered in this paper consists of a set of heterogeneous clusters, denoted by $CL = \{cl_1, cl_2, \ldots, cl_M\}$, where M is the number of heterogeneous clusters. Each cluster of cores has a certain computation capability depending on the configuration of cores in the cluster. Clusters are connected with each other through communication links with various communication capacities. Cores located in the same cluster are fully connected. The data communication between clusters takes much longer time and much higher cost than that within the same cluster. Fig. 1(a) shows an example of this kind of architectural model with three clusters.

When data communication transfers between various clusters, the communication time and communication cost are different. We define the communication time of unit data volume for communication links as a function $CT(cl_i, cl_j)$, representing the time of transferring unit data volume from cluster cl_i to cluster cl_j. We define the communication cost of unit data volume for communication links as a function $CC(cl_i, cl_j)$, representing the cost of transferring unit data volume from cluster cl_i to cluster cl_j.

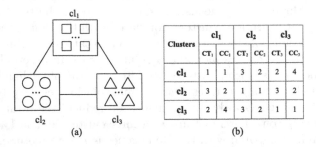

Fig. 1. (a) An architectural model. (b) Communication time and cost of unit data volume among various clusters in (a).

The table in Fig. 1(b) shows values of communication time and cost for unit data volume between each pair of clusters in Fig. 1(a). For example, the cell of column "CT_3" and row "cl_2" represents that the communication time of unit data volume from cluster cl_2 to cluster cl_3 is 3 time units.

2.2   Task Model

In this section, we use Communication Data Flow Graph (CDFG) to model tasks to be executed on a heterogeneous multicore system. A CDFG $G =< V, E, CL, T, C, D >$ is a node-weighted and edge-weighted directed acyclic graph (DAG), where $V =< v_1, v_2, \ldots, v_N >$ is a set of nodes, and $E \subseteq V \times V$ is a set of edges. Each node $v \in V$ represents a task. An edge $(u, v) \in E$ represents the dependency between node u and node v. It indicates that task u has to be executed before task v. A set $CL = \{cl_1, cl_2, \ldots, cl_M\}$ represents a set of M heterogeneous clusters.

When a task is assigned to different clusters, its execution time and cost shows different values. We define the following functions for execution time and cost on various clusters. We define a node-weighted execution time function $T(v_i, cl_j)$ to represent the execution time of task v_i when it is assigned to cluster cl_j. Similarly, we define a node-weighted execution cost function $C(v_i, cl_j)$ to represent the execution cost of task v_i when it is assigned to cluster cl_j. The volume of data communication between node v_i and node v_j is represented by an edge-weighted function $D(v_i, v_j)$.

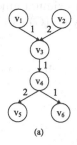

Tasks	cl₁		cl₂		cl₃	
	T_1	C_1	T_2	C_2	T_3	C_3
v_1	3	9	5	4	8	2
v_2	1	7	2	5	3	1
v_3	1	6	3	5	4	1
v_4	1	10	2	4	3	2
v_5	2	10	3	6	4	1
v_6	3	11	5	7	7	1

(a)   (b)

Fig. 2. (a) A DAG. (b) Values of execution time and cost for tasks in (a) on various clusters.

Fig. 2(a) shows a simple example of CDFG. There are six task nodes $v_1, v_2, \cdots$, v_6 to be assigned to three heterogeneous clusters shown in Fig. 1(a). As shown in Fig. 2(a), numbers on edges indicate data communication volume. For example, the volume of data communication from node v_1 to node v_3 is 1 unit. Values of execution time and cost functions for each task are provided in the table in Fig. 2(b). For example, the value in the cell of column "T_2" and row "v_1" indicates that the execution time of task v_1 is 5 time units when it is assigned to cluster cl_2; the value in the cell of column "C_2" and row "v_1" indicates that the execution cost of task v_1 is 4 cost units when it is assigned to cluster cl_2.

For a given CDFG $G =< V, E, CL, T, C, D >$, we define a task assignment function $A : V \longrightarrow CL$, where $v \in V$ is a task assigned to a cluster $cl_i \in CL$. For example, the assignment function $A(v_1) = cl_3$ indicates that node v_1 is assigned to cluster cl_3.

For a given CDFG $G =< V, E, CL, T, C, D >$, we use a function $\alpha((u,v), (A(u), A(v)))$ to compute communication time and a function $\beta((u,v), (A(u), A(v)))$ to compute communication cost on an edge (u, v) under a task assignment function A. Functions α and β can be computed in advance for different communication links. In some simple cases, the communication time can be computed as $D(u, v) \times CT(A(u), A(v))$. The communication cost can be computed as $D(u, v) \times CC(A(u), A(v))$. These formulas are used to compute the total communication time and cost in our motivational example in the next section and in our experiments.

Given a path $p : v_i \leadsto v_j$ and a task assignment function A for all the nodes in p, the total completion time of path p under assignment A, denoted by $T_A(p)$, is the summation of all the execution time and communication time occurred on path p. Providing the parallel execution on heterogeneous cluster model, the total completion time of CDFG G define to be the completion time of a critical path p in G.

$$T_A(G) = \sum_{v \in p} T(v, A(v)) + \sum_{(u,v) \in p} \alpha((u,v), (A(u), A(v))). \tag{1}$$

Where p is a path whose completion time is the maximum among all paths in G. Similarly, the total cost of CDFG G, denoted by $C_A(G)$ can be computed as follows:

$$C_A(G) = \sum_{v \in V} C(v, A(v)) + \sum_{(u,v) \in E} \beta((u,v),(A(u),A(v))). \tag{2}$$

2.3 Problem Definition

The problem of Heterogeneous Task Assignment with Communication (HTAC) is defined as follows: Given a CDFG $G = < V, E, CL, T, C, D >$, and a time constraint L, the HTAC problem is to find an assignment $A(v)$ for each task $v \in V$ such that the completion time of the CDFG G satisfies the inequality $T_A(G) \leq L$, and the total cost $C_A(G)$ is minimized.

The general HTAC problem is NP-complete. The heterogeneous assignment problem has been proved to be NP-complete [12]. The heterogeneous assignment problem defined by Shao et al. in [12] can be reduced to the HTAC problem in polynomial time. Thus, the HTAC problem is also NP-complete.

3 Motivational Example

In this section, we present a motivational example to show that different task assignment results affect completion time and the total system cost significantly on the heterogeneous multicore system.

The example uses the architectural model shown in Fig. 1(a). Suppose that cluster cl_1 provides the best performance with the highest execution cost, and cluster cl_3 the worst performance with the lowest execution cost, values of communication time and cost of unit data volume transferred between any two clusters are provided in Fig. 1(b).

The CDFG G considered in this example is a DAG as shown in Fig. 2(a). Values of execution time and execution cost for each task executed on various clusters are shown in Fig. 2(b). The volume of data transferred on each edge is represented by edge weight.

Table 1 shows four different assignment solutions considering a time constraint $L = 23$. In solution "1", all six tasks are assigned to cluster cl_3. The completion time of G is 25 with a total cost of 15. Solution "1" has the lowest cost, but its completion time exceeds the time constraint. Therefore, it is an invalid assignment. In solution "2", all six tasks are assigned to cluster cl_2 with a total cost 38 and a completion time 18. Although solution "2" achieves the shortest completion time, its total cost is high. In order to reduce the total system cost, we can assign some tasks to different clusters with different computation capacities as shown in solution "3" and solution "4". Solution "3" assigns tasks v_1, v_2, v_3 to cluster cl_2, and tasks v_4, v_5, v_6 to cluster cl_3. The total system cost is reduced by 31.6% compared with the result generated by solution "2" which assigns all tasks to one cluster. Meanwhile, time constraint is satisfied. Solution

"3" is generated by our Ratio Greedy Assign algorithm which will be presented in Section 5 in details. Solution "4" is an optimal assignment obtained by the ILP method with minimal total system cost. Solution "3" and solution "4" show that the total system cost can be reduced by exploring task assignment on a heterogeneous multicore system while the time constrain is satisfied.

Table 1. Four assignment solutions for the task graph in Fig. 2(a) with time constraint $L = 23$

Solution	Assignment	Completion Time	Total Cost	Reduction (%)
1	assign all six tasks to cl_3	25	15	*Invalid*
2	assign all six tasks to cl_1	18	38	–
3	assign v_1, v_2, v_3 to cl_2 assign v_4, v_5, v_6 to cl_3	23	26	31.6
4	assign v_1 to cl_1 assign v_2, v_3, v_4, v_5, v_6 to cl_3	21	25	34.2

4   ILP Formulation for the HTAC Problem

In this section, we construct the ILP formulation for the HTAC problem. First, we introduce notations for the ILP formulation. Then, a theorem is presented for formulating a logic statement in ILP. Last, the objective function and constraints for the HTAC problem are derived.

We define a binary variable $S_{v,i}$ indicating whether node v is assigned to cluster cl_i. The value of $S_{v,i}$ equals to 1 if and only if node v is assigned to cluster cl_i. Also, a binary variable $B_{u,v,i,j}$ is defined for each edge (u, v). The value of $B_{u,v,i,j}$ equals to 1 if and only if there is a dependency edge between node u and node v, while node u is assigned to cluster cl_i and node v is assigned to cluster cl_j. Variable F_v represents the total execution and communication time when node v is finished.

Before we present the ILP formulation for HTAC problem, we prove the following theorem for transforming an "if and only if" logic statement to linear inequalities.

Theorem 1. *The statement " For three binary variables x, y and z, $x = 1$ and $y = 1$ if and only if $z = 1$" can be modeled by the following linear inequalities:*

$$2z - 1 \leq x + y - 1 \leq z \tag{3}$$

Proof. To prove **"if"** statement, we need to prove the statement "For three binary variables x, y and z, if $z = 1$ and the linear inequality $2z-1 \leq x+y-1 \leq z$ holds, then $x = 1$ and $y = 1$". When $z = 1$, the linear inequality can be written as $1 \leq x + y - 1 \leq 1$, that is $2 \leq x + y \leq 2$. Because x and y are binary variables, it's clear that $x = 1$ and $y = 1$. To prove **"only if"** statement, we prove the statement "For three binary variables x, y and z, according to the linear inequality $2z - 1 \leq x + y - 1 \leq z$, only if $z = 1$, then $x = 1$ and $y = 1$". This means "If $z \neq 1$, according to the linear inequality $2z - 1 \leq x + y - 1 \leq z$, x and y can not equal to 1 at the same time". If $z \neq 1$, $z = 0$, then the linear inequality can be written as $-1 \leq x + y - 1 \leq 0$, that is $0 \leq x + y \leq 1$. When $x = 1$ and $y = 1$, the inequality $x + y > 1$ holds. Therefore, x and y can not equal to 1 at the same time.

In the following, we derive constraints for the HTAC problem.

Constraint 1: Each node can be only assigned to one cluster at any time.

$$\sum_{cl_i \in CL} S_{v,i} = 1 \qquad \forall v \in V \tag{4}$$

Constraint 2: Data communication exists if and only if there exists an edge $(u, v) \in E$, node u is assigned to cluster cl_i, and node v is assigned to cluster cl_j. We use Theorem 1 to obtain the following inequalities.

$$2B_{u,v,i,j} - 1 \leq S_{u,i} + S_{v,j} - 1 \leq B_{u,v,i,j}$$
$$\forall (u, v) \in E, cl_i \in CL, cl_j \in CL, 1 \leq i, j \leq M \tag{5}$$

Constraint 3: Each node has to follow the precedence relationship defined by CDFG G. That is, a node v can not be executed until all the ancestors and all the incoming data communications are finished.

$$F_u + \sum_{cl_i \in CL} \sum_{cl_j \in CL} [B_{u,v,i,j} \times \alpha((u, v), (A(u), A(v)))]$$
$$+ \sum_{cl_i \in CL} [S_{v,i} \times T(v, cl_i)] \leq F_v \qquad \forall (u, v) \in E, 1 \leq i, j \leq M \tag{6}$$

where $\alpha((u, v), (A(u), A(v)))$ is a function representing the communication time between node u and node v, and $T(v, cl_i)$ represents the execution time of node v when it is assigned to cluster cl_i.

Constraint 4: The earliest execution time of a node with no parent node is 0.

$$\sum_{cl_i \in CL} [S_{v,i} \times T(v, cl_i)] \leq F_v \qquad \forall v \in V \tag{7}$$

Constraint 5: All the nodes in CDFG G must be finished before a given time constraint L.

$$F_v \leq L \qquad \forall v \in V \tag{8}$$

The objective function of the HTAC problem computes the total execution and communication cost when all the nodes in the given task model are assigned to clusters. It is formulated as follows:

$$\min \sum_{(u,v) \in E} \sum_{cl_i \in CL} \sum_{cl_j \in CL} [B_{u,v,i,j} \times \beta((u, v), (A(u), A(v)))]$$
$$+ \sum_{v \in V} \sum_{cl_i \in CL} [S_{v,i} \times C(v, cl_i)] \tag{9}$$

where $\beta((u, v), (A(u), A(v)))$ is a function that computes the communication cost between node u and node v with their assignments, and $C(v, cl_i)$ represents the execution cost of node v when it is assigned to cluster cl_i.

The ILP formulation presented above computes the optimal solution for the HTAC problem. The development of ILP formulation is important since it guarantees optimal results. We can also use the optimal results generated by ILP to evaluate the effectiveness of our heuristic which will be present in Section 5.

5   The Ratio Greedy Assign Algorithm for the HTAC Problem

In this section, we propose a polynomial time heuristic, the Ratio Greedy Assign (RGA) algorithm, for solving the HTAC problem. The RGA algorithm aims to find a solution of heterogeneous task assignment that satisfies a given time constraint with the minimal total cost.

Provided that there are enough computation and communication resources, a *critical path* (CP) in G is defined as a path $p : u \rightsquigarrow v$ with the longest execution and communication time among all paths in G. Thus, the completion time of CDFG G is equal to the completion time of the critical path p. The completion time of G should be less than or equal to a given time constraint in the HTAC problem.

Given a set of heterogeneous clusters and their connections, the RGA algorithm starts with assigning all the nodes to a cluster cl_k. If the completion time of G under the initial assignment exceeds the time constraint, the algorithm iteratively finds a critical path $p \subseteq G$ and tries to reduce the completion time of p by moving one node to a cluster with a shorter latency than the current assignment. The decision of reassigning a node is made based on a cost-to-time ratio computed as follows:

$$Ratio(v_i, cl_j) \leftarrow \frac{DiffCost(v_i, cl_j)}{DiffTime(v_i, cl_j)} \tag{10}$$

where $DiffCost(v_i, cl_j)$ is the difference of cost when node v_i is moved from the current assigned cluster to a new cluster cl_j, and $DiffTime\ (v_i, cl_j)$ is the difference of time when node v_i is moved from the current assigned cluster to a new cluster cl_j. In order to obtain the minimal total cost and satisfy the time constraint, the RGA algorithm always selects a node with the the the lowest cost-to-time ratio $Ratio(v_i, cl_j)$ to be moved to a cluster cl_j. For the same amount of reduction on completion time, a smaller cost-to-time ratio indicates a smaller increase of cost. After adjusting the assignment of a critical path is done, the algorithm tries to find a new critical path in G and attempts to reduce its completion time till the time constraint is satisfied, or the completion time of G can not be reduced any more.

Otherwise, if the completion time of G under the initial assignment satisfies the time constraint, the algorithm tries to reduce the total system cost by moving a node with the lowest cost-to-time ratio to a new cluster. In this case, the cost-to-time ratio indicates the benefit of cost reduction with a sacrifice on time

---

Algorithm 5.1. *Ratio Greedy Assign (RGA)* Algorithm

Require: A given $CDFG$ $G = <V, E, CL, T, C, D>$, and a time constraint L.
Ensure: Assignment for each node in G.
1: **for** each cluster cl_k, $1 \leq k \leq M$ **do**
2:     $A(v_i) \leftarrow cl_k$, $\forall v_i \in V$;
3:     **if** $T_A(G) > L$ **then**
4:         **repeat**
5:             Find a critical path $p : v_i \rightsquigarrow v_j$ in G;
6:             $V_{cp} \leftarrow$ all nodes in critical path p;
7:             **for** $\forall v_i \in V_{cp}$ **do**
8:                 **for** $\forall cl_j \in CL$ **do**
9:                     **if** cl_j is a new cluster for v_i and $DiffTime(v_i, cl_j) < 0$ **then**
10:                        Compute $Ratio(v_i, cl_j)$ by Equation (10);
11:                    **end if**
12:                **end for**
13:            **end for**
14:            $Ratio(v_i, cl_j) \leftarrow$ the minimal ratio of nodes in critical path p;
15:            $A(v_i) \leftarrow cl_j$;
16:        **until** $T_A(G) \leq L$ or $T_A(G)$ can not be reduced;
17:    **else**
18:        **repeat**
19:            **for** $\forall v_i \in V$ **do**
20:                **for** $\forall cl_j \in CL$ **do**
21:                    **if** cl_j is a new cluster for v_i, $DiffCost(v_i, cl_j) < 0$ and $T_A(G) \leq L$
                            then
22:                        Compute $Ratio(v_i, cl_j)$ by Equation (10);
23:                    **end if**
24:                **end for**
25:            **end for**
26:            $Ratio(v_i, cl_j) \leftarrow$ the minimal ratio of all the nodes in V;
27:            $A(v_i) \leftarrow cl_j$;
28:        **until** $C_A(G)$ can not be reduced;
29:    **end if**
30: **end for**
31: $A(G) \leftarrow$ assignment with the minimum total system cost from all solutions.

---

performance. After reassigning a node, the algorithm tries to find another node and continues to make such attempts till the total system cost of G can not be reduced any more. The RGA algorithm iteratively tries each cluster to find an assignment with the minimum total system cost.

The time complexity for computing the cost-to-time ratio for all the nodes on a critical path is $O(|V| * M * (|E| + |V|))$. The algorithm iterates M times. Therefore, the time complexity of the Ratio Greedy Assign algorithm is $O(|V| * M^2 * (|E| + |V|))$, where $|V|$ is the number of nodes, M is the number of clusters, and $|E|$ is the number of edges.

6   Experiments

The effectiveness of our algorithm is evaluated by running a set of benchmarks on a simulation environment. We use the following applications in our experiments: Differential equation solver, Allpole filter, Floyd-Steinberg algorithm, RLS-languerre lattice filer, Elliptic filter, 10-4stage lattice filter and 20-4stage lattice filter. All the benchmarks are from the DSPstone benchmark [13].

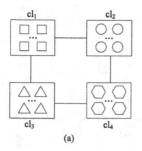

Clusters	cl_1		cl_2		cl_3		cl_4	
	CT_1	CC_1	CT_2	CC_2	CT_3	CC_3	CT_4	CC_4
cl_1	1	1	2	3	2	2	5	4
cl_2	2	3	1	1	4	5	3	2
cl_3	2	2	4	5	1	1	2	2
cl_4	5	4	3	2	2	2	1	1

(a)   (b)

Fig. 3. (a) An architecture with four clusters. (b) Communication time and cost of unit data volume among various clusters in (a).

The experiments are conducted on two different heterogeneous cluster architectures. The first one is composed of three completely connected clusters as shown in Fig. 1(a). The second one consists of four connected clusters as shown in Fig. 3(a). Values of communication time and cost for unit data volume between each pair of clusters are shown in Fig. 1(b) and Fig. 3(b), respectively. Values of execution time and execution cost are different when a node is assigned to various clusters. Values of execution time and cost are given for all the nodes in CDFG. Also, data volume transferred on each edge is pre-determined. All the experiments are conducted by a simulator on an Intel® Core™2 Duo Processor E7500 2.93G processor.

In our experiments, we use three different methods to generate task assignments for various benchmarks with different time constraints. The Homogeneous Assign (HA) method assigns all the nodes to a cluster such that the time constraint can be satisfied with the minimal total cost. The Ratio Greedy Assign (RGA) algorithm generates a task assignment with the minimal cost using a greedy strategy on the ratio of cost to time gain. The ILP method computes the optimal results.

Table 2 and Fig. 4 show the experimental results and comparison of total system cost on the architecture with three clusters as shown in Fig. 1(a). Table 3 and Fig. 5 show the experimental results and comparison of total system cost on the architecture with four clusters as shown in Fig. 3(a).

In Table 2 and Table 3, column "Time Constr." lists various time constraints in ascending order for each benchmark. Column "HA Cost" shows execution costs of benchmarks with task assignments generated by the Homogeneous Assign method. Column "Cost" under "RGA" shows execution costs produced

Table 2. Experimental results for benchmarks of DAGs with various time constraints on the architecture with three clusters as shown in Fig. 1(a)

Bench.	Num. of Nodes	Time Constr.	HA Cost	RGA		ILP		
				Cost	Reduc. vs. HA(%)	Cost	Reduc. vs. HA(%)	Reduc. vs. RGA(%)
Diff. Eq.	11	40	150	135	10.0	135	10.0	0.0
		55	150	91	39.3	91	39.3	0.0
		70	77	77	0.0	77	0.0	0.0
		85	77	68	11.7	60	22.1	11.8
Allpole	15	45	251	190	24.3	182	27.5	4.2
		60	251	158	37.1	128	49.0	19.0
		75	143	83	42.0	83	42.0	0.0
		90	143	75	47.6	75	47.6	0.0
Floyd	16	75	211	174	17.5	164	22.3	5.7
		90	211	148	29.9	144	31.8	2.7
		105	121	121	0.0	116	4.1	4.1
		120	121	115	5.0	107	11.6	7.0
RLS-lang.	19	40	334	223	33.2	203	39.2	9.0
		60	334	202	39.5	174	47.9	13.9
		80	173	168	2.9	146	15.6	13.1
		100	173	146	15.6	132	23.7	9.6
Elliptic	34	120	511	382	25.2	343	32.9	10.2
		140	511	314	38.6	302	40.9	3.8
		160	287	281	2.1	276	3.8	1.8
		180	287	270	5.9	253	11.8	6.3
10-4lattice	260	100	3723	2671	28.3	×	×	×
		140	3723	2035	45.3	×	×	×
		180	2193	1706	22.2	×	×	×
		220	2193	1572	28.3	×	×	×
20-4lattice	520	180	7508	4591	38.9	×	×	×
		230	7508	3943	47.5	×	×	×
		280	4448	3441	22.6	×	×	×
		330	4448	3176	28.6	×	×	×
Ave. Reduction(%)					24.6		26.2	6.1

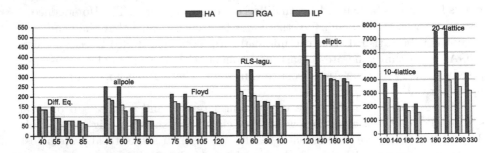

Fig. 4. Total system cost generated by three methods for each benchmark with various time constraints on the architecture with three clusters as shown in Fig. 1(a)

Table 3. Experimental results for benchmarks of DAGs with various time constraints on the architecture with four clusters as shown in Fig. 3(a)

Bench.	Num. of Nodes	Time Constr.	HA Cost	RGA		ILP		
				Cost	Reduc. vs. HA(%)	Cost	Reduc. vs. HA(%)	Reduc. vs. RGA(%)
Diff. Eq.	11	40	219	201	8.2	201	8.2	0.0
		60	219	175	20.1	146	33.3	16.6
		80	146	122	16.4	118	19.2	3.3
		100	118	90	23.7	90	23.7	0.0
		120	118	80	32.2	79	33.1	1.3
Allpole	15	50	350	255	27.1	248	29.1	2.7
		80	242	163	32.6	163	32.6	0.0
		110	242	130	46.3	130	46.3	0.0
		140	149	109	26.8	109	26.8	0.0
		170	149	93	37.6	91	38.9	2.2
Floyd	16	75	312	270	13.5	253	18.9	6.3
		100	312	238	23.7	205	34.3	13.9
		125	222	156	29.7	156	29.7	0.0
		150	222	113	49.1	113	49.1	0.0
		175	191	97	49.2	92	51.8	5.2
RLS-lang.	19	40	456	317	30.5	307	32.7	3.2
		60	456	261	42.8	254	44.3	2.7
		80	295	182	38.3	180	39.0	1.1
		100	295	145	50.8	144	51.2	0.7
		120	247	114	53.8	114	53.8	0.0
Elliptic	34	100	724	634	12.4	605	16.4	4.6
		140	724	551	23.9	493	31.9	10.5
		180	500	433	13.4	407	18.6	6.0
		220	423	342	19.1	319	24.6	6.7
		260	423	277	34.5	265	37.4	4.3
10-4lattice	260	100	5225	3814	27.0	×	×	×
		150	5225	2710	48.1	×	×	×
		200	3695	1945	47.4	×	×	×
		250	2975	1499	49.6	×	×	×
		300	2975	1298	56.4	×	×	×
20-4lattice	520	180	10426	6547	37.2	×	×	×
		240	10426	4887	53.1	×	×	×
		300	7366	3886	47.2	×	×	×
		360	7366	3228	56.2	×	×	×
		420	5926	2852	51.9	×	×	×
Ave. Reduction(%)					35.1		33.0	3.6

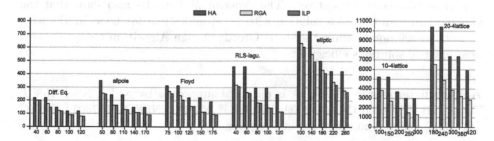

Fig. 5. Total system cost generated by three methods for each benchmark with various time constraints on the architecture with four clusters as shown in Fig. 3(a)

by the Ratio Greedy Assign algorithm. Compared with the Homogeneous Assign method, the Ratio Greedy Assign algorithm reduces the system cost by 24.6% and 35.1% on average for all the benchmarks on two different cluster architectures, respectively. Column "Cost" under "ILP" shows execution costs generated by the ILP method. The ILP method produces the optimal task assignment results. However, it cannot finish the computation within hours for large-sized benchmarks, such as 10-4lattice filter with 260 nodes. Each "×" in Table 2 and Table 3 indicates that the running time of the corresponding experiment is longer than ten hours. The "Reduc. vs. HA(%)" colume shows reduction rates on the total system cost by comparing ILP method against Homogeneous Assign method. The "Reduc. vs. RGA(%)" colume shows reduction rates on system cost by comparing ILP method with the Ratio Greedy Assign algorithm. Although the ILP model obtains optimal results on some of the benchmarks, the computation time of the ILP method grows exponentially with increasing size of benchmarks. Our experimental results show that it takes a long time to get results even for a medium-sized CDFG with more than 200 nodes. For example, on the architecture with three clusters as shown in Fig. 1(a), the ILP model takes 441 seconds to compute the assignment result for an elliptic filter with time constraint $L = 180$, while our Ratio Greedy Assign algorithm takes only 0.016 second to produce a near optimal solution. Also, the ILP formulation cannot generate a solution for 10-4lattice filter and 20-4lattice filter within 10 hours. The computation time of the ILP method is unacceptable for large-sized CDFGs. The Ratio Greedy Assign algorithm, on the other hand, can always generate near optimal solutions efficiently for all the benchmarks.

7   Conclusion

In this paper, we propose a novel heuristic, Ratio Greedy Assign algorithm, to generate task assignments on heterogeneous multicore systems with minimal total system cost considering both execution and communication loads. The ILP formulation of Heterogeneous Task Assignment problem with Communications (HTAC) is also presented. The experimental results show that the Ratio Greedy Assign algorithm reduces the total system cost by 24.6% and 35.1% on average compared with the homogeneous assign method, on two different heterogeneous cluster architectures respectively. The experimental results also show that the ILP method cannot find a solution with acceptable time for benchmarks with more than 200 nodes, while the Ratio Greedy Assign Algorithm always obtains near-optimal solutions efficiently.

Acknowledgments. This work is partially supported by NSF CNS-1015802, Texas NHARP 009741-0020-2009, HK GRF 123609, NSFC 61173014, NSFC 61133005, China Thousand-Talent Program.

References

1. Chen, T., Raghavan, R., Dale, J.N., Iwata, E.: Cell broadband engine architecture and its first implementation - a performance view. IBM Journal of Research and Development 51(5), 559–572 (2007)
2. Nvidia Corporation, http://www.nvidia.com/object/tegra-3-processor.html
3. Ucar, B., Aykanat, C., Kaya, K., Ikinci, M.: Task assignment in heterogeneous computing systems. Journal of Parallel and Distributed Computing 66(1), 32–46 (2006)
4. Attiya, G., Hamam, Y.: Task Allocation for Minimizing Programs Completion Time in Multicomputer Systems. In: Laganá, A., Gavrilova, M.L., Kumar, V., Mun, Y., Tan, C.J.K., Gervasi, O. (eds.) ICCSA 2004. LNCS, vol. 3044, pp. 97–106. Springer, Heidelberg (2004)
5. Yin, P.Y., Yu, S.S., Wang, P.P., Wang, Y.T.: Task allocation for maximizing reliability of a distributed system using hybrid particle swarm optimization. Journal of Systems and Software 80(5), 724–735 (2007)
6. Shen, C.C., Tsai, W.H.: A graph matching approach to optimal task assignment in distributed computing systems using a minimax criterion. IEEE Transactions on Computers C-34(3), 197–203 (1985)
7. Ito, R., Parhi, K.: Register minimization in cost-optimal synthesis of dsp architectures. In: IEEE Signal Processing Society [Workshop on] VLSI Signal Processing, VIII, pp. 207–216 (October 1995)
8. Martinez, J., Ipek, E.: Dynamic multicore resource management: A machine learning approach. IEEE Micro 29(5), 8–17 (2009)
9. Ma, Y.C., Chen, T.F., Chung, C.P.: Branch-and-bound task allocation with task clustering-based pruning. Journal of Parallel and Distributed Computing 64(11), 1223–1240 (2004)
10. Kang, Q., He, H., Song, H.: Task assignment in heterogeneous computing systems using an effective iterated greedy algorithm. Journal of Systems and Software 84(6), 985–992 (2011)
11. Sivanandam, S.N., Visalakshi, P.: Multiprocessor scheduling using hybrid particle swarm optimization with dynamically varying inertia. International Journal of Computer Science and Applications 4(5), 95–106 (2007)
12. Shao, Z., Zhuge, Q., Xue, C., Sha, E.M.: Efficient assignment and scheduling for heterogeneous dsp systems. IEEE Transactions on Parallel and Distributed Systems 16(6), 516–525 (2005)
13. Zivojnovic, V., Martinez, J., Schlager, C., Meyr, H.: Dspstone: A dsp-oriented benchmarking methodology. In: Proc. of ICSPAT 1994, Dallas (October 1994)

Budget Constrained Resource Allocation for Non-deterministic Workflows on an IaaS Cloud

Eddy Caron[1], Frédéric Desprez[1], Adrian Muresan[1], and Frédéric Suter[2]

[1] UMR CNRS - ENS Lyon - UCB Lyon 1 - INRIA 5668
46, allée d'Italie, 69364 Lyon Cedex 7, France
{ecaron,desprez,amuresan}@ens-lyon.fr
[2] IN2P3 Computing Center, CNRS, IN2P3
43, bd du 11 novembre 1918, 69622 Villeurbanne, France
fsuter@cc.in2p3.fr

Abstract. Many scientific applications are described through workflow structures. Due to the increasing level of parallelism offered by modern computing infrastructures, workflow applications now have to be composed not only of sequential programs, but also of parallel ones. Cloud platforms bring on-demand resource provisioning and pay-as-you-go billing model. Then the execution of a workflow corresponds to a certain budget. The current work addresses the problem of resource allocation for non-deterministic workflows under budget constraints. We present a way of transforming the initial problem into sub-problems that have been studied before. We propose two new allocation algorithms that are capable of determining resource allocations under budget constraints and we present ways of using them to address the problem at hand.

1 Introduction

Many scientific applications from various disciplines are structured as *workflows*. Informally, a workflow can be seen as the composition of a set of basic operations that have to be performed on a given input data set to produce the expected scientific result. The interest for workflows mainly comes from the need to build upon legacy codes that would be too costly to rewrite. Combining existing programs is also a way to lead to new results that would not have been found using each component alone. For years, such program composition was mainly done by hand by scientists, that had to run each program one after the other, manage the intermediate data, and deal with potentially tricky transitions between programs. The emergence of Grid Computing and the development of complex middleware components [6,7,9,11,12,15,18] automated this process.

The evolution of architectures with more parallelism available, the generalization of GPUs, and the main memory becoming the new performance bottleneck, motivate a shift in the way scientific workflows are programmed and executed. A way to cope with these issues is to consider workflows composing not only

Y. Xiang et al. (Eds.): ICA3PP 2012, Part I, LNCS 7439, pp. 186–201, 2012.

sequential programs but also parallel ones. This allows for the simultaneous exploitation of both the task and data-parallelisms exhibited by an application. It is thus a promising way toward the full exploitation of modern architectures. Each step of a workflow is then said to be *moldable* as the number of resources allocated to an operation is determined at scheduling time. Such workflows are also called Parallel Task Graphs (PTGs).

In practice, some applications cannot be modeled by classical workflow or PTG descriptions. For such applications the models are augmented with special semantics that allow for exclusive diverging control flows or repetitive flows. This leads to a new structure called a *non-deterministic* workflow. For instance, we can consider the problem of gene identification by promoter analysis [2,20] as described in [12], or the GENIE (Grid ENabled Integrated Earth) project that aims at simulating the long term evolution of the Earth's climate [14].

Infrastructure as a Service (IaaS) Clouds raised a lot of interest recently thanks to an elastic resource allocation and pay-as-you-go billing model. A Cloud user can adapt the execution environment to the needs of his/her application on a virtually infinite supply of resources. While the elasticity provided by IaaS Clouds gives way to more dynamic application models, it also raises new issues from a scheduling point of view. An execution now corresponds to a certain budget, that imposes certain constraints on the scheduling process. In this work we detail a first step to address this scheduling problem in the case of non-deterministic workflows. Our main contribution is the design of two original allocation strategies for non-deterministic workflows under budget constraints. We target a typical IaaS Cloud and adapt some existing scheduling strategies to the specifics of such an environment in terms of resource allocation and pricing.

This paper is organized as follows. Section 2 discusses related work. Section 3 describes our application and platform models and gives a precise problem statement. Section 4 details the proposed algorithms for resources allocation of non-deterministic workflows on an IaaS Cloud, which is evaluated in Section 5. Finally, Section 6 summarizes our contribution and presents some future work.

2   Related Work

The problem of scheduling workflows has been widely studied by the aforementioned workflow management systems. Traditional workflows consist of a deterministic DAG structure whose nodes represent compute tasks and edges represent precedence and flow constraints between tasks. Some workflow managers support conditional branches and loops [4], but neither of them target elastic platforms such as IaaS Clouds nor address their implications.

Several algorithms have been proposed to schedule PTGs, *i.e.*, deterministic workflows made of moldable tasks, on various non-elastic platforms. They usually decompose the scheduling in two phases: (i) determine a resource allocation for each task; (ii) map the allocated tasks on the compute resources. Among the existing algorithms, we based the current work on the CPA [17] and biCPA [8] algorithms. We refer the reader to [8] for details and references on other scheduling algorithms.

The flexibility provided by elastic resource allocations offers great opportunities as shown by the increasing body of work on resource management for elastic platforms. In [10], the authors give a proof of concept for a chemistry-inspired scientific workflow management system. The chemical programming paradigm is a nature-inspired approach for autonomous service coordination [19]. Theirs results make this approach encouraging, but still less performing than traditional workflow management systems. In contrast to the current work, they do not aim at conditional workflows or budget constraints. An approach to schedule workflows on elastic platforms under budget constraints is given in [13], but is limited to traditional workflows that have no conditional structures.

3   Problem Statement

3.1   Platform and Application Models

We consider an IaaS Cloud as a provider of a possibly infinite set of virtual resources, each having three well defined of features from a catalog: i) number of equivalent virtual CPUs, $nCPU$, which allows for comparing the relative performance of different resources; ii) the network *bandwidth* of the virtual machine; iii) monetary cost per running hour, *cost*, fractional numbers of hours being rounded up, as in most commercial cloud providers. We define the catalog as:

$$\mathcal{C} = \{vm_i = (nCPU_i, bandwidth_i, cost_i) | i \geq 1\}.$$

We consider that all virtual CPUs in the IaaS Cloud have the same computing speed s. Instances of the same type are then homogeneous, while the complete catalog is a heterogeneous set. We also consider that a virtual CPU can communicate with several others simultaneously under the *bounded multi-port* model. All the concurrent communication flows share the bandwidth of the communication link that connects this CPU to the remaining of the IaaS Cloud.

Our workflow model is inspired by previous work [1,14]. We define a non-deterministic workflow as a directed graph $\mathcal{G} = (\mathcal{V}, \mathcal{E})$, where $\mathcal{V} = \{v_i | i = 1, \ldots, V\}$ is a set of V vertexes and $\mathcal{E} = \{e_{i,j} | (i, j) \in \{1, \ldots, V\} \times \{1, \ldots, V\}\}$ is a set of E edges representing precedence and flow constraints between tasks. Without loss of generality we assume that $\mathcal{G}$ has a single entry task and a single exit task. The vertexes in $\mathcal{V}$ can be of different types. A **Task** node represents a (potentially parallel) computation. Such nodes can have any number of predecessors, *i.e.*, tasks that have to complete before the execution of this task can start and any number of successors, *i.e.*, tasks that wait for the completion of this task to proceed. We consider that each edge $e_{i,j} \in \mathcal{E}$ has a weight, which is the amount of data, in bytes, that task v_i must send to task v_j.

Traditional workflows are made of task nodes only. The relations between a task node and its predecessors and successors can be represented by control structures, that we respectively denote by **AND-join** and **AND-split** transitions as seen in Figure 1(a). Task nodes are moldable and can be executed on any numbers of virtual resource instances. We denote by $Alloc(v)$ the set of instances allocated to task v for its execution. The total number of virtual CPUs in this set is then: $p(v) = \sum_j nCPU_j | vm_j \in Alloc(v)$. This allows us to estimate $T(v, Alloc(v))$, the execution time of task v on a given allocation. In practice, this time can be measured via benchmarking for several allocations or it can be calculated via a performance model. In this work, we rely on Amdahl's law. This model claims that the speedup of a parallel application is limited by its strictly serial part α. The execution time of a task is given by

$$T(v, Alloc(v)) = \left(\alpha + \frac{(1 - \alpha)}{p(v)} \right) \times T(v, 1),$$

where $T(v, 1)$ is the time needed to execute task v on a single virtual CPU. The overall execution time of $\mathcal{G}$, or *makespan*, is defined as the time between the beginning of $\mathcal{G}$'s entry task and the completion of $\mathcal{G}$'s exit task.

To model non-deterministic behavior, we add the following control nodes to our model. An **OR-split** node has a single predecessor and any number of successors, that represent mutually-exclusive branches of the workflow. The decision of which successor to run is taken at runtime. Conversely an **OR-join** node has any number of predecessors and a single successor. If any of the parent sub-workflows reaches this node, the execution continues with the successor.

Finally, our model of non-deterministic workflows can also include **Cycle** constructs. This is an edge joining an OR-split node and one OR-join ancestor. A cycle must contain at least one OR-join node to prevent deadlocks. Figure 1 gives a graphical representation of these control nodes and constructs.

Figure 1(c) is a simple representation of the Cycle construct. $p_{2,3}$ and $p_{4,2}$ are not edges of the workflow, but paths leading from v_2 to v_3 and from v_4 to v_2 respectively. These paths are a weak constraint that ensure the creation of a cycle in the graph, in combination with the OR-join and OR-split nodes v_2 and

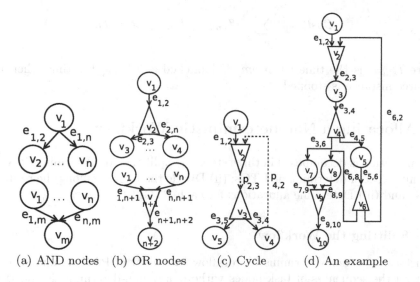

(a) AND nodes   (b) OR nodes   (c) Cycle   (d) An example

Fig. 1. Non-deterministic workflow control nodes and constructs

v_4. However, a Cycle can contain any number of OR-split or OR-join nodes and even an unbound number of edges leading to other parts of the workflow.

We give a more complex example of functional workflow in Figure 1(d), in which the path deriving from the edge $e_{6,2}$ comprises an OR-split node (v_4). This implies that the Cycle construct does not determine the number of iterations of the cycle path by itself, as in a loop construct for instance. Decisions taken at runtime for v_4 may make the execution flow exit the cycle before reaching v_6.

3.2   Metrics and Problem Statement

The problem of determining allocations for a single non-deterministic workflow amounts to allocating resource instances to the tasks of this workflow so as to minimize its makespan while respecting a given budget constraint. An additional issue is to deal with the non-determinism of the considered workflows. At scheduling time, all the possible execution paths have to be considered. But at runtime, some sub-workflows will not be executed, due to the OR-split construct, while others may be executed several times, due to the Cycle construct. This raises some concerns related to the budget constraint. Our approach is to decompose the workflow into a set of deterministic sub-workflows with non-deterministic transitions between them. Then, we fall back to the well studied problem of determining allocations for multiple Parallel Task Graphs (PTGs).

We denote by B the budget allocated to the execution of the original workflow and by B^i the budget allocated to the ith sub-workflow. These budgets are expressed in a currency-independent manner. Finally, $Cost^i$ is the cost of a schedule $\mathcal{S}^i$ built for the ith sub-workflow on a dedicated IaaS Cloud. It is defined as the sum of the costs of all the resource instances used during the schedule. Due to the pricing model, we consider every started hour as fully paid.

$$Cost^i = \sum_{\forall vm_j \in \mathcal{S}^i} \lceil T_{end_j} - T_{start_j} \rceil \times cost_j,$$

where T_{start_j} is the time when vm_j is launched and T_{end_j} the time when this resource instance is stopped.

4   Allocating a Non-deterministic Workflow

Our algorithm is decomposed in three steps: (i) Split the non-deterministic workflow into a set of deterministic PTGs; (ii) Divide the budget among the resulting PTGs and (iii) Determine allocations for each PTG.

4.1   Splitting the Workflow

Transforming a non-deterministic workflow into a set of PTGs amounts to extract all the sequences of task nodes without any non-deterministic construct. The OR-split nodes define the sub-workflow boundaries. An OR-split node leads

to $n + 1$ sub-workflows, one ending with the predecessor of the node and n starting with each of the successors of the OR-split node. It is worth noting that
OR-join nodes do not actually lead to the creation of new sub-workflows since
they do not have a non-deterministic nature and therefore they do not lead to
non-deterministic transitions. What they actually do is to preserve the number
of sub-workflows coming from their inwards transitions. Each of these transitions should come from a different sub-workflow *i.e.*, from a different outwards
transition of an OR-split. These principles are illustrated in Figure 2.

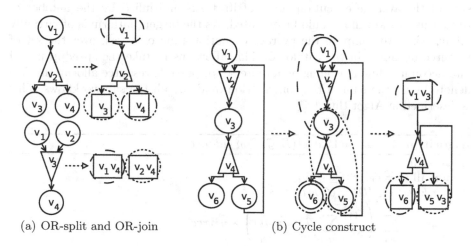

(a) OR-split and OR-join   (b) Cycle construct

Fig. 2. Extracting sub-workflows from OR-splits, OR-joins and Cycles

Extracting sub-workflows from a Cycle node is simple if we consider that
a Cycle is actually a construct composed of one or more OR-split nodes and a
feedback loop. Then we fall back to the rules of splitting OR-split nodes, as shown
in Figure 2(b). Here we extract three sub-workflows containing two instances of
task v_3. One is a result of executing task v_1 and the other derives from following
the cycle branch. Task v_5 is the predecessor of this second instance.

More details and examples on workflow splitting can be found in [5].

4.2 Distributing Budget to Sub-workflows

We must decide what part of the budget we can dedicate to each sub-workflow.
Because of the non-deterministic transitions between them, we first have to estimate the odds and number of times of execution for each of them.

The number of executions of a sub-workflow is described completely by the
number of transitions of the edge connecting its parent OR-split to its start node
since there is only one non-deterministic transition that triggers its execution.
We model this behavior by considering that the number of transitions of each
outwards edge of an OR-split is described by a random variable with a *normal
distribution* D^i. We also consider a parameter *Confidence* $\in [0, 1)$ that we use to

express the level of confidence with which the algorithm can guarantee that each sub-workflow will be executed a determined number of times. More formally, the expected maximum number of executions of a $\mathcal{G}^i$ is

$$nExec^i \leftarrow CDF_{D^i}^{-1}(Confidence)$$

where $CDF_{D^i}^{-1}$ is the reverse *Cumulative Distribution Function* (CDF) of D^i.

For each sub-workflow we allocate a part of the budget that is proportional to its contribution. We determine the contribution ω^i of sub-workflow $\mathcal{G}^i$ as the sum of the average execution times of its tasks multiplied by the number of times this sub-workflow could be executed. As the target platform is of virtually infinite size, we compute the average execution time of a task over the set of resource instances in the catalog $\mathcal{C}$. This allows us to take the speedup model into account, while reasoning on a finite set of possible resource allocations. We denote by ω^* the sum of the contribution made by all the sub-workflows. This is described in Algorithm 1.

Algorithm 1. Share_Budget($B, \mathcal{G}, Confidence$)

1: $\omega^* \leftarrow 0$
2: **for all** $\mathcal{G}^i = (\mathcal{V}^i, \mathcal{E}^i) \subseteq \mathcal{G}$ **do**
3:     $nExec^i \leftarrow CDF_{D^i}^{-1}(Confidence)$
4:     $\omega^i \leftarrow \sum_{v_j \in \mathcal{V}^i} \left(\frac{1}{|\mathcal{C}|} \sum_{vm_k \in \mathcal{C}} T(v_j, vm_k) \right) \times nExec^i$
5:     $\omega^* \leftarrow \omega^* + \omega^i$
6: **end for**
7: **for all** $\mathcal{G}^i \subseteq G$ **do**
8:     $B^i \leftarrow B \times \frac{\omega^i}{\omega^*} \times \frac{1}{nExec^i}$
9: **end for**

4.3   Determining PTG Allocations

Now we have to determine which combination of virtual instances from the resource catalog leads to the best compromise between the reduction of the makespan and the monetary cost for each sub-workflow, *i.e.*, for each PTG.

We base our work on the allocation procedures of two two-step algorithms, named CPA [17] and biCPA [8], that were designed to schedule PTGs on homogeneous clusters. We adapt them to the specifics of IaaS Cloud platforms.

The biCPA algorithm is an improvement of the original CPA algorithm. It starts by allocating one CPU to each task in the PTG. Then it iterates and allocates one extra CPU to a task from the critical path of the application that benefits the most until the average work T_A becomes greater than the length of the critical path T_{CP}. The definition of the average work used by the CPA algorithm was $T_A = \frac{1}{P} \sum_{i=1}^{|\mathcal{V}^i|} W(v_i)$ where $W(v_i)$ is the work associated to task v_i, *i.e.*, the product of its execution time by the number of CPUs in its allocation, and P the total number of CPUs in the target platform. In biCPA, the value of

P is iterated over from one to the size of the target platform and its semantics is changed to represent the total number of CPUs of any task allocation.

The definition of the length of the critical path was $T_{CP} = max_i BL(v_i)$ where $BL(v_i)$ represents the *bottom level* of task v_i *i.e.,* its distance until the end of the application. For the current work we keep this definition for T_{CP}. On an IaaS Cloud the size of the target platform is virtually infinite. Thus we propose to reason in terms of budget and average cost of an allocation. Moreover, the pricing model implies that each started hour is fully paid, even though the application has finished its execution. Then, some *spare time* may remain for a virtual resource instance at the end of an execution of a task of the workflow.

When building an allocation, we do not know yet in which order the tasks will be executed. Then we cannot make any strong assumption about reusing spare time. As we aim at building an allocation for $\mathcal{G}^i$ that costs less than B^i, a conservative option would be to consider that this spare time is never reused.

Overestimating the costs allows us to guarantee that the produced allocation will not exceed the allowed budget. However, it can have a devastating impact on makespan depending on how much spare time is lost. We just have to consider a situation in which tasks have small running time (a lot smaller than 1 hour). In such situations, the amount of spare time not reused is a lot bigger then the actual useful time used. The overestimation of the costs would make this approach useless for such tasks, as they will be unschedulable for small budgets.

To hinder the effect of this overestimation, we can assume that the spare time left by each task has one in two chance to be reused by another task. The risk inherent to such an assumption is that we do not anymore have a strong guarantee that the resulting allocation will fall short of the allowed budget once scheduled. Nevertheless, we can define $cost(v_i)$ as:

$$cost(v_i) = \frac{\lceil T(v_i, Alloc(v_i)) \rceil + T(v_i, Alloc(v_i))}{2} \times \sum_{vm_j \in Alloc(v_i)} cost_j.$$

Then we defined T_A^{over} as:

$$T_A^{over} = \frac{1}{B'} \times \sum_{j=1}^{|\mathcal{V}^i|} \left(T(v_j, Alloc(v_j)) \times cost(v_j) \right),$$

Based on this definition, we propose a first allocation procedure detailed in Algorithm 2. This procedure determines one allocation for each task in a sub-workflow while trying to find a good compromise between the length of the critical path (the completion time) and the time-cost area as defined by T_A^{over}.

Since the purpose of this algorithm is to determine only one allocation, we need to estimate the value of B' such that the values of T_A^{over} and T_{CP} will converge at the end of the allocation. At convergence time, the two values are equal. B' is the maximum cost of running any single task at convergence time and B^i is the total cost of the allocation. As a heuristic to determine B' we assume that the proportion between the total work area and the maximum work area is constant. We can therefore calculate these areas for an initial iteration and determine the value of B' when convergence occurs.

$$\frac{B'}{B^i} = \frac{\sum_{j=1}^{|\mathcal{V}^i|} \left(T(v_j, Alloc^{init}(v_j)) \times cost^{init}(v_j) \right)}{T_{CP}^{init} \times \sum_{j=1}^{|\mathcal{V}^i|} cost^{init}(v_j)}$$

$Alloc^{init}$ represents the initial allocation in which we give a VM instance of the smallest type to every task.

Algorithm 2. Eager-allocate($\mathcal{G}^i = (\mathcal{V}^i, \mathcal{E}^i), B^i$)

1: **for all** $v \in \mathcal{V}^i$ **do**
2:     $Alloc(v) \leftarrow \{\min_{vm_i \in \mathcal{C}} CPU_i\}$
3: **end for**
4: Compute B'
5: **while** $T_{CP} > T_A^{over} \cap \sum_{j=1}^{|\mathcal{V}^i|} cost(v_j) \leq B^i$ **do**
6:     **for all** $v_i \in$ Critical Path **do**
7:         Determine $Alloc'(v_i)$ such that $p'(v_i) = p(v_i) + 1$
8:         $Gain(v_i) \leftarrow \frac{T(v_i, Alloc(v_i))}{p(v_i)} - \frac{T(v_i, Alloc'(v_i))}{p'(v_i)}$
9:     **end for**
10:    Select v such that $Gain(v)$ is maximal
11:    $Alloc(v) \leftarrow Alloc'(v)$
12:    Update T_A^{over} and T_{CP}
13: **end while**

Each task's allocation set is initialized with the number of CPUs of the smallest virtual instance in the catalog. Then, we determine which task belonging to the critical path would benefit the most from an extra virtual CPU, and increase the allocation of this task. We iterate this process until we find a compromise between makespan reduction and estimated cost increase. Note that the determination of $Alloc'(v_i)$ (line 7) may mean either adding a new instance with one virtual CPU to the set of resource instances already composing the allocation, or switching to another type of instance from the catalog.

In practice it is worth continuing the allocation process only while T_{CP} decreases. We have added an extra stop condition, called T_{CP} *cut-off*, that is triggered if T_{CP} cannot be reduced by more than one second.

As this first procedure may produce allocations that do not respect the budget limit, we propose an alternate approach based on the biCPA algorithm. Instead of just considering the allocation that is eventually obtained when the trade-off between the length of the critical path and the average cost is reached, we keep track of intermediate allocations build as if the allowed budget was smaller. Once all these candidate allocations are determined, we build a schedule for each of them on a dedicated platform to obtain a precise estimation of the makespan they achieve and at which cost. Then it is possible to choose the "best" allocation that leads to the smallest makespan for the allowed budget.

In this second procedure, we can rely on a tighter definition of the average time-cost area that does not take spare time into account. If some spare time exists, it will be reused (or not) when the schedule is built. Since we select the final allocation based on the resulting scheduling, we do not have to consider spare time in the first step. Essentially, we are underestimating the cost of the execution of a task when determining allocations. Our second allocation procedure will then rely on T_A^{under}, which is identical to T_A^{over} in all aspects but one, it uses the following definition for cost:

$$cost_{under}(v_j) = T(v_j, Alloc(v_j)) \times \sum_{vm_k \in Alloc(v_j)} cost_k$$

that includes the exact estimation of execution time of v_j. In this approach, B' allows us to mimic the variable size of the cluster used by the biCPA algorithm, and represents the maximum budget allowed to determine any one task's allocation. Its value will grow along with the allocation procedure, starting from the largest cost of running any task from the initial allocation and up to B^i. The use of B' has a direct impact on the computation of the average time-cost area and will lead to several intermediate trade-offs and corresponding allocations. We refer the reader to [8] for the motivations and benefits of this approach.

Algorithm 3. Deferred-allocate($\mathcal{G}^i = (\mathcal{V}^i, \mathcal{E}^i), B^i$)

1: **for all** $v \in \mathcal{V}^i$ **do**
2:     $Alloc(v) \leftarrow \{\min_{vm_i \in C} CPU_i\}$
3: **end for**
4: $k \leftarrow 0$
5: $B' \leftarrow \max_{v \in \mathcal{V}^i} cost_{under}(v)$
6: **while** $B' \leq B^i$ **do**
7:     $T_A^{under} = \frac{1}{B'} \times \sum_{j=1}^{|\mathcal{V}^i|} (T(v_j, Alloc(v_j))) \times cost_{under}(v_j))$
8:     **while** $T_{CP} > T_A^{under}$ **do**
9:         **for all** $v_i \in$ Critical Path **do**
10:            Determine $Alloc'(v_i)$ such that $p'(v_i) = p(v_i) + 1$
11:            $Gain(v_i) \leftarrow \frac{T(v_i, Alloc(v_i))}{p(v_i)} - \frac{T(v_i, Alloc'(v_i))}{p'(v_i)}$
12:        **end for**
13:        Select v such that $Gain(v)$ is maximal
14:        $Alloc(v) \leftarrow Alloc'(v)$
15:        Update T_A^{under} and T_{CP}
16:     **end while**
17:     **for all** $v \in \mathcal{V}^i$ **do**
18:        Store $Allocs^i(k, v) \leftarrow Alloc(v)$
19:     **end for**
20:     $B' \leftarrow \max_{v \in \mathcal{V}^i} cost_{under}(v)$
21:     $k \leftarrow k + 1$
22: **end while**

This second allocation procedure is detailed in Algorithm 3. A first difference is on lines 5 and 20 where we determine and update the value of B' to be the maximum cost of running any one task. The main difference with our first allocation procedure lies in the outer while loop (lines 6-22). This loop is used to set the value of T_A^{under} that will be used in the inner loop (lines 8-16). This inner loop actually corresponds to an interval of iterations of our first allocation procedure. Each time $T_{CP} \leq T_A^{under}$, the current allocation is stored for each task (lines 17-19). At the end of this procedure, several candidate allocations are associated with each task in the PTG.

In a second step, we have to get an estimation of the makespan and total cost that can be achieved with each of these allocations. To obtain these performance indicators, we rely on a classical list scheduling function. Tasks are considered by decreasing bottom-level values, *i.e.*, their distance in terms of execution time to the end of the application. For each task, we convert an allocation into a mapping to a set of virtual resource instances, while trying to minimize the finish time of the scheduled task and favor reuse of spare time to reduce the schedule's cost.

We achieve this in two steps. First, we estimate the finish time a task will experience by launching only new instances to satisfy its resource request, so that its cost is minimum, *i.e.*, favor big and cheap instances from the catalog. However, we do not make any assumption about spare time reuse for this mapping. Hence, its cost is computed by rounding up the execution time of the task. This provides us a baseline both in terms of makespan and cost for the current task. Second, we consider all the running instances to see if some spare time can be reused and thus save cost. We sort these instances by decreasing amount of spare time (from the current time) and then by decreasing size. Then we select instances from this list in a greedy way until the allocation request is fulfilled, and estimate the finish time of the task on this allocation, as well as its cost.

Of these two possible mappings we select the candidate that leads to the earliest finish time for the task or the cheapest one in case of equality.

The algorithms for these two steps can be found in [5].

5   Experimental Evaluation

To validate our claims we have chosen to use synthetic workloads as they allow us to test workflow patterns of various application types quickly and against a large volume of workflows. We have used a total of 864 generated synthetic PTGs based on three application models: Fast Fourier Transform (FFT), Strassen matrix multiplication and random workloads that allow us to explore a wider range of possible applications. For more details related to the synthetic workloads and their generation we would like to refer the reader to [8], section V. As a basis for our simulator we have used the SIMGRID toolkit [16].

5.1   Platform Description

Throughout our experiments we have used Amazon EC2 [3] as a reference IaaS Cloud. Our virtual resource catalog is inspired by its available virtual resource types as described in Table 1. Given that the network bandwidth information for the *m1*, *m2* and *c1* type instances is not given, we have considered 1 and 10 Gigabit Ethernet for *moderate* and respectively *high* network performance.

Table 1. Amazon EC2's virtual resource types

Name	#VCPUs	Network performance	Cost / hour
m1.small	1	*moderate*	0.09
m1.med	2	*moderate*	0.18
m1.large	4	*high*	0.36
m1.xlarge	8	*high*	0.72
m2.xlarge	6.5	*moderate*	0.506
m2.2xlarge	13	*high*	1.012
m2.4xlarge	26	*high*	2.024
c1.med	5	*moderate*	0.186
c1.xlarge	20	*high*	0.744
cc1.4xlarge	33.5	10 Gigabit Ethernet	0.186
cc2.8xlarge	88	10 Gigabit Ethernet	0.744

As no network bandwidth information is given for *m1*, *m2* and *c1* type instances, we assume that *high* network performance corresponds to a 10 Gigabit Ethernet network and *moderate* corresponds to a 1 Gigabit Ethernet network.

5.2   Comparison of Allocation Times

A first way to compare the proposed procedures is by measuring the time needed to build an allocation. As the Deferred allocation procedure builds and schedules many candidate allocations, it is clearly outperformed by the Eager procedure. On a 16-core Intel Xeon CPU running at 2.93GHz we have obtained the average running time of 21 ms for Eager and 350 ms for Deferred. Eager produces allocations up to an order of magnitude faster than Deferred.

5.3   Simulation Results

We made the budget limit for all the input PTGs vary from 1 to 50 units. With regard to the cost of the cheapest VM type (0.0084 unit per CPU per hour) from the catalog in Table 1, this corresponds to a testing interval from a minimum of 11 CPU hours to a maximum of 5914 CPU hours. Such a range allows bigger PTG to manifest their influence over time to produce a more general trend. It also stresses the algorithms to find out their best operating parameters.

Figure 3 shows plots of aggregated results of makespan and cost after task mapping, for all three application types. The results are presented in box-and-whiskers fashion. The box represents the inter-quartile range (IQR), *i.e.*, , all the values comprised between the first (25%) and third (75%) quartiles, while the whiskers show values up to 1.5 the IQR. The horizontal line within the box indicates the median, or second quartile, value.

First we can see that up to a certain budget value Eager exceeds the budget limit. This means that our initial assumption of 50% VM spare time reuse is too optimistic. Moreover, Eager reaches a point of "saturation", *i.e.*, a point after which makespan does not decrease, due to the T_{CP} *cut-off* strategy after a certain budget limit. This means that, from this point, the same allocation will be produced hence the same task mapping. In the case of Eager, in our test cases this happens on average between the budget values of 20 and 25.

While the T_{CP} cut-off strategy also applies to Deferred, this procedure always underestimates the costs while performing allocations. Then the actual costs of the allocations produced by Deferred will be a lot higher than the budget limit and the actual saturation level will also be higher. In our test cases this happens between the budget values of 25 and 30. However, in combination with the list-scheduling algorithm, Deferred will always select an allocation that, after task mapping, is within the budget limit. In combination with a high saturation level this yields the behavior seen in Figure 3(b). The only moment when Deferred produced allocations that are not in the budget limit is when the budget limit is too tight to accommodate all the tasks in the workflow.

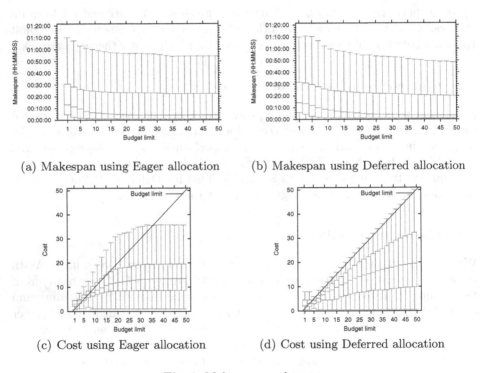

(a) Makespan using Eager allocation   (b) Makespan using Deferred allocation

(c) Cost using Eager allocation   (d) Cost using Deferred allocation

Fig. 3. Makespans and costs

Figure 4 eases the comparison of both procedures. For small budgets, Eager produces shorter yet more expensive schedules than Deferred. As the budget increases, both cost of Eager allocations and length of Deferred schedules decrease. However, the difference is slighter for large budgets than for small budgets.

For small budgets, *i.e.,* while task parallelism can be exploited, Eager outperforms Deferred in terms of makespan by a median of as much as 12%. However, Deferred outperforms Eager in terms of cost by a median of as much as 26% and

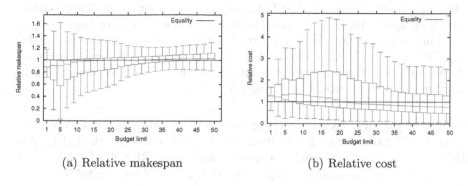

(a) Relative makespan   (b) Relative cost

Fig. 4. Relative makespan and cost ($\frac{Eager}{Deferred}$)

never exceeds the budget limit. The situation changes once task parallelism is fully exploited. The two algorithms then yield the same makespan with a median difference of 2%. Yet, Eager outperforms Deferred in terms of cost by as much as 23%. We can conclude that for small applications and small budgets Deferred should be preferred. When the size of the applications increases or the budget limit approaches task parallelism saturation, using Eager is preferable.

6 Conclusion and Future Work

The elastic allocations offered by IaaS Clouds opened the way for more flexible scheduling approach. Notably, applications modeled by a structure more complex than classic DAG workflows are a good candidate to benefit of an elastic allocation model. Scheduling of Parallel task graph on Grids or Clouds has been widely studied. However, none of the previous works addressed both elastic allocations and non-DAG workflows simultaneously.

In this article we present a first step towards the scheduling of non-deterministic workflows on Clouds under budget constraints. Our approach is to transform this scheduling problem into a set of smaller and well studied sub-problems. Concretely, we split the input non-deterministic workflow into deterministic sub-workflows. Then present two original allocation procedures, *Eager* and *Deferred*, built on the specifics of an IaaS Cloud and provide an algorithm for selecting the most interesting of these allocations such that the budget limit is not reached. We compared these procedures with regard to their execution time, clearly in favor of Eager. When the budget constraint is tight, Eager leads to shorter yet more expensive schedules that usually pass the budget limit. In contrast, Deferred always keeps withing the budget limit when possible, but results in longer makespan schedules. Conversely, for looser budget constraints, that allows for a full exploitation of task parallelism, the difference between the two algorithms in terms of the quality of the resulting schedules is relatively small (median of 2%). Eager is the preferred solution here due to its fast running time.

The take home message is that Deferred is more suited to small applications or small budgets, while Eager is preferred for large applications or large budgets.

As long term goal we plan on integrating the current work into an existing Open Source IaaS Cloud platform. A good improvement will be to determine automatically which is the tipping point up to which Deferred should be used and after which Eager would be the best fit.

Acknowledgments. Experiments presented in this paper were carried out using the Grid'5000 experimental testbed, being developed under the INRIA AL-ADDIN development action with support from CNRS, RENATER and several Universities as well as other funding bodies (see https://www.grid5000.fr).

References

1. van der Aalst, W., Barros, A., ter Hofstede, A., Kiepuszewski, B.: Advanced Workflow Patterns. In: Proc. of the 7th Intl. Conference on Cooperative Information Systems, pp. 18–29 (2000)
2. Altintas, I., Bhagwanani, S., Buttler, D., Chandra, S., Cheng, Z., Coleman, M., Critchlow, T., Gupta, A., Han, W., Liu, L., Ludäscher, B., Pu, C., Moore, R., Shoshani, A., Vouk, M.A.: A modeling and execution environment for distributed scientific workflows. In: Proc. of the 15th Intl. Conference on Scientific and Statistical Database Management, pp. 247–250 (2003)
3. Amazon Elastic Compute Cloud, Amazon EC2 (2012), http://aws.amazon.com/ec2/instance-types/
4. Bahsi, E.M., Ceyhan, E., Kosar, T.: Conditional Workflow Management: A Survey and Analysis. Scientific Programming 15(4), 283–297 (2007)
5. Caron, E., Desprez, F., Muresan, A., Suter, F.: Budget Constrained Resource Allocation for Non-Deterministic Workflows on a IaaS Cloud. Research report (May 2012), http://hal.inria.fr/hal-00697032
6. Couvares, P., Kosar, T., Roy, A., Weber, J., Wenger, K.: Workflow Management in Condor. In: Taylor, I., Deelman, E., Gannon, D., Shields, M. (eds.) Workflows for e-Science, pp. 357–375. Springer (2007)
7. Deelman, E., Singh, G., Su, M.H., Blythe, J., Gil, Y., Kesselman, C., Mehta, G., Vahi, K., Berriman, G.B., Good, J., Laity, A., Jacob, J., Katz, D.: Pegasus: a Framework for Mapping Complex Scientific Workflows onto Distributed Systems. Scientific Programming Journal 13(3), 219–237 (2005)
8. Desprez, F., Suter, F.: A Bi-Criteria Algorithm for Scheduling Parallel Task Graphs on Clusters. In: Proc. of the 10th IEEE/ACM Intl. Symposium on Cluster, Cloud and Grid Computing, pp. 243–252 (2010)
9. Fahringer, T., Jugravu, A., Pllana, S., Prodan, R., Seragiotto Jr., C., Truong, H.L.: ASKALON: a Tool Set for Cluster and Grid Computing. Concurrency - Practice and Experience 17(2-4), 143–169 (2005)
10. Fernandez, H., Tedeschi, C., Priol, T.: A Chemistry Inspired Workflow Management System for Scientific Applications in Clouds. In: Proc. of the 7th Intl. Conference on E-Science, pp. 39–46 (2011)
11. Glatard, T., Montagnat, J., Lingrand, D., Pennec, X.: Flexible and Efficient Workflow Deployment of Data-Intensive Applications on GRIDS with MOTEUR. Intl. Journal of High Performance Computing Applications 3(22), 347–360 (2008); Special Issue on Workflow Systems in Grid Environments

12. Ludäscher, B., Altintas, I., Berkley, C., Higgins, D., Jaeger, E., Jones, M., Lee, E.A., Tao, J., Zhao, Y.: Scientific Workflow Management and the Kepler System. Concurrency and Computation: Practice and Experience 18(10), 1039–1065 (2006)
13. Mao, M., Humphrey, M.: Auto-Scaling to Minimize Cost and Meet Application Deadlines in Cloud Workflows. In: Proc. of the Conference on High Performance Computing Networking, Storage and Analysis (SC 2011) (2011)
14. Mayer, A., McGough, S., Furmento, N., Lee, W., Newhouse, S., Darlington, J.: ICENI Dataflow and Workflow: Composition and Scheduling in Space and Time. In: UK e-Science All Hands Meeting, pp. 627–634. IOP Publishing Ltd. (2003)
15. Oinn, T., Greenwood, M., Addis, M., Alpdemir, N., Ferris, J., Glover, K., Goble, C., Goderis, A., Hull, D., Marvin, D., Li, P., Lord, P., Pocock, M., Senger, M., Stevens, R., Wipat, A., Wroe, C.: Taverna: Lessons in Creating a Workflow Environment for the Life Sciences. Concurrency and Computation: Practice and Experience 18(10), 1067–1100 (2006)
16. Quinson, M.: Simgrid: a generic framework for large-scale distributed experiments. In: Peer-to-Peer Computing, pp. 95–96 (2009)
17. Radulescu, A., van Gemund, A.: A Low-Cost Approach towards Mixed Task and Data Parallel Scheduling. In: Proc. of the 15th Intl. Conference on Parallel Processing (ICPP), pp. 69–76 (2001)
18. Taylor, I., Shields, M., Wang, I., Harrison, A.: The Triana Workflow Environment: Architecture and Applications. In: Workflows for e-Science, pp. 320–339 (2007)
19. Viroli, M., Zambonelli, F.: A Biochemical Approach to Adaptive Service Ecosystems. Information Sciences 180(10), 1876–1892 (2010)
20. Werner, T.: Target Gene Identification from Expression Array Data by Promoter Analysis. Biomolecular Engineering 17(3), 87–94 (2001)

On a Wideband Fast Fourier Transform Using Piecewise Linear Approximations: Application to a Radio Telescope Spectrometer

Hiroki Nakahara[1], Hiroyuki Nakanishi[2], and Tsutomu Sasao[3]

[1] Faculty of Engineering, Kagoshima University, Japan
[2] Faculty of Science, Kagoshima University, Japan
[3] Department of Creative Informatics, Kyushu Institute of Technology, Japan

Abstract. In a radio telescope, a spectrometer analyzes radio frequency (RF) received from celestial objects at the frequency domain by performing a fast fourier transform (FFT). In radio astronomy, the number of points for the FFT is larger than that for the general purpose one. Thus, in a conventional design, the twiddle factor memory becomes too large to implement. In this paper, we realize a twiddle factor by a piecewise linear approximation circuit consisting of a small memory, a multiplier, an adder, and a small logic circuit. We analyze the approximation error for the piecewise liner approximation circuit for the twiddle factor part. We implemented the 2^{30} points FFT by the $R2^k FFT$ with the piecewise linear approximation circuits. Compared with the SETI spectrometer for 2^{27}-FFT, the eight parallelized proposed circuit for 2^{27}-FFT is 41.66 times faster, and that for 2^{30}-FFT is 5.20 times faster. Compared with the GPU-based spectrometer for 2^{27}-FFT, the proposed one is 8.75 times faster and dissipates lower power.

1 Introduction

1.1 Spectrometer on a Radio Telescope

Radio astronomy, which is a subfield of astronomy, studies celestial objects at the radio frequency (RF). In 1931, Karl Jansky, who was an engineer at Bell Telephone Laboratories, observed the RF (14.6 meter wave length) coming from the Milky Way. Since then, observation of the RF by the radio telescope found that celestial objects take a different stance in the RF from the visible light. The development in radio astronomical observatory is expected to help us learn more about the newborn Galaxy in early universe, a birth of a star, an evolution of materials in space, and so on.

Fig. 1 shows the operations in a typical radio telescope. First, the antenna receives the RF coming from the celestial objects. Second, the feedhone sends the electromagnetic wave to the receiver through the waveguide. Third, the receiver transforms it to the intermediate frequency (IF) by using the amplifier and the mixer. Finally, **the spectrometer** converts the voltage wave to the power spectrum. The early spectrometer used the filter bank consisting of many analog filters for the specified frequency. However, in the spectrometer using filter bank, the bandwidth is too narrow. After that, the acoustooptical spectrometer (AOS) based on the diffraction of light at ultrasonic waves was

Y. Xiang et al. (Eds.): ICA3PP 2012, Part I, LNCS 7439, pp. 202–217, 2012.

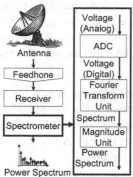

Fig. 1. Ratio Telescope and
Digital Spectrometer

Table 1. Comparison of the number of points N

	Application	N
General Purpose [25]	Baseband 3GPP	2^{10}-2^{11}
	OFDM	2^8
	CT scanner	2^{10}-2^{13}
	High Quality Sound	2^9
Radio Telescope	Zeeman effect in the OH emission	2^{20}
	SETI Spectrometer	2^{27}

developed. However, in the AOS, adjusting non-linear characteristics in the analog device (such as piezo element) is difficult. Nowadays, digital spectrometers are used for a wide range of radio telescopes. Fig. 1 also shows operations of the digital spectrometer. First, the analog-to-digital converter (ADC) converts the IF voltage wave to the digital signal. Then, the Fourier transform unit performs **the fast Fourier transform (FFT)** to obtain the spectrum. Finally, the magnitude unit calculates the power spectrum. The computation of magnitude is a light task, while that of Fourier transform is a heavy task. Thus, in the digital spectrometer, hardware for the Fourier transform is indispensable.

1.2 Requirement of Radio Telescope

Wideband Analysis: Benefits for the wideband analysis of the RF are as follows [16]: The first benefit is the expansion of measurement range of physical parameter. For example, by obtaining spectrum for atoms, and bright lines from ionized gas, we can investigate new gas component and perform measurement of temperature between the stars. The second benefit is the improvement of sensitivity of the radio telescope. The noise of the measurement data is proportional to $\frac{1}{\sqrt{f}}$, where f is the bandwidth. Thus, an increase of f enhances the sensitivity. As a result, we can detect more dark stars.

Table 1 compares numbers of points N for the radio telescope with that for general purpose FFTs. The FPGA implementation of the conventional FFT requires $O(\log_2 N)$ multipliers and $O(N\log_2 N)$ bits of memory [26]. Table 1 implies that, for the radio telescope, in the conventional implementation of FFT, the memory would be too large to implement.

High-Speed Operation: In the radio telescope, the aperture synthetic radar technology produces a high resolution data from multiple radio telescopes. Thus, the high-speed operation is required

Limited Space: Since the RF from celestial objects is absorbed by water molecules and oxygen molecules, the radio telescope should be located at the altitude of 4,000-5,000 meters summit of mountains such as Mauna Kea on the island of Hawaii, Atacama desert of the Andes Mountains[1]. Also, since the RF with long wavelength is reflected at ionization layer, a satellite measurement at outer space is necessary. In 1997, the radio telescope satellite HALCA (Highly Advanced Laboratory for Communications and Astronomy) was on a mission [6]. In the satellite, the super computer requiring huge space is unacceptable.

Low Power Consumption: At the summit of mountains or outer space, the power source is also limited. Thus, low-power consumption is required. For example, NASA's MARVEL (Mars Volcano Emission and Life) mission requires a circuit that dissipates less than 10 W power [14]. Although the GPU outperforms the FPGA [8], it dissipates much higher power. Thus, the GPU-based method is unacceptable.

Therefore, we use the FPGA board to implement the spectrometer.

1.3   Related Works

The Square Kilometer Array (SKA) is developing the next generation radio telescope with a large collecting area (a square kilometer) for the RF [20]. The SERENDIP (Search for Extraterrestrial Radio Emissions from Nearby Developed Intelligent Populations project), which is one of a SETI (Search for Extra-Terrestrial Intelligence) project [21], uses **the SETI spectrometer** analyzing $f = 200$ MHz bandwidth with $\Delta f = 2$ Hz in one second [17]. In this case, the 2^{27}-point FFT operations are necessary.

Cooley and Tukey proposed **the fast Fourier transform (FFT)** based on radix two [3]. Duhamel et al. proposed the split-radix FFT [4]. Radix 3, 2^2, 4, 5, and 8 FFTs were proposed in [13,10,5]. As for the FFT implementation, He et al. proposed the radix 2^2 single delay path feedback FFT [7]. Knight and Rabiner analyzed error with respect to the fixed point FFT [12,18]. Zhou et al. analyzed the amount of hardware [26]. To implement the twiddle factor part, the pipelined CORDIC [1] and the piecewise linear approximations [9,22,19] were considered. Kondo et al. implemented the equivalent SETI spectrometer on the NVIDIA's Tesla S1070 utilizing four GPUs [11].

Since the amount of embedded memory is a bottleneck, related works could not realize the wide-band spectrometer. In this paper, we propose the reduction technique for the embedded memory on the FPGA.

1.4   Contribution of This Paper

Due of the constraints in the space and the power consumption, we adopt a single-FPGA board for the wideband FFT. In the FFT, we need the twiddle factor memory and the transform memory. First, we extend the radix of the FFT to 2^k to reduce the number of transform memories. We realize the transform memory by the DDR2SDRAM. Second, we replace the twiddle factor memory with the piecewise linear approximation using the memory. In this way, we implemented the wideband FFT. Contributions of this paper are as follows:

---

[1] Currently, ALMA (Atacama Large Millimeter/submeter Array) project is going to build a new radio telescope at the Andes Mountains.

Analysis of the Area of a Conventional FFT: We analyze the area of a conventional FFT, then show that the memory size of the twiddle factor is a bottleneck.

Realization of the Wideband and Compact FFT Circuit Using Piecewise Linear Approximation Circuits: We implement the 2^{27}-FFT on the FPGA board, and show its performance and area. Then, we compare the FPGA-based FFT with the GPU-based FFT.

The rest of the paper is organized as follows: Chapter 2 shows the radix 2^k FFT and its area complexity; Chapter 3 replaces the twiddle factor memory with the piecewise linear approximation circuit; Chapter 4 shows the experimental results; and Chapter 5 concludes the paper.

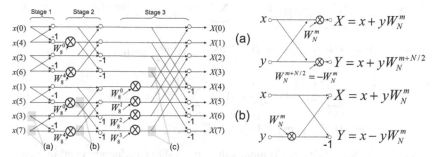

Fig. 2. Dataflow for 8-DFT   **Fig. 3.** Butterfly operator

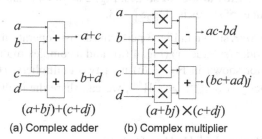

(a) Complex adder   (b) Complex multiplier

Fig. 4. Complex operators

2 Radix 2^k Fast Fourier Transform ($R2^k FFT$)

2.1 N-Point Discrete Fourier Transform

Let $x(n), (n = 0, 1, \ldots, N-1)$ be the input signal. **The N-point discrete Fourier transform (N-DFT) is**

$$X(m) = \sum_{n=0}^{N-1} x(n) W_N^{nm}, (m = 0, 1, \ldots, N-1), \qquad (1)$$

where W_N^{nm} **is a twiddle factor**. It is defined as

$$W_N^{nm} = e^{-j\frac{2\pi}{N}nm} = \cos(\frac{2\pi}{N}nm) + j\sin(\frac{2\pi}{N}nm), \qquad (2)$$

where j is the imaginary unit. In this paper, we assume that the input signal $x(n)$ is a complex number, N is a power of two, and $\frac{k}{N} \in [0, 1.0)$.

2.2 N-Point Fast Fourier Transform (FFT)

Cooley and Tukey proposed **the N-point fast Fourier transform (N-FFT)** that reduces the number of multipliers to $O(N\log_2 N)$. In this paper, we adopt **the decimation-in-time N-FFT**.

Here, we convert the N-DFT into the N-FFT. In Expr. (1), suppose that N input signals are partitioned into odd indices and even ones, then we have

$$X(m) = \sum_{n=0}^{N/2-1} x(2n)W_N^{2nm} + \sum_{n=0}^{N/2-1} x(2n+1)W_N^{(2n+1)m}.$$

Since $W_N^{2mn} = e^{-j(2\pi/N)2mn} = e^{-j(2\pi/(N/2))mn} = W_{N/2}^{mn}$, we have

$$X(m) = \sum_{n=0}^{N/2-1} x(2n)W_{N/2}^{nm} + W_N^m \sum_{n=0}^{N/2-1} x(2n+1)W_{N/2}^{nm} \qquad (3)$$

$$= DFT_{even}(m) + W_N^m DFT_{odd}(m),$$

where $m = 0, 1, \ldots, \frac{N}{2} - 1$. Expr. (3) means that the N-DFT is decomposed into two $\frac{N}{2}$-DFTs. By applying Expr. (3) to the N-DFT $s = \log_2 N$ times recursively, we have the N-FFT, where s is **the number of stages**. Fig. 2 shows the dataflow of the 8-FFT. In this case, the number of stages is $\lceil \log_2 8 \rceil = 3$.

The Butterfly Operator. shown in Fig. 3 performs a basic operation in N-FFT. It consists of a complex adder (subtracter) (Fig. 4 (a)) and a complex multiplier (Fig. 4 (b)). The butterfly operator shown in Fig. 3 (a) uses two multipliers. However, by using the symmetric property $W_N^{m+N/2} = -W_N^m$, we can share the multiplier as shown in Fig. 3 (b).

2.3   Radix 2^k Butterfly ($R2^k Butterfly$)

The butterfly operator can be realized by adders and multipliers on an FPGA. The twiddle factors are stored in **the twiddle factor memory**. We assign the stage numbers as $1, 2, \ldots, \log_2 N$ from the input to the output. In the stage 1, the inputs for the butterfly operation are applied to the adjacent points, and the results are sent to the adjacent points (Fig. 2 (a)). In the stage 2, the inputs for the butterfly operation are applied to the distance-two points, and the results are sent to distance-two points (Fig. 2 (b)). In the stage 3, the inputs for the butterfly operation are applied to the distance-four points, and the results are sent to distance-four points (Fig. 2 (c)). Since these operations are done sequentially from the top to the bottom, **the timing adjuster** is necessary between adjacent stages. **The radix-2^k butterfly unit** for the N-FFT can be realized by the timing adjuster, the butterfly operator, and the twiddle factor memory [7].

Example 2.1. *Fig. 5 shows the radix-2^3 butterfly unit realizing the 8-FFT shown in Fig. 2.*   ∎

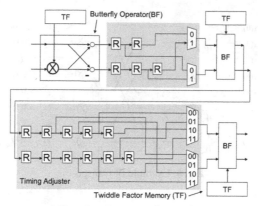

Fig. 5. Radix 2^3 butterfly unit ($R2^3 Butterfly$) for 8-FFT

Here, we analyze the amount of hardware for the radix-2^k butterfly unit. Let $s = \log_2 N$ be the number of stages for the N-FFT. In the radix-2^k butterfly unit for N-FFT, the number of multipliers is $\log_2 N$. Fig. 4 (b) shows that a complex multiplier is realize by four integer multipliers. Thus, the number of integer multipliers Mul_{R2^k} is

$$Mul_{R2^k} = 4s = 4\lceil \log_2 N \rceil.$$

Fig. 3 shows that a butterfly operator consists of a complex multiplier and two complex adders. Two integer adders are necessary for a complex multiplier, and four integer adders are necessary for two complex adders. Thus, the number of integer adders Add_{R2^k} is

$$Add_{R2^k} = (4+2)s = 6\lceil \log_2 N \rceil.$$

For stage i, the number of necessary registers is $2^i + 2^{i-1} - 1$. Note that, the stage 1 uses no register. Thus, the total number of registers Reg_{R2^k} is

$$Reg_{R2^k} = \sum_{i=2}^{s}(2^i + 2^{i-1} - 1).$$

We assume that the selector consists of multiplexers with two data inputs (2-MUXs),. For stage i, a pair of selectors consisting of $2^{i-1} - 1$ copies of 2-MUXs are necessary. Thus, the total number of 2-MUXs is

$$Mux_{R2^k} = 2 \times \sum_{i=2}^{s}(2^{i-1} - 1).$$

The amount of the twiddle factor memory $TwiddleMem_{R2^k}$ is

$$TwiddleMem_{R2^k} = Ns.$$

Therefore, for the radix-2^k butterfly unit, registers and 2-MUXs will be the bottlenecks for the implementation.

For radix-2^k butterfly units, since different stages handle points with different distances, numbers of registers and 2-MUXs increase. By applying **the transpose**

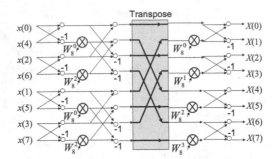

Fig. 6. Example of transpose

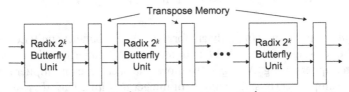

Fig. 7. Radix-2^k FFT with transpose ($R2^k FFT$).

operation replacing indices between adjacent stages, we can adjust the points of the inputs for the butterfly operators. As a result, numbers of registers and 2-MUXs can be reduced. **The transpose memory** performs such a transpose operation.

Example 2.2. *Fig. 6 shows an example of applying transpose operation between stage 2 and stage 3 on the dataflow shown in Fig. 2. In this case, since the inputs for the butterfly operators become adjacent points, no timing adjuster is necessary.* ∎

Consider an N-FFT with $s = \lceil \log_2 N \rceil$ stages. Fig. 7 shows **the radix 2^k FFT with transpose memory**. The R2^{k}FFT has $q = \frac{s}{k}$ radix-2^k butterfly units, and q transpose memories. Thus, increasing k decreases the number of transpose memories.

The number of multipliers $Mul_{R2^k FFT}$ for the $R2^k FFT$ is

$$Mul_{R2^k FFT} = 4s = 4\lceil \log_2 N \rceil.$$

The number of adders $Add_{R2^k FFT}$ for the $R2^k FFT$ is

$$Add_{R2^k FFT} = 6s = 6\lceil \log_2 N \rceil.$$

The number of registers $Reg_{R2^k FFT}$ for the $R2^k FFT$ is

$$Reg_{R2^k FFT} = q \sum_{i=2}^{k} (2^i + 2^{i-1} - 1). \tag{4}$$

In this case, since k is assume to be a large number, we have $q \ll \log_2 N$. The number of 2-MUXs $Mux_{R2^k FFT}$ for the $R2^k FFT$ is

$$Mux_{R2^k FFT} = q \sum_{i=2}^{k} (2^{i-1} - 1). \tag{5}$$

The amount for the transpose memory $TransMem_{R2^kFFT}$ for the $R2^kFFT$ is

$$TranMem_{R2^kFFT} = Nq. \tag{6}$$

When $k \simeq s$, $TransMem_{R2^kFFT}$ is $O(N)$. For the given number of stages s, Exprs. (4) and (5) show that, the increase of k increases numbers of registers and 2-MUXs. Thus, we must find the suitable k that is feasible for given hardware. In our implementation, k is obtained experimentally[2]. The amount of the twiddle factor memory $TwiddleMem_{R2^k}$ for the $R2^kFFT$ is

$$TwiddleMem_{R2^kFFT} = Ns. \tag{7}$$

From above analysis, in the $R2^kFFT$, the amount of memory for the twiddle factor memory is the bottleneck.

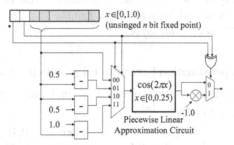

Fig. 8. Circuit for $\cos(x)$

3   Twiddle Factor Circuit Using Piecewise Linear Approximation

3.1   Piecewise Linear Approximation Circuit

From Expr. (2), the twiddle factors consist of $\cos(2\pi x)$ and $\sin(2\pi x)$, where $x \in [0, 1.0)$. A straightforward method to realize the twiddle factors is to use a single memory, where the address is the binary representation of x and the content of that address is the corresponding value of the twiddle factor. However, with this simple approach, the memory size can be very large. **The piecewise linear approximation** implements such function, and its hardware tends to be small [9,22]. First, the domain for x is divided into **segments**. Then, in each segment, the function is approximated by the linear function $c_0 x + c_1$. In this way, the number of memory locations is reduced to the number of segments. Although we need to store two numbers, c_1 and c_0, the total memory needed is much lower. In the piecewise linear approximation, the approximation error occurs. In [19], the number representation and precision are defined.

Definition 3.1. **The binary fixed-point representation** *of a value r has the form $(d_{l-1},$ $d_{l-2}, \ldots, d_1, d_0. d_{-1}, d_{-2}, \ldots, d_{-m})_2$, where $d_i \in \{0, 1\}$, l is the number of bits for the integer part, and m is the number of bits for the fractional part of r. This representation is two's complement and, so, $r = -2^{l-1}d_{l-1} + \sum_{i=-m}^{l-2} 2^i d_i$.*

---

[2] In the implementation, we set $k = \lceil \frac{s}{3} \rceil$.

Definition 3.2. Error *is the absolute difference between the exact value and the value produced by the hardware.* **Approximation error** *is the error caused by a function approximation.* **Rounding error** *is the error caused by a binary fixed-point representation. It is the result of truncation or rounding, whichever is applied. However, both operations yield an error that is called rounding error.* **Acceptable error** *is the maximum error that an approximation may assume.* **Acceptable approximation error** *is the maximum approximation error that a function approximation may assume.*

Definition 3.3. Precision *is the total number of bits for a binary fixed-point representation. Specially,* n**-bit precision** *specifies that* n *bits are used to represent the number, that is,* $n = l + m$. *An* n**-bit precision** *approximation function has an* n*-bit input.*

Definition 3.4. Accuracy *is the number of bits in the fractional part of a binary fixed-point representation. Specially,* m**-bit accuracy** *specifies that* m *bits are used to represent the fractional part of the number. In this paper,* **an** m**-bit accuracy approximation** *is an approximation with an* m*-bit fractional part of the input, an* m*-bit fractional part of the output, and a* 2^{-m} *acceptable error.*

3.2 Reduction of Approximation Error for Trigonometric Functions

In the FFT, the twiddle factors consists of $\cos(2\pi x)$ and $\sin(2\pi x)$, where $x \in [0, 1.0)$. By using the symmetry property, we have

$$
\cos(2\pi x) = \begin{cases} \cos(2\pi x) & \text{when } x \in [0, 0.25), \\ -\cos(2\pi(0.5 - x)) & \text{when } x \in [0.25, 0.5), \\ -\cos(2\pi(x - 0.5)) & \text{when } x \in [0.5, 0.75), \\ \cos(2\pi(1.0 - x)) & \text{when } x \in [0.75, 1.00). \end{cases}
$$

Similarly, we have

$$
\sin(2\pi x) = \begin{cases} \cos(2\pi(0.25 - x)) & \text{when } x \in [0, 0.25), \\ \cos(2\pi(x - 0.25)) & \text{when } x \in [0.25, 0.5), \\ -\cos(2\pi(0.75 - x)) & \text{when } x \in [0.5, 0.75), \\ -\cos(2\pi(x - 0.75)) & \text{when } x \in [0.75, 1.00). \end{cases}
$$

These functions are realized by $\cos(2\pi x)$ where $x \in [0, 0.25)$. Fig. 8 shows the circuit for $\cos(2\pi x)$. Note that cosine function is monotone decreasing when $x \in [0, 0.25)$.

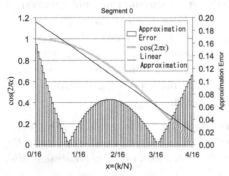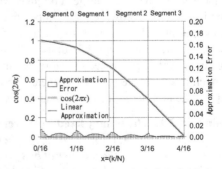

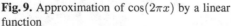

Fig. 9. Approximation of $\cos(2\pi x)$ by a linear function

Fig. 10. Approximations of $\cos(2\pi x)$ by four linear functions

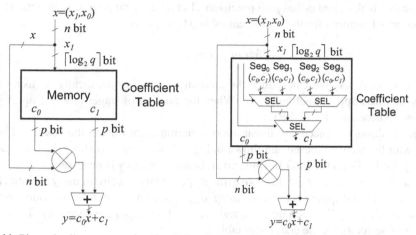

Fig. 11. Piecewise linear approximation using the memory

Fig. 12. Piecewise linear approximation using the selector

Example 3.3. *Fig. 9 illustrates the approximation of $cos(2\pi x)$, where $x \in [0, 0.25)$, by a linear function. Fig. 10 divides the domain into four segments uniformly, and approximates each segments by a linear function. In Fig. 10, these segments are approximated by*

$$f_{seg_0} = -0.003390x + 1.012637,$$
$$f_{seg_1} = -0.009659x + 1.152129,$$
$$f_{seg_2} = -0.014456x + 1.365152, and$$
$$f_{seg_3} = -0.017052x + 1.536663.$$

Obviously, the increase of segments decreases the approximation error. ∎

The piecewise linear approximation circuit is realized by **the coefficient table**, the adder, and the multiplier. To approximate the function for given x, first, the coefficient table generates c_0 and c_1 corresponding the segment for x [3]. Then, the adder and the multiplier computes $c_0 \times x + c_1$. Two types realizations of the coefficient table exist: One is the memory-based, and the other is the selector-based. Fig. 11 shows the piecewise linear approximation circuit using the memory.

We analyze the area for the piecewise linear approximation circuit using the memory. From Fig. 11, the number of multipliers Mul_{Linear} is

$$Mul_{Linear} = 1.$$

The number of adders Add_{Linear} is

$$Add_{Linear} = 1.$$

---

[3] As shown in Example 3.3, for $x \in [0, 0.25)$, since $c_0 < 0.00$, the coefficient table need not store the sign bit. Also, since $1.00 < c_1 < 2.00$, it need not store the integer bit.

Assume that both c_0 and c_1 has p bit precision[4]. Let q be the number of segments. Then, the amount of memory for the coefficient table Mem_{coef} is

$$Mem_{coef} = 2pq \qquad (8)$$

Since $p < q \ll N$, we can reduce the amount of memory drastically by using the piecewise linear approximation circuit. When the number of stages is $s = \lceil \log_2 N \rceil$, s circuits are necessary for N-FFT.

Fig. 12 shows the piecewise linear approximation circuit using the selector. Compared with the memory-based one shown in Fig. 11, this circuit realizes the coefficient table by the LUTs on the FPGA. Thus, no embedded memory is necessary.

We analyze the area for the piecewise linear approximation circuit using the selector. The number of multipliers is the same as Mul_{Linear}, also, the number of adders is the same as Add_{Linear}. For each bit of c_0 and c_1, $q - 1$ selectors are necessary. Thus, the number of selectors for the coefficient table Sel_{coef} is

$$Sel_{coef} = 2p(q - 1). \qquad (9)$$

When the number of stages is $s = \lceil \log_2 N \rceil$, s circuits are necessary for N-FFT.

3.3   Analysis of the Approximation Error

Since the piecewise linear approximation circuit approximates the original function, it causes the approximation error. When the piecewise linear approximation circuit has n bit precision, the internal circuit must compute p bit, where $p > n$. Example 3.3 shows that, in the piecewise linear approximation circuit, the increase of the number of segments q decreases the approximation error. Also, the increase of p decreases it. However, Exprs (8) and (9) show that large q and p increase the hardware. The optimal values for q and p are desired.

Table 2. Approximation error (2^{-18} acceptable error) with respect to numbers of internal bits p and number of segments q

Internal	Number of segments q		
bit p	128	256	512
18	.00029756	.00028991	.00025177
19	.00016021	.00014495	.00013732
20	.00007629	.00007522	.00007437
21	.00003851	.00003514	.00003513
22	.00001525	.00001525	.00001525
23	.00000762	.00000762	.00000762
24	.00000762	.00000000	.00000000

In this paper, we obtain q and p experimentally. Since the SETI spectrometer, which treats the largest wideband, uses 18 bit fixed point precision, we assumed that the acceptable approximation error is 2^{-18}. Then, we obtained q and p for $\cos(x)$ and $\sin(x)$

---

[4] Although, c_0 and c_1 may have different precisions, to make the discussion simple, we assume that both have the same precisions.

that satisfies the acceptable one. Table 2 shows that the approximation error with respect to q and p. From Table 2, when $q = 256$ and $p = 24$, it satisfies the acceptable approximation error. We implement the piecewise linear approximation circuit with these values.

4   Experimental Results

4.1   Implementation Environment

We implemented the R2^{k}FFT on the Altera's DE4 development and education board (FPGA: Altera's Stratix IV GX530, ALUTs 424,960, REGs: 424,960, M9ks: 1,280, and 18×18 DSP blocks: 1,024). This board has two DDR2SO-DIMMs, one PCI Express ($\times 8$), and two HSMCs (high-speed connector) to connect the high-speed AD converter. We used the Altera's Quartus II version 11.0 to synthesize, and the Altera's MegaCore Function to generate the DDR2SO-DIMM controller and the PCI Express controller.

Exprs. (4) and (5) show that, numbers of registers and 2-MUXs increase with $O(2^k)$. The DE4 FPGA board has two DDR2SO-DIMMs. We implemented the R2^{k}FFT consisting of three radix-2^k butterfly units, where $k = \lceil \frac{log_2 N}{3} \rceil$. We used the ADC1x5000-8

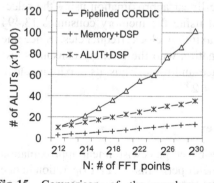

Fig. 13. Comparison of the numbers of M9ks (Available: 1,280)

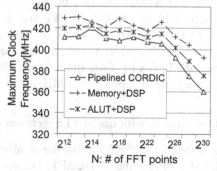

Fig. 14. Comparison of the numbers of DSP blocks (Available: 1,024)

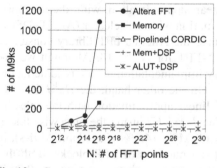

Fig. 15. Comparison of the numbers of ALUTs (Available: 424,960)

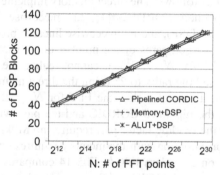

Fig. 16. Comparison of the maximum clock frequencies

(dual 2.5 Giga sample per second, 4bit). The implemented FFT extended to 36-bit fixed point two's complement complex numbers (18-bit real and 18-bit imaginary). In the butterfly operation in each stage of the FFT, the width grows by 1 bit by the addition and subtraction. This may yield ($\log_2 N + w$)-bit outputs for w-bit data [5,18]. To avoid an overflow, the scaling schedule is used to divide the values by a factor of $2^{\lceil (4+N-w/k)\rceil}$ in each $R2^k$ butterfly operator. Although this produces the scaling error, the radio astronomy requires high-speed and wideband operations rather than the precision. To avoid overflow in the FFT operations, we used the rounding and saturation unit (RSU) in each DSP block. The SETI spectrometer also uses 36-bit fixed point two's complement complex numbers in the FFT part. To reduce hardware of the FFT part, the SETI spectrometer partitions the frequency band to r sub-bands by using FIR filters, and uses smaller $\frac{N}{r}$-FFTs [17]. On the other hand, our FFT directly performs the FFT operation. Thus, our FFT has a smaller error margin than the SETI spectrometer.

4.2   Comparison with Other FFT Libraries

We compared the $R2^k FFT$ with the Altera's MegaCore Function library ($R2^k FFT$) with respect to the amount of hardware (M9ks, ALUTs, and DSPs) and the maximum clock frequency. In the $R2^k FFT$, we implemented four types of twiddle factor part as follows: The direct memory implementation (Memory); the pipelined CORDIC (Pipelined CORDIC) [1]; the piecewise linear approximation with the memory (Mem+DSP); and the piecewise linear approximation with the selector (ALUT+DSP). Fig. 13 compares of the number of M9ks. Since the Altera's FFT library consumes 93.7% for $N = 2^{16}$, it cannot realize the 2^N-FFT for $N > 16$. Although we increased the radix to 2^k using the direct memory implementation for the twiddle factor part, it cannot realize the FFT for $N \geq 2^{18}$. On the other hand, the $R2^k FFT$ using the pipelined CORDIC and the piecewise linear approximation with the selector for the twiddle factor part requires no M9k. The $R2^k FFT$ using the piecewise linear approximation with the memory requires only 60 M9ks (4.6% of available M9Ks), it fits on a modern FPGA. Fig. 14 compares of the numbers of DSP blocks. Both the pipelined CORDIC and the piecewise linear approximation circuits consume 120 DSP blocks (9.4% of available DSP blocks) for 2^{30}-FFT. They fits on the FPGA. Fig. 15 compares required numbers of ALUTs. For $N = 2^{30}$, the pipelined CORDIC consumes 101,814 ALUTs (23.9%), the piecewise linear approximation using the selector consumes 35,304 ALUTs (8.3%), and that using the memory consumes 13,494 ALUTs (3.1%). Fig. 16 compares of the maximum clock frequencies. Since the $R2^k FFT$ using the piecewise linear approximation with the memory consumes less hardware, the FPGA has extra space for the place-and-route. Thus, its maximum clock frequency was the highest (395.27 MHz for $N = 2^{30}$).

4.3   Comparison with the SETI Spectrometer

We compared the $R2^k FFT$ using the memory-based piecewise linear approximation with the SETI spectrometer. The SETI spectrometer performs 2^{27} FFT operation in one second. For 2^{27}-FFT, the eight parallel proposed FFTs consumed 93,032 ALUTs, 416 M9ks, and 832 DSP blocks. Its maximum clock frequency was 372.1 MHz. To run the

Table 3. Comparison of GPUs with the proposed method for 2^{27}-FFT

Method	Time for 2^{27}-FFT [sec]	Additional Hardware
1GPU	0.442	
2GPU	0.295	Sharing PCI Express
4GPU	0.210	Sharing PCI Express
Eight parallel $R2^k FFT$	0.024	two DDR2SDRAMs

DDR2SO-DIMM[5] at 667 MHz, we set the system clock frequency to 333 MHz by using the PLL. Since the one FFT handles two points per one clock (333 MHz), it handles per $\frac{1}{333 \times 2^{20}}$ second. Thus, the operation time to handle 2^{27} points was $\frac{2^{27}}{333 \times 2^{20}} \times \frac{1}{16} = 0.024$ second. Therefore, our FFT utilizing eight parallel FFTs is 41.66 times faster than the SETI spectrometer.

For 2^{30}-FFT, our FFT utilizing eight parallel FFTs consumed 107,952 ALUTs, 480 M9ks, and 960 DSP blocks. Its maximum clock frequency was 342.7 MHz. We also set the system clock frequency to 333 MHz for the DDR2SO-DIMM. The operation time to handle 2^{30} points was $\frac{2^{30}}{333 \times 2^{20}} \times \frac{1}{16} = 0.192$ second. Therefore, our FFTs utilizing eight parallel FFTs is 5.20 times faster than the SETI spectrometer, and performs eight times wider bandwidth FFT than the SETI spectrometer.

4.4 Comparison with GPUs

With respect to the 2^{27}-FFT used for the SETI spectrometer, we compared our FFT with the GPU-based spectrometer (NVIDIA Corp. Tesla S1070 GPU computing system, four GPUs, total VRAM: 16 GB, Power: 800 W) [23]. Table 3 shows that, our FFT is 8.75 times faster than the four GPUs, is 12.29 times faster than the two GPUs, and is 18.41 times faster than the single GPU. Since the power consumption for the FFT board used in our implementation is less than 10 W, our FFT dissipates much lower power than the GPU-based ones. As for the space, our FFT uses PCI slot, while the Tesla S1070 requires one rack unit. Thus, our FFT is smaller than the GPU-based one. These comparisons show that out FFT is superior to GPU-based one for the radio telescope. Note that, for the precision, the GPU uses 32-bit floating point, while out FFT uses 36-bit fixed point. Although the GPU-based one has more accuracy than our FFT, in the radio telescope, the high-speed and compact realization is more important than the accuracy. In fact, the SETI spectrometer adopts 36 bits fixed point as same as our system.

5   Conclusion

This paper showed wideband $R2^k$FFT with a piecewise linear approximation circuits. The piecewise linear approximation circuit divide the domain of a function into segments, and approximates the function by linear functions. It consists of a multiplier, an adder, and a coefficient table. We consider two types of realizations of the coefficient

---

[5] In our implementation, we used PC2-5300 DDR2SDRAM (dual channel), its bandwidth is 10.666 Giga Bytes per second. It has eight banks, and we used posted-CAS operation.

table; memory-based and selector-based. We implemented the 2^{27} FFT with piecewise linear approximation circuits using the memory on the Altera's FPGA. Compared with the Altera's FFT library, our implementation has 2^{14} times wider band. Compared with the FFT with the pipelined CORDIC, as for the number of ALUTs, our implementation is 7.54 times smaller. Compared with the $R2^k$FFT using a selector-based one, as for the number of ALUTs, the memory-based FFT is 2.61 times smaller. Although the $R2^k$FFT with the memory-based piecewise linear approximation consumes 4.6% of available memory, it is feasible. Also, compared with the SETI spectrometer, realizing the same numbers of points of the FFT, our implementation is 41.66 times faster. Compared with the GPU-based spectrometer, our implementation is 8.75 times faster and dissipates much lower power. Thus, our FFT circuit is suitable for a radio telescope.

Acknowledgments. This research is supported in part by the grant of Young Researcher Overseas Visits Program for Vitalizing Brain Circulation, and subsidy for Young Researchers by Kagoshima University.

References

1. Andraka, R.: A survey of CORDIC algorithms for FPGA based computers. In: FPGA 1998, pp. 191–200 (1998)
2. Altera Corp., FFT MegaCore Function v11.0 (2011)
3. Cooley, J.W., Tukey, J.W.: An algorithm for the machine computation of complex fourier series. Mathematics of Computation 19, 297–301 (1965)
4. Duhamel, P., Hollmann, H.: Split-radix FFT algorithm. Electron. Lett. 20, 14–16 (1984)
5. Goedecker, S.: Fast radix 2,3,4 and 5 kernels for fast fourier transformations on computers with overlapping multiply-add instructions. SIAM Journal Sci. Compt. 18, 1605–1611 (1997)
6. HALCA: Highly Advanced Laboratory for Communications and Astronomy, http://www.vsop.isas.jaxa.jp/top.html
7. He, S., Torkelson, M.: A new approach to pipeline FFT processor. In: IPPS 1996, pp. 766–770 (1996)
8. Jones, D.H., Powell, A., Bouganis, C.S., Cheung, P.Y.K.: GPU Versus FPGA for High Productivity Computing. In: FPL 2010, pp. 119–124 (2010)
9. Jain, V.K., Wadekar, S.A., Lin, L.: A universal nonlinear component and its application to WSI. IEEE Trans. Components, Hybrids, and Manufacturing Technology 16(7), 656–664 (1993)
10. Karner, H., et al.: Multiply-add optimized FFT kernels. Math. Models and Methods in Appl. Sci. 11, 105–117 (2001)
11. Kondo, H., Heien, E., Okita, M., Werthimer, D., Hagihara, K.: A multi-GPU spectrometer system for real-time wide bandwidth radio signal analysis. In: ISPA 2010, pp. 594–604 (2010)
12. Knight, W.R., Kaiser, R.: A Simple Fixed-Point Error Bound for the Fast Fourier Transform. IEEE Trans. Acoustics, Speech and Signal Proc. 27(6), 615–620 (1979)
13. Linzer, E.N., Feig, E.: Implementation of efficient FFT algorithms on fused multiply-add architectures. IEEE Trans. Signal Processing 41, 93–107 (1993)
14. Mars Scout Program, http://www.nasa.gov/
15. Muller, J.M.: Elementary function: algorithms and implementation, 2nd edn. Birkhauser Boston, Inc., New York (2006)

16. Hirota, A., Kuno, N., Sato, N., Nakanishi, H., Tosaki, T., Sorai, K.: Variation of molecular gas properties across the spiral arms in IC 342: Large-scale 13CO (1-0) emission. PASJ (62), 1261–1275 (2010)
17. Parsons, A., et al.: PetaOp/Second FPGA signal processing for SETI and radio astronomy. In: Proc. of the Asilomar Conference on Signals, Systems, and Computers (2006)
18. Rabiner, L.R., Gold, B.: Theory and Application of Digital Signal Processing. Prentice-Hall Inc. (1975)
19. Sasao, T., Nagayama, S., Butler, J.T.: Numerical function generators using LUT cascades. IEEE Trans. on Comput. 56(6), 826–838 (2007)
20. SKA: Square Kilometre Array, http://www.skatelescope.org/
21. SERENDIP: The Search for extra terrestrial intelligence at UC Berkeley, http://seti.berkeley.edu/SERENDIP/
22. Schulte, M.J., Stine, J.E.: Approximating elementary functions with symmetric bipartite tables. IEEE Trans. Comput. 48(8), 842–847 (1999)
23. Nvidia Corp., TESLA S1070 GPU Computing System, http://www.nvidia.com/
24. Volder, J.E.: The CORDIC trigonometric computing technique. IRE Trans. on Electronic Computers, 330–334 (1959)
25. Xilinx Inc., LogiCORE IP fast fourier transform v7.1 (2011)
26. Zhou, B., Peng, Y., Hwang, D.: Pipeline FFT architectures optimized for FPGAs. Int'l Journal of Reconfigurable Computing (2009)

A Verified Library of Algorithmic Skeletons on Evenly Distributed Arrays

Wadoud Bousdira[1], Frédéric Loulergue[1], and Julien Tesson[2]

[1] LIFO, University of Orléans, France
{Wadoud.Bousdira,Frederic.Loulergue}@univ-orleans.fr
[2] Kochi University of Technology, Japan
tesson.julien@kochi-tech.ac.jp

Abstract. To make parallel programming as widespread as parallel architectures, more structured parallel programming paradigms are necessary. One of the possible approaches are algorithmic skeletons. They can be seen as higher order functions implemented in parallel. Algorithmic skeletons offer a simple interface to the programmer without all the details of parallel implementations as they abstract the communications and the synchronisations of parallel activities. To write a parallel program, users have to combine and compose the skeletons.

Orléans Skeleton Library (OSL) is an efficient meta-programmed C++ library of algorithmic skeletons that manipulate distributed arrays. A prototype implementation of OSL exists as a library written with the function parallel language Bulk Synchronous Parallel ML (BSML). In this paper we are interested in verifying the correctness of a subset of this prototype implementation. To do so, we give a functional specification of a subset of OSL and we prove the correctness of the BSML implementation with respect to this functional specification, using the Coq proof assistant. To illustrate how the user could use these skeletons, we prove the correctness of two applications implemented with them.

Keywords: Parallel programming, algorithmic skeletons, program specification, program verification, proof assistant.

1 Introduction

While parallel architectures are now everywhere, parallel programming is not so widespread. The most widespread models are very related to the architectures for which they have been conceived: threads and locks for shared memory and message passing for distributed memory. In the sequential case, unstructured programming was abandoned and structured programming preferred. This is also desirable for parallel programming: in this respect, send/receive communications could be considered as unstructured [11].

This calls for more structured models of parallel programming. Algorithmic skeletons, introduced at the end of the eighties [5], are such a form of structured parallelism. Skeletons belong to a finite set of higher-order functions or patterns that can be run in parallel. To write a parallel program, users have

Y. Xiang et al. (Eds.): ICA3PP 2012, Part I, LNCS 7439, pp. 218–232, 2012.

to combine and compose the existing skeletons. Usually the programming semantics of a skeleton is similar to the functional semantics of a corresponding sequential pattern (for example the application of a function to all the elements of a collection) and the execution semantics remains implicit or informal. Thus the skeletons abstract the communication and synchronisation details of parallel activities. Skeletons are not in general any parallel operations, but try to capture the essence of well-known techniques of parallel programming such as parallel pipeline, master-slave algorithms, the application of a function to distributed collections, parallel reduction, *etc.* Various libraries and languages are based on programming with algorithmic skeletons. A recent survey is [10].

Orléans Skeleton Library [15] is an efficient C++ library of parallel algorithmic skeletons (on top of MPI) that uses expression templates for optimisation. In the design of a new version of OSL, we aimed at improving the safety of the library while preserving its expressivity. In [16] we presented the prototyping of the new OSL library with a parallel functional programming language that follows the BSP [25] model: Bulk Synchronous Parallel ML [20], an extension of the OCaml language [17]. Moreover the languages of proof assistants such as Coq [24] or Isabelle/HOL contain as a subset a pure functional programming language, as well as a subset close to usual mathematical logic. This is therefore possible to use this prototype as a basis for a Coq development where all the parallel implementations of the skeletons are proved correct. This is the contribution of the paper.

The paper is organised as follows. We first review related work on the semantics of algorithmic skeletons (section 2). We then present informally the considered subset of OSL skeletons as well as the formal functional specification in Coq (section 3). This functional specification is used to program and prove the correctness of two applications: a heat diffusion simulation and the maximum segment sum problem (section 4). In order to describe the implementation of the skeletons we present briefly the parallel functional language Bulk Synchronous Parallel ML (section 5). The implementation and the proof that it is correct with respect to the functional specification are addressed in section 6. We conclude and give further research direction in section 7.

2   Related Work

In the algorithmic skeletons literature, the *programming model* i.e. the semantics given to the user of the skeleton library or language is a *functional* semantics. It is not per se a formal semantics, but usually an unambiguous definition of the skeleton is given using very often an Haskell-like [13] notation making these definitions executable. The *execution model*, i.e. how the skeletons are executed on a parallel machine often remains implicit or at least very informally defined, usually using figures. This is the case for the work that coined the name "algorithmic skeleton" [5] and other subsequent work.

Nevertheless there is few work about the formal semantics of skeletons, with, to some extent, parallel aspects in these semantics. In [4] the work seems to be the first one where some skeletons are formalised using abstract state machines. In [7] the authors present a data-parallel calculus of multi-dimensional arrays, but it is a formal semantics without any related implementation. This is mostly a programming model but distribution is modelled in the semantics. Lithium is an algorithmic skeleton library for Java that is stream-based. In [1] a programming model and a (high-level) execution model for Lithium are proposed in a single formalism. The skeletons of [8] are also stream-based but the semantics is used rather as a guideline for the design of the meta-programmed optimisation of the skeletons in C++. It is a formal execution model of the considered skeleton library. There is no proof of equivalence with a programming model.

The semantics of the Calcium library is described in [3]: the focus in on a programming model semantics (operational semantics) as well as a static semantics (typing) and the proof of the subject reduction property (the typing is preserved during evaluation). In this work the semantics of the skeletons are detailed, but not the semantics of what the authors call the "muscles" i.e. the sequential arguments of the skeletons (the semantics of the host language of the library, in the particular case Java).

Orléans Skeleton Library (OSL) [15] has a formal, and *mechanised* in Coq [14], programming model but that handles the distribution of the data structure manipulated with the skeletons. Moreover this formal semantics is not declarative as the functional specification of the skeletons given in section 3: this is an operational semantics, not very suitable for user program verification.

Apart from OSL, none of these semantics have been used as the basis of proofs of program correctness, but are rather formal reference manuals for the libraries. Moreover, none have been formalised using a proof assistant.

Eden [19] and BSML [20] are two parallel functional languages that are often used for implementing algorithmic skeletons. The former has a formal semantics on paper [12]. Therefore we could indirectly obtain an execution model for the skeletons implemented in Eden. BSML has a semantics axiomatised in Coq [23] that allows to write parallel BSML programs within Coq (and extract them to real BSML programs that can be compiled and run on parallel machines).

To our knowledge the use of BSML as an implementation language of algorithmic skeletons and the proof that these implementations indeed are correct with respect to a functional semantics in a proof assistant, is unique. In this respect we have both a programming model (the "sequential" functional version) and an execution model (the BSML implementation) and a proof of their equivalence. This was already done for a new algorithmic skeleton called BH that is used in a framework for deriving programs written in BH from specifications [9]. The current work continues this line of research and concerns a verified prototype implementation of SkeTo's [22] skeletons on distributed arrays (SkeTo offers skeletons on other data structures), that is also a subset of OSL skeletons on evenly distributed arrays.

3   Specification of Algorithmic Skeletons

3.1   An Overview of OSL Programming Model

OSL programs are similar to sequential programs but operate on a distributed data structure called distributed array. At the time of the creation of the array, data is distributed among the processors. Distributed arrays are implemented as a template class `DArray<A>`. Internally, a distributed array consists of partitions distributed on the processors, each being an array of elements of type `A`. In the considered subset of OSL distributed array constructors and skeletons, all distributed arrays are evenly distributed.

The following table gives an informal semantics for the main OSL skeletons together with their signatures. A distributed array of type `DArray<A>` can be seen "sequentially" as an array $[t_0, \ldots, t_{t.size-1}]$ where $t.size$ is the global size of the distributed array t:

Skeleton	Signature
	Informal semantics
map	`DArray<B> map(B f(A), DArray<A> t)`
	$\mathrm{map}(f, [t_0, \ldots, t_{t.size-1}]) = [f(t_0), \ldots, f(t_{t.size-1})]$
zip	`DArray<C> zip(C f(A,B), DArray<A> t, DArray<B> u)`
	$\mathrm{zip}(f, [t_0, \ldots, t_{t.size-1}], [u_0, \ldots, u_{t.size-1}]) = [f(t_0, u_0), \ldots, f(t_{t.size-1}, u_{t.size-1})]$
reduce	`<A> reduce(A ⊕(A,A), DArray<A> t)`
	$\mathrm{reduce}(\oplus, [t_0, \ldots, t_{t.size-1}]) = t_0 \oplus t_1 \oplus \ldots \oplus t_{t.size-1}$
shift	`DArray<A> shift(int offset, A f(int), DArray<A> t)`
	$\mathrm{shift}(\mathrm{offset}, f, [t_0, \ldots, t_{t.size-1}]) = [f(0), \ldots, f(\mathrm{offset}-1), t_0, \ldots, t_{t.size-1-\mathrm{offset}}]$

In additional to these skeletons, there are constructors of distributed arrays. For the sake of coherence with the formal model of the skeletons in the remaining of the paper, we will consider here constructors as two specific skeletons: `empty` is the empty distributed array (its size is 0), `init_da` creates a distributed array of a given size with its elements given by applying a function from indices to values. Its C++ signature would be: `DArray<A> (A f(int), int size)`.

As already said, the OSL library uses evenly distributed arrays. They are distributed arrays in which all the processors have roughly the same number of values. This subset corresponds to the skeletons of the Sketo [22] library on arrays. In an evenly distributed array, if the size is not divided by the number of processors, the processors with a low process identifier may have one additional element. `empty` and `init_da` give an evenly distributed array. The skeletons `map`, `zip` and `shift` do not change the distribution of their arguments.

`map` takes two arguments, an unary function `f` and a distributed array. It applies the function to every element of the distributed array and returns the resultant distributed array. As `map` applies the function to each element independently, there is no need of communicating anything. `zip` is an extension to the `map` skeleton. It accepts a binary function and two distributed arrays. The application of the function to the input arrays is similar to that of `map`.

The `shift` skeleton takes three arguments: the number `d` of elements to be shifted (positive the elements are shifted to the right, negative they are shifted to the left), a function `f` and a distributed array. As the shifting is not circular, the function `f` is used to fill the holes at the beginning (resp. the end) of the distributed array.

`reduce` applies the reduction operator over the elements of the distributed array. Unlike `map` and `zip`, the result of the `reduce` operation is a single element. Every processor after reducing its local data communicates the result to a given processor (or to all other processors according to the reduce algorithm). Then this processor reduces the local results to get the final result and performs a broadcast if required. So, for this skeleton, the communications are needed after the computation of the local results.

3.2   Specification in Coq

For the user of the library, distributed arrays are specified without showing parallelism. A distributed array is an indexed structure on which higher order functions are defined.

Our specification is defined using the formalism of Coq's module system, which provides a tool for more rigorous development of generic theorems. This feature system is similar to OCaml's module system. **Module Type** name groups, in the module name, concrete and abstract types with operations over those types, as well as properties. In the same way it is possible to define functors, which are functions from modules to modules (or modules parameterised by other modules).

The module DA (figure 1) captures the essence of a distributed array. A distributed array consists of a carrier set DArray and the operations which are listed after. Furthermore, we specify that DArray is generic: it takes as parameter a type T and returns the type of distributed arrays of elements of type T, noted DArray T (instead of `DArray<T>` in C++).

The distributed arrays are defined as an abstract datatype. We have two operations on this datatype: an operation size that returns the number of elements contained in the distributed array, and an operation get that given a distributed array da and a position (N is the type of natural numbers in Coq) returns the element of the distributed array at this position. This operation takes an additional argument d that stands for the default element: the element that is returned if the position is not a valid position (above the size of the distributed array). These two operations should satisfy two properties omitted here: get returns the same value whatever the default argument is when the position is valid, and get returns the default value when the position is invalid.

The signatures of these operations do not seem very usual. In C++ notation, the signature of the first one would be: `template<A> int size(DArray<A> da)`. In Coq $\forall(A:\textbf{Type})$ means that the function is polymorphic and the type argument is called A. As the type of the second argument depends on the first argument, in Coq we shall use a universal quantification. The last expression is the return type. A usual abbreviation in Coq is to write $\forall(a\ b:A)(c:C)$ instead of $\forall(a:A),\forall(b:A),\forall(c:C)$: this notation is used but for the two first operations. It is sometimes possible to omit the types and write $\forall a\ b\ c$. The Coq system infers the appropriate types. However as it is less readable we avoid this notation as much as possible.

After the two operators on distributed arrays, used to specify the behaviour of the real constructors and skeletons on arrays, come the constructors. For empty, the return type is also very unusual but should be read as a usual mathematical notation. empty returns a distributed array da' of type Darray A such that its size

Module Type DA.
  Parameter DArray: **Type** →**Type**.
  Parameter size: ∀(A:**Type**), ∀(da:DArray A), N.
  Parameter get: ∀(A:**Type**), ∀(da:DArray A), ∀(pos:N), ∀(d:A), A.

  Parameter empty: ∀(A:**Type**), { da' : DArray A | size (da') = 0}.

  Parameter init: ∀(A:**Type**), ∀(f:N→A), ∀(size:N),
   { da': DArray A | size (da') = size ∧
                ∀(d:A)(pos:N), get(da',pos,d)= **if** (pos<size(da')) **then** f(pos) **else** d }.

  Parameter map: ∀(A B:**Type**)(f:A→B)(da: DArray A),
   { da':DArray B | ∀(d:A)(pos:N), get(da',pos,f(d)) = f(get(da,pos,d)) }.

  Parameter zip: ∀(A B C:**Type**)(f:A→B→C)(da1:DArray A)(da2:DArray B)
             {H:compatible da1 da2},
   { da':DArray C | ∀(d1:A)(d2:B)(pos:N), get(da',pos,f(d1,d2)) =
                       f(get(da1,pos,d1),get(da2,pos,d2)) }.
  Parameter reduce: ∀(A:**Type**)(op: A→A→A)(e:A){monoid: Monoid op e}(da:DArray A),
   { a : A | ∀(d:A), a = List.fold_left(op, List.map(fun i⇒get(da,i,d), seq(0,size(da)), e) }.

  Parameter shift: ∀(A:**Type**)(offset: Z)(f: N→A)(da: DArray A),
   { da' : DArray A | size (da') = size (da) ∧
    ∀(d:A)(pos:N), get(da',pos,d) =
      if (pos<size(da))
     then if (offset=0)
        then get(da,pos,d)
       else if (offset>0 ∧ offset≤pos) ∨ (offset<0 ∧ pos<size(da)+offset)
          then get(da, pos−offset, d)
          else f(pos)
     else d }.
End DA.

Fig. 1. Functional Specification of OSL Skeletons in Coq

is 0. For the init constructor the return type is even richer as we specify the content of the distributed array using the get operation. For reader familiar with functional programming or the Coq proof assistant, please note that we chose to write all the functions in uncurried form (more familiar for most readers) whereas they are in curried form in the formalisation

The map skeleton specification is very close to its informal description. The shift skeleton specification is a more involved as all the cases for sign of the offset, and the comparison of the offset and the position should be taken into account.

zip skeleton has an additional argument: a proof that both arrays are "compatible". Two distributed arrays are compatible if they have same distribution. In the case of an even distribution, it is enough to show that they have the same size. This is the definition of the compatibility property for evenly distributed arrays. The use of class types in Coq allows in most cases to build automatically the compatibility proof. Thus, this avoids the user to give it explicitly.

The specification of the reduce skeleton needs a monoid with a composition law op and a neutral element e. It is defined using the fold_left function of the List library of Coq. fold_left(op,[v_1;...;v_n], e) = op(... (op(op(e,v_1),v_2)...),v_n). Here, the list [v_1;...;v_n] is obtained by applying the map function on the list of elements of the distributed array. This list is the result of the application of the get function over the list of distributed array indices ([0;...;da$_{size-1}$]).

Using this functional specification, it is possible to write skeletal programs, and to reason about them. We illustrate this in the next section.

4   Applications Using the Specification

4.1   One Dimensional Heat Equation

We now illustrate how the skeletons in OSL can be used to specify a scientific application. The heat equation describes the variation in temperature over time in a given material. It can be used to simulate the evolution of the distribution of heat in a material. We will consider here the one dimensional heat equation:

$$\frac{\delta u}{\delta t} - \kappa \frac{\delta^2 u}{\delta^2 x} = 0 \qquad u(0,t) = l \qquad u(1,t) = r$$

where $u(x,t)$ gives the temperature in position x at time t, κ is the thermal diffusivity of the material, and l and r are the constant temperatures outside the material. Using a discretization method on time and space using steps dx and dt we obtain the following equation:

$$u(x,t+dt) = \frac{\kappa \times dt}{dx^2} \times \big(u(x+dx,t) + u(x-dx,t) - 2 \times u(x,t)\big) + u(x,t)$$

plus boundary conditions. To build a simulation program of heat diffusion, the values of function u at the discretisation points are stored in an array and this equation is further approximated by considering floating point numbers instead of real numbers. The specification of our program will thus be:

$$\text{step}(u)[i] = \frac{\kappa \times dt}{dx^2} \times \big(u[i+1] + u[i-1] - 2 \times u[i]\big) + u[i] \qquad (1)$$

where step is the function that is supposed to compute the temperatures for the bar at the next time step, and where we omitted the boundary conditions. The formal Coq development [21], where u is modelled as a list rather than an array, gives all the details.

The Coq program, named OSLstep, that implements the computation of one step of the simulation could be written as follows. This function step takes five arguments of type number and a sixth argument that is a distributed array of numbers and returns a distributed array of numbers:

Definition OSLstep (kappa dx dt l r:number)(u: DArray number) : DArray number :=
   zip((+),
       map((*) ((kappa*dt)/(dx*dx))),
           zip((−), zip((+), shift(−1, (fun _⇒l), u), shift(1, (fun _⇒r), u))
                 zip((+), u, u)))
   u).

where (+), (*), (/), (−) represent the usual operators but as binary functions, (*)((kappa*dt)/(dx*dx)) is the partial application of the function (*) to ((kappa*dt)/(dx*dx)) i.e. the function: $y \mapsto \frac{\kappa \times dt}{dx^2} \times y$, and fun _ ⇒l is the constant function that returns always the value l. It is to be noticed that u is not an array but a *distributed* array.

As the function step manipulates a distributed array but that (1) deals with an array (a list in the Coq formalisation) it is necessary to have the functions toList (resp. ofList) that transforms a distributed array (resp. a list) to a list (resp. a distributed array). We then can prove that the function:

fun kappa dx dt l r u ⇒toList(step(kappa,dx,dt,leftBound,rightBound,ofList(u)))

actually fulfills specification (1). The proof proceeds in three steps: (a) we use the fact that the skeletons commute with toList, for example for the map skeleton we have: ∀(A B:**Type**)(f:A→B)(u:DArray A),   toList(map(f,u)) = List.map(f,toList(u)) where List.map is the usually sequential map function on lists (predefined in the Coq library). (b) We use the fact that: ∀(A:**Type**)(l:list A), toList(ofList l) = l. (c) We conclude by case reasonning on i to take into account boundary conditions.

4.2 Maximum Segment Sum

We now consider the maximum segment sum problem [2], which is to compute the maximum value among the sums of all the possible sub-arrays of an integers array. The sum for the empty segment is supposed to be zero, thus any maximum segment sum will be positive or null. For instance, supposing mss is the function that solves the problem and ↑ gives the maximum of two values, we have:

$$mss[1, -1, 2] = 1 \uparrow (1 + (-1)) \uparrow (1 + (-1) + 2) \uparrow -1 \uparrow (-1 + 2) \uparrow 2 = 2$$

Coq specification. In order to specify the result of the maximum segment sum problem, we use a function segments which computes all the segments of the list corresponding to a given distributed array, then we map a function sum on this list of segments to get the list of segments sums, then we iterate on the list to get its maximum element. The Coq specification of the problem is as follows:

Definition mss_spec (da : DArray number) : number :=
   fold_left(max,List.map(sum,segments(toList(da)))),zero).

Maximum Segment Sum Definition Using Skeletons. In [6], Cole gives an operator to solve this problem using the reduce skeleton. The idea is to solve the problem for an array by solving it for contiguous sub-arrays and then merging the results. The maximum segment sum for the concatenation of two arrays is the maximum value among the maximum segment sum (mss) of the first array, or the maximum segment sum of the second array, or the sum of the maximum concluding segment sum (mcs) of the first array and the maximum initial segment sum (mis) of the second array.

To be able to cut an array at multiple places, we also have to compute the maximum initial (respectively concluding) segment sum for the concatenation of the two arrays. This can be computed from the maximum initial (respectively concluding) segment sum of the arrays and their total sum.

To summarise, for each sub-array we have to compute four values: the maximum segment sum, the maximum initial segment sum, the maximum concluding segment sum and the total sum. These values are gathered in a quadruplet of numbers and the operator can be defined as follows:

$$(\text{mssx, misx,mcsx,tsx}) \oplus (\text{mssy, misy,mcsy,tsy}) =$$
$$(\text{mssx} \uparrow \text{mssy} \uparrow (\text{mcsx+misy}) \,, \text{misx} \uparrow (\text{tsx+misy}) \,, (\text{mcsx+ tsy}) \uparrow \text{mcsy} \,, \text{tsx+tsy}).$$

As the maximum segment sum is positive, the values mss, mis and mcs can be restricted to positive or null values. In that case, the operator $\oplus$ is associative and (0, 0, 0, 0) is a neutral for this operator. Thus, it forms a monoid and the operator $\oplus$ can be used as a parameter of reduce.

In our Coq development, we define the operator op_mss, for which the arguments are quadruplet of value together with a proof that those values satisfy the positive or null condition on mss, mis and mcs. The operator returns a quadruplet computed using $\oplus$ together with a proof that it satisfies the same property.

Before applying reduce on a distributed array, each element has to be transformed into a value usable by the op_mss operator. This is done with the skeleton map applied on the distributed array with a function buildTupleWithInvariant that, for a given number n, returns (n $\uparrow$ 0, n $\uparrow$ 0, n $\uparrow$ 0, n) decorated with the adequate proof. The maximum segment sum is computed with our skeletons as follow :

Program Definition mss (da : DArray number) : number :=
   fst4(reduce(op_mss,op_mss_neutral,map(buildTupleWithInvariant(da)))).

where fst4 returns the first element of a quadruplet which corresponds there to the maximum segment sum and op_mss_neutral is the neutral element for op_mss.

Proof of correctness. The correctness of this implementation is stated by:

Lemma mms_correct: $\forall$da, mss(da) = mss_spec(da).

It is proved in three steps: (a) We use the reduce specification and the fact that skeletons commute with toList to have an application of skeletons sequential equivalents on toList da. (2) We generalise the lemma by adding the fact that the projection on the second element of the result gives the maximum over prefix sum of the list. (3) We prove this generalised lemma by induction on the list corresponding to toList da. This proof relies on the facts that numbers are totally ordered, that (+) distribute over ($\uparrow$) and that both are associative.

5   Bulk Synchronous Parallel ML

Bulk Synchronous Parallel ML is a functional programming language designed to write BSP (Bulk Synchronous Parallel) algorithms [25]. BSML [20] is currently implemented as a library for the OCaml language [17] and is axiomatised as a Coq module type [23].

A BSML program is built as a sequential program on parallel vectors. A parallel vector has type 'a par (or par A in Coq) and embeds p values of any type 'a at each of the p different processors in the parallel machine. We will write informally $\langle v_0, \ldots, v_{p-1} \rangle$ for a parallel vector containing value v_i at processor i. Parallel vectors are handled through the use of four different primitives that constitute the core of BSML. Two asynchronous ones (**mkpar, apply**) corresponding to local access to values inside each member of the vector, and two synchronous ones that perform communications (**proj, put**). Their informal semantics follows:

$$\mathbf{mkpar}(f) = \langle f(0), \ldots, f(p-1) \rangle$$
$$\mathbf{apply}(\langle f_0, \ldots, f_{p-1} \rangle, \langle v_0, \ldots, v_{p-1} \rangle) = \langle f_0(v_0), \ldots, f_{p-1}(v_{p-1}) \rangle$$
$$\mathbf{proj}(\langle v_0, \ldots, v_{p-1} \rangle) = \mathbf{fun}\ i \to v_i$$
$$\mathbf{put}(\langle f_0, \ldots, f_{p-1} \rangle) = \langle \mathbf{fun}\ i \to f_i(0), \ldots, \mathbf{fun}\ i \to f_i(p-1) \rangle$$

The **proj** primitive transforms a parallel vector into a sequential function. The **put** primitive is used for any BSP communication pattern. A function f_i at a processor i encodes the messages to be sent to other processor. For example $f_i(j)$ is the message to be sent from processor i to processor j (could possibly be an empty message). In the result, other functions encode the received messages.

In the following section we use a Coq axiomatisation of BSML for a BSML implementation of the skeletons presented in section 3. Using the Coq extraction mechanism it is then possible to extract actual OCaml+BSML programs to be run on parallel machines.

6   Verified Implementation of Algorithmic Skeletons

Now, in order to have a correct implementation of OSL based on BSML, we propose to define an implementation of distributed arrays and skeletons. Using the proof assistant Coq, we verify that the implementation of the algorithmic skeletons is correct with respect to the functional specification given in section 3.

Implementation of the Evenly Distributed Arrays. The data structure manipulated by the skeletons of our prototype library are evenly distributed arrays. In BSML such a data structure could be implemented as a parallel vector of arrays. However it is convenient, and more efficient, to store some additional information rather than to compute on demand:

- the start index of each processor with respect to the global array: each processor contains one array, but this array is a sub-array of the distributed array considered as a whole array; computing it from the parallel vector of arrays would require communications,

- the global length (size) of the distributed array: if it is not stored then a parallel reduction is needed to compute it from the parallel vector of arrays,
- the distribution: each processor knows the local length of the other local arrays without having to communicate; we store the distribution in a list of integers of size p.

In the definition below,

- we note v[i] the *ith* element of the parallel vector v; list A designs a data structure list of elements of type A and A par denotes a parallel vector of elements of type A.
- scanl takes a binary operator op and its neutral e and a list $[a_0; \ldots; a_k]$, and returns the list $[op(e,a_0); op(op(e,a_0),a_1); \ldots; op(\ldots(op(op(e,a_0),a_1)\ldots),a_k)]$.
- fold_right and nth are both functions of the List library of Ocaml.
  fold_right(f, $[a_1; \ldots; a_k]$, e) returns the value $f(a_1,f(a_2,\ldots,f(a_k,e)\ldots))$.
  nth(l, i) returns the i-th element of the list l.

The type for distributed arrays of elements of type A (da A for short) is defined (in "pseudo" Coq for sake of clarity) as the following record. The two first fields are local, (one value per processor) and the two last are global data. The last field integrates a coherence property that garantees a correct distributed array. For sake of clarity, we give the definition in "pseudo" Coq. Note that this definition holds for any distributed array, not necessarily evenly distributed. Let us recall p is the number of processors we have in the BSP computer.

The type for distributed arrays of elements of type A (i.e. DArray A) is thus defined as a first step with:

```
Record da (A:Type) := make_da {
    da_content: par (list A);
    da_firstLocalIndex: par N;
    da_length: N;
    da_distribution: list N;
    da_coherence:
        length (da_distribution)=p ∧ da_length=List.fold_right( (+), 0, da_distribution ) ∧
        ∀pid, get (da_firstLocalIndex[pid]) = scanl ( (+), 0, da_distribution) ∧
        ∀pid, length (get (da_content[pid])) = List.nth(da_distribution, pid)
}.
```

A record definition is similar to a struct in C with several fields. In the case of Coq, the type of a field such as da_coherence could be complex: its type is a logical formula. make_da is the name of the function that should be used to create record values: this function has five arguments.

The other fields are more usual: da_length and da_distribution are not parallel vectors but have usual sequential types. This makes clear that these fields cannot have a different value on two different processors. On the contrary da_firstLocalIndex is a parallel vector: at each processor it contains the start index of the local component in the global array. It is also possible to choose da_firstLocalIndex to be the array of the first indices of all the local components. However, for all skeletons but one, it is not necessary for a processor to know the first indices of other processors: therefore it is better to save memory by having only one integer value per processor for da_firstLocalIndex rather than having a replicated array of size p (than in practice is p integer values on each processor).

The value for the da_coherence field is a proof that guarantees the coherence between the other fields. It includes checking the equality between the number of processors and the length of the global array. It also verifies that the number of local elements is equal to the distribution local value, and that at each processor the first index of the local component is equal to the partial sum of the distribution field. Finally, the coherence checks that the length of the global array is the sum of all local values of the distribution field.

As an example, suppose we have 4 processors, and let string_of_int be the function that converts an integer to string, then the evaluation of the expression:

- init(string_of_int,10) returns the distributed array of figure 2 (top),
- shift(2,fun i⇒"−1",da) returns the distributed array of figure 2 (bottom).

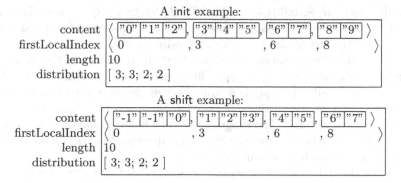

Fig. 2. Examples of Distributed Arrays

Finally, using reduce, we can for example compute the sum of the square of da's elements with the expression reduce((fun (x,y) ⇒$x+y*y$),0,da)

In a second step, we need to specify that we deal only with evenly distributed arrays. An even distribution is characterized by the following property:

Definition evenlyDistributed {A:**Type**}(d : da A) : Prop :=
  ∀(pid:processor), length (get(da_content(d)[pid])) =
                if pid<(length(d) mod p) **then** (length(d)/p)+1 **else** length(d)/p.

Consequently, an evenly distributed array is defined in this way:

Definition DArray (A:**Type**) := { d : da A | evenlyDistributed(d) }.

If we extract [18] OCaml code from these Coq definitions we would obtain an OCaml record type definition but with only the four first fields of da: the other field and the evenlyDistributed property being in the logical realm, they are removed to yield only a pure computational code.

As already mentioned, if two arrays are evenly distributed, using type classes mechanism of Coq, we define the compatibility property that is true if both arrays have the same length.

Class compatible {A B:**Type**}(da1: DArray A)(da2: DArray B) :=
  { compatibleProperty: length (da1) = length (da2) }.

Verified Implementation of a Skeleton. We refer to [21] to obtain the full development in Coq. For the sake of conciseness we only give here an overview of how we can obtain a verified implementation of a skeleton with the example of the empty constructor:

Program Definition empty (A:**Type**) : {da' : DArray A | length(da') = 0} :=
  make_da(A, replicate([]), replicate(0), 0, LIFO.List.replicate(p,0), _).

replicate is a BSML parallel function taking one argument x and returning a parallel vector in which all processors have the value x. Then replicate([]) (resp. replicate(0)) is a parallel vector in which all the values are the empty list [] (resp. 0). To build an empty distributed array, we use the make_da function that returns a record in which da_content field (resp. da_firstLocalIndex) is the result of replicate([]) (resp. replicate(0)), and the field da_length is equal to 0. To set the value of the field da_distribution, we invoke replicate function of our List library, which returns the list of size p in which all values are 0.

Finally, we use the _ notation to indicate that the definition of the value of the fifth field is delayed to the next step. The careful ready may have noticed that make_da returns a value of type da A. But the specification of section 3 indicates that empty should return a value d of type DArray A and that this value d should be such that its length is 0. The **Program** keyword before **Definition** indicates that all these missing parts, that are proofs of logical properties will be handled with the proof (or tactics) language of Coq.

Therefore the definition of empty in Coq generates three *proof obligations* resulting from the definition of the type of da A, DArray A and the specification of empty.

The first one is the coherence property in the definition of the type da: to prove it we use some properties over lists such that the following lemma:

Lemma replicateLength: $\forall$(A:**Type**) (n:nat) (a:A), length(LIFO.List.replicate(n,a)) = n.

The proof of this obligation yields the definition of a value named empty_obligation_1 that is the value given to the fifth field. Therefore the following value (we name it d) of type da A is defined:

  {| da_content := replicate([]); da_firstLocalIndex := replicate(0); da_length := 0;
     da_distribution := LIFO.List.replicate(p,0); da_coherence := empty_obligation_1(A) |}.

The second obligation has to be proved to verify that the empty definition builds an evenly distributed array: $\forall$(A:**Type**), evenlyDistributed(d) (i.e. a value of type DArray A). We achieve the proof by unfolding the definition of evenlyDistributed, and simplifying the obligation since $\forall$(pid:processor),length(get(da_content(d)[pid])) is equal to 0. With this proof (named empty_obligation_2) a value of type DArray A, that we name ed, is defined as:

exist((fun(d':da A)$\Rightarrow$evenlyDistributed(d')),d, empty_obligation_2(A))

that means that ed contains the value d and the proof that d is evenly distributed.

The third obligation derives from the specification of empty, which specifies that the length of an empty distributed array is equal to 0: $\forall$(A:**Type**), length(ed)=0. This obligation is trivial according to the definition of length that is defined by: **Definition** length (A:**Type**)(d:DArray A):=da_length(d).

7   Conclusion and Perspectives

Algorithmic skeletons are a parallel programming paradigm that could make parallel programming mainstream. It is important to offer skeletal parallelism for widespread programming languages such as Java and C++ for example. However it is also very important to provide robust parallel libraries to mainstream programmers. This is why the development of our Orléans Skeleton Library for C++ is backed by a prototype implementation with the functional parallel programming language Bulk Synchronous Parallel ML. The contribution of the paper is that this prototype implementation was proved correct with respect to a functional specification of the skeletons. This specification was used as a basis for the proof of correctness of two applications.

In the current subset we consider only skeletons that do not change the distribution of the manipulated distributed arrays and constructors that only build evenly distributed arrays: therefore only evenly distributed arrays are manipulated. However this hinders the expressivity of the library. The full OSL library supports non evenly distributed arrays using additional skeletons: we shall verify them too. The next step is to verify the C++ library rather than the prototype implementation. We will first address the formalisation of a minimal subset of C++ necessary to verify the correct implementation of the expression template technique in OSL.

Acknowledgements. This work is supported by ANR (France) and JST (Japan) (project PaPDAS ANR-2010-INTB-0205-02).

References

1. Aldinucci, M., Danelutto, M.: Skeleton-based parallel programming: Functional and parallel semantics in a single shot. Computer Languages, Systems and Structures 33(3-4), 179–192 (2007)
2. Bentley, J.: Programming Pearls. Addison-Wesley (1986)
3. Caromel, D., Henrio, L., Leyton, M.: Type safe algorithmic skeletons. In: EuroMicro PDP, pp. 45–53. IEEE Computer Society (2008)
4. Cavarra, A., Riccobene, E., Zavanella, A.: A formal model for the parallel semantics of P3L. In: ACM Symposium on Applied Computing, pp. 804–812. ACM (2000)
5. Cole, M.: Algorithmic Skeletons: Structured Management of Parallel Computation. MIT Press (1989), http://homepages.inf.ed.ac.uk/mic/Pubs
6. Cole, M.: Parallel Programming, List Homomorphisms and the Maximum Segment Sum Problem. In: Joubert, G.R., Trystram, D., Peters, F.J., Evans, D.J. (eds.) ParCo 1993, pp. 489–492. Elsevier (1994)

7. Di Cosmo, R., Pelagatti, S., Li, Z.: A calculus for parallel computations over multidimensional dense arrays. Computer Language Structures and Systems 33(3-4), 82–110 (2007)
8. Falcou, J., Sérot, J.: Formal Semantics Applied to the Implementation of a Skeleton-Based Parallel Programming Library. In: Bischof, C.H., Bücker, H.M., Gibbon, P., Joubert, G.R., Lippert, T., Mohr, B., Peters, F.J. (eds.) ParCo 2007, pp. 243–252. IOS Press (2007)
9. Gesbert, L., Hu, Z., Loulergue, F., Matsuzaki, K., Tesson, J.: Systematic Development of Correct BSP Programs. In: PDCAT, pp. 334–340. IEEE (2010)
10. González-Vélez, H., Leyton, M.: A survey of algorithmic skeleton frameworks: high-level structured parallel programming enablers. Software, Practrice & Experience 40(12), 1135–1160 (2010)
11. Gorlatch, S.: Send-receive considered harmful: Myths and realities of message passing. ACM TOPLAS 26(1), 47–56 (2004)
12. Hidalgo-Herrero, M., Ortega-Mallén, Y.: An Operational Semantics for the Parallel Language Eden. Parallel Processing Letters 12(2), 211–228 (2002)
13. Hutton, G.: Programming in Haskell. Cambridge University Press (2007)
14. Javed, N., Loulergue, F.: A Formal Programming Model of Orléans Skeleton Library. In: Malyshkin, V. (ed.) PaCT 2011. LNCS, vol. 6873, pp. 40–52. Springer, Heidelberg (2011)
15. Javed, N., Loulergue, F.: Parallel Programming and Performance Predictability with Orléans Skeleton Library. In: HPCS, pp. 257–263. IEEE (2011)
16. Javed, N., Loulergue, F., Tesson, J., Bousdira, W.: Prototyping a Library of Algorithmic Skeletons with BSML. In: PDPTA 2011, pp. 520–526. CSREA Press (2011)
17. Leroy, X., Doligez, D., Frisch, A., Garrigue, J., Rémy, D., Vouillon, J.: The OCaml System release 3.12 (2010), http://caml.inria.fr
18. Letouzey, P.: Extraction in Coq: An Overview. In: Beckmann, A., Dimitracopoulos, C., Löwe, B. (eds.) CiE 2008. LNCS, vol. 5028, pp. 359–369. Springer, Heidelberg (2008)
19. Loogen, R., Ortega-Mallen, Y., Pena-Mari, R.: Parallel functional programming in eden. Journal of Functional Programming 3(15), 431–475 (2005)
20. Loulergue, F., Gava, F., Billiet, D.: Bulk Synchronous Parallel ML: Modular Implementation and Performance Prediction. In: Sunderam, V.S., van Albada, G.D., Sloot, P.M.A., Dongarra, J. (eds.) ICCS 2005. LNCS, vol. 3515, pp. 1046–1054. Springer, Heidelberg (2005)
21. Loulergue, F., Tesson, J., Bousdira, W.: Certified BSML and Verified OSL Prototype version 0.3 (April 2012), http://traclifo.univ-orleans.fr/BSML
22. Matsuzaki, K., Iwasaki, H., Emoto, K., Hu, Z.: A Library of Constructive Skeletons for Sequential Style of Parallel Programming. In: InfoScale 2006. ACM Press (2006)
23. Tesson, J., Loulergue, F.: A Verified BSML Heat Diffusion Simulation. In: ICCS. Procedia Computer Science, pp. 36–45. Elsevier (2011)
24. The Coq Development Team: The Coq Proof Assistant, http://coq.inria.fr
25. Valiant, L.G.: A bridging model for parallel computation. CACM 33(8), 103 (1990)

Performance Measurement of Parallel Vlasov Code for Space Plasma on Various Scalar-Type Supercomputer Systems

Takayuki Umeda[1] and Keiichiro Fukazawa[2]

[1] Solar-Terrestrial Environment Laboratory, Nagoya University,
Nagoya 464-8601, Japan
umeda@stelab.nagoya-u.ac.jp
[2] Research Institute for Information Technology, Kyushu University,
Fukuoka 812-8581, Japan
fukazawa@cc.kyushu-u.ac.jp

Abstract. Computer simulations with the first-principle (kinetic) model are essential for studying multi-scale processes in space plasma. We develop numerical schemes for Vlasov simulations for practical use on currently-existing supercomputer systems. The weak-scaling benchmark test shows that our parallel Vlasov code achieves a high performance and a high scalability. Currently, we use more than 1000 cores for parallel computations and apply the present parallel Vlasov code to various cross-scale processes in space plasma, such as a first-principle global simulation of solar-wind-magnetosphere interactions.

1 Space Plasma Simulations

No less than 99.9% of the matter in the visible Universe is in the plasma state. The plasma is a gas in which a certain portion of the particles are ionized, which is considered to be the "fourth state" of the matter. The Universe is filled with plasma particles ejected from the upper atmosphere of stars. The stream of plasma is called the stellar wind, which also carries the intrinsic magnetic field of the stars. Our solar system is also filled with plasma particles from the Sun. Neutral gases in the upper atmosphere of the Earth are also ionized by a photoelectric effect due to absorption of energy from sunlight.

Computer simulation has now becomes an essential approach in studies of space plasma. Since the number density of plasma particles in space is low, and the mean free path between collisions is large, the word "space plasma" is generally equivalent to collisionless plasma. For an example, the number density far above the Earth's ionosphere is $\sim 100\text{cm}^{-3}$ or much less, and a typical mean-free path of solar-wind plasma is about 1AU (Astronomical Unit: the distance from the Sun to the Earth; 1AU $\sim 150,000,000\text{km}$). In the case of long collision length, the scale of plasma variability is set by the Debye length, which varies from a few millimeters at the low-Earth orbit to a kilometer or so in tenuous plasma. Motion of plasma is affected by electromagnetic fields. The change in the

Y. Xiang et al. (Eds.): ICA3PP 2012, Part I, LNCS 7439, pp. 233–240, 2012.

motion of plasma results in an electric current, which can modify the surrounding electromagnetic fields. The plasma behaves as a dielectric medium with strong nonlinear interactions between plasma particles and electromagnetic fields.

There are numerous types of self-consistent computer simulations that treat space plasma according to various approximations. The global-scale dynamics are commonly described by magneto-hydro-dynamic (MHD), Hall-MHD and multi-fluid models, while electron-scale processes are described by the kinetic model, i.e., the Maxwell equations and either the Newton-Lorentz equation for charged particles or the Vlasov (collisionless Boltzmann) equation. Hybrid methods treat ions as particles and electrons as a fluid for ion-scale processes.

Conventionally, MHD simulations have been widely used for numerical modeling of global-scale problems such as magnetospheres of stars and planets. The MHD or fluid equations are derived by taking the zeroth, first, and second moments of the kinetic Vlasov equations with the zeroth, first, and second moments being the conservation laws of the density, momentum, and energy, respectively. Thus, the MHD simulations need diffusion coefficients, which are essentially due to kinetic processes that are eliminated in the framework of the MHD approximation. These coefficients are essentially due to first-principle kinetic processes that are eliminated in the framework of the fluid approximations. Recent high-resolution in-situ observations have also suggested that fluid scale and kinetic scale in space plasma are strongly coupled with each other, which is called cross-scale coupling. To understand the cross-scale coupling in space plasma, it is important to include full kinetics in global-scale simulations, which is a final goal of space plasma physics.

In the present study, we develop numerical schemes for Vlasov simulations for practical use on currently-existing supercomputer systems. There are several hyper-dimensional (>3D) Vlasov simulations of the magnetic reconnection [1,2,3], the Kelvin-Helmholtz instability[4]. Currently, we use 256-1024 cores for parallel computations and apply the present parallel Vlasov code to "global" simulation on the interaction of solar/stellar winds with unmagnetized dielectric bodies [5,6] and weakly-magnetized small bodies (Fig.1). This paper gives a performance measurement study of our parallel Vlasov code on various scalar-type multi-core systems and massively-parallel supercomputers.

2   Overview of Numerical Schemes

The Vlasov model solves the kinetics equations of space plasma, i.e., the Maxwell equations (1) and the Vlasov (collisionless Boltzmann) equation (2),

$$\left.\begin{array}{c} \nabla \times \mathbf{B} = \mu_0 \mathbf{J} + \dfrac{1}{c^2}\dfrac{\partial \mathbf{E}}{\partial t} \\[2mm] \nabla \times \mathbf{E} = -\dfrac{\partial \mathbf{B}}{\partial t} \end{array}\right\} \tag{1}$$

$$\frac{\partial f_s}{\partial t} + \mathbf{v}\frac{\partial f_s}{\partial \mathbf{r}} + \frac{q_s}{m_s}\left[\mathbf{E} + \mathbf{v}\times\mathbf{B}\right]\frac{\partial f_s}{\partial \mathbf{v}} = 0 \tag{2}$$

where $\mathbf{E}$, $\mathbf{B}$, $\mathbf{J}$, ρ, μ_0, ϵ_0 and c represent electric field, magnetic field, current density, charge density, magnetic permeability, dielectric constant and light speed,

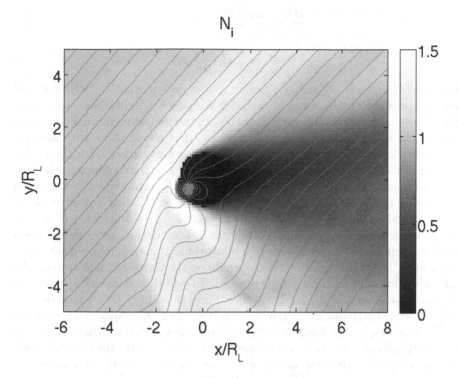

Fig. 1. Structures of bow shock and wake tail formed as a result of the interaction between a weakly-magnetized object and the solar wind. Spatial profile of ion density together with the configuration of magnetic field lines obtained by a global Vlasov simulation.

respectively. The Vlasov equation (2) describes the development of the distribution functions by the electromagnetic (Lorentz) force, with the collision term in the right hand side set to be zero. The distribution function $f_s(\mathbf{r}, \mathbf{v}, t)$ is defined in position-velocity phase space with the subscript s being the species of singly-charged particles (e.g., $s = i, e$ for ions and electrons, respectively). The Maxwell equations and the Newton-Lorentz equations or the Vlasov equation are coupled with each other via the current density $\mathbf{J}$ that satisfies the continuity equation for charge

$$\frac{\partial \rho}{\partial t} + \nabla \cdot \mathbf{J} = 0 \tag{3}$$

These equations are regarded as the "first principle" of the collisionless plasma.

The Vlasov equation (2) consists of two advection equations with a constant advection velocity and a rotation equation by a centripetal force without diffusion terms. To simplify the numerical time-integration of the Vlasov equation, we adopt a modified version of the operator splitting [7],

$$\frac{\partial f_s}{\partial t} + \mathbf{v}\frac{\partial f_s}{\partial \mathbf{r}} = 0 \tag{4}$$

$$\frac{\partial f_s}{\partial t} + \frac{q_s}{m_s} \mathbf{E} \frac{\partial f_s}{\partial \mathbf{v}} = 0 \tag{5}$$

$$\frac{\partial f_s}{\partial t} + \frac{q_s}{m_s} [\mathbf{v} \times \mathbf{B}] \frac{\partial f_s}{\partial \mathbf{v}} = 0 \tag{6}$$

Equations (4) and (5) are scalar (linear) advection equations in which $\mathbf{v}$ and $\mathbf{E}$ are independent of $\mathbf{r}$ and $\mathbf{v}$, respectively. We adopt a multidimensional conservative semi-Lagrangian scheme [7] for solving the multidimensional advection equations. In the full electromagnetic method, it is essential to use conservative schemes for satisfying the continuity equation for charge. With the multidimensional conservative semi-Lagrangian scheme, the continuity equation for charge (3) is exactly satisfied. In the present study, we compute the numerical flux by using the multi-dimensional advection scheme [7] with a positive, non-oscillatory and conservative limiter [8,9] for stable time-integration of advection equations. Equation (6), on the other hand, is a multi-dimensional rotation equation which follows a circular motion of a profile at constant speed by a centripetal force. For stable rotation of the profile on the Cartesian grid system, the "back-substitution" technique [10] is applied. In addition, Maxwell's equations are solved by the implicit Finite Difference Time Domain (FDTD) method.

The velocity distribution function has both configuration-space and velocity-space dimensions, and defined as a hyper-dimensional (>3D) array, There are some additional communications overhead in parallelizing over the velocity-space dimensions since a reduction operation is required to compute the charge and current densities (the zeroth and first moments) at a given point in configuration space. Thus we adopt the "domain decomposition" only in configuration space, where the distribution functions and electromagnetic fields are decomposed over the configuration-space dimensions. This involves the exchange of ghost values for the distribution function and electromagnetic field data along boundaries of each procession element. The non-oscillatory and conservative scheme [8,9] uses six grids for numerical interpolation, and three ghost grids are exchanged by using the "Mpi_Sendrecv()" subroutine in the standard message passing interface (MPI) library for simplicity and portability [11]. We also use the "Mpi_Allreduce()" subroutine for the convergence check on each iteration of the implicit FDTD method. Note that the code allows thread parallelization over the velocity-space dimensions via OpenMP.

3   Performance Evaluation

We conduct the performance measurement test of our parallel Vlasov code with a phase-space grid of $(N_{v_x}, N_{v_y}, N_{v_z}, N_x, N_y) = (30, 30, 30, 40, 20)$ on one core, which corresponds to a weak-scaling test with 1GB/core.

We use Hitachi HA8000 at the University of Tokyo, Fujitsu FX1 at Nagoya University, Fujitsu HX600 at Nagoya University, Fujitsu RX200S6 at Kyushu University, and DELL PowerEdge R815 at Solar-Terrestrial Environment Laboratory, Nagoya University. The details of these systems are described in Table 1. Note that most of the systems does NOT allow the use of all computational resources.

Table 1. Details of computer systems

System	HA8000	HX600	FX1
Site	Univ. of Tokyo	Nagoya Univ.	Nagoya Univ.
CPU	Opteron 8356	Opteron 8380	SPARC64 VII
Num. of Cores	4	4	4
Clock	2.3GHz	2.5GHz	2.5GHz
L2	512KB/core	512KB/core	6MB/CPU
L3	6MB/CPU	6MB/CPU	
Num. of sockets	4	4	1
Memory per node	32GB	64GB	32GB
Theoretical Performance	36.8GFlops	40.0GFlops	10.0GFlops
Number of nodes	952	160	768
Inter-node connection	Myrinet-10G × 4 1.25GB/s per link	DDR InfiniBand × 4 2GB/s per link	DDR InfiniBand ×1 2GB/s per link

System	RX200S6	R815-1	R815-2
Site	Kyushu Univ.	STE Lab.	STE Lab.
CPU	Xeon X5670	Opteron 6174	Opteron 6276
Num. of Cores	6	12	16*
Clock	2.93GHz	2.2GHz	2.3GHz
L2 cache	512KB/core	512KB/core	2MB/module
L3 cache	12MB/CPU	12MB/CPU	16MB/CPU
Num. of sockets	2	4	4
Memory per node	48GB	96GB	128GB
Theoretical Performance	70.32GFlops	422.4GFlops	665.6GFlops
Number of nodes	392	48	1
Inter-node connection	QDR InfiniBand × 1 5GB/s per link	QDR InfiniBand × 1 5GB/s per link	N/A

*8 modules.

3.1 Performance on Multi-core Systems

Figure 2 shows the computational performance on these systems on a single node. The peak performances (performance efficiencies) of the Vlasov code with one core is 1.61GFlops (17.5%) on the AMD Opteron 8356 processor of HA8000, 1.74GFlops (17.4%) on the AMD Opteron 8380 processor of HX600, 1.42GFlops (14.2%) on the SPARC64 VII processor of FX1, 2.60GFlops (22.2%) on the Intel Xeon X5670 processor of RX200S6, 1.57GFlops (17.9%) and 2,71 GFlops (14.7%) on the AMD Opteron 6174 and 6276 processors of R815. The computational speed of the Xeon X5670 processor and the Opteron 6276 processor is very similar, and the computational speed of the other four processors is also similar. The performance efficiency of the Xeon X5670 processor is very high (>20%), while the performance efficiency of the previous-generation Opteron processors (Barcelona, Shanghai, and Magny-Cours) is 16−18%. The performance efficiency of the SPARC64 VII processor is lower (∼14%) with our code. It should be

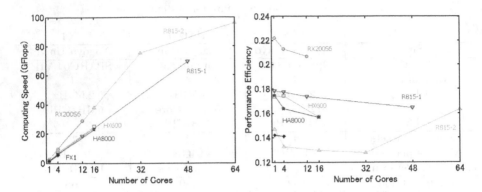

Fig. 2. Performance of different multi-core systems with scalar processors. (left) Computational speed and (right) performance efficiency as a function of the number of cores. The star, asterisk, square, circle, up-pointing- and downward-pointing-triangle marks represent the results on the HA8000, FX1, HX600, RX200S6, R815-1 and R815-2, respectively.

noted that the Opteron 6276 processor has 8 Bulldozer modules on a CPU. One Bulldozer module has a capability of 8 flop per cycle and is a shared with 2 cores. Thus the theoretical performance of this CPU with 32 cores and 64 cores are same. Thus the performance efficiency is lower up to 32 cores but becomes higher with 64 cores.

3.2 Scaling on Massively Parallel Supercomputers

Figure 3 shows the inter-node parallel performance on these systems. Note that the computational performance is measured by using the hardware counter installed on the Fujitsu FX1 system, and the performances on other systems are estimated based on the result with the FX1. The peak performances (performance efficiencies) of the parallel Vlasov code are 8.19TFlops on the HA8000 with 8192 cores, 3.17TFlops on the HX600 with 2048 cores, 4.10TFlops on the FX1 with 3072 cores, and 1.80TFlops on the RX200S6 with 768 cores, 2.95TFlops on the R815 with 2304 cores. As seen, we obtained a high scalability of ~90% with 1000 cores. The scalability of the FX1 is very high (more that 95%) with up to 2048 cores. The scalability of the R815 with up to 1152 cores is higher than that of HX600, because of the inter-node communication device. However, the scalability becomes worse when the all computational resources (3072 cores on FX1 and 2304 cores on R815) are used. The Myrinet-10G internode-connection device of the HA8000 system also gives a high scalability of ~80% up to 2048 cores. However, the scalability becomes worse with more cores because of the network bandwidth capacity.

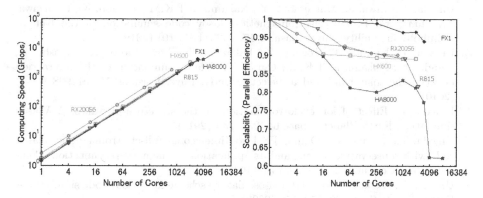

Fig. 3. Performance of different supercomputer systems with scalar processors. (left) Computational speed and (right) scalability as a function of the number of cores. The star, asterisk, square, circle, and downward-pointing-triangle marks represent the results on the HA8000, FX1, HX600, RX200S6, and R815-1. respectively.

4   Conclusion

In this paper, we have made performance measurements of a new Vlasov-Maxwell code on different types of scalar computer systems, which are the Hitachi HA8000, Fujitsu HX600, Fujitsu FX1, Fujitsu RX200S6, and DELL R815 systems. These systems consist of AMD Opteron (64bit x86) processors, SPARC64VII processors and Intel Xeon (64bit x86) processors. The weak-scaling benchmark test shows that our parallel Vlasov code achieves a high performance (>14%) and a high scalability (>80%) with more than 1000 cores.

As a future study, we make performance measurements on new supercomputer systems with Xeon-E5 26xx processors and Sparc64 IX processors, which will be installed in 2012.

Acknowledgement. The authors are grateful to Yosuke Ito, Yasuhiro Nariyuki, and Tatsuki Ogino for discussions. This work was supported by MEXT/JSPS under Grant-in-Aid for Young Scientists (B) No.23740367. The computational resources are provided as a STEL computational joint research program, a Nagoya University HPC program, and a JHPCN program.

References

1. Silin, I., Büchner, J.: Three-dimensional Vlasov-code simulations of magnetopause-like current sheets. Adv. Space Res. 37, 1354–1362 (2006)
2. Schmitz, H., Grauer, R.: Kinetic Vlasov simulations of collisionless magnetic reconnection. Phys. Plasmas 13, 092309 (p. 9) (2006)
3. Umeda, T., Togano, K., Ogino, T.: Structures of diffusion regions in collisionless magnetic reconnection. Phys. Plasmas 17, 052103 (p. 6) (2010)

4. Umeda, T., Miwa, J., Matsumoto, Y., Nakamura, T.K.M., Togano, K., Fukazawa, K., Shinohara, I.: Full electromagnetic Vlasov code simulation of the Kelvin-Helmholtz instability. Phys. Plasmas 17, 052311 (p. 10) (2010)
5. Umeda, T., Kimura, T., Togano, K., Fukazawa, K., Matsumoto, Y., Miyoshi, T., Terada, N., Nakamura, T.K.M., Ogino, T.: Vlasov simulation of the interaction between the solar wind and a dielectric body. Phys. Plasmas 18, 012908 (p. 7) (2010)
6. Umeda, T.: Effect of ion cyclotron motion on the structure of wakes: A Vlasov simulation. Earth Planets Space 64, 231–236 (2012)
7. Umeda, T., Togano, K., Ogino, T.: Two-dimensional full-electromagnetic Vlasov code with conservative scheme and its application to magnetic reconnection. Comput. Phys. Commun. 180, 365–374 (2009)
8. Umeda, T.: A conservative and non-oscillatory scheme for Vlasov code simulations. Earth Planets Space 60, 773–779 (2008)
9. Umeda, T., Nariyuki, Y., Kariya, D.: A non-oscillatory and conservative semi-Lagrangian scheme with fourth-degree polynomial interpolation for solving the Vlasov equation. Comput. Phys. Commun. 183, 1094–1100 (2012)
10. Schmitz, H., Grauer, R.: Comparison of time splitting and backsubstitution methods for integrating Vlasov's equation with magnetic fields. Comput. Phys. Commun. 175, 86–92 (2006)
11. Umeda, T., Fukazawa, K., Nariyuki, Y., Ogino, T.: A scalable full electromagnetic Vlasov solver for cross-scale coupling in space plasma. IEEE Trans. Plasma Sci. 40, 1421–1428 (2012)

Ultrasound Simulation on the Cell Broadband Engine Using the Westervelt Equation

Andrew A. Haigh[1], Bradley E. Treeby[2], and Eric C. McCreath[1]

[1] Research School of Computer Science, The Australian National University
[2] Research School of Engineering, The Australian National University
ahaigh1@gmail.com
{bradley.treeby,eric.mccreath}@anu.edu.au

Abstract. The simulation of realistic medical ultrasound imaging is a computationally intensive task. Although this task may be divided and parallelized,
temporal and spatial dependencies make memory bandwidth a bottleneck on
performance. In this paper, we report on our implementation of an ultrasound
simulator on the Cell Broadband Engine using the Westervelt equation. Our approach divides the simulation region into blocks, and then moves a block along
with its surrounding blocks through a number of time steps without storing intermediate pressures to memory. Although this increases the amount of floating
point computation, it reduces the bandwidth to memory over the entire simulation
which improves overall performance. We also analyse how performance may be
improved by restricting the simulation to regions that are affected by the transducer output pulse and that influence the final scattered signal received by the
transducer.

Keywords: ultrasound simulation, Westervelt equation, Cell Broadband Engine,
parallelization.

1 Introduction

The simulation of realistic ultrasound signals is important in a number of fields, including ultrasound system design and development [1], the delivery of therapeutic ultrasound [2], and the registration of diagnostic ultrasound images with other imaging
modalities [3]. However, ultrasound simulation is a computationally intensive task due
to the large number of grid points and time steps required to accurately replicate typical biomedical scenarios. For example, the central frequency of a diagnostic ultrasound
transducer can range from $2 - 15$ MHz, with depth penetrations from cms to tens of
cms. To discretize domains of this size, a 2 dimensional finite-difference time-domain
(FDTD) simulation can require grid sizes in excess of 1000×1000 grid points [4,5].
Similarly, the simulation of a single scan line in which waves propagate from the transducer into the medium and back can require more than 6000 time steps [6]. This is
increased further if the simulation of nonlinear harmonics is required, or if the simulations are performed in 3 dimensions. This is to the point where merely storing the
pressure values at each grid point becomes difficult on modern desktop computing systems. The computational task is challenging both from the perspective of the number of
floating point operations, and also the transfer of data to and from the CPU.

Y. Xiang et al. (Eds.): ICA3PP 2012, Part I, LNCS 7439, pp. 241–252, 2012.

Recently, nonlinear ultrasound simulation on general-purpose graphics processing units (GPGPUs) have been attracting attention [5,6,7]. This has helped with the floating point operations, however, memory bandwidth is still a bottleneck. Our research extends the GPGPU implementation discussed by Karamalis et al. [6], and explores how the Westervelt Equation could be used to simulate ultrasound on the Cell processor. In this case, the Westervelt equation is solved with a FDTD scheme which can take advantage of important aspects of the Cell's hardware, including multiple cores, SIMD calculations, and asynchronous memory retrieval/storage. We have designed and implemented a simulator on the Cell hardware, and explored how the memory transfers may be reduced by dividing the region up into blocks of pressure samples and stepping these multiple steps in time. This approach is shown to improve the performance and we believe is novel within the ultrasound simulation field. We have also explored how the number of grid points used in the simulation can be limited to those that are affected by the ultrasound signal transmitted by the transducer, or that influence the scattered ultrasound signal that is subsequently received.

We have evaluated our approaches on the Cell microprocessor as it has been shown that the Cell can be used effectively for computation-intensive applications [8,9,10]. In particular the Cell has been used effectively for FDTD calculations [11,12]. However, the approaches presented in this paper are not limited to the Cell and may be applied to other architectures such as GPGPUs or more standard multi-core/cluster architectures. We envisage that similar improvements in performance would also be gained on these systems.

This paper is organised as follows. In Section 2 we give the Westervelt equation along with the finite difference discretization used in our implementation. In Section 3 we overview the salient features of the Cell processor. Section 4 gives the approach taken in implementing our simulation. In Section 5 our results are reported. These focus on understanding the improvements gained by applying the multiple time steps and only simulating required regions. Finally in Section 6 we provide a conclusion along with a discussion of possible future research.

2 Westervelt Equation

The lossy Westervelt Equation for a thermoviscous fluid is given by [13]

$$\nabla^2 p - \frac{1}{c^2}\frac{\partial^2 p}{\partial t^2} + \frac{\delta}{c^4}\frac{\partial^3 p}{\partial t^3} + \frac{\beta}{\rho_0 c^4}\frac{\partial^2 p^2}{\partial t^2} = 0, \tag{1}$$

where p is the acoustic pressure (Pa), c is the propagation speed (m s^{-1}), ρ_0 is the ambient density (kg m^{-3}), δ is the diffusivity of sound (m^2 s^{-1}), and β is the coefficient of nonlinearity. The first two terms are equivalent to the conventional linearized wave equation, the third term accounts for thermoviscous absorption, and the fourth term accounts for cumulative nonlinear effects.

Here, this equation is solved numerically using the FDTD method on a rectangular grid. The grid has spacing Δx and Δy in the x and y dimensions (m), where $\Delta x = \Delta y$. The time steps are equally spaced and given by Δt (s). $p_{i,j}^n$ denotes the variation from the background acoustic pressure at time step n at grid point (i, j). The gradients are approximated using finite differences that are fourth-order accurate in space and second-order accurate in time [14]. This is the same as the schemes used in [6,15]. The finite differences generated by this algorithm and used in the code are:

$$\frac{\partial^2 p}{\partial t^2} \approx \frac{1}{\Delta t^2}\left(p_{i,j}^{n+1} - 2p_{i,j}^n + p_{i,j}^{n-1}\right), \tag{2}$$

$$\frac{\partial^3 p}{\partial t^3} \approx \frac{1}{2\Delta t^3}\left(3p_{i,j}^{n+1} - 10p_{i,j}^n + 12p_{i,j}^{n-1} - 6p_{i,j}^{n-2} + p_{i,j}^{n-3}\right), \tag{3}$$

$$\frac{\partial^2 p}{\partial x^2} \approx \frac{1}{12\Delta x^2}\left(-p_{i+2,j}^n + 16p_{i+1,j}^n - 30p_{i,j}^n + 16p_{i-1,j}^n - p_{i-2,j}^n\right), \tag{4}$$

$$\frac{\partial^2 p}{\partial y^2} \approx \frac{1}{12\Delta y^2}\left(-p_{i,j+2}^n + 16p_{i,j+1}^n - 30p_{i,j}^n + 16p_{i,j-1}^n - p_{i,j-2}^n\right). \tag{5}$$

The $\frac{\partial^2 p^2}{\partial t^2}$ term is calculated by making use of the chain rule and product rule:

$$\frac{\partial^2 p^2}{\partial t^2} = 2\left(\left(\frac{\partial p}{\partial t}\right)^2 + p\frac{\partial^2 p}{\partial t^2}\right), \tag{6}$$

where the temporal gradients are respectively computed using explicit third-order and second-order accurate backward finite differences

$$\frac{\partial p}{\partial t} \approx \frac{1}{\Delta t}\left(\frac{11}{6}p_{i,j}^n - 3p_{i,j}^{n-1} + \frac{3}{2}p_{i,j}^{n-2} - \frac{1}{3}p_{i,j}^{n-3}\right), \tag{7}$$

$$\frac{\partial^2 p}{\partial t^2} \approx \frac{1}{\Delta t^2}\left(2p_{i,j}^n - 5p_{i,j}^{n-1} + 4p_{i,j}^{n-2} - p_{i,j}^{n-3}\right), \tag{8}$$

(the use of a backward difference avoids $p_{i,j}^{n+1}$ (etc) terms and makes solving the final equation easier). Combining these equations with (1) using a second-order accurate finite difference scheme for the remaining temporal derivative then gives

$$\begin{aligned}
p_{i,j}^{n+1} = &\left(c^{-2}\Delta t^{-2} - \frac{3}{2}\delta c^{-4}\Delta t^{-3}\right)^{-1}\left(\nabla^2 p + p_{i,j}^n(2c^{-2}\Delta t^{-2} - 5\delta c^{-4}\Delta t^{-3})\right.\\
&+ p_{i,j}^{n-1}(6\delta c^{-4}\Delta t^{-3} - c^{-2}\Delta t^{-2}) - p_{i,j}^{n-2}(3\delta c^{-4}\Delta t^{-3})\\
&\left.+ p_{i,j}^{n-3}(\frac{1}{2}\delta c^{-4}\Delta t^{-3}) + \frac{\beta}{\rho_0 c^4}\frac{\partial^2 p^2}{\partial t^2}\right),
\end{aligned} \tag{9}$$

where in 2 dimensions $\nabla^2 p = \frac{\partial^2 p}{\partial x^2} + \frac{\partial^2 p}{\partial y^2}$. Note that c is actually dependent on (i,j) as it varies depending on the properties of the medium at each position. For simplicity we assume reflecting boundary conditions (i.e. $p_{i,j}^n = 0$ for all (i,j) which lie outside the grid.)

3   The Cell and the PS3

The Cell processor and the PS3 have been extensively described in articles such as [16]. A brief overview of the salient aspects is now given. The PS3 has a 3.2GHz Cell processor along with 256MB of main memory which is Rambus XDR DRAM. The Cell Broadband Engine (CBE) is a microprocessor developed by Sony, Toshiba and IBM [16] which contains 9 cores. These cores are composed of a single Power processor element (PPE) intended to be used for coordinating the actions of the other cores, and eight Syngergistic processor elements (SPEs) which are RISC SIMD processor elements and are optimised for numerical computation [17, p. 34].

The PPE is a two-way multi-threaded core with 512kB of L2 cache. Linux may be installed and run on the PS3, although a hypervisor restricts access to the RSX 'Reality Synthesizer' graphics processing unit and also disables 2 of the 8 SPEs [18, p. 7]. Ubuntu gutsy (7.10) running Linux 2.6.20 64 bit SMP version has been installed on our test machine. Figure 1 depicts a block diagram of the effective architecture when the system is run with the hypervisor.

Each SPE has 128 128-bit registers which can be used to perform SIMD calculations. The SIMD instruction set [19, Section 2] contains a large number of useful instructions. These include operations that may be performed on vectors of 4 floats (contained in a single 128-bit register). An example of such an operation is to construct a new vector using 2 floats from one vector and 2 floats from another vector. These operations are pipelined and may be issued on every clock cycle. The arithmetic/logic operations are done in the even side of the pipeline. The odd side of the pipeline includes operations such as load/store between registers and the local store (LS). A multiply-add operation enables a maximum of 8 floating point operations per cycle thus giving a maximum of 25.6GFlops per SPE, although for most operations this maximum is 12.8GFlops.

The Cell has an internal bus, called the Element Interconnect Bus (EIB), which enables the SPEs to communicate with each other, the PPE, and the memory interface. The effective bandwidth of the EIB is 96 bytes per cycle [16, Figure 1].

Each SPE contains 256kB of LS to be used for data, instructions and stack and this is the only memory that can be accessed directly by each SPE; of this storage, 240kB is available for data. Data is transferred between main memory and local store via Direct Memory Access (DMA) requests [16, p. 595]. These accesses can be initiated by either the SPE or PPE and are asynchronous and can be barriered/fenced against each other [19, p. 57]. Each request can transfer at most 16kB.

Each SPE channel to the EIB is limited to 25.6GB/s, moreover, the transfers between the EIB and main memory is also limited to 25.6GB/s, this becomes a bottleneck when only a few operations are needed to be performed on each float that is transferred to/from main memory. A particular type of request that we make heavy use of is a 'scatter and gather' request where multiple discontiguous area of main memory are loaded into a contiguous area of local storage. Correct alignment of data is important for the performance of the system.

4   Approach

Solving the FDTD scheme is performed solely by the (available) SPEs, with the PPE responsible for delegating tasks to the SPEs and coordinating their actions. Initially the PPE allocates 1/6th of the total spatial region (consisting of a large number of smaller square regions we call 'blocks') to each SPE during the process of thread creation.

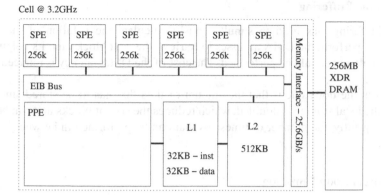

Fig. 1. Block diagram of the PS3 architecture

Mailboxes are used for synchronisation; each SPE places a message in its outbound mailbox when it has completed an entire timestep in its allocated region and then waits for a message in its inbound mailbox before restarting the calculations for the same region (moved on by a number of timesteps). Although this minimizes the amount of synchronisation and simplifies the implementation, a downside of this approach is that the load on SPEs may become unbalanced due to contention of main memory accesses, resulting in some SPEs waiting while other still have calculations to perform.

The SPE performs the calculation for a single block at a time. The pressures at all grid points for the previous 4 timesteps in that block and all 8 neighbouring blocks are loaded. The pressures are then stepped forwards by as many timesteps as possible. The final pressures and the pressure at the transducers for all intermediate timesteps (i.e. the received signal) are stored in main memory.

Our implementation uses a number of standard techniques [9,12,10] to help improve performance, these include SIMD, double buffering, and loop unrolling. In addition to these standard approaches, we also explore how multiple timesteps (Section 4.4) and ignoring regions (Section 4.5) may be used to improve performance. The various techniques used in the implementation are now given.

4.1 SIMD

It is relatively straightforward to use the Cell's SIMD capabilities to improve the performance of the calculations. Since our calculations are performed in single precision, four floats can fit in a single register and so the FDTD scheme can be solved at four grid points simultaneously. The SIMD instruction set contains fused multiply and add instructions which are used in the main computation loop.

There is some extra overhead (compared to the scalar version) due to permute-style operations which are required to approximate the $\frac{\partial^2 p}{\partial y^2}$ term. The permute operations are required because misaligned (not on 128 bit boundary) loads can not be performed directly.

4.2 Double Buffering

Double buffering was used to simultaneously calculate the solution of the FDTD scheme and perform the DMA accesses to retrieve the next block (and its neighbours) where calculation should be performed. The cost of the DMA latency is reduced in this way.

However, the downside is that the amount of data that has to be stored simultaneously in the local storage is doubled, which reduces the size of blocks that can be used, and consequently, the number of timesteps that can be performed in between memory accesses.

4.3 Manual Loop Unrolling

A technique that was found to be effective in improving performance was to manually unroll the main computation loop (that performs the solving of the FDTD scheme) by a factor of 3. This allows extra instructions to be interleaved during compiler optimization and reduces stalls due to dependencies.

4.4 Multiple Timesteps in between Memory Access

In order to minimize the amount of DMA required, the scheme is solved for multiple time steps in a single block before writing the result back to main memory. An area of 3×3 blocks ($3d \times 3d$ grid points) is loaded into main memory, with the intention of calculating the pressures for the central block ($d \times d$ grid points) over a number of timesteps. Under a fourth-order spatially accurate scheme, no more than $\lfloor \frac{d}{2} \rfloor$ timesteps can be calculated at a time, since the region that can be stepped forward in time shrinks 2 grid points with each time step (since pressures cannot be calculated on the boundary of the region).

Other CBE programmers (including [9]) have found it necessary to ensure that large amounts of work is performed on data that is loaded from main memory to avoid being limited by the memory bandwidth. Work on performing linear algebra computations on the CBE [8] uses similar techniques.

Using this timestep approach, it is advantageous to do calculations on blocks that are as big as possible. This maximizes the number of timesteps that can be performed in between memory accesses. Here, blocks of size 24 x 24 were used, allowing 12 time steps to be performed in between memory accesses. Taking into account double buffering, the amount of memory used in our implementation to store the pressures and an index to wavespeeds at an SPE is the equivalent of 51840 floats, or about 210 kB (out of the total 240 kB local storage that is available).

Performing multiple timesteps comes at the cost of extra computation (since some pressures are calculated more than once). Let t denote the number of time steps performed in between memory accesses. Then $d \geq 2t$, and ideally $t = \frac{d}{2}$. The total number of times we apply the FDTD formula in between memory accesses is:

$$W = \sum_{i=0}^{t-1} (d + 2 \times 2i)^2 = d^2 t + 4dt(t-1) + \frac{8t}{3}(t-1)(2t-1) \qquad (10)$$

compared to td^2 for the same amount of useful work if only one timestep is performed at a time. It can be shown that the relative amount of extra work that is done is bounded by

$$\frac{\text{extra work}}{\text{total work}} = \frac{W - d^2 t}{d^2 t} \leq \frac{10}{3} \tag{11}$$

i.e., for large t, the extra work done is about three times the amount of work performed if a single timestep is performed in between memory accesses.

Let T be the number of timesteps backward required to solve the FDTD scheme (this depends on the FDTD scheme used; $T = 4$ in our case). In this implementation the calculation requires that $9d^2(T+1)$ floats are loaded to calculate t timesteps forward in some block. If one timestep is performed at a time, $(T+1)(d+4)^2$ floats are loaded to calculate one timestep forward in some block. Therefore, the amount of loads performed is reduced for $t \geq 9$ by a factor of approximately $\frac{9}{t}$. In our case, for $t = 12$, the total amount of loads is reduced by about $1/4$.

After each block of t timesteps is completed, the previous $T \leq t$ timesteps worth of pressures at each point must be stored in main memory. When a single timestep is performed at a time, 1 timestep worth of pressures at each point must be stored (since the previous ones have not changed). This means that the total amount of stores that are performed is reduced by a factor of $\frac{t}{T}$ under the new scheme (a factor of 3 in our case). In our implementation stores are more costly than loads because the individual stores operate on quite small pieces of data.

4.5   Ignore Empty Regions

Regions in which the acoustic pressure is approximately zero, or where the local waveforms cannot affect the final signal received by the transducer do not have to be considered in the calculations. At the start and end of the computation, only regions very near the transducer need to be simulated. Since the number of time steps is chosen to be roughly enough for a pulse to reflect off the furthest wall and return, only a small fraction of the timesteps require the entire region to be simulated. Here, this is implemented conservatively by increasing the height of the simulated region by one grid point per timestep, until the entire grid is being simulated, and reversing this process toward the end of the simulation. The effective width of the grid remains constant because in our implementation the array of transducers is aligned in this direction.

5   Results

The proposed method was implemented in C. The code that runs on the PPE (and organises the calculation) is about 400 lines of code in total. The SPE code which performs the actual calculation (including memory accesses and double buffering) is about 350 lines.

For the simulation we used $\Delta x = \Delta y = 5.0 \times 10^{-5}$m and $\Delta t = 3.0 \times 10^{-9}$s giving a CFL number[1] of ~ 0.1, this provides a good balance between accuracy and performance.

---

[1] The Courant-Friedrichs-Lewy (CFL) number is calculated by $(\Delta t\ c_{max})/\Delta x$, it measures the number of spatial grid points the fastest wave travels in one time step. Normally this will be a small fractional number and is dictated by stability constraints.

A 3 cycle tone burst with a centre frequency of 3 MHz was used. This provides 10 grid points per wavelength at the centre frequency. The medium parameters were set to $\beta = 6$, $\rho_0 = 1100\,\mathrm{kg\,m^{-3}}$, $\delta = 4.5 \times 10^{-6}\,\mathrm{m^2\,s^{-1}}$. For comparison with [6], the results reported below are for the simulation of 6000 time steps (the equivalent of one scan line computation) using a grid of size of 2064×2064.[2] The sound speeds within the medium were defined using a numerical phantom of a fetus [20]. This contained a small number of large homogeneous regions and other regions consisting of sub-wavelength scatterers. A snapshot showing the wave field as it propagates through the phantom is shown in Figure 2.

Fig. 2. Snapshot of an ultrasound wave propagating through a numerical phantom of a fetus

Parallelisation (via use of multiple SPEs) of the code improves the performance of the code by approximately a factor of 5. The time required to perform this calculation when only one SPE is used is 284 seconds, compared to 57 seconds when all six of the available SPEs are used.

Figure 3 shows how the time taken to compute one scan line changes as the number of steps between memory synchronisation increases. These results are calculated by repeating the execution 10 times for each measurement and reporting the average (the standard error on all these estimations is less than 0.9s). When the maximum amount of time steps (12) are calculated in between memory accesses, the time taken to calculate

---

[2] [6] used a grid size of 2048×2048, however, as our grid dimensions needed to be a multiple of 24 we simulated on a slightly larger grid.

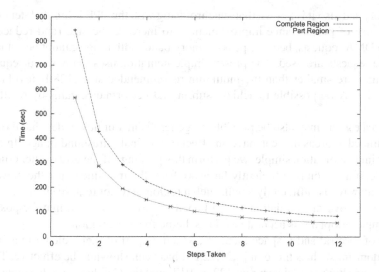

Fig. 3. Time required to compute a scan line (in seconds) vs number steps taken by a block

one scan line is 57 seconds. In [6], 192 scan lines (with the same grid size and number of timesteps) are computed in 55 minutes, approximately 17 seconds per scan line. Figure 3 also shows the improvement gained by restricting the simulation region, this shows an improvement of 32% over simulating the entire region over all time steps (for the maximum amount of time steps between memory synchronisation).

The performance of our code corresponds to an average main memory bandwidth usage of 7.2 GB/s, which is below the theoretically possible of 25.6 GB/s main memory bandwidth. Although, clearly there is room for improvement, such a figure is typical for applications like this.

6   Conclusion and Future Research

In this paper we described an implementation of nonlinear ultrasound simulation based on the Westervelt equation using the Cell Broadband Engine. The simulation time required is of the same order of magnitude as recent results achieved using GPGPUs [6] and avoids the need to use PC clusters, an approach used in other work [4]. The simulation of one scanline, which requires 57 seconds on the Cell, requires about 17 minutes when performed on a desktop PC with an Intel Core i7-2600K 3.40 GHz processor with 3 GB RAM. We have also shown the performance gained by doing multiple timesteps between memory sychronisation. It would be interesting to explore how this approach may be applied to other architectures such as a GPGPU.

A number of aspects of our implementation affect performance detrimentally. As mentioned above, it may be advantageous to allocate work to the SPEs using a work queue instead of allocating a fixed amount of work. This approach is used to do FDTD simulation in [11]. Performance may be also improved by communicating data and synronisation events between SPEs. This has the potential of saving DMA bandwidth to main memory and also it is known that synchronising with the PPE is highly latent [10]. Another source of performance improvement is to increase the size (and reduce the number of) DMA requests, because peak memory bandwidth usage cannot be achieved unless large requests are used. The present implementation uses many small requests, some of which are smaller than the minimum recommended size (128 bytes) [17, p. 455]. Thus, it may be possible to achieve substantial performance gains by rectifying these issues.

Performance gains may also be possible by generalising our novel idea that the simulation is limited to areas that can have an effect of the final ultrasound image. In order to keep our implementation simple, we perform this pruning (of the grid) rather crudely. For example, if a region is sufficiently far away from the transducer and the power of the ultrasound wave is sufficiently small, such a region may not require simulation calculations for the overall simulation to still be sufficiently accurate. It may be possible to, for example, adopt a less accurate FDTD scheme for those regions.

The use of spectral and k-space methods, which do part of their calculations in the frequency domain, such as those in [5,21,22,23] has been shown to be effective. These methods provide high spatial accuracy [22, p. 917] and the Cell has already shown that it can efficiently perform the FFT [9,10] which is required to implement these spectral and k-space methods. Thus it would be interesting to explore the effectiveness of these method on the Cell.

More realistic modelling may be achieved by substituting the thermoviscous absorption term in the Westervelt equation with a more general integro-differential operator that can account for power law absorption [24,5]. It would be worth understanding and evaluating the exact performance costs of such modelling improvements.

Our promising results indicate that implementing a 3D ultrasound simulation on this hardware may be worthwhile. The implementation of absorbing boundary conditions (such as Berenger's PML adapted for ultrasound in [4]) would be necessary in order to accurately compare results with those gained from experimental data.

While the Cell processor is perhaps a non-standard computing platform (particularly in the ultrasound area), the push towards large-scale simulations requires both novel hardware and numerical approaches to make the calculations tractable. Moreover, emerging parallel architectures such as APUs or the Cell are likely to form an integral part of high performance computing clusters in the future. For example, a number of Cell clusters already exist, including the well known Roadrunner super computer.[3] Our research provides a good starting point for tackling much bigger ultrasound problems using a Cell cluster.

In summary, ultrasound simulation on the Cell can be performed much faster than using a standard single threaded desktop CPU and comparable to that of a GPGPU. Moreover, lessons learnt in our research are almost certainly transferable to any new architecture that emerges in the next decade.

Acknowledgements. We would like to thank the College of Engineering and Computer Science at The Australian National University for supporting this work through

---

[3] The Roadrunner includes 12,240 PowerXCell 8i processor and was the world's fastest computer in 2008-2009; see http://www.lanl.gov/roadrunner/ .

the summer scholar program. Bradley Treeby is supported by the Australian Research Council/Microsoft Linkage Project LP100100588.

References

1. Matte, G.M., Van Neer, P.L.M.J., Danilouchkine, M.G., Huijssen, J., Verweij, M.D., de Jong, N.: Optimization of a phased-array transducer for multiple harmonic imaging in medical applications: frequency and topology. IEEE Trans. Ultrason. Ferroelectr. Freq. Control 58(3), 533–546 (2011)
2. Huang, J., Holt, R.G., Cleveland, R.O., Roy, R.A.: Experimental validation of a tractable numerical model for focused ultrasound heating in flow-through tissue phantoms. J. Acoust. Soc. Am. 116(4), 2451–2458 (2004)
3. Wein, W., Brunke, S., Khamene, A., Callstrom, M.R., Navab, N.: Automatic CT-ultrasound registration for diagnostic imaging and image-guided intervention 12(5), 577–585 (2008)
4. Pinton, G., Dahl, J., Rosenzweig, S., Trahey, G.: A heterogeneous nonlinear attenuating full-wave model of ultrasound. IEEE Transactions on Ultrasonics, Ferroelectrics and Frequency Control 56(3), 474–488 (2009)
5. Treeby, B.E., Tumen, M., Cox, B.T.: Time Domain Simulation of Harmonic Ultrasound Images and Beam Patterns in 3D Using the k-space Pseudospectral Method. In: Fichtinger, G., Martel, A., Peters, T. (eds.) MICCAI 2011, Part I. LNCS, vol. 6891, pp. 363–370. Springer, Heidelberg (2011)
6. Karamalis, A., Wein, W., Navab, N.: Fast Ultrasound Image Simulation using the Westervelt Equation. Medical Image Computing and Computer-Assisted Intervention, 243–250 (2010)
7. Varray, F., Cachard, C., Ramalli, A., Tortoli, P., Basset, O.: Simulation of ultrasound nonlinear propagation on GPU using a generalized angular spectrum method. EURASIP Journal on Image and Video Processing 17 (2011)
8. Bader, D., Agarwal, V., Madduri, K., Kang, S.: High performance combinatorial algorithm design on the Cell Broadband Engine processor. Parallel Computing 33(10-11), 720–740 (2007)
9. Chow, A., Fossum, G., Brokenshire, D.: A programming example: Large FFT on the Cell Broadband Engine (Online accessed January 24, 2012)
10. Bader, D., Agarwal, V.: FFTC: Fastest Fourier transform for the IBM Cell Broadband Engine. High Performance Computing, 172–184 (2007)
11. Xu, M., Thulasiraman, P.: Parallel Algorithm Design and Performance Evaluation of FDTD on 3 Different Architectures: Cluster, Homogeneous Multicore and Cell/BE. In: 10th IEEE International Conference on High Performance Computing and Communications, pp. 174–181. IEEE (2008)
12. Li, B., Jin, H., Shao, Z.: Two-Level Parallel Implementation of FDTD Algorithm on CBE. In: IEEE International Conference on Networking, Sensing and Control, pp. 1812–1817. IEEE (2008)
13. Hamilton, M.F., Blackstock, D.T. (eds.): Nonlinear Acoustics. Acoustical Society of America, Melville (2008)
14. Fornberg, B.: Generation of Finite Difference Formulas on Arbitrarily Spaced Grids. Mathematics of Computation 51(184), 699–706 (1988)
15. Hallaj, I., Cleveland, R.: FDTD simulation of finite-amplitude pressure and temperature fields for biomedical ultrasound. Acoustical Society of America 105, 7–12 (1999)
16. Kahle, J., Day, M., Hofstee, H., Johns, C., Maeurer, T., Shippy, D.: Introduction to the Cell multiprocessor. IBM Journal of Research and Development 49(4.5), 589–604 (2005)

17. IBM: Cell Broadband Engine Programming Handbook (2008) (Online accessed January 24, 2012)
18. Koranne, S.: Practical computing on the Cell Broadband Engine. Springer, New York (2009)
19. IBM: C/C++ Language Extensions for Cell Broadband Engine Architecture. vol. 2.4 (March 2007)
20. Jensen, J.A., Munk, P.: Computer phantoms for simulating ultrasound B-mode and cfm images. In: 23rd Acoustical Imaging Symposium, pp. 75–80 (1997)
21. Daoud, M., Lacefield, J.: Parallel three-dimensional simulation of ultrasound imaging. In: 22nd International Symposium on High Performance Computing Systems and Applications, pp. 146–152. IEEE (2008)
22. Liu, Q.: Large-scale simulations of electromagnetic and acoustic measurements using the pseudospectral time-domain (PSTD) algorithm. IEEE Transactions on Geoscience and Remote Sensing 37(2), 917–926 (1999)
23. Tabei, M., Mast, T., Waag, R.: A k-space method for coupled first-order acoustic propagation equations. The Journal of the Acoustical Society of America 111, 53–63 (2002)
24. Purrington, R.D., Norton, G.V.: A numerical comparison of the westervelt equation with viscous attenuation and a causal propagation operator. Mathematics and Computers in Simulation 82(7), 1287–1297 (2012)

Study on the Data Flow Balance in NFS Server with iSCSI

Nianmin Yao, Yong Han, Shaobin Cai, and Qilong Han

College of Computer Science and Technology,
Harbin Engineering University, China
{yaonianmin,hanyong,caishaobin,hanqilong}@hrbeu.edu.cn

Abstract. With the developing of the architecture of networked storage, a new type of storage servers acting as the data conduits over the network emerge, which is called pass-through servers. A typical example is the NFS servers based on iSCSI whose one end is connected to NFS clients and the other is connected to iSCSI storage device. As a store-and-forward device, the NFS servers experience heavy load, which includes protocols and data copying overhead, so a lot of CPU resource is consumed. In this paper, we build a mathematical model for the flow of data in pass-through servers using queuing theory and put forward a scheme of CPU time distribution. This scheme can allocate time of CPU to the service of iSCSI and NFS reasonably. Consequently, the flow rate of data inside servers is accelerated and the system performance is enhanced. We carry out both simulation experiments and real experiments to prove the conclusions. The results show that, if we properly adjust the CPU time distribution ratio according to different request sizes and different ratios of read/write requests, the system can improve the throughput more than 17% compared to the original one and can greatly reduce the mean response time of the data forwarding tasks.

Keywords: iSCSI; NFS; *SimPy*; SAN; pass-through server; Queuing Theory; flow balance; cpu time distribution.

1   Introduction

With the development of high-speed LAN technologies (e.g., Gigabit Ethernet), the IP-networked client-server storage architecture has become more and more common. The emerging of 10 Gb/s Ethernet will further accelerate this trend. Speaking from a broad sense, IP-based network storage is defined to be any approaches which permit remote data to be accessed over IP. A traditional method uses NFS (Network File System) [1], where the server provides clients a subset of local available namespace and clients use RPC (Remote Procedure Call) protocol to access meta-data and files on the server. Another approach which is used to access remote data is the IP-based storage area networking protocol iSCSI (Internet Small Computer System Interface) [2]. With this method, a portion of the remote disk's storage space is exported to a client.

Y. Xiang et al. (Eds.): ICA3PP 2012, Part I, LNCS 7439, pp. 253–272, 2012.

NFS and iSCSI are fundamentally in different data sharing semantics [3]. Since NFS can enable files of server machine to be shared among multiple client machines, it is inherently suitable for data sharing. However, the storage capacity provided by one single NFS server is limited. In contrast, iSCSI protocol supports a single client for one or several volumes of iSCSI server to permit applications of client machines to share remote data. Consequently, it is not directly suitable for sharing data across machines. However, iSCSI can use storage virtualization management technologies to make all the individual and scattered storage devices into a single SAN storage. So it provides users the logical capacity rather than the physical capacity, and brings the advantage of scalability and facility. A good distributed file system should combine both the advantage of data sharing feature of NFS and storage virtualization feature of iSCSI. Pass-through servers should accord with this demand.

Pass-through servers relay data between its two external parties. When data flow through the server, the system needs to do a great deal of protocol conversion and memory copying. As shown in Fig. 1, a typical example of these servers is a NFS server relying on network storage devices such as iSCSI or Fiber-Channel storage. Its main job is to pass data between NFS clients and iSCSI storage devices. The server uses two network interfaces to send and receive data by iSCSI protocol or NFS protocol respectively. Therefore, once data packets reach one of the network interfaces, the corresponding protocol would decapsulate the packets to fetch effective data and then it would be encapsulated by another protocol through the remaining interface. This process includes much work of protocol processing and memory copying. When the system operates at full capacity, all the work above will make the CPU busy working, so that the system can't provide abundant CPU time for both iSCSI module and NFS module. So it's obvious that the reasonable CPU time distribution to the service of iSCSI and NFS within the pass-through server is an important issue.

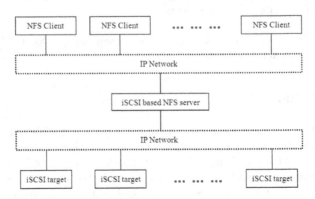

Fig. 1. Topology of storage system with iSCSI-based NFS server

In this paper, we design a scheme of CPU time distribution for pass-through servers that allocate CPU time to the iSCSI service and the NFS service reasonably. By presenting the data flow of a standard iSCSI based NFS server and its system overhead of memory copying and protocol processing, we build a mathematical model for the data flow in pass-through servers by queuing theory to provide the theory basis for our design. The potential performance gain of the proposed approach is demonstrated through measurements with the improved scheme compared to the original system.

The rest of this paper is structured as follows. Section 2 discusses related work. Section 3 introduces the overview of the iSCSI processing and the NFS processing. Section 4 presents the data flowing procession of the standard iSCSI based NFS server. Section 5 presents the theoretical model of the procession within the server. Section 6 discusses the measurement and performance evaluation of the mechanism. This paper is concluded in Section 7.

2   Related Work

The VISA architecture is well-known for such concept—SCSI over IP [4]. At the same period, CMU also proposed two innovative architectures which used networks to explore scalability and performance of block storage devices [5]. The iSCSI protocol [6,7] is a combination of the SCSI protocol and the traditional TCP/IP protocol. In view of the potential bottleneck caused by overhead of TCP/IP protocol and iSCSI protocol, optimization is usually performed with respect to data check, data copy and data encapsulation [8]. iSCSI protocol uses the software method for long division to calculate the CRC32 Field, which, as a result, consume a significant amount of CPU resource. Abhijeet [9] achieves CRC check calculation by the method of SB8 (Slicing-8) which is about three times faster than the traditional method. iSCSI layer hands over iSCSI PDUs to TCP/IP protocol stack buffer in the manner of memory copying. Ogawara [10] uses virtual memory remap technology to reach the goals of zero-copy, which makes CPU seizure rate brought down from 39.4% to 30.8%, but this method now remains in the field of laboratory study. If the length of data transmitted on a conventional Ethernet is in excess of 1500 bytes, it needs to be split and encapsulated anew. Gigabit Ethernet introduce jumbo frame whose size is 9000 bytes, in order to minimize the influence on CPU resource caused by the operation of split and encapsulation. And several other studies focus on the data path overheads and latency of the iSCSI protocol [11,12].

The study above is accomplished by scholars for the purpose of improving the performance of iSCSI protocol. Similarly there are also many scholars persevering in an effort to improve that of NFS. Some studies focus on the performance and cache consistency of network file-access protocols [13,14,15]. And in [15], a workload is used to evaluate the benefits of meta-data caching in a distributed file system. Recently Batsakis [16] accomplishes the CA-NFS (Congestion-Aware Network File System) with congestion pricing mechanism. It accelerates, defers, or cancels asynchronous requests in order to make the NFS server and all the clients coordinating with each other to use the various resources of the system.

All the work mentioned above aim at improving the performance of the iSCSI or NFS respectively, but not both. Reference [17] first puts forward a comparison of block-access and file-access protocols in the late eighties. Differing from the efforts which focus solely on NFS or iSCSI performance, [12] compares iSCSI to SMB, and

[18] uses meta-data intensive benchmarks to compare a commercial iSCSI target implementation and NFS. For designing IP-networked storage, [3] examines the suitability of the different layers (block-level and file-level) implementation by comparing iSCSI and NFS along several dimensions such as protocol interactions, network latency and sensitivity to different workloads.

After the pass-through servers have arisen, we should also study the problem emerging with the combination. Gang Peng [19] makes a case for network-centric buffer cache organization for the iSCSI based NFS servers. Since it eliminate any data copying between the network stack and the buffer/page cache, the system eliminates redundant data copying operations greatly when the data forwards through the server, increasing the capability of data transmission in pass-through servers. But this approach requires significant modifications to the file system underlying the NFS server. So its compatibility and portability are weak. By contrast, our scheme which can allocate time of CPU to the service of iSCSI and NFS reasonably is easier to be realized. To allocate CPU time to tasks according to special proportion is a basic function of modern operating system, so it can be achieved through simple settings with strong maneuverability.

3   Overview of iSCSI and NFS Processing

3.1   SCSI Initiator Processing

iSCSI [6,7] is a storage networking standard which uses IP Networks as its basis for accessing remote storage devices. How an iSCSI initiator processes a data PDU is demonstrated in [9]. We take iSCSI read operations for an example to show that.

An iSCSI PDU has a default size of 8KB, so it can span multiple TCP segments. As the NIC (Network Interface Card) receives these segments, the processing associated at the TCP/IP layer and below strips off the Eth/IP/TCP headers and queues the segment payloads into socket descriptor structures. The next, processing is associated with the iSCSI layer. The iSCSI header consists of a fixed 48 byte basic header, a header CRC, and in some cases additional header bytes. The iSCSI layer first reads the iSCSI header from the socket layer into an internal scratch buffer, and then it computes a CRC over the header and compares this value with the CRC attached to the header. A tag value included in the header is used for identifying the buffer/page cache where the data PDU should be placed. The iSCSI layer creates a scatter-list pointing to the buffer/page cache and passes it to the socket layer. Then the socket layer copies the iSCSI PDU payload from the TCP segments into the buffer/page cache. Finally, the data CRC is computed and validated over the entire PDU payload.

The iSCSI processing mainly involves three main components – CRC generation, data memory copy, and data structure manipulation. The CRC generation includes iSCSI header CRC calculation and entire iSCSI PDU payload CRC calculation. The data memory copy is the data transmission between buffer/page cache and network stack. The data structure manipulation runs through the whole processing.

In order to get the system time cost of each component mentioned above, we use a machine with a 1.7 GHz Intel Pentium processor and a single channel DDR-333 memory subsystem to perform the test. In the experiment, the maximum value of iSCSI PDU is set to be 8KB. Header digest and data digest adopt CRC32c standard. The results of the experiment showed that, when performing read processing, for each iSCSI PDU, no matter how great the PDU payload is, its data structure manipulation cost remains constant and it is about 1500 cycles. The total CRC generation cost and the total data memory copy cost are directly proportional to the effective PDU data payload. Using byte as a basic unit of analysis, the CRC generation cost is about 5.2 cycles per byte, while the data memory copy cost is about 1.8 cycles per byte. When performing write processing, its data structure manipulation cost is smaller than the cost of read processing and it is about 1400 cycles. The CRC generation cost and the data memory copy cost are the same per byte as those of read processing. If the effective data payload of an iSCSI PDU is δKB, then for each byte the cost of read (or write) processing can be expressed as:

$$Cost\_iscsi\_read\,(or\ write)_{\_per\_byte} = 5.2 + 1.8 + \frac{1500(or\ 1400)}{1024 \times \delta}\ (cycle)$$

So, when the effective PDU data payload becomes larger, The CRC generation cost and the data memory copy cost are significantly more than the data structure manipulation cost, and the both cost almost completely dominate the iSCSI protocol processing cost.

3.2   NFS Server Processing

There are four generations of the NFS protocol. NFS v3 [20] supports asynchronous writes and we assume that it takes TCP as its transport protocol here. For simplicity, in the following narrative, we will no longer introduce the processing associated at the TCP/IP layer and below. Next, We take the processing of read request for an example to show how NFS server works.

On the NFS server, the daemon process "nfsd" keeps on inquiring if there are requests from clients arriving. When NFS clients send a NFS read request to the NFS server, the daemon process first accepts the request and hands it over to the RPC (Remote Procedure Call), then the RPC uses the function "nfsd_dispatch" to call the read procedure "nfsd_proc_read". Before calling the read procedure, the function "nfsd_dispatch" uses a decoding function to convert the parameters from clients into a format which can be understood by the server. The NFS read handling function is unable to complete the whole read process by itself, so it must call the read function of underlying file system through VFS (Virtual File System) interface-the file read operation pointer "f_op→read" to perform the practical file read operating. This operation first searches the requested data from the buffer/page cache in the local file system. If the content happens to be cached in the buffer/page cache, the local file system copies the data directly to the NFS server module. Otherwise, it gets the data from the storage device firstly into the buffer/page cache, and then into the NFS server module. Then, when sending data to NFS clients, NFS server module converts the data into certain data format through XDR (eXternal Data Representation) protocol, and uses RPC to transmit it to network. This process incurs data copying from the NFS server module to the network stack once again.

The NFS processing mainly involves three main components – XDR conversion, data memory copy, function and procedure call. The XDR conversion performs coding process when sending data to clients, and performs decoding process when receiving written data from clients. The data memory copy includes two parts: one is the data transmission between buffer/page cache and NFS server module, and the other is the data transmission between NFS server module and network stack. The function and procedure call involves the RPC and all kinds of abstract NFS services, which constructs the whole framework of the NFS processing.

In addition, the abstract file operations provided by NFS are truly accomplished by the functions of underlying file system. These operations either read data from storage devices into buffer/page cache or write read data from buffer/page cache into storage devices. However, within an iSCSI based NFS server, all this work is accomplished by the iSCSI processing. So, we don't consider this part as one component of NFS processing here.

To get the system time cost of each component of NFS processing and compare these with the iSCSI processing, we still use the machine which performs the test for the iSCSI processing. In the experiment, we use NFS v3 and the parameters "*rsize*" and "*wsize*" which indicate the maximum length of the read/write data are set as 32KB. The results of the experiment showed that, when handling each read/write request, no matter how large the read/write data requested is, its function and procedure call cost remains constant and it is about 2200 cycles. The total XDR conversion cost and the total data memory copy cost are directly proportional to the size of the requested data. The sum of the two costs is about 4.4 cycles per byte. If the size of the data for a NFS read/write request is δ KB, then for each byte the cost of the processing handling read (or write) request can be expressed as:

$$Cost\_nfs\_read(or\ write)_{\_per\_byte} = 4.4 + \frac{2200}{1024 \times \delta}\ (cycle)$$

So, The larger the size of the data for the NFS read/write request is, the higher the percentage of the whole NFS processing that the server pays for the XDR conversion cost and the data memory copy cost.

3.3   Comparison and Summary

We don't discuss the overhead of the TCP/IP protocol above. Because in the following performance evaluation experiments, in order to release the CPU resource as much as possible, we will use NAC (Network Accelerator Card) to implement the TCP/IP processing, which is not only a NIC but also with the TOE (TCP offload engine). That means the iSCSI processing and the NFS processing are handled by the processor, and the TCP/IP processing is dealt with by the NAC to cut down the load on the CPU. So, we don't consider the overhead of the TCP/IP processing as an important issue here.

Now lets begin to compare the cost of the iSCSI processing with that of the NFS processing. The experiments above show that, under the environment with our machine, the calculation of CRC32 is the part which uses the most system time. The system spends 6.5 circles on the operations of that procession per byte, and 2.2 circles on the operations of memory copying per byte. Comparing with the iSCSI protocol, the NFS protocol does not include the computation-intense operations of data check, so the service provided by the NFS server spends almost all the CPU time on the two memory copy operations and the XDR conversion. In that case, when the data being transmitted is large, in order to complete the forwarding of one byte, the iSCSI processing needs approximately 7.0 cycles, and the NFS server processing needs approximately 4.4 cycles.

These analyses of the both processing costs indict that, when the size of the data requested is smaller or it is a meta-data read/write operation, the per-packet cost (which means the data structure manipulation cost in iSCSI or means the function and procedure call cost in NFS) dominates the whole processing cost. As the request size increases, the per-packet cost is gradually diluted and the per-byte cost (which means the CRC generation and the data memory copy cost in iSCSI or the XDR conversion and the data memory copy cost in NFS) plays an increasingly more important role. Therefore, different workloads have different effects on both the processing costs.

4   A Standard iSCSI-Based NFS Server's Data Flow

An iSCSI based NFS server's software structure is shown in Fig. 2, which indicates that each module copies data to the module contiguously. The solid lines with arrows describe the data flowing across different software modules within an iSCSI-based NFS server. These operations of memory copying and protocol processing are necessary because different modules need store data in different formats. For example, in case of the Linux kernel, data in network stack is stored in the format of *sk_buff*, but as contiguous buffer chunks in the buffer/page cache.

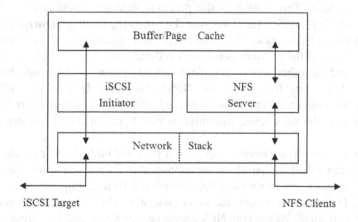

Fig. 2. An iSCSI-based NFS server's software structure and its data flowing path

When a NFS reading request reaches the NFS server, the server accepts the request and calls the read function of underlying file system to perform the practical file read operating. This operation first searches the data requested in the buffer/page cache in the local file system. If the data needed is found, the data would be copied directly to the NFS server by local file system. If not, the system sends a disk access request to the iSCSI initiator in order to retrieve the data from the iSCSI target which stores the requested data. While the iSCSI initiator receiving the requested data over the network, it gets iSCSI PDUs from TCP/IP protocol stack buffer and then decapsulates the PDUs to fetch effective data which would be firstly saved in buffer/page cache and then copied from the buffer/page cache to the NFS server. In case the NFS server module gets the requested data, it issues an NFS reply and sends it out to the NFS client through RPC protocol, which includes the XDR coding operations and the data copying from the NFS server module to the network stack.

When the NFS server copes with write requests, as the operations incurred by the processing for read requests, the same number of data copying and protocol processing operations are performed. With the XDR decoding operations, the written data is firstly copied from the network stack into the NFS server module, and then copied from the NFS server into the buffer/page cache of the local file system. If there are some dirty pages in the NFS server need to be flushed, the system issues disk requests to the iSCSI initiator in order to writes them back to the remote iSCSI target. When sending data to iSCSI target, the iSCSI initiator encapsulates the data in buffer/page cache to be iSCSI PDUs and copies them into the network stack, and then transmits the PDUs to IP network through TCP/IP protocol.

Thus it can be seen that, buffer/page cache becomes the communication hinge of the data flowing in an iSCSI-based NFS server. While performing the operations of writing, iSCSI module transfers the data from the network stack into the buffer/page cache with protocol processing and data format converting, while NFS server copying the data from buffer/page cache to the network stack. If the former's data transmitting rate is higher than the latter, the data in the buffer/page cache would be held up and waiting to be sent. This consumes the precious memory resource and affects the completion of the following tasks, because the following reading or writing tasks also need to perform a large amount of memory copying operations and they have to wait to be executed until the memory is released, reducing the data throughout rate within the server. And the other way round, if the latter is faster, iSCSI would become the bottleneck of the data forwarding and NFS server module would be idle, which produces a bad effect too. The same as writing, the process of reading is also facing the problems of the unmatched transmission rate between iSCSI module and NFS module.

Obviously, if we just provide ample CPU time for both iSCSI module and NFS module, we can avoid the problems mentioned above by accelerating the course of both ends' protocol processing and data format converting, improving the flow rate of data inside servers. However, the main task of an iSCSI based NFS server is to transport data from iSCSI target to NFS clients or vice versa, and it is pressurized by a heavy workload of memory copying in this process. In addition, there are other CPU-consuming tasks including network interrupt handling, TCP processing, NFS protocol handling, iSCSI processing and other related system tasks. All the tasks will make the CPU busy working, so that the system can't provide abundant CPU time for both iSCSI module and NFS module. For this reason, according to the data processing ability of CPU now available, a practical method of improving the performance of the iSCSI based NFS server is to allocate time of CPU to the service of iSCSI and NFS reasonably, which make both ends' rates of data forwarding match up to each other, in order to improve the data throughput of the server.

5   Theoretical Model of the Data Flow within the Server

Below we build the theoretical model of The data flow within the standard iSCSI based NFS server. In order to study the ideal state, we neglect the data forwarding bottleneck caused by the restriction of network bandwidth. Our purpose is to observe the whole process of the read/write tasks, so we now consider the case without the situation that the data requested is found directly in the buffer/page cache in the local file system of the server when the task of reading is carried out, and without the situation that the data written is saved in the dirty pages of the server until they are flushed when the task of writing is carried out.

It is observed that when the task of reading is carried out, the process of data flowing within a standard iSCSI based NFS server mainly includes two stages. In the stage one, the data stored in the network stack from the remote storage device is copied to the buffer/page cache, with iSCSI protocol decapsulation processing and data format converting. In the stage two, NFS server converts the data copied from the buffer/page cache into certain date format through XDR protocol, and then uses RPC to transmit the data to network by copying it from NFS server to the network stack. We assume that, with τ CPU clock cycles, the stage one can process and forward s_1 size of data, and the size of that the stage two can handle is s_2.

Similarly, the process of writing task is the reverse of the operations of reading task and its data flow also includes two stages. Specifically, the operations performed in the stage three and the stage four are the reverse of the stage two and the stage one. Assuming that, if the number of CPU clock cycles allocated is τ, the size of the data that the stage three can transfer is s_3 and the stage four can transfer is s_4.

In that case, if the number of CPU clock cycles allocated to the stage one by the system is $c_1\tau$, the size of the data the stage one can process and forward is $c_1 s_1$. Similarly, if the numbers of CPU clock cycles allocated to the stage two, the stage three and the stage four are $c_2\tau, c_3\tau$ and $c_4\tau$, within the corresponding CPU time, the sizes of data the three stages can process are $c_2 s_2$, $c_3 s_3$, $c_4 s_4$ respectively. That is to say, if we consider

$$T = (c_1 + c_2 + c_3 + c_4)\,\tau \tag{1}$$

as a basic CPU time cycle, by using the CPU clock cycles allocated to them within a basic cycle, each stage can forward $c_1 s_1$, $c_2 s_2$, $c_3 s_3$, $c_4 s_4$ sizes of data respectively.

In the theoretical model, we suppose that the arrival rate of read/write tasks reaching the NFS server obeys *Poisson* distribution with parameter λ, and the size of the data that read/write tasks request obeys *Exponential* distribution with parameter s. As shown in Fig. 3, all the tasks wait in the queue L_S. The proportion of read tasks to all tasks is α and the proportion of write tasks is β ($\alpha + \beta = 1$). S is the service counter in charge of receiving the requests of the tasks. In order to focus on the overhead of data transmitting, the overhead of receiving the requests is considered negligible. So we suppose that the service time of S is zero. And thus, when reaching S, L_S is divided into the read tasks queue L_1 and the write tasks queue L_3 immediately without any time wasted.

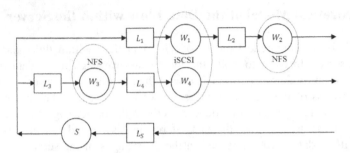

Fig. 3. Queueing model of the data flow within the server

Firstly, lets analyze the process of reading. The arrival rate of reading tasks reaching the queue L_1 obeys *Poisson* distribution with parameter $\alpha\lambda$. After waiting in the queue L_1, the task gets its operations of the stage one from the service counter W_1. Within a cycle T, the number of CPU clock cycles allocated to the stage one is $c_1\tau$, and the size of the data that the stage one can process and forward is c_1s_1. So the average number of the tasks that W_1 can complete per T is c_1s_1/s, and then the service rate of W_1 is represented as an equation

$$\mu_1 = c_1s_1/sT \tag{2}$$

Next, the tasks go on to wait in the queue L_2, in order to get the service of W_2 to completes the process of the stage two. In a two stage tandem queuing network, the arrival rate reaching the second queue is the same as the preceding [21], so the arrival rate for L_2 is $\alpha\lambda$ too. As the first stage, W_2 provides the service rate

$$\mu_2 = c_2s_2/sT \tag{3}$$

Then, it is writing task's turn to be observed. With the same rule as reading, the arrival rate of write tasks reaching the queue L_3 obeys *Poisson* distribution with parameter $\beta\lambda$ and so does the arrival rate reaching the queue L_4. the service counter W_3 and the service counter W_4 provide the service of the stage three and the stage four respectively. Obviously, W_3 provides the service rate $\mu_3 = c_3s_3/sT$ and W_4 provides the service rate $\mu_4 = c_4s_4/sT$.

The average queue length of read tasks expressed as L_r is the sum of the average length of the queue L_1 and that of L_2, which is showed as the equation:

$$L_r = \alpha\lambda/(\mu_1 - \alpha\lambda) + \alpha\lambda/(\mu_2 - \alpha\lambda) \tag{4}$$

So it is with the average queue length of write tasks represented by L_w, which is the sum of the average length of the queue L_3 and that of L_4. That means:

$$L_w = \beta\lambda/(\mu_3 - \beta\lambda) + \beta\lambda/(\mu_4 - \beta\lambda) \tag{5}$$

So the mean response time (the sum of waiting time and service time) of read tasks is represented as $W_r = 1/(\mu_1 - \alpha\lambda) + 1/(\mu_2 - \alpha\lambda)$ and that of write tasks is represented as $W_w = 1/(\mu_3 - \beta\lambda) + 1/(\mu_4 - \beta\lambda)$. The mean response time of all tasks is denoted as $W = \alpha W_r + \beta W_w$, and furthermore, that can be showed as following:

$$W = 1/((\mu_1/\alpha) - \lambda) + 1/((\mu_2/\alpha)) - \lambda) + 1/((\mu_3/\beta) - \lambda) + 1/((\mu_4/\beta) - \lambda) \tag{6}$$

We analyze the process of the read task and the write task in isolation. But in fact, both W_2 and W_3 offer the corresponding services of the NFS server module, although they implement the operation of data forwarding in the opposite directions. Similarly, W_1 and W_4 work together to perform the functions of the iSCSI module. W_4 use iSCSI protocol to encapsulate the data and then transfer it by memory copying, and W_1 provide the service with the decapsulation of iSCSI protocol processing. In the practical application, it's hard to split the function of the entire module into parts absolutely. So next, we study on the holistic indicator of each module. Within a cycle T, the number of CPU clock cycles allocated to W_1 by the system is $c_1\tau$, and that allocated to W_4 is $c_4\tau$, so the total CPU time allocated to the iSCSI module within the cycle is represented as

$$A\tau = (c_1 + c_4)\tau \tag{7}$$

In like manner, within the fixed time T, the total CPU time allocated to the iSCSI module is represented as

$$B\tau = (c_2 + c_3)\tau \tag{8}$$

Now lets study the relation between the numerical value of s_1 and that of s_4, and do the same to s_2 and s_3. Basically, while in the two processes of data forwarding in the opposite directions which belong to the same module, for the same amount of CPU time, the data that can be handled with the operation of memory copying and protocol processing by the two processes are the same of size. So it is approximatively expressed by the equations

$$s_4 = s_1, s_2 = s_3 \tag{9}$$

We insert (7) (8) (9) into (6) to calculate the mean response time of all tasks:

$$W = \frac{1}{(\frac{c_1 s_1}{sT\alpha})-\lambda} + \frac{1}{(\frac{(B-c_3)s_2}{sT\alpha})-\lambda} + \frac{1}{(\frac{c_3 s_3}{sT\beta})-\lambda} + \frac{1}{(\frac{(A-c_1)s_4}{sT\beta})-\lambda} = \frac{1}{(\frac{c_1 s_1}{sT\alpha})-\lambda} + \frac{1}{(\frac{(A-c_1)s_1}{sT\beta})-\lambda} +$$
$$\frac{1}{(\frac{(B-c_3)s_2}{sT\alpha})-\lambda} + \frac{1}{(\frac{c_3 s_2}{sT\beta})-\lambda} \tag{10}$$

Let the function $f(c_1) = 1/((c_1 s_1/sT\alpha) - \lambda) + 1/(((A - c_1) s_1/sT\beta) - \lambda)$. When $c_1 = A/2 + \lambda(\alpha - \beta)sT/2s_1$, $c_4 = A/2 + \lambda(\beta - \alpha)sT/2s_1$ are fulfilled, the function $f(c_1)$ can get the minimum value.

Let the function $f(c_3) = 1/(((B - c_3) s_2/sT\alpha) - \lambda) + 1/((c_3 s_2/sT\beta) - \lambda)$. When $c_3 = B/2 + \lambda(\alpha - \beta)sT/2s_2$, $c_2 = B/2 + \lambda(\beta - \alpha)sT/2s_2$ are fulfilled, the function $f(c_3)$ can get the minimum value.

So when

$$c_1 = A/2 + \lambda(\alpha - \beta)sT/2s_1$$
$$c_2 = B/2 + \lambda(\beta - \alpha)sT/2s_2 \qquad\qquad (11)$$
$$c_3 = B/2 + \lambda(\alpha - \beta)sT/2s_2$$
$$c_4 = A/2 + \lambda(\beta - \alpha)sT/2s_1$$

are fulfilled, the function $W = f(c_1) + f(c_3)$ can get its minimum value. In other words, now, we make the mean response time of all tasks the shortest.

When executing the read tasks, in order to ensure that the tasks could be carried out smoothly through the two service counters W_1 and W_2 arranged in tandem, both the average length of the queue L_1 and that of L_2 ought to have the same value, which is showed as the equation: $\alpha\lambda/(\mu_1 - \alpha\lambda) = \alpha\lambda/(\mu_2 - \alpha\lambda)$. Only in this way can the service counters be neither idle nor too busy. Similarly, when executing the write tasks, both the average length of L_3 and that of L_4 ought to have the same value and this means $\beta\lambda/(\mu_3 - \beta\lambda) = \beta\lambda/(\mu_4 - \beta\lambda)$. The equations above are calculated to get the following result:

$$s_1/s_2 = c_2/c_1 = c_3/c_4 \qquad\qquad (12)$$

We solve the equations consisting of formula (11) and formula (12) to get the equation:

$$A/B = s_2/s_1 \qquad\qquad (13)$$

which ensure that the operations of data forwarding can be performed smoothly and the mean response time of all tasks can get the minimum value. Thus it can be seen that, no matter what the proportion of read tasks or write tasks is, to allocate time of CPU to the service of iSCSI and NFS reasonably in the ratio of s_2/s_1 can improve the performance of the system.

This deduction has great significance. On enterprise systems, reading usually is much more than writing unless it is a data collection system of some sort. Database systems assume something like a 60/40 split reading/writing historically. For supercomputing scratch systems, it has heavy writing for checkpoint restarts. Developer machines have heavy writing due to code compilation of intermediate files. General end user machines are very heavy for reading since users generally consume rather than create data. With this deduction, there will be no need to collect data about the proportion of writing and reading requests.

However, this conclusion is acquired from assumed ideal status. We just study the data flow within the iSCSI based NFS server without considering the impact of the network transmission and the asynchronous read/write operations. More importantly, we should test and verify that with different kinds of workloads. Therefore, in the following experiments, based on an overall consideration of above various factors, we will further investigate this conclusion.

6   Setup and Performance Evaluation

This section describes the system setup used by our experiments and our storage performance evaluation. For better proving the conclusions, we carry out both simulation experiments and real experiments. In the simulation experiments, we make the request arrival rate and the request size obey the assumed ideal distributions of Section 5, without considering the impact of the factors including the network latency, the asynchronous operations and the workloads. In the real experiments, based on an overall consideration of various factors mentioned above, we test the performance of a real storage system to verify the conclusions.

6.1   System Setup

The storage testbed used in our experiments consists of four NFS clients, an iSCSI based NFS server, and an iSCSI storage server. The NFS clients are 1 GHz Pentium-III machines with 512MB main memory. The iSCSI based NFS server is a machine with a 1.7 GHz Intel Pentium processor and a single channel DDR-333 memory subsystem which has 1 GB main memory. The iSCSI storage server connects an Adaptec Serve RAID adapter card to a Dell PowerVault disk pack with fourteen SCSI disks and the storage system is configured as RAID-0. All machines are equipped with Intel Pro/1000 MT Server Gigabit Ethernet adapters and are connected to a Gigabit switch. To avoid network link performance bottleneck, the iSCSI based NFS server machine uses two Ethernet adapters to serve the NFS clients and the iSCSI storage server respectively.

The operating system on all machines is RedHat Linux 9 with kernel version 2.4.20. The default file system used in our experiments is *ext3* and the block size is set to be 4 KB. The NFS server is based on NFS v3 and it uses TCP as the transport protocol [20]. We choose an open-source iSCSI implementation UNH_iSCSI.1.6.00 [22]. The TCP/IP checksum offloading support on the Ethernet card is enabled.

6.2   Simulation Evaluation

The experiments are performed under the simulation scenarios constructed by *SimPy* in accordance with the requirements of Section 5 to imitate the process of the read/write tasks. In the course of implementation, the ratio of read tasks to write tasks is 50%, and the arrival rate of tasks obeys *Poisson* distribution with parameter λ, and the size of the data that read/write tasks request obeys *Exponential* distribution with parameter s.

Now lets begin to analyze the proportion of the data size processed by the iSCSI module to that processed by the NFS module within the same CPU time. From the analysis of Section 3 we learn that, for data-intensive applications with large data requested, the proportion of the data forwarding rate of iSCSI module to that of NFS server module is about 4.4/7.0. Therefore the improved system should allocate time of CPU to the iSCSI module and the NFS server module in the ratio of $7.0/4.4 = 1.6$.

When the value of parameter s with which the request size obeys *Exponential* distribution is set at 512 KB, we measured the performance of the NFS server throughput and the mean response time of tasks for varying parameter λ. The performance comparison is done for eight CPU time distribution configurations in Fig. 4 and Fig. 5. The horizontal abscissas of all the following figures denote the CPU time distribution ratio of iSCSI to NFS. The parameter λ ranges from 96 to 288. Each curve corresponds to a certain value of the request arrival rate parameter λ.

As shown in Fig. 4, when λ has a small value, the CPU workload is low, and as the CPU time distribution ratio varies, the mean response time of tasks shows no significant changes. With the increasing of the value of λ, the CPU workload increases gradually and the distribution effectively exerts more positive influence on the system performance, which makes the mean response time of tasks get its minimum value at the optimal distribution ratio point. In terms of throughput whose result is shown in Fig. 5, when λ value is small, the CPU is not saturated by data processing. The same as the mean response time of tasks, when the CPU operates below capacity, the distribution does not enhance the throughput performance obviously. When the value of λ comes to the larger numbers, the CPU operates at an overload. In such circumstances, the throughput of the server reaches the limit and gets its maximum value at the optimal distribution ratio point. Thus it can be seen that, when the CPU operates at full capacity, the allocation mechanism can exploit its advantages to use the limited CPU resources more effectively.

Each curve in Fig. 6 and in Fig. 7 corresponds to a certain combination value of parameters s and $λ$ which just push the CPU to its limit and make it working almost at full capacity. And the two parameters are in inverse proportion to each other.

As shown in Fig. 6, in the full load states established by combination value of two parameters, the optimal distribution ratio point has the lowest value of mean response time of tasks. Moreover, with the increasing of the value of s, the mechanism develops its advantage more conspicuously. Fig. 7 shows that when the system runs at full capacity, the server has a sustained maximum throughput as high as around 80MB/s at the optimal distribution ratio point.

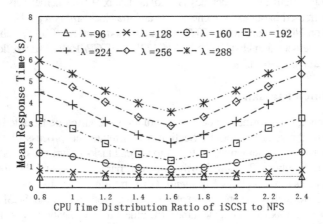

Fig. 4. Mean response time of requests with parameter s value of 512KB for different parameter $λ$ value

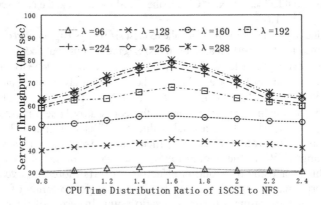

Fig. 5. Throughput of NFS server with parameter s value of 512KB for different parameter $λ$ value

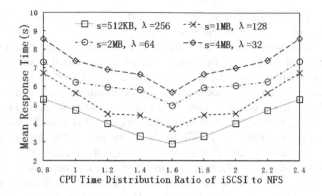

Fig. 6. Mean response time of requests for different combination value of two parameters

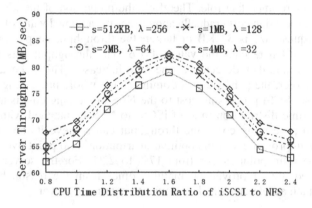

Fig. 7. Throughput of NFS server for different combination value of two parameters

6.3 Real Evaluation

6.3.1 Impact of Workloads

In the simulation experiments, we have the simulation testing and the performance analyzing on the data-intensive applications with large data requested. In this section, we test the performance of a real storage system. Besides, we ought to also study the situation for data-intensive applications with small data requested and metadata-intensive applications.

For the purpose of our research is how to allocate time of CPU to the service of iSCSI and NFS reasonably, we only observe the *all-miss* workloads, which means all NFS requests miss in the buffer/page cache of the local file system in the NFS server machine. In the course of implementation, the ratio of NFS read and write requests is maintained at the value 6:1. The workloads comprise of requests of size from 1 KB to 256 KB. The number of NFS server daemons is adjusted to reach the best performance.

Fig. 8 shows the throughput when all NFS requests miss in the server's buffer cache. Each curve corresponds to a certain size of the NFS requests. Once the NFS request is accepted, it is the first for the NFS client to get the meta-data. So, data-intensive applications with small data requested can be considered as metadata-intensive applications.

When a meta-data read/write operation is performed, iSCSI incurs a quite higher overhead than NFS. In case of NFS, a single packet is sufficient to invoke a file system operation on a path name. In contrast, in case of iSCSI the path name must be completely resolved before the operation can proceed, which results in additional packet overhead. Furthermore, the meta-data packet size in iSCSI is higher than that of NFS. For iSCSI is a block access protocol, the granularity of reads and writes in iSCSI is a disk block while RPCs allow NFS to read or write smaller chunks of data.

As shown in Fig. 8, when the size of the data requested is smaller than 4 KB, as the CPU time distribution ratio of iSCSI to NFS increases, the throughput becomes increasingly higher and higher. This is because when the request size is smaller, the meta-data cost dominates the whole processing cost, and the meta-data cost of iSCSI is much higher than that of NFS. So, the more CPU time is allocated to the iSCSI processing, the higher the throughput achieves. However, as the request size increases, the meta-data cost and the per-packet cost is gradually diluted, and the per-byte cost plays an increasingly more important role. Therefore, the proportion of the iSCSI processing cost to the NFS processing cost gradually approaches the assumed value of 1.6.

When the request size is 32 KB or larger, the throughput keeps going up as the ratio increases until it reaches the value of 1.6. The throughput gets its maximum value at this point and then descends as the ratio increases. This is because when the request size is larger, the per-byte cost dominates the whole processing cost, and the proportion of the iSCSI processing cost to the NFS processing cost is about 1.6. So, when the CPU time distribution ratio of iSCSI to NFS is matched with the practical ratio of the two processing costs, the throughput can achieve its best performance. The throughput improvement of the optimal distribution ratio point over the half-and-half distribution ratio point ranges from 17% to 22%. For the server CPU always remains saturated, this improvement mainly comes from the reasonable CPU time distribution, which accelerates the data flow rate within the server.

6.3.2   Impact of Asynchronous Operations
The previous section studies the impact of the CPU time distribution on the throughput under workloads with different request sizes. In this section, we carry out further studies for workloads with different ratio of read/write requests.

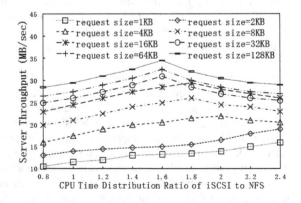

Fig. 8. Throughput of NFS server for different request sizes

Reference [3] finds that NFS v3 and iSCSI are comparable for read-intensive workloads. However, iSCSI significantly outperforms NFS v3 for write-intensive workloads. The higher performance of iSCSI is due to the asynchronous writes in the *ext3* file system. NFS v3 also supports asynchronous writes, but it specifies a limit on the number of pending writes in the cache at the NFS client. For write-intensive workloads, this limit is quickly reached, causing the write-back cache to degenerate into a write-through cache. Since iSCSI appears to issue very large write requests (mean request size is 128KB as opposed to 4.7KB in NFS), the number of messages in iSCSI is significantly smaller than NFS. Consequently, the total NFS packet cost is significantly higher than iSCSI.

We run the *all-miss* workloads with the requests of size 128 KB. Fig. 9 shows the throughput when all NFS requests miss in the server's buffer cache. Each curve corresponds to a certain ratio of NFS read/write requests. As shown in Fig. 9, as the ratio of NFS read/write requests decreases, the maximum throughput for each ratio gradually increases too.

When the ratio of NFS read/write requests is smaller than 1.0, the differences of the asynchronous write performance between NFS and iSCSI are not embodied obviously and the per-byte cost holds a leading post. So, when the CPU time distribution ratio of iSCSI to NFS is matched with the theory value of 1.6, the throughput can achieve its best performance. When the ratio is equal to or larger than 1.0, the CPU time distribution ratio of value 1.4 can get the maximum throughput. This is because that, the iSCSI processing may pay for one packet cost to accomplish a data forwarding task, while the NFS processing needs several packet costs for the same work, which is caused by the differences of performance for asynchronous write operations. As the proportion of write request increases, the total exceeding packet costs of the NFS over the iSCSI becomes increasingly higher and higher. Consequently, now to allocate a little more CPU time to the NFS than assumed above can achieve better performance. When the write requests take a large proportion, the throughput improvement of the optimal practical distribution ratio point over the optimal theoretical distribution ratio point ranges between 6% to 8%.

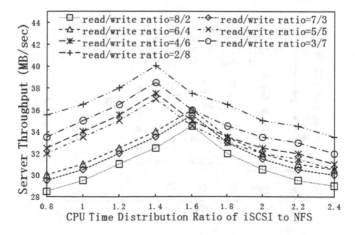

Fig. 9. Throughput of NFS server for different read/write request ratios

6.3.3   Impact of Network Latency

In the experiments above, we assume a Gigabit Ethernet LAN under the condition of light load, and the RTT (Round-Trip Time) is very small (<1ms). In practice, the latency between the NFS clients and the iSCSI based NFS server, and the latency between the iSCSI based NFS server and the iSCSI storage server, can vary from a few milliseconds to tens of milliseconds, determined by the distance between the machines. Consequently, in this section, we vary the network latency and study the impact of the CPU time distribution on the throughput under different RTTs. We vary the RTT from 10ms to 80ms to simulate wide-area conditions.

When performing read operations, the network latency has a great impact on the performance of both the NFS and the iSCSI. In case of write operations, for the pseudo-synchronous nature of writes, the performance of the NFS is impacted and increases with the latency. However, due to the asynchronous write nature, the performance of the iSCSI is almost not affected by the network latency. So, when the latency is high, write operations cause more performance differences on the both applications than read operations. Therefore, in the experiments of this section, to make the study more representative, we set the ratio of NFS read and write requests to be maintained at the value 1:4.

We run the *all-miss* workloads with the requests of size 128 KB. Fig. 10 shows the throughput when all NFS requests miss in the server's buffer cache. Each curve corresponds to a certain value of RTT. As shown in Fig. 10, when the RTT is lower than 30 ms, the CPU time distribution has an effect on the throughput distinctly.

Then, as the RTT increases, the impact of the CPU time distribution on the throughput gradually decreases. And when the RTT is equal to or higher than 80 ms, the CPU time distribution hardly has any influence on the throughput. This is because when the network latency is higher, the number of the packets processed by the server is smaller, and therefore the CPU is made working under low workload. So, no matter how the CPU time is allocated, the service time provided for both the iSCSI module and the NFS module is sufficient. Consequently, when the latency is high, the CPU time distribution only has a small influence on the throughput.

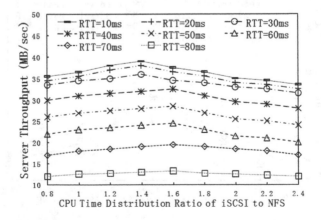

Fig. 10. Throughput of NFS server for different RTTs

7   Conclusion

In this paper, first we analyze the data flowing procession of the standard iSCSI based NFS server and the system overhead within the procession, then analyze the proportion of the data forwarding rate of iSCSI module to that of NFS server module in specified hardware circumstances. Next, we build a mathematical model for the whole data forwarding process of the NFS server by queuing theory, which is used as the theory basis of the improved CPU time allocation mechanism, finally carry out both simulation experiments and real experiments to have the performance test.

We use *SimPy* to construct the simulation scenarios to imitate the process of the read/write requests, and the experimental results basically tally with the theoretical analysis. The system experiments results indicate that, when the system operates at full capacity, with the optimal distribution ratio it can effectively use the limited CPU resources, making the mean response time of tasks decrease conspicuously and improving the throughput by 25% than the half-and-half distribution ratio point.

In the real experiments, based on an overall considering the impact of various factors including the workloads, the asynchronous operations and the network latency, we test the performance of a real storage system to verify the conclusions. The distribution ratio mentioned below means the CPU time distribution ratio of iSCSI to NFS. When the data-intensive applications with large data requested take read operations as the dominant factor, the system can achieve its best performance at the optimal distribution ratio point, and as the proportion of write operations increases, this distribution ratio ought to be brought down appropriately to maintain the best performance. While for the situation of data-intensive applications with small data requested and metadata-intensive applications, in order to achieve the best throughput performance, the distribution ratio ought to be enhanced gradually with the decrease of the size of the requested data. When the latency is high, the CPU is made working under low workload and so the CPU time distribution only has a small influence on the throughput. Consequently, we should properly adjust the distribution ratio according to different request sizes and different ratios of read/write requests to get the best storage system performance.

References

[1] Sandberg, R., Golgberg, D., Kleiman, S., Walsh, D., Lyon, B.: Design and implementation of the Sun network filesystem. In: Innovations in Internetworking, pp. 379–390. Artech House, Inc., Norwood (1988)

[2] Sarkar, P., Voruganti, K.: IP Storage: The Challenge Ahead. In: Proceedings of the 19th IEEE Symposium on Mass Storage Systems, College Park, MD, pp. 35–42 (April 2002)

[3] Radkov, P., Li, Y., Goyal, P., Sarkar, P., Shenoy, P.: A Performance Comparison of NFS and iSCSI for IP-Networked Storage. In: Proceedings of the 3rd USENIX Conference on File and Storage Technologies (FAST 2004), pp. 101–114. USENIX Association, Berkeley (2004)

[4] Meter, R.V., Finn, G.G., Hotz, S.: VISA: Netstation's virtual Internet SCSI adapter. In: Proceedings of the 8th International Conference on Architectural Support for Programming Languages and Operating Systems (ASPLOS-VIII), pp. 71–80. ACM, New York (1998)

[5] Gibson, G.A., Nagle, D.F., Amiri, K., Butler, J., Chang, F.W., Gobioff, H.: A cost-effective, high-bandwidth storage architecture. In: Proceedings of the 8th International Conference on Architectural Support for Programming Languages and Operating Systems (ASPLOS-VIII), pp. 92–103. ACM, New York (1998)

[6] Meth, K.Z., Satran, J.: Design of the iSCSI Protocol. In: Proceedings of the 20th IEEE/11th NASA Goddard Conference on Mass Storage Systems and Technologies (MSS 2003), p. 116. IEEE Computer Society, Washington, DC (2003)

[7] Satran, J., Meth, K., Sapuntzakis, C., Chadalapaka, M., Zeidner, E.: Internet Small Computer Systems Interface (iSCSI). IBM, Inc. (April 2004),
http://www.ietf.org/rfc/rfc3720.txt

[8] Tan, Z., Wan, J.: Review of iSCSI Performance Improvement Aproaches. Journal of Computer Science 36, 16–18 (2009) (in Chinese)

[9] Joglekar, A., Kounavis, M.E., Berry, F.L.: A scalable and high performance software iSCSI implementation. In: Proceedings of the 4th Conference on USENIX Conference on File and Storage Technologies (FAST 2005), p. 20. USENIX Association, Berkeley (2005)

[10] Tomonori, F., Masanori, O.: Performance of optimized software implementation of the iSCSI protocol. In: Proceedings of the International Workshop on Storage Network Architecture and Parallel I/Os (SNAPI 2003), pp. 1–10. ACM, New York (2003)

[11] Aiken, S., Grunwald, D., Pleszkun, A.R., Willeke, J.: A Performance Analysis of the iSCSI Protocol. In: Proceedings of the 20th IEEE/11th NASA Goddard Conference on Mass Storage Systems and Technologies (MSS 2003), p. 123. IEEE Computer Society, Washington, DC (2003)

[12] Lu, Y., Du, D.: Performance Study of iSCSI-Based Storage Subsystems. IEEE Communications Magazine 41, 76–82 (2003)

[13] Howard, J.H., Kazar, M.L., Menees, S.G., Nichols, D.A., Satyanarayanan, M., Sidebotham, R.N., West, M.J.: Scale and performance in a distributed file system. ACM Transactions on Computer Systems 6, 51–81 (1988)

[14] Pawlowski, B., Juszczak, C., Staubach, P., Smith, C., Lebel, D., Hitz, D.: NFS Version 3: Design and Implementation. In: Proceedings of USENIX Summer, pp. 137–152 (June 1994)

[15] Shirriff, K., Ousterhout, J.: A Trace-Driven Analysis of Name and Attribute Caching in a Distributed System. In: Proceedings of USENIX Winter, pp. 315–331 (January 1992)

[16] Batsakis, A., Burns, R., Kanevsky, A., Lentini, J., Talpey, T.: CA-NFS: A congestion-aware network file system. ACM Transactions on Storage 5 (December 2009)

[17] Ramakrishnan, K.K., Emer, J.S.: Performance Analysis of Mass Storage Service Alternatives for Distributed Systems. IEEE Transactions on Software Engineering 15, 120–133 (1989)

[18] Performance Comparison of iSCSI and NFS IP Storage Protocols. Technical report, TechnoMages, Inc.

[19] Peng, G., Sharma, S., Chiueh, T.: Network-Centric Buffer Cache Organization. In: Proceedings of the 25th IEEE International Conference on Distributed Computing Systems (ICDCS 2005), pp. 219–228. IEEE Computer Society, Washington, DC (2005)

[20] Callaghan, B., Pawlowski, B., Staubach, P.: RFC1813: NFS Version 3 Protocol Specification. Sun Microsystems, Inc. (June 1995),
http://www.faqs.org/rfcs/rfc1813.html

[21] Sheng, Y.: Queue Theory and Its Application in Computer Communication. Beijing University of Posts and Telecommunications Press, Beijing (2000)

[22] UNH-iSCSI Initiator and Target for Linux,
http://sourceforge.net/projects/unh-iscsi/

Performance, Scalability, and Semantics of Concurrent FIFO Queues*

Christoph M. Kirsch, Hannes Payer, Harald Röck, and Ana Sokolova

Department of Computer Sciences
University of Salzburg, Austria
{Christoph.Kirsch,Hannes.Payer,Harald.Röck,Ana.Sokolova}@cs.uni-salzburg.at

Abstract. We introduce the notion of a k-FIFO queue which may dequeue elements out of FIFO order up to a constant $k \geq 0$. Retrieving the oldest element from the queue may require up to $k + 1$ dequeue operations (bounded lateness), which may return elements not younger than the $k + 1$ oldest elements in the queue (bounded age) or nothing even if there are elements in the queue. A k-FIFO queue is starvation-free for finite k where $k + 1$ is what we call the worst-case semantical deviation (WCSD) of the queue from a regular FIFO queue. The WCSD bounds the actual semantical deviation (ASD) of a k-FIFO queue from a regular FIFO queue when applied to a given workload. Intuitively, the ASD keeps track of the number of dequeue operations necessary to return oldest elements and the age of dequeued elements. We show that a number of existing concurrent algorithms implement k-FIFO queues whose WCSD are determined by configurable constants independent from any workload. We then introduce so-called Scal queues, which implement k-FIFO queues with generally larger, workload-dependent as well as unbounded WCSD. Since ASD cannot be obtained without prohibitive overhead we have developed a tool that computes lower bounds on ASD from time-stamped runs. Our micro- and macrobenchmarks on a state-of-the-art 40-core multiprocessor machine show that Scal queues, as an immediate consequence of their weaker WCSD, outperform and outscale existing implementations at the expense of moderately increased lower bounds on ASD.

1 Introduction

We are interested in designing and implementing concurrent FIFO queues that provide high performance and positive scalability on shared memory, multiprocessor and multicore machines. By performance we mean throughput measured in queue operations per second. Scalability is performance as a function of the number of threads in a system. The ideal result is linear scalability and high performance already with few threads. This is nevertheless an unlikely outcome on multicore hardware where shared memory access is typically orders of magnitude slower than core computation. A still challenging yet more realistic outcome and our goal in particular is positive scalability, i.e., increasing performance with an increasing number of threads, up to as many

* This work has been supported by the Austrian Science Fund (National Research Network RiSE on Rigorous Systems Engineering S11404-N23 and Elise Richter Fellowship V00125) and the National Science Foundation (CNS1136141).

Y. Xiang et al. (Eds.): ICA3PP 2012, Part I, LNCS 7439, pp. 273–287, 2012.
© Springer-Verlag Berlin Heidelberg 2012

threads as possible, and high performance already with few threads. Achieving both performance and scalability is important since positive scalability but low performance with few threads may be even worse than negative scalability.

The key to high performance and positive scalability is parallelization with low sequential overhead. Earlier attempts to improve the performance and scalability of simple, lock-based FIFO queues include the lock-free Michael-Scott FIFO Queue [13] and, more recently, the Flat-Combining FIFO Queue [11], which we have both implemented for our experiments. Both algorithms tend to provide better performance and scale to more threads than lock-based FIFO queues. Another two recent examples of algorithms that aim at improving performance and scalability are the Random Dequeue Queue [1] and the Segment Queue [1], which we have also implemented and study here. An important difference to the former two algorithms is that the latter two provide only relaxed FIFO semantics in the sense that elements may be returned out of FIFO order. The goal is to increase parallelism further while the challenge is to maintain bounds on the relaxation of semantics.

Based on the same principle of improving performance and scalability at the expense of strict FIFO semantics we propose Scal queues for implementing FIFO queues with relaxed semantics. The idea is to maintain (a distributed system of) p instances of a regular FIFO queue (we chose Michael-Scott for our experiments) and then select, upon each enqueue or dequeue operation, one of the p instances before performing the operation on the selected instance without further coordination with the other instances. Thus up to p queueing operations may be performed in parallel. Selection is done by a load balancer whose implementation has an immediate impact on performance, scalability, and semantics. In particular, the load balancer determines how close the semantics of the Scal queue is to the semantics of a regular FIFO queue. We have implemented a variety of load balancers for our experiments to study the trade-off between performance, scalability, and semantics with Scal queues relative to the previously mentioned queues.

With the straightforward metric of operation throughput in place for measuring performance, the only remaining challenge is to quantify and to measure difference in semantics. For this purpose, we introduce the notion of semantical deviation as a metric for quantifying the difference in semantics between a queue with relaxed FIFO semantics and a regular FIFO queue. Intuitively, when running a given queue implementation on some workload, semantical deviation keeps track of the number of dequeue operations necessary to return oldest elements and the age of dequeued elements. However, measuring actual semantical deviation on existing hardware is only possible indirectly and approximatively through time-stamping invocation and response events of operations online, and then computing offline, using a tool that we developed, an approximation of the actual run that took place. The approximation is a sequence of linearization points that leads to a lower bound on the actual semantical deviation.

Here a key observation is that there exist upper bounds on semantical deviation independent of at least all workloads in a given class (e.g. with a fixed number of threads) for most of the implementations we consider. It turns out that these implementations are instances of the notion of a k-FIFO queue for different $k \geq 0$ where $k + 1$ is their worst-case semantical deviation from a regular FIFO queue. A k-FIFO queue may dequeue elements out of FIFO order up to k. In particular, retrieving the oldest element from

$$enqueue_k(e)(q,l) = (q \cdot e, l)$$

$$
dequeue_k(e)(q,l) =
\begin{cases}
(\varepsilon, 0) & \text{if } e = null, q = \varepsilon & \text{(L1)} \\
(q, l+1) & \text{if } e = null, q \neq \varepsilon, \text{(C1) } l < k & \text{(L2)} \\
(q', 0) & \text{if } q = e \cdot q' & \text{(L3)} \\
(e_1 \ldots e_{i-1} e_{i+1} \ldots e_n, l+1) & \text{if } e = e_i, q = e_1 \ldots e_n, & \text{(L4)} \\
& \quad 1 < i \leq n, \text{(C2) } l < k, \\
& \quad \text{(C3) } i \leq k+1-l \\
error & \text{otherwise} & \text{(L5)}
\end{cases}
$$

Fig. 1. Sequential specification of a k-FIFO queue (a FIFO queue w/o lines (L2), (L4); a POOL w/o conditions (C1), (C2), (C3))

the queue may require up to $k+1$ dequeue operations (bounded lateness), which may return elements not younger than the $k+1$ oldest elements in the queue (bounded age) or nothing even if there are elements in the queue. Depending on the implementation k may or may not depend on workload characteristics such as number of threads or may even be probabilistic. The non-determinism in the choice of elements to be returned provides the potential for performance and scalability which, in our benchmarks, tend to increase with increasing k.

We summarize the contributions of this paper: (1) the notion of k-FIFO queues (previously presented in a brief announcement [12]), (2) Scal queues, (3) the notion of semantical deviation, and (4) micro- and macrobenchmarks showing the trade-off between performance, scalability, and semantics.

In Section 2, we formally define k-FIFO queues and then discuss the existing concurrent algorithms we consider. In Section 3, we introduce Scal queues along with the load balancers we have designed and implemented. Semantical deviation is defined in Section 4. Related work is discussed in Section 5, our experiments are presented in Section 6, and conclusions are in Section 7.

2 k-FIFO Queues

We introduce the notion of a k-FIFO queue where $k \geq 0$. Similar to a regular FIFO queue, a k-FIFO queue provides an enqueue and a dequeue operation but with a strictly more general semantics defined as follows. Let the tuple (q, l) denote the state of a k-FIFO queue where q is the sequence of queue elements and l is an integer, called lateness, that counts the number of dequeue operations since the most recent dequeue operation removed the oldest element. The initial, empty state of a k-FIFO queue is $(\varepsilon, 0)$. The enqueue operation of a k-FIFO queue is a function from queue states and queue elements to queue states. The dequeue operation is a function from queue states and queue elements or the *null* return value to queue states. The formal definition of the semantics (sequential specification) of a k-FIFO queue is shown in Figure 1. In order to keep the definition simple we assume, without loss of generality, that queue elements are unique, i.e., each element will only be enqueued once and discarded when dequeued.

A k-FIFO queue is a queue where an enqueue operation, as usual, adds an element to the queue tail. A dequeue operation, however, may either return nothing (*null*) although there could be elements in the queue, or else remove one of the $k+1-l$ oldest elements from the queue with $l < k$ again being the number of invoked dequeue operations since the most recent dequeue operation that removed the oldest element from the queue. Retrieving the oldest element from the queue may require up to $k+1$ dequeue operations (bounded lateness), which may return *null* or elements not younger than the $k+1-l$ oldest elements in the queue (bounded age) and which may be interleaved with any number of enqueue operations. Thus k-FIFO queues are starvation-free for finite k and a 0-FIFO queue is a regular FIFO queue.

The standard definition of a regular FIFO queue can be obtained from Figure 1 by dropping lines (L2) and (L4). Just dropping line (L2) provides the definition of a k-FIFO queue without *null* returns if non-empty, which is a special case that we have implemented for some queues. Other combinations may also be meaningful, e.g. dropping conditions (C1), (C2), and (C3) defines the semantics of a POOL. In other words, a POOL is equivalent to a k-FIFO queue with unbounded k.

2.1   Implementations

We study different implementations of k-FIFO queues with k independent from any workload as well as k dependent on workload parameters such as the number of threads. In particular, k may or may not be configurable for a given implementation.

The following queues implement regular FIFO queues: a standard lock-based FIFO queue (LB), the lock-free Michael-Scott FIFO queue (MS) [13], and the flat-combining FIFO queue (FC) [11]. LB locks a mutex for each data structure operation. With MS each thread uses at least two compare-and-swap (CAS) operations to insert an element into the queue and at least one CAS operation to remove an element from the queue. FC is based on the idea that a single thread performs the queue operations of multiple threads by locking the whole queue, collecting pending queue operations, and applying them to the queue.

The Random Dequeue Queue (RD) [1] is a k-FIFO queue where $k = r$ and r defines the range $[0, r-1]$ of a random number. RD is based on MS where the dequeue operation was modified in a way that the random number determines which element is returned starting from the oldest element. If the element is not the oldest element in the queue it is marked as dequeued and returned but not removed from the queue. If the element is already marked as dequeued the process is repeated until a not-dequeued element is found or the queue is empty. If the element is the oldest element the queue head is set to the first not-dequeued element and all elements in between are removed. Hence RD may be out-of-FIFO order by at most r and always returns an element when the queue is not empty. RD was originally not defined as a k-FIFO queue but introduced in the context of relaxing the consistency condition linearizability [1].

The Segment Queue (SQ) [1] is a k-FIFO queue implemented by a non-blocking FIFO queue of segments. A segment can hold s queue elements. An enqueue operation inserts an element at an arbitrary position of the youngest segment. A dequeue operation removes an arbitrary element from the oldest segment. When a segment becomes full a new segment is added to the queue. When a segment becomes empty it is removed from the queue. A thread performing a dequeue operation starts looking for an element in the oldest segment. If the segment is empty it is removed and the thread checks

the next oldest segment and so on until it either finds an element and returns that, or
else may return *null* if only one segment containing up to $s - 1$ elements remains in
the queue. The thread returns *null* if other threads dequeued the up to $s - 1$ elements
before the thread could find them. Hence, $k = s$ for SQ. SQ was originally not defined
as a k-FIFO queue but introduced in the context of relaxing the consistency condition
linearizability [1].

Next, we discuss new implementations of k-FIFO queues where k depends not only
on constant numbers but also on the workload such as the number of threads or is even
unbounded and may only be determined probabilistically.

3 Scal Queues

Scal is a framework for implementing k-FIFO queues as well as potentially other concurrent data structures such as relaxed versions of stacks and priority queues that may
provide bounded out-of-order behavior. In this paper we focus on k-FIFO queues and
leave other concurrent data structures for future work. In the sequel we refer to k-FIFO
queues implemented with Scal as Scal queues.

Scal is motivated by distributed systems where shared resources are distributed and
access to them is coordinated globally or locally. For implementing k-FIFO queues
Scal uses p instances of a regular FIFO queue, so-called partial FIFO queues, and a
load balancer that distributes queueing operations among the p partial FIFO queues.
Upon the invocation of a queueing operation the load balancer first selects one of the
p partial FIFO queues and then calls the actual queueing operation on the selected
queue. The value of p and the type of load balancer determine k, as discussed below,
as well as the performance and scalability of Scal queues, i.e., how many queueing
operations can potentially be performed concurrently and in parallel, and at which cost
without causing contention. Moreover, in our Scal queue implementations selection and
queueing are performed non-atomically for better performance and scalability. Thus
k with Scal queues depends on the number of threads in the system since between
selection and queueing of a given thread all other threads may run. The semantics of
Scal queues may nevertheless be significantly closer to FIFO semantics than what the
value of k may suggest because of the low probability of the worst case, as shown in
Section 6. Note that p and the load balancer may be configured at compile time or
dynamically at runtime with the help of performance counters. For example, a load
balancer may be chosen with $p = 1$ under low contention and with increasing p as
contention increases. Dynamic reconfiguration is future work.

Round-Robin Load Balancing. We have implemented a round-robin load balancer (RR)
for Scal that selects partial FIFO queues for enqueue and dequeue operations in round-
robin fashion. Two global counters keep track on which of the p partial FIFO queues the
last enqueue and the last dequeue operation was performed. The counters are accessed
and modified using atomic operations, which can cause contention. However, scalability
may still be achieved under low contention since the load balancer itself is simple. A
Scal queue using RR implements a k-FIFO queue with $k = t \cdot (p - 1)$ where t is an
upper bound on the number of threads in the system. Note that k comes down to $p - 1$
if selection and queueing are performed atomically.

Randomized Load Balancing. Another approach is to use a randomized load balancer (RA) for Scal that randomly distributes operations over partial FIFO queues. Randomized load balancing [4,16,6] has been shown to provide good distribution quality if the random numbers are distributed independently and uniformly. However, generating such random numbers may be computationally expensive. Therefore, it is essential to find the right trade-off between quality and overhead of random number generation. We use an efficient random number generator that produces evenly distributed random numbers [15]. The value of k for RA Scal queues is unbounded but may be determined probabilistically as part of future work. A first step is to determine the maximum imbalance of the partial FIFO queues. Suppose that t threads have performed m operations each on p partial FIFO queues using RA. Then, with a probability of at least $1 - O\left(\frac{1}{p}\right)$, the maximum difference (imbalance) between the number of elements in any partial FIFO queue and the average number of elements in all partial FIFO queues is $\Theta\left(\sqrt{\frac{t \cdot m \cdot \log p}{p}}\right)$ [16] if selection and queueing are performed atomically. However, as previously mentioned, selection and queueing are performed non-atomically in our implementation. The presented maximum imbalance is anyway relevant for a comparison with a refined version of RA discussed next.

In order to improve the load balancing quality of RA, d partial FIFO queues with $1 < d \leq p$ may be chosen randomly. Out of the d partial FIFO queues the queue that contributes most to a better load balance is then selected. More precisely, enqueue and dequeue operations are performed on the partial FIFO queues that contain among the d partial FIFO queues the fewest and the most elements, respectively. We refer to such a load balancer as d-randomized load balancer (dRA). The runtime overhead of dRA increases linearly in d since the random number generator is called d times. Thus d allows us to trade off balancing quality and global coordination overhead. Here, again the value of k for dRA is unbounded. However, again with a probability of at least $1 - O(\frac{1}{p})$, the maximum difference (imbalance) between the number of elements in any partial FIFO queue and the average number of elements in all partial FIFO queues is now $\Theta\left(\frac{\log \log p}{d}\right)$ [6] if selection and queueing are performed atomically. Again, determining the maximum imbalance for the case when selection and queueing are performed non-atomically, as in our implementation, is future work. However, the presented maximum imbalance shows an important difference to RA Scal queues. It is independent of the state of the Scal queue, i.e., the history of enqueue and dequeue operations. In particular, $d = 2$ leads to an exponential improvement in the balancing quality in comparison to RA. Note that $d > 2$ further improves the balancing quality only by a constant factor [6] at the cost of higher computational overhead.

Hierarchical Load Balancing. With hierarchical load balancing p partial FIFO queues are partitioned into $0 < h \leq p$ non-overlapping subsets. In this paper we use a two-level hierarchy where the high-level load balancer chooses the subset and the low-level load balancer chooses one of the partial FIFO queues in the given subset. For partitioning we take the cache architecture of the system into account by making the subsets processor-local, i.e., h is here the number of processors of the system. For the high-level load balancer we use a weighted randomized load balancer where the thread running on processor i chooses the processor-local subset i with a given probability w while one of the remaining subsets is chosen with probability $1 - w$. This allows us to increase cache utilization and reduce the number of cache misses. On the lower level we use a randomized (H-RA) or 2-randomized (H-2RA) load balancer to choose the actual partial FIFO queue. Note that in principle multiple hierarchies of load balancers could be used and in each hierarchy a different load balancer could run. The value of k for H-RA and H-2RA Scal queues is again unbounded but may be determined probabilistically similar to the value of k for RA and 2RA Scal queues, respectively.

Backoff Algorithm. We have implemented two so-called backoff algorithms for dequeue operations to avoid *null* returns on non-empty Scal queues. In particular, we have implemented a perfect backoff algorithm (no *null* returns if queue is non-empty) based on the number of elements in a Scal queue as well as a heuristic backoff algorithm (no *null* returns, if queue is non-empty, with high probability given a sufficiently high retry threshold).

In the perfect backoff algorithm a global counter holds the number of elements in a Scal queue. The counter is incremented after a successful enqueue operation and decremented after a successful dequeue operation. If a dequeue operation ends up at an empty partial FIFO queue the backoff algorithm inspects the counter. If it indicates that the Scal queue is not empty the load balancer selects another partial FIFO queue. Updating and inspecting the global counter requires synchronization and can lead to cache conflicts, which may limit performance and scalability.

The heuristic backoff algorithm may simply retry a given number of times determined at compile-time before having the dequeue operation return *null*. The average number of retries depends on different factors such as the application workload. In the experiments in Section 6 we use a heuristic backoff algorithm with a maximum retry threshold set high enough to avoid *null* returns on non-empty Scal queues.

4   Semantical Deviation

We are interested in what we call the semantical deviation of a k-FIFO queue from a regular FIFO queue when applied to a given workload. Semantical deviation captures how many dequeue operations it took to return oldest elements (lateness) and what the age of dequeued elements was. Since semantical deviation cannot be measured efficiently without introducing prohibitive measurement overhead we propose lower and upper bounds of which the lower bounds can be computed efficiently from time-stamped runs of k-FIFO queue implementations. Our experimental results show that the lower bounds at least enable a relative, approximative comparison of different implementations in terms of their actual semantical deviation. Computing the upper bounds remains future work.

We represent a workload applied to a queue by a so-called (concurrent) history H, which is a finite sequence of invocation and response events of enqueue and dequeue operations [10]. We work with complete histories, i.e., histories in which each operation has a corresponding invocation and response event and the invocation is before the response event. By $\langle op$ and by $op \rangle$ we denote the invocation and response events of the operation op, respectively. Two operations op_1 and op_2 in a history H are overlapping if the response event $op_1\rangle$ is after the invocation event $\langle op_2$ and before the response event $op_2\rangle$, or vice versa. An operation op_1 precedes another operation op_2 in a history H, if the response event $op_1\rangle$ is before the invocation event $\langle op_2$. Two histories are equivalent if the one is a permutation of the other in which precedences are preserved (only events of overlapping operations may commute). A history H is sequential if the first event of H is an invocation event and each invocation event is immediately followed by a matching response event [10]. Equivalently, a sequential history is a sequence of enqueue and dequeue operations.

Given a sequential specification C (here FIFO, k-FIFO, or POOL), an execution sequence corresponding to a sequential history $H_S = op_1 \ldots op_m$ is a sequence of states $C(H_S) = s_0 s_1 \ldots s_m$ starting from the initial state s_0 with $s_{j+1} = op_{j+1}(s_j)$ for $j = 0, \ldots, m-1$. The sequential history H_S is valid with respect to the sequential specification C if no s_i in $C(H_S)$ is the error state $error$.

In particular, for a sequential history $H_S = op_1 \ldots op_m$, $\mathrm{FIFO}(H_S)$ is the sequence of FIFO queue states obtained from the sequential specification of Figure 1 without lines (L2) and (L4), where $s_0 = (\varepsilon, 0)$ and $s_j = (q_j, l_j)$ with $l_j = 0$ for $j = 0, \ldots, m$; k-$\mathrm{FIFO}(H_S)$ is the sequence of k-FIFO queue states obtained from the sequential specification of Figure 1, where $s_0 = (\varepsilon, 0)$. If H_S is valid with respect to FIFO, FIFO-valid for short, i.e., if no queue state in $\mathrm{FIFO}(H_S)$ is the error state $error$, then each dequeue operation in H_S returns the head of the queue or $null$ if the queue is empty. Similarly, if H_S is valid with respect to k-FIFO, k-FIFO-valid for short, then each dequeue operation in H_S returns one of the $k + 1 - l$ oldest elements in the queue (or $null$) and queue heads are always returned in H_S in at most $k + 1$ steps. Every FIFO-valid sequential history is k-FIFO-valid.

We next define the notion of semantical deviation of a sequential history and characterize validity in terms of it. In order to do that we need the sequential specification of a POOL. Given a sequential history $H_S = op_1 \ldots op_m$,

$$\mathrm{POOL}(H_S) = (q_0, l_0)(q_1, l_1) \ldots (q_m, l_m)$$

is the sequence of POOL states obtained from the sequential specification of Figure 1 without the conditions (C1), (C2), and (C3), where $(q_0, l_0) = (\varepsilon, 0)$.

From $\mathrm{POOL}(H_S)$ we quantify bounded fairness through (maximum) lateness of H_S, denoted $L(H_S)$, which is the maximum number of dequeue operations it ever took in H_S to return an oldest element, i.e.,

$$L(H_S) = max_{1 \leq j \leq m}(l_j).$$

The average lateness $ML(H_S)$ is the mean of the number of dequeue operations it took to return all oldest elements in H_S, i.e.,

$$ML(H_S) = mean(\{l_{j-1} \mid l_j = 0, j \in \{1, \ldots, m\}\}).$$

From $\mathrm{POOL}(H_S)$ we also define the sequence of (inverse) ages $a_0 a_1 \ldots a_m$ of H_S by

$$a_j = \begin{cases} i - 1 & \text{if } q_j = e_1 \ldots e_n, q_{j+1} = e_1 \ldots e_{i-1} e_{i+1} \ldots e_n \\ 0 & \text{otherwise} \end{cases}$$

The (minimum inverse) age of H_S, denoted $A(H_S)$, is the (inverse) age of the youngest element ever returned in H_S, i.e.,

$$A(H_S) = max_{1 \leq j \leq m}(a_j).$$

The average (inverse) age $MA(H_S)$ is the mean of the (inverse) ages of all elements returned in H_S, i.e.,

$$MA(H_S) = mean_{1 \leq j \leq m}(a_j).$$

Finally, the (maximum) semantical deviation of H_S, denoted $SD(H_S)$, is the maximum of the sums of the lateness and (inverse) age pairs obtained from POOL(H_S), i.e.,

$$SD(H_S) = max_{1 \leq j \leq m}(l_j + a_j).$$

Similarly, the average semantical deviation is

$$MSD(H_S) = mean_{1 \leq j \leq m}(l_j + a_j).$$

We are now ready to present the characterization of k-FIFO validity in terms of lateness, age, and semantical deviation.

Proposition 1. *A sequential history H_S is k-FIFO-valid if and only if $L(H_S) \leq k$, $A(H_S) \leq k$, and $SD(H_S) \leq k+1$.*

Finally, we recall the notion of linearizability [10] before introducing the remaining concepts. Given a history H and a sequential specification C, $lin(H,C)$ denotes the set of all sequential histories that are equivalent to H and valid with respect to C. If $lin(H,C)$ is not empty, H is said to be linearizable with respect to C [10]. Hence, H is linearizable with respect to FIFO if there is a sequential history H_S equivalent to H that is FIFO-valid; it is linearizable with respect to k-FIFO if there is a sequential history H_S equivalent to H that is k-FIFO-valid. Note that every history linearizable with respect to FIFO is linearizable with respect to k-FIFO as well. A concurrent implementation of a sequential specification is said to be linearizable if all histories that can be obtained with the implementation are linearizable [10]. Linearizability is thus a consistency condition for specifying the semantics of objects in the presence of concurrency. The implementations of all (k-FIFO) queues discussed in this paper are linearizable.

In general, $lin(H,C)$ may contain more than one sequential history if H is linearizable with respect to C. However, we are only interested in the sequential history H_A in $lin(H,C)$ that represents the run that was actually performed. In particular, we are interested in the actual semantical deviation $SD(H_A)$ of H (ASD for short), and similarly in $L(H_A)$ and $A(H_A)$. Unfortunately, H_A cannot be determined on existing hardware without introducing prohibitive overhead. In practice, only H can be obtained efficiently by time-stamping the invocation and response events of all operations. We therefore propose to approximate H_A by computing two sequential histories H_L and H_H in $lin(H,C)$ such that

$$L(H_L) = min(\{L(H_S)|H_S \in lin(H,C)\})$$
$$A(H_L) = min(\{A(H_S)|H_S \in lin(H,C)\})$$
$$SD(H_L) = min(\{SD(H_S)|H_S \in lin(H,C)\})$$

and, similarly for H_H with *min* replaced by *max*, holds.

The following proposition is a consequence of Proposition 1 and the definition of a k-FIFO queue.

Proposition 2. *For all histories H of a linearizable implementation of a k-FIFO queue we have that*

$$L(H_L) \leq L(H_A) \leq L(H_H) \leq k$$
$$A(H_L) \leq A(H_A) \leq A(H_H) \leq k$$
$$SD(H_L) \leq SD(H_A) \leq SD(H_H) \leq k+1$$

and $SD(H_H) = 0$ for $k = 0$.

We therefore call k the worst-case lateness (WCL) and worst-case age (WCA), and $k+1$ for $k > 0$ and 0 for $k = 0$ the worst-case semantical deviation (WCSD) of a k-FIFO queue.

4.1 Computing H_L

We have designed and implemented a tool that computes H_L from a given history H without enumerating $lin(H, C)$ explicitly (assuming that the sequential specification C is POOL not knowing any k in particular). The tool scans H for invocation events of dequeue operations in the order of their appearance in H to construct H_L in a single pass (and POOL(H_L) to keep track of the queue states and lateness). For each invocation event $\langle op$ of a dequeue operation op the following computation is performed until a linearization point for op has been created: (1) if op returns *null* remember the (inverse) age for op as zero, otherwise compute and remember the (inverse) age for op assuming that the linearization point of the enqueue operation that matches op is as far in the past as possible under the precedence constraints in H, (2) repeat (1) for all dequeue operations that overlap with op and are not preceded by any other dequeue operations that also overlap with op, (3) among the dequeue operations considered in (1) and (2) find the dequeue operation op' that returns an element other than *null* and has the minimum remembered (inverse) age (any such op' will do if multiple exist), or else if only dequeue operations that return *null* have been considered in (1) and (2) then take any of those as op', and finally (4) create a linearization point in H_L for the enqueue operation that matches op' and move that point under the precedence constraints in H as far into the past as possible and create a linearization point for op' in H_L right before the invocation event $\langle op$. Note that after creating a linearization point for an operation its invocation and response events are not considered anymore in subsequent computations. The key insight for correctness is that bringing operations forward with minimum (inverse) age also minimizes lateness and thus produces H_L. In contrast to H_L, computing H_H may require exploring all possible permutations of overlapping operations, which is computationally expensive, in particular for histories obtained from k-FIFO queue implementations with large or even unbounded k.

5 Related Work

We relate the notions of a k-FIFO queue and semantical deviation as well as the concept, design, and implementation of Scal queues to other work.

The topic of this paper is part of a recent trend towards scalable but semantically weaker concurrent data structures [17] acknowledging the intrinsic difficulties of implementing deterministic semantics in the presence of concurrency [3]. The idea is to address the multicore scalability challenge by leveraging non-determinism in concurrent data structure semantics for better performance and scalability. In the context of concurrent FIFO queues, the notion of a k-FIFO queue is an attempt to capture the degree of non-determinism and its impact on performance and scalability in a single parameter. Many existing implementations of concurrent FIFO queues (with or without relaxed semantics) are instances of k-FIFO queues. The implementations we consider here [13,11,1] are only a subset of the available choices [9]. Other implementations such as work stealing queues which may return the same element multiple times before removing it are not instances of k-FIFO queues but are anyway related in high-level objective and principle [14]. The concept of Scal queues can be seen as an example of best-effort computing [7] where inaccuracies introduced on a given level in a system may lead to better overall performance but must then be dealt with on a higher level.

The notion of semantical deviation is a metric for quantifying the difference in semantics between a queue with relaxed FIFO semantics and a regular FIFO queue. Another approach for relaxing the sequential specification is quasi-linearizability [1]. As opposed to relaxing the sequential specification of a concurrent object one can also relax the consistency condition. An example of a more relaxed consistency condition than linearizability is quiescent consistency [2], for which concurrent data structure implementations exist which may provide superior performance in comparison to their linearizable counterparts. A comprehensive overview of variants of weaker and stronger consistency conditions than linearizability can be found in [9].

6 Experiments

We evaluate performance, scalability, and semantics of the k-FIFO queue implementations described in Section 2.1 and Section 3. All experiments ran on an Intel-based server machine with four 10-core 2.0GHz Intel Xeon processors (40 cores, 2 hyperthreads per core), 24MB shared L3-cache, and 128GB of memory running Linux 2.6.39.

We study the LB, MS, FC, RD, SQ, and Scal queues (with the RR, RA, 2RA, H-RA, and H-2RA load balancers without backoff as well as the RR-B, RA-B, 2RA-B, H-RA-B, and H-2RA-B load balancers with backoff). The partial FIFO queues of the Scal queues are implemented with MS. For the RD, SQ, and Scal queues we use $r = s = p = 80$. For the hierarchical load balancers we use $h = 4$ (number of processors) and $w = 0.9$.

All benchmarked algorithms are implemented in C and compiled using gcc 4.3.3 with -O3 optimizations. In all experiments the benchmark threads are executed with real-time priorities to minimize system jitter. The threads are scheduled by the default Linux scheduler and not pinned to cores. Each thread pre-allocates and touches a large block of memory to avoid subsequent demand paging, and then allocates and deallocates thread-locally all queue elements from this block to minimize cache misses and to avoid potential scalability issues introduced by the underlying memory allocator.

6.1 Microbenchmarks

We designed and implemented a framework to microbenchmark and analyze different queue implementations under configurable contention. The framework emulates a
multi-threaded producer-consumer setup where each thread enqueues and dequeues in
alternating order an element to a shared queue. The framework allows to specify the
number of threads, the number of elements each thread enqueues and dequeues, how
much computation is performed between queueing operations, and which queue implementation to use. We focus on two microbenchmark configurations: 1. a high contention configuration where no computational load in between queueing operations is
performed and 2. a low contention configuration where in between any two queueing
operations additional computational load is created by executing an iterative algorithm
that calculates in 500 loop iterations an approximation of π which takes in total on
average 1130ns.

We evaluate each queue implementation with an increasing number of threads and
determine its performance, scalability, and semantics. Performance is shown in number
of operations performed per millisecond. Scalability is performance with an increasing
number of threads. Semantics is average semantical deviation as computed by our tool
described in Section 4.

Figure 2(a) depicts the performance result of the high contention benchmark. The
throughput of LB, MS, FC, RD, and SQ decreases with an increasing number of threads.
RR does not scale but performs better then the non-Scal queues. The non-backoff Scal
queues provide better performance then their backoff counterparts. This is due to the
fact that in the non-backoff case a Scal queue may return *null* if no element is found
in the selected partial FIFO queue whereas in the backoff case it has to retry. The best
performance is provided by the hierarchical Scal queues which scale up to the number
of hardware threads in the system, due to better cache utilization. For all other instances
the number of L3 cache misses significantly increases between 20 and 32 threads.

The average semantical deviation of the experimental runs or the high contention
benchmark are depicted in Figure 2(b). Note that the graphs for regular FIFO queues,
i.e., LB, MS, and FC, are not visible since their semantical deviation is always zero.
Using a backoff algorithm for Scal queues generally improves the average semantical
deviation by an order of magnitude, except for RR and RR-B. Scal queues that show
higher average semantical deviation clearly outperform the other queues in terms of
performance and scalability. The Scal queue with H-2RA load balancing appears to
offer the best trade-off between performance, scalability, and semantics on the workload
and hardware considered here.

Figures 2(c) and 2(d) depict the performance result of the low contention benchmark.
The LB, MS, FC, RD, and SQ queues scale for up to 8 threads. Between 8 to 16 threads
throughput increases only slightly. With more than 16 threads scalability is negative.
The RR Scal queue scales for up to 16 threads and then maintains throughput. The
other Scal queues provide scalability up to the number of hardware threads in the system. The performance difference between backoff and non-backoff is less significant in
the presence of additional computational load. The best performance and scalability is
still provided by the hierarchical Scal queues but the difference to the non-hierarchical
versions is significantly smaller. The number of L3 cache misses are similar to the high

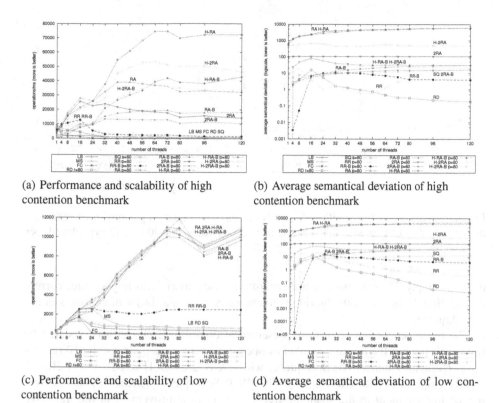

(a) Performance and scalability of high contention benchmark

(b) Average semantical deviation of high contention benchmark

(c) Performance and scalability of low contention benchmark

(d) Average semantical deviation of low contention benchmark

Fig. 2. High and low contention microbenchmarks with an increasing number of threads on a 40-core (2 hyperthreads per core) server

contention case. Again, the hierarchical Scal queues have the lowest number of L3 cache misses. The additional computational load between queueing operations does not change average semantical deviation significantly on the workload considered here, see Figure 2(d).

6.2 Macrobenchmarks

We ran two macrobenchmarks with parallel versions of transitive closure and spanning tree graph algorithms [5] using random graphs consisting of 1000000 vertices where 1000000 unique edges got randomly added to the vertices. All threads start operating on the graph at different randomly determined vertices. From then on each thread iterates over the neighbors of a given vertex and tries to process them (transitive closure or spanning tree operation). If a neighboring vertex already got processed by a different thread then the vertex is ignored. Vertices to be processed are kept in a global queue (which we implemented with a representative selection of our queue implementations). When a vertex is processed, then it is removed from the queue and all its unprocessed neighbors are added to the queue. The graph algorithm terminates when the global

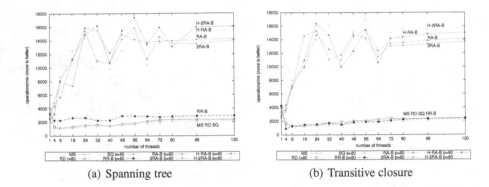

(a) Spanning tree   (b) Transitive closure

Fig. 3. Performance and Scalability of macrobenchmarks on a random graph with 1000000 vertices and 1000000 edges with an increasing number of threads on a 40-core (2 hyperthreads per core) server

queue is empty. Thus we need to use backoff in these experiments to guarantee correct termination. Note that both algorithms tolerate any particular order of elements in the global queue.

The macrobenchmark results are presented in Figure 3. Each run was repeated 10 times. We present the average number of operations per milliseconds of the 10 runs as our performance metric. The Scal queues with RA-B, 2RA-B, H-RA-B, and H-2RA-B clearly outperform MS, RD, and SQ. The RR-B Scal queue provides a small performance improvement in the spanning tree case and no improvement in the transitive closure case. Both algorithms may produce high cache-miss rates since accessing the neighbors of a vertex may result in disjoint cache line accesses. A graph representation that takes hardware features into account may improve scalability further.

7   Conclusions

We have introduced the notion of a k-FIFO queue which may dequeue elements out of FIFO order up to k. Several existing queue implementations are instances of k-FIFO queues for different k. We have also introduced Scal queues, which aim at improving performance and scalability of FIFO queue implementations through load balancing by distributing queueing operations across multiple, independent queue instances. Load balancing directly determines performance, scalability, and semantics of Scal queues, in particular how close the queueing behavior is to FIFO. In order to quantify the difference between actual and regular FIFO semantics, we have introduced the notion of semantical deviation, which captures how many dequeue operations it took to return oldest elements (lateness) and what the age of dequeued elements was. Our experiments show that Scal queues with a memory-hierarchy-aware combination of randomized and queue-size-based load balancing (H-2RA) offer the best trade-off between performance, scalability, and semantics on the considered workloads and hardware.

We see many interesting directions for future work. Which applications tolerate semantical deviation to what extent? Is the parameter k the right choice of information that should be exposed to application programmers for performance-oriented multicore programming (rather than, e.g. the memory hierarchy)? Can concurrent data structures other than FIFO queues be relaxed in a similar way? In recent collaboration [8] we have developed a framework for quantitative relaxation of concurrent data structures which covers FIFO queues but also stacks, priority queues, and other examples.

References

1. Afek, Y., Korland, G., Yanovsky, E.: Quasi-Linearizability: Relaxed Consistency for Improved Concurrency. In: Lu, C., Masuzawa, T., Mosbah, M. (eds.) OPODIS 2010. LNCS, vol. 6490, pp. 395–410. Springer, Heidelberg (2010)
2. Aspnes, J., Herlihy, M., Shavit, N.: Counting networks. Journal of the ACM 41, 1020–1048 (1994)
3. Attiya, H., Guerraoui, R., Hendler, D., Kuznetsov, P., Michael, M., Vechev, M.: Laws of order: expensive synchronization in concurrent algorithms cannot be eliminated. In: Proc. of Principles of Programming Languages (POPL), pp. 487–498. ACM (2011)
4. Azar, Y., Broder, A.Z., Karlin, A.R., Upfal, E.: Balanced allocations (extended abstract). In: Proc. Symposium on Theory of computing (STOC), pp. 593–602. ACM (1994)
5. Bader, D., Cong, G.: A fast, parallel spanning tree algorithm for symmetric multiprocessors (smps). Journal of Parallel and Distributed Computing 65, 994–1006 (2005)
6. Berenbrink, P., Czumaj, A., Steger, A., Vöcking, B.: Balanced allocations: The heavily loaded case. SIAM Journal on Computing 35(6), 1350–1385 (2006)
7. Chakradhar, S., Raghunathan, A.: Best-effort computing: re-thinking parallel software and hardware. In: Proc. Design Automation Conference, pp. 865–870. ACM (2010)
8. Henzinger, T., Kirsch, C., Payer, H., Sezgin, A., Sokolova, A.: Quantitative relaxation of concurrent data structures. Technical Report 2012-03. Department of Computer Sciences. University of Salzburg (May 2012)
9. Herlihy, M., Shavit, N.: The Art of Multiprocessor Programming. Morgan Kaufmann Publishers Inc. (2008)
10. Herlihy, M., Wing, J.: Linearizability: a correctness condition for concurrent objects. ACM Transactions on Programming Languages and Systems (TOPLAS) 12(3), 463–492 (1990)
11. Incze, D.H.I., Shavit, N., Tzafrir, M.: Flat combining and the synchronization-parallelism tradeoff. In: Proc. Symposium on Parallelism in Algorithms and Architectures (SPAA), pp. 355–364. ACM (2010)
12. Kirsch, C., Payer, H., Röck, H., Sokolova, A.: Brief announcement: Scalability versus semantics of concurrent FIFO queues. In: Proc. Symposium on Principles of Distributed Computing (PODC). ACM (2011)
13. Michael, M., Scott, M.: Simple, fast, and practical non-blocking and blocking concurrent queue algorithms. In: Proc. Symposium on Principles of Distributed Computing (PODC), pp. 267–275. ACM (1996)
14. Michael, M., Vechev, M., Saraswat, V.: Idempotent work stealing. In: Proc. Principles and Practice of Parallel Programming (PPoPP), pp. 45–54. ACM (2009)
15. Park, S., Miller, K.: Random number generators: good ones are hard to find. Communications of the ACM 31(10), 1192–1201 (1988)
16. Raab, M., Steger, A.: "Balls into Bins" - A Simple and Tight Analysis. In: Rolim, J.D.P., Serna, M., Luby, M. (eds.) RANDOM 1998. LNCS, vol. 1518, pp. 159–170. Springer, Heidelberg (1998)
17. Shavit, N.: Data structures in the multicore age. Communications ACM 54, 76–84 (2011)

Scalable Distributed Architecture for Media Transcoding

Horacio Sanson, Luis Loyola, and Daniel Pereira

SkillupJapan Corp.

Abstract. We present a highly scalable distributed media transcoding system that reduces the time required for batch transcoding of multimedia files into several output formats. To implement this system we propose a fully distributed architecture that leverages proven technologies to create a highly scalable and fault-tolerant platform. Also a new task-oriented parallel processing framework that improves on MapReduce is developed in order to express transcoding tasks as distributed processes and execute them on top of the distributed platform. Preliminary results show a significant reduction in time resources required to transcode large batches of media files with little effects on the quality of the output transcoded files.

1 Introduction

The proliferation of mobile devices with video playback capabilities and Internet connectivity have increased the number of distribution channels for digital content. This, in turn, has created a burden to content creators that must support all different combinations of devices and channels to reach a larger audience. A recent example of this is the new HTTP Live Streaming protocol [1] from Apple Inc. that recommends at least six different versions of the same content with different resolutions and bitrates to deliver it to iOS mobile devices.

To address this increasing number of transcoding tasks we implemented a distributed transcoding platform capable of reducing the time and human resources required to handle them. To this end we implemented a fully distributed and fault-tolerant architecture and developed a new task-oriented parallel processing framework that allows easy execution of transcoding tasks in a distributed fashion. The distributed architecture builds on top of proven technologies in distributed computing like distributed queues and storage. This resulted in a robust platform on which we could execute parallel processes without worrying about fault-tolerance, synchronization and availability issues. On top of the platform we needed a parallel processing framework that would allow us to model complex problems as smaller sub-tasks that could be executed in parallel. Unfortunately state of the art in parallel processing frameworks like MapReduce [2] and Dryad [3] lack the expressiveness required to model complex tasks, such as multimedia transcoding, forcing us to develop our own task-oriented framework. This new task-oriented parallel processing framework improves over MapReduce by adding a task primitive on top of the map/reduce semantics.

Y. Xiang et al. (Eds.): ICA3PP 2012, Part I, LNCS 7439, pp. 288–302, 2012.

In section 2 we present related work on distributed and cloud transcoding, sections 3 and 4 present detailed description of our distributed platform architecture and details on our improved task-oriented parallel processing framework respectively. On section 5 we elaborate on the model for transcoding process using the proposed parallel processing framework and explain how it is executed on the distributed platform. Section 6 presents transcoding experiments using the system and elaborate on its performance. Finally, in section 7, we remark the important points of this work and give an overview of our future work.

2 Related Work

This paper is inspired by the work in [4] that presents a high-speed distributed transcoding platform. The authors focus on the optimal segmentation of media files that generates lower degradation on the transcoded file; then propose a simple centralized architecture with a round-robin scheduler to handle the distribution of transcoding tasks among several transcoding servers. This architecture works on the assumption that all segments are equal and have the same encoding time. Unfortunately, even in a controlled environment as ours, there exist differences in transcoding server capacity, network conditions and varied media source complexity that invalidates such assumptions.

To mitigate the effects of such a heterogeneous environment, the authors in [5] propose a scheduling algorithm that takes into account the estimated transcoding time of each source and the capabilities of the transcoding servers. The new scheduling results in a more linear scalability and better load distribution among the transcoding servers, which shows the importance of distributed scheduling. However the proposed scheduler requires global knowledge and must also calculate transcoding time estimates of tasks in order to properly schedule them. This estimation can be inaccurate due to the variable complexity of source materials and require complex operations that may choke the scheduler, jeopardizing the scalability of the system.

Other authors [6,7] have proposed P2P architectures, however, transcoding poses high CPU and network I/O requirements that combined with the unreliability of low availability of P2P clients makes it difficult to envision a real implementation of such systems.

3 Architecture and Implementation

3.1 Centralized Architecture

Figure 1 shows the classic distributed transcoding architecture common in previous research [4,8]. The architecture is composed of a **storage** system where media files are stored, a **transcoder manager** that is the center of the system and the **transcoding workers** that are one or more machines dedicated to transcode video segments. The **transcoder manager** contains the intelligence of the system and is composed of these sub-systems:

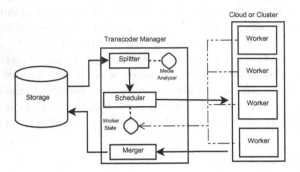

Fig. 1. Centralized Transcoding Architecture

- Splitter: The splitter is in charge of analysing the source media files on the storage and split them in segments. The decision of the segments split points and the size must be done carefully since it affects the quality, load balancing and scheduling performance of the whole system. Splitting in large files may result in better quality movies but in less distributable loads and vice versa.
- Scheduler: The scheduler must take decisions on which segments should be sent to each available worker. If all workers and all segments are equal in capacity/requirements then a simple First Come First Serverd (FCFS) scheduler is optimal. Unfortunately in a real scenarios both, the segments and the workers, have different requirements/capabilities that demands for more intelligent scheduling algorithms.
- Merger: A separate server or process receives the transcoded segments from transcoding servers to create the final transcoded video.

This architecture presents obvious scalability issues on several points. Firstly, the only channel which the workers can use to receive and return media segments is through the **transcoder manager**. This limits the network capacity of the whole system to that of the manager. Secondly, the scalability of the manager to handle high input load and more workers greatly depends on the complexity of the splitting and the scheduling algorithms used. Additionally the manager must track media segments states (encoded, waiting) and workers states (loaded, idle, failed) in order to make scheduling decisions.

3.2 Distributed Architecture

By taking advantage of recent advances in distributed storage, databases and parallel processing we decided to shift radically from the classical centralized architecture and implemented a fully distributed architecture as depicted in Figure 2. When compared to the centralized approach, we can observe that the central manager no longer exists and the sub-systems it contained are now inside the workers themselves. This way, the load that was handled before on

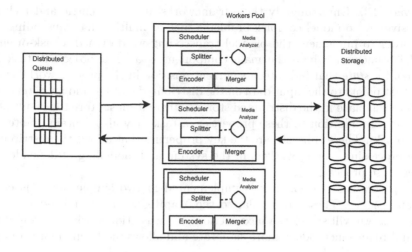

Fig. 2. Distributed Transcoding Architecture

the central manager is now distributed along with the actual transcoding among all workers in the system. Since scheduling and splitting decisions are made by workers there is no need to keep track of each workers capabilities and state, thus reducing even further the complexity of the system.

Transcoding tasks are submitted to the system by pushing them to a distributed queue. The workers scheduler poll this queue for new tasks and select which task to execute from the available tasks in the queue. Depending on the queue structure and the way worker's schedulers select tasks from it, it is possible to implement different scheduling strategies. In our architecture the distributed queue is built on top of Redis DB [9]. Redis is a scalable and fault-tolerant database that supports atomic operations which are an important property to avoid synchronization issues in distributed systems.

In order to transcode the media files the workers need a way to access them. We implemented this in our architecture using GlusterFS [10] that is a distributed storage with replication and stripping support. With replication and stripping the source files are stored in replicated stripes over several storage servers. This greatly improves the fault-tolerance and read performance of the whole system by distributing the reading load among all available storage servers.

4 Task-Oriented Parallel Processing

By leveraging known technologies in distributed queuing and storage, we implemented a distributed architecture for our transcoding platform. The main problem resides now on how to implement the workers logic that orchestrate all the different sub-systems to transcode media files in a distributed manner. Our first attempt was to apply parallel processing frameworks like MapReduce or Dryad [2,3]. Unfortunately these frameworks are data-centric and lack the expressiveness to model complex problems such as multimedia transcoding.

In order to implement the parallel transcoding we designed a task-oriented parallel framework where the main component is a **task** object. A task has by default a *state* that indicates its current position in the process workflow, an *input* that points to the input data on the distributed storage and an *output* that points to the place in the distributed storage where it must store the result of its processing. In addition to these properties, a task may also contain pointers to two subtasks. These subtasks are the key properties that allows the distribution of the processing among workers in the system and modelling of dependencies among those processes.

The processing of each task is implemented in two simple methods called map and reduce. These are similar to the MapReduce map and reduce methods but, as we will see in the next section, the execution workflow around our map and reduce methods is more elaborate and allows modelling more complex problems.

4.1   Worker Execution Workflow

When a worker acquires a task from the distributed queue, it follows a simple execution workflow as shown in Figure 3. If the task is in *pending* state it means it is a new task so the worker invokes the *map* method on it and moves the task to the *map* state. If the input data is not splittable then the task result is stored in the output path and the task changes to the *complete* state. If on the other hand the input data is splittable the map method may split it into two equal parts. This splitting will push to the distributed queue two new sub-tasks with those parts as inputs and move the current task to the *waiting* state.

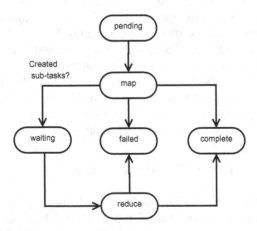

Fig. 3. Worker Parallel Processing Execution Workflow

If the reserved task is in *waiting* state it means the task has subtasks it is waiting for. In this case the worker checks the state of the subtasks and if these are completed then the worker invokes the *reduce* method with the subtasks outputs as inputs. The reduce method, then merges these inputs and produce the task's output.

5 Modelling the Distributed Transcoding Problem

With the task-oriented parallel processing framework presented in section 4 we can now model each step of a transcoding process in a parallel fashion and execute it on top of our distributed platform. The model is easy to visualize if we think about transcoding as a group of smaller processes: demuxing, decoding, filtering, encoding and muxing. As previous research shows [4,8], the encoding process can be divided further in smaller processes using video segmentation. These processes have precedence dependencies (e.g. encoding cannot start if demuxing is not finished) but for the most part they can be executed in parallel.

Based on this premise we can model the transcoding problem with three simple task classes: **TranscodeTask**, **VideoTask** and **AudioTask** (see Listings 1.1,1.2 and 1.3).

The process execution flow of these tasks is depicted in Figure 4. When a user requires to transcode a media file he submits a TranscodeTask into the distributed queue. A worker, that acquires this new task, sees it is in pending

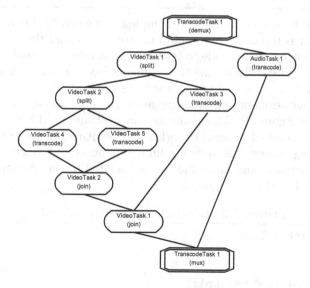

Fig. 4. Distributed Transcoding Model Flow

state and invokes its map method. The map method of the TranscodeTask (see Listing 1.1) demuxes the input data into the audio and video components and creates two new sub-tasks: a VideoTask and an AudioTask with the corresponding video and audio components as inputs. After the map method finishes, the worker marks the TranscodeTask as waiting and pushes it back to the queue.

Later during the parallel processing, when both the VideoTask and AudioTask are completed, a worker will acquire the waiting TranscodeTask from the queue and find if its sub-tasks are completed. This will prompt the worker to execute the reduce method on the TranscodeTask that as shown in Listing 1.1 muxes back the outputs of the sub-tasks (transcoded video and audio) into the final transcoded file.

Listing 1.1. TranscodeTask simplified pseudocode

```
class TranscodeTask < Task

  def map
    [audiofile,videofile] = demux(input)
    left = VideoTask.new(videofile)
    right = AudioTask.new(audiofile)
  end

  def reduce
    output = mux(left, right)
  end
end
```

The VideoTask map method is more complex as it can take two different paths. If the task input is too large and would take too long under the workers current load, then the worker may decide to split the input into two equal segments and create two new VideoTasks for the two segments (see VideoTask 1 on Figure 4). Any worker that acquires one of these sub-tasks can further split the segment into even smaller segments distributing more the load among all workers (see VideoTask 2 on Figure 4). This splitting can continue until a max number of allowed splits is reached or until a worker decides it can handle the processing without splitting. When this splitting limit is reached the worker proceeds to transcode the segment and mark the task associated to the segment completed (VideoTasks 3, 4, and 5 on Figure 4).

Listing 1.2. VideoTask simplified pseudocode

```
class VideoTask < Task

  def map
    if split_count < max_split
      [segment1, segment2] = cut(input)
      left = VideoTask.new(segment1)
      right = VideoTask.new(segment2)
```

```
      else
        output = encode_video(input)
      end
   end

   def reduce
     output = join(left, right)
   end
end
```

As segments are transcoded the VideoTask reduce methods are called with the transcoded outputs backtracking all the way to the initial VideoTask. On each reduce call the transcoded segments are joined to recreate the whole transcoded video stream that can then be muxed with the transcoded audio stream (see VideoTasks 2 and 1 at bottom of figure 4).

The example on Listing 1.2 is very simple and uses a hard limit on the max number of segments a video stream can be split. We could add on the workers more complex logic that considers the segment size (in frames or seconds), video complexity (slow or fast action scenes), the workers capabilities (CPU/RAM), and the network conditions (error rate, bandwidth) to decide either to further segment the task or transcode it.

Listing 1.3. AudioTask simplified pseudocode

```
class AudioTask < Task
  def map
    output = encode_audio(input)
  end
end
```

For completeness we also present a simple implementation of the AudioTask class. Since audio trancoding uses less resources the map method always decides to transcode the audio (AudioTask 1 on Figure 4). This does not mean that audio transcoding cannot be distributed. We could, for example, transcode different audio tracks (e.g. languages, formats) or channels in parallel using our system.

6   Evaluation

In this section we evaluate our distributed architecture and the task-oriented parallel processing framework presented in Sections 3 and 4 respectively by performing some transcoding jobs on the system using the model we described on Section 5.

6.1   Sample Media

For evaluation purposes, we transcoded a batch of 45 media files into 6 different output formats (Table 1) used for HTTP live streaming to mobile devices. Table

Table 1. Transcoding output formats

Name	Dimensions	Bitrate	FPS
HLS0	1024x768	2Mbps	max 30
HLS1	854x640	1.5Mbps	max 30
HLS2	576x432	1Mbps	max 30
HLS3	426x320	600Kbps	max 30
HLS4	384x288	400Kbps	max 15
HLS5	384x288	200Kbps	max 15

Table 2. Sample Media Distribution

	Short	Medium	Long
FHD	20%	0%	0%
HD	7%	2%	2%
SD	12%	44%	13%

2 shows the batch of movies we used. The batch contains a variety of source media files with different sizes: FHD (1440x1080), HD (1280x720) and SD (720x480) and durations: Short clips (¡10 min), Medium clips ($\approx$ 20 min), and Long clips (¿ 1 hour).

The transcoding cluster consists of four transcoding servers with Intel Xeon iCore7 3.2GHz CPU and 6GByte RAM. Each server is running six instances of the transcoding worker that gives us a total of 24 transcoding workers in the cluster. Two small virtual servers running Redis in master-slave mode serve as our distributed queue and two 24TB storage servers with GlusterFS in replication 2 with four stripes per replica.

6.2 Transcoding Speed

To evaluate the speed improvements of distributed transcoding, we submitted each transcode task, one at the time, to the distributed system. This is done to measure the transcoding time of each task when it has all the system resources available to it. We repeated and measured the test for each source media and output format combination for one (no splitting) and sixteen segments max. We accumulated the transcode times for each output format and plotted it against the source media duration in Figure 5. It is clear from the plot that splitting the source media and transcoding each segment in parallel reduces the time it takes to finish all tasks. We can also observe that the longer the source media duration the larger the benefits obtained from segmenting it. To give a concrete example; a DVD source that takes 6.48 hours to transcode with no splitting, takes around 28.5 minutes to transcode when splitted in sixteen segments and processed in parallel.

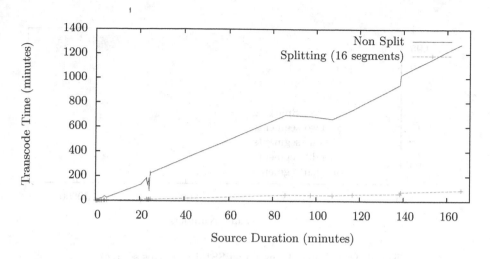

Fig. 5. Transcoding speed improvement of split transcoding vs non split transcoding

6.3 Transcoding Quality

Segmentation and parallel transcoding of a video along the time axis usually results in quality discontinuity and degradation around the segment cut points [4]. One way to avoid this problem is to always split the clip at GOP boundaries of the source media [8]. In Figure 7 we plot the Structural Similarity Index Metric (SSIM) between a source file and the corresponding transcoded files with no splitting and with two, four, eight and sixteen segments splitting. It can be seen that all lines overlap which means there is no difference in quality when transcoding with no splitting or when splitting in sixteen segments separately.

A problem we found with this approach is that in case of non exact frame rates (e.g. 29.97fps) splitting the source at exact frame boundaries can be inefficient and difficult due to limitations in the used transcoding tools. Figure 6 shows the same similarity index test but with a source media that has a 29.97 frame rate. We can observe some frames that present a very low similarity index (¡ 0.80) that would indicate a large degradation on the resulting video; however a careful frame by frame comparison of the source media and the transcoded files, show that this degradation was due to a shift in the frames ordering on the output. Again this frame shifting is due to the inhability of our splitting tools to correcly cut at exact frame boundaries on the source. Fortunately, at sixteen segments, subjective tests show a negligible difference in output quality and no audible effects on the audio synchronization.

6.4 Task Scheduling

The system becomes overloaded when the transcoding task demands exceeds by far the available transcoding resources. In this case scheduling of tasks plays

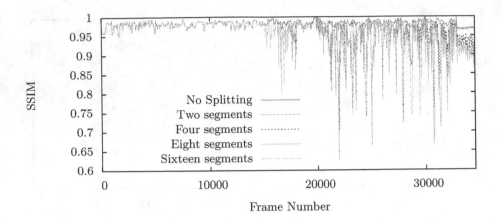

Fig. 6. Distributed Transcoding SSIM (29.97fps source)

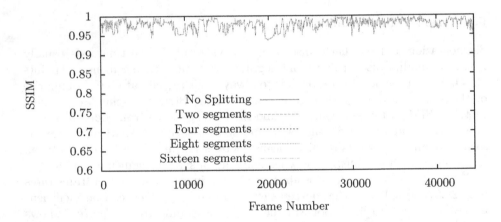

Fig. 7. Distributed Transcoding SSIM (30fps source)

an important role that affects the overall system performance and user quality perception. Scheduling, centralized or distributed, is a known hard problem [11,12,5,13,14] and is a topic on our list of future research. Therefore in this section we will only evaluate two simple distributed schedulers: First Come First Served (FCFS) scheduler and a Random scheduler, both on a 24-worker system. In the FCFS scheduler tasks are submitted to the distributed queue and workers acquire them in the order they are submitted. In the Random scheduler workers take a random task from the queue with uniform probability. Using both schedulers we submitted the batch of 270 transcoding tasks using splitting (16

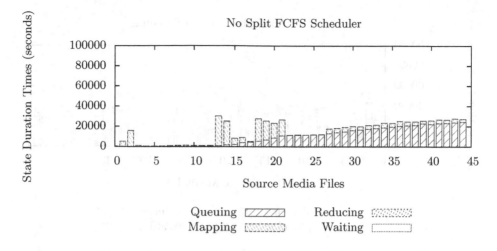

Fig. 8. No split FCFS Scheduler

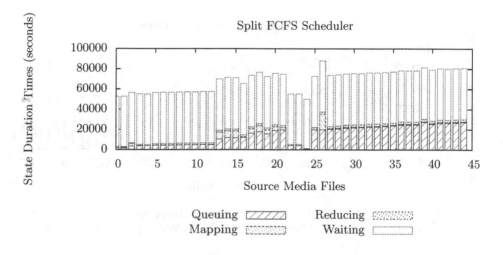

Fig. 9. Split (16 segments) FCFS Scheduler

segments) and no splitting, and measured the time each source file spent on each of the states: queuing, mapping, reducing and waiting.

Figure 8 shows the FCFS scheduler with no splitting. The y axis shows the stacked times each media file spends in each state of the transcoding process and the x axis corresponds to the transcoding tasks in the order they were submitted to the system. As expected from FCFS, the tasks that are submitted later have larger queuing times, because latter tasks must wait for all previous tasks to finish, before they can be taken by a worker. The same Figure 8 also shows how

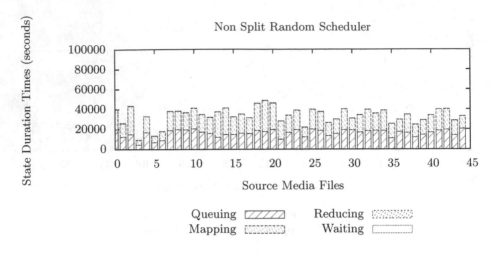

Fig. 10. No Split Random Scheduler

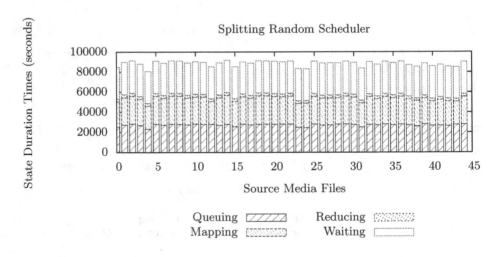

Fig. 11. Split (16 segments) Random Scheduler

a few heavy tasks (e.g. long mapping times) at the middle cause large delays on the following smaller tasks. The splitting case, using FCFS and depicted in Figure 9, shows no improvement in queuing times and further increases on the waiting time of each transcoding task. This is expected if we consider how our parallel processing framework works. When a task creates sub-tasks, they are pushed back to the queue resulting in longer waiting times for the parent task.

As shown in figures 10 and 11 the random scheduler does a better job spreading the load among the available workers. This results in a better overall system throughput but at the cost of longer completion times per task. The reduced performance in completion times is aggravated when we use splitting, because each split increases the number of tasks in the queue, thus increasing the number of processes competing for resources. This is an expected trade off, given the naive schedulers tested, between throughput and performance in distributed systems [15]. Completion time of a task corresponds to the sum of all state times: queuing, mapping, reducing and waiting.

7   Conclusions and Future Work

We have presented and evaluated a distributed transcoding platform that can be used to speed up the process of batch transcoding into different formats and sizes. Our results show significant performance improvements, in terms of transcoding completion times, on different input sources with little impact on the resulting quality of the output under normal conditions. Under overloaded conditions, the increased number of tasks generated by splitting combined with both naive schedulers results in larger completion times than the no-split cases. This indicates that further research on distributed scheduling, that can better accommodate the available worker resources to the factorial number of possible task allocations, is required. Likewise, other video stream segmentation approaches that do not affect output quality and are independent of the source properties (e.g. FPS, codec, GOP) must be investigated.

References

1. Pantos, A.I.R., May, E.W.: HTTP Live Streaming - draft (September 2011) (expires: April 2, 2012)
2. Dean, J., Ghemawat, S.: Mapreduce: simplified data processing on large clusters. Commun. ACM 51, 107–113 (2008)
3. Isard, M., Budiu, M., Yu, Y., Andrew, B., Fetterly, D.: Dryad: Distributed data-parallel programs from sequential building blocks. In: European Conference on Computer Systems, EuroSys (March 2007)
4. Sambe, Y., Watanabe, S., Yu, D., Nakamura, T., Wakamiya, N.: High-speed distributed video transcoding for multiple rates and formats. IEICE Transactions on Information and Systems 88(8), 1923–1931 (2005)
5. Dongmahn, S., Jongwoo, K., Inbum, J.: Load distribution algorithm based on transcoding time estimation for distributed transcoding servers. In: International Conference on Inforamtion Science and Applications (ICISA), pp. 1–8 (April 2010)
6. Yang, C., Chen, Y., Shen, Y.: The research on a p2p transcoding system based on distributed farming computing architecture. Knowledge Engineering and Software Engineering (KESE), 55–58 (December 2009)
7. Ravindra, G., Kumar, S., Chintada, S.: Distributed media transcoding using a p2p network of set top boxes. In: Consumer Communcications and Networking Conference (CCNC), pp. 1–2 (January 2009)
8. Deneke, T.: Scalable Distributed Video Transcoding Architecture, Master's thesis. Åbo Akademi University (2011)

9. Redis key-value database, http://redis.io
10. Gluster file system architecture, tech. rep., http://download.gluster.com/pub/gluster/documentation/Gluster_Architecture.pdf
11. Isard, M., Prabhakaran, V., Currey, J., Wieder, U., Talwar, K., Goldberg, A.: Quincy: fair scheduling for distributed computing clusters. In: Proceedings of the ACM SIGOPS 22nd Symposium on Operating Systems Principles, SOSP 2009, pp. 261–276. ACM, New York (2009)
12. Zaharia, M., Borthakur, D., Sen Sarma, J., Elmeleegy, K., Shenker, S., Stoica, I.: Delay scheduling: a simple technique for achieving locality and fairness in cluster scheduling. In: Proceedings of the 5th European Conference on Computer Systems, EuroSys 2010, pp. 265–278. ACM, New York (2010)
13. Beaumont, O., Carter, L., Ferrante, J., Legrand, A., Marchal, L., Robert, Y.: Centralized versus distributed schedulers for bag-of-tasks applications. IEEE Transactions on Parallel and Distributed Systems (May 2008)
14. Ghatpande, A., Nakazato, H., Beaumont, O.: Scheduling of divisible loads on heterogeneous distributed systems. In: Ros, A. (ed.) Parallel and Distributed Computing, pp. 179–202. In-Tech (2010)
15. Raman, R., Livny, M., Solomon, M.: Matchmaking: Distributed resource management for high throughput computing. In: Proceedings of the Seventh IEEE International Symposium on High Performance Distributed Computing, pp. 28–31 (1998)

GPU-Accelerated Restricted Boltzmann Machine
for Collaborative Filtering

Xianggao Cai[1], Zhanpeng Xu[1], Guoming Lai[2], Chengwei Wu[1], and Xiaola Lin[1]

[1] School of Information Science and Technology
Sun Yat-sen University Guangzhou, 510275, China
[2] Department of Computer Application and Technology
Hanshan Normal University Chaozhou, 521041, China
{is03cxg,xuzhanp}@mail2.sysu.edu.cn, laigm@mail3.sysu.edu.cn,
wuchengw@mail2.sysu.edu.cn, linxl@mail.sysu.edu.cn

Abstract. Collaborative Filtering (CF) is an important technique for recommendation systems which model and analyzes the preferences of customers for giving reasonable advices. Recently, many applications based on Restricted Boltzmann Machine (RBM) have been developed for a large variety of learning problems. RBM-based model for Collaborative Filtering (RBM-CF) is able to deal with large scale data sets and obtains good recommendation performance. However, the computation of RBM becomes problematic when using large number of hidden features to improve the recommendation accuracy. Although RBM has great potential for parallelism, it is still a challenge to develop a parallel implementation of RBM-CF on GPU, since the data sets for CF are always large and sparse. In this paper, we propose a parallel implementation of RBM-CF on GPU using CUDA. We first present how to transform the computation of RBM-CF into matrix-based operation on GPU, and three CUDA kernels for sparse matrix-matrix multiplication to further improve the computational efficiency of RBM-CF for modeling large scale and sparse data sets. Experimental results show that significant speedups are achieved by our parallel implementation on GPU.

1   Introduction

Recommender system plays an important role in e-commerce applications. Although much research work has been done on recommendation techniques recently, Collaborative Filtering (CF) has been known to be one of the most successful recommendation approaches. CF works through building a database of preference for items given by users, and then makes recommendations to help them find items that they would like.

However, most of the existing CF approaches are incapable of dealing with large scale data sets. In order to overcome that, Salakhutdinov et al. developed an extended model of Restricted Boltzmann Machine (RBM) [1] for Collaborative Filtering (RBM-CF) in [2]. RBM is a type of promising machine learning tool which has been applied to many learning applications including object recognition [3] and document

Y. Xiang et al. (Eds.): ICA3PP 2012, Part I, LNCS 7439, pp. 303–316, 2012.

classification [4] due to its strong power of representation. One of the advantages of RBM is its inherent high-degree parallelism. Much work to improve the computational performance has been done on GPU [5] [6] [7] and FPGA [8] [9] [10] [11] [12] with significant performance benefits over CPU.

For the rating database is often very large and sparse [13] [14] [15], if we parallelize the computation of RBM-CF the same way with that of standard RBM, there would be lots of unnecessary computation tying up GPU's processing power. Thus, implementing the computation of RBM-CF on GPU is still a challenge.

The remainder of this paper is organized as follows. Section 2 briefly states the basic concepts of RBM and how to apply RBM to CF. Section 3 presents how to transform the computation of RBM-CF into matrix-matrix operations. Section 4 proposes how to improve the computational efficiency of the Matrix-Matrix Multiplications (MMMs) on GPU with consideration on the sparsity of data set. In Section 5, experiments are carried out to evaluate the speedup performance.

For easy reference, we list the symbols used in Table 1.

Table 1. Symbols used in this paper

Symbol	Meaning
$\mathbf{v},\mathbf{h}$ [1]	the visible units and hidden units (features) of RBM, both of them are column vector
$\mathbf{W}$	the connection weight matrix
$\mathbf{b},\mathbf{c}$	the visible biases and hidden biases respectively
I,J	the number of visible units (items) and the number of hidden units respectively
$\mathrm{tr}(\mathbf{A})$, $\mathbf{A}_{i\cdot}$, $\mathbf{A}_{\cdot j}$	the transpose matrix, i th row and j th column of $\mathbf{A}$ respectively,
η	the learning rate
ρ	the sparsity rate of the data set
$\mathrm{sigm}(x)$	$1/(1+e^{-x})$
K	the maximumn rating number
$\mathbf{v}^{k}$	corresponding to the k th row of the softmax matrix of RBM-CF, $\mathbf{v}^{k}$ is a column vector
$\mathbf{b}^{k}$	the biases of $\mathbf{v}^{k}$
$\mathbf{W}^{k}$	the connection weight matrix between $\mathbf{h}$ and $\mathbf{v}^{k}$
M	the size of mini-batch
$\bar{\mathbf{a}}$	the augmented $\mathbf{a}$ for mini-batch
T	the thread number in each block, it may be different in different kernels

---

[1]   The matrices and vectors listed above are all stored by column.

2   Background

In this section, we first briefly introduce the basic ideas of RBM, and then present how to apply RBM to CF.

2.1   Restricted Boltzmann Machine

Restricted Boltzmann Machine (RBM) is a type of stochastic recurrent neural network that consists of visible layer and hidden layer without visible-visible and hidden-hidden connections. Figure **1** illustrates a standard RBM with two layers. Samples of RBM can be obtained by running a Monte Carlo Markov Chain (MCMC) to convergence, using Gibbs sampling as the transition operator of the chain.   Given the states of the hidden units, all the visible units are independent of each other, and vice versa. Therefore, the Gibbs sampling can be performed layer-wise rather than unit-wise, which makes it possible to improve the computational efficiency on parallel environment such as GPU.

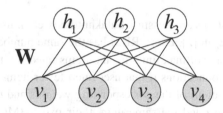

Fig. 1. A Restricted Boltzmann Machine with 3 hidden units and 4 visible units

The conditional probabilities of the visible units and the hidden units are given as follows,

$$p(v_i = 1 \mid \mathbf{h}) = \text{sigm}(b_i + \mathbf{W}_{i.}\mathbf{h}). \tag{1}$$

$$p(h_j = 1 \mid \mathbf{v}) = \text{sigm}\left[c_j + \text{tr}(\mathbf{W}_{.j})\mathbf{v}\right]. \tag{2}$$

2.2   Restricted Boltzmann Machine for CF

In order to apply RBM to CF, the first thing is to replace the visible binary unit with the composite binary units to model ratings of items given by users. The augmented unit consisting of these multiple binary units is called softmax unit [2]. The extended model is represented by RBM-CF (RBM-based model for Collaborative Filtering) in this paper as shown in Figure **2**. Assume that we have I items, and ratings are given as integer values on a scale from 1 to K. The input of RBM is augmented to a $K \times I$ matrix. The k th binary unit of the i th softmax unit is set to one only if the user rated the item i as with k. Note that there is only one binary unit in the softmax unit that would be set to one. The connections from hidden units to softmax units consist of K weight matrices $\mathbf{W}^1 \sim \mathbf{W}^K$.

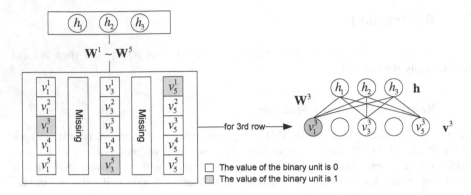

Fig. 2. A RBM-CF with binary hidden units and softmax visible units with $K=5$. For each user, the RBM only includes softmax units for the items that user has rated. In addition to the symmetric weights between each hidden unit and each of the 5 values of a softmax unit, there are 5 biases for each softmax unit and 1 bias for each hidden unit.

When most of the ratings are missing, Salakhutdinov et al. use a different RBM for each user (see Figure **2**) in [2]. Every RBM has the same number of hidden units, but an RBM only has visible softmax units for the items rated by its corresponding user, so an RBM has fewer connections if that user rated fewer items. Each RBM only has a single training case, but all of the corresponding weights and biases are tied together, so if two users have rated the same item, their two RBMs must share the same weights between the hidden units and the softmax visible unit for that item. The binary states of the hidden units, however, can be quite different for different users.

Let $\mathbf{v}^k$ be an $I \times 1$ observed column binary vector corresponding to the k th row of the softmax matrix. The value of v_i^k is defined as follows,

$$v_i^k = \begin{cases} 1 & \text{if the user rated movie } i \text{ as } k \\ \text{x} & \text{if missing (0 in computation)} \\ 0 & \text{otherwise} \end{cases} \tag{3}$$

where x represents the missing data, and $1 \le k \le K$. The conditional probabilities of hidden units and softmax units are given by,

$$p(v_i^k = 1 \mid \mathbf{h}) = \exp\left(b_i^k + \mathbf{W}_{i\cdot}^k \mathbf{h}\right) / \sum_{l=1}^{K} \exp\left(b_i^l + \mathbf{W}_{i\cdot}^l \mathbf{h}\right), \tag{4}$$

$$p(h_j = 1 \mid \mathbf{v}^1 \sim \mathbf{v}^K) = \text{sigm}\left[b_j + \sum_{k=1}^{K} \text{tr}(\mathbf{W}_{\cdot j}^k) \mathbf{v}^k\right]. \tag{5}$$

```
initialize all the parameters
for each training epoch do
    for each mini-batch update do
        load M samples to construct  v̄¹ ~ v̄ᴷ
        for k=1 to K do
            compute  h̄ᵏ = tr(Wᵏ)×v̄ᵏ+c̄  (1)
        endfor
        compute  h̄ ~ σ(∑ᵏ₌₁ᴷ h̄ᵏ)
        h̄' = h̄
        for each sampling step do
            for k=1 to K do
                compute  v̄ᵏ' = Wᵏh̄'+b̄ᵏ  (2)
            endfor
            compute  v̄ᵏ' ~ exp(v̄ᵏ')/∑exp(v̄ᵏ')
            compute  h̄' at the same way
        endfor
        for k=1 to K do
            compute  ΔWᵏ = v̄ᵏ×tr(h̄)-v̄ᵏ'×tr(h̄')  (3)
            compute  Wᵏ = Wᵏ+η×avg(ΔWᵏ)
            compute  Δb̄ᵏ = η(v̄ᵏ-v̄ᵏ')  and update  b̄ᵏ
        endfor
        update  c̄ at the same way
    endfor
endfor
```

Fig. 3. The matrix-based algorithm of training RBM-CF. (1) ~ (3): three main types of MMMs in the matrix-based algorithm, which should take the sparsity issues of data sets into consideration

The steps of making recommendation for a user u on item i after training are: 1) Load the rating sample of the user onto the softmax matrix. 2) Compute $\hat{p}_j = p(h_j = 1 | \mathbf{v}^1 \sim \mathbf{v}^K)$ for all hidden units j. 3) Compute $p(v_i^k = 1 | \hat{\mathbf{p}})$ for $k = 1, ..., K$. 4) Take the expectation $\sum_{k=1}^{K} p(v_i^k = 1 | \hat{\mathbf{p}}) \times k$ as the prediction.

3   Matrix-Based Training Algorithm for RBM-CF

The free parameters of RBM-CF can be learnt from the data by using Contrastive divergence (CD) algorithm [16]. The learning rule of RBM-CF can be written as follows,

$$\Delta W_{ij}^k \propto \left(<v_i^k h_j>_{data} - <v_i^k h_j>_{recon} \right),$$ (6)

$$\Delta b_i \propto \left(<v_i>_{data} - <v_i>_{recon} \right),$$ (7)

$$\Delta c_j \propto \left(<h_j>_{data} - <h_j>_{recon} \right),$$ (8)

where $\langle \cdot \rangle_{data}$ is the expectation with respect to the data distribution, and $\langle \cdot \rangle_{reconn}$ is the expectation of k-step re-construction, which is obtained by Markov Chain Monte Carlo (MCMC). The CD algorithm initializes the chain with a training sample and does not wait for the chain to converge. The reconstructed samples are obtained only after k-steps Gibbs sampling. In practice, k=1 has been shown to work well.

For increasing the update rate, we reduce the number of training observations in each update by splitting them into mini-batches and transforming the computation into matrix-matrix operations such as Matrix-Matrix Multiplication (MMM). The size of mini-batch is denoted as M, the augmented matrix of $\mathbf{v}^k$ as $\overline{\mathbf{v}}^k = (\overline{\mathbf{v}}_1^k, \overline{\mathbf{v}}_2^k, ..., \overline{\mathbf{v}}_M^k)$, so does $\mathbf{h}$. For the sake of representation, we also augment $\mathbf{b}^k$ to $\overline{\mathbf{b}}^k = (\overline{\mathbf{b}}_1^k, \overline{\mathbf{b}}_2^k, ..., \overline{\mathbf{b}}_M^k)$ and have $\overline{\mathbf{b}}_{m_1}^k = \overline{\mathbf{b}}_{m_2}^k$ where $1 \leq m_1, m_2 \leq M$, so does $\mathbf{c}$. However, we do not actually augment $\mathbf{b}^k / \mathbf{c}$ in practice due to the memory issue in the case of large scale data sets.

Figure **3** illustrates a matrix-based training algorithm of RBM-CF with mini-batch. Since we have transformed most of the computation into matrix-based operations, the parallelization of the training can be performed by developing simple efficiency CUDA (Compute Unified Device Architecture) [17] kernels and utilizing CUBALS (CUDA BLAS) [18] on GPU.

4   Parallel Implementation with Sparse MMM Kernels

For most of the time consuming operations of RBM-CF are several types of MMMs, it is clear that high performance of speedup would be obtained by utilizing CUBLAS on GPU. Furthermore, the speedup performance of these MMMs in RBM-CF can be further improved by taking the sparsity of $\overline{\mathbf{v}}^k$ into consideration.

The three essential types of MMMs are shown in Table **2**. Obviously, MMM 1 and MMM 3 should take account of the sparsity of $\overline{\mathbf{v}}^k$. Since the product of $\mathbf{W}^k \times \overline{\mathbf{h}}'$ is used to reconstruct $\overline{\mathbf{v}}^k$ (namely $\overline{\mathbf{v}}^{k'}$), there is no need to compute all elements of the product in MMM 2. Therefore, developing kernels for "sparse" MMMs is the essential part of the parallel implementation of RBM-CF. However, popular sparse MMM frameworks on GPU such as CUSP (http:// code.google.com/p/cusp-library/) are not fit for RBM-CF due to storage issues, which will be detailed in the following subsection. In addition, these frameworks are not able to deal with MMM 2, since the left matrix and right matrix in MMM 2 are dense but the product is sparse.

Table 2. Three essential MMMs

	Left Matrix		Right Matrix		Product [2]	
	Symbol	Dim	Symbol	Dim	Symbol	Dim
MMM 1	$\mathrm{tr}(\mathbf{W}^k)$	$J \times I$	$\bar{\mathbf{v}}^k$ (CSC)	$I \times M$	$\bar{\mathbf{h}}^k$	$J \times M$
MMM 2	$\mathbf{W}^k$	$I \times J$	$\bar{\mathbf{h}}'$	$J \times M$	$\bar{\mathbf{v}}^{k'}$ (COO)	$I \times M$
MMM 3	$\bar{\mathbf{v}}^k$ (CSR)	$I \times M$	$\mathrm{tr}(\bar{\mathbf{h}})$	$M \times J$	$\Delta \mathbf{W}^k$	$I \times J$

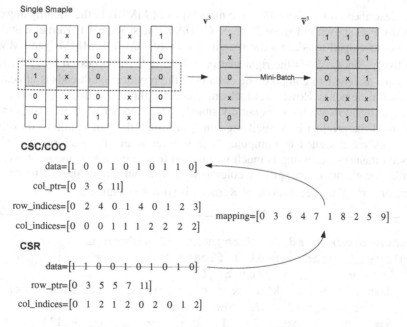

Fig. 4. An example of storage format for $\bar{\mathbf{v}}_k$

4.1   Sparse Matrix Formats

To develop kernels for these sparse MMMs, the first important step is to choose or design sparse matrix format for $\bar{\mathbf{v}}^k$. Just as shown in Table **2**, the position of $\bar{\mathbf{v}}^k$ in

---

[2] For the sake of presentation, the products are represented as $\bar{\mathbf{h}}^k$, $\bar{\mathbf{v}}^{k'}$, $\Delta \mathbf{W}^k$ respectively.

different MMMs is different. Therefore, two sparse instances are created to access $\bar{v}^k$ in our CUDA kernels. The first instance is constructed by Compressed Sparse Column (CSC) with an extra array of row indices (row coordinates), which is also a Coordinate (COO) instance. The other instance is based on Compressed Sparse Row (CSR) format. For the second instance, it accesses its data from the data array of the first instance through a mapping array rather than really store its own data array.

In order to save the computation time of compression at each Gibbs sampling step and facilitate programming while developing CUDA kernels, the elements of value zero are also stored in those instances. Another advantage of storing zero elements is that all the indices, coordinates and mapping information can be shared by all $\bar{v}^k$ and

$\bar{v}^{k'}$ in the same mini-batch. Therefore, there is only one copy of the instances except for data array in one mini-batch. An example of our combined format is illustrated in Figure 4.

4.2   CUDA Kernels

Just as described above, there are three main types of MMMs in the training algorithm of RBM-CF as shown in Figure 3. Three CUDA kernels: Kernel 1, Kernel 2 and Kernel 3 are developed to address the sparsity issues of MMM 1, MMM 2 and MMM 3 respectively. Since $\bar{v}^k$ is the right matrix in MMM 1, it is accessed by CSC indices. Blocks are assigned to compute one column of the product and threads is allocated to compute the elements. However, blocks may contain threads with nothing to do at the end of computation while J is not divisible by T. Another scheme is splitting the elements of the product into small segments, of which the size should be divisible by T. Blocks are assigned to compute these segments. For the performance of non-coalesced memory accessing is much worse than that of coalesced memory accessing on GPU, the elements are split by column-wise to avoid non-coalesced memory accessing of $\bar{v}^k$. The pseudo-code of Kernel 1 is shown in Figure 5.

```
//each block handles a segment of hidden unit
__global__ void kernel_1(float* W, int* v_data, int* v_col-
ptr, int* v_row-indices, float* h) {
    int pos = blockIdx.x * blockDim.x + threadIdx.x;
    int col = pos / J, row = pos % J;
    int begin = v_col-ptr[col], end = v_col-ptr[col + 1];
    float result = 0.0f;
    for (int i = begin; i < end; i++) {
        if (v_data[i] > 0.5)
            result += W[v_row-indices[i] * J + row];
    }
    h[pos] = result;
}
```

Fig. 5. Kernel 1 is designed to compute $\bar{q}^k = tr(W^k) \times \bar{v}^k$

For Kernel 2, threads are not allocated to compute visible elements of the product directly of the kernel, because the rows of $\mathbf{W}^k$ needed by each thread are different from one thread to another, which leads to non-coalesced memory accessing. In order to improve the performance of memory accessing, one block is assigned to compute only one nonmissing element. The nonmissing elements are accessed by COO indices directly. For each block, threads are allocated to compute the inner product of $\mathbf{W}_{i\cdot}^k$ and $\mathbf{h}_{\cdot j}$. Shared memory is used to store the intermediate results of each thread. When all the threads finishing its multiplication tasks, parallel sum reduction is performed to obtain the final result of the inner product.

```
// each block handles an element of visible unit
__global__ void kernel_2(float* W, float* h, float*
v_data, int* v_col-ptr, int* v_col-indices, int* v_row-indices, int
segment_ptr) {
    int tid = threadIdx.x;
    int pos = blockIdx.x + segment_ptr;
    int col = v_col-indices[pos], row = v_row-indices[pos];
    float result = 0.0f;
    // intermediate result
    __shared__ float sdata[128];
    for (int i = 0; i < J; i += blockDim.x){
        if (h[col * J + i]>0.5)
            result += W[row * J + i];
    }
    sdata[tid] = result;
    __syncthreads();
    // the size of threads is set 128
    int threads = 128/2;
    if (J >= (threads<<1) && tid < threads)
        sdata[tid] += sdata[tid + threads];
    // no __syncthreads() in the same warp
    if (tid < 32) {
        while (threads > 1) {
            thread = threads>>1;
            if (J >= (threads<<1) && tid < threads)
                sdata[tid] += sdata[tid + threads];
        }
    }
    if(tid == 0)
        v_data[pos] = sdata[0];
}
```

Fig. 6. The pseudo-code of Kernel 2 for compute $\bar{\mathbf{v}}^{k'} = \mathbf{W}^k \times \bar{\mathbf{h}}'$

For threads in a block are launched by warps (32 threads), the threads within the same warp are no need to be synchronized. Thus, the performance of the parallel sum reduction in Kernel 2 can be improved by employing this feature. In addition, the number of synchronizing threads operations depends on the size of block threads and would affect the performance of the whole kernel especially when J is small. For example, assume $J = 1024$, taking $T = 256$, each thread performs less multiplications but the kernel needs one more synchronizing thread operations in the parallel sum reduction comparing to $T = 128$. In practice, T is pre-evaluated by experiments and basically set to 128 according to the experiment results. The pseudo-code of Kernel 2 is given in Figure **6**.

One important trick used in Kernel 1 and Kernel 2 to improve the computational efficiency is transforming the multiplication between two elements into addition, for the value of elements in $\overline{\mathbf{v}}^k / \overline{\mathbf{h}}$ can only be 1 or 0. Therefore, better performance would be obtained since the cost of performing addition on GPU is much lower.

In MMM 3, $\overline{\mathbf{v}}^k$ is in the left matrix and should be arranged by row, therefore, the data array of $\overline{\mathbf{v}}^k$ is accessed by using CSR indices and the mapping array. Blocks are assigned to compute rows of the product directly, and consecutive threads are allocated to update consecutive elements in each row of the product. The pseudo-code of Kernel 3 is shown in Figure **7**.

```
//each block handles one row of visible unit
__global__ void kernel_3(float* v_data, int* v_row-ptr, int*
v_col_indices, int* Mapping, int* h, float* W) {
    int tid = threadIdx.x;
    int begin = v_row-ptr[blockIdx.x];
    int end = v_row-ptr[blockIdx.x + 1] - 1;
    for (int j = tid; j < J; j += blockDim.x) {
        float delta = 0.0f;
        for (int i = begin; i < end; i++) {
            int pos = Mapping[i], col = v_col_indices[i];
            delta += v_data[pos] * h[j+J*col];
        }
        // coalesced memory access
        W[blockIdx.x * J + j] = delta;
    }
}
```

Fig. 7. Kernel 3 is designed to compute $\Delta \mathbf{W}^k = \overline{\mathbf{v}}^k \times tr(\overline{\mathbf{h}})$ or $\Delta \mathbf{W}^k = \overline{\mathbf{v}}^{k\prime} \times tr(\overline{\mathbf{h}}')$

5   Experiments

Several experiments are carried out in this section. We investigate the speedup performance of our parallel implementation with different number of hidden units. The comparison results between our sparse MMM kernels and CUBLAS are also given.

5.1   Research Data

We adopt the Netflix data set as our research data. The data were collected between 1998/10 and 2005/12. Only about 1.2% of the ratings are available, which are split up by the organizers as training and probe set. The available dataset contains ratings given by 480189 users on 17770 movies, and its sparsity (nonmissing) rate is about 1.2%.

5.2   Experiment Setting

All the experiments are conducted on a system with an Intel(R) Xeon(R) CPU E5620 @ 2.40GH with 16 processors, 48GB RAM, and graphic card of NVIDIA C2050. The specification of C2050 is given in Table 3. In our experiment settings, the elements of the weight matrices are randomly initialized, and the biases b^k and c are initialized to 0. We implement the framework with JAVA programming language using a JNI library called JCUDA (http://www.jcuda.org). In order to accelerate the convergence of the training, the momentum mechanism is adopted. The comparison benchmark is the optimized version of the matrix-based algorithm on GPU, which has taken sparsity into consideration. The runtime performance of non-optimized CPU version is not given due to its low efficiency.

Table 3. The hardware specification about NVIDIA C2050

Property	Specification
Number of CUDA Core	448
Clock speed	1.15 GHz
Peak performance	515 GFLOPS
Memory	3 GB
Memory bandwidth	144 GB/sec
Graphics bus	PCI Express x16 Generation 2.0

5.3   Results

To begin with, we evaluate the performance of our parallel implementation with different hidden units. Figure   8 shows the speedup achieved by our implementation and CUBLAS. As illustrated in the figure, the benefits become larger with the number of hidden units incrementing. The large reduction in the execution time is mainly due to a larger J that helps hiding communication latency of GPU. The speedup performance of our approach with sparse MMM kernels are about 51 over CPU. The speedups achieved by CUBLAS are only about 13, since the benchmark is the optimized version of the training algorithm on CPU.

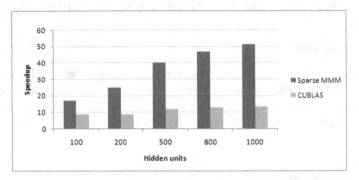

Fig. 8. The speedup performance of RBM-CF with different number of hidden units

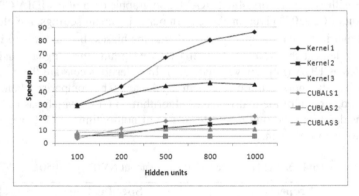

Fig. 9. The speedup performance of the three main sparse MMM kernels, compared with those of CUBLAS

Then, we investigate the speedup performance of the three types of MMMs achieved by our CUDA kernels and CUBLAS with different hidden units in detail as shown in Figure 9. As a consequence, our kernels perform much better than that of CUBLAS, since many unnecessary calculations are ignored. The speedups of both our sparse MMM kernels and CUBLAS are basically improving when J is increasing, because larger J would benefit more in hiding communication latency. For Kernel 3, it has achieved its best speedup performance when the number of hidden units is about 800. The gap of speedup between Kernel 2 and CUBLAS 2 is not as significant as other pairs. Since the inner product of $\mathbf{W}_{i.}^{k}$ and $\mathbf{h}_{.j}$ is computed by one block and the dimension of the vectors is only J, the speedup would be limited when J is too small (≤ 1000).

6   Conclusion

With the scale of the machine learning problem becoming larger and larger, many learning tools encounter the computational problem. RBM-CF also has this problem when dealing with large scale data sets. Therefore, it is important to develop an efficiency parallel algorithm to accelerate the computation. In this paper, we detail how to parallelize the RBM-CF on GPU for large and sparse data sets such as Netflix. The experiments indicate that our optimized implementation on GPU yields higher performance of speedups comparing with that on CPU. Our future work is to parallelize the computation of RBM on GPU-accelerated cluster to model much larger scale problems.

Acknowledgment. This work is supported in part by the National Natural Science Foundation of China under Grant No. 61073055, 985-III fund, and Natural Science Foundation of Guangdong Province, China under Grant No.10152104101000004.

References

1. Smolensky, P.: Information processing in dynamical systems: Foundations of harmony theory. Parallel Distributed Processing: Explorations in the Microstructure of Cognition 1, 194–281 (1986)
2. Salakhutdinov, R., Mnih, A., Hinton, G.: Restricted boltzmann machines for collaborative filtering. In: Proceedings of the 24th International Conference on Machine Learning, pp. 791–798. ACM (2007)
3. Salakhutdinov, R., Hinton, G.: Deep boltzmann machines. In: Proceedings of the International Conference on Artificial Intelligence and Statistics, vol. 5, pp. 448–455 (2009)
4. Ranzato, M., Szummer, M.: Semi-supervised learning of compact document representations with deep networks. In: Proceedings of the 25th International Conference on Machine Learning, pp. 792–799. ACM (2008)
5. Ly, D., Paprotski, V., Yen, D.: Neural networks on gpus: Restricted boltzmann machines. Tech. rep., Technical Report, Department of Electrical and Computer Engineering, University of Toronto (2008)
6. McAfee, L.: Design and analysis of blas, gpu, and sparse multithreaded acceleration methods for restricted b oltzmann machine training
7. Raina, R., Madhavan, A., Ng, A.: Large-scale deep unsupervised learning using graphics processors. In: Proceedings of the 26th Annual International Conference on Machine Learning, pp. 873–880. ACM (2009)
8. Kim, S., McAfee, L., McMahon, P., Olukotun, K.: A highly scalable restricted boltzmann machine FPGA implementation. In: International Conference on Field Programmable Logic and Applications, FPL 2009, pp. 367–372. IEEE (2009)
9. Kim, S., McMahon, P., Olukotun, K.: A large-scale architecture for restricted boltzmann machines. In: 2010 18th IEEE Annual International Symposium on Field-Programmable Custom Computing Machines (FCCM), pp. 201–208. IEEE (2010)

10. Ly, D., Chow, P.: A high-performance FPGA architecture for restricted boltzmann machines. In: Proceeding of the ACM/SIGDA International Symposium on Field Programmable Gate Arrays, pp. 73–82. ACM (2009)

11. Ly, D., Chow, P.: A multi-fpga architecture for stochastic restricted boltzmann machines. In: International Conference on Field Programmable Logic and Applications, FPL 2009, pp. 168–173. IEEE (2009)

12. Le Ly, D., Chow, P.: High-performance reconfigurable hardware architecture for restricted boltzmann machines. IEEE Transactions on Neural Networks 21(11), 1780–1792 (2010)

13. Lekakos, G., Giaglis, G.: Improving the prediction accuracy of recommendation algorithms. Approaches Anchored on Human Factors. Interacting with Computers 18(3), 410–431 (2006)

14. Roh, T., Oh, K., Han, I.: The collaborative filtering recommendation based on som cluster-indexing cbr. Expert Systems with Applications 25(3), 413–423 (2003)

15. Shih, Y., Liu, D.: Product recommendation approaches: Collaborative filtering via customer lifetime value and customer demands. Expert Systems with Applications 35(1), 350–360 (2008)

16. Hinton, G.: Training products of experts by minimizing contrastive divergence. Neural Computation 14(8), 1771–1800 (2002)

17. Nvidia, C.: Compute unified device architecture programming guide, vol. 83, p. 129. NVIDIA, Santa Clara (2007)

18. Nvidia, C.: Cublas library, vol. 15. NVIDIA Corporation, Santa Clara (2008)

STM Systems:
Enforcing Strong Isolation between Transactions and Non-transactional Code

Tyler Crain[1], Eleni Kanellou[1], and Michel Raynal[1,2]

[1] IRISA, Université de Rennes 35042 Rennes Cedex, France
[2] Institut Universitaire de France
{tyler.crain,eleni.kanellou,michel.raynal}@irisa.fr

Abstract. Transactional memory (TM) systems implement the concept of an atomic execution unit called *transaction* in order to discharge programmers from explicit synchronization management. But when shared data is atomically accessed by both transaction and non-transactional code, a TM system must provide *strong isolation* in order to overcome consistency problems. Strong isolation enforces ordering between non-transactional operations and transactions and preserves the atomicity of a transaction even with respect to non-transactional code. This paper presents a TM algorithm that implements strong isolation with the following features: (a) concurrency control of non-transactional operations is not based on locks and is particularly efficient, and (b) any non-transactional read or write operation always terminates (there is no notion of commit/abort associated with them).

Keywords: Transactional Memory, Strong Isolation, Atomicity.

1 Introduction

STM Systems. Transactional Memory (TM) [9,18] has emerged as an attempt to allow concurrent programming based on sequential reasoning: By using TM, a user should be able to write a correct concurrent application, provided she can create a correct sequential program. The underlying TM system takes care of the correct implementation of concurrency. However, while most existing TM algorithms consider applications where shared memory will be accessed solely by code enclosed in a transaction, it still seems imperative to examine the possibility that memory is accessed both inside and outside of transactions.

Strong vs Weak Isolation. TM has to guarantee that transactions will be isolated from each other, but when it comes to transactions and non-transactional operations, there are two paths a TM system can follow: it may either act oblivious to the concurrency between transactions and non-transactional operations, or it may take this concurrency into account and attempt to provide isolation guarantees even between transactional and non-transactional operations. The

Y. Xiang et al. (Eds.): ICA3PP 2012, Part I, LNCS 7439, pp. 317–331, 2012.

first case is referred to as *weak isolation* while the second case is referred to as *strong isolation*. (This distinction of guarantees was originally made in [12], where reference was made to "weak atomicity" versus "strong atomicity".)

While weak isolation violates the isolation principle of the transaction abstraction, it could nevertheless be anticipated and used appropriately by the programmer, still resulting in correctly functioning applications. This would require the programmer to be conscious of eventual race conditions between transactional and non-transactional code that can change depending on the STM system used.

Desirable Properties. In order to keep consistent with the spirit of TM principles, however, a system should prevent unexpected results from occurring in presence of race conditions. Furthermore, concurrency control should ideally be implicit and never be delegated to the programmer [2,13]. These are the reasons for which strong isolation is desirable. Under strong isolation, the aforementioned scenarios, where non-transactional operations violate transaction isolation, would not be allowed to happen. An intuitive approach to achieving strong isolation is to treat each non-transactional operation that accesses shared data as a "mini-transaction", i.e., one that contains a single operation. In that case, transactions will have to be consistent (see Sect. 2) not only with respect to each other, but also with respect to the non-transactional operations. However, while the concept of the memory transaction includes the possibility of abort, the concept of the non-transactional operation does not. This means that a programmer expects that a transaction might fail, either by blocking or by aborting. Non-transactional accesses to shared data, though, will usually be read or write operations, which the programmer expects to be atomic. While executing, a read or write operation is not expected to be de-scheduled, blocked or aborted.

Content of the Paper. This paper presents a TM algorithm which takes the previous issues into account. It is built on top of TM algorithm TL2 [6], a word-based TM algorithm that uses locks. More precisely, TL2 is modified to provide strong isolation with non-transactional read and write operations. However, the algorithm is designed without the use of locks for non-transactional code, in order to guarantee that their execution will always terminate. To achieve this, two additional functions are specified, which substitute conventional read or write operations that have to be performed outside of a transaction. Possible violations of correctness under strong isolation are reviewed in Sect. 2. The TL2 algorithm is described in Sect. 3. Section 4 describes the proposed algorithm that implements strong isolation for TL2, while Sect. 5 concludes the paper by summarizing the work and examining possible applications.

2   Correctness and Strong Isolation

Consistency Issues. Commonly, consistency conditions for TM build on the concept of *serializability* [15], a condition first established for the study of database transactions.

A concurrent execution of transactions is serializable, if there exists a serialization, i.e., a legal sequential execution equivalent to it. Serializability refers only to committed transactions, however, and fails to take into account the possible program exceptions that a TM transaction may cause - even if it aborts - when it observes an inconsistent state of memory.

Opacity [7], a stricter consistency condition for TM, requires that both committed as well as aborted transactions observe a consistent state of shared memory. This implies that in order for a concurrent execution of memory transactions to be opaque, there must exist an equivalent, legal sequential execution that includes both committed transactions and aborted transactions, albeit reduced to their read prefix. Other consistency conditions have also been proposed, such as *virtual world consistency* [10]. It is weaker than opacity while keeping its spirit (i.e., it depends on both committed transactions and aborted transactions).

Transaction vs Non-transactional Code. In a concurrent environment, shared memory may occasionally be accessed by both transactions as well as non-transactional operations. Traditionally, however, transactions are designed to synchronize only with other transactions without considering the possibility of non-transactional code; a program that accesses the same shared memory both transactionally and non-transactionally would be considered incorrect. A TM system that implements opacity minimally guarantees consistency between transactional accesses, however, consistency violations may still be possible in the presence of concurrent non-transactional code. Given this, it can still be acceptable to have concurrent environments that may be prone to some types of violations, as is the case with systems that provide weak isolation [12,19]. Under weak isolation, transactional and non-transactional operations can be concurrent, but the programmer has to be aware of how to handle these. Interestingly, this possibility of *co-existence of two different paradigms* between strong and weak isolation reveals two different interpretations of transactional memory: On one hand considering TM as an implementation of shared memory, and, on the other hand, considering TM as an additional way of achieving synchronization, to be used alongside with locks, fences, and other traditional methods.

Under weak isolation, transactions are considered to happen atomically only with respect to other transactions. It is possible for non-transactional operations to see intermediate results of transactions that are still live. Conversely, a transaction may see the results of non-transactional operations that happened during the transaction's execution. If this behavior is not considered acceptable for an application, then the responsibility to prevent it is delegated to the programmer of concurrent applications for this system. However, in order to spare the programmer this responsibility, both the transactional memory algorithm as well as the non-transactional read and write operations must be implemented in a way that takes their co-existence into account. Such an implementation that provides synchronization between transactional and non-transactional code is said to provide strong isolation.

Providing Strong Isolation. There are different definitions in literature for strong isolation [12,11,8]. In this paper we consider strong isolation to be the following:

(a) non-transactional operations are considered as "mini" transactions which never abort and contain only a single read or write operation, and (b) the consistency condition for transactions is opacity.

This definition implies that the properties that are referred to as *containment* and *non-interference* [12] are satisfied. Containment is illustrated in the left part of Fig. 1. There, under strong isolation, we have to assume that transaction T_1 happens atomically, i.e., "all or nothing", also with respect to non-transactional operations. Then, while T_1 is alive, no non-transactional read, such as R_x, should be able to obtain the value written to x by T_1. Non-interference is illustrated in the right part of Fig. 1. Under strong isolation, non-transactional code should not interfere with operations that happen inside a transaction. Therefore, transaction T_1 should not be able to observe the effects of operations W_x and W_y, given that they happen concurrently with it, while no opacity-preserving serialization of T_1, W_x and W_y can be found. Non-interference violations can be caused, for example, by non-transactional operations that are such as to cause the ABA problem for a transaction that has read a shared variable x. An additional feature of strong isolation, implemented in this paper, is that non-transactional read and write operations never block or abort. For this reason, it is termed *terminating strong isolation*.

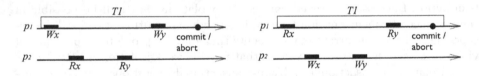

Fig. 1. Left: *Containment* (operation R_x should not return the value written to x inside the transaction). Right: *Non-Interference* (wile it is still executing, transaction T_1 should not have access to the values that were written to x and y by process p_2).

Privatization/Publication. A discussion of the co-existence of transactional and non-transactional code would not be complete without mentioning the *privatization problem*. An area of shared memory is privatized, when a process that modified it makes it inaccessible to other concurrent processes[1] with the purpose being that the process can then access the memory without using synchronization operations [21]. A typical example of privatization would be the manipulation of a shared linked list. The removal of a node by a transaction T_i, for private use, through non-transactional code, by the process that invoked T_i, constitutes privatization. Then, T_i is called privatizing transaction. While the privatization is not visible to all processes, inconsistencies may arise, given that for T_i's process the node is private but for other processes, the node is still seen as shared. Several solutions have been proposed for the privatization problem such as [17,1,5].

---

[1] Conversely, a memory area is made public when it goes from being exclusively accessible by one process to being accessible by several processes [20] . This is referred to as the *publication problem* and the consistency issues that arise are analogous.

A system that provides *strong isolation* has the advantage of inherently also solving the privatization problem, because it inherently imposes synchronization between transactional and non-transactional code.

3 A Brief Presentation of TL2

TL2, aspects of which are used in this paper, has been introduced by Dice, Shalev and Shavit in 2006 [6]. The word-based version of the algorithm is used, where transactional reads and writes are to single memory words.

Main Features of TL2. The shared variables that a transaction reads form its *read set*, while the variables it updates form the *write set*. Read operations in TL2 are *invisible*, meaning that when a transaction reads a shared variable, there is no indication of the read to other transactions. Write operations are *deferred*, meaning that TL2 does not perform the updates as soon as it "encounters" the shared variables that it has to write to. Instead, the updates it has to perform are logged into a local list (also called *redo log*) and are applied to the shared memory only once the transaction is certain to commit. Read-only transactions in TL2 are considered efficient, because they don't need to maintain local copies of a read or write set and because they need no final read set validation in order to commit. To control transaction synchronization, TL2 employs locks and logical dates.

Locks and Logical Date. A lock is associated with each shared variable. When a transaction attempts to commit it first has to obtain the locks of the variables of its write set, before it can update them. Furthermore, a transaction has to check the logical dates of the variables in its read set in order to ensure that the values it has read correspond to a consistent snapshot of shared memory. TL2 implements logical time as an integer counter denoted GVC. When a transaction starts it reads the current value of GVC into local variable, rv. When a transaction attempts to commit, it performs an increment-and-fetch on GVC, and stores the return value in local variable wv (which can be seen as a write version number or a version timestamp). Should the transaction commit, it will assign its wv as the new logical date of the shared variables in its write set. A transaction must abort if its read set is not valid. Its read set is valid if the logical date of every item in the set is less than the transaction's rv value. If, on the contrary, the logical date of a read set item is larger than the rv of the transaction, then a concurrent transaction has updated this item, invalidating the read.

4 Implementing Terminating Strong Isolation

A possible solution to the problem of ensuring isolation in the presence of non-transactional code consists in using locks: Each shared variable would then be associated with a lock and both transactions as well as non-transactional operations would have to access the lock before accessing the variable.

Locks are already used in TM algorithms - such as TL2 itself - where it is however assumed that shared memory is only accessed through transactions. The use of locks in a TM algorithm entails blocking and may even lead a process to starvation. However, it can be argued that these characteristics are acceptable, given that the programmer accepts the fact that a transaction has a duration and that it may even fail: The fact that there is always a possibility that a transaction will abort means that the eventuality of failure to complete can be considered a part of the transaction concept.

On the contrary, when it comes to single read or write accesses to a shared variable, a non-transactional operation is understood as an event that happens atomically and completes. Unfortunately strong isolation implemented with locks entails the blocking of non-transactional read and write operations and would not provide termination.

Given that this approach would be rather counter-intuitive for the programmer (as well as possibly detrimental for program efficiency), the algorithm presented in this section provides a solution for adding strong isolation which is not based on locks for the execution of non-transactional operations. This algorithm builds on the base of TM algorithm TL2 and extends it in order to account for non-transactional operations. While read and write operations that appear inside a transaction follow the original TL2 algorithm rather closely (cheap read only transactions, commit-time locking, write-back), the proposed algorithm specifies non-transactional read and write operations that are to be used by the programmer, substituting conventional shared memory read and write operations. TM with strong isolation has also been proposed in software [16,19] in hardware [14], and has been suggested to be too costly [4]. This work differs from other implementations in that it is terminating and is implemented on top of a state-of-the-art STM in order to avoid too much extra cost.

4.1 Memory Set-Up and Data Structures

Memory Set-up. The underlying memory system is made up of atomic read/write registers. Moreover some of them can also be accessed by the the following two operations. The operation denoted Fetch&increment() atomically adds one to the register and returns its previous value. The operation denoted C&S() (for compare and swap) is a conditional write. C&S(x, a, b) writes b into x iff $x = a$. In that case it returns *true*. Otherwise it returns *false*.

The proposed algorithm assumes that the variables are of types and values that can be stored in a memory word. This assumption aids in the clarity of the algorithm description but it is also justified by the fact that the algorithm extends TL2, an algorithm that is designed to be word-based.

As in TL2, the variable GVC acts as global clock which is incremented by update transactions. Apart from a global notion of "time", there exists also a local one; each process maintains a local variable denoted *time*, which is used in order to keep track of when, with respect to the GVC, a non-transactional operation or a transaction was last performed by the process. This variable is then used during non-transactional operations to ensure the (strict) serialization of operations is not violated.

In TL2 a shared array of locks is maintained and each shared memory word is associated with a lock in this array by some function. Given this, a memory word directly contains the value of the variable that is stored in it. Instead, the algorithm presented here, uses a different memory set-up that does not require a lock array, but does require an extra level of indirection when loading and storing values in memory. Instead of storing the value of a variable directly to a memory word, each write operation on variable *var*, transactional or non-transactional, first creates an algorithm-specific structure that contains the new value of *var*, as well as necessary meta-data and second stores a pointer to this structure in the memory word. The memory set-up is illustrated in Fig. 2. Given the particular memory arrangement that the algorithm uses, pointers are used in order to load and store items from memory. [2]

T-record and NT-record. These algorithm-specific data structures are shared and can be of either two kinds, which will be referred to as T-records and NT-records. A T-record is created by a transactional write operation while an NT-record is created by a non-transactional write operation.

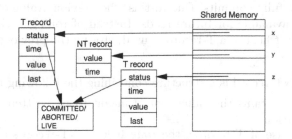

Fig. 2. The memory set-up and the data structures that are used by the algorithm

New T-records are created during the transactional write operations. Then during the commit operation the pointer stored at *addr* is updated to point to this new T-record. During NT-write operations new NT-records are created and the pointer at *addr* is updated to point to the records.

When a read operation - be it transactional or non-transactional - accesses a shared variable it cannot know beforehand what type of record it will find. Therefore, it can be seen in the algorithm listings, that whenever a record is accessed, the operation checks its type, i.e., it checks whether it is a T-record or an NT-record (for example, line 02 in Fig. 3 contains such a check. A T-record is "of type T", while an NT-record is "of type NT").

---

[2] The following notation is used. If *pt* is a pointer, $pt \downarrow$ is the object pointed to by *pt*. if *aa* is an object, $\uparrow aa$ is a pointer to *aa*. Hence $((\uparrow aa) \downarrow = aa$ and $\uparrow (pt \downarrow) = pt$.

T-record. A T-record is a structure containing the following fields.

status This field indicates the state of the transaction that created the T-record. The state can either be LIVE, COMMITTED or ABORTED. The state is initially set to LIVE and is not set to COMMITTED until during the commit operation when all locations of the transaction's write set have been set to point to the transaction's T-records and the transaction has validated its read set. Since a transaction can write to multiple locations, the *status* field does not directly store the state, instead it contains a pointer to a memory location containing the state for the transaction. Therefore the *status* field of each T-record created by the same transaction will point to the same location. This ensures that any change to the transaction's state is immediately recognized at each record.

time The *time* field of a T-record contains the value of the GVC at the moment the record was inserted to memory. This is similar to the logical dates of TL2.

value This field contains the value that is meant to be written to the chosen memory location.

last During the commit operation, locations are updated to point to the committing transaction's T-records, overwriting the previous value that was stored in this location. Failed validation or concurrent non-transactional operations may cause this transaction to abort after it updates some memory locations, but before it fully commits. Due to this, the previous value of the location needs to be available for future reads. Instead of rolling back old memory values, the *last* field of a T-record is used, storing the previous value of this location.

NT-record. An NT-record is a structure containing the following fields.

value This field contains the value that is meant to be written to the chosen memory location.

time As in the case of T-records, the *time* field of NT-records also stores the value of the GVC when the write took place.

Due to this different memory structure a shared lock array is no longer needed, instead of locking each location in the write set during the commit operation, this algorithm performs a compare and swap directly on each memory location changing the address to point to one of its T-records. After a successful compare and swap and before the transactions status has been set to COMMITTED or ABORTED, the transaction effectively owns the lock on this location. Like in TL2, any concurrent transaction that reads the location and sees that it is locked ($status = $ LIVE) will abort itself.

Transactional Read and Write Sets. Like TL2, read only transactions do not use read sets while update transactions do. The read set is made up of a set of tuples for each location read, $\langle addr, value \rangle$ where *addr* is the address of the location read and *value* is the value. The write set is also made up of tuples for each location written by the transaction, $\langle addr, item \rangle$ where *addr* is the location to be written and *item* is a T-record for this location.

Discussion. One advantage of the TL2 algorithm is in its memory layout. This is because reads and writes happen directly to memory (without indirection) and the main amount of additional memory that is used is in the lock array. Unfortunately this algorithm breaks that and requires an additional level of indirection as well as additional memory per location. While garbage collection will be required for old T- and NT-records, here we assume automatic garbage collection such as that provided in Java, but additional solutions will be explored in future work. These additional requirements can be an acceptable trade-off given that they are only needed for memory that will be shared between transactions. Still, in the technical report [3] we present two variations of the algorithm that trade off different memory schemes for different costs to the transactional and non-transactional operations.

4.2   Description of the Algorithm

The main goal of the algorithm is to provide strong isolation in such a way that the non-transactional operations are never blocked. In order to achieve this, the algorithm delegates most of its concurrency control and consistency checks to the transactional code. Non-transactional operations access and modify memory locations without waiting for concurrent transactions and it is mainly up to transactions accessing the same location to deal with ensuring safe concurrency. As a result, this algorithm gives high priority to non-transactional code.

4.3   Non-transactional Operations

Algorithm-specific read and write operations shown in Fig. 3 must be used when a shared variable is accessed accessed outside of a transaction. This be done by hand or applied by a complier.

Non-transactional Read. The operation non_transactional_read() is used to read, when not in a transaction, the value stored at *addr*. The operation first dereferences the pointer stored at *addr* (line 01). If the item is a T-record that was created by a transaction which has not yet committed then the *value* field cannot be immediately be read as the transaction might still abort. Also if the current process has read (or written to) a value that is more recent then the transaction (meaning the process's *time* field is greater or equal to the T-records *time*, line 03) then the transaction must be directed to abort (line 04) so that opacity and strong isolation (containment specifically) is not violated. From a T-record with a transaction that is not committed, the value from the *last* field is stored to a local variable (line 06) and will be returned on operation completion. Otherwise the *value* field of the T- or NT-record is used (line 07).

Next the process local variable *time* is advanced to the maximal value among its current value and the logical date of the T- or NT-record whose value was read. Finally if *time* was set to ∞ on line 11 (meaning the T- or NT-record had yet to set its *time*), then it is updated to the *GCV* on line 12. The updated *time* value is used to prevent consistency violations. Once these book-keeping operations are finished, the local variable *value* is returned (line 13).

```
operation non_transactional_read(addr) is
(01)    tmp ← (↓ addr);
(02)    if ( tmp is of type T ∧(↓ tmp.status) ≠ COMMITTED )
(03)       then if (tmp.time ≤ time ∧ (↓ tmp.status) = LIVE)
(04)          then C&S(tmp.status, LIVE, ABORTED) end if;
(05)          if ((↓ tmp.status) ≠ COMMITTED)
(06)             then value ← tmp.last
(07)             else value ← tmp.value
(08)          end if;
(09)       else value ← tmp.value
(10)    end if;
(11)    time ← max(time, tmp.time)
(12)    if (time = ∞) then time = GCV end if;
(13)    return (value)
end operation.

operation non_transactional_write(addr, value) is
(14)    allocate new variable next_write of type NT;
(15)    next_write ← (addr, value, ∞);
(16)    addr ← (↑ next_write)
(17)    time ← GVC;
(18)    next_write.time ← time;
end operation.
```

Fig. 3. Non-transactional operations for reading and writing a variable

Non-transactional Write. The operation non_transactional_write() is used to write to a shared variable *var* by non-transactional code. The operation takes as input the address of the shared variable as well as the value to be written to it. This operation creates a new NT-record (line 14), fills in its fields (line 15) and changes the pointer stored in *addr* so that it references the new record it has created (line 16). Unlike update transactions, non-transactional writes do not increment the global clock variable GCV. Instead they just read GCV and set the NT-record's time value as well as the process local *time* to the value read (line 17 and 18). Since the GCV is not incremented, several NT-records might have the same *time* value as some transaction. When such a situation is recognized where a live transaction has the same time value as an NT-record the transaction must be aborted (if recognized during an NT-read operation, line 04) or perform read set validation (if during a transactional read operation, line 23 of Fig. 4). This is done in order to prevent consistency violations caused by the NT-writes not updating the GCV.

4.4   Transactional Read and Write Operations

The transactional operations for performing reads and writes are presented in Fig. 4.

Transactional Read. The operation transactional_read() takes *addr* as input. It starts by checking whether the desired variable already exists in the transaction's write set, in which case the value stored there will be returned (line 19). If the variable is not contained in the write set, the pointer in *addr* is dereferenced (line 20) and set to *tmp*. Once this is detected to be a T- or NT-record some checks are then performed in order to ensure correctness.

In the case that *tmp* is a T-record the operation must check to see if the status of the transaction for this record is still LIVE and if it is the current transaction is aborted (line 29). This is similar to a transaction in TL2 aborting itself when a locked location is found. Next the T-record's *time* field is checked, and (similar to TL2) if it greater then the process's local *rv* value the transaction must abort (line 32) in order to prevent consistency violations. If this succeeds without aborting then the local variable *value* is set depending on the stats of the transaction that created the T-record (line 29-30).

In case *tmp* is an NT-record (line 21), the operation checks whether the value of the *time* field is greater or equal to the process local *rv* value. If it is, then this write has possibly occurred after the start of this transaction and there are several possibilities. In the case of an update transaction validation must be preformed, ensuring that none of the values it has read have been updated (line 23). In the case of a read only transaction, the transaction is aborted and restarted as an update transaction (line 24). It is restarted as an update transaction so that it has a read set that it can validate in case this situation occurs again. Finally local variable *value* is set to be the value of the *value* field of the *tmp* (line 26).

It should be noted that the reason why the checks are performed differently for NT-records and T-records is because the NT-write operations do not update the global clock value while update transaction do. This means that the checks must be more conservative in order to ensure correctness. If performing per value validation or restarting the transaction as an update transaction is found to be too expensive, a third possibility would be to just increment the global clock, then restart the transaction as normal.

Finally to finish the read operation, the $\langle addr, value \rangle$ is added to the read set if the transaction is an update transaction (line 34), and the value of the local variable *value* is returned.

Transactional Write. The transactional_write() operation takes *addr* as input value, as well as the value to be written to *var*. As TL2, the algorithm performs commit-time updates of the variables it writes to. For this reason, the transactional write operation simply creates a T-record and fills in some of its fields (lines 37 - 38) and adds it to the write set. However, in the case that a T-record corresponding to *addr* was already present in the write set, the *value* field of the corresponding T-record is simply updated (line 39).

Begin and End of a Transaction The operations that begin and end a transaction are begin_transaction() and try_to_commit(), presented in Fig. 5. Local variables necessary for transaction execution are initialized by begin_transaction(). This includes *rv* which is set to *GCV* and, like in TL2, is used during transactional reads to ensure correctness, as well as *status* which is set to LIVE and the read and write sets which are initialized as empty sets. (lines 41-43).

After performing all required read and write operations, a transaction tries to commit, using the operation try_to_commit(). Similar to TL2, a try_to_commit() operation starts by trivially committing if the transaction was a read-only one

```
operation transactional_read(addr) is
(19)    if addr ∈ ws then return (item.value from addr in ws) end if;
(20)    tmp ← (↓ addr);
(21)    if (tmp is of type NT)
(22)    then if (tmp.time >= rv)
(23)        then if this is an update transaction then validate_by_value()
(24)            else abort() and restart as an update transaction end if;
(25)        end if;
(26)        value ← tmp.value;
(27)    else if (tmp is of type T)
(28)        if ((status ← (↓ tmp.status)) ≠ COMMITTED )
(29)        then if (status = LIVE) then abort() else value ← tmp.last end if;
(30)            else value ← tmp.value
(31)        end if;
(32)        if (tmp.time > rv) then abort() end if;
(33)    end if;
(34)    if this is an update transaction then add ⟨addr, value⟩ to rs end if;
(35)    return (value)
end operation.

operation transactional_write(addr, value) is
(36)    if addr ∉ ws
(37)    then allocate a new variable item of type T;
(38)        item ← (value, (↑ status), ∞); ws ← ws ∪ ⟨addr, item⟩;
(39)    else set item.value with addr in ws to value
(40)    end if;
end operation.
```

Fig. 4. Transactional operations for reading and writing a variable

(line 44) while an update transaction must announce to concurrent operations what locations it will be updating (the items in the write set). However, the algorithm differs here from TL2, given that it is faced with concurrent non-transactional operations that do not rely on locks and never block. This implies that even after acquiring the locks for all items in its write set, a transaction could be "outrun" by a non-transactional operation that writes to one of those items causing the transaction to be required to abort in order to ensure correctness. As described previously, while TL2 locks items in its write set using a lock array, this algorithm compare and swaps pointers directly to the T-records in its write set (lines 45-53) while keeping a reference to the previous value. The previous value is stored in the T-record before the compare and swap is performed (lines 48-49) with a failed compare and swap resulting in the abort of the transaction. If while performing these compare and swaps the transaction notices that another LIVE transaction is updating this memory, it aborts itself (line 48). By using these T-records instead of locks concurrent operations have access to necessary metadata used to ensure correctness.

The operation then advances the GVC, taking the new value of the clock as the logical time for this transaction (line 54). Following this, the read set of the transaction is validated for correctness (line 54). Once validation has been performed the operation must ensure that non of its writes have been concurrently overwritten by non-transactional operations (lines 55-58) if so then the transaction must abort in order to (line 57) to ensure consistency. During this check the transaction updates the *time* value of its T-records to the transactions

```
operation begin_transaction() is
(41)    determine whether transaction is update transaction based on compiler/user input
(42)    rv ← GVC; Allocate new variable status;
(43)    status ←LIVE;  ws ← ∅; rs ← ∅
end operation.

operation try_to_commit() is
(44)    if (ws = ∅) then return (COMMITTED) end if;
(45)    for each (⟨addr, item⟩ ∈ ws) do
(46)       tmp ← (↓ addr);
(47)       if (tmp is of type T ∧ (status ← (↓ tmp.status)) ≠ COMMITTED )
(48)          then if (status = LIVE) then abort() else item.last ← tmp.last end if;
(49)          else item.last ← tmp.value
(50)       end if;
(51)       item.time ← tmp.time;
(52)       if (¬C&S(addr, tmp, item)) then abort() end if;
(53)    end for;
(54)    time ← increment&fetch(GVC); validate_by_value();
(55)    for each (⟨addr, item⟩ ∈ ws) do
(56)       item.time ← time;
(57)       if (item ≠ (↓ addr)) then abort() end if;
(58)    end for;
(59)    if C&S(status, LIVE, COMMITTED)
(60)       then return (COMMITTED)
(61)       else abort()
(62)    end if;
end operation.
```

Fig. 5. Transaction begin/commit

logical time (line 56) similar to the way TL2 stores time values in the lock array so that future operations will know the serialization of this transaction's updates.

Finally the transaction can mark its updates as valid by changing its *status* variable from LIVE to COMMITTED (line 59). This is done using a compare and swap as there could be a concurrent non-transactional operations trying to abort the transaction. If this succeeds then the transaction has successfully committed, otherwise it must abort and restart.

Transactional Helping Operations. Apart from the basic operations for starting, committing, reading and writing, a transaction makes use of helper operations to perform aborts and validate the read set. Pseudo-code for this kind of helper operations is given in Fig. 6.

Operation validate_by_value() is an operation that performs validation of the read set of a transaction. Validation fails if any location in *rs* is currently being updated by another transaction (line 67) or has had its changed since it was first read by the transaction (line 71) otherwise it succeeds. The transaction is immediately aborted if validation fails (lines 67, 71). Before the validation is performed the local variable *rv* is updated to be the current value of *GVC* (line 63). This is done because if validation succeeds then transaction is valid at this time with a larger clock value possibly preventing future validations and aborts.

When a transaction is aborted in the present algorithm, the status of the current transaction is set to ABORTED (line 73) and it is immediately restarted as a new transaction.

```
operation validate_by_value() is
(63)     rv ← GVC;
(64)     for each ⟨addr, value⟩ in rs do
(65)         tmp ← (↓ addr);
(66)         if (tmp is of type T ∧ tmp.status ≠ COMMITTED)
(67)             then if (tmp.status = LIVE ∧ ⟨addr, tmp⟩ ∉ ws) then abort() end if;
(68)                 new_value ← tmp.last;
(69)             else new_value ← tmp.value
(70)         end if;
(71)         if new_value ≠ value then abort() end if;
(72)     end for;
end operation.

operation abort() is
(73)     status ← ABORTED;
(74)     the transaction is aborted and restarted
```

Fig. 6. Transactional helper operations

5   Conclusion

This paper has presented an algorithm that achieves non-blocking strong isolation "on top of" a TM algorithm based on logical dates and locks, namely TL2. In the case of a conflict between a transactional and a non-transactional operation, this algorithm gives priority to the non-transactional operation, with the reasoning that while an eventual abort or restart is part of the specification of a transaction, this is not the case for a single shared read or write operation. Due to this priority mechanism, the proposed algorithm is particularly appropriate for environments in which processes do not rely heavily on the use of especially large transactions along with non-transactional write operations. In such environments, terminating strong isolation is provided for transactions, while conventional read and write operations execute with a small additional overhead.

Acknowledgements. The research leading to these results has received funding from the European Union Seventh Framework Programme (FP7/2007-2013) under grant agreement nr. 238639, ITN project TRANSFORM.

References

1. Afek, Y., Avni, H., Dice, D., Shavit, N.: Efficient Lock Free Privatization. In: Lu, C., Masuzawa, T., Mosbah, M. (eds.) OPODIS 2010. LNCS, vol. 6490, pp. 333–347. Springer, Heidelberg (2010)
2. Crain, T., Imbs, D., Raynal, M.: Towards a Universal Construction for Transaction-Based Multiprocess Programs. In: Bononi, L., Datta, A.K., Devismes, S., Misra, A. (eds.) ICDCN 2012. LNCS, vol. 7129, pp. 61–75. Springer, Heidelberg (2012)
3. Crain, T., Kanellou, E., Raynal, M.: Enforcing Strong Isolation. Irisa Technical Report (2012)

4. Dalessandro, L., Scott, M.: Strong Isolation is a Weak Idea. In: Proc. Workshop on Transactional Memory, TRANSACT 2009 (2009)

5. Dice, D., Matveev, A., Shavit, N.: Implicit privatization using private transactions. In: Proc. Workshop on Transactional Memory, TRANSACT 2010 (2010)

6. Dice, D., Shalev, O., Shavit, N.N.: Transactional Locking II. In: Dolev, S. (ed.) DISC 2006. LNCS, vol. 4167, pp. 194–208. Springer, Heidelberg (2006)

7. Guerraoui, R., Kapalka, M.: On the correctness of transactional memory. In: Proc. 13th ACM SIGPLAN Symposium on Principles and Practice of Parallel Programming (PPoPP 2008), pp. 175–184. ACM Press (2008)

8. Harris, T., Larus, J., Rajwar, R.: Transactional Memory, 2nd edn. Synthesis Lectures on Computer Architecture. Morgan & Claypool Publishers (2006)

9. Herlihy, M., Moss, J.M.B.: Transactional memory: architectural support for lock-free data structures. In: Proc. of the 20th annual Int'l Symposium on Computer Architecture (ISCA 1993), pp. 289–300. ACM Press (1993)

10. Imbs, D., Raynal, M.: A versatile STM protocol with invisible read operations that satisfies the virtual world consistency condition. Theoretical Computer Science 444, 113–127 (2012)

11. Maessen, J.-W., Arvind, M.: Store Atomicity for Transactional Memory. Electronic Notes on Theoretical Computer Science 174(9), 117–137 (2007)

12. Martin, M., Blundell, C., Lewis, E.: Subtleties of Transactional Memory Atomicity Semantics. IEEE Computer Architecture Letters 5(2) (2006)

13. Matveev, A., Shavit, N.: Towards a Fully Pessimistic STM Model. In: Proc. Workshop on Transactional Memory, TRANSACT 2012 (2012)

14. Minh, C., Trautmann, M., Chung, J., McDonald, A., Bronson, N., Casper, J., Kozyrakis, C., Olukotun, K.: An effective hybrid transactional memory system with strong isolation guarantees. SIGARCH Comput. Archit. News 35(2), 69–80 (2007)

15. Papadimitriou, C.H.: The Serializability of Concurrent Updates. Journal of the ACM 26(4), 631–653 (1979)

16. Schneider, F., Menon, V., Shpeisman, T., Adl-Tabatabai, A.: Dynamic optimization for efficient strong atomicity. ACM SIGPLAN Noticers 43(10), 181–194 (2008)

17. Scott, M.L., Spear, M.F., Dalessandro, L., Marathe, V.J.: Delaunay Triangulation with Transactions and Barriers. In: Proc. 10th IEEE Int'l Symposium on Workload Characterization (IISWC 2007), pp. 107–113. IEEE Computer Society (2007)

18. Shavit, N., Touitou, D.: Software transactional memory. Distributed Computing 10(2), 99–116 (1997)

19. Shpeisman, T., Menon, V., Adl-Tabatabai, A.R., Balensiefer, S., Grossman, D., Hudson, R.L., Moore, K.F., Saha, B.: Enforcing isolation and ordering in STM. ACM SIGPLAN Noticers 42(6), 78–88 (2007)

20. Spear, M.F., Dalessandro, L., Marathe, V.J., Scott, M.L.: Ordering-Based Semantics for Software Transactional Memory. In: Baker, T.P., Bui, A., Tixeuil, S. (eds.) OPODIS 2008. LNCS, vol. 5401, pp. 275–294. Springer, Heidelberg (2008)

21. Spear, M.F., Marathe, V.J., Dalessandro, L., Scott, M.L.: Privatization techniques for software transactional memory. In: Proc. 26th Annual ACM Symposium on Principles of Distributed Computing (PODC 2007), pp. 338–339. ACM Press (2007)

A Dependency Aware Task Partitioning and Scheduling Algorithm for Hardware-Software Codesign on MPSoCs

Chunsheng Li [1,2], Xi Li [1], Chao Wang [1], Xuehai Zhou [1], and Fangling Zeng [2]

[1] School of Computer Science, University of Science and Technology of China
{cslee,sanitwc}@mail.ustc.edu.cn,{llxx,xhzhou}@ustc.edu.cn
[2] Key Laboratory of Electric Restriction, Electronic Engineering Institute
zella@ustc.edu.cn

Abstract. Hardware-Software partitioning and scheduling are the crucial steps in HW-SW codesign of MPSoC since they have a strong effect on the performance, area, power and the system. Considered as NP-complete problem, the involvement of inter-task data dependencies have posed a serious challenge on the MPSoC based embedded application domain. In this paper, we propose an efficient algorithm for dependent task HW-SW codesign with Greedy Partitioning and Insert Scheduling Method (GPISM) by task graph. For hardware tasks, the critical path with maximum sum of benefit-to-area ratio can be achieved and implemented in hardware while the total area occupation in this path fitting global hardware constraint; after that, the task graph is updated by removing tasks in the critical path iteratively until the available hardware area doesn't fit. For software tasks, the longest communication time path can be obtained from the updated task graph and assigned to software implementation integrally, then second path will be located if it does exist. For task scheduling, rest scatter nodes are inserted into hardware/software implementation list by scheduling criterion. Simulation results demonstrate that GPISM algorithm has a polynomial time complexity without affordable computation; meanwhile it can greatly improve system performance even in the case of generation large communication cost, and efficiently facilitate the researchers to partition and schedule embedded applications on MPSoC hardware architectures.

Keywords: Hardware-Software Partitioning, Dependent Task Scheduling, Task Graph, DAG, MPSoC.

1 Introduction

The tremendous invasion of Multi-Processor Systems-on-Chip (MPSoC) has brought numerous computation abilities to heterogeneous platforms in the past decades. However, it still poses significant challenges to partition and schedule tasks to different function units, especially for tasks with data dependencies. Task partitioning and scheduling problems are intractable in many applications by its NP-complete characters [1, 2], especially in Hardware-Software (HW-SW) Codesign. It is well known that efficient partitioning and scheduling algorithms have a central impact on

Y. Xiang et al. (Eds.): ICA3PP 2012, Part I, LNCS 7439, pp. 332–346, 2012.

global performance improvement, for instance, energy, power, area, acceleration, etc. MPSoC, which has emerged for decades, now is dominating and will eventually become the pervasive computing model. It has both hardware and software cores and needs high performance task partitioning and scheduling algorithms.

The object of partitioning is to decide whether the task should be implemented in hardware or software. Generally, software implementation is flexible and sequentially in execution; in contrast, hardware implementation is fixable and parallel. Hence, performance- or power- critical tasks of the system should be realized in hardware, while noncritical components can be done in software alternatively, in this way, an optimal tradeoff among cost, power, and performance can be achieved [3]. The aim of scheduling is to minimize the overall execution time of the parallel applications by properly allocating and rearranging the execution order of the tasks on the cores without violating the precedence constraints among the tasks [4, 5].

In order to attack the above problems, this paper proposes a task partitioning and scheduling method which can access an efficient utilization with polynomial time. We claim following contributions:

(1)   Combine partitioning and scheduling together with both of their advantages. Take into account the critical paths and the scattered tasks with greedy strategy, then just simple insert operations in the basic orderly queue.

(2)   A $O(V+E)$ polynomial time complexity with facile computations, most of them can be operated at initialization, and need a little space complexity.

(3)   Computation cost, area constraint and communication ratio are all considered simultaneously, while the algorithm has a good scalability for large-scale problems and other MPSoC platforms.

The rest of this paper is organized as follows: Related work can be seen in section 2. Section 3 gives some statements, utilizing system model. In section 4, we discuss partitioning and scheduling algorithms. Illustrative examples will be presented in section 5. Section 6 shows the simulation experiment results and analysis. Finally section 7 draws the work conclusion and future work.

2   Related Work

There have been many state-of-the-art research works reported in this field, focusing on different aspects in the HW-SW partitioning and task scheduling. Traditional HW-SW partitioning approaches include software-oriented [6] and hardware-oriented [7]. The distinction between the two methods depends on which (SW/HW) is initialization first and iteratively moving to the other (HW/SW) with the performance constraints. Many approaches pay attention to the algorithm aspects, i.e., accurate algorithms, including Dynamic Programming [8], Integer Linear Programming [9], Branch and Bound [10], which suit small-scale problems; another heuristic algorithms like Genetic Algorithms [11], Simulated Annealing [12], Tabu Search [13], Greedy Strategy [14], are more proper for large-scale questions. Most of these algorithms are based on static strategy; there are also some dynamic methods [15, 16].

Partitioning has a close relationship with scheduling and they are problem-architecture- dependent [17]. In particular, many researchers consider scheduling as a part of partitioning [14, 18], whereas others don't [19]. Recently, a trend in HW-SW codesign on MPSoC Combines partitioning with scheduling together. Scheduling First Partitioning Later (SFPL) is one method[4, 5, 20], paper [4] uses A-star algorithm for scheduling dependent tasks onto homogeneous processors, then chooses the longest schedule length converting to hardware implement, the time complexity is $O(p(V^3-V^2)/2)$; the channel conflict is handled by graph coloring technique in paper [5]. The time complexity of this algorithm is large and no area constraint is considered in [4, 5]. Here A-star algorithm is an extension of Dijkstra's algorithm, which achieves better performance by using heuristics with cost functions. Paper [20] improves the A-star algorithm time complexity to $O(pV^2)$ in scheduling and introduces benefit-to-area ratio as the priority in partitioning, cost functions in A-star algorithm still need to be calculated many times. Another method is Partitioning First Scheduling Later (PFSL) [17, 21], in which three heuristic search partitioning methods are compared with each other [21], the result shows Tabu Search is the best one of the three. Paper [17] introduces the new benefit function for partitioning, then uses critical-path and communication combined scheduler (CPCS) algorithm for scheduling. Both of the papers choose hardware-implementation tasks like Breadth First Search (BFS), the hardware nodes are always scattered, not in a full deeply path; meanwhile both the hardware/Software implementation is just in one core. It isn't a good way for dependent tasks especially when there are large frequent communication times.

The advantages of SFPL and PFSL are combined in this paper: deeply critical or longest paths are calculated by SFPL, while scattered hardware/software nodes are found by PFSL and inserted with greedy scheduling. We name this approach Greedy Partitioning and Insert Scheduling Method (GPISM) detailed in section 4 and 5.

3   Target System and Graph Model

3.1   MPSoC Architecture

Today, there are variety of MPSoC architecture and platform for different purposes. The target system architecture in this paper is illustrated in figure 1 based on Xilinx FPGAs. There is a main-control CPU in charge of task partitioning and scheduling, it deals with the generated tasks graph into software or hardware cores. Software cores and hardware logic unit communicate via bus connection, while each core (software or hardware) has its own local memory (LM) for inter-task communication destined in the same core. In order to provide data communications between processors, one shared memory block is implemented.

Xilinx FPGAs are the most widely used programmable silicon foundation for Targeted Design Platforms, which deliver integrated software and hardware components. For the ease of the IP based modular and scalable architecture design, Xilinx FPGA supplies PowerPC、MicroBlaze/PicoBalze cores and advanced DSP slices in one chip, and distribute RAM and block RAM are used for memory storage. The utilization of hardware resources, like Configurable Logic Blocks (CLBs) for FPGA in particular, plays a vital role during the evaluation and metrics of programmable devices. In this paper, we select Xilinx FPGA as the foundation of abstract architecture platform and measure the equipped CLBs for area constraint evaluations.

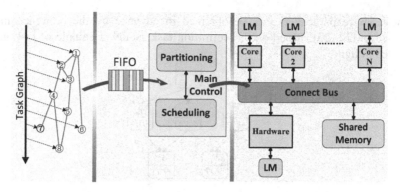

Fig. 1. MPSoC Architecture Constructed in Xilinx FPGA

Throughout this paper, we define the term "task" as a coarse grained set of computation or function unit, and pick up a static strategy for partitioning and scheduling. Tasks are modeled as nodes in the graph and can be paralyzed either in hardware implementation or sequentially in software implementation. We put the limitations into assumption preliminaries as follows:

1) Each selected task in the task graph can be virtualized only to one specific core, the selection of homogeneous/heterogeneous core according to the task performance.
2) Tasks can be implemented either by software or hardware. Software can handle a single task at a time by sequentially executed; while the number of tasks paralyzed execution in hardware according to the area constraint of the system.
3) Once the task starts execution, it cannot be interrupted.
4) Connect bus has enough bandwidth for handling the conflicts.
5) Communication time is the total time including read, write and so on.
6) Communications between tasks in one core are cost free.

3.2 Task Graph Model

The task graph model is generated by the Data Flow Graph (DFG), and usually expressed as the Directed Acyclic Graph (DAG). In this paper we give the six-group expression as follow:

$$G = (V \,|\, (Sw, Hw, A), \ E \,|\, C)$$

V : The set of nodes in DAG, which represent dependent tasks;

Sw : The execution time of tasks (node V) by software;

Hw : The execution time of tasks (node V) by hardware;

A : The area consumption of tasks implemented by hardware;

E : The set of edges in DAG, which refers to inter-task data communication between tasks;

C : The communication time between two tasks.

These above parameters can be obtained in advance by the reference methods described in [22, 23]. Based on the definition task model, a sample of task graph is presented in figure 2.

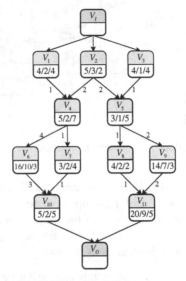

Fig. 2. Task Graph Example

The demonstrative task graph example in figure 2 is originated from input task V_I and end up with the final output task V_O. Between the input and output tasks, 11 tasks are generated, and each of them is illustrated in the square box. The top part of the task refers to the ID assigned during initialization, while the bottom part indicates the tuples including Sw, Hw and A. The digit on each edge represents the communication overheads between the two tasks connected by the edge.

In particular, we define following terms:

Definition 1: V refers to the tasks set $\{V_1, V_2, ..., V_n\}$. Considering all the nodes in DAG, if there exists a path between two nodes which is presented as $V_i \xrightarrow{C(V_i,V_j)} V_j$ in DAG, V_i is the predecessor of V_j; meanwhile V_j is the successor of V_i.

$$\begin{cases} P\_Set(V) = \{V' | (V',V) \in E\} \\ S\_Set(V) = \{V' | (V,V') \in E\} \end{cases} \quad (1)$$

The value of C_r (V_i, V_j) denotes the "real" communication time between two dependent tasks.

$$C_r(V_i,V_j) = \begin{cases} 0 & if \;\; V_i,V_j \;\; on \;\; same \;\; core \\ C(V_i,V_j) & if \;\; V_i,V_j \;\; on \;\; different \;\; cores \end{cases} \quad (2)$$

Definition 2: A task V_i can be executed iff all the tasks in $P\_Set(V_i)$ are finished and the data communication is ready, so the finish time of task V_i is:

$$T_f(V_i) = \begin{cases} \max\{T_f(P\_Set(V_i)) + C_r(P\_Set(V_i), V_i)\} + Sw(V_i) & \text{if } V_i \text{ is a softeware task} \\ \max\{T_f(P\_Set(V_i)) + C_r(P\_Set(V_i), V_i)\} + Hw(V_i) & \text{if } V_i \text{ is a hardware task} \end{cases} \quad (3)$$

Definition 3:   The virtual Input Task V_I and Output Task V_O are added into the set of tasks for the convenience of DAG algorithms.

$$V_I : \begin{cases} P\_Set(V_I) = \varnothing \\ C(V_I, S\_Set(V_I)) = 0 \\ T_f(V_I) = 0 \end{cases} \quad (4)$$

$$V_O : \begin{cases} S\_Set(V_O) = \varnothing \\ C(P\_Set(V_O), V_O) = 0 \end{cases}$$

According to the definitions above, $T_f(V_O)$ indicates the time when all the tasks (nodes in DAG) are finished. Hence the design object of task partitioning and scheduling is to find a minimum of $T_f(V_O)$.

4   Algorithm

4.1   Greedy Partitioning

1. Benefit Function

For each task (node in DAG), following characters are taken into consideration: hardware execution time, software execution time and area constraints. All these factors are limited by the utility of Graph Theory. In order to leverage the influences of the parameters, we combine these factors into benefit-to-area function as [20].

Definition 4: For each task V in DAG, the benefit-to-area function is defined as bellow.

$$B(V) = \frac{Sw(V) - Hw(V)}{A(V)} \quad (5)$$

$B(V)$ denotes the time saved on the unit area. We use subtraction instead of division (acceleration) because the time subtraction on the unit area not only reflects saved time, but also reflects the area constraint. The benefit value can be calculated at beginning and the time complexity is $O(V)$.

2. Critical Hardware Path

To identify the critical hardware path, our object is to find an orderly path from V_I to V_O, in which the sum of tasks' benefits is max, and the area occupation of these tasks fitting global hardware constraint, critical hardware path is defined as follow:

Definition 5: The Critical Hardware Path is an orderly path in the DAG, in which the sum of tasks' benefit-to-area values achieves the peak, while the total area occupation of tasks in this candidate path doesn't exceed the global area limitations. An orderly list is presented in (6):

$$Hw_{order}:\left\{V_I \to V_i \to V_j \to \cdots \to V_O \left| \max \sum B(V_i) \quad and \quad \sum A(V_i) \leq A_{all} \right.\right\} (6)$$

DAG is updated by removing nodes and edges between them except V_I and V_O, and then new critical path will be searched if it exists in the updated DAG, which means this operation can be done repeatedly by searching and updating. Otherwise, some scatter nodes can be found just according to area occupation and ordered by benefit value, which is called "hard-like" nodes:

$$Hw_{like}:\left\{ \begin{array}{l} V_j \left| A(V_j) \leq A_{all} - \sum A_{path} \right. \\ V_i, V_j \quad if \quad A(V_i) < A(V_j) \quad or \quad B(V_i) > B(V_j) \,|\, A(V_i) = A(V_j) \end{array} \right\} (7)$$

These "hard-like" nodes aren't removed in the updated DAG.

3. Longest Software Path

We use communication time (edge value) to find the longest software path in the updated DAG from previous part 2. Similar to the hardware paths, a software path is an orderly line too.

Definition 6: The Longest Software Path is an orderly path in the DAG; the sum of communication time between nodes in this path is the biggest among other paths:

$$Sw_{order}:\left\{V_I \to V_m \to V_n \to \cdots \to V_O \left| \max \sum C(V_i) \right.\right\} \qquad (8)$$

If this path has some "hard-like" nodes like "$V_m \to V_{hwlike} \to V_n$", a comparison is operated to choose the path or node options.

$$\left\{ \begin{array}{l} C(V_m,V_{hwlike})+Hw(V_{hwlike})+C(V_{hwlike},V_n) > Sw(V_{hwlike}), \quad keep \quad path \quad and \quad remove \quad node \qquad (9)\\ C(V_m,V_{hwlike})+Hw(V_{hwlike})+C(V_{hwlike},V_n) \leq Sw(V_{hwlike}), \quad remove \quad path \quad and \quad keep \quad node \end{array} \right.$$

We may get multiple longest software paths by updating DAG, the "hard-like" nodes in Hw_{like} are renewed by formula (9) operations. Furthermore, when there is no complete paths from V_I to V_O in the updated DAG, add the rest nodes in the set:

$$Sw_{rest}:\left\{V_n \left| V_n \in V - Hw_{order} - Hw_{like} - Sw_{order} \right.\right\} \qquad (10)$$

The key step of this algorithm is to find the longest path in DAG. The method is similar to the critical path exploration in Activity On Edge network (AOE), therefore the time complexity of the path exploration is $O(V+E)$. Due to the largest comparing time of $O(V)$, the total time complexity of orderly partitioning is $O(V+E)$ $+O(V+E)+O(V)=O(V+E)$.

4.2   Insert Scheduling

Four sets of tasks (section 4.1) are further divided into two categories: paths set (may be more than one path) and nodes set. According to definition 2, the task's order in these paths cannot be modified afterwards. Single node can be inserted into these orderly paths at a proper position to shorten the total execution time as much. To be specific, following criterions are taken into account:

1) Hardware tasks can be executed in parallel.
2) Every node can enter execution stage once all of its parent nodes are finished.

3) Software tasks can be put in multiple cores indicated by longest edge path.

4) Scatter software tasks can be put in an independent core if there are enough available cores and no tasks are being executed simultaneously

5) The node which has more successors' hardware tasks will be appointed to a higher priority of execution, comparing with the same level nodes before insertion.

6) When similar tasks at the same level, the one with the shortest execution time should be executed first.

The purpose of Insert Scheduling is to find an optimal execution time and maintain the overall system utilization, the scatter tasks can be inserted into an orderly path (already existed core) or just kept into a new independent core, the numbers of needed cores are added according to platform constraints and insert criterions above. The upper bound of cores is in line with conclusion of [4] that scheduling length of optimal task assignment to $P+1$ processors is always no bigger than the one to P processors. The time complexity of insert scheduling is $O(V)$, because only some scatter nodes need to be compared, and the maximum of compared nodes is V.

4.3   Algorithm Flow Chart

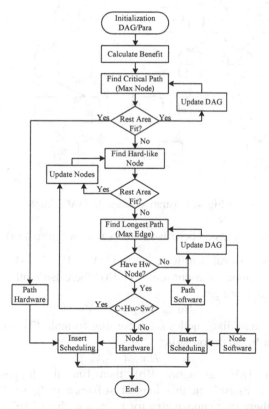

Fig. 3. Algorithm Flow Chart

The algorithm flow chart is described in figure 3. First, the benefit value of each task is calculated as the reference for task partitioning, the critical path, which have maximum sum of tasks' benefit values and total area occupation fitting the requirements will be chosen. Meanwhile the global area constraint is updated by subtracting this critical path area occupation and the DAG is also updated by removing nodes and edges between them in this critical path. Then greedy strategy is used for rest paths until all the "hard-like" nodes are found. Second, the longest path and rest nodes will be found by the same way, meanwhile "hard-like" nodes will be renewed according to comparing with computation and communication time. Finally the orderly tasks in the critical or longest path will be assigned to alternative hardware or software core, scatter nodes are inserted according to insert scheduling criterions.

5   Illustrative Example

In order to demonstrate the effectiveness of our proposed algorithm, we run a test case in figure 4, similar to paper [17]. For better describing the algorithm, the nodes V_I and V_O are omitted for simplicity.

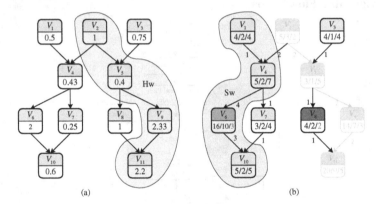

Fig. 4. Illustrative Example-DAG Graph

Step 1: Calculate every task's benefit-to-area value as figure 4 (a).

Step 2: Find the critical hardware path is $V_2 \to V_5 \to V_9 \to V_{11}$, the sum of area occupation is 15 (global area constraint is 18), there isn't other critical path in the updated DAG, and so we get:

$$Hw_{order}\{ V_2 \to V_5 \to V_9 \to V_{11} \}$$

Step 3: Find the "hard-like" nodes set according formula (7), the area occupation of V_8 is smaller than V_6, so the order is:

$$Hw_{like}\{ V_8, V_6 \}$$

Step 4: Updated DAG as figure 4(b), then find the longest software path is $V_1 \to V_4 \to V_6 \to V_{10}$, V_8 isn't in this longest software path, so V_8 can be made by hardware. Then there isn't enough area for V_6, renew "hard-like" nodes set as follow:

$$Hw_{like}\{ V_8 \}$$

If the area occupation of V_8 is assumed to be 3, we can get "hard-like" nodes set $Hw_{like}\{\ V_6,V_8\ \}$ by formula (7). There is a node V_6 in the set of Hw_{like}, according to formula (9), 4+10+3>16, so keep this longest path and V_6 should be removed from "hard-like" nodes set.

There isn't other longest path in the updated DAG (by removing found longest software path $V_1{\rightarrow}V_4{\rightarrow}V_6{\rightarrow}V_{10}$), we can get:

$$Sw_{order}\{\ V_1{\rightarrow}V_4{\rightarrow}V_6{\rightarrow}V_{10}\}$$

Step 5: Find the rest nodes set:

$$Sw_{rest}\{\ V_3,V_7\}$$

The above steps are Greedy Partitioning as shown in figure 4. Shaded area in figure 4 (a) is the critical hardware path; while the longest software path is shown in figure 4 (b). The node V_6 (red in b) is the "hard-like" node in the temp calculation process and finally is deleted from the set of "hard-like" nodes. The node V_8 (blue in b) is the end result of "hard-like" node.

The rest steps are Insert Scheduling, and the results can be represented by Gantt chart.

Step 6: Insert V_8 into the hardware implementation set, which can be executed in parallel with V_9 as soon as V_5 is finished. Tasks in the longest path (Sw_{order}) are assigned into one software core, while the rest software nodes assigned into another core, like Gantt chart in figure 5.

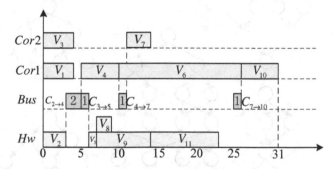

Fig. 5. Illustrative Example-Gantt Chart (2 cores)

Step 7: If there is only one software core, all the tasks that implemented by software should be inserted into this core. According to criterion (5), the successor of V_3 is hardware, so V_3 is first to execute than V_1, which successor is software; V_7 should be executed before V_6 according to criterion (6). The procedure is presented in figure 6.

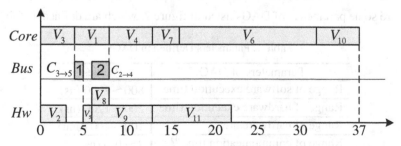

Fig. 6. Illustrative Example-Gantt Chart (1 core)

The whole execution time is *31* in figure 5 (two software cores) and *37* in figure 6 (one software core). Taking the CPCS strategy [17] into consideration, the hardware-implementation tasks are V_2, V_6, V_8, V_9 and V_{11}, in this case the whole execution time is *42* and it needs more calculations as well as longer communication time.

6   Experimental Results and Analysis

There is a broad range of applications with different scheduling and partitioning algorithms. The assumptions, preconditions and benchmarks are varying from each other. So it is hard to tell which application-oriented algorithm has a better performance than others. The evaluation of the algorithm performance in this paper depends on the platform configuration and application utilization presented in [17, 21].

DAGs used in this paper are randomly generated task graphs with a uniform distribution and commonly encountered structure: in-tree, out-tree, fork-joint, mean value analysis and FFT (figure 7). These five kinds of DAGs are randomly generated by Task Graphs For Free (TGFF) [24], which provides a flexible and standard way of generating pseudo-random task-graphs during the scheduling and allocation research.

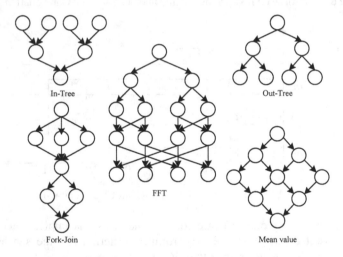

Fig. 7. Five kinds of task graphs (DAGs)

There are some parameters of DAGs listed in figure 2, which are defined as follow:

Table 1. Parameters Defined in DAGs

Parameters of DAG	Values
Range of software execution time	800~2000 (ns)
Range of hardware execution time	200~1200 (ns)
Range of hardware area	100~400 (unit)
Range of communication time[1]	2~100 (ns)
Range of communication time[2]	20~800(ns)

The last two rows in the table are the different communication time cases: case (1) is similar to the presentation in paper [16] and [20], while (2) improves the communication cost in the total execution time. In contrast to the "hopts" and "hardware task in percentage" definitions in the article [16], we define "Acceleration Ratio (AR)" and "Area Percentage (AP)" as follow:

Definition 7: Assume there are n tasks in the DAG, denoted as V_i $(i=1:n)$, and every task occupies $A(V_i)$ unit area. The global area constraint takes p percentage of all tasks' area occupation, which is defined as AP (Area Percentage):

$$AP = \left[p \times \sum_{i=1}^{n} A(V_i) \right] \quad (p = \frac{1}{5}, \frac{2}{5}, \frac{1}{3}, \frac{1}{2}, \frac{3}{5}, \frac{2}{3}, \frac{4}{5})$$ (11)

Definition 8: If only one software core is available in the platform, we assume that all the tasks are implemented by software, and then the communication time is free. In this situation the longest execution time is defined as the sum of all software time, and the AR (Acceleration Ratio) for one software core is in (12):

$$AR_{one} = \frac{Assume \ \ longest \ \ time}{Algorithm \ \ time} = \frac{\sum_{i=1}^{n} Sw(V_i)}{Algorithm \ \ time}$$ (12)

Definition 9: If there are more than one software cores used in the platform, we assume DAG has l levels and the communication time isn't free. So the longest execution time is defined as the sum of maximum of software time and communication time level by level. The AR (Acceleration Ratio) for multi software cores is:

$$AR_{multi} = \frac{\sum_{i=1}^{l} Max\{Sw(V_i), \ \ C(V_i) \ \ in \ \ one \ \ level\}}{Algorithm \ \ time}$$ (13)

Still take figure 2 as illustrative example, where the AP is $18 = [2/5 \times all \ area]$. The AR is $83/37=2.2432$ for single software core situation, while $55/31=1.7741$ for a multi-core scenario.

In this paper, the output is described by AR not by scheduling length because results of scheduling length are dominantly affected by random parameters under different conditions, which cannot reflect the performance of the algorithm.

The input is random DAGs with dependent tasks by TGFF, the parameters such as software time, hardware time, area occupation and communication time are randomly generated according to table 1. We use average of 30×5 (5 kinds of DAGs in figure 7) experiments by computer simulation.

Figure 8 depicts the comparison between the GPISM with the state-of-the art CPCS. The chart is based on the communication time case (1). X-axis in the figure represents Area Percentage, while Y-axis refers to the change of Acceleration Ratio according to AP. The numerical result of figure 8 (a) is slight higher than (b), because figure 8 (a) is single software core that all the software tasks should be executed in

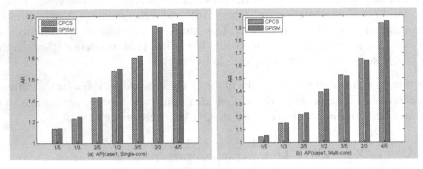

Fig. 8. AR with AP (case 1)

sequential, when the tasks are changed into hardware implementation, the results should be more obviously. These results have an upper bound to reach the theoretical speedup, which is the division between the time that all tasks are implemented by software and all hardware execution time. From this figure, we can see that the performance of these two algorithms is very close to each other, because the proportion of communication time is less than calculation time, but GPISM needs less computation workloads than CPCS method with similar performance.

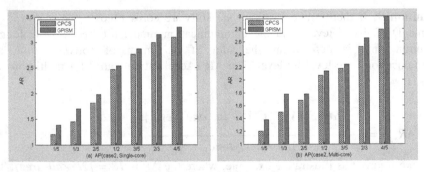

Fig. 9. AR with AP (case 2)

Furthermore, figure 9 presents the Acceleration Ratio changes with communication time case (2), and simulates run time comparison with two algorithms in the same configuration and environment. The overall performance increase ratio of GPISM than CPCS is about 15% in our average of 30×5 experiments with specific parameters. As the DAGs and their parameters are randomly generated, maybe this result changes according to different conditions, such as random communication cost by statistical information. We believe that when the communication cost scales, The AR with GPISM is larger than CPCS algorithm, because the latter searched for scattered tasks may lead to more communication time than the former one. Meanwhile, the performance of GPISM still maintained at a stable level with the expansion of the scale of the problem for its efficient utilization. GPISM makes leverage between algorithm complicity and system performance, and this algorithm can be extended to complex MPSoC environments.

7   Conclusion and Future Work

In this paper, we have proposed a highly efficient Greedy Partitioning and Insert Scheduling Method on Hardware-Software partition problem. The timing complexity of the proposed approach is a polynomial time $O(V+E)$. Meanwhile the algorithm can be applied to the situation with considerable communication cost and the performance keeps stable. Simulation results on sample applications demonstrate that the algorithm makes a tradeoff between computation complexity and optimal results. Although the platform architecture in this paper has only one hardware zone according to Xilinx FPGA limitations, we believe that the method can be extended to multiple hardware cores with changeable communication configurations.

In spite of the promising results, there are a lot of directions worth pursuing. On one hand, random DAGs with different parameters have a great impact on the performance of algorithms, rigorous experimental design and scientific evaluation are needed for further exploration and research; on the other hand, since the reconfigurable heterogeneous MPSoC has been regarded as one of the major trends in the future, our next step is to extend this method to reconfigurable FPGA, in order to take benefits of run time partial reconfiguration features and technical supports from FPGA research communities.

Acknowledgements. This paper is supported by the grant of Jiangsu provincial Natural Science Foundation "Study of Task Parallelization on Service-oriented Heterogeneous Reconfigurable Multiprocessor System-on-chip".

References

1. Garey, M.R., Johnson, D.S.: Computers and intractability: a guide to the theory of NP-completeness. W.H. Freeman (1979)
2. Graham, R.L.: Bounds on multiprocessing timing anomalies. SIAM Journal on Applied Mathematics 17, 416–429 (1969)
3. Wu, J., Srikanthan, T., Guang, C.: Algorithmic Aspects of Hardware/Software Partitioning: 1D Search Algorithms. IEEE Transactions on Computers 59(4), 532–544 (2010)
4. Youness, H., et al.: A high performance algorithm for scheduling and hardware-software partitioning on MPSoCs. In: 4th International Conference on Design & Technology of Integrated Systems in Nanoscal Era, DTIS 2009 (2009)
5. Youness, H., et al.: Efficient partitioning technique on multiple cores based on optimal scheduling and mapping algorithm. In: Proceedings of 2010 IEEE International Symposium on Circuits and Systems, ISCAS (2010)
6. Vahid, F., Gajski, D.D.: Clustering for improved system-level functional partitioning. In: Proceedings of the Eighth International Symposium on System Synthesis (1995)

7. Niemann, R., Marwedel, P.: Hardware/software partitioning using integer programming. In: Proceedings of European Design and Test Conference, ED&TC 1996 (1996)
8. Wu, J., Srikanthan, T.: Low-complex dynamic programming algorithm for hardware/software partitioning. Information Processing Letters 98(2), 41–46 (2006)
9. Shiann-Rong, K., Chin-Yang, C., Ren-Zheng, L.: Partitioning and Pipelined Scheduling of Embedded System Using Integer Linear Programming. In: Proceedings of 11th International Conference on Parallel and Distributed Systems (2005)
10. Chatha, K.S., Vemuri, R.: Hardware-software partitioning and pipelined scheduling of transformative applications. IEEE Transactions on Very Large Scale Integration (VLSI) Systems 10(3), 193–208 (2002)
11. Yi, Z., Zhenquan, Z., Huanhuan, C.: HW-SW partitioning based on genetic algorithm. In: Congress on Evolutionary Computation, CEC 2004 (2004)
12. Lanying, L., Yanbo, S., Ming, G.: A new genetic simulated annealing algorithm for hardware-software partitioning. In: 2010 2nd International Conference on Information Science and Engineering, ICISE (2010)
13. Lanying, L., Min, S.: Software-Hardware Partitioning Strategy Using Hybrid Genetic and Tabu Search. In: International Conference on Computer Science and Software Engineering (2008)
14. Chatha, K.S., Vemurl, R.: MAGELLAN: multiway hardware-software partitioning and scheduling for latency minimization of hierarchical control-dataflow task graphs. In: Proceedings of the Ninth International Symposium on Hardware/Software Codesign, CODES 2001 (2001)
15. Le-jun, F., et al.: An Approach for Dynamic Hardware /Software Partitioning Based on DPBIL. In: Third International Conference on Natural Computation, ICNC 2007 (2007)
16. Stitt, G., Lysecky, R., Vahid, F.: Dynamic hardware/software partitioning: a first approach. In: Proceedings of Design Automation Conference (2003)
17. Jigang, W., Srikanthan, T., Jiao, T.: Algorithmic aspects for functional partitioning and scheduling in hardware/software co-design. Design Automation for Embedded Systems 12(4), 345–375 (2008)
18. Lopez-Vallejo, M., Lopez, J.C.: On the hardware-software partitioning problem: System modeling and partitioning techniques. ACM Trans. Des. Autom. Electron. Syst. 8(3), 269–297 (2003)
19. Vahid, F.: Partitioning sequential programs for CAD using a three-step approach. ACM Trans. Des. Autom. Electron. Syst. 7(3), 413–429 (2002)
20. Hong-lei, H.A.N., et al.: An Efficient Algorithm of Hardware/Software Partitioning and Scheduling on MPSoC. Computer Engineering and Science 33(9) (2011)
21. Wiangtong, T., Cheung, P.Y.K., Luk, W.: Comparing Three Heuristic Search Methods for Functional Partitioning in Hardware-Software Codesign. Design Autom. for Emb. Sys. 6(4), 425–449 (2002)
22. Hong-xing, M.A., Xue-hai, Z., Yan-yan, G.A.O.: Algorithm for hardware/software task partitioning and scheduling on reconfigurable computing platform. Systems Engineering and Electronics 32(11) (2010)
23. Madsen, J., et al.: LYCOS: the Lyngby Co-Synthesis System. Design Automation for Embedded Systems 2(2), 195–235 (1997)
24. Dick, R.P., Rhodes, D.L., Wolf, W.: TGFF: task graphs for free. In: Proceedings of the Sixth International Workshop on Hardware/Software Codesign, CODES/CASHE 1998 (1998)

Power Efficiency Evaluation of Block Ciphers on GPU-Integrated Multicore Processor

Naoki Nishikawa, Keisuke Iwai, and Takakazu Kurokawa

Departmemt of Computer Science and Engineering
National Defense Academy of Japan
1-10-20 Hashirimizu, Yokosuka-shi, Kanagawa-ken, 239-8686, Japan
{ed11001,iwai,kuro}@nda.ac.jp

Abstract. Computer systems with discrete GPUs are expected to become the standard methodology for high-speed encryption processing, but they require large amounts of power consumption and are inapplicable to embedded devices. Therefore, we have specifically examined a new heterogeneous multicore processor with CPU–GPU integration architecture. We first implemented three 128-bit block ciphers (AES, Camellia, and SC2000) from several symmetric block ciphers in an e-government recommended ciphers list by CRYPTREC in Japan using OpenCL on AMD E-350 APU with CPU–GPU integration architecture and two traditional systems with discrete GPUs. Then we evaluated their respective power efficiencies. Result showed that performance per watt of AES-128 on the APU including 80 cores were 743.0 Mbps/W and 44.0 % increases compared with those on a system equipped with a discrete AMD Radeon HD 6770 including 800 cores. This paper is the first to describe a study to evaluate the per-watt performance of block ciphers on GPUs.

Keywords: Power efficiency, Block cipher, GPGPU, OpenCL, Heterogeneous multicore processor.

1 Introduction

This paper presents a discussion of a performance evaluation of symmetric block ciphers on GPUs, with emphasis on their power efficiencies.

Small and inexpensive portable devices such as smartphones and tablet PCs have become adopted explosively into widespread use, which has increased the necessity for high-speed cryptographic technology for use with such large amounts of data. Especially, the capacity of their data storage has become much greater. People often carry personal and business data in these devices. However, the battery capacity of the devices has not kept pace with their storage capacity. These facts indicate that the security countermeasures against these devices take on a decisive necessity of the compatibility between high-performance and low power consumption. However, in reality, the encryption processing is conducted on CPUs in those devices despite their low processing speed and bad power efficiency. To date, some researchers have suggested systems equipped with discrete

Y. Xiang et al. (Eds.): ICA3PP 2012, Part I, LNCS 7439, pp. 347–361, 2012.

GPUs for high-speed encryption processing with a good cost-performance ratio. Systems with discrete GPUs can gain a several-fold increase in throughput, but they are not competitive in terms of power efficiency. In short, this methodology is difficult to apply for portable electronic devices because of their high power consumption.

New heterogeneous multicore processors with CPU–GPU integration architecture are a recent arrival to the market. Their developer claims that this new processor maintains a balance between high performance and low power consumption. Therefore, this processor can become a standard of high-speed cryptographic processor for embedded devices. Moreover, this new processor presents the possibility of solving the performance deterioration because the bottleneck of the data transfer between the CPU and GPU memory spaces is assigned in the same memory module. Regarding the encryption processing on discrete GPUs, some previous reports have clarified that the data transfer rate holds a dominant position of the overall processing time. Currently, both memory spaces are separated using a partition of the new processor. In the near future, this partition is expected to be eliminated by the improvement of the memory controller.

As described in this paper, we implemented three 128-bit block ciphers (AES, Camellia, and SC2000) from several symmetric block ciphers in an e-government recommended ciphers list by CRYPTography Research and Evaluation Committees (CRYPTREC)[1] project in Japan using OpenCL on AMD Fusion E-350 APU with CPU–GPU integration architecture and two traditional systems with discrete GPUs. Then we evaluated these systems in terms of throughput per watt.

2   Current Status of Heterogeneous Multicore Processors

Some leading processor vendors have been shifting the development of processors with CPU and GPU integration architecture into the same silicon die. In March 2012, Intel Corp. released a processor with Ivy Bridge architecture containing both a CPU and a GPU together, which supports GPGPU based on OpenCL[2]. Nvidia Corp. released the Tegra 250 processor[3] containing both an ARM Cortex A9 CPU and an 8-core GPU together. The processor does not currently support GPGPU, but considering Nvidia's position as a leading GPGPU company development, it can be readily anticipated that next Tegra series will support GPGPU technology soon. Apple Computer Inc. also presented an A4 processor containing both an ARM Cortex A8 CPU and a PowerVR SGX 535 GPU[4]. This embedded GPU does not support GPGPU, but GPUs in Apple's next-generation processor are expected to support the acceleration technology at some future date.

3   AMD Fusion APU

AMD Corp. released its Accelerated Processing Unit (APU) with a CPU–GPU integration architecture[5]. This processor already supports GPGPU using OpenCL[6].

The AMD Fusion APU architecture is displayed in Fig. 1. In the APU, x86 CPU cores and GPU are integrated together in the interior of a silicon die through the High Performance Bus. The embedded GPU is identified as a Compute Device in OpenCL and then used as a co-processor of x86 CPU cores. The GPU has several Compute Units with a processor comprising multiple Stream Cores, an L1 cache, and a Local Data Store (LDS). A Stream Core is a processor with Very Long Instruction Words (VLIWs) with five operation instruction units, one branch instruction unit, and numerous registers. These five instruction units are identified as Processor Elements in OpenCL. An LDS is memory with small capacity, but low access latency. Moreover, the memory for x86 CPU cores and the global memory for a Compute Device, partitioning for each other purpose, are located in the same memory module. Currently, each memory space is separated completely: the CPU and GPU can not access the space of the other.

Parallel processing using OpenCL on AMD GPUs is attributed to many-thread parallelism. Many threads are managed as several blocks of threads. In OpenCL, thread and thread blocks are designated respectively as work-item and work-group. Work-groups are assigned to Compute Units respectively. Then work-items in the work-group are assigned to Stream Cores. If the instructions for a work-item have instruction-level parallelism, then they are executed on Processor Elements in a Stream Core in parallel as VLIW instructions. The number of work-items per work-group is recommended to set as a multiple of 64 to extract higher performance in a GPU[7]. In cases where Stream Cores stall by memory access instruction of a work-group, the execution is changed to another work-group to hide the memory access latency. Consequently, to use Compute Units with high usability, the number of work-groups should be set as a multiple of the number of Compute Units in a GPU.

4 Symmetric Block Ciphers

The CRYPTREC project in Japan publishes an e-government recommended cipher list, including several excellent block ciphers. We selected three 128-bit block ciphers among the several block ciphers: AES, Camellia, and SC2000. Because the data randomization structure of AES, Camellia, and SC2000 are, respectively, SPN, Feistel, and the hybrid of SPN and Feistel. In addition, AES and Camellia are recommended by New European Schemes for Signatures, Integrity and Encryption (NESSIE)[8], which is a European research project to identify secure cryptographic primitives.

In the three block ciphers, the secret key size can be selected with three options, 128-bit, 192-bit, and 256-bit. Generally, although the number of rounds in the cipher algorithms varies depending on the size, it becomes the same number in 192-bit and 256-bit key size of Camellia and SC2000.

4.1 AES

As for AES, the developers presented a high-speed implementation style for software[9]. The round process can be combined into a transformation simply

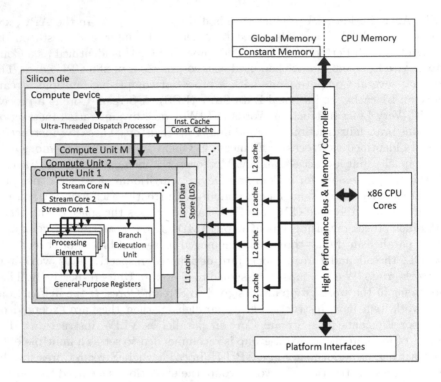

Fig. 1. Architecture of AMD Fusion APU

using 16 S-table substitutions and XOR operations. Letting a be the round input, which is divided into four inputs a_0, a_1, a_2, a_3, each of which consists of 32 bits, the round output e is represented as

$$e_j = T_0[a_{0,j}] \oplus T_1[a_{1,j+1}] \oplus T_2[a_{2,j+2}] \oplus T_3[a_{3,j+3}] \oplus k_j,$$

where T_0, T_1, T_2, T_3, are S-tables and k_j is the j-th columns of a roundkey.

4.2   Camellia

For Camellia, the optimization method for software implementation is presented in the specification document[10]. In Camellia, an F-function is executed in the round. In the F-function, the 64-bit input are transformed simply using eight S-table substitutions with 8-bit input and 32-bit output and XOR operations. The FL and FL^{-1} functions, consisting of 32-bit AND, OR, XOR, and cyclic left shift, are inserted per six rounds.

4.3   SC2000

As for SC2000, the optimization for software implementation is shown in the specification document[11]. Each round executes five transformations in sequence: I, B, I, R, and R-function. In the R-function, the 32-bit input is separated into several fragments of arbitrary size, for example (6-bit, 5-bit, 5-bit, 5-bit, 5-bit, 6-bit) or (11-bit, 10-bit, 11-bit). Then they are replaced by S_6 and S_5-table or S_{11} and S_{10}-table, etc.

5   Related Works

5.1   Performance Study of AMD Fusion APUs

Daga et al. analyzed the effectiveness of the AMD Fusion APU using four benchmarks as well as a PCI-Express bandwidth test[12]. Their benchmarks showed that the APU produces a 1.7–6.0-fold higher data transfer rate than a discrete Radeon HD 5870. Moreover, if the data transfer is included, then a reduction benchmark on the APU with 80 cores achieved a 3.5-fold higher rate of processing than the discrete GPU with 1600 cores. Additionally, the authors inferred that the next generation of APUs is expected to merge the partition between of the x86 cores and the GPU.

Hetherington et al. evaluated Memcached, a high-performance distributed memory cache server system, on two AMD Fusion APUs and a system with a discrete GPU[13]. They reported that the performance including the data transfer between a CPU and a GPU on an A8-3580 APU exhibits about nine times increased performance compared with the trivial GPGPU system.

5.2   Symmetric Block Ciphers on Discrete GPU System

No research has been reported of the evaluation of block ciphers on processors with CPU–GPU integration architecture. However, because the architecture of the embedded GPU in an AMD Fusion APU is the same as that of traditional GPU, previous works are sufficiently helpful for analyzing the optimization methodology for implementation of a block cipher on GPUs.

Biagio et al. implemented counter mode AES (AES-CTR) on an Nvidia Geforce 8800 GT using CUDA[14]. The authors of this paper achieved 12.5 Gbps with an input size of 128 MB considering processing granularity.

Iwai et al. implemented AES on CUDA with different granularities and various memory allocation styles[15]. For the AES encryption module, they contrived what bytes should be mapped to each thread, granularity, as one component to increase its performance. They defined the following four ways of granularity: 16 Bytes/Thread and the other granularities. In 16 Bytes/Thread, a thread is in charge of encryption of a plaintext block. They concluded that 16 Bytes/Thread tended to show higher throughput than the other granularities because this granularity requires no synchronization between threads in parallel processing.

Nishikawa et al. implemented AES-128, Camellia-128, and SC2000-128 in ECB mode and achieved about 27.5 Gbps, 27.5 Gbps, and 28.0 Gbps, respectively, with data transfer and overlapping function on a Nvidia Tesla C2050[16]. Aside from our study, no other works for the implementation of SC2000 have been reported.

Gervasi et al. implemented AES-192 and achieved about 38.6 Mbps at 2 KB file size without data transfer using OpenCL on a AMD Firestream 9270 with 800 cores[17]. Moreover, the throughput of their AES-192 with data transfer was about 31.9 Mbps. Wang et al. implemented AES-256 in XTS mode at 828.8 MB/s using OpenCL on a AMD Radeon HD 5970 with 3200 cores[18]. Moreover, they claimed that the best parameters of work-groups and work-items per work-group were 120 and 256, respectively. They stored the S-box and key into local memory to decrease the latency of accessing memory. However, the weak point of these researches is that whether or not optimized and high-speed AES with T-box was adopted for evaluation of the algorithm on GPUs is unclear. For a pertinent evaluation of the throughput on GPUs, Section 4.1 shows that programmers should make the most of optimized AES for software[9].

6   Implementation

6.1   Granularity

In 128-bit symmetric block ciphers, the input data are separated specifically to 128-bit block size and are then encrypted. Section 6.4 shows that 128-bit parallelism can be extracted in the case of some parallelizable encryption modes. For this reason, in this paper, we set the computation granularity to 128-bit per thread in parallel encryption processing on GPUs. Compared with the other granularities, this granularity has the benefit of no synchronization instruction during parallel processing by multiple threads.

Moreover, Section 3 shows that each Compute Unit has multiple Stream Cores and the number of work-items per work-group in multiples of 64 engenders high efficiency of GPU. Therefore, we tentatively set the number of work-items per work-group in multiples of 64 and subsequently adjusted the optimum values manually.

6.2   Memory Allocation

Generally in optimized software implementation of block ciphers, the same substitution tables are referred multiple times. Therefore, storage of the table and extended key stored in local memory with low access latency engender higher performance than that achieved with those stored in global memory. We stored substitution tables and keys into local memory to decrease the access latency.

6.3   Overlapping GPU Processing and Memory Copy

Generally, countermeasures against data transfer to extract higher performance are substantial, occupying large overhead in GPGPU applications. However, transfer of a large amount of data such as plaintext and ciphertext between a CPU and a GPU is unavoidable during implementation of cipher algorithms on GPUs. Therefore, if the data transfer is not included into the whole encryption processing time, then it does not indicate the real processing time at all.

Fortunately, AMD GPUs provide a function of overlapping data transfer (memory copy) and processing. Here, it is noteworthy that the memory spaces of a CPU and a GPU are separated by the partition in the system memory of current AMD Fusion APUs, as presented in Section 3. However, the overlapping function described above is also available for the APU like discrete AMD GPUs.

For this reason, we implemented the encoding process of each cipher algorithm with overlapping transferring plaintext to (and ciphertext from) the off-chip memory of GPU and the GPU's encoding process. Fig. 2 presents the overlapping diagram in the case of data division into two plaintext blocks. Fig. 3 is the code corresponding to the diagram presented in Fig. 2. This overlapping process is known as pipeline processing between data transfer and processing. To optimize this pipeline, a tradeoff exists between block size, which is the dividing size of plaintext as the pipeline stage, and the pipelined overhead. This pipeline optimization is expected to achieve good performance when the data transfer time and processing time are balanced.

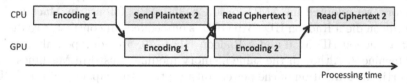

Fig. 2. Overlapping GPU encryption processing and plaintext copy

```
/* offset is the pointer of plaintext in each command queue */
/* plaintextmobj is the memory object of plaintext */
clEnqueueWriteBuffer(queue[0], plaintextmobj, CL_FALSE, FILESIZE/2*0,
        FILESIZE/2, (void*)&plaintext[offset*0], 0, NULL, NULL);
clEnqueueWriteBuffer(queue[1], plaintextmobj, CL_FALSE, FILESIZE/2*1,
        FILESIZE/2, (void*)&plaintext[offset*1], 0, NULL, NULL);
clEnqueueNDRangeKernel(queue[0], kernel[0], 1, NULL, &global_item_size,
        &local_item_size, 0, NULL, NULL);
clEnqueueReadBuffer(queue[0], ciphertextmobj, CL_FALSE, FILESIZE/2*0,
        FILESIZE/2, (void*)&ciphertext[offset*0], 0, NULL, NULL);
clEnqueueNDRangeKernel(queue[1], kernel[1], 1, NULL, &global_item_size,
        &local_item_size, 0, NULL, NULL);
clEnqueueReadBuffer(queue[1], ciphertextmobj, CL_FALSE, FILESIZE/2*1,
        FILESIZE/2, (void*)&ciphertext[offset*1], 0, NULL, NULL);
```

Fig. 3. Code corresponding to the diagram presented in Fig. 2

6.4   Encryption Modes

Electronic Code Book (ECB), CountTeR (CTR), or Xor-encrypt-xor Tweakable code book mode with ciphertext Stealing (XTS)[19] are known as parallelizable modes in block cipher. ECB use a single key applied to all plaintexts, and CTR uses a key stream generated from a secret key and combined to plaintexts. In the CTR mode, the generation of the key stream is conducted in the same manner as ECB. In the XTS mode, plaintexts are encrypted using two ECB modes. Therefore, we discussed only ECB mode to evaluate the parallel processing of symmetric block ciphers.

7   Evaluation

7.1   Evaluation Environment

Evaluation environments are presented in Table 1. As heterogeneous multicore processors, we adopted an AMD Fusion E-350 APU for use in Machine 1, in whose silicon die a Radeon HD 6310 GPU is embedded. In contrast, two discrete GPUs, a Radeon HD 5450 and a Radeon HD 6770, are equipped alternatively with Machine 2. Although the same memory module is used in Machines 1 and 2 for pertinent evaluation of the power consumption, the capacity of the GPU in Machine 1 is not 4 GB because of the partitioning separation. The specifications of the tested GPUs are presented in Table 2.

In our manual optimization to extract higher throughput, the combinations of the number of work-groups and work-items per work-group were respectively (10, 128), (10, 128), (160, 256) for E-350, Radeon HD 5450, and Radeon HD 6770, whose values were common to all three block ciphers.

The part of encryption processing runs through the entire code one hundred times, disregarding the first 10 iterations to avoid the effects of cold instruction cache misses.

Table 1. Machine specifications

	Machine 1	Machine 2	
CPU	AMD E-350 (2 cores available)	AMD Phenom II X6 1100T (6 cores available)	
Motherboard	J&W MINIX E350-GT	ASUS M5A99X EVO	
Memory	Silicon Power, SP004GBLTU133V01 DDR3 PC3-10600 4 GB		
OS	CentOS 6.0 (Kernel version 2.6.32-71)		
Compiler	GCC version 4.4.4 (Option -O3)		
Power supply	SilverStone Strider Gold SST-ST1200-G (1200 watt output)		
GPU	**Radeon HD 6310 (Embedded)**	**Radeon HD 5450 (Discrete)**	**Radeon HD 6770 (Discrete)**
GPU driver	AMD Catalyst 12.2 Proprietary Linux x86 Display Driver		

Table 2. GPU specifications

	Radeon HD 6310 (Embedded)	Radeon HD 5450 (Discrete)	Radeon HD 6770 (Discrete)
Process technology		40 nm	
Engine speed	492 MHz	650 MHz	850 MHz
# Compute Units	2	2	10
# Stream Cores	16	16	160
# Processing Elements	80	80	800
# Work-items (1 dimension)	Up to 256	Up to 128	Up to 128
LDS capacity	32 KB	32 KB	32 KB
Global memory capacity	192 MB	256 MB	1024 MB
Memory type	DDR3	DDR3	GDDR5
Memory speed	533 MHz	800 MHz	1200 MHz
12 volt auxiliary line	Not equipped	Not equipped	Equipped

7.2 Evaluation of Throughput

The encryption throughput values of AES, Camellia, and SC2000 with 128-bit key size using GPGPU are shown respectively in Figs. 4 – 6. In each figure, the horizontal and vertical axes respectively portray the input size of plaintexts and the throughput. In the graph legend, Kernel, Overlap, and Non-overlap respectively indicate the throughput without data transfer, the throughput with data transfer and overlapping, and the throughput with data transfer and non-overlapping. Moreover, throughput of AES with a 128-bit key in Machine 1 with 80 GPU cores was 75.1 % of Machine 2 equipped with a Radeon HD 5450 with the same number of the cores, but this main reason results from the difference in GPU engine speed. Here, we omitted the graph with 192-bit and 256-bit key sizes because the throughput's tendency with various input size was almost identical to that obtained with the 128-bit key. In addition, the maximum throughput values with 128, 192, and 256-bit key with data transfer and overlapping, the real throughput, are shown in Fig. 7. However, as for Camellia and SC2000, the 256-bit version is eliminated in Fig. 7 because the number of rounds in the version is the same as that in the 192-bit version.

Figs. 4 – 6 show that the performance deterioration including the data transfer represents that the data transfer rate holds a dominant position in GPGPU, even if the processing speed of GPU is extremely fast. For example, although the throughput results of AES-128, Camellia-128, and SC2000-128 without the data transfer on a Radeon HD 6770 in Machine 2 show a difference in performance, the throughput including the data transfer deteriorated to an equal degree of about 20 Gbps, as shown in Fig. 7(c). This reason is that the differences in throughput are absorbed because of the low transfer rate of the PCIe bus.

Moreover, as the reference of the evaluation, we presented the throughput on multicore CPUs, as shown in Fig. 8. As might be readily apparent from the comparison of Fig. 7(b) and Fig. 8(b), the throughput on multicore CPU is

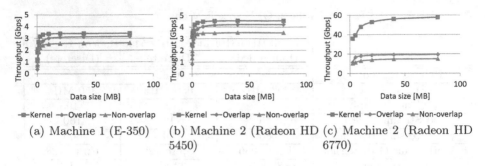

(a) Machine 1 (E-350)   (b) Machine 2 (Radeon HD (c) Machine 2 (Radeon HD
                          5450)   6770)

Fig. 4. AES-128 Throughput

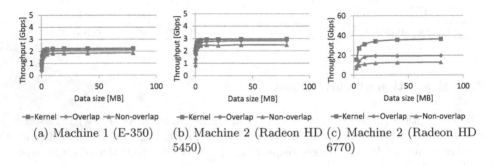

(a) Machine 1 (E-350)   (b) Machine 2 (Radeon HD (c) Machine 2 (Radeon HD
                          5450)   6770)

Fig. 5. Camellia-128 Throughput

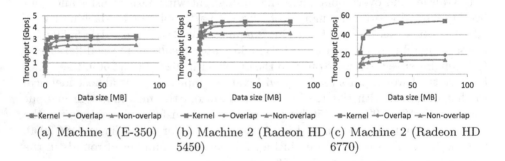

(a) Machine 1 (E-350)   (b) Machine 2 (Radeon HD (c) Machine 2 (Radeon HD
                          5450)   6770)

Fig. 6. SC2000-128 Throughput

higher than that on the equipped GPU in the case of combination of high-end CPU and low-end GPU.

7.3   Evaluation of Power Consumption

Section 1 shows that for encryption processing on GPUs in small portable devices, throughput per watt becomes extremely important.

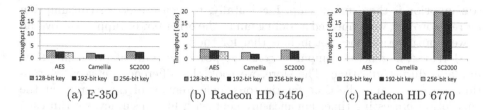

Fig. 7. Throughput values achieved with data transfer and overlapping; real values including data transfer overhead

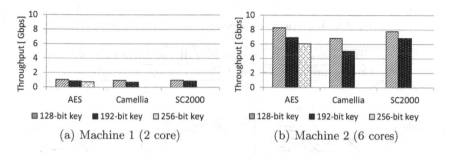

Fig. 8. Throughput value achieved with each multicore CPU

Power Consumption Measurement. Generally, in a system with discrete GPUs, power is supplied to GPUs through a PCIe bus and 12 V auxiliary lines when needed. In some previous studies, voltage or current from a PCIe bus and auxiliary lines are measured. Then the power consumption is calculated [20][21][22]. A riser card is inserted between a GPU and a PCIe connector to measure voltage or current only from the bus to the GPU. This approach is certainly effective for a system with a discrete GPU. However, in Machine 1, the approach described above is not available because a silicon die already has a built-in GPU.

For this reason, to obtain the power consumption of each Machine, we measured current through 3.3 V, 5 V, and two 12 V lines from a ATX power supply to a motherboard using the devices depicted in Table 3, as presented in Fig. 9. In addition, for the measurement in Machine 2 equipped with a Radeon HD 6770, we measured an extra current through a 12 V auxiliary line. In general, computers drive receiving power through a 24-pin main power supply line and a 4-pin or an 8-pin of the auxiliary line, which is common to both Machines 1 and 2. Therefore, this measuring approach is a consolidated means for pertinent evaluation of Machines 1 and 2. Another merit of this approach is that the power consumption of the whole system at the encryption processing can be measured rigorously. During encryption processing, not only the GPU but every peripheral drive receiving power from the motherboard. Consequently, for the acquisition of power consumption, we multiplied the measured current with the rated voltage of 12 V, 3.3 V, or 5 V. The amount of respective power consumption is then summed up. Incidentally, to measure power consumption more rigorously, we connected a cooling fan to the other power supply; the overall power consumption does not include that for the fan.

Moreover, in general, computers consume power not only at processing time but also during idle time. Therefore, we took the difference between encryption processing and idle time for rigorous measurement of the current at the encryption processing time. For measurement with high-accuracy, we run each encryption program for more than 10 consecutive seconds to obtain enough observational data and then measured current using a high-accuracy current probe during 10 seconds with 25,000/second sampling frequency.

Table 3. Devices to measure power consumption

Digital oscilloscope	Iwatsu DS-4354ML 500 MHz 1 GS/S
Current probe	LeCroy CP015 15 ampere 50 MHz

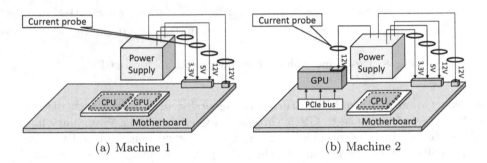

(a) Machine 1   (b) Machine 2

Fig. 9. Power consumption measurement environments

Measurement Results of Power Consumption. First, measurement results of power consumption in each environment are presented in Table 4. In Machines 1 and 2, the power consumption of encryption processing on multicore CPUs was much higher than that on GPUs. Moreover, the power consumption of AES is slightly higher than that of the other block ciphers. Irrespective of block cipher algorithms, the three key sizes show almost no difference in power consumption. However, comparing the power consumption of Machine 1 as embedded Radeon HD 6310 with a system with a discrete Radeon HD 5450, the former is 2 watts less than the latter, mainly because of no PCIe bus in Machine 1 as well as lower GPU engine speed than Machine 2.

7.4   Evaluation of Power Efficiency

Next, throughput values in Fig. 7 divided by the power consumptions displayed in Table. 4, the throughput values per watt, are presented in Fig. 10. Results show

Table 4. Summary of power consumptions; the difference between encryption processing and idle time

	Machine 1		Machine 2		
	CPU	Radeon HD 6310 (Embedded)	CPU	Radeon HD 5450 (Discrete)	Radeon HD 6770 (Discrete)
AES-128 [Watt]	7.3	4.4	119.7	6.7	38.6
AES-192 [Watt]	7.3	4.0	119.0	6.4	38.7
AES-256 [Watt]	7.2	4.0	118.7	6.2	39.1
Camellia-128 [Watt]	7.0	3.8	109.0	6.1	38.8
Camellia-192 [Watt]	6.9	3.6	106.8	5.8	37.5
SC2000-128 [Watt]	6.8	4.0	106.4	6.4	36.6
SC2000-192 [Watt]	6.8	3.9	105.6	6.1	36.9

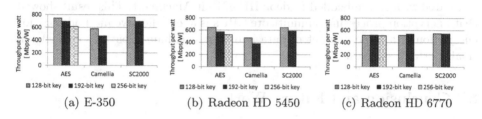

(a) E-350   (b) Radeon HD 5450   (c) Radeon HD 6770

Fig. 10. Comparison of the throughput values per watt with data transfer and overlapping. The per-watt throughput of E-350 represents much higher than that on a system with discrete GPUs.

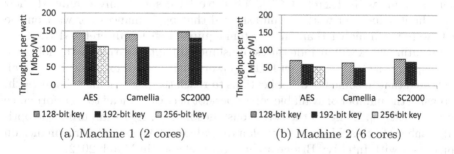

(a) Machine 1 (2 cores)   (b) Machine 2 (6 cores)

Fig. 11. Comparison of the throughput values per watt on each multicore CPU. Multicore CPUs are less-effective methodology for encryption of large amount of data.

that the per-watt throughput of AES-128 using an embedded Radeon HD 6310 with 80 cores in Machine 1 was 743.0 Mbps/W, representing an approximately 44.0 % increase over that obtained using a discrete Radeon HD 6770 with 800 cores in Machine 2. In contrast, the per-watt performance of AES-128 on the embedded Radeon HD 6310 was 15.6 % increased over that of a system with a discrete Radeon HD 5440.

Additionally, the system memory is currently separated to the CPU and GPU memory space exhaustively. Therefore, trivial data transfer between CPU and GPU memory space is required. Hereinafter, improvement of the memory controller in the Fusion APU is expected to eliminate the partition and the data transfer between a CPU and a GPU. Under the expected improvement for APU, for example, the per-watt throughput of AES-128 is expected to achieve 805.5 Mbps/W and 56.1 % increase compared with the system with a Radeon HD 6770 because the data transfer time will become negligible.

Here, as a reference of the throughput per watt, we present that for multicore CPUs. The preceding section described that ignoring the power consumption, encryption processing on high-end multicore CPUs gained the throughput at the same degree and more of that on GPUs. However, given the power consumption, the throughput of AES-128 per watt on the multicore CPU in Machine 2 was extremely low 70.7 Mbps/W and merely 9.6 % of the performance per watt compared with the embedded Radeon HD 6310 in Machine 1. This result showed that encryption processing on multicore CPUs is a less-effective methodology for encryption of a large amount of data and that it exhausts battery capacity in small portable devices.

8   Conclusion and Future Works

Power consumption is a primary deterrent for high-speed encryption processing with a large anout of data on all pervasive small portable devices. Therefore, in this paper, we implemented three 128-bit block ciphers (AES, Camellia, SC2000) on AMD E-350 APU with CPU-GPU integration architecture and two traditional systems with discrete GPUs. Then we have specifically examined their throughput values per watt. Results showed that performances per watt on the APU were much higher than on a system equipped with a discrete GPU.

Our future work will include the establishment of optimization methodology of block ciphers on GPUs to extract higher power efficiency. For example, Hong et al. illustrated that in some GPU applications to reach the peak memory bandwidth, increasing the number of available cores does not necessarily lead to a performance improvement[23]: Using all the cores consumes more energy than using the optimal number of cores. Moreover, we plan to evaluate the per-watt performance on a processor with Intel Ivy Bridge architecture released in March 2012.

References

1. Cryptography Research and Evaluation Committees,
   http://www.cryptrec.go.jp/english/index.html
2. Intel Corporation: Intel SDK for OpenCL Applications 2012 Release Notes (2012)
3. NVIDIA Corporation: Bringing High-End Graphics to Handheld Devices (2011)
4. Imagination Technologies: PowerVR SGX Series5 IP Core Family (2011)
5. AMD Corporation: AMD Fusion. Family of APUs: Enabling a Superior, Immersive PC Experience (2011)

6. Khronos Group: Open Compute Language, http://www.khronos.org/
7. AMD Corporation: AMD Accelerated Parallel Processing OpenCL Programming Guide Revision 2.1b (2012)
8. New European Schemes for Signatures, Integrity and Encryption, https://www.cosic.esat.kuleuven.be/nessie/
9. Daemen, J., Rijmen, V.: The Design of Rijndael: AES - The Advanced Encryption Standard. Springer, Heidelberg (2002)
10. Aoki, K., Ichikawa, T., Kanda, M., Matsui, M., Moriai, S., Nakajima, J., Tokita, T.: Camellia: A 128-Bit Block Cipher Suitable for Multiple Platforms - Design and Analysis. In: Stinson, D.R., Tavares, S. (eds.) SAC 2000. LNCS, vol. 2012, pp. 39–56. Springer, Heidelberg (2001)
11. Shimoyama, T., Yanami, H., Yokoyama, K., Takenaka, M., Itoh, K., Yajima, J., Torii, N., Tanaka, H.: The Block Cipher SC2000. In: Matsui, M. (ed.) FSE 2001. LNCS, vol. 2355, pp. 312–327. Springer, Heidelberg (2002)
12. Daga, M., Aji, A.M., Feng, W.C.: On the Efficacy of a Fused CPU+GPU Processor (or APU) for Parallel Computing. In: Proceedings of the 2011 Symposium on Application Accelerators in High-Performance Computing, Washington, DC, USA, pp. 141–149 (2011)
13. Hetherington, T.H., Rogers, T.G., Hsu, L., O'Connor, M., Aamodt, T.M.: Characterizing and Evaluating a Key-value Store Application on Heterogeneous CPU-GPU Systems. In: Balasubramonian, R., Srinivasan, V. (eds.) ISPASS, pp. 88–98. IEEE (2012)
14. Biagio, A.D., Barenghi, A., Agosta, G., Pelosi, G.: Design of a parallel AES for graphics hardware using the CUDA framework. In: The 23rd International Parallel and Distributed Processing Symposium, pp. 1–8 (2009)
15. Iwai, K., Nishikawa, N., Kurokawa, T.: Acceleration of AES encryption on CUDA GPU. International Journal of Networking and Computing 2(1), 131–145 (2012)
16. Nishikawa, N., Iwai, K., Kurokawa, T.: Implementation of Symmetric Block Ciphers using GPGPU. In: 7th International Conference on Information Warfare and Security, Seattle, USA, pp. 222–232 (March 2012)
17. Gervasi, O., Russo, D., Vella, F.: The AES Implantation Based on OpenCL for Multi/many Core Architecture. In: 2010 International Conference on Computational Science and Its Applications, pp. 129–134 (2010)
18. Wang, X., Li, X., Zou, M., Zhou, J.: AES finalists implementation for GPU and multi-core CPU based on OpenCL. In: Proceedings of the 2011 IEEE International Conference on Anti-Counterfeiting, Security and Identification, ASID 2011, pp. 38–42 (2011)
19. The IEEE Security in Storage Working Group: XTS block cipher-based mode (XEX-based tweaked-codebook mode with ciphertext stealing), http://siswg.net/
20. Ma, X., Dong, M., Zhong, L., Deng, Z.: Statistical Power Consumption Analysis and Modeling for GPU-based Computing. In: Proc of ACM SOSP Workshop on Power Aware Computing and Systems Hot Power (2009)
21. Nagasaka, H., Maruyama, N., Nukada, A., Endo, T., Matsuoka, S.: Statistical power modeling of GPU kernels using performance counters. In: The First International Green Computing Conference, pp. 115–122 (2010)
22. Zhang, Y., Hu, Y., Li, B., Peng, L.: Performance and Power Analysis of ATI GPU: A Statistical Approach. In: Proceedings of the 2011 IEEE Sixth International Conference on Networking, Architecture, and Storage, NAS 2011, pp. 149–158 (2011)
23. Hong, S., Kim, H.: An integrated gpu power and performance model. In: Proceedings of the 37th Annual International Symposium on Computer Architecture, ISCA 2010, pp. 280–289. ACM, New York (2010)

Experiments in Parallel Matrix Multiplication on Multi-core Systems

Joeffrey Legaux, Sylvain Jubertie, and Frédéric Loulergue

LIFO, University of Orléans, France
{Joeffrey.Legaux,Sylvain.Jubertie,Frédéric.Loulergue}@univ-orleans.fr

Abstract. Matrix multiplication is an example of application that is both easy to specify and to provide a simple implementation. There exist numerous sophisticated algorithms or very efficient complex implementations. In this study we are rather interested in the design/programming overhead with respect to performance benefits. Starting from the naive sequential implementation, the implementation is first optimised by improving data accesses, then by using vector units of modern processors, and we finally propose a parallel version for multi-core architectures. The various proposed optimisations are experimented on several architectures and the trade-off software complexity versus efficiency is evaluated using Halstead metrics.

Keywords: matrix multiplication, memory accesses, SIMD unit, shared-memory parallelism, software metrics.

1 Introduction

Parallel architectures are now pervasive. However parallel programming is not as widespread as parallel processors. High level parallel programming approaches are a necessity. Such high-level approaches include algorithmic skeletons [2,7]. We are interested in having very efficient and extended versions of the OSL library [9] but for multi-core programming (CPU, GPU and hybrid) instead of distributed memory. One of our goal is to find the right balance between the ease of programming for the non-specialist of parallel programming, and the possibility for the more skilled programmer to obtain more performances.

However it is difficult to evaluate the advantages of such high-level approaches with respect to more widespread but lower level approaches in terms of productivity and ease of programming. As a first step to obtain a methodology for such comparisons, we investigate how a programmer could optimise her program from a naive version to more efficient ones using widespread shared memory parallel and programming libraries. We use software metrics to measure the complexity of the code, especially the *effort* of Halstead set of metrics, that is supposed to be proportional to the time needed for the development of the software. Having such measures we can then evaluate the efficiency / effort trade-off.

For this study, we chose matrix multiplication: the problem and the naive solutions are quite simple, but very complex algorithms and very efficient and

Y. Xiang et al. (Eds.): ICA3PP 2012, Part I, LNCS 7439, pp. 362–376, 2012.

complex implementations exist. We are not aiming at providing more efficient algorithms or implementations, but rather to see if not too complicated optimisations could lead to good improvements. We believe a certain point, the increase of the complexity of the code no longer matches the increase of efficiency. This would guide the design and implementation of a high-level programming library that should allow optimisations up to this point, but going beyond could not be possible without breaking the ease of programming.

Matrix multiplication is a conceptually simple task, however it is a core mechanism when dealing with linear algebra, which is widely used in many applications such as image processing, physical or economical simulations, and can represent most of the computational load of such applications. Standard benchmarks such as the reference LINPACK [6] used to establish the well-known top500 list[1] rely heavily on this sort of computation.

The algorithm is pretty straightforward. Given a matrix A of size m (lines) by k (columns) and a matrix B of size k by n, the resulting matrix C of their multiplication is obtained by computing the dot product between all lines of A with all columns of B.

$$C_{i,j} = \left(AB \right)_{i,j} = \sum_{k=1}^{n} A_{i,k} \times B_{k,j} \tag{1}$$

To compute a single element of C (equation 1), we have to conduct k multiplications and $k - 1$ additions. As C contains $m \times n$ elements this leads to a total of $m \times n \times (2k - 1)$ operations, thus if n, m, and k are of the same order, the algorithmic complexity is $O(n^3)$.

Other algorithms have been researched in order to reduce this cubic complexity. The first was Strassen's algorithm [13] which has a mathematical complexity of $O(n^{2.81})$. However, this algorithm applies a recursive division of the matrix into sub-matrices, thus, it only works on square matrices and adds several memory operations to create the recursive blocks. As we will see in the following sections, memory accesses tend to be the main bottleneck for this algorithm and Strassen's algorithm accesses to the data have poor locality, thus we may not be able to easily improve the memory operations and parallelise the computations. Experimental results [4] show that this algorithm starts to become more efficient on a single processor only for large matrices (at least a few million elements). Coppersmith-Winograd [3] designed another algorithm that has been recently improved to a complexity of $O(n^{2.3727})$, but this complexity involves a huge constant that renders it only useful for matrices of unrealistic sizes.

In this paper we proceed as follows. First we optimise the simple algorithm by improving data accesses (section 2), then by using vector units of modern processors, (section 3), and we finally propose a parallel version for multi-core architectures (section 4). The performances of the various proposed optimisations are experimented on several architectures (section 5). In section 6 we present

---

[1] www.top500.org

Halstead's metrics and the methodology for their use. With these metrics, we evaluate the design/programming overhead with respect to performance benefits. Finally, we conclude and give future research directions (section 7).

2   A Sequential Implementation

The naive implementation is simple: we need two nested loops of size m and n to cover all the elements of C. Then for each element we need a loop of size k to conduct the dot product between the corresponding line of A and column of B, as described in listing 1.1.

Listing 1.1. Matrix multiplication

```
1      for (int i = 0; i < C->_height; i++) {
2       for (int j = 0; j < C->_width; j++) {
3         for (int k = 0; k < A->_width; k++)
4         C->data(i,j) = C->data(i,j) + A->data(i,k) * B->data(k,j);
5         }
6       }
7       }
```

This approach is very inefficient mainly because of the memory access pattern: for each iteration of the inner loop, we have three read accesses and one write access to the memory, and only two arithmetic operations. On current hardware architectures (CPUs as well as GPUs), arithmetic operations are considered fast (a few cycles of the processing unit) while memory accesses are very slow (up to hundreds of cycles). Although the compiler's optimisations and the cache memories may somewhat reduce the impact of those memory accesses, the processing unit will still spend most of its time waiting for the data to be available as the ratio of mathematical operations on memory operations is very low. Thus our main goal will be to reduce the amount of those memory operations in order to get the most of the processing unit's computational power.

2.1   First Optimisation

If we consider the innermost loop, the $C_{i,j}$ element being processed contains the result of the dot product processed during all the iterations. We do not have to store all the partial sums in memory, instead we may accumulate them in a processor register. A register is a small amount of very fast memory located inside the processor which can be read or written without latency. By doing this, we only have to write the content of the register once after the last iteration of the loop ended, and we do not have to read the matrix C anymore. Thus, the number of read accesses is divided by a third, and the number of memory writes is divided by k.

2.2   Exploiting Memory Cache: The Blocked Algorithm

We have reduced the number of memory accesses to the matrix C to the minimum, since we cannot do less than writing each element once, but we may improve the accesses to A and B with the help of cache memory.

A cache is a small amount of very fast memory which is close to the processor. While accessing data in memory can take up to hundreds of processor cycles, a cache read occurs in less than a dozen cycles. If we keep data in the cache, after the first slow read in main memory (which is still mandatory to bring the data in the cache) the following accesses will be very fast.

Another interesting feature of cache memory is that it automatically retrieves data from the main memory by "cache lines", i.e. when you read a value in memory, it copies a whole block containing it (usually 64 bytes on current architectures). This means that the first time you read a value, it takes the whole main memory latency, but when you access the following values of the block they are already in the cache and are accessed with a very low latency. As we access A's elements by line we automatically benefit from this mechanism, but we access B's elements by column, which are not contiguous in memory. However when reading an element of B, the cache still gets the including line which contains the elements of the following columns, so we also may benefit from this mechanism.

If A and B completely fit into the cache, then these mechanisms solve our problem: each element will be read only once from the main memory, and all subsequent accesses will occur at the cache's low latency. However, cache memory is relatively small (typically 32 to 64 kB on current architectures for the fastest cache level), limiting us to matrices of only a few thousands elements. A solution is to split the matrices into sub-matrices that fit into cache memory.

The idea behind blocked matrix multiplication [5] is quite simple: instead of considering C as an group of number obtained by multiplying a line of A with a column of B, we will consider it as a group of smaller sub-matrices obtained by multiplying a line of sub-matrices of A with a column of sub-matrices of B. If the sub-matrices are small enough to fit in the cache, their multiplication will be fully performed inside the cache. So, even though the whole matrices won't be accessed optimally, their sub-matrices will be, which will efficiently reduce the global amount of memory operations. For example, if C has 1600 lines, the single element algorithm will read each column of B 1600 times. If we use the blocked algorithm with blocks of 16 lines, each block of B will be read only 100 times.

The drawback of this approach is that we have to copy the blocks as independent matrices. However, for sufficiently large matrices, blocks will be reused several times, so the gains obtained will largely compensate the copy cost. Simply copying the data of the main matrices into blocks each time we need them already leads to a consequent speedup. However this still produces a lot of unnecessary memory operations, thus creating a structure in memory that keeps the blocks when they are created is much more beneficial: even though we will still have to read the whole blocks at each call, we will only have to write them once. Moreover, we have several levels of cache memory available on recent processors, those are being slower than the level 1 cache, but are much larger (up to a few megabytes) and still faster than the main memory, so if we keep the blocks in memory, chances are that they will be present in the higher-level caches. As we will see in the parallelisation section, higher-level caches may also be shared between computing cores, which will also be beneficial if those cores need to access the same blocks.

We have applied several generic optimisations for the current processor architectures. There is still room for architecture-specific tuning. Optimisations presented here lead to significant gains on any current architecture (see section 5), although some tuning (such as block size which may be adjusted to the available cache size) have to be done for every target processor. Still, those are only sequential optimisations, and current architectures offer powerful parallelisation capabilities and the next section will deal with those.

3   A SIMD Implementation

In the previous sections, we have operated on the matrices in a scalar way, i.e. one element at a time, but modern processors have internal SIMD (Single Instruction on Multiple Data) units [12] that allow to process data in a vectorial way, i.e. to apply the same instruction on several data at the same time. We will focus on the SSE (Streaming SIMD Extensions) units which are present on modern x86 processors [14].

SSE units have dedicated 128 bit registers used, for example, to store 4 single-precision floating point numbers, or 2 double precision numbers or integral values. There are 8 such registers available on x86 processors using them, and 16 on the x86-64 architecture. SSE units also provide an instruction set to move data between registers and memory, and to perform arithmetic and logical operations between registers. These instructions have similar execution times than their FPU counterparts, thus, using SSE units may lead to a computational speedup of 4 when operating on 4 single-precision floating point values.

SSE instructions are available through compiler intrinsic functions operating on 128-bits data types representing SSE registers. Instrinsic functions are named according to the following scheme: _mm_instr_suffix, where instr is the name of the instruction, and where suffix describe the type of data and if the instruction is to be applied to the whole register or only to a single value. Data types are named _m128, _m128d, _m128i, to represent respectively registers containing 4 single-precision floating point values, 2 double floating-point values, or integral values. For example, the function _mm_add_ps(_m128 r1, _m128 r2) performs the addition of ps values i.e. packed floating-point single precision values stored in registers r1 and r2.

3.1   Memory Alignment and Padding

Working with SSE instructions adds a few constraints if we want to get the best performance from them. The first constraint is to align data in memory along 16-byte boundaries to optimise data exchanges between registers and memory since memory buses are physically designed to optimise these accesses. Instructions to access unaligned data are also available but are less efficient.Functions like posix_memalign or _mm_malloc provide a way to allocate aligned data in memory. This ensures that the first line of our matrices will be correctly aligned, but, as we store the matrix linearly in memory, the following lines may not be aligned if the first line does not contain a multiple of four floating-point numbers (16 bytes). We can solve this by padding the lines with zeros i.e. adding one to three zeros at the end of each line to keep them correctly aligned. This padding can be considered negligible on matrices containing millions of elements, and allows to use the same SSE operations on 4 elements all along the whole lines, as the added zeros do not affect the multiplications and additions used to perform the dot product of a line by a column.

3.2 Transposition

Accessing the elements of B is still an issue as we need to read them by column, in a non-contiguous pattern. SSE units provide an intrinsic function to access a single element in memory, but this would be very detrimental to performance. Instead, we may load 4 contiguous elements in 4 subsequent lines, thus effectively loading a 4×4 submatrix in 4 SSE registers with 4 aligned memory accesses. This 4×4 submatrix is stored by lines inside the registers, but we can rearrange them to be stored in columns with a few register swapping instructions. The intrinsics already provide a macro _MM_TRANSPOSE4_PS which performs the transposition of a 4×4 matrix loaded into 4 registers. This local transposition has a minimal cost since it occurs completely inside the registers. Although using a blocking algorithm may reduce the impact of those accesses by keeping data into the cache memory, internal registers of the processor are still the fastest memory we can access.

3.3 Algorithm

Listing 1.2. SSE matrix multiplication

```
1    _m128 vA, vB[4], accumulator[4];
2    for(unsigned int i = 0 ; i < C−>height() ; i++) {
3      for(unsigned int j = 0 ; j < C−>width() ; j+=4) {
4        for(unsigned int k = 0 ; k < A−>width() ; k+=4) {
5          for(unsigned int l = 0 ; l < 4 ; l++)
6            vB[l] = _mm_load_ps(&B[k+l][j]);
7          _MM_TRANSPOSE4_PS(vB[0], vB[1], vB[2], vB[3]);
8          vA = _mm_load_ps(&A[i][k]);
9          for(unsigned int l = 0 ; l < 4 ; l++)
10           accumulator[l] = _mm_add_ps(accumulator, _mm_mul_ps(vA, vB[l]));
11         }
12         for(unsigned int l = 0 ; l < 4 ; l++) {
13           accumulator[l] <− _mm_hadd_ps(_mm_hadd_ps(accumulator[l]));
14           _mm_store_ss(C[i][j+l], accumulator[l]);
15         }
16       }
17    }
```

Our SSE algorithm is presented in listing 1.2 and is described below. The main loop iterates over elements of matrix C. As we obtain 4 columns after the transposition in B, we are able to treat 4 elements of C at each iteration. The innermost loop iterates over the elements of a line in A and also treats 4 elements of

A at a time. At each iteration, a submatrix of 4 elements of 4 columns of B is loaded into 4 registers (listing 1.2, line 5,6) and is then transposed (line 7) as described in section 3.2. Then, 4 elements of a line in A are loaded into a single register vA (line 8). Since required data are available in registers, we can multiply vA with each of the vB with the _mm_mul_ps instruction. We then add (instruction _mm_add_ps) the results of those multiplications to 4 accumulator registers (line 9,10) that were originally set to zeros (instruction _mm_set_zero_ps). At the end of the line, we have for each of the 4 columns of B an accumulator containing 4 values which are a partial dot product, we then have to add those 4 values to obtain the complete product. The horizontal addition operator _mm_hadd_ps allows us to add the values inside a register 2 by 2, so we need to apply it twice (line 13). We can finally write the final value of the first element of each accumulator register in C (line 14).

In the end, for a line length of k elements in A, we have applied $(k - 1)$ additions, k multiplications, 3 horizontal additions, $k \times (4 + 1)$ memory reads, 1 memory write. So we have calculated 4 values of C with $2 \times k + 3$ mathematical operations and $5k + 1$ memory operations, which respectively represents roughly 25% and 62.5% of the number of operations needed in the sequential implementation.

However, the transpose macro consists in 8 swapping instructions between the registers. As we have to load and transpose every 4×4 submatrix of B for every line of A, we introduce an important workload although these instructions have a lower latency than the 4 additions and multiplications that will occur in the same iteration (on the AMD K10 architecture: 3 cycles for the move instructions, but 4 cycles for addition and multiplication). Keeping the result of this transposition over several lines would be very beneficial, and does not require much modifications in the code. If we want to treat N lines, the outermost loop will advance by N lines at each iteration instead on a single one, and inside the innermost loop, after reading and transposing the 4×4 submatrix of B, we will have to add another loop of size N which will read 4 elements in each of the N lines of A and proceed to their multiplication with vB and addition to the accumulators. Of course, we will now need $N \times 4$ accumulators. We have a limited number of SSE registers (16 in the x86-64 architecture), but the accumulators of a line may be written into cache memory and then retrieved later when we will work on this line again, leading to a minimal performance loss.

Empirical results show that this approach is very efficient: using $N = 4$ leads to twice the performance of $N = 1$, and it keeps increasing as we set N bigger and seems to peak at around a few dozens (such as 40, but it varies slightly according to the problem size and hardware), with a resulting speedup of around 8.

Next, we may combine this approach with the blocked algorithm. We will apply the exact same algorithm as detailed in the sequential section, our new SSE implementation being applied at each subsequent sub-matrices multiplication.

We also tried to apply the transposition directly when creating the blocks, so we would not have to do it several times inside the main loop. However, it appeared that the compiler generates a code with a good overlap between those operations and the data loads from matrix A, which leads to no noticeable performance loss, thus eliminating the transposition from the loop didn't produce any practical gain.

As both the blocked algorithm and the SSE implementation already optimise the use of cache memory, we cannot expect a multiplicative total speedup when combining them. However those are complementary as the SSE implementation addresses very local optimisation, while the blocked algorithm works on the whole matrix. On sufficiently large matrices (6400×6400), applying the blocked algorithm on the SSE implementation leads to a speedup of around 2, but on smaller matrices the cost of blocks creation overrides its advantages, and the unblocked algorithm may prove to be more efficient. This was already the case with the sequential algorithm, but as the SSE instructions provides a consequent memory access optimisation, we need bigger matrices to reach the point of efficiency.

4   A Shared-Memory Parallel Implementation

We have shown several optimisations by exploiting the cache memory and local parallelism with SSE instructions. However, we have only worked on the sequential code, and there is still room to explore the global parallelism. This may be very beneficial, as most of the computers nowadays have multi-core processors, and the current trend evolves towards more and more on-chip parallelism.

Converting an algorithm from sequential to parallel is not a simple task, however there are software libraries such as OpenMP that facilitates the creation and management of multiple threads inside a program. To keep the correctness of our algorithm, we have to ensure that our data stays consistent between all the threads. Our input matrices A and B are never modified, so only the writes in C may be problematic. As we will have to compute at least several thousands of values for the smallest matrices, we decide that the computation of each element of C will not be split over several threads. If each thread writes distinct elements in C, we avoid all possible conflicts.

Creating a thread for every element in C is not the best choice to obtain good performance, though, as we are unlikely to have as much computing cores as elements in C and creating threads is an expensive operation. Ideally, we will have the same number of threads as the number of cores in the machine. In OpenMP, we define the number of execution threads in an environment variable, thus we can easily launch evaluation batches with a varying amount of threads to evaluate how the program execution time scales with the number of execution cores.

Parallelising a C/C++ loop with OpenMP is simple. Basically, we only have to add the following pragma :

`#pragma omp parallel for`

before a loop, and the threading mechanism will be generated at compile time.

For performance reasons, we choose to parallelise the outermost loop of the algorithm, thus giving to each thread several lines to multiply will all the columns. We could have parallelised the loop on the columns, which would have led to the creation of several threads for each line, and each thread would have managed several columns but only for a single line. This would lead to a similar subdivision of the work across the processors, but with a bigger number of threads created, which is costly.

Parallelising the blocked algorithm is similar, but instead of parallelising the inside multiplication of two blocks, we parallelise the global algorithm, thus any single processor will compute the multiplication of two blocks at any given time, which will keep the advantage of having the whole blocks in their local cache memory. In a shared memory context, we want to create the blocks only once and share them between the threads. Keeping the block creation inside the loop will parallelise their creation, but we need to be sure that only a single processor will write a given block. Once again, OpenMP provides a simple solution : by enclosing a piece of code between the two pragmas

```
#pragma omp critical
....
#pragma omp end critical
```

we ensure that only a single thread may execute this code at any moment.

4.1   Improving Scalability

A side effect of the blocked algorithm is that it reduces the number of iterations of the main loop by the size of the blocks. We originally split the work between threads by dividing the lines of blocks between the processing cores. However the algorithm has a cubic complexity, thus the increase in the number of lines will be much slower than the full load increase, and we already divided the number of iterations by the block size. In the extreme case, we may end up with more processors available than lines of blocks, of very poor work splitting. For example, our test machine has 48 cores. If we consider matrices of size 6400×6400 split in blocks of size 64×64, we will have 100 lines to iterate over. Each processor will do the first two iterations, which will make 96 iterations in total. This will leave 4 iterations, so 44 cores will be idle during these last iterations, wasting 30 percent of the resources over the whole algorithm.

This can be easily improved by redesigning the loops. We have a loop iterating over the columns inside a loop iterating over the lines, but as all the lines and columns computations are independent, we can merge them in a single loop which will iterate on the number of blocks in the matrix only by modifying the variables that count the indexes. We parallelise this loop with OpenMP the same way as before, however the number of iterations will now scale exactly as the matrix size does, allowing for a better work splitting. If we consider the previous example on our test machine, it would now lead to ten thousands iterations to split between the 48 cores. They would each do 208 full iterations, then 32 processors will be idle on the last iteration, thus leading to a minimal waste of 0.36 percent of the whole available processing time.

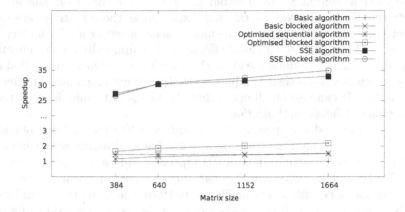

Fig. 1. Measured speedups of the various algorithms on a single processor

5 Experiments

The speedup times are statistically evaluated using the procedure described in [15]. Every execution on a given set of algorithms and parameters are independently repeated 30 times, then a statistical evaluation is performed between two sets of execution times to compute a median speedup and a confidence level in that speedup. All the results presented in this section were validated with a minimum confidence level of 95%.

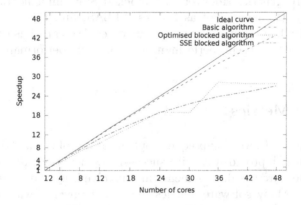

Fig. 2. Relative scaling of the various parallel algorithms on a multi-core system

We measured the speedup times obtained by our optimisations on various matrix sizes. These measures were first conducted on a Intel Core2 Duo T9300 processor running at 2.50GHz, using a core. We observe in figure 1 that all our modifications always lead to at least a minimal speedup, thus we can effectively consider them as optimisations. The blocked versions of the algorithms are not very effective for small matrices, this was expected as those matrices are small enough to already benefit from the memory cache, however as the matrix size increases they become more and more effective. We empirically found well-suited sizes for the blocks by running the algorithms with square blocks that fitted into the lowest cache level and then by adjusting their sizes with increments of the size of a cache line. It can also be observed that the use of SSE units is consistently the single most efficient optimisation.

Next, we measured the speedup time obtained when parallelising our algorithms over several computing cores (figure 2). These measures were conducted on our 48 cores test machine (four AMD Opteron dodeca-core processors running at 2.2GHz). The basic algorithm has almost a perfect linear scaling. As it accesses the memory with a very inefficient pattern, the memory bus and cache hierarchy can easily feed all the processors with the data they need to process. The blocked algorithm show good scaling at the beginning, but worsens as the number of computing cores increases. This was expected since, as the number of cores increases, we will be more likely to have several cores trying to access the memory at the same time. A solution to improve this situation would be to create a mechanism to finely control the placement of the blocks in order to maximise their reuse inside the various level of caches, but this would be very specific to the architecture. Although the blocked algorithms do not scale as well as the basic one, it should be noted that the single core SSE blocked algorithm is already faster than the basic algorithm parallelised over 48 cores.

We compared our results with the ATLAS [16] library. This is a high-performance linear algebra library which implements very hardware-specific code and auto-tuning. Our implementations could not be expected to run as fast, as our optimisations are generic. However, the blocked SSE implementation showed to be between a third and half as fast as ATLAS, and this result appeared to be consistent when scaling over numerous cores. We can thus consider that this algorithm offers decent performances in a high performance multi-core environment.

6   Software Metrics

We have implemented several subsequent optimisations of the matrix multiplication algorithm which provided us with successively increased speedups. Now we would like to measure the development time involved, by the mean of a suited software metric. Many software metrics exist that cover a wide range of usages. High-level tools such as function point analysis [1] of the constructive cost model [10] are often used in software conception in order to estimate the development cost needed to create an application based on the functionalities it will provide to its target user. This does not suite us as we want to compare several implementations which provide exactly the same functionality but with different performances. Other metrics analyse the actual behaviour of the application, such as the cyclomatic complexity [11] which builds a graph of the possible flows of execution and exhibit some characteristic measures of this graph. Again, this does not really well suit us as we may expect to have very few – if none at all – differences in the graph of the various implementation of a same algorithm. What we need here is a metric that measures the actual code written for each implementation. Some basic metrics such as the number of lines of code (LOC) or the number of machine instructions can measure this, but they only give a very rough estimate. Halstead [8] proposed a set of metrics that apply to the source code of a program and give an estimate of the difficulty to write it. We will use these metrics, as they directly target our needs.

Halstead's metrics are based on the count of operators and operands in the code. However, there is no standardised definition of what is exactly considered as an operand or operator for any given language. We used a reasonable definition for C++ that may be summarises as this: Operands are typename, constant and user-defined identifiers. Operators are storage class specifiers (**static**, **virtual**, **inline**, ...), type qualifiers (**const**, **friend**, ...), C++ reserved instructions (for, if, struct,namespace, typename, ...) and all the usual arithmetic and logical operators (**+**, **==**, **&&**, **->**, ...). The delimiter ; and pairs of parenthesis are also considered operators, as well as all function calls.

We can apply those definitions on each implementation to obtain four basic measures (table 1). Given those measures, we can calculate the set of Halstead metrics (table 2). The last metric, Effort (E), gives a value that is directly proportional to the estimated development time. Applying those metrics on each implementation of the algorithm gives the results in table 3.

Table 1. Halstead measures

N_1	total number of operators
N_2	total number of operands
η_1	number of distinct operators
η_2	number of distinct operands

Table 2. Halstead metrics

η	$\eta_1 + \eta_2$	Program vocabulary
N	$N_1 + N_2$	Program length
V	$N \times \log_2 \eta$	Volume
D	$\frac{\eta_1}{2} \times \frac{N_2}{\eta_2}$	Difficulty
E	$D \times V$	Effort

As expected, the basic algorithm is straightforward and has a really low cost. Its optimized version is in the same order of magnitude, which is coherent as only a temporary variable is added and used. The SSE algorithm needs an effort several dozen times higher than the basic algorithm. This value is coherent with the amount of work needed to implement this algorithm, and can even be considered underestimated. Indeed, this set of metrics was designed with languages such as fortran or assembler in mind which had a limited vocabulary that could be assumed to be mastered by the developer. We can assume that the standard C++ operators are mastered by the developer, but using SSE instructions often requires some additional learning, and conceiving an efficient algorithm using them is more difficult due to their parallel nature. In our particular case, we also tried different variants of the algorithm, but we could have their cost accounted for if we measured them separately. On the other hand, parallelising those algorithms with OpenMP has a minimal cost since we just have to parallelise the

Table 3. Metrics applied

Algorithm	η_1	η_2	η	N_1	N_2	N	V	D	E
Seq*	16 (+2)	11 (+3)	27 (+5)	52 (+2)	33 (+3)	85(+5)	404 (450)	24,0 (23,1)	9k (10k)
Seq opti	17 (+2)	14 (+3)	31 (+5)	60 (+2)	40 (+3)	100(+5)	495 (543)	24,3 (24,0)	12k (13k)
SSE	26 (+2)	24 (+3)	50 (+5)	408 (+2)	328 (+3)	736(+5)	4154 (4284)	177,7 (171,6)	738k (735k)
Blocked algorithms									
Seq	26 (+3)	27 (+5)	53 (+8)	224 (+9)	177 (+28)	401 (+37)	2297 (2598)	85,2 (92,9)	196k (241k)
Seq opti	27 (+3)	30 (+5)	57 (+8)	232 (+9)	184 (+28)	416 (+37)	2426 (2728)	82,8 (90,9)	201k (248k)
SSE	36 (+3)	40 (+5)	76 (+8)	580 (+9)	572 (+28)	1152 (+37)	7198 (7600)	257,4 (260,0)	1852k (1976k)
Blocking	24 (+3)	24 (+5)	48 (+8)	172 (+7)	144 (+25)	316 (+32)	1765 (2021)	72,0 (78,7)	127k (159k)

* In parenthesis: additional cost of OMP version.

outermost loop by adding a single pragma. The calculated effort is even a bit smaller for the SSE algorithm, this is a little bias of the metric: the Difficulty value depends on the ratio $\frac{N_2}{\eta_2}$ and adding three operands that will occur only once has a bigger relative impact on η_2 than N_2. The blocked versions of the three algorithms need a much bigger effort than their unblocked counterparts, which was quite predictible. However, if we consider the blocking algorithm that divides the matrices into blocks and multiplies them, it is completely separated from the previous algorithms which are called to multiply the blocks. We can thus consider only the effort needed to produce the blocking algorithm, as it adds on top of the existing algorithms. If taken alone, the blocking algorithm needs an effort approximately ten times higher than the optimized sequential algorithm, but this is still only a fraction of the effort needed for the SSE. Parallelising it with OpenMP has an non-negligible cost (25% more effort) ; this is coherent since in addition to parallelising the main loop, we also have to set up critical sections to solve concurrent write accesses to the blocks.

We can then put in comparison the development costs and the obtained speedups. The optimisation on the sequential algorithm is reasonably efficient, as the effort needed to develop it is minor, while providing around 50% more performance. The blocking algorithm, doesn't seem as efficient : it needs ten times the effort while only providing a 40% increase in performance. Moreover, when combined with SSE we only obtain those gains with big matrices (3000*3000 or bigger). Although, this algorithm allows a good scaling when parallelising with OpenMP, so it is still worth the effort in this case. A more interesting comparison is between the SSE and OpenMP codes, which provide two different and complementary ways of parallelism. The SSE algorithm has a very consequent cost, 80 times more than the optimized sequential algorithm, but provides speedups in the same order of magnitude around 30. On the other hand, converting the algorithms to OpenMP has a very low cost and scales very well. On our 48 cores test machine, we obtained speedups between 28 to 42 (depending on the algorithm being parallelized), which are similar to the gains obtained with the SSE algorithm. If someone has access to a computer with several computing cores, the speedup obtained by parallelising with OpenMP is much more efficient than developing an SSE algorithm if we consider the development time involved.

During the development phase, we intuitively started by optimising the computations through SSE, then we considered cache optimisation with the blocked algorithm, and finally parallelised it with OpenMP. With hindsight, our results show that this approach was not the most efficient. Over a large number of cores, parallelising the algorithm with OpenMP provides the best speedup, while also having the lowest development cost. Optimising the basic sequential algorithm is the next most efficient move as it provides some speedup at an almost negligible cost. Then we should implement the SSE algorithm as it provides a huge speedup despite its developmenet cost. The blocking algorithm as a lower cost than the SSE, but provides only a small fraction of its speedup and thus should be implemented lastly.

7   Conclusion and Future Work

We have described the algorithm of matrix multiplication and have applied several optimisations in order to render it efficient for high performance computing on many-cores architectures. These optimisations are generic and portable: all processors have been fitted with cache memory for a long time, and this will continue due to the ever widening gap between processors and memory speed. Vector units are also a strong trend (such as the AVX units recently introduced on Intel's processors), so are the multi-core processors which have even reached low-power hand-held devices. These optimisations can be understood without deep knowledge of the target architecture and represent a reasonable amount of code (according to the Halstead software metrics) while providing sensible speedups : several dozen times faster execution on a single CPU, and more than a thousand when parallelised over 48 cores.

We will continue this work by implementing this algorithm for GPUs using CUDA and OpenCL in order to investigate how those architectures compares with many-core CPUs and the difficulty involved. We will also study if they may be combined in an efficient hybrid implementation at a reasonable development cost.

As stated in the introduction 1, this work is a basis for our bigger project. The next major step will be to embed our linear algebra algorithms – as well as other common problems in scientific computations such as Fast Fourier Transform or N-bodies interactions – in a high-level language. Our final goal is to provide good performance for the user while minimising its development effort. We are planning to achieve this by extending the OSL library [9].

Acknowledgements. Joeffrey Legaux is supported by a PhD grant from the *Conseil Général du Loiret*. This work is partly supported by the SPEED project[2], funded by the *Conseil Général du Loiret*.

---

[2] http://traclifo.univ-orleans.fr/SPEED/

References

1. Albrecht, A.: Measuring Application Development Productivity. In: Press, I.B.M. (ed.) IBM Application Development Symp., pp. 83–92 (October 1979)
2. Cole, M.: Algorithmic Skeletons: Structured Management of Parallel Computation. MIT Press (1989), http://homepages.inf.ed.ac.uk/mic/Pubs
3. Coppersmith, D., Winograd, S.: Matrix multiplication via arithmetic progressions. Journal of Symbolic Computation 9(3), 251–280 (1990), http://www.sciencedirect.com/science/article/pii/S0747717108800132
4. D'Alberto, P., Nicolau, A.: Adaptive strassen and atlas's dgemm: A fast square-matrix multiply for modern high-performance systems. In: Proceedings of the Eighth International Conference on High-Performance Computing in Asia-Pacific Region. HPCASIA 2005, p. 45. IEEE Computer Society, Washington, DC (2005), doi:10.1109/HPCASIA.2005.18
5. Dongarra, J.J., Du Croz, J., Hammarling, S., Duff, I.S.: A set of level 3 basic linear algebra subprograms. ACM Trans. Math. Softw. 16(1), 1–17 (1990), http://doi.acm.org/10.1145/77626.79170
6. Dongarra, J.J., Luszczek, P., Petitet, A.: The linpack benchmark: past, present and future. Concurrency and Computation: Practice and Experience 15(9), 803–820 (2003), doi:10.1002/cpe.728
7. Gonzáalez-Vélez, H., Leyton, M.: A survey of algorithmic skeleton frameworks: highlevel structured parallel programming enablers. Software, Practrice & Experience 40(12), 1135–1160 (2010)
8. Halstead, M.H.: Elements of Software Science. Operating and programming systems series. Elsevier Science Ltd. (1977)
9. Javed, N., Loulergue, F.: Parallel Programming and Performance Predictability with Orléans Skeleton Library. In: International Conference on High Performance Computing and Simulation (HPCS), pp. 257–263. IEEE (2011)
10. Kemerer, C.F.: An empirical validation of software cost estimation models. Commun. ACM 30(5), 416–429 (1987)
11. Mccabe, T.J.: A complexity measure. In: ICSE 1976: Proceedings of the 2nd International Conference on Software Engineering. IEEE Computer Society Press, Los Alamitos (1976)
12. Peleg, A., Weiser, U.: MMX technology extension to the intel architecture. IEEE Micro 16(4), 42–50 (1996)
13. Strassen, V.: Gaussian elimination is not optimal. Numerische Mathematik 13, 354–356 (1969), doi:10.1007/BF02165411, 10.1007/BF02165411
14. Strey, A., Bange, M.: Performance Analysis of Intel's MMX and SSE: A Case Study. In: Sakellariou, R., Keane, J.A., Gurd, J.R., Freeman, L. (eds.) Euro-Par 2001. LNCS, vol. 2150, pp. 142–147. Springer, Heidelberg (2001)
15. Touati, S.A.A., Worms, J., Briais, S.: The Speedup Test. Tech. Rep. inria-00443839, INRIA Saclay - Ile de France (2010), http://hal.inria.fr/inria-00443839
16. Whaley, R.C., Petitet, A., Dongarra, J.J.: Automated empirical optimization of software and the ATLAS project. Parallel Computing 27(1-2), 3–35 (2001); also available as University of Tennessee LAPACKWorking Note #147, UT-CS-00-448 (2000), www.netlib.org/lapack/lawns/lawn147.ps

Fault Tolerance Logical Network Properties of Irregular Graphs

Christophe Cérin[1], Camille Coti[1], and Michel Koskas[2]

[1] Université Paris 13 - PRES Sorbonne Paris Cité, LIPN UMR CNRS 7030,
99 avenue Jean-Baptiste Clément, F-93430 Villetaneuse, France
{cerin,coti}@lipn.fr
[2] Institut National de la Recherche en Agronomie, Département de mathématique,
UMR 518 (MIA. INRA), 16, rue Claude Bernard, F-75231 Paris Cedex 05, France
michel.koskas@agroparistech.fr

Abstract. Assume a desktop grid middleware or a deployed cloud in-frastructure that are both based on a large number of volunteers for computational-intensive applications or business applications. In this case, the Internet is the communication layer; hence, the communication graph is not regular. Scalability and fault tolerance issues are implicitly present on any platform. For instance, the overlay network that must be built to control the application as part of the run-time support system needs to be scalable and fault tolerant. In this paper, we compute fault tolerance properties of large, irregular graphs that may be used as models for the Internet. In a previous work, we presented algorithms and a framework for computing fault tolerance properties of different variants of randomly-generated binomial regular graphs (BMG). In the present paper we compute the metrics of the Node and Link connectivities and the fault diameter for four benchmarks. We also compare our implementation of the diameter computation with the work of Magnien *et al.*

Keywords: Large scale systems, models for overlay networks, fault tolerance, performance evaluation, performance measurement, graph algorithms.

1 Introduction

1.1 Context

Desktop Grids and Volunteer Computing are well-known terms related to the notion of computing on loosely connected resources, usually personal computers over the Internet but also sometimes clusters, that are controlled by their own-ers. These terms appeared in the Internet and research community at the end of the 90s. Nowadays, this type of computing platform forms one of the largest dis-tributed computing systems, and currently provides scientists with PetaFLOPS from hundreds of thousands of hosts[1].

---

[1] Check the list of available BOINC projects on the Web at
http://boinc.berkeley.edu/projects.php.

Y. Xiang et al. (Eds.): ICA3PP 2012, Part I, LNCS 7439, pp. 377–391, 2012.
© Springer-Verlag Berlin Heidelberg 2012

SlapOS [20] is an open-source grid operating system for distributed cloud computing. SlapOS combines grid computing and Enterprise Resource Planning (ERP) to provide Infrastructure as a Service (IaaS), Platform as a Service (PaaS) and Software as a Service (SaaS) through a simple, unified API that everyone can learn in a couple of minutes. SlapOS opens new perspectives for research in the area of resilience and security on the Cloud because it is based on similar concepts than Desktop Grids. Indeed, the data centers are located on the home PCs of volunteers.

The extremely large number of nodes implies that faults (for instance hardware component failures) should be handled at any layer of the software stack (middleware, programming libraries, algorithmic level). Distributed problems on a large number of volatile resources with asynchronous communications are difficult to handle; some of them have even been proved impossible.

In traditional, tightly-coupled parallel applications, the survivability of the application is dependent upon the survivability of *all the resources* used by the application. When a single node fails, the application fails; on the other hand, in Desktop Grid computing the failure of a single client has no impact on the survivability of the other clients. The main reason is that Desktop Grid applications are follow the Bag-of-Tasks pattern (independent tasks) that are duplicated in order to tolerate failures. But, what happens if a major disaster appears, for instance if floods devastate eastern Europe and a large zone becomes disconnected from the Internet. For example in 2011, whole of Armenia was disconnected from the Internet by a simple copper wire theft[2].

In this context, we propose in this article, algorithms and techniques to evaluate the 'quality' of the virtual topology we use in Distributed applications or in some flavors of Cloud applications. We compute metrics that define the quality according to usual definitions [9, 3, 8, 12]. Among the most useful properties, we compute the Node and Link connectivity and the fault diameters. Experiments are performed on large irregular graphs and we explain why it is challenging.

1.2   Motivations and Paper'S Organization

Failures are inherent to large scale systems [17]. Let s be the number of successful executions and f be the number of failures. Let $n = s + f$ be the number of executions we start on a large scale system. Then the probability of failure is $\frac{f}{s+f}$. As the number of hardware components increases when using large scale systems, so does the probability of failure, for a same n. Researchers made the observation that to ensure an efficient and safe execution of applications on large scale systems, a scalable and fault tolerance framework ought to be used.

Consider now an example. Parallel applications are supported by a run-time environment, which is in charge of deploying, supporting and monitoring the application on remote computing resources. The basic services it provides to the

---

[2] http://www.guardian.co.uk/world/2011/apr/06/
georgian-woman-cuts-web-access

application include deploying the processes on the available resources, enabling communications between processes, I/O forwarding and monitoring.

This run-time environment is a distributed overlay network spanning over the available computing resources that can route out-of-band messages (*i.e.,* signaling messages) for peer-to-peer or collective communications. These communications are not directly used by the parallel application, but they are used internally to support the application. Hence, the core of a run-time environment is a communication infrastructure used to communicate these control and signaling messages between nodes.

Scalable and fault tolerant framework [3] may concern the run-time environment or the applications themselves. Implementing a scalable and fault tolerant component in connection with the application is not a good idea because this leads to develop a component for each application. It is preferable to develop it as a component of the run-time environment, and if possible inside a run-time environment that supports the communication library, such as MPI (Message Passing Interface [6, 7], which is the *de facto* standard for programming parallel applications).

Hence, the run-time environment can be extended to feature fault tolerance capabilities. The overlay network itself must be able to recover its state from failures and maintain an acceptable quality of service during the recovery phase (self-healing property). It also needs to provide the application with some features that will allow it to recover from the failure and proceeds with an application-based fault tolerance mechanism.

Scalable and fault tolerant framework even for Desktop Grid applications may also concern the building of dedicated "control signaling networks" for collecting or monitoring information (which node is alive? what is the energy consumption of these nodes? what is the load of node X?), for gathering simulation results, for saving checkpoint information.

Hence, the topology of the communication infrastructure of the overlay network is highly critical. It determines the efficiency of peer-to-peer communications, the scalability of the overlay network itself, and the resilience or self-healing properties it can have.

The aim of this paper is to propose efficient parallel algorithms and use cases for computing fault tolerant properties of irregular topologies that cannot be analyzed by exact methods. Those topologies are modeling a communication and control infrastructure network, and re not exclusively dedicated for massively parallel applications or for Desktop Grid applications. For the engineer, and regarding how much control or how many signaling processes he wants, some fault tolerance properties can be more or less relaxed. For instance, the diameter of the graph may be a more important criteria when we have to collect information about the temperature of a machine occasionally than when we want to implement a collective communication primitive or an efficient deployment framework on top of the Internet.

Thus, the contributions of this paper are new mathematical results concerning the fault tolerance properties of benchmarks that map to large irregular graphs and also parallel algorithms for computing the relevant metrics. The objectives are: how "good" are the topologies regarding fault tolerance and how to compute efficiently the metrics.

The organization of this paper is as follows. Section 2 recalls the useful definitions. Section 3 gives details about the fault tolerance properties we are studying in this paper. In this section we also give refinements of algorithms initially introduced in [5] and we compare the approach of Magnien *et al* in [16] for computing the diameter with our approach. Section 4 presents experiments with large irregular graphs. Section 5 concludes the paper.

2   Binomial Graphs for Introducing the Problems

2.1   Introduction

In [5] we presented the computation of fault tolerant properties of one class of regular graphs, namely, binomial graphs. Originally, the binomial graph logical structure was introduced in [4, 2] with the purpose of satisfying fault tolerant requirements for the communication layer of run-time environments. In general, scalable logical topologies ought to meet the following requirements: (a) low degree – the degree of a node is the number of links incident to the node; (b) regular graph – every node has the same degree such that a 'single' algorithm should be designed to route message for instance; (c) low diameter – the diameter of a graph is the longest shortest path between any two nodes and it gives a bound on the complexity of routing messages; (d) symmetric graph – the average inter-nodal distance should be the same from any source node; (e) no restriction in terms of numbers of nodes to support large scale application.

A BMG (Binomial Graph) is an undirected graph $G = (V, E)$ where V is a set of Vertices ; $|V| = n$ and E is a set of links (edges) ; $|E| = m$. Each node $i \in V$, and $i = 1, 2, \cdots n$ has links to a set of nodes U, where $U = i \pm 1, i \pm 2, \cdots, i \pm 2^k | 2^k \leq n$ in circular space *i.e.*, node i is connected to its right and to its left to a node at distance 2^k for all $0 \leq k \leq \lfloor \log n \rfloor$.

In [5] we have introduced a variant of binomial graphs. Formally, a probabilistic BMG is a graph where we randomly select n vertices, then from each vertex, we graft links according to a logarithmic method. Intuitively, we try to keep as much as possible the good properties of BMG regarding its structure, whereas some of them are relaxed. In [5] we consider three methods for generating the graphs:

1. Model 0 is the original BMG;
2. Model 1: we graft exactly as with the original BMG. Node i, randomly selected, has links to a set of nodes U, where $U = i \pm 1, i \pm 2, \cdots, i \pm 2^k | 2^k \leq n$ in circular space. The fact is that since we do trials for the choice of the node, this kind of BMG has no more links than the original BMG;
3. Model 2: the process is as with Model 1, but we select less links when we have to graft links. The number of nodes is divided by two at each iteration. With this process, we get less links than with Model 1;

Notice that to avoid to have more than one connected component in the graphs, we also connect, for processes 1 and 2, each node to its neighbor, the one at its right and the one at its left (node i is connected to $i - 1$ and $i + 1$).

2.2 Terminology about the Structures of Graphs

The minimum degree δ_{min} of a graph is the smallest node degree, while the maximum degree δ_{max} of a graph is the largest node degree. If every node has the same degree ($\delta_{min} = \delta_{max}$) the graph is *regular*. A regular graph also means that all the nodes are equivalent and for each node, we can use symmetrically the same routing and fault-handling algorithms instead of managing special cases. However, notice that the graph of the Internet is obviously not a regular one. The original BMG graph is a regular graph but not the graphs produced with models 1 and 2.

One important question is: how to compute some properties of graphs with a large number of nodes and vertices? One interesting property is the diameter, which gives a bound on the number of steps required to route a message between two nodes. Computing the diameter of a graph is time-consuming, as we explain in the next section which is devoted to the setting of properties of our graphs.

3 Fault Tolerant Properties and New Mathematical Results

3.1 Preliminary Remark

A mathematical computation of properties describing the graph, for instance the diameter, may consider the shortest path length computation which is difficult for the following reason: the stochastic model we have used in model 1 and 2 implies that many parameters of the graph (average degree and others structural properties) have no closed form that could be estimated easily, in average and in the worst case. This explains why we have introduced in [5] heuristics for the various computations. Some of them are bounded (with lower and upper bounds).

3.2 Definition of the Properties

We now explain the computation of specific metrics related to fault tolerance, such as connectivity and fault diameter of large scale graphs.

The *Node connectivity* κ of a graph is defined as the minimum number of nodes of which removal can result in a graph with at least two connected components.

The Node connectivity metric can be computed according to the following optimizations: when we remove a vertex we have also to adjust the adjacency lists of the nodes that are present in the adjacency list of the node we remove. If we maintain an ordered list of vertices and another ordered list for the adjacency lists, we can accomplish the work according to a logarithmic factor in the size of the adjacency lists and also in $\log(n)$. Moreover, instead of renumbering the whole graph after removing a vertex, which would require an $\mathcal{O}(n^2)$ time complexity, it is sufficient that the nodes be marked as not present. This marking is done in constant time.

As you can notice, many programming optimizations are possible and they are dependent of the initial choice of the graph's representation. We do not give more details here and we invite the reader to examine the codes[3] corresponding to the metrics.

The *Link connectivity* λ of a graph is defined as the minimal number of links of which removal can result in disconnecting the network. The algorithm presented in [5] is introduced as algorithm 1 in this paper.

Algorithm 1. Link connectivity as published in [5]
___
1: **for** $i = 1$ to δ_{min} **do**
2:     **for** NumChoice $= 1$ to MaxChoiceLinks **do**
3:         choose i links;
4:         remove the links;
5:         **if** graph is not connected **then**
6:             **return** i
7:         **end if**
8:     **end for**
9: **end for**

Note that in Algorithm 1, we can stop the iteration at δ_{min} which is low in practice with BMG like graphs.

The *fault diameter* F is the largest diameter of the network when there are $\kappa - 1$ node failures (a maximum number of failure nodes before the network becomes bipartite, κ being the node connectivity).

Algorithm 2. Fault diameter as published in [5]
___
1: **for** NumChoice $= 1$ to MaxChoiceDiameter **do**
2:     choose $\kappa - 1$ vertices;
3:     remove the vertices and compute the diameter;
4:     keep the maximal value for diameters;
5: **end for**

Note that Algorithm 2 does not implies exhaustive searches, so it is not an exact method for computing the associated metric. In general, the exact time for executing the computation depends on a parameter describing the graph (for

---

[3] The current release of our implementation is available on
http://www.lipn.fr/~cerin/code.tar.bz2

instance the minimal degree in the Link connectivity algorithms). In practice for BMGs, since the degree is small comparing to n, we may drastically decrease the execution time of the computation comparing to a full enumeration of combinations over all the vertices or links. Algorithms provide an estimate of the associated metric: it is an heuristic method, bounded by δ_{min} for instance.

Here again, it seems difficult to have a closed formula for the different complexities. However, the exact computation of the Node connectivity metric for the initial algorithm can be bounded by the sum of binomial coefficient computation (because we have to compute n times the choice of i vertices among n in all possible ways) times the time complexity of detecting if we have at least 2 connected components. The complexity is exponential and we cannot expect to solve the problem by exhaustive searches, hence our heuristics that do sampling over all the combinations are more realistic.

The last property we encounter in the papers related to the domain is about resilience. There are two classes of graph G distinguished by the relationship between the fault diameter F and the diameter D of the graph [13], called *strongly resilient* and *weakly resilient*. A graph is considered strongly resilient if there exists a constant ϕ such as $F(G) \leq D(G) + \phi$ for all graph sizes n, where $n \in \mathbb{N}$. A graph is considered weakly resilient if there exists a constant ϕ such as $F(G) \leq D(G) \times \phi$ for all graph sizes n, where $n \in \mathbb{N}$. The original BMG is considered as strongly resilient by Angskun, Bosilca and Dongarra [2] with $\phi = 2$. Note that the proof is made with experiments and it is not a formal one. Under the experimental conditions of the paper, the result indicates that, even under faulty conditions, the performance of BMG will not be severely degraded.

3.3 Computational Issues and Related Work for Diameter Computation

In this section, we explain one important computational issue and solutions. The distance $d(i, j)$ between a node i and a node j in a graph is defined as the length of the shortest path from i to j in the graph. The diameter D of a graph is given by $\max\{d(i, j)\}$ over all possible pairs (i, j) of nodes in the graph. The diameter D is the longest shortest path between any two nodes in the graph.

It is not difficult to see that in the case of BMG, which is a regular graph, the diameter is in $\mathcal{O}(\log n)$, and as pointed out in [4, 2], the BMG has the lowest diameter among Hypercube [15], Chord [21], 4-ary Hypercube topologies [?, 8]. This property explains why we have studied, initially, the BMG.

But computing all distances from one vertex to all the others has $\Theta(m)$ time and space costs using a breadth-first search (BFS). In order to compute the diameter, one has to compute the distance between all pairs of vertices, which therefore involve a $\Theta(nm)$ time and a $\Theta(m)$ space cost using a BFS. Using matrix products, one may achieve the computation in $\mathcal{O}(n^{2.376}\text{polylog } n)$ time and $\mathcal{O}(n^2)$ space [1, 19]. Therefore, BFS approach is too slow for graphs with a large number of vertices, and matrix approach has also a supplementary and prohibitive space cost.

Different solutions have been proposed in a recent past as well as implementations to solve this problem. We can mention [11, 10] but we do prefer to introduce the work and the implementation [16] done by Magnien, Latapy and Habib. The key points in the methods used by Magnien is to compute lower and upper bounds and to iterate them from different initial vertices in order to obtain tighter bounds, with a linear cost for each step. Authors also use heuristics to choose in an intelligent way the vertices able to provide with a tight bound.

Notice that to our knowledge, the metrics, in particular the computation of the metrics related to fault tolerance has not been investigated in the context of large scale non-regular graphs.

3.4   New Approaches and Results for Computing the Fault Tolerant Metrics

In this section, we first improve the algorithms for Node Connectivity and Link Connectivity according to a dichotomous approach as follows then we focus on the diameter computation.

At the beginning of the Node and Link Connectivity algorithms, we remove $n/2$ vertices. If the graph is not connected, then we check the connectivity property between 1 and $n/2$ vertices. If the graph is still connected, we check the property on the interval $n/2$ and n vertices. As with any dichotomous approach, we stop the process as soon as the 'lower bound' crosses the 'upper bound'. The corresponding algorithm is Algorithm 3. In doing this we limit the use of arbitrary constants to bound the iterations number.

Notice that with Algorithm 3, we can replace the word 'vertices' by 'edges' when we have to remove objects in order to get the Link connectivity. Technically speaking, we have also to replace the call for replacing a vertex by the call for replacing an edge.

Notice that for the computation of Link and Node Connectivity we have to check if the graph is connected. We have implemented this operation as follows. The key ideas of the Algorithm 4 and the forthcoming algorithms are in the intensive use of the BFS (Breadth First Search) algorithm slightly modified.

The idea is to start from a vertex and to consider its neighbors and their neighbors and so on. But the seen vertices are pruned of the list of vertices that we have to visit. So we stop the process when there is no new neighbor. The new algorithm for computing the connected components of a graph is the Algorithm 4.

Starting with this idea, we have also implemented the IAmconnected() procedure for checking if a graph is connected. Here again, the idea is to start from a (random) vertex and we visit its connected component according to the previous technique. If all the vertices have been visited, we return True, otherwise we return False.

We have also revisited the computation of the diameter done by Magnien in [16] according to the following algorithm (see Algorithm 5).

Algorithm 3. New Node connectivity algorithm

Require: Low = 1 ; Up = MAX.
Require: (MAX = NbVertices or MinDegree).
1: set $K = \log n$
2: **while** $Up - Low > 1$ **do**
3:    m = (Low + Up) / 2
4:    **repeat**
5:       Remove m vertices (or edges) randomly
6:       **if** graph not connected **then**
7:          Up = m
8:       **end if**
9:    **until** K times
10:   **if** all graphs are connected **then**
11:      Low = m
12:   **end if**
13: **end while**
14: return Low + 1

Algorithm 4. New implementation for checking if a graph is connected

1: Start with the first non visited vertex
2: Visit its connected component according to the previous technique
3: Restart until there is no more vertice to visit
4: (that is to say that all vertices have been visited)
5: The number of times we do step 3 = number of connected components

Algorithm 5. New algorithm for the diameter

1: set $Diameter = 0$
2: **repeat**
3:    Select randomly a vertex, name it 'current vertex'
4:    and mark it as visited. Set 'Current diameter' to 0
5:    **while** current vertices have non visited neighbors **do**
6:       a) Compute the non visited neighbors of current vertices
7:       b) Replace the current vertices by their non visited vertices
8:       c) Add 1 to 'Current diameter'
9:    **end while**
10:   **if** 'Current diameter' > 'Diameter' **then**
11:      'Diameter' = 'Current diameter'
12:   **end if**
13: **until** 'some' vertices have been visited
14: return 'Diameter'

Here again, the tricky part is to accelerate the computation in visiting the neighbors of the neighbors that have not yet been visited. It is a strategy similar to the 'doubling strategy' for the PRAM (Parallel Random Access Memory) paradigm.

The diameter computation is used in the fault diameter computation that is not modified since our initial approach in [5]. See Algorithm 2 for the fault diameter computation.

4   Experimental Results

We used the data set available online[4] and provided by Clémence Magnien and Matthieu Latapy. The online data set is composed of 4 files that lead to a wide variety of real-world graphs coming from different contexts. It may be considered as representative of the variety of cases that we found in complex network studies [14].

We use the following four benchmark files:

- An Internet topology graph (inet) obtained from traceroutes ran daily in 2005 by Skitter[5] from several scattered sources to almost one million destinations, leading to 1,719,037 vertices and 11,095,298 edges; The number of connected components is 23,378 and the largest one has 1,694,616 vertices and 11,094,209 edges. We compute the fault tolerant properties for that component characterized by a minimum degree of 1 and a maximum degree of 35455 and also after pruning vertices with a degree lower of equal to 1 (in this case, the graph has a number of vertices equal to 1,463,934 and the edge number is 10,863,527).
- A peer-to-peer graph (p2p) in which two peers are linked if one of them provided a file to the other in a measurement conducted on a large eDonkey server for a period of 47 hours in 2004[6], leading to 5,792,297 vertices and 142,038,401 edges; The number of connected components is 411,757 and the largest one has 5,380,491 vertices and 142,038,351 edges. We compute the fault tolerant properties for that component characterized by a minimum degree of 1 and a maximum degree of 15115 and also after pruning vertices with a degree lower of equal to 1 (in this case, the graph has a number of vertices equal to 4,705,668 and the edge number is 141,363,528, a minimum degree of 2 and a maximal degree of 15092).
- A web graph (web) containing the 39,459,925 web pages (vertices) and 783,027,125 links (edges) collected in the .uk domain during a measurement conducted in 2005 by WebGraph[7]; The number of connected components is 12,906 and the largest one has 39,252,879 vertices and 781,439,892 edges. We compute the fault tolerant properties for that component characterized

---

[4] See: http://data.complexnetworks.fr/Diameter/
[5] http://www.caida.org/tools/measurement/skitter/
[6] http://www-rp.lip6.fr/~latapy/P2P_data/
[7] http://webgraph.dsi.unimi.it/

by a minimum degree of 1 and a maximum degree of 1,776,858 and also after pruning vertices with a degree lower of equal to 1 (in this case, the graph has a number of vertices equal to 35,156,004 vertices and the edge number is 77,7343,017, a minimum degree of 2 and a maximal degree of 1,776,858).

– A traffic graph (ip) obtained from MetroSec[8] that captured each ip packet header routed by a given router during 24 hours, two ip addresses being linked if they appear in a packet as sender and destination, leading to 2,250,498 vertices and 19,394,216 edges; The number of connected components is 45 and the largest one has 2,250,046 vertices and 19,393,724 edges. We compute the fault tolerance properties for that component characterized by a minimum degree of 1 and a maximal degree of 259905; We also compute the properties after pruning the vertices of degree 1, leading to a graph with 417,189 vertices and 1,756,0867 edges. This last graph has a minimal degree of 2 and a maximal degree of 11,4826.

Table 1 shows the results for the diameter estimation in comparing our estimate with the estimates of Magnien and Latapy in [16]. We present two numbers, one for the diameter including all the vertices and one, between braces, corresponding to a pruning of vertices with a degree lower or equal to 1. Vertices of degree 1 are vertices corresponding to "end-users" so that pruning them may correspond to the study of the core-network topology. In fact, our code allows to study graphs pruned such that the degree of each node is greater to a given parameter. It is a refinement for the user.

Since Magnien and Latapy provide five bounds, we give them explicitly in Table 1. Lowest values are for lower bounds, highest values are for upper bounds on the diameter. We found that in any case, our estimates fit between the lower and upper bounds of Magnien because we try with only 15 vertices.

The originality of the Magnien's approach lies in the fact that there is a guarantee that the actual diameter is within the bounds they find, but there is no guarantee on the tightness of these bounds. The tricky part of Magnien's implementation is to start the estimate with vertices with low degrees because in that way, the underlying BFS tree has a much greater height than if we start with vertices with high degree. In another words, we have more chance to extend the distance between vertices.

We have also implemented this heuristic in our code. Our implementation is based on a quicksort-based algorithm for finding the k best degrees among all the vertices that have a degree lower or equal to a given bound. After this first step, we pick randomly k vertices for which we compute the diameter.

Table 2 presents our estimates on the major fault tolerance metrics, namely the Link and Node connectivity and the fault diameter when nodes with a degree equal to one are eliminated. As expected, the Link connectivity is low, showing that the graphs are not resilient. For instance, The value returned for the Link-connectivity by our algorithm is `LowerBound + 1` with `Lowerbound = 1 = ` δ_{min} hence the values equal to 2 (see the `Graph::LinkConnectivity ()` implementation). In fact, we are computing a lower bound and not a mean value.

---

[8] http://www2.laas.fr/METROSEC/

Table 1. Comparison between estimated diameters

	Magnien and Latapy results [16] tlb - dslb - hdtub - rtub - tub	Our results
inet	29-31-34-34-38	25 (24)
p2p	8-9-10-10-10	8 (7)
web	26-32-33-33-34	22 (23)
ip	9-9-9-9-10	8 (7)

Table 2. Metrics for Fault Tolerance ($\delta_{min} > 1$)

	Link co.	Node co.	Fault diameter
inet	2	18	24
p2p	2	1054	7
web	2	36	23
ip	2	391	7

The expected fault diameters would be estimated to the values of the diameters. The column for the Node connectivity parameters represents mean values. Hence, Table 2 demonstrates that the Node connectivity is a discriminant measure of fault-tolerance for Internet graphs.

Moreover, it is important to notice that our algorithms run in few hours (except for the web graph) for computing **all** the parameters of a single graph on a computing platform based on a node equipped with 512GB of RAM and with 40 cores (4 Intel Xeon E7-4850 at 2GHZ with 10 cores each). Memory usage of the fours programs running in parallel is about 96GB of RAM. The last version of our code is available upon request. It has been parallelized with OpenMP pragmas but experiments we made show that the main parts of our algorithms are intrinsically sequential.

At least, note that it is the first time, to our knowledge, that the metrics presented in this paper are computed for Internet graphs. As a consequence we do not provide a broad comparison in terms of execution times. We are only able to show some results about the diameter in terms of returned bounds provided by our method versus Magnien's method.

Moreover, we can also parameterize our code in such a way that all vertices with a degree lower than a given bound are eliminated before computing the metrics. In doing this, we offer to the user the possibility to examine the metrics of a graph representing what he considers as being the core of the network.

5   Conclusion

This paper presents estimators for two very useful graph metrics: diameter and connectivity. Then, we use these metrics in conjunction with previous research related to fault tolerance properties of different types of graphs. With these estimators, we compare the estimators against other published results using a publicly available suite of sample graphs, which represent various network topologies.

Some experimental results were expected, for instance the Link connectivity of the benchmark which is low for Internet. Fault diameters are quite similar to the diameters and the Node connectivity metrics, which is computed as a mean value, gives a good estimate of how the benchmarks are fault tolerant.

The algorithms described in this paper are for large, and irregular graphs, and are parallel probabilistic algorithms. Experimental results presented in Section 4 demonstrate that the algorithms work and compare favorably to previous approaches that required higher computational complexity.

It is the first time, to the best of our knowledge, that fault tolerant properties are exhibited for the benchmarks that map to large scale graphs. In particular we conducted the experiments on real life graphs extracted from the Internet.

The initial objective of this work is to evaluate the suitability of any regular topologies to be used as a basis for a resilient, scalable communication infrastructure. Examples of such infrastructure are the run-time environment of a parallel, distributed system on top of the Internet or any controlling network (for monitoring loads, temperature of CPUs). In this paper, we demonstrate that our implementation is also good for working on irregular structures and large scale graphs.

Based on our experiments, we conclude that our methods and algorithms are operational for estimating the metrics of fault tolerant overlay networks. One issue would be to compute them in a distributing way, we mean with local interaction, only.

The core objective of this work is related to Internet computing. In the future we will focus on a holistic approach to explore and to understand the 'behaviors' of complex systems such as clouds or large scale grids in case of disasters. The work will focus on one aspect of safety (the condition of being protected against physical, social, financial, political, or consequences of failure, damage, error, accidents) in Cloud industry. Safety is part of the security area. The scenario we envision is the following one: floods devastate eastern Europe. Internet is no longer available in Dresden area. Data centers are destroyed.

Some rescue missions are sent with tablet PCs or Net PCs. How can we restore access to the Cloud despite such disaster? How to measure the quality of the network being reconstructed? The issue is about resilience which is the ability of a system or network architecture to continue to operate in case of failure and the computational methods of this article will serve to estimate and to drive the rebuilding of a new topology.

References

[1] Alon, N., Galil, Z., Margalit, O., Naor, M.: Witnesses for boolean matrix multiplication and for shortest paths. In: FOCS, pp. 417–426. IEEE (1992)

[2] Angskun, T., Bosilca, G., Dongarra, J.: Binomial Graph: A Scalable and Fault-Tolerant Logical Network Topology. In: Stojmenovic, I., Thulasiram, R.K., Yang, L.T., Jia, W., Guo, M., de Mello, R.F. (eds.) ISPA 2007. LNCS, vol. 4742, pp. 471–482. Springer, Heidelberg (2007)

[3] Angskun, T., Fagg, G.E., Bosilca, G., Pješivac–Grbović, J., Dongarra, J.: Scalable Fault Tolerant Protocol for Parallel Runtime Environments. In: Mohr, B., Träff, J.L., Worringen, J., Dongarra, J. (eds.) PVM/MPI 2006. LNCS, vol. 4192, pp. 141–149. Springer, Heidelberg (2006)

[4] Angskun, T., Fagg, G.E., Bosilca, G., Pjesivac-Grbovic, J., Dongarra, J.: Self-healing network for scalable fault-tolerant runtime environments. Future Generation Comp. Syst. 26(3), 479–485 (2010)

[5] Cérin, C., Koskas, M., Lei, Y.: Computing properties of large scalable and fault-tolerant logical networks. In: De Souza, A.F., Catabriga, L. (eds.) IEEE SBAC. IEEE (2011)

[6] Message Passing Interface Forum. MPI: A message-passing interface standard. Technical Report UT-CS-94-230, Department of Computer Science, University of Tennessee, Tue, May 22, 101 17:44:55 GMT (April 1994)

[7] Geist, A., Gropp, W.D., Huss-Lederman, S., Lumsdaine, A., Lusk, E.L., Saphir, W., Skjellum, A., Snir, M.: MPI-2: Extending the Message-Passing Interface. In: Fraigniaud, P., Mignotte, A., Bougé, L., Robert, Y. (eds.) Euro-Par 1996. LNCS, vol. 1123, pp. 128–135. Springer, Heidelberg (1996)

[8] Ghafoor, A., Bashkow, T.R.: A study of odd graphs as fault-tolerant interconnection networks. IEEE Transactions on Computers 40(2), 225–232 (1991)

[9] Labarta, B.M.J., Miller, B.P., Schulz, M.: Program development for extreme-scale computing. Technical report, Dagstuhl Seminar 10181 (2010), http://www.dagstuhl.de/10181

[10] Kang, U., Tsourakakis, C.E., Appel, A.P., Faloutsos, C., Leskovec, J.: Radius plots for mining tera-byte scale graphs: Algorithms, patterns, and observations. In: SDM, pp. 548–558. SIAM (2010)

[11] Kang, U., Tsourakakis, C.E., Faloutsos, C.: Pegasus: mining peta-scale graphs. Knowl. Inf. Syst. 27(2), 303–325 (2011)

[12] Kim, J.-S., Lee, H.-O.: Comments on a study of odd graphs as fault-tolerant interconnection networks. IEEE Transactions on Computers 57(6), 864 (2008)

[13] Krishnamoorthy, M.S., Krishnamurthy, B.: Fault diameter of interconnection networks. Computers & Mathematics with Applications 13(5-6), 577–582 (1987)

[14] Latapy, M., Magnien, C.: Complex network measurements: Estimating the relevance of observed properties. In: INFOCOM, pp. 1660–1668. IEEE (2008)

[15] Louri, A., Weech, B., Neocleous, C.: A spanning multichannel linked hypercube: A gradually scalable optical interconnection network for massively parallel computing. IEEE Trans. Parallel Distrib. Syst. 9(5), 497–512 (1998)

[16] Magnien, C., Latapy, M., Habib, M.: Fast computation of empirically tight bounds for the diameter of massive graphs. ACM Journal of Experimental Algorithmics 13 (2008)

[17] Reed, D.A., da Lu, C., Mendes, C.L.: Reliability challenges in large systems. Future Generation Computer Systems 22(3), 293–302 (2006)

[18] Saad, Y., Schultz, M.H.: Topological properties of hypercubes. IEEE Transactions on Computers 37, 867–872 (1988)
[19] Seidel, R.: On the all-pairs-shortest-path problem. In: STOC, pp. 745–749. ACM (1992)
[20] Smets-Solanes, J.-P., Cérin, C., Courteaud, R.: Slapos: A multi-purpose distributed cloud operating system based on an erp billing model. In: Jacobsen, H.-A., Wang, Y., Hung, P. (eds.) IEEE SCC, pp. 765–766. IEEE (2011)
[21] Stoica, I., Morris, R., Karger, D., Kaashoek, M.F., Balakrishnan, H.: Chord: A scalable peer-to-peer lookup service for internet applications. In: Proceedings of the 2001 Conference on Applications, Technologies, Architectures, and Protocols for Computer Communications, SIGCOMM 2001, pp. 149–160. ACM, New York (2001)

Fault Recovery Technique for TMR Softcore Processor System Using Partial Reconfiguration

Makoto Fujino, Hiroki Tanaka, Yoshihiro Ichinomiya*, Motoki Amagasaki, Morihiro Kuga, Masahiro Iida, and Toshinori Sueyoshi

Graduate School of Science and Technology, Kumamoto University,
2-39-1 Kurokami, Chuoh-ku, Kumamoto 860-8555, Japan
{fujino,tanaka,ichinomiya}@arch.cs.kumamoto-u.ac.jp,
{amagasaki,kuga,iida,sueyoshi}@cs.kumamoto-u.ac.jp
http://www.arch.cs.kumamoto-u.ac.jp/

Abstract. System LSI is used for the dependable system, such as in-vehicle system. However, the miniaturization of semiconductor manufacturing process degrades the system dependability. We focus attention on SRAM-based FPGAs (Field Programmable Gate Arrays) which can implement the arbitrary circuits. However, FPGAs are vulnerable to a soft-error, which is induced by the radiation effects. Therefore, we propose the reliable system which can recover both soft-error and hard-error. As a result, we can design the reliable system for both soft-error and hard-error.

Keywords: FPGA, Dependability, Partial Reconfiguration, Fault Recovery.

1 Introduction

System LSI (Large Scale Integration) is widely used in various systems. These days, it is used also the dependable system, such as in-vehicle system. However, the miniaturization of semiconductor manufacturing process degrades the system dependability[1][2]. Therefore, improving the system dependability is required. We focus attention on SRAM-based FPGAs (Field Programmable Gate Arrays) which can implement the arbitrary circuits. FPGAs can implement the various circuits by reconfiguration. FPGAs are very popular due to their capability of implementing complex circuits in a short turn around time. Because FPGAs also have a lot of redundant wires, it can avoid the hard-error part by rerouting. However, FPGAs are vulnerable to a soft-error, which is induced by the radiation effects[3]. It corrupts the data of SRAM cell, because FPGAs consist of a huge amount of configuration memory bits in SRAM cell. Whereat soft-error induces the function error on FPGA. The soft-error occurs once a week in the space environment or once in several months at the ground level. Therefore, System on FPGA requires improving dependability to soft-error. We propose the reliable system design which can recover both soft-error and hard-error.

---

* Research Fellow of the Japan Society for the Promotion of Science

Y. Xiang et al. (Eds.): ICA3PP 2012, Part I, LNCS 7439, pp. 392–404, 2012.

The remainder of the present paper is organized as follows. Section 2 describes related work. Sections 3 and 4 describe the proposed system and the recovery process from soft-error and hard-error, respectively. Section 5 describes the verification of recovery process. Section 6 describes the evaluation of the proposed system. Finally, the conclusions are presented in Section 7.

2   Related Work

This section presents traditional reliable implementation techniques for FPGA.

The common reliable implementation technique is redundancy technique such as DMR (Dual Module Redundancy) and TMR (Triple Module Redundancy)[3]. However, DMR cannot identify soft-error affected module. Therefore, it is difficult to recover system using DMR dynamically. This is undesirable for the system by which continuous operation is required. Consequently, we focus on the TMR implementation technique.

The basic concept of the TMR scheme is that the robustness of a circuit against soft-error. Although, TMR only mitigate a soft-error or a hard-error, and cannot recover the circuit altered or corrupted by those. Scrubbing is the reliable technique which can recover the circuit altered by soft-error[4]. The combination of TMR and Scrubbing can deal with most soft-error in combinational circuit. However, they are insufficient for the reliability of sequential circuit such as processor, because they cause context mismatches. The context synchronization is necessary to ensure the reliability of a sequential circuit[5]. Above techniques can deal with most soft-error dynamically. The reliable technique for hard-error is to replace and reroute the circuit avoiding the hard-error part. It requires stopping the system. The reliable technique which dynamically avoids hard-error part isn't indurated.

3   Proposed System

This section presents the proposed system construction.

We used Plasma as the target processor element[6]. It is the small 32-bit RISC microprocessor, and executes all MIPS I(TM) user mode instructions except unaligned load and store operations. The reason using Plasma is that it is open source CPU and can flexibly accommodate to the reliable design and verification. We use BRAM (Block RAM) which is Xilinx FPGA embedded memory as the main memory of system, and UART (Universal Asynchronous Receiver Transmitter) as the external interface. BRAM is protected by ECC (Error Correcting Code) using hamming code.

Fig. 1 shows proposed system. It is constructed on the basis of TMR. And we add RC (Recovery Controller), RM (Recovery Module), spare region, and Selector. RC and RM control reconfiguration process. The spare region is the region to avoid hard-error. Processor or peripheral is designed as the target of hard-error avoidance. Memory controller, UART, and RC are evacuated in spare region together.

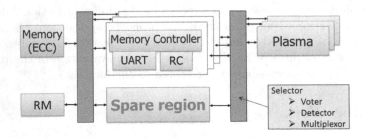

Fig. 1. Proposed system

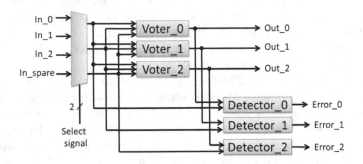

Fig. 2. The selector construnction

We explain about RM, RC, and Selector which are the composition circuits of the proposed system. RM consist of ICAP (Internal Configuration Access Port), FrameECC, and BRAM which store the configuration data performed read-back from FPGA[7][8]. ICAP is hard macro implemented in the Xilinx FPGA, and port to access to configuration memory from within FPGA. FrameECC is IP (Intellectual Property) core provided from Xilinx, corrects the one bit error, and detects the two bit errors by using the read-back value from FPGA.

RC controls Scrubbing, the hard-error avoidance, and the context synchronization in the processor. Scrubbing means recovery process using the partial reconfiguration from breakdown by soft-error.

Fig. 2 shows Selector construction. The Selector consists of Voter, Detector, and Multiplexer. The Voter decides the correct output by majority voting the three outputs from redundant modules. The Detector identifies the module where error occurs. The Multiplexer selects the module hard-error occurs. If an error occurs in Plasma or Peripherals, the Voter can conceal the error effects. And, the Detector detects the error module, and sends the error signal to RC. While RC recovers the system, the error effect is concealed by the Voter. Therefore, we can recover the system from hard and soft error dynamically.

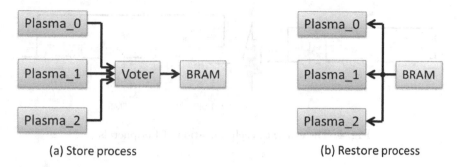

Fig. 3. The context synchronization of Plasma

4   Recovery Process

This section presents recovery process in the proposed system. Hereinafter, we explain about soft-error recovery process and hard-error recovery process.

4.1   Soft-Error Recovery Process

We apply TMR, Scrubbing, and the context synchronization to the proposed system to recovery from soft-error. TMR scheme can mitigate a soft-error, and Scrubbing can eliminate the soft-error from configuration memory. However, they are insufficient for the reliability of sequential circuit such as processor, because they cause context mismatches. The context synchronization is necessary to ensure the reliability of a sequential circuit.

Proposed system performs Scrubbing by FrameECC and ICAP. RM reads back one frame in the configuration data through the ICAP, and store it in BRAM. And, FrameECC detects the error part particularly. If an error is detected, configuration data is read back from FPGA, and is recovered by FrameE-CC. Recovered configuration data is rewritten on the same frame address through ICAP. Then, read-back is performed once again, and if the error isn't detected, the next frame is read back. Scrubbing means that these processes are performed in all frames. Scrubbing doesn't influence to the context in the system because it only reconfigure the configuration data. Therefore, the context synchronization is required.

The context synchronization of Plasma and Peripherals is performed by different methods. Fig. 3 shows the context synchronization of Plasma. It is performed by storing the context of Plasma in BRAM, and then restoring the context in Plasma[5]. The context synchronization begins by sending the interrupt signal from RC after Scrubbing. Plasma receives the interrupt signal, and the context in Plasma is first stored in BRAM through the Voter. Because Voter can conceal an error, the correct context is stored in BRAM. Then, the context stored in BRAM is restored in Plasma. As a result, the context in Plasma can be synchronized.

Fig. 4 shows the context synchronization of Peripheral. The context synchronization of Peripherals is automatically performed by feeding back the context

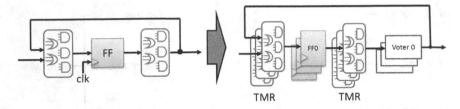

Fig. 4. The context synchronization of Peripherals

of Peripherals[9]. The circuit having the context in proposed system is FF (Flip Flop). FF having the feedback construction may remain the error after Scrubbing. Therefore, the output of FF is fed back through the Voter. As a result, the context in Peripheral can be automatically synchronized.

4.2   Hard-Error Recovery Process

The recovery process from hard-error is performed by evacuating in the spare region. Fig. 5 shows dynamic hard error recovery process. While the Voter conceals an error, the corrupted module, which is Plasma or Peripheral, is evacuated in spare region. Evacuation is performed by using partial reconfiguration to spare region. After evacuation to spare region, the context synchronization is performed, and spare module synchronize with correct modules. Then, RC controls the Selector, and cut off the corrupted module. TMR construction is restructured by using the spare region. The spare region in proposed system has the input-output of both Plasma and Peripheral. Therefore, either one of the Plasma or Peripherals is evacuated only once in the spare region.

Commonly, partial reconfiguration bitstream is ready required to perform partial reconfiguration. Because the memory capacity in FPGA is small, the partial reconfiguration bitstream is stored in off-chip memory. It is not a good idea because of its cost. Therefore, we discuss the reuse of bitstream by using the equivalent design in partial reconfigurable region[10]. By using equivalent design, the circuit information of Plasma or Peripheral in partial reconfiguration region will be read back and be directly reconfigured in the spare region. As a result, the proposed system will be able to avoid the hard-error without using off-chip memory.

4.3   Recovery Flow

Fig. 6 shows recovery flow. When Detector detects the error, it sends error detection signal to RC, and the recovery process begins. In soft-error recovery process, Scrubbing and the context synchronization are performed. After the context synchronization, the state of RC transits from recovery process state to standby state. While the state of RC is standby state, if Detector detects the error and error part is the same as the part detected before recovery process, it is judged that the error is the hard-error. If Detector didn't detect the error, the

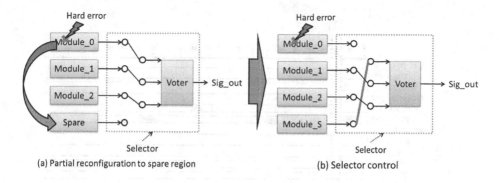

Fig. 5. Hard-error Recovery Process

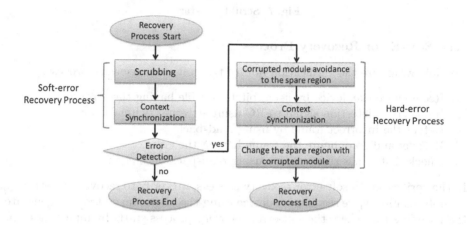

Fig. 6. Recovery flow

state of RC returned to normal state. In hard-error recovery process, hard-error avoidance is performed by using the spare region. After hard-error avoidance, the context synchronization is performed. Then the spare region is changed with corrupted module, and recovery process ends.

5   Verification of Recovery Process

This section presents verification of recovery process in the proposed system. We verified the recovery process using ChipScope Pro which is an application of ISE (Integrated Software Environment)13.3.

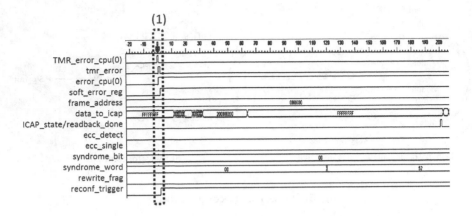

Fig. 7. Scrubbing start

5.1   Soft-Error Recovery Process

The followings are the verification flow of the soft-error recovery process.

1. Reconfigure the device by using bitstream file having the error.
2. Input error detection signal to RC using external switch.
3. Detect the incorrect frame by using read-back.
4. Recover and reconfigure the frame having the error.
5. Check that it has recovered by using read-back once again.

In the verification of soft-error recovery process, we verify to recover soft-error by Scrubbing. Firstly, we reconfigure device using the bitstream edited to ingenerate the pseudo error. Then, the soft-error recovery process starts by inputting error detection signal to RC. We use the external switch as the error detection signal to RC to simplify the verification.

Fig. 7 shows the waveform of Scrubbing start. The tmr_error_cpu is error detection signal of Detector, the tmr_error is the trigger of recovery process using detection signal, and the error_cpu is the register storing the location of incorrect module. The Frame_address is the target frame address in read-back, the data_to_icap is the input signal to ICAP, the ecc_detect is the error detection signal in read-back, and the ecc_single is error detection signal which is asserted only at the time of one bit error detection. The ecc_detect and ecc_single is updated whenever the frame is read back. That is, when being ecc_detect='1' and ecc_single='1', it means that two bits error occur in one frame. The reconf_trigger is the status register which shows that the system is performing the recovery process. In Fig. 7(1), the error detection signal is input to RC from Detector. The reconf_trigger is asserted, the data_to_icap is input to ICAP, and read-back starts.

Fig. 8 shows the waveform of error recovery by Scrubbing. In Fig. 8(1), the read-back of frame address "01228F" starts. The ecc_detect is asserted and the

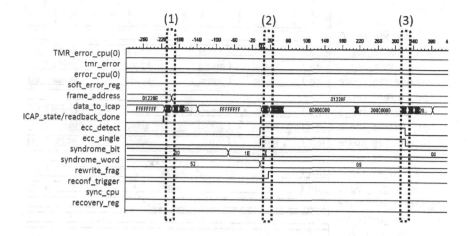

Fig. 8. Error recovery by Scrubbing

error are detected during read-back. And, the syndrome value is fetched. In Fig. 8, the error exists in thirty first bit(0x1E) of ninth word(0x09) of frame. In Fig. 8(2), the frame reconfiguration is performed by using read-back data and syndrome. Then, in Fig. 8(3), the read-back is performed once again, and we check that the error is recovered. As a result, we found that the error is recovered by Scrubbing after soft-error detection.

5.2 Hard-Error Recovery Process

The followings are the verification flow of the soft-error recovery process.

1. Reconfigure the device by using bitstream file having the error.
2. Partially reconfigure the spare region by using the circuit which accommodate to the corrupted module.
3. Change to the corrupted module with spare module by controlling the Selector.
4. Perform the context synchronization.
5. Check that it has recovered.

In the verification of hard-error recovery process, we verify to evacuate both Plasma and Peripherals to the spare region. In this verification, reconfiguration to the spare region and the context synchronization are controlled not by RC but by the external switch. Therefore, this recovery flow is different from recovery flow in 4.3, and the context synchronization is performed after Selector change. The reason is that we check the context assent by the context synchronization. Selector is also controlled by Detector output, and isn't re-changed after module change.

Firstly, we verify the hard-error recovery process of Plasma. We perform partial reconfiguration to Plasma0 using black box module to break Plasma0. Black

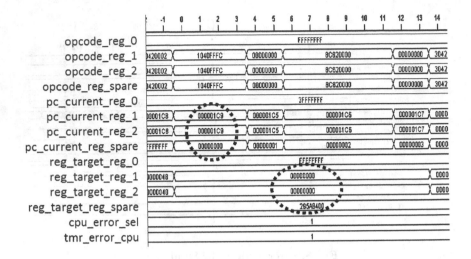

Fig. 9. Partial reconfiguartion using Plasma to the spare region

box module is clear module not having the logic circuit. Then, we reconfigure Plasma in the spare region, check that Selector change to spare module from Plasma0. Finally, the context synchronization is performed, and we check that the action of spare Plasma correspond with that of Plasma1 and Plasma2.

Fig. 9 shows the waveform at the time of performing partial reconfiguartion using Plasma to the spare region. The opcode_reg is the instruction register, the pc_current_reg is program counter, and reg_target_reg is the output signal of the using register. The cpu_error_sel is the control signal of Selector, and tmr_error_cpu is error detection signal. When tmr_error_cpu is '01', '10', '11', the Plasma0, 1, or 2 is incorrect, respectively. In Fig. 9, because the register of Plasma0 is different from the others, Plasma0 is incorrect. Also, because cpu_error_sel is '01' and the register of Plasma spare runs, we found that Plasma is reconfigured in spare region. However, because the context synchronization is performed, the context of Plasma0 is different from the others.

Fig. 10 shows the waveform of the context synchronization of Plasma. The left-side of Fig. 10 is the waveform before the context synchronization, and right-side of that is waveform after the context synchronization. Before the context synchronization, the context of spare region Plasma is different from the other Plasmas, and we find the spare region Plasma is incorrect because tmr_error_cpu is '01'. After the context synchronization, the context of spare region Plasma corresponds to the other Plasmas, and we found that the hard-error is avoided because tmr_error_cpu is '00'. Although we don't show all registers of Plasma in this figure, we checked that all registers are synchronized. Thereby, we found that Plasma can avoid to the spare region after error detection.

Secondly, we verify the hard-error recovery process of Peripherals. Just like Plasma verification, we also perform partial reconfiguration of Peripherals using black box module to break Peripherals0. We perform partial reconfiguration

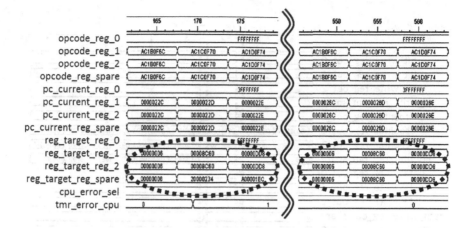

Fig. 10. The context syncronization of Plasma

in spare region, and check that Selector changes to the spare module from Peripheral0. Then, the context synchronization is performed, and we check that Peripheral behavior of spare region corresponds to the others.

Fig. 11 shows the result of hard-error recovery process of Plasma. The bit_write_reg_out, counter_reg_out, data_write_reg_out, and delay_write_reg_out are a part of register outputs in Peripherals. The error_peri is the error detection signal at the time the error occurs in Peripherals. When error_peri is '01', '10', '11', the Peripheral0, 1, or 2 is incorrect, respectively. In Fig. 11, because error_peri is '01' and each reg_out is different from the others, Peripheral0 breaks down. In Fig. 11(1), the partial reconfiguration to the spare region ends. After partial reconfiguration, Peripherals of the spare region run, and the context synchronization is automatically performed in Fig. 11(2). Although we don't show all registers of Peripherals in this figure, we checked that all registers are synchronized. Thereby, we found that Peripherals can avoid to the spare region after error detection.

As mentioned above, we checked the hard-error recovery process of Plasma and Peripherals.

6   Evaluation of Proposed System

6.1   Implementation Environment

Table 1 shows system implementation environment. We used ML605 board with Xilinx Virtex-6 XC6VLX240T, and Xilinx ISE13.3 as the development tool. When we implement the system, we disable "Register Duplication", "Equivalent Register Removal", and "LUT Combining" which are the logic synthesis option. The clock constraint is 50MHz. We used PlanAhead which is ISE application to design partial reconfiguration. Evaluation items are the resource usage and the maximum operating frequency. Evaluation targets are base system which isn't

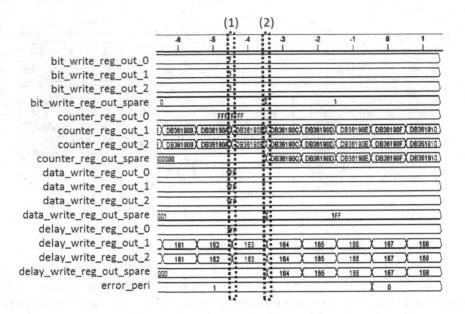

Fig. 11. Hard-error recovery process

Table 1. Implementation Environment

Board	ML605 Evaluation Kit FPGA : Virtex-6 XC6VLX240T
Tool	ISE(Integrated Software Environment) 13.3

performed reliable design, TMR which shares the memory and external pin, and proposed system. The spare region of proposed system isn't partial reconfiguration region, and implement Plasma simply. The reason is that the width of spare region fits in the larger module of evacuating modules. The resource usage and maximum operating frequency is referred to ISE implementation report.

6.2   Implemantation Result

Table 2 shows implementation result. Firstly, we discuss the resource usage. We compare "TMR" with "base" to analyze resource increase of TMR. "TMR" requires 4.04 times the slices compared with "base". The reason that "TMR" is constructed from three "base" and one Voter. It is thought that four more times resource usage depend on the influence of optimization. Then, we compare proposed system with "TMR" to analyze resource increase of TMR. Proposed system requires about 1,200 larger slices than "TMR". RC requires about 400 slices, Selector requires about 100 slices, and the spare region requires about 600

Table 2. Evaluation Result

	Slices iutilizationj	Maximum operating frequencyiMHzj
base system	606(2%)	85.609
TMR	2,450(7%)	58.302
proposed system	3,640(9%)	64.691

slices. Thus, the total number of slice is about 1,200 slices. We think that the resource which can't identify from report depend on the influence of optimization. In fact, in order to set up the partial reconfiguration region, we think that the resource usage increase to add communication circuits between static region and partial reconfiguration.

Secondly, we discuss the maximum operating frequency. The evaluated systems satisfied a clock timing constraint of 20 ns, which corresponds to a frequency of 50 MHz. The maximum operating frequency of "TMR" decreased to about 31.9% compared with "base". This reason is that the wire routing becomes long since "TMR" shares BRAM. Also, the critical path of "base" and "TMR" is between BRAM and CPU, and that of "TMR" is longer than that of "base" to add the Voter between BRAM and CPU. Thus, the maximum operating frequency of "TMR" decrease. The maximum operating frequency of proposed system increased to about 10.9% of that of "TMR". The additional circuit such as RC, Selector, and the context synchronization doesn't influence to the critical path. Therefore, we thought that this improvement is fudge factor. In fact, in order to set up the partial reconfiguration region, we think that the maximum operating frequency decrease by the critical increase.

6.3   Reliability

Improving the reliability to the soft-error is performed by TMR, Scrubbing, and the context synchronization. Therefore, even if a soft-error occurred in TMR module, it could be recovered. The case proposed system break down by soft-error is the case two or more soft-error occurs in TMR modules or a soft-error occurs in non-TMR modules. Since those probabilities are very low, the probability that system break down by the soft-error is very low similarly.

Improving the reliability to the hard-error is performed by evacuating the corrupted module to spare region. Therefore, even if a hard-error occurred in Plasma or Peripherals, it could be avoided once. While the system halt by maintenance, re-design is performed avoiding hard-error part. By construct the TMR and the spare region once again, we can use the same device for a long time. As a result, we think that proposed system has reliability to both soft-error and hard-error. Aftertime, we will quantitatively evaluate proposed system by fault injection.

7   Conclusion

We proposed the reliable system which perform both soft-error and hard-error recovery process. We applied TMR, Scrubbing, and the context synchronization to the proposed system to recovery from soft-error. And, the hard-error recovery process is performed by evacuating the corrupted module in the spare region. Aftertime, we will apply equivalent design to decrease BRAM usage. And, we will quantitatively evaluate the proposed system by fault injection. Then, we will discuss availability of the proposed system.

References

1. Teramoto, A., et al.: Time-dependent dielectric breakdown of SiO_2 films in a wide electric field range. Microelectronics Reliability 41(1), 47–52 (2001)
2. Schimschak, M., Krug, J.: Surface Electromigration as a Moving Boundary Value Problem. PRL 78, 278 (1997)
3. Kastensmidt, F.L., et al.: Fault-Tolerance Techniques for SRAM-based FPGAs, p. 180. Vishwani D. Agrawal Springer, Netherlands (2006)
4. Carmichael, C., et al.: Correcting Single-Event Upsets Through Virtex Partial Configuration. Xilinx Application Note, XAPP216 (v1.0), June 1 (2000)
5. Ichinomiya, Y., et al.: Improving the Soft-error Tolerability of a Softcore Processor on an FPGA using Triple Modular Redundancy and Partial Reconfiguration. JNIT: Jounal of Next Generation Information Technology 2(3), 35–48 (2011)
6. Plasma - most MIPS(TM) opcode: Overview: OpenCores,
   `http://opencores.org/project,plasma,overview`
7. Xilinx Inc., SEU Strategies for Virtex-5 Devices, XAPP864(v2.0) (April 2010)
8. Xilinx, Virtex-6 FPGA Configuration User Guide, UG360 (v3.2), November 1 (2010)
9. Fujino, M., et al.: Reliable Softcore Processor System using TMR and Dynamic Reconfiguration. In: JCEEE 2011, September 26 (2011)
10. Usagawa, S., et al.: Relocation of Partial Reconfiguration Data for Dynamic Reconfigurable System. IEICE Technical Report RECONF2011-30, September 26, pp. 49–54 (2011) (in Japanese)
11. Xilinx Inc., PlanAhead Reconfiguration Tutorial, UG743(v13.3) (October 2011)

Non-Blocking Atomic Commitment in Asynchronous Distributed Systems with Faulty Processes

Sung-Hoon Park and Seon-Hyong Lee

School of Electrical and Computer Engineering,
Chungbuk National Unvi. Cheongju ChungBuk 361-763 Korea
spark@chungbuk.ac.kr, bblsh1689@hanmail.net

Abstract. This paper defines the Non-Blocking Atomic Commitment problem in a message-passing asynchronous system and determines a failure detector to solve the problem. This failure detector, which we call the modal failure detector star, and which we denote by M*, is strictly weaker than the perfect failure detector P but strictly stronger than the eventually perfect failure detector $\diamond$P. The paper shows that at any environment, the problem is solvable with M*.

1   Introduction

We address the fault-tolerant *Non-Blocking Atomic Commitment* problem, simply NB-AC, in an asynchronous distributed system where the communication between a pair of processes is by a message-passing primitive, channels are reliable and processes can fail by crashing. In distributed systems, to ensure transaction failure atomicity in a distributed system, an agreement problem must be solved among a set of participating processes. This problem, called the Atomic Commitment problem (AC) requires the participants to agree on an outcome for the transaction: commit or abort [1,2,15]. When it is required that every correct participant eventually reach an outcome despite the failure of other participants, the problem is called Non-Blocking Atomic Commitment (NB-AC) [1,2].

The problem of Non-Blocking Atomic Commitment becomes much more complex in distributed systems (as compared to single-computer systems) due to the lack of both a shared memory and a common physical clock and because of unpredictable message delays. Evidently, the problem cannot be solved deterministically in a crash-prone asynchronous system without any information about failures. There is no way to determine that a process is crashed or just slow. Clearly, no deterministic algorithm can guarantee Non-Blocking Atomic Commitment simultaneously. In this sense, the problem stems from the famous impossibility result that consensus cannot be solved deterministically in an asynchronous system that is subject to even a single crash failure [7].

1.1   Failure Detectors

In this paper, we introduced a *modal failure detector M** and showed that the Non-Blocking Atomic Commitment problem is solvable with it in the environment with

Y. Xiang et al. (Eds.): ICA3PP 2012, Part I, LNCS 7439, pp. 405–413, 2012.

majority correct processes. The concept of (unreliable) failure detectors was introduced by Chandra and Toueg [3,4], and they characterized failure detectors by two properties: completeness and accuracy. Based on the properties, they defined several failure detector classes: perfect failure detectors P, weak failure detectors W, eventually weak failure detectors $\Diamond$W and so on. In [3] and [4] they studied what is the "weakest" failure detector to solve Consensus. They showed that the weakest failure detector to solve Consensus with any number of faulty processes is $\Omega+\Sigma$ and the one with faulty processes bounded by $\lceil n/2 \rceil$ (i.e., less than $\lceil n/2 \rceil$ faulty processes) is $\Diamond$W. After the work of [8], several studies followed. For example, the weakest failure detector for stable leader election is the perfect failure detector P [4], and the one for Terminating Reliable Broadcast is also P [1,3].

Recently, as the closest one from our work, Guerraoui and Kouznetsov showed a failure detector class for mutual exclusion problems that is different from the above weakest failure detectors [16]. The failure detector, called the Trusting failure detector, satisfies the three properties, i.e., strong completeness, eventual strong accuracy and trusting accuracy so that it can solve the mutual exclusion problem in asynchronous distributed systems with crash failure. And they used the bakery algorithm to solve the mutual exclusion problem with the trusting failure detector.

1.2   Contributions

How about the Non-Blocking Atomic Commitment problem? More precisely, what is the *weakest* failure detector to solve the Non-Blocking Atomic Commitment problem? The mutual exclusion algorithm is completely different from the NB-AC in which the order of getting the critical section is decided based on a ticket order. In contrast to the mutual exclusion algorithm, the NB-AC algorithm should receive the messages from all members of a group to make a decision.

In general, Non-Blocking Atomic Commitment algorithms assume that the system is either a failure-free model [1,2,8,15] or a synchronous model in which (1) if a process crash, it is eventually detected by every correct process and (2) no correct process is suspected before crash [8,15]: with the conjunction of (1) and (2), the system is assumed to equipped with the capability of the *perfect* failure detector P [3]. In other words, the perfect failure detector P is *sufficient* to solve the Non-Blocking Atomic Commitment problem. But is *P necessary*? For the answer to the question, we present a *modal failure detector star M**, that is a new failure detector we introduce here, which is strictly weaker than P (but strictly stronger than $\Diamond P$, the *eventually perfect* failure detector of [3]). We show that the answer is "no" and we can solve the problem using the *modal* failure detector star M^*.

Roughly speaking, failure detector M^* satisfies (1) eventual strong accuracy and (2) strong completeness together with (3) modal accuracy, i.e., initially, every process is suspected, after that, any process that is once confirmed to be correct is not suspected before crash. If M^* suspects the confirmed process again, then the process has crashed. However, M^* might suspect temporarily every correct process before confirming it's alive as well as might not suspect temporarily a crashed process before confirming it's crash. Intuitively, M^* can thus make at least one mistake per every correct process and algorithms using $M*$ are, in terms of a practical distributed system view, more useful than those using P.

We here present the algorithm to show that $M*$ is sufficient to solve Non-Blocking Atomic Commitment and it is inspired by the well-known Non Blocking Atomic Commit Protocols of D. Skeen [15].

1.3   Road Map

The rest of the paper is organized as follows. Section 2 addresses motivations and related works and Section 3 overviews the system model. Section 4 introduces the Modal failure detector star $M*$. Section 5 shows that $M*$ is sufficient to solve the problem, respectively. Section 6 concludes the paper with some practical remarks.

2   Motivations and Related Works

Actually, the main difficulty in solving the Non-Blocking Atomic Commitment problem in presence of process crashes lies in the detection of crashes. As a way of getting around the impossibility of Consensus, Chandra and Toug extended the asynchronous model of computation with unreliable *failure detectors* and showed in [4] that the FLP impossibility can be circumvented using failure detectors. More precisely, they have shown that Consensus can be solved (deterministically) in an asynchronous system augmented with the failure detector $\lozenge S$ *(Eventually Strong)* and the assumption of a majority of correct processes. Failure detector $\lozenge S$ guarantees *Strong Completeness*, i.e., eventually, every process that crashes is permanently suspected by every process, and *Eventual Weak Accuracy*, i.e., eventually, some correct process is never suspected. Failure detector $\lozenge S$ can however make an arbitrary number of mistakes, i.e., false suspicions.

A Non-Blocking Atomic Commitment problem, simply NB-AC, is an agreement problem so that it is impossible to solve in asynchronous distributed systems with crash failures. This stems from the FLP result which mentioning the consensus problem can't be solved in asynchronous systems. Can we also circumvent the impossibility of solving NB-AC using some failure detector? The answer is of course "yes". The NB-AC algorithm of D. Skeen [15] solves the NB-AC problem with assuming that it has the capability of the failure detector P *(Perfect)* in asynchronous distributed systems. This failure detector ensures *Strong Completeness* (recalled above) and *Strong Accuracy*, i.e., no process is suspected before it crashes [3]. Failure detector P does never make any mistake and obviously provides more knowledge about failures than $\lozenge S$.

But it is stated in [9,10] that Failure detector $\lozenge S$ cannot solve the NB-AC problem, even if only one process may crash. This means that NB-AC is strictly harder than Consensus, i.e., NB-AC requires more knowledge about failures than Consensus. An interesting question is then "What is the weakest failure detector for solving the NB-AC problem in asynchronous systems with unreliable failure detectors?" In this paper, as the answer to this question, we show that there is a failure detector that solves NB-AC weaker than the Perfect Failure Detector. This means that the weakest failure detector for NB-AC is not a Perfect Failure Detector P.

3   Model

We consider in this paper a crash-prone asynchronous message passing system model augmented with the failure detector abstraction [3].

3.1   The Non-Blocking Atomic Commitment Problem

Atomic commitment problems are at the heart of distributed transactional systems. A transaction originates at a process called the Transaction Manager (abbreviated TM) which accesses data by interacting with various processes called Data Managers abbreviated DM. The TM initially performs a begin transaction operation, then various write and read operations by translating writes and reads into messages sent to the DM and initially an end-transaction operation. To ensure the so-called failure atomicity property of the transaction, all DMs on which write operations have been performed, must resolve an Atomic Commitment problem as part of the end-transaction operation. These DMs are called participants in the problem. In this paper we assume that the participants know each other and know about the transactions [1].

The atomic commitment problem requires the participants to reach a common outcome for the transaction among two possible values: *commit* and *abort*. We will say that a participant AC-decides commit (respectively AC-decides abort). The write operations performed by the DMs become permanent if and only if participants AC-decide commit. The outcome AC-decided by a participant depends on votes (*yes* or *no*) provided by the participants. We will say that a participant votes *yes* (respectively votes *no*). Each vote reflects the ability of the participant to ensure that its data updates can be made permanent.

We do not make any assumption on how votes are defined except that they are not predetermined. For example, a participant votes *yes* if and only if no concurrency control conflict has been locally detected and the updates have been written to stable storage. Otherwise the participant votes no. A participant can AC-decide commit only if all participants vote yes. In order to exclude trivial situations where participants always AC-decide abort, it is generally required that commit must be decided if all votes are yes and no participant crashes [2]. We consider the Non-Blocking Atomic Commitment problem, NB-AC, in which a correct participant AC-decides even if some participants have crashed, NB-AC is specified by the following conditions:

— Uniform-Agreement: No two participants AC-decide different outcomes.
— Uniform-Validity: If a participant AC-decides commit, then all participants have voted yes.
— Termination: Every correct participant eventually AC-decides.
— Non-Triviality: If all participants vote yes and there is no failure, then every correct participant eventually AC-decides commit.

Uniform-Agreement and Uniform-Validity are safety conditions. They ensure the failure atomicity property of transactions. Termination is a liveness condition which guarantees non-blocking. Non-Triviality excludes trivial solutions to the problem where participants always AC-decide abort. This condition can be viewed as a liveness condition from the application point of view since it ensures progress, i.e. transaction commit under reasonable expectations when no crash and no participant votes no.

4   The Modal Failure Detector Star M*

Each module of failure detector $M*$ outputs a subset of the range 2^Π. Initially, every process is suspected. However, if any process is once confirmed to be correct by any correct process, then the confirmed process id is removed from the failure detector list of $M*$. If the confirmed process is suspected again, the suspected process id is inserted into the failure detector list of $M*$. The most important property of $M*$, denoted by *Modal Accuracy*, is that a process that was once confirmed to be correct is not suspected before crash. Let H_M be any history of such a failure detector $M*$. Then $H_M(i,t)$ represents the set of processes that process i suspects at time t. For each failure pattern F, $M(F)$ is defined by the set of all failure detector histories H_M that satisfy the following properties:

- *Strong Completeness:* There is a time after which every process that crashes is permanently suspected by every correct process:
  - $\forall i,j \in \Omega$, $\forall i \in correct(F)$, $\forall j \in F(t)$, $\exists t''$: $\forall t' > t''$, $j \in H(i, t')$.

- *Eventual Strong Accuracy:* There is a time after which every correct process is never suspected by any correct process. More precisely:
  - $\forall i,j \in \Omega$, $\forall i \in correct(F)$, $\exists t$: $\forall t' > t$, $\forall j \in correct(F)$, $j \notin H(i, t')$.

- *Modal Accuracy:* Initially, every process is suspected. After that, any process that is once confirmed to be correct is not suspected before crash. More precisely:
  - $\forall i,j \in \Omega$: $j \in H(i,t_0)$, $t_0 < t < t'$, $j \notin H(i,t) \land j \in \Omega - F(t') \Rightarrow j \notin H(i, t')$

Note that *Modal Accuracy* does not require that failure detector $M*$ keeps the Strong Accuracy property over every process all the time t. However, it only requires that failure detector $M*$ never makes a mistake before crash about the process that was confirmed at least once to be correct.

If process $M*$ outputs some crashed processes, then $M*$ accurately knows that they have crashed, since they had already been confirmed to be correct before crash. However, concerning those processes that had never been confirmed, $M*$ does not necessarily know whether they crashed (or which processes crashed).

5   Solving NB-AC Problem with $M*$

We give in Figure 1 an algorithm solving NB-AC using $M*$ in any environment of group where at least one node is available. The algorithm uses the fact that eventual strong accuracy property of $M*$. More precisely, with such a property of $M*$ and the assumption of at least one node being available, we can implement our algorithm of Figure 1.

Var *status*: {*rem*, *try*, *ready* } initially rem
Var *coordinator* : initially NULL
Var *token* : initially empty list
Var *group*$_i$: set of processes

Periodically(τ) **do**
    request $M*$ for H_M

1.   **Upon received** (*trying, upper_ layer*)
2.   **if** not (status = *try*) **then**
3.   wait until $\forall j \in group_i : j \notin H_M$
4. $status_i := try$
5.   **send** (*ready*, *i*) to $\forall j \in group_i$

6.   **Upon received** (*ok*, *j*)
7. $token := token \cup \{\, j\,\}$
8.   **If** $group = token$ **then**
9.   **send** (*commit*, *i*) to $\forall j \in Q_k$
10.   *status:= rem*
11. **Upon received** (*ready*, *j*)
12.   **if** status = *rem* **then**   **send** (*ok*, *i*) to *j*
13.   *coordinator:=i*
14.   *status:= ready*
15.   **else send** (*no*, *i*) *to j*

16. **Upon received** (*no*, *j*)
17.   **if** *status=try* **then send** (*abort*, *i*) to$\forall j \in$ *group*
18.   *status:= rem*

19. **Upon received** (*abort*, *j*)
20.   **if** *status=ready* **then** **do** *abort*()
21.   *status:= rem*

22. **Upon received** (*commit*, *j*)
23.   **if** *status=ready* **then**   *commit-transaction()*
24.   *status:= rem*

25. **Upon received** H_M from M_i
26.   **if** (*status=try and* $\exists i \in$ *my_group and* H_M)
        then send (*abort*, *i*) to to $\forall j \in$ *my_group*
        abort-transaction()
27.   *status:= rem*
28.   **if** (*status=ready and coordinator* $\in H_M$)
        then *coordinator:=NULL*
        abort-transaction()
29.   *status:= rem*

Fig. 1. NB-AC algorithm using $M*$: process *i*

We give in Figure 1 an algorithm solving NB-AC using M^* in any environment E *of a group* with any number of correct processes ($f < n$). Our algorithm of Figure 1 assumes:

- Each process i has access to the output of its modal failure detector module M_i^*;
- At least one process is available;

In our algorithm of Figure 1, each process i has the following variables:

1. A variable status, initially rem, represents one of the following states {*rem, try, ready*};
2. A variable *coordinator$_i$*, initially NULL, which denotes the coordinator when i send its *ok* message to other node;
3. A list *token$_i$*, initially empty, keeping the ok messages that i has received from each member of the group.

Description of [Line 1-5] in Figure 1; the idea of our algorithm is inspired by the well-known NB-AC algorithm of D. Skeen [15]. That is, the processes that wish to try their Atomic Commitment first wait for the group whose members are all alive based on the information H_M from its failure detector M^*. Those processes eventually know the group by the eventual strong accuracy property of M^* in line 3 of Figure 1 and then sets its *status* to "*try*", meaning that it is try to commit. It sets the variable *group* with all members and send the message "(*ready, i*)" to all nodes in the group.

Description of [Line 6-10] in Figure 1; the coordinator asking for a ready to proceed an atomic commitment from every process of the group does not take steps until the all "ok messages" are received from the group. But it eventually received ok or no messages from the group, and it will commits or aborts the transaction.

Description of [11-15] in Figure 1; On received "ready message from the coordinator, the node sends "*ok*" to the coordinator and it set its status with "*ready*" meaning that it is in ready state to wait a decision that is "commit" or "abort".

Description of [16-18] in Figure 1; If the coordinator received the message "*no*" from a node of group, it sends the "abort" message to every member of the group and after that it remains in "rem" state again.

Description of [19-21] in Figure 1; The node i, received "*abort*" from coordinator j, if it is in ready state, aborts the transaction.

Description of [22-24] in Figure 1; The node i, received "*commit*" from coordinator j, if it is in ready state, commits the transaction.

Description of [25-27] in Figure 1; When the node i received the failure detector history H_M from M^*, if it is a coordinator and knows that a node of group died, it sends the abort message to all members of group.

Description of [28-29] in Figure 1; Upon received the failure detector history H_M from M^*. If it is a node waiting a decision from the coordinator and it knows that the coordinator died, it aborts the transaction.

Now we prove the correctness of the algorithm of Figure 1 in terms of two properties: *Uniform-Agreement* and *Uniform-Validity*. Let R be an arbitrary run of the algorithm for some failure pattern $F \in E$ (f<n). Therefore we prove Lemma 1 and 2 for R respectively.

Lemma 1. (*Uniform-Agreement*) *No two participants atomic-commit decide different outcomes.*

Proof: By contradiction, assume that i and j ($i \neq j$) have made a different decision, one is commit and other is abort at time t'. According to the line 7-9 of the algorithm 1, the process i sends "ok" message and j sends "no" message to the coordinator. Without loss of generality, one of the following events occurred before t'' at every member of a group:

1. Assume the event that i received "commit" message from the coordinator. Then all participants of group eventually received the "commit" message" from the coordinator: a contradiction.
2. Assume the event that j received "abort" message from the coordinator. Then all participants of group eventually received the "abort" message" from the coordinator: a contradiction.

Hence, Uniform-Agreement is guaranteed.

Lemma 2. (*Uniform-Validity*) *If a participant atomic decides commit, then all participants have voted yes.*

Proof: Assume that a correct process i sends "no" message but commits the transaction at time t', and all correct processes except i send "ok" message to the coordinator after t'. According to the algorithm, after t', the coordinator eventually receives the messages from the group including process i and make a decision: *commit* or *abort*. But the coordinator received at least one "no" message from the participant of group. It would send "abort" message to all member of group. So it is contradiction.

Theorem 1. *The algorithm of Figure 1 solves NB-AC using M*, in any environment E of a group with $f < n$, combining with two lemmas 1 and 2.*

6   Concluding Remarks

Is it beneficial in practice to use a Non-Blocking Atomic Commitment algorithm based on M^*, instead of a traditional algorithm assuming P? The answer is "yes". Indeed, if we translate the very fact of not trusting a correct process into a *mistake*, then M^* clearly tolerates mistakes whereas P does not. More precisely, M^* is allowed to make up to n^2 mistakes (up to n mistakes for each module M_i, $i \in \Pi$). As a result, M^*'s implementation has certain advantages comparing to P's (given synchrony assumptions).

For example, in a possible implementation of M^*, every process i can gradually increase the timeout corresponding to a heart-beat message sent to a process j until a response from j is received. Thus, every such timeout can be flexibly adapted to the current network conditions. In contrast, P does not allow this kind of "fine-tuning" of timeout: there exists a maximal possible timeout, such that i starts suspecting j as soon as timeout exceeds. In order to minimize the probability of mistakes, it is normally chosen sufficiently large, and the choice is based on some a priori assumptions about current network conditions.

This might exclude some remote sites from the group and violate the properties of the failure detector. Thus, we can *implement* $M*$ in a more effective manner, and an algorithm that solves NB-AC using $M*$ exhibits a smaller probability to violate the requirements of the problem, than one using P, i.e., the use of $M*$ provides more resilience.

References

1. Babaoglu, O., Toueg, S.: Non_Blocking Atomic Commitment. In: Mullender, S. (ed.) Distributed Systems, pp. 147–166. ACM Press (1993)
2. Bernstein, P.A., Hadzilacos, V., Goodman, N.: Concurrency Control and Recovery in Database Systems. Addison Wesley (1987)
3. Chandra, T.D., Hadzilacos, V., Toueg, S.: The weakest failure detector for solving consensus. Journal of the ACM 43(4), 685–722 (1996)
4. Chandra, T.D., Toueg, S.: Unreliable failure detectors for reliable distributed systems. Journal of the ACM 43(2), 225–267 (1996)
5. Coan, B., Welch, J.: Transaction commit in a realistic timing model. Distributed Computing 4(2), 87–103 (1990)
6. Dolev, D., Strong, R.: A Simple Model For Agreement in Distributed Systems. In: Simons, B., Spector, A.Z. (eds.) Fault-Tolerant Distributed Computing. LNCS, vol. 448, pp. 42–50. Springer, Heidelberg (1990)
7. Fischer, M., Lynch, N., Paterson, M.: Impossibility of Distributed Consensus with One Faulty Process. Journal of the ACM 32, 374–382 (1985)
8. Gray, J.: A Comparison of the Byzantine Agreement Problem and the Transaction Commit Problem. In: Simons, B., Spector, A.Z. (eds.) Fault-Tolerant Distributed Computing. LNCS, vol. 448, pp. 10–17. Springer, Heidelberg (1990)
9. Guerraoui, R., Larrea, M., Schiper, A.: Non_Blocking Atomic Commitment with an Unreliable Failure Detector. In: Proceedings of the 14th IEEE Symposium on Reliable Distributed Systems (1995)
10. Guerraoui, R., Schiper, A.: The Decentralized Non-Blocking Atomic Commitment Protocol. To appear in Proceedings of the 7th IEEE Sysmposium on Parallel and Distributed Processing (1995)
11. Guerraoui, R., Schiper, A.: Transaction Model vs Virtual Synchrony Model: Bridging the Gap. In: Birman, K.P., Mattern, F., Schiper, A. (eds.) Dagstuhl Seminar 1994. LNCS, vol. 938, pp. 121–132. Springer, Heidelberg (1995)
12. Hadzilacos, V.: On the Relationship Between the Atomic Commitment and Consensus Problems. In: Simons, B., Spector, A.Z. (eds.) Fault-Tolerant Distributed Computing. LNCS, vol. 448, pp. 201–208. Springer, Heidelberg (1990)
13. Sabel, L., Marzullo, K.: Election Vs. Consensus in Asynchronous Systems. Technical Report TR-951488, Cornell Univ. (1995)
14. Schiper, A., Sandoz, A.: Primary Partition "Virtually-synchronous Communication" Harder than Consensus. In: Tel, G., Vitányi, P.M.B. (eds.) WDAG 1994. LNCS, vol. 857, pp. 39–52. Springer, Heidelberg (1994)
15. Skeen, D.: Non-Blocking Commit Protocols. In: Proceedings of the ACM SIGMOD International Conference on Management of Data, pp. 133–142. ACM Press (1981)

On Modelling and Prediction of Total CPU Usage for Applications in MapReduce Environments

Nikzad Babaii Rizvandi[1,2], Javid Taheri[1], Reza Moraveji[1,2], and Albert Y. Zomaya[1]

[1] Centre for Distributed and High Performance Computing
School of IT, University of Sydney, Australia
[2] National ICT Australia (NICTA), Australian Technology Park
nikzad@it.usyd.edu.au

Abstract. Recently, businesses have started using MapReduce as a popular computation framework for processing large amount of data, such as spam detection, and different data mining tasks, in both public and private clouds. Two of the challenging questions in such environments are (1) choosing suitable values for MapReduce configuration parameters – e.g., number of mappers, number of reducers, and DFS block size–, and (2) predicting the amount of resources that a user should lease from the service provider. Currently, the tasks of both choosing configuration parameters and estimating required resources are solely the users' responsibilities. In this paper, we present an approach to provision the total CPU usage in clock cycles of jobs in MapReduce environment. For a MapReduce job, a profile of total CPU usage in clock cycles is built from the job past executions with different values of two configuration parameters e.g., number of mappers, and number of reducers. Then, a polynomial regression is used to model the relation between these configuration parameters and total CPU usage in clock cycles of the job. We also briefly study the influence of input data scaling on measured total CPU usage in clock cycles. This derived model along with the scaling result can then be used to provision the total CPU usage in clock cycles of the same jobs with different input data size. We validate the accuracy of our models using three realistic applications (WordCount, Exim MainLog parsing, and TeraSort). Results show that the predicted total CPU usage in clock cycles of generated resource provisioning options are less than 8% of the measured total CPU usage in clock cycles in our 20-node virtual Hadoop cluster.

Keywords: total CPU usage in clock cycles, MapReduce, Hadoop, Resource provisioning, Configuration parameters, input data scaling.

1 Introduction

Recently, businesses have started using MapReduce as a popular computation framework for processing large amount of data in both public and private clouds; e.g., many web-based service providers like Facebook is already utilizing MapReduce to analyse its core business as well as to extract information from their produced data.

Y. Xiang et al. (Eds.): ICA3PP 2012, Part I, LNCS 7439, pp. 414–427, 2012.
© Springer-Verlag Berlin Heidelberg 2012

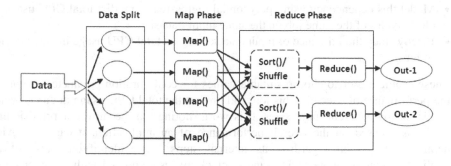

Fig. 1. MapReduce workflow

Therefore, understanding performance characteristics in MapReduce-style computations brings significant benefit to application developers in terms of improving application performance and resource utilization.

One of the regular user jobs – running experiments on MapReduce environment – is to frequently process and analysis almost relatively fixed-size data. For example, system administrators are always interested to frequently analysis system log files (such as Exim MainLog files[1]). As these log files are captured with fix sampling rate, their sizes do not usually change for specific period of times – e.g., for each month. Another example is Seismic imaging data where fix number of ultrasound senders/receivers produce earth underground information in a specific region; therefore, the size of output file – usually in the order of terabyte – is usually consistent [2]. The other example is to find a sequence matching between a new RNA and RNAs in a database [3], where the size of such databases (such as NCBI [4]) is almost unchanged over adjacent periods of time. These applications, which generally heavily consume resources, repeatedly show same execution pattern over their frequently deployments. As a result, any improvement in their resource utilisation can significantly improve the overall performance of such systems.

Two typical performance questions in MapReduce environments are: (1) how to estimate the required resources for a job, and (2) how to automatically tweak/tune MapReduce configuration parameters to improve execution of a job; these two questions are important as they directly influence the performance of MapReduce jobs. Moreover, users are solely responsible to properly set these configuration parameters to achieve desirable performances. Although there are a few recent methodologies to estimate resource provisioning of MapReduce jobs (mostly on execution time prediction [5-8]), to best of our knowledge, there is no practice to study the dependency between performance of executing a job and the configuration parameters. The technique in this paper is our first attempt to study and model this dependency between two major configuration parameters – e.g., number of mappers, and number of reducers– and total CPU usage in clock cycles of jobs in MapReduce environment.   Briefly, our contributions in this paper are:

- Study the influence of configuration parameters on the performance of executing a job (here, total CPU usage in clock cycles) in MapReduce environments.

- Model this dependency using polynomial regression to predict total CPU usage in clock cycles of the same job on the same input data size.
- Briefly study the influence of input data scaling on total CPU usage in clock cycles of jobs.

These enable a user to choose suitable values for configuration parameters, improve the performance of executing his job, and predict the total CPU usage in clock cycles of his job on different input sizes. It is worth noting that because our provisioning model is focused on the overall performance of an application, it cannot provide detailed information regarding its internal steps –e.g., identifying parts of an application that are more CPU usage in clock cycles compared with its other parts. Moreover, complexity degree of an application along with a proper model selection can significantly influence accuracy of our model; thus, results are expected to be less accurate for highly complex applications. It should be noted that all realistic jobs selected for provision validation are moderate/high CPU intensive jobs. This is because analysing of total CPU usage in clock cycles is the most important factor in CPU intensive jobs; while for I/O jobs, I/O utilization should be studied.

2   Related Work

Early works on analysing/improving MapReduce performance started almost since 2005; such as an approach by Zaharia et al [7] that addressed problem of improving the performance of Hadoop for heterogeneous environments. Their approach was based on the critical assumption in Hadoop that only targets homogeneous cluster nodes; i.e., Hadoop assumes homogenous nodes to schedule its tasks and stragglers. A statistics-driven workload modelling was introduced in [9] to effectively evaluate design decisions in scaling, configuration and scheduling. Their framework was used to make practical suggestions to improve energy efficiency of MapReduce applications. Authors in [10] proposed a theoretical study on the MapReduce programming model which characterizes the features of mixed sequential and parallel processing in MapReduce.

Performance prediction in MapReduce has been another important issue. In [11], the variation effect of Map and Reduce slots on the performance has been studied. Also, it was observed that different MapReduce applications may result in different CPU and I/O patterns. Then a fingerprint based method is utilized to predict the performance of a new MapReduce application based on the studied applications. The idea of pattern matching was used in [12] to find the similarity between CPU time patters of a new application and applications in database. Then it was concluded that if two applications show high similarity for several setting of configuration parameters it is very likely their optimal values of configuration parameters also be the same. Authors in [5] also used historical execution traces of applications on MapReduce environment for profiling and performance modelling and prediction. A modelling method was proposed in [9] to predict the total execution time of a MapReduce application; they used Kernel Canonical Correlation Analysis to obtain the correlation between the performance feature vectors extracted from MapReduce

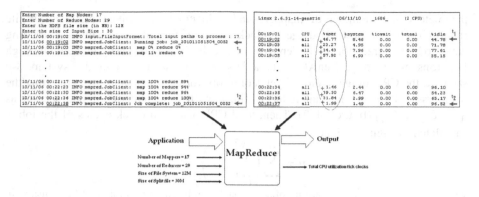

Fig. 2. The flow of the MapReduce job in Hadoop (left) and CPU usage time series extracted from actual system (right). This value is then converted to total CPU usage in clock cycle based on the platform's operating frequency.

job logs, and map time, reduce time, and total execution time. These features were acknowledged as critical characteristics for establishing any scheduling decisions. Authors in [13, 14] reported a basic model for MapReduce computation utilizations. Here, at first, the map and reduce phases were modelled using dynamic linear programming independently; then, these phases were combined to build a global optimal strategy for MapReduce scheduling and resource allocation. Another study in [8] proposed a resource provisioning framework to predict how much resources a user job needs to be completed by a certain time. This work also studied the impact of failures on the job completion time. To the best of our knowledge, most of resource provisioning methodologies in MapReduce environment address predicting of execution time of jobs; there is no specific research on studying (1) CPU, memory, and I/O cost of such jobs, and (2) dependency between configuration parameters of MapReduce environment and performance of execution of jobs (e.g., execution time, CPU usage in clock cycles). In sections 3.1 and 4.2, the importance of these two issues will be further explained.

3   Application Modelling in MapReduce

In commercial clouds (such as Amazon EC2), the problem of allocating appropriate number of machines for a proper time frame strongly depends on an application; user is responsible to set these values properly [15]. Thus, to estimate how much resource (in CPU cost, I/O cost, and Memory cost) a job requires in total enables user to make educated decisions to hire appropriate number of machines. In MapReduce environments, this problem becomes more important as number of machines cannot be changed after starting a job.

3.1   Profiling Total CPU Usage in Clock Cycles

For each application, we generate a set of jobs –i.e., an experiment of application on MapReduce environment– with different values of two MapReduce configuration parameters –i.e., number of mappers and reducers– on a given platform. While running each job, the CPU usage in clock cycles of the job is gathered –as training data– to build a trace for future deployments; such data can be easily gathered through functions provided in XenAPI with almost no overhead. Within the system, we sampled the CPU usage in clock cycles of a job, for each machine, from the time the mappers start to the time all reducers finish with time interval of one second as $\{C_{t_0}, C_{t_1}, \ldots, C_{t_N}\}$ (figure 2-left). Then, total CPU usage in clock cycles of the job is calculated as (figure 2-right):

$$ncpu = \sum_{k=1}^{M} \left(\sum_{i=1}^{N} C_{t_i,k} \right) \times f_{clock,k}$$

where M, N, and $f_{clock,k}$ are number of machines in cluster, number of CPU usage in clock cycles per seconds, and CPU clock frequency of k-th machine in cluster, respectively; for homogenous cluster, CPU clock frequency of all machines are the same.

Total CPU usage in clock cycles is an independent metric from number of machines in cluster. This means total CPU usage in clock cycles of a job should not significantly change on two clusters with different number of the same machines and configuration. For a cluster with R machines, and a job with T execution time, the following statements should be almost correct:

- A cluster with $\frac{R}{2}$ machines, the same configuration, and with the same CPU clock frequency should finish the job in $2T$ time.
- A cluster with R machines, and the same configuration but half CPU clock frequency should finish the job at $2T$ time.

Total CPU usage in clock cycles on a job on the same clusters, however, can change for different values of configuration parameters – the purpose of this study.

3.2   Total CPU Usage in Clock Cycles Model Using Polynomial Regression

The next step is to create a model for an application on MapReduce environment by characterizing the relationship between a set of MapReduce configuration parameters and CPU usage in clock cycles metric. The problem of such a modeling –based on linear regression– involves choosing of suitable coefficients for the model to better approximate a real system response time [16, 17].

Consider the linear algebraic equations for K different jobs of an application (φ_i) with different sets of two configuration parameters values as follows:

$$\begin{cases} ncpu_{\varphi_i}^{(1)} = a_{0,\varphi_i} + a_{1,\varphi_i}M^{(1)} + a_{2,\varphi_i}(M^{(1)})^2 + a_{3,\varphi_i}R^{(1)} + a_{4,\varphi_i}(R^{(1)})^2 \\ ncpu_{\varphi_i}^{(2)} = a_{0,\varphi_i} + a_{1,\varphi_i}M^{(2)} + a_{2,\varphi_i}(M^{(2)})^2 + a_{3,\varphi_i}R^{(2)} + a_{4,\varphi_i}(R^{(2)})^2 \\ \qquad\qquad\qquad\qquad\qquad \vdots \\ ncpu_{\varphi_i}^{(k)} = a_{0,\varphi_i} + a_{1,\varphi_i}M^{(k)} + a_{2,\varphi_i}(M^{(k)})^2 + a_{3,\varphi_i}R^{(k)} + a_{4,\varphi_i}(R^{(k)})^2 \end{cases} \quad (1)$$

where $ncpu_{\varphi_i}^{(i)}$ is the actual value of total CPU usage in clock cycles of the application φ_i in the jth job on MapReduce environment and $S^{(j)} = (M^{(j)}, R^{(j)})$ are the MapReduce configuration parameters; $M^{(j)}$ as the number of mappers, and $R^{(j)}$ as the number of reducers. Using the above definition, the approximation problem turns into estimating values of $\overline{a_{0,\varphi_l}}, \overline{a_{1,\varphi_l}}, \overline{a_{2,\varphi_l}}, \overline{a_{3,\varphi_l}}, \overline{a_{4,\varphi_l}}$ to optimize a cost function between the approximation values and the actual values of total CPU usage in clock cycles. An approximated total CPU clock tick $(\widehat{ncpu_{\varphi_l}})$ of the application for an unseen job with configuration parameters (M_*, R_*) is predicted as:

$$\widehat{ncpu_{\varphi_l}} = \overline{a_{0,\varphi_l}} + \overline{a_{1,\varphi_l}} M_* + \overline{a_{2,\varphi_l}} M_*^2 + \overline{a_{3,\varphi_l}} R_* + \overline{a_{4,\varphi_l}} R_*^2 \qquad (2)$$

There are a variety of well-known mathematical methods in the literature to calculate the variables $(\overline{a_{0,\varphi_l}}, \overline{a_{1,\varphi_l}}, \overline{a_{2,\varphi_l}}, \overline{a_{3,\varphi_l}}, \overline{a_{4,\varphi_l}})$. One widely used in many application domains is the Least Square Regression which calculates the parameters in Eqn.2 by minimizing the following error:

$$error = \sqrt{\sum_{j=1}^{K} (\widehat{ncpu_{\varphi_l}^{(j)}} - ncpu_{\varphi_i}^{(j)})^2}$$

Least Square Regression theory claims that if:

$$H_{model} = \begin{bmatrix} 1 & M^{(1)} & (M^{(1)})^2 & R^{(1)} & (R^{(1)})^2 \\ 1 & M^{(2)} & (M^{(2)})^2 & R^{(2)} & (R^{(2)})^2 \\ & & \vdots & & \\ 1 & M^{(k)} & (M^{(k)})^2 & R^{(k)} & (R^{(k)})^2 \end{bmatrix}, H_{actual,\varphi_i} = \begin{bmatrix} ncpu_{\varphi_i}^{(1)} \\ ncpu_{\varphi_i}^{(2)} \\ \vdots \\ ncpu_{\varphi_i}^{(k)} \end{bmatrix},$$

$$A = \begin{bmatrix} \overline{a_{0,\varphi_l}} \\ \overline{a_{1,\varphi_l}} \\ \vdots \\ \overline{a_{4,\varphi_l}} \end{bmatrix} \qquad (3)$$

then the model satisfying the above error will be calculated as [17]:

$$A = (H_{model}^T H_{model})^{-1} H_{model}^T H_{actual,\varphi_i} \qquad (4)$$

where $(.)^T$ denotes a transpose matrix. The set of configuration parameters values $\overline{a_{0,\varphi_l}}, \overline{a_{1,\varphi_l}}, \overline{a_{2,\varphi_l}}, \overline{a_{3,\varphi_l}}, \overline{a_{4,\varphi_l}}$ is the model that approximately describes the relationship between total CPU usage in clock cycles of an application to two MapReduce configuration parameters.

4   Experimental Validation

In this section, we evaluate the effectiveness of our models using three realistic applications.

4.1   Experimental Setting

Three realistic applications are used to evaluate the effectiveness of our method. Our method has been implemented and evaluated on a private Cloud with the following specifications:

- Physical H/W: includes five servers, each one is an Intel Genuine with 3.00GHz clock, 1GB memory, 1GB cache and with 50GB of shared SAN hard disk.
- For virtualization, Xen cloud platform (XCP) has been used on top of the physical H/W. The XenAPI [18] provides functionality to directly manage virtual machines inside XCP. It provides binding in high level languages like Java, C# and Python. Using these bindings, it was possible to measure the performance of all virtual machines in a datacentre and live-migrate them.
- Virtual nodes are implemented on top of the XCP. The number of virtual nodes is chosen 20 with Linux image (Debian). The virtual nodes run Hadoop version 0.20.2 – i.e., Apache implementation of MapReduce developed in Java [19]. The XenAPI package is executed in background to monitor/extract the CPU utilization time series of applications (in the native system) [20]. For an experiment with a specific set of MapReduce configuration parameters values, statistics are gathered from "running job" stage to the "job completion" stage (arrows in Figure 2-left) with sampling time interval of one second. All CPU usages samples are then combined to form CPU utilization time series of an experiment.

In the training phase of our modelling, $64\,sets$ of jobs for each application are conduced where the number of mappers and reducers are integers with a value in $[4,8,12,16,20,24,28,32]$; the size of input data is fixed to $12G$. To overcome temporal changes, each job is repeated ten times. Then in the prediction phase, the accuracy of the application model is evaluated with 30 new/unseen jobs on the same input data size where the number of mappers and reducers are randomly selected from the integers $[4 \ldots 32]$.

Our benchmark applications are WordCount (used by leading researchers in Intel [21], IBM [6], MIT [22], and UC-Berkeley [7]), TeraSort (as a standard benchmark in the international TeraByte sort competition [23, 24] as well as many researchers in IBM [25, 26], Intel [21], INRIA [27] and UC-Berkeley [28]), and Exim Mainlog parsing [12, 29]. These benchmarks are used due to their striking differences as well as their popularity among MapReduce applications.

4.2   Evaluation Criteria

We evaluate the accuracy of the fitted models, generated from regression based on a number of metrics [30]: Mean Absolute Percentage Error (MAPE), PRED(25) , Root Mean Squared Error (RMSE) and R2 Prediction Accuracy .

4.2.1   Mean Absolute Percentage Error (MAPE)
The Mean Absolute Percentage Error[30] for a prediction model is described as:

$$MAPE = \frac{\sum_{i=1}^{N} \frac{\left| ncpu_{\varphi_k}^{(i)} - \widetilde{ncpu_{\varphi_k}}^{(i)} \right|}{ncpu_{\varphi_i}^{(i)}}}{N}$$

where $ncpu_{\varphi_k}^{(i)}$ is the actual total CPU usage in clock cycles of application φ_k, $\widetilde{ncpu_{\varphi_k}}^{(i)}$ is the predicted total CPU usage in clock cycles and N is the number of observations in the dataset. The smaller MAPE value indicates the better fit of the prediction model.

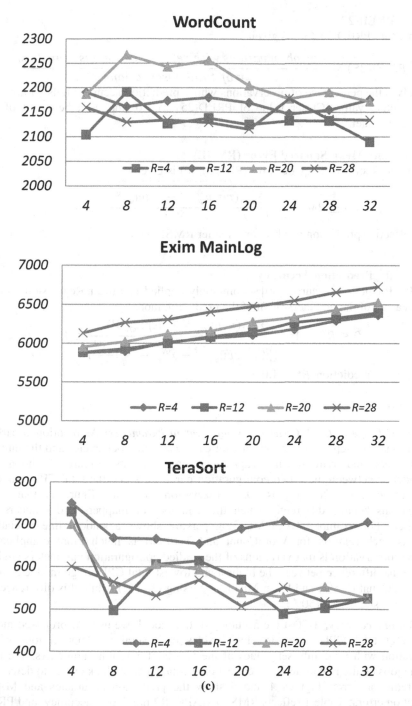

Fig. 3. The dependency between number of mappers and reducers and total CPU usage in clock cycle of jobs. The X-axis is number of mappers and Y-axis is total CPU usage(in tera clock cycle).

4.2.2   PRED(25)

The measure PRED(25)[30] is given as:

$$PRED(25) = \frac{\#\ of\ observations\ with\ relative\ error\ less\ than\ 25\%}{\#\ of\ total\ observations}$$

It involves the percentage of observations whose prediction accuracy falls within 25% of the actual value. Closer value of PRED(25) to 1.0 implies a better fit of the prediction model.

4.2.3   Root Mean Squared Error (RMSE)

The metric Root Mean Square Error (RMSE)[30] is given by:

$$0 \leq RMSE = \sqrt{\frac{\sum_{i=1}^{N}(ncpu_{\varphi_k}^{(i)} - n\widehat{cpu}_{\varphi_k}^{(i)})^2}{N}} \leq 1$$

More effective prediction results from smaller RMSE value.

4.2.4 R^2 Prediction Accuracy

The R^2 Prediction Accuracy[30] – commonly applied to Linear Regression models as a measure of the goodness-of-fit of the prediction model– is calculated as:

$$0 \leq R^2 = 1 - \frac{\sum_{i=1}^{N}(ncpu_{\varphi_k}^{(i)} - n\widehat{cpu}_{\varphi_k}^{(i)})^2}{\sum_{i=1}^{N}(n\widehat{cpu}_{\varphi_k}^{(i)} - \sum_{r=1}^{N}\frac{ncpu_{\varphi_k}^{(r)}}{N})} \leq 1$$

For a perfect prediction, $R^2 = 1.0$.

4.3   Results

Total CPU Usage in Clock Cycles and Configuration Parameters: As mentioned earlier, there is a strong dependency between total CPU usage in clock cycles and the number of mappers and reducers in MapReduce environments. Figure 3 shows the dependency between these two configuration parameters and the total CPU usage in clock cycles for different jobs. One observation from this figure is that these applications behave differently when their number of mappers and reducers are increased. For example, Exim MainLog parsing shows a smooth linear relation, whereas such relation for WordCount and TeraSort is much more complicated. Another observation is that variations of the studied configuration parameters slightly change the difference between the highest and lowest total CPU usage in clock cycles for WordCount (9.5%) and Exim MianLog parsing (15.5%), while this difference for TeraSort is significant (50%).

Prediction Accuracy: To test the accuracy of the model, we use our proposed model to predict total CPU usage in clock cycles of several new/unseen jobs of an application with randomly set values of the two configuration parameters. We then ran the jobs on the real system and collect their total CPU in clock cycles to determine the prediction error. Figures 4 and 5 show the prediction accuracies and MAPE prediction errors; Table 1 reflects RMSD, MAPE, R2 prediction accuracy, and PRED for these.

We found that most prediction evolution criteria are well satisfied for both

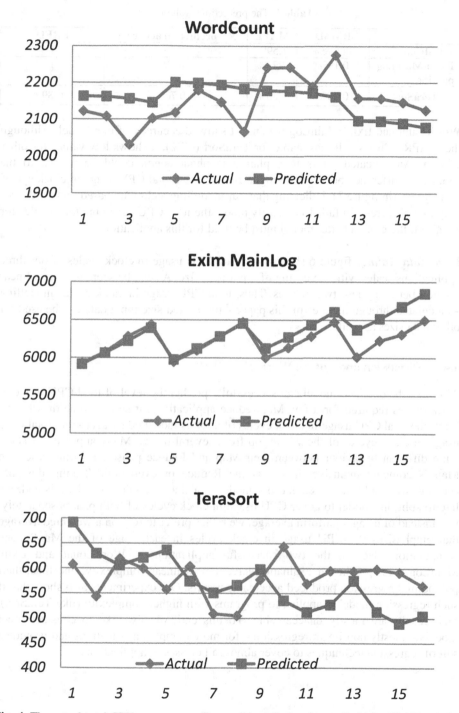

Fig. 4. The actual total CPU usage verses the model prediction for studied jobs. The X-axis is job ID and Y-axis is total CPU usage (in tera clock cycle).

Table 1. The prediction evalution

	RMSD	MAPE	R^2 prediction accuracy	PRED
WordCount	0.208%	1.59%	0.851	1
Exim MainLog parsing	0.19%	2.28%	0.99	1
TeraSort	0.28%	7.26%	0.76	0.89

WordCount and Exim MainLog parsing; it showed accuracy of our model. Although the MAPR value is still reasonable for TeraSort (~7%), it shows low values for other criteria. An educated guess to explain this phenomenon could be related to the significant difference between the highest and lowest total CPU usage in clock cycles of TeraSort (in figure 3), indicating that our modelling technique based on two-degree polynomial regression fails to correctly model the total CPU usage in clock cycles for TeraSort; therefore a better model must be used for this application.

Input data scaling: figure 6 shows how total CPU usage in clock cycles of our three applications scales with increasing of input data size. As can be seen, there is a linear relation between these two metrics. Thus, total CPU usage in clock cycles modelling – calculated through the idea of this paper – for a fixed-size input data can be used for other data sizes as well.

4.4   Discussion and Future Work

Although the obtained model can successfully predict the level of total CPU usage in clock cycles required for a few MapReduce applications, it shows some drawbacks. First, the total CPU usage in clock cycles of a job is modelled by averaging total CPU usage in clock cycles of the whole job from several traces. Many applications show quite different behaviour between their Map and Reduce phases: in some cases the Map is compute intensive, in others the Reduce or even both. Taking this into account, we would like to extend our model to a finer granular one. To this end, we like to split this model to cover CPU usage in clock cycles of both phases separately; i.e., instead of using a uniform average, we rather prefer to rely on a weighted average that emphasizes the CPU usage in clock cycles in each stage of the MapReduce computation. Second, the two successful applications – WordCount and Exim MainLog parsing – in our evaluation have almost linear complexity; and thus, their polynomial regression produced acceptable results. Our experiments also show that if such regression model is applied to programs with higher complexity (like TeraSort), their results are mostly unacceptable. To this end, we also like to consider other models – mostly non-linear regression – for more complex applications and provide a suit of regression techniques to cover almost all classes of applications.

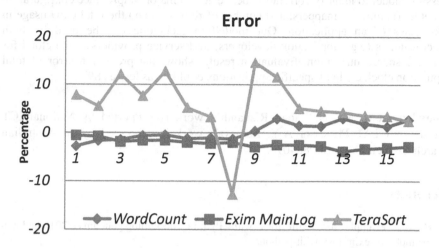

Fig. 5. The error between actual total CPU usage in clock cycle and the model prediction. The X-axis is job ID while Y-axis is percentage of error.

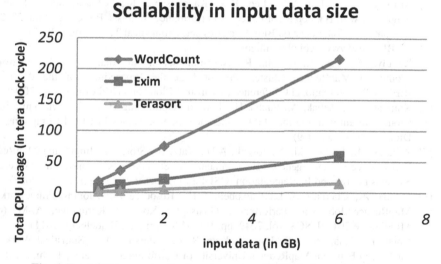

Fig. 6. Total CPU usage in clock cycles and scalability in input data size.

5   Conclusion

In this work we proposed an accurate modelling technique to predict total CPU usage in clock cycles of jobs in MapReduce environment before their actual deployment on clusters and/or clouds. Such prediction can greatly help both application performance and effective resource utilization. To achieve this, we have presented an approach to model/profile total CPU usage in clock cycles of applications and applied polynomial regression model to identify correlation between two major MapReduce configuration parameters (number of mappers, and number of reducers) and the total CPU usage in clock cycles of an application. Our modelling technique can be used by both users/consumers (e.g., application developers) and service providers in the cloud for effective resource utilization. Evaluation results show that prediction error of total computation clock cycle of specific applications could be as less as 8%.

Acknowledgment. Mr. N. Babaii Rizvandi's work is supported by National ICT Australia (NICTA). Professor A.Y. Zomaya's work is supported by an Australian Research Council Grant LP0884070.

References

[1] Hadoop example for Exim logs with Python, http://blog.gnucom.cc/2010/hadoop-example-for-exim-logs-with-python/

[2] Rizvandi, N.B., Boloori, A.J., Kamyabpour, N., Zomaya, A.: MapReduce Implementation of Prestack Kirchhoff Time Migration (PKTM) on Seismic Data. Presented at the The 12th International Conference on Parallel and Distributed Computing, Applications and Technologies (PDCAT), Gwangju, Korea (2011)

[3] Arumugam, K., Tan, Y.S., Lee, B.S., Kanagasabai, R.: "Cloud-enabling Sequence Alignment with Hadoop MapReduce: A Performance Analysis. Presented at the 2012 4th International Conference on Bioinformatics and Biomedical Technology (2012)

[4] NCBI, http://www.ncbi.nlm.nih.gov/

[5] Kavulya, S., Tan, J., Gandhi, R., Narasimhan, P.: An Analysis of Traces from a Production MapReduce Cluster. Presented at the Proceedings of the 2010 10th IEEE/ACM International Conference on Cluster, Cloud and Grid Computing (2010)

[6] Kambatla, K., Pathak, A., Pucha, H.: Towards Optimizing Hadoop Provisioning in the Cloud. Presented at the the 2009 Conference on Hot Topics in Cloud Computing, San Diego, California (2009)

[7] Zaharia, M., Konwinski, A., Joseph, A.D., Katz, R., Stoica, I.: Improving MapReduce Performance in Heterogeneous Environments. In: 8th USENIX Symposium on Operating Systems Design and Implementation (OSDI 2008), December 18, pp. 29–42 (2008)

[8] Verma, A., Cherkasova, L., Campbell, R.H.: Resource Provisioning Framework for MapReduce Jobs with Performance Goals. In: Kon, F., Kermarrec, A.-M. (eds.) Middleware 2011. LNCS, vol. 7049, pp. 165–186. Springer, Heidelberg (2011)

[9] Chen, Y., Ganapathi, A.S., Fox, A., Katz, R.H., Patterson, D.A.: Statistical Workloads for Energy Efficient MapReduce. University of California at Berkeley, Technical Report No. UCB/EECS-2010-6 (2010)

[10] Karloff, H., Suri, S., Vassilvitskii, S.: A model of computation for MapReduce. Presented at the Proceedings of the Twenty-First Annual ACM-SIAM Symposium on Discrete Algorithms, Austin, Texas (2010)

[11] Kambatla, K., Pathak, A., Pucha, H.: Towards optimizing hadoop provisioning in the cloud. Presented at the Proceedings of the 2009 Conference on Hot Topics in Cloud Computing, San Diego, California (2009)

[12] Rizvandi, N.B., Taheri, J., Zomaya, A.Y., Moraveji, R.: A Study on Using Uncertain Time Series Matching Algorithms in Map-Reduce Applications. In: Concurrency and Computation: Practice and Experience (2012)

[13] Wieder, A., Bhatotia, P., Post, A., Rodrigues, R.: Brief Announcement: Modelling MapReduce for Optimal Execution in the Cloud. Presented at the Proceeding of the 29th ACM SIGACT-SIGOPS Symposium on Principles of Distributed Computing, Zurich, Switzerland (2010)

[14] Wieder, A., Bhatotia, P., Post, A., Rodrigues, R.: Conductor: orchestrating the clouds. Presented at the 4th International Workshop on Large Scale Distributed Systems and Middleware, Zurich, Switzerland (2010)

[15] Oprescu, A.-M., Kielmann, T.: Bag-of-Tasks Scheduling under Budget Constraints. Presented at the IEEE Second International Conference on Cloud Computing Technology and Science (CloudCom), Indianapolis, IN, U.S.A (2010)

[16] Wood, T., Cherkasova, L., Ozonat, K., Shenoy, P.D.: Profiling and Modeling Resource Usage of Virtualized Applications. In: Issarny, V., Schantz, R. (eds.) Middleware 2008. LNCS, vol. 5346, pp. 366–387. Springer, Heidelberg (2008)

[17] Rizvandi, N.B., Nabavi, A., Hessabi, S.: An Accurate Fir Approximation of Ideal Fractional Delay Filter with Complex Coefficients in Hilbert Space. Journal of Circuits, Systems, and Computers 14, 497–506 (2005)

[18] Chisnall, D.: The definitive guide to the xen hypervisor, 1st edn. Prentice Hall Press (2007)

[19] Hadoop-0.20.2, http://www.apache.org/dyn/closer.cgi/hadoop/core

[20] Sysstat-9.1.6, http://perso.orange.fr/sebastien.godard/

[21] Optimizing Hadoop Deployments, Intel Corporation (2009)

[22] Mao, A., Morris, R., Kaashoek, M.F.: Optimizing MapReduce for Multicore Architectures. Massachusetts Institute of Technology (2010)

[23] Babu, S.: Towards automatic optimization of MapReduce programs. Presented at the 1st ACM Symposium on Cloud Computing, Indianapolis, Indiana, USA (2010)

[24] Sort Benchmark Home Page, http://sortbenchmark.org/

[25] Wang, G., Butt, A.R., Pandey, P., Gupta, K.: A Simulation Approach to Evaluating Design Decisions in MapReduce Setups. Presented at the MASCOTS (2009)

[26] Wang, G., Butt, A.R., Pandey, P., Gupta, K.: Using realistic simulation for performance analysis of mapreduce setups. Presented at the Proceedings of the 1st ACM Workshop on Large-Scale System and Application Performance, Garching, Germany (2009)

[27] Moise, D., Trieu, T.-T.-L., Boug, L., #233, Antoniu, G.: Optimizing intermediate data management in MapReduce computations. Presented at the Proceedings of the First International Workshop on Cloud Computing Platforms, Salzburg, Austria (2011)

[28] Gillick, D., Faria, A., DeNero, J.: MapReduce: Distributed Computing for Machine Learning, http://www.icsi.berkeley.edu/~arlo/publications/gillick_cs262a_proj.pdf2008

[29] Rizvandi, N.B., Taheri, J., Zomaya, A.Y.: On using Pattern Matching Algorithms in MapReduce Applications. Presented at the The 9th IEEE International Symposium on Parallel and Distributed Processing with Applications (ISPA), Busan, South Korea (2011)

[30] Islam, S., Keung, J., Lee, K., Liu, A.: Empirical prediction models for adaptive resource provisioning in the cloud. Future Generation Comp. Syst. 28, 155–162 (2012)

The Impact of Global Communication Latency at Extreme Scales on Krylov Methods

Thomas J. Ashby[1,2], Pieter Ghysels[1,3], Wim Heirman[1,4], and Wim Vanroose[3]

[1] Intel/Flanders Exascience Lab, Leuven, Belgium
[2] Imec, Leuven, Belgium
[3] Universiteit Antwerpen, Antwerp, Belgium
[4] Universiteit Gent, Ghent, Belgium

Abstract. Krylov Subspace Methods (KSMs) are popular numerical tools for solving large linear systems of equations. We consider their role in solving sparse systems on future massively parallel distributed memory machines, by estimating future performance of their constituent operations. To this end we construct a model that is simple, but which takes topology and network acceleration into account as they are important considerations. We show that, as the number of nodes of a parallel machine increases to very large numbers, the increasing latency cost of reductions may well become a problematic bottleneck for traditional formulations of these methods. Finally, we discuss how *pipelined KSMs* can be used to tackle the potential problem, and appropriate pipeline depths.

Keywords: Krylov methods, extreme scaling, global communication, reduction latency, pipelining, latency hiding.

1 Introduction

Krylov Subspace Methods (KSMs), such as GMRES, CG, BICGSTAB and numerous other variants, are widely used numerical tools for solving linear systems of equations $Ax = b$. They are popular because they are easy to parallelize, meaning that they can be run quickly, and they do not require direct manipulation of the matrix A, only matrix–vector products Av, and so can be used easily with sparse matrices without memory capacity problems. They are the tool of choice for solving extremely large sparse systems of equations on parallel distributed memory machines.

The general trend in large scale parallel computing is towards more cores per node, and more nodes. Because KSMs are such important tools, it is therefore a valuable exercise to model the future performance of the algorithms assuming this machine architecture trend will continue into the future. The potential parallel inefficiency of the KSMs at extreme scales on distributed memory machines is the problem we investigate in this paper.

The dependency structures of the KSM basic operations when vector elements are distributed across a parallel machine are given in Table 1. If the work per node is fixed, then of these operations the only ones which must *necessarily* get

Y. Xiang et al. (Eds.): ICA3PP 2012, Part I, LNCS 7439, pp. 428–442, 2012.

more costly as the number of machine nodes increases are the scalar products. Reduction operations on distributed memory machines are dominated by their latency cost, and have necessarily rather poor parallel efficiency for the non-local parts of the computation. Consequently the relative cost of this operation to the others and what the schedule of operations will end up looking like are both important to gauge the overall parallel efficiency as the scalar products get more expensive.

Pipelined (a.k.a. *Communication-Hiding*) KSMs have been proposed as an alternative formulation of KSMs to tackle the case when scalar products become an efficiency bottleneck [7]. The approach requires modifying the algorithms of the KSMs to alter their dependency structure. The extra scheduling freedom thus introduced is then used to implement a form of pipelining that can significantly improve the parallel efficiency of the algorithms.

The contribution of this paper is to show in detail how reduction latencies may become a problem on future exascale machines, and give a first quantification of what degree of pipelining in the KSMs may be required to avoid that latency becoming a bottleneck.

2   Example Problem

As the sparsity pattern, and thus form of the matrix–vector product, is problem specific, we choose a specific instance to make discussion easier. For our example problem we take a simple finite difference stencil, being the nearest neighbour in each direction on a regular 3D grid. The layout is the natural one, with contiguous sub-cubes of the grid allocated to each machine node. Although this problem is relatively simple, it is a reasonable approximation to sparse matrices that have a relatively low degree of connections between grid points. As there are many problems that use grids derived from physical problems with low spatial connectivity, including many finite element problems, this is a useful yardstick.

We stick to cubic grids for simplicity. We have chosen four local grid sizes; 1, 50^3, 100^3 and 200^3 per machine node (this amount is then further subdivided over sockets/cores). The largest size gives around 8 million Degrees of Freedom (DoFs). Although these numbers are not large for full problem sizes, there are several cases when they are relevant. Firstly, particle-mesh simulations often have high particle to mesh ratios resulting in thinly spread linear systems. Secondly, the use of multigrid for preconditioning (or as a solver) is interesting in that KSMs have been used for the "bottom solve" in a U-cycle, that is to solve the system once further restriction steps are abandoned as the resulting system will suffer from too much parallel inefficiency [8]; if the bottom solve requires enough iterations then pipelining can be useful. Thirdly, strong scaling can lead to thinly spread problems. The smallest problem size (i.e. 1) is intended to show the limit case for the problem rather than being a practical grid size.

3 Available Parallelism in *Krylov Subspace Methods*

KSM basic operations and their dependencies on a distributed memory machine are given in Table 1. The total available parallelism of a KSM is determined by the dependencies within and between these basic operations.

Table 1. Krylov Subspace Method basic operations

Operation	Notation	Dependencies
Matrix-vector multiplication	Ax	Depends on sparsity of A and machine topology; usually localised
Scalar products	$< v, w >, \|v\|$	Global tree
Vector operations	$\alpha v, v \pm w$	Local (element wise)

3.1 Parallelism within Operations

The two classes of operations with dependencies that result in communication are the matrix-vector multiplication and the scalar products. KSMs are popular for use with sparse linear systems. Of particular interest are those systems where the sparsity can be modelled by a graph with a low number of edges that approximates a grid structure.

When mapping such a problem and associated matrix onto a parallel machine, it is a natural mapping to distribute the graph on the machine such that a small graph neighbourhood becomes a small machine neighbourhood wherever possible, e.g. in our example problem, grid neighbours become machine neighbours. If the machine network supports low latency communication for all resulting neighbourhoods, then the cost of the matrix-vector product is either fixed or dominated by data transmission cost, and this doesn't change if the problem size is increased by weak scaling. Such an operation can in principle be weakly scaled to arbitrary problem sizes without significantly changing its parallel efficiency.

The reduction operations on the other hand, do not have a fixed level of parallelism. Their non-local operation structure is one large binary tree of operations where the leaves are the vector elements. As the number of input values grows, the height of the tree also grows, albeit slowly. Higher levels of the tree have many fewer operations than available computational resources, thus reductions have bad parallel efficiency, which gets worse as the machine gets larger; the ratio of computation to number of communication events is very low, and the amount of data sent is also low, so the whole operation is dominated by network latency costs, with most of the computing elements spending most of the time idle waiting for values to arrive.

3.2 Parallelism between Operations

In the standard KSM algorithms, scalar products are used in such a way that their parallel efficiency will be affected at extreme scales, and potentially before.

The start of an algorithm iteration involves applying the matrix (also called applying the stencil, as our sparse matrix is in stencil form) to produce a new vector, then calculating some scalar products on that new vector. The result of the scalar products are used to construct the input for the next stencil operation, and so there is a dependency cycle between stencil and scalar product operations. This pattern of dependencies occurs in all the methods in one form or other. Thus, the ratio of the reduction time vs. the time required to do the communication necessary for a stencil operation is a proxy to gauge general parallel efficiency of standard KSMs, from the point of view of communication costs. Note that in some methods, i.e. GMRES, there is a dependent sequence of at least two scalar products per stencil.

The validity of the stencil communication time vs. reduction time metric depends on some assumptions about local operations. As well as the two acts of communication (with associated computation for the reduction), a KSM iteration requires the local part of the stencil operation and some purely local vector operations to be performed. The relationship of these to the reduction time and stencil communication time is discussed in sec. 6; it suffices here to say that in some circumstances the reduction time dominates. When this holds, a reasonable portion of the schedule can be spent waiting for the latency dominated and parallel-inefficient non-local scalar products.

4 Relative Cost of KSM Operations at Extreme Scales

We start by modelling the off-node communication costs in this section. Although our model is relatively simple, we note that the problem we are analysing results from the value of the ratios. As such, the absolute values we use in our model may be wrong, but the conclusions that we come to will still be valid provided the actual ratios (now, at exascale or later) are similar to the ones we report on.

A formula for the relative cost of the communicating operations at extreme scale is given below:

$$\frac{\delta_r}{\delta_s} = \frac{\beta + \sum_{i=0}^{T}(\lambda_r^i + \delta_n)}{\lambda_s + (D_{\text{face}}/\theta_s)} \tag{1}$$

where δ_r and δ_s are the total time taken for the reduction and stencil operations respectively. We assume that the reduction takes the form of a series of non-local communication steps, where data is transmitted on the network, and local reduction steps where the operations are actually carried out on the data present. T is the height of the tree of non-local reduction steps, λ_r^i is the latency of traversing the network links and switches for reduction step i, and δ_n is the time for executing the local reduction operations on a compute node or network switch to make an intermediate or final result. β is the cost of broadcasting the reduction result. λ_s is the maximum latency for traversing the network links and switches to logically neighbouring nodes for a single stencil step, D_{face} is the volume of data to transfer to a neighbour, representing the face of the local grid cube, and θ_s is the per-face bandwidth available over the links used for the stencil operation. Our choice of stencil means that what gets communicated to neighbours are the six faces of the locally allocated sub-cube of the problem grid, with the longest time taken to communicate any face determining δ_s. Stating the bandwidth parameter as "per face" allows us to model different network topologies by deriving the per face bandwidth from the network link bandwidth and the topology.

The reduction operations we consider are of type *all-reduce*, meaning that the result of the operation should be made available to all cores. There are several ways to implement such all-to-all operations. We have chosen a reduction to a single value followed by a broadcast for the following reasons. True N-to-N broadcast and butterfly networks of high radix are unlikely to be implemented for a very large number of nodes due to the prohibitive equipment cost. Also, mapping such algorithmic approaches on to the network topologies we consider here is unlikely to gain much if anything in terms of the latency cost after taking switch contention into account.

4.1   Applying the Model

To use formula 1 we need to fill in the parameters; these, and associated assumptions, are given below.

Nodes: Node count estimates for future exascale systems vary, from around 100,000 for "fat nodes" to around 1,000,000 for "thin nodes" [13]. By *node* we mean the parts of a machine with their own separate network interfaces (usually containing several *sockets* and/or *accelerators*, each supporting multiple *cores* or *CPUs*). On the assumption that we will get there eventually, at exascale or shortly thereafter, we take the larger number to illustrate the problem of latency when scaling to larger node counts.

Network: The latency costs λ_s and λ_r^i depend on the corresponding cable lengths, a per switch latency, which we assume is the same for all switches in a given network, and an at-node network to user-process (and vice versa) transfer latency. Our basic model for cables is based on a square warehouse of densely packed cabinets each measuring $1m^2$, with maximum 500 nodes per cabinet. Cable distance for longer cables is calculated using Manhattan distance between cabinets, and cable latency is based on signals propagating at the speed of light. We reduce cable latency within a cabinet to zero to simplify the model (cable latency costs are dominated by the longer links). We derive the link bandwidth (Eqn. 2) and router latency (Eqn. 3) from a simple model of a router, based on the bi-directional router bandwidth and network radix (i.e. number of in or out ports):

$$\text{link}_{BW} = \text{router}_{BW}/(2 \times \text{radix}) \tag{2}$$

$$\text{router}_{latency} = 10ns + 5 \times log_2(\text{radix}) \tag{3}$$

The constant (10 nanoseconds) in Eqn. 3 is to take account of SerDes and signalling. The factor 2 Eqn. 2 is to turn a network radix into the total number of I/O ports on a network router (for bi-directional bandwidth). All router chips in a given model have the same bandwidth. In the case of multiple networks, the number of I/O ports can be different for each network. We set the local node latency cost to move data from a network interface into a user process or back the other way according to machine type (details below). The height of the non-local reduction tree, T, is given by the number of nodes (given above) and the non-local reduction tree radix.

4.2 Machine Architecture

Although for our case the scalar products are the limiting factor for available parallelism in KSMs as the size of a problem grows, the mapping of the KSMs onto a machine architecture needs to be taken into account to understand actual parallel efficiency. The main concerns here are the network topology and the available bandwidth. To apply the model, we take two example machine architectures. The first is a machine where the grid embeds in such a way that nearest neighbour communication links are available, and there is a separate Accelerated Reduction Tree (ART) for reductions; this is a close match with the program dependencies. An ART is a separate network where the switches are capable of buffering the incoming values and executing a reduction operation on them directly before sending the result further up the tree. The reduction requires one trip up the ART to compute the result, and one trip down it to make it available to all cores. Machines with accelerated reduction networks include [2,4,3].

The second is a machine with a single high-radix fat-tree network; this represents a machine where a different network has been chosen due to cost and flexibility issues, and the network architecture is a less good fit to the dependencies. In the case of a standard indirect tree-like network with no in-built acceleration, the logical form of the reduction would still be a tree of a certain radix, but where the local reduction steps are carried out at the leaves of the tree network. Note that the individual links in the operation tree would be mapped onto various sets of links in the machine tree network, and thus would have different total switch latency costs, unlike the ART where only cable length varies.

After using the parameters and assumptions in sec. 4.1, we need per face bandwidth θ_s, non-local reduction step tree radix, local reduction cost δ_n, and broadcast latency β to derive a value from our model. These values are either specific to the machine architecture, or used as range parameters to generate plots.

θ_s is derived from the router bandwidth. The bi-directional router bandwidth is a free parameter which we vary in the plots from 0.5 to 5 TBytes/s. The local reduction costs are based on an assist circuit serially executing floating point operations at 2 GHz. To get the height of the tree of non-local reduction steps, we need a radix. We fix this radix based on the machine architecture. For an ART, the machine ART radix thus becomes a plot parameter. For a fat-tree, we

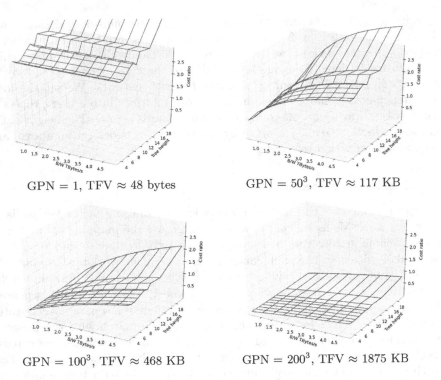

GPN = 1, TFV ≈ 48 bytes   GPN = 50^3, TFV ≈ 117 KB

GPN = 100^3, TFV ≈ 468 KB   GPN = 200^3, TFV ≈ 1875 KB

Fig. 1. δ_r/δ_s for **mesh + ART**. The x-axis is router bandwidth (0.5 to 5 TBytes/s), y-axis is increasing ART height (i.e. the different heights given by the radices in the range 200 to 2), and z-axis is the resulting δ_r/δ_s. GPN is Grid Points per Node, TFV is Total Face data Volume (i.e. per face volume ×6).

make the radix of the non-local reduction tree the same as the network radix, so there is again a single architecture radix parameter. We use the radix parameter to generate different tree heights, and plot the tree height and router bandwidth against the resulting ratio of reduction to stencil time cost.

Mesh and ART. We take the link latency for the stencil operation on the mesh network, λ_s, based on a cable to each neighbouring node at most 1 metre long, and the assumption that each node has a Network Interface Controller (NIC) that also acts as the switch for the mesh network. We assume the bandwidth to the NIC from the cores is at least as much as the total off-node bandwidth, and we divide the router chip bandwidth between the off-node links only. We assume that the face exchange can be done in parallel, so that all torus router links are used simultaneously at full link bandwidth.

The local reduction latency δ_n is a function of the local operations in the ART. We assume that the ART supports broadcast directly with no at-switch copy overhead, so β is just derived from switch and cable crossing costs on the way down the tree. The core-to-NIC cost is 100ns, based on reported numbers for a specialised low overhead system [6], which is in line with design choices such as reduction acceleration hardware.

In Fig. 1 we plot the relative cost of the two operations, where the parameters are ART height and bi-directional router bandwidth. The number of bits for a cube face varies from figure to figure; the maximum is $200^2 \times 64$ bits, that is the face of a local 3D cube of double precision floats that has dimension 200^3, and the minimum is 1×64, the case where the local cube is a single point.

The model shows that the ratio δ_r/δ_s gets worse with taller tree heights and increased router bandwidth, with the exception that the results for the smallest face volume are not affected by the bandwidth parameter. Whilst the ratios are mostly under 1 for the largest problem size (200^3), they are mostly above 1 for the other sizes, and there is a significant amount of the design space above 1.5 for both 50^3 and 100^3.

We consider ratios less than 0.25 to be largely irrelevant for pipelining, on the basis that a chain of two such scalar products still only costs at most half as much as a stencil in a standard KSM, and thus the parallel efficiency is already reasonable. This occurs for very few points, suggesting that for the *mesh + ART* the standard KSMs should show a reasonable benefit from pipelining to improve parallel efficiency for these problem sizes.

Fat-tree. For the fat-tree the nearest neighbour latency cost for the stencil, λ_s, will be the full cost of a trip via the top node of the tree. Thus the radix and resulting height of the fat-tree will affect the stencil time δ_s. Cable latencies are again derived from the tree layout model, with longer cables now affecting both operations. Given that each node has one cable link to its immediate parent switch, which is not attached to any node, the bandwidth available for parallel face exchange in the stencil operation is one sixth that of the network link bandwidth (as the stencil is 3D); this is different from the *mesh + ART* case. We use a core-to-NIC cost of 800ns for this architecture, based on reported numbers for hardware that would be used in a commodity cluster ([1] reports a one-way MPI latency of $1.6\mu s$, giving a maximum of 800ns per core).

A reduction on a network without full acceleration gives rise to a more complicated calculation for δ_r. As the local reduction of each stage must be computed at the network leaves, the length of the path taken by the operands through the network will change; for example, the operands for the first stage of the reduction could pass through one switch to a neighbouring node, but the operands for the last stage of the reduction must pass through the top of the tree (and get back to a leaf node). Due to the latency cost of getting information from the NIC on to the sockets, we assume that the actual reduction operation itself is done by an assist processor on the NIC to avoid this; for a current example of such an approach, see [12]. We assume that the final broadcast is supported by the switches, so that the cost for it (β) is the same latency as a trip up and down the tree network. Note that the lack of acceleration means that it is not a good fit for the reduction, which must use multiple trips through the tree.

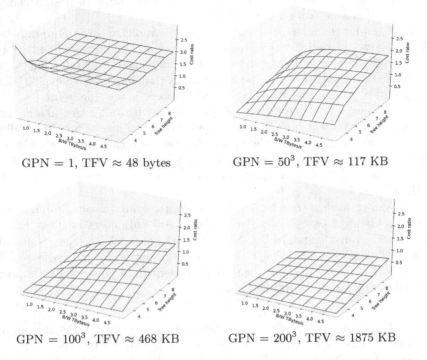

GPN = 1, TFV ≈ 48 bytes   GPN = 50^3, TFV ≈ 117 KB

GPN = 100^3, TFV ≈ 468 KB   GPN = 200^3, TFV ≈ 1875 KB

Fig. 2. δ_r/δ_s for **fat-tree**. The x-axis is router bandwidth (0.5 to 5 TBytes/s), y-axis is increasing fat-tree height (i.e. the different heights given by the radices in the range 500 to 5), and z-axis is the resulting δ_r/δ_s. GPN is Grid Points per Node, TFV is Total Face data Volume (i.e. per face volume ×6).

In Fig. 2 we give plots of the relative cost of the two operations, where the parameters are fat-tree height and router bandwidth. The calculations for the fat-tree bear some similarity to the *mesh + ART* results. However, the ratio values tend to be less. For 200^3, roughly half the space is < 0.25, and thus unlikely to profit much from pipelining. Similarly, the lower tree heights, which are more likely for a low diameter network, are quite often under 0.25 for 100^3. However, 50^3 problem sizes will almost definitely benefit from pipelining. The increase in reduction cost for lower router bandwidth for size 1 is a quirk that probably results from a contested fat-tree down-link to the nodes that perform the reduction calculations at each step.

5   Reduction Times, Bandwidth and Pipeline Depth

The reduction times computed from the model are given in Fig. 3. The per link one-directional bandwidth varies from 155 GBits/s to 1.55 TBits/s for the torus network as the router chip bandwidth changes, and from 18 GBits/s to 3.7 TBits/s for the fat-tree as both the router bandwidth and tree radix changes.

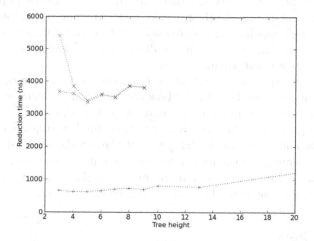

Fig. 3. Reduction times. x-axis is tree network height, y-axis is total all-reduce time in nanoseconds. The bottom line (blue) is for the **mesh + ART**, the top two lines (green and red) are for the minimum and maximum **fat-tree** reduction times respectively (as the radix varies).

Measured reduction times for large clusters are difficult to find in the literature. [6] states that a barrier on a full size machine is expected to take about $6\mu s$. It is reasonable to suppose that a reduction will also take roughly this amount of time. Our model gives results which are less that this due to significantly lower assumed latency in the routers, use of tree networks reducing the number of hops, and the fact that the barrier time in [6] is somewhat larger than the value expected from extrapolating directly from their per-hop reduction costs. If our predictions are overly optimistic, then larger values for reduction times at exascale will make scalar products more expensive relative to stencil operations, and deeper pipelines will be necessary.

The required pipeline depths for methods with two reductions per matrix product are (the ceiling of) twice the ratios given in the result plots. Thus, a pipeline depth of at least 1 should be applied to everything except the low bandwidth/low tree height parts of 200^3 for the *mesh + ART*, and many parameter points for the 100^3 and 50^3 problem sizes would benefit from pipeline depths of 3 or 4. Depths are somewhat less for the fat-tree, but depths 1 and 2 are still common, and reasonable parts of the parameter space benefit from 3.

6   Off-Node vs. On-Node Costs

We consider on-node costs for a stencil or an iteration of a KSM as the floating point operations (flop) and transfers from memory that are required. Instruction bandwidth is unlikely to be important as the algorithms are concise. The amount of non-floating point operations and their throughput is heavily dependant on code implementation details and the features of the core micro-architecture (such as how many integer pipelines there are and how fast they run compared to the floating point vector unit etc), and thus is difficult to include in the model in an unbiased way; thus we omit them.

Rather than very specific predictions of on-node resources, we consider here the general scaling of on-node costs and how technology advancement may affect this in the future. In our example problem, each node is allocated a cube of data to represent its portion of the grid, which is then further subdivided over the different sockets and cores. In the language of the KSMs, each such grid is a (local part of a) *vector*, and the basic operations manipulate these vectors. First we consider when off-node costs dominate for a stencil as a function of the size of the local grid, then we extend this reasoning to the KSMs.

6.1   Stencil Costs

Computational Bandwidth. Given the latencies of the reduction operations calculated from the model, the first comparison is against the computational throughput on the node. Estimates of node performance for exascale vary. Here we take the "fat" node estimate from [13], which predicts 10 TFlop/s per node.

The number of flops required per element of a centred difference stencil operation is $2n + k$, where n is the dimensionality of the hypercube and k is some fixed number to take into account the centre point and any normalisation etc.; $n = 3$ in our running example, and we take $k = 3$ to allow for normalisation. For a local cube of side length g, this gives a total number of flops as $9g^3$. This number grows rapidly as g increases. Similarly, the on-node cost for the local part of a reduction is $2g^3$.

The node is not computationally limited provided that the flop rate is sufficient to process the appropriate local cube size in the time taken to perform the corresponding communication. In our example, this means executing $(9 + 2)g^3$ flops in the time taken to perform an off-node all-reduce, when the all-reduce is the longest of the communications. Compute times for the various problem sizes are given in table 2. The figures suggest that the computational bandwidth will start to be a bottleneck shortly before $g = 100$ for the *mesh + ART* and shortly afterwards for the fat-tree topology. We are wary of making any hard claims here due to the fairly wide error margins on the calculations from the model and the predictions of effective future computational bandwidth. Nonetheless is reasonable to suppose that pipelining is likely to be useful for $g \leq 100$, which is also what the δ_r/δ_s ratios show. Due to the cube growth of flops required with g, it is unlikely that $g = 200$ will not be computational-bandwidth bound.

Memory Bandwidth. Computing a stencil requires $2n + 1$ reads and 1 writes per element. If we assume modest cache capacities that can capture the reuse of the values between different element read accesses (which is reasonable for low n), then this becomes 1 read and 1 write to main memory per element. An inner-product requires 1 read and 1 write per element. Thus, the number of off-chip memory transfers to compute a local stencil and scalar product when the vector objects do not fit entirely in cache is $4g^3$.

Although the number of transfers from memory required to compute a stencil is less than the number of flops needed, the factor of difference is small; only 2.75. By contrast, the flop to bandwidth ratio in current and predicted future machines is much larger than this. The ratio of computational bandwidth to memory bandwidth given in [13] is 20:1. The implication of this trend is that a problem size that is mostly out-of-cache will be much sooner memory bandwidth bound than computational bandwidth bound. Thus, the problem should fit (almost) entirely in-cache for pipelining to be relevant, or future memory bandwidth would have to be substantially larger than current predictions.

Table 2. Data sizes and local compute times as local cube side length g varies

g	Volume per vector	Total volume GMRES(10)	Compute stencil + reduce	Compute GMRES
1	8 bytes	88 bytes	$< 10ns$	$< 10ns$
50	976.5 kB	10.4 MB	137ns	662ns
100	7812.5 kB	83.9 MB	1100ns	5300ns
200	62500 kB	671.3 MB	8800ns	$42.4\mu s$

6.2   KSM Costs

To extend this sort of calculation to a whole KSM algorithm, we need to take into account the change in algorithm resource requirements. A prototypical long recurrence algorithm, truncated GMRES(m), requires $m + 1$ vectors of storage, where m is chosen to balance rough estimates of iteration cost vs. the number of iterations needed for convergence. GMRES(m) requires $2m + 8$ memory transfers and $2n + 4m + 7$ flops per grid element. We show an analysis for GMRES(10). Note that GMRES requires two scalar products, so we are comparing against 2× the reduction costs given in Fig. 3.

Computational Bandwidth. The local GMRES(10) computation times are given in table 2. This suggests that, for this recurrence length, pipelining will be interesting for $g \leq 60$ for the *mesh + ART*. As the recurrence length increases, this number will drop, but relatively slowly as the recurrence gives a linear increase in resource requirements. For the fat-tree, pipelining is relevant for $g \approx 100$ for the fastest predicted reduction time. The same caveat for the reduction times derived from the model applies here; a relatively small error in the model could make $g = 100$ a candidate for pipelining GMRES, but the estimates would have to be an order of magnitude off for it to be worthwhile for $g = 200$.

Memory Bandwidth. The ratio of required computational bandwidth to data bandwidth for GMRES(10) is 53:28 ($\approx 1.8 : 1$), which is worse than the ratio required for the simple stencil test. Thus, GMRES is even more prone to being memory bandwidth limited. Added to this, the total storage required is $m + 1$ vectors, thus for GMRES(10) the cache should be $100^3 \times 11 \approx 83$MB. Although this is somewhat out of the range of current standard nodes (e.g. 4 sockets $\times$ 10MB L3 cache per socket), a doubling of L3 cache size would be enough to keep virtually all the problem in cache. Thus, $g = 100$ could well still benefit from pipelining on exascale machines if cache capacities increase modestly. However, caches would have to grow by a factor of 15 to fit $200^3 \times 11 \approx 671$MB; this is less likely, but not impossible if capacity follows Moore's law.

Relevant recurrence lengths for GMRES are clearly quite small due to cache capacities when considering pipelining. Pipelining is mostly targeted at short recurrence KSMs though, as they suffer the worst from strong scaling parallel inefficiency.

7 Technology Factors

It is very difficult to predict exactly what the machines will look like at exascale and afterwards due to the jump effects of the introduction of different technologies. The ratios of the resources may be significantly different. For example, the computation to DRAM bandwidth ratio may change in the medium term due to 3D stacking of DRAM and CPU, and/or optical interconnects [16,15]. Any relative increase in DRAM bandwidth will close the gap somewhat between computational and memory bandwidth, and may make pipelining relevant for problem sizes that are currently memory bandwidth limited due to limited cache capacity.

Note that implementing pipelined KSMs requires simultaneous execution of communicating parts of the algorithm that occur together, and thus they must be multiplexed onto the network resources. At the very least it must be possible to execute a stencil whilst waiting for a reduction to complete. We omit a discussion on these details due to lack of space, and refer to [10] for ongoing work on asynchronous reductions in e.g. MPI.

8 Related Work

8.1 Rescheduling

There have been various projects looking at how to combine and schedule basic KSM operations, without altering the dependency structure of the algorithms themselves, and/or the resulting performance; some examples include [5], which considers rescheduling for bandwidth reduction, and [14], which uses careful ordering of the operations of variants of the two-sided KSMs to allow scalar products to be executed at the same time as one of the matrix-vector products; this amounts to a partial pipelining approach. Our work is differs as we consider the future impact of an algorithm that does more extensive reordering.

8.2 Partial Pipelining of Gram-Schmidt Orthogonalization

In [9] the authors improve the scalar product latency tolerance of two iteration Iterated Classical Gram-Schmidt (ICGS(2)) by doing the first iteration of orthogonalization and normalisation as usual, and then launching the second iteration in parallel with the creation of the next basis vector. They report moderate speed-up improvements over standard ICGS, but do not attempt to extrapolate to future computing technology. The context of the work is KSM–based eigensolvers.

9 Conclusions and Future Work

This paper has given the motivation for the study of pipelined KSMs [7] based on a performance model of exascale machines. We have shown how the lack of parallelism could affect the performance of KSM algorithms mapped onto different parallel architectures for smaller problem sizes that occur as a result of strong scaling or use of multigrid. We have also given estimates of the extent of pipelining that will be needed; depths of 1 are likely to be common, and depths up to 4 could easily be needed.

Our work can be expanded in a number of ways. A missing component of our model is OS noise [11] and synchronisation jitter, which would have the effect of increasing the cost of all-reduce operations and make δ_r/δ_s larger, and pipelines thus longer. Secondly, although it is impossible to validate our model (as exascale hardware has not been built yet), we plan to adjust our model parameters to reflect current hardware to see whether pipelining could already be used. Finally, the scheduling freedom introduced to tolerate all-reduce latencies in pipelined KSMs could also be used to improve the temporal locality of access to vector entries. This may have an important impact for larger, memory bandwidth limited problems even when reduction latency itself is not problematic. We will investigate the performance of the algorithms for this size of problem in future work.

Acknowledgements. This work is funded by Intel and by the Institute for the Promotion of Innovation through Science and Technology in Flanders (IWT). Thanks to Karl Meerbergen for his input.

References

1. Retrieved from MVAPICH2 website (2012),
   http://mvapich.cse.ohio-state.edu/performance/interNode.shtml (2011)
2. Adiga, N., et al.: An overview of the BlueGene/L supercomputer. In: ACM/IEEE 2002 Conference on Supercomputing, p. 60 (November 2002)
3. Ajima, Y., Sumimoto, S., Shimizu, T.: Tofu: A 6D mesh/torus interconnect for exascale computers. Computer 42(11), 36–40 (2009)
4. Arimilli, B., et al.: The PERCS high-performance interconnect. In: IEEE HOTI 2010, pp. 75–82 (August 2010)

5. Ashby, T.J., O'Boyle, M.: Iterative collective loop fusion. In: Mycroft, A., Zeller, A. (eds.) CC 2006. LNCS, vol. 3923, pp. 202–216. Springer, Heidelberg (2006)
6. Chen, D., Eisley, N.A., Heidelberger, P., Senger, R.M., Sugawara, Y., Kumar, S., Salapura, V., Satterfield, D.L., Steinmacher-Burow, B., Parker, J.J.: The IBM BlueGene/Q interconnection network and message unit. In: Proceedings of 2011 International Conference for High Performance Computing, Networking, Storage and Analysis. SC 2011, pp. 26–27. ACM, New York (2011)
7. Ghysels, P., Ashby, T.J., Meerbergen, K., Vanroose, W.: Hiding global communication latency in the GMRES algorithm on massively parallel machines (to be published, 2012)
8. Gmeiner, B., Gradl, T., Köstler, H., Rüde, U.: Analysis of a flat highly parallel geometric multigrid algorithm for hierarchical hybrid grids. Technical report, Dept. Comp. Sci., Universität Erlangen-Nürnberg (2011)
9. Hernández, V., Román, J.E., Tomás, A.: A parallel variant of the Gram-Schmidt process with reorthogonalization. In: PARCO, pp. 221–228 (2005)
10. Hoefler, T., Lumsdaine, A.: Overlapping communication and computation with high level communication routines. In: Proceedings of the 8th IEEE Symposium on Cluster Computing and the Grid (CCGrid 2008) (May 2008)
11. Hoefler, T., Schneider, T., Lumsdaine, A.: Characterizing the influence of system noise on large-scale applications by simulation. In: ACM/IEEE Supercomputing 2010, pp. 1–11 (2010)
12. Moody, A., Fernandez, J., Petrini, F., Panda, D.K.: Scalable NIC-based reduction on large-scale clusters. In: ACM/IEEE Supercomputing 2003, pages 59 (2003)
13. Stevens, R., White, A., et al.: Architectures and technology for extreme scale computing. Technical report, ASCR Scientic Grand Challenges Workshop Series (December 2009)
14. Tianruo Yang, L., Brent, R.: The improved Krylov subspace methods for large and sparse linear systems on bulk synchronous parallel architectures. In: IEEE IPDPS 2003, p. 11 (April 2003)
15. Udipi, A.N., Muralimanohar, N., Balasubramonian, R., Davis, A., Jouppi, N.P.: Combining memory and a controller with photonics through 3D-stacking to enable scalable and energy-efficient systems. In: ISCA 2011, pp. 425–436 (2011)
16. Woo, D.H., Seong, N.H., Lewis, D., Lee, H.-H.: An optimized 3D-stacked memory architecture by exploiting excessive, high-density TSV bandwidth. In: IEEE HPCA 2010, pp. 1–12 (January 2010)

Fast Parallel Algorithms for Blocked Dense Matrix Multiplication on Shared Memory Architectures

G. Nimako, E.J. Otoo, and D. Ohene-Kwofie

School of Computer Science
The University of the Witwatersrand
Johannesburg, South Africa
{gideonnimako,papaotu,danielkwofie}@gmail.com

Abstract. The current trend of multicore and Symmetric Multi-Processor (SMP), architectures underscores the need for parallelism in most scientific computations. Matrix-matrix multiplication is one of the fundamental computations in many algorithms for scientific and numerical analysis. Although a number of different algorithms (such as Cannon, PUMMA, SUMMA etc), have been proposed for the implementation of matrix-matrix multiplication on distributed memory architectures, matrix-matrix algorithms for multicore and SMP architectures have not been extensively studied. We present two types of algorithms, based largely on blocked dense matrices, for parallel matrix-matrix multiplication on shared memory systems. The first algorithm is based on blocked matrices whiles the second algorithm uses blocked matrices with the MapReduce framework in shared memory. Our experimental results show that, our blocked dense matrix approach outperforms the known existing implementations by up to 50% whiles our MapReduce blocked matrix-matrix algorithm outperforms the existing matrix-matrix multiplication algorithm of the Phoenix shared memory MapReduce approach, by about 40%.

Keywords: Matrix-Matrix Multiplication, High Performance Computing, Shared Memory Algorithm.

1 Introduction

Matrix-Matrix multiplication is one of the most important linear algebra operation in many scientific and numeric computations. Over the last few decades, a significant number of different matrix-matrix multiplication algorithms have been proposed for distributed memory architectures. Examples of such algorithms include the Cannon algorithm [1], Parallel Universal Matrix Multiplication Algorithm (PUMMA) [2], Scalable Universal Matrix Multiplication Algorithm (SUMMA) [3] and Matrix Multiplication Algorithm Suitable for Clusters (SRUMMA) [4]. These algorithms are best suited for grid of processors. Usually, the matrices are divided into blocks of horizontal and vertical slices of sub-matrices. Consider the simple matrices $C[M][N], A[M][K], B[K][N]$ depicted in

Y. Xiang et al. (Eds.): ICA3PP 2012, Part I, LNCS 7439, pp. 443–457, 2012.
© Springer-Verlag Berlin Heidelberg 2012

Figure 1, where $C = A \times B$. A horizontal slice from A and its multiplicative vertical slice from B are assigned to a node or processor within the grid. Usually a 2-dimensional grid is used. Now since a node has only two blocks, one from each of the two input matrices, the other blocks within the horizontal and vertical slices need to be transferred. The performance of these distributed algorithms is usually dependent on the efficient parallel organisation of the grid of processors.

However, such distributed matrix-matrix algorithms are not suitable for multicore and SMP architectures. Symmetric multiprocessing (SMP) involves a multiprocessor computer hardware architecture where two or more identical processors are connected to a single shared main memory and are controlled by a single Operating System (OS) instance. In multicore architectures, memory is shared and data accesses are performed through a hierarchy of caches. As a result, algorithms based on these architectures should take advantage of data locality in order to minimise the data movements encountered in distributed memory algorithms. Unfortunately, parallel matrix-matrix algorithms for such shared memory architectures have received little attention. Although SRUMMA [4] was designed for both distributed and shared memory architectures, it incurs an initial overhead of recording and sorting a *task list* to determine and optimise the locality references. This involves mapping the task list to use shared memory to access parts of the matrices held in processors within the same domain and use other access techniques such as Random Memory Access (RMA), to access parts of the matrices outside the local shared memory. In cases where A, B and C reside in the same local domain, the initialization stage only involves mapping the task list to use the shared memory. This paper presents our first algorithm, as a fast blocked matrix parallel algorithm that outperforms SRUMMA and other existing algorithms for shared memory architectures.

MapReduce, a functional programming model for processing large dataset on large-scale cluster of machines, has been adopted in areas such as distributed pattern-based searching, distributed sorting, document clustering and machine learning. This is due to its simplicity and applicability to practical problems. Although it was initially created for distributed systems, it can be implemented on multicore architectures [5]. The Phoenix API [5] [6] is an implementation of MapReduce model on shared-memory systems based on the original Google MapReduce model [7]. Although it uses parallel threads for both the Map and Reduce tasks, since it uses shared-memory buffers, it incurs some overhead in data copying. Our second algorithm is a MapReduce Algorithm for blocked matrix-matrix multiplication that outperforms the Phoenix algorithm for matrix multiplication.

1.1   Problem Motivation

Current state-of-the-art of linear algebra libraries such as ScaLAPACK [8] and LAPACK [9] incurs performance deterioration on multicore processors and multi-socket systems of multi-core processors often referred to as Symmetric Multi-Processor (SMP) architectures due to their inability to fully exploit thread-level parallelism and data locality [10].

This problem is twofold. Achieving high peak performance on these emerging architectures is a major challenge that calls for new algorithms and data structures. Reimplementing already existing code based on new programming models is another major challenge, particularly in the domain of high performance scientific computing.

Although some efforts have been made to redesign and implement current matrix multiplication algorithms for shared memory systems using programming models such as OpenMP and Cilk, these approaches do not achieve high peak performance. In this paper, we present two fast parallel algorithms for blocked dense matrix-matrix multiplication. The dense matrices used in our algorithms are always partitioned into blocks as depicted in Figure 2.

1.2 Contributions

The major contribution of this paper is the development and implementation of fast algorithms for general matrix multiplication (specifically DGEMM) for shared memory architectures. The main results being reported include:

- the development and implementation of a blocked-based parallel algorithm for dense matrix multiplication.
- the development and implementation of a MapReduce algorithm for dense matrix multiplication.
- an analytical and experimental performance analyses of our algorithms with existing algorithms such as the Phoenix API, SRUMMA and PLASMA DGEMM.

1.3 Organisation of the Paper

The remainder of this paper is organised as follows. Section 2 gives a brief survey of existing matrix multiplication algorithms for shared memory environments. In Section 3, we give some detailed descriptions of our matrix multiplication algorithms. We provide discussions of the blocked matrix-matrix multiplication algorithm and the MapReduce version. Section 4 gives an overview of our experimental setup. We give the results of some experiments conducted and some comparative analysis of our algorithms with existing algorithms. We summarise the work of this paper in Section 6, and give some directions for future work, namely implementing the two algorithms on GPU architectures.

2   Background and Related Work

A number of techniques for parallelizing matrix-matrix algorithms on SMP and multi-core architectures have been developed. In [11], a double precision general matrix multiplication routine using OpenMP was developed. The implementation (called ODGEMM) was integrated into GAMESS, a software suite for quantum chemistry. In order to improve the performance of all routines within the suit that had numerous calls to BLAS DGEMM, they provided wrapper routines that use OpenMP to parallelize the matrix multiplication. However, simply using OpenMP *pragmas* to parallelize matrix multiplication algorithms is not enough to gain high peak performance.

Another work that used OpenMP to parallelize matrix-matrix multiplication is given in [12]. The work focuses on the optimisation of numerical libraries such as MKL (Intel Math Kernel Library) and SGI SCSL (Scientific Computing Software Library) on the SGI Altix 3700 architecture using OpenMP. Again the optimisation is based on OpenMP pragmas and not on an optimal or elegant matrix multiplication algorithm.

To address the critical performance issues facing linear algebra libraries such as LAPACK and ScaLAPACK on multi-core architectures, Jakub et. al in [10] looked at the scheduling and implementation of linear algebra (LU Factorisation and Matrix Multiplication) workloads, using dynamic data-driven execution. However the emergence of shared- memory and multi-core systems calls for new algorithms that have good performance on such platforms. In the next section we give a detailed description of two parallel algorithms for matrix-matrix multiplication based primarily on blocked dense matrices.

3   Matrix-Matrix Algorithm

The BLAS specification [13], defines general matrix multiplication as $C \leftarrow \alpha AB + \beta C$ where α, β are scalars and A, B and C are $M \times K$, $K \times N$ and $M \times N$ matrices respectively. The main computation in the BLAS specification is $C \leftarrow AB$. Given

$$A_{M,K} = \begin{pmatrix} a_{1,1} & a_{1,2} & \cdots & a_{1,K} \\ a_{2,1} & a_{2,2} & \cdots & a_{2,K} \\ \vdots & \vdots & \ddots & \vdots \\ a_{M,1} & a_{M,2} & \cdots & a_{M,K} \end{pmatrix}$$

and

$$B_{K,N} = \begin{pmatrix} b_{1,1} & b_{1,2} & \cdots & b_{1,N} \\ b_{2,1} & b_{2,2} & \cdots & b_{2,N} \\ \vdots & \vdots & \ddots & \vdots \\ b_{K,1} & b_{K,2} & \cdots & b_{K,N} \end{pmatrix}$$

then for $C \leftarrow AB$, $c_{i,j} = \sum_{k=1}^{K} a_{i,k} b_{k,j}$. A parallel implementation of the matrix multiplication will be to assign a row i of A and a column j of B to a process to compute $c_{i,j}$ of C. This approach however is not scalable as the number of processes required to compute all $c_{i,j}$ in C is MN. Assuming that there are $m \times n$ processes (or processors/cores), the block sizes in A, B and C will be $\frac{M}{m} \times \frac{K}{k}$, $\frac{K}{k} \times \frac{N}{n}$ and $\frac{M}{m} \times \frac{N}{n}$ respectively. Process $P_{i,j}$ computes all $c_{i,j}$ in block $C_{i,j}^+$, where C^+ denotes a block in matrix C. Similarly, blocks in matrices A and B are denoted as A^+ and B^+ respectively.

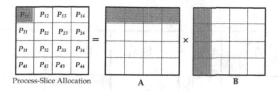

Process-Slice Allocation   A   B

Fig. 1. *SRUMMA Matrix Slicing: In a 4 × 4 processes, process P_{11} computes elements in block C_{11} using blocks $A_{11} \rightarrow A_{14}$ and blocks $B_{11} \rightarrow B_{41}$*

Hence $P_{i,j}$ is assigned a horizontal slice of blocks $A_{i,1}^+, A_{i,2}^+, ..., A_{i,k}^+$ from matrix A and a vertical slice of block $B_{1,j}^+, B_{2,j}^+, ..., B_{k,j}^+$ from matrix B as illustrated in Figure 1. In our blocked matrix-matrix multiplication algorithm, A and B are blocked in a similar fashion as described above but the computation uses more processes.

3.1   Blocked Matrix-Matrix Algorithm

As the number of cores, the speed and memory sizes of multi-core architectures keep increasing, scientific computations that require matrix multiplication of large matrix sizes can be ported conveniently to these architectures. We exploit these features in our blocked matrix-matrix algorithm.

To compute $C \leftarrow \alpha AB + \beta C$, where A, B and C are $M \times K$, $K \times N$ and $M \times N$ matrices respectively, we partition the three matrices into sub-matrices denoted by $A_{i,p}^+$, $B_{p,j}^+$ and $C_{i,j}^+$. If μ represent the beginning index i, of block $A_{i,p}^+$ and ρ represent the ending index j, of block $B_{p,j}^+$, then the results (partial sums) from these blocks will be targeted at block $C_{\mu,\rho}^+$ (i.e. $C_{i,j}^+$). This forms the basis for the blocked matrix algorithm. Let m denote the number of row partitions in A and C, and let k denote the number of column partitions in A as well as the row partitions in B. Let n be the number of column partitions in B and C. Then the number of processor needed for parallel computation of $C \leftarrow \alpha AB + \beta C$ is mkn. Let

$$mSize = \left\lceil \frac{M}{m} \right\rceil, \text{ maximum rows per } A \text{ and } C \text{ block}$$

$$kSize = \left\lceil \frac{K}{k} \right\rceil, \text{ max. columns per } A \text{ block and rows per } B \text{ block} \qquad (3.1)$$

$$nSize = \left\lceil \frac{N}{n} \right\rceil, \text{ maximum columns per } B \text{ and } C \text{ block}$$

and

$$1 \leq i \leq m$$
$$1 \leq p \leq k \qquad (3.2)$$
$$1 \leq j \leq n$$

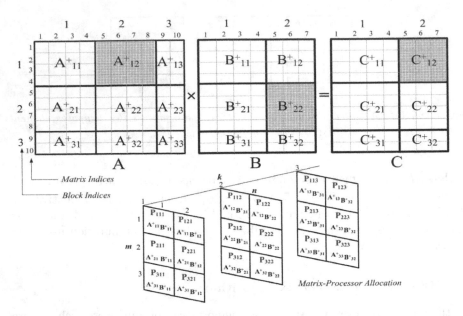

Fig. 2. Blocked Matrix-Matrix Allocation

then we define:

$A^+_{i,p}$ as a block of A consisting of :
  row $(mSize * (i - 1) + 1)$ to $min(mSize * i, M)$
  column $(kSize * (p - 1) + 1)$ to $min(kSize * p, K)$

$B^+_{p,j}$ as a block of B consisting of :
  rows $(kSize * (p - 1) + 1)$ to $min(kSize * p, K)$
  columns $(nSize * (j - 1) + 1)$ to $min(nSize * j, N)$

$C^+_{i,j}$ as a block of B consisting of :
  rows $(mSize * (i - 1) + 1)$ to $min(mSize * i, M)$
  columns $(nSize * (j - 1) + 1)$ to $min(nSize * j, N)$

The blocking scheme, illustrated in Figure 2 allows for optimal allocation of blocks to processors. In contrast to most matrix-matrix algorithms, we do not assume that M, K and N are respective integral multiples of m, k and n. Further, A, B, C need not be square matrices. The algorithm involves two levels of computations. At the first level (the allocation level), block $A^+_{i,p}$ of matrix A and block $B^+_{p,j}$ of matrix B are assigned to processor $P_{i,j,p}$. This is illustrated in Algorithm 1.

An example of our allocation scheme is illustrated in Figure 2. Suppose we wish to multiply a 10×10 matrix A by a 10×7 matrix B ($M = 10$, $K = 10$ and

---

Algorithm 1: Blocks Allocation

---

input : $A_{[M][K]}, B_{[K][N]}, C_{[M][N]}, m, k, n, \alpha, \beta$
output: $C_{[M][N]}$
begin
  Initialise:
  $P \leftarrow m * k * n;$
  for $i \leftarrow 1$ **to** m **do**
    for $j \leftarrow 1$ **to** n **do**
      for $p \leftarrow 1$ **to** k **do**
        $P_{i,j,p} \leftarrow MatMult(i, p, j, M, K, N, m, k, n, \alpha, \beta);$

$N = 7$). If we chose $m = 3$, $k = 3$ and $n = 2$, then we need $mnk = 3 * 3 * 2 = 18$ processors. We then have $mSize = \lceil \frac{10}{3} \rceil = 4$, $kSize = \lceil \frac{10}{3} \rceil = 4$ and $nSize = \lceil \frac{7}{2} \rceil = 4$. Once $mSize$, $kSize$ and $nSize$ have been computed, the boundaries of each block $A_{i,p}^+$, in A and block $B_{p,j}^+$, in B can be define. For instance block $A_{1,2}^+$ in A consists of row $(4 * (0) + 1) = 1$ to row $min(4 * 1, 10) = 4$ and column $(4 * (1) + 1) = 5$ to column $min(4 * 2, 10) = 8$. Similarly, block $B_{2,2}^+$ in B consists of row $(4 * (1) + 1) = 5$ to row $min(4 * 2, 10) = 8$ and column $(4 * (1) + 1) = 5$ to column $min(4 * 2, 7) = 7$. These two are assigned to processor $P_{1,2,2}$ and the partial sums from this processor will be accumulated in block $C_{1,2}^+$ in C.

At the second level, all assigned processors compute their respective $C_{i,j}^+ \leftarrow \alpha(A_{i,p}^+ * B_{p,j}^+) + \beta C_{i,j}^+$ in parallel as illustrated Algorithm 2. The bounds (or sizes) and starting indices of $A_{i,p}^+$ and $B_{p,j}^+$ in processor $P_{i,j,p}$ are computed using Algorithm 4 and Algorithm 3 respectively. We utilise the operation atomicAdd() for synchronised additions to *sum*.

3.2   The MapReduce Version

In the MapReduce framework [7], the *Map* function processes the input task by dividing it into smaller sub-tasks and distributing them to the *workers* or processors. Every mapper emits a partial result of the required complete result. The *Reduce* function collects all the partial results from the mappers and merges them using unique keys. Primarily, there are four stages in the MapReduce algorithm: the *splitting* stage, the *mapping* stage, the *reduction* stage and the *merging* stage as illustrated in Figure 3.

3.2.1   Splitting Stage

The *Map* function is initiated after the input matrices A and B have been chunked into sub-matrices (preferably called *blocks*). We require an appropriate blocking schemes to partition the input matrices. We use same blocking scheme as illustrated in Figure 2. Once the matrices have been blocked, the individual blocks are assigned to the mappers. Block $A_{i,p}^+$ of matrix A and block $B_{p,j}^+$ of matrix B are assigned to the mapper $P_{i,j,p}$ using Algorithm 1.

Algorithm 2: Concurrent $MatMult$

---

input : $i, p, j, M, K, N, m, k, n, \alpha, \beta$

output: $partialC_{i,j}^{+}$

begin

    Initialise:

    $mSize \leftarrow blockSize(M, m, i)$;

    $kSize \leftarrow blockSize(K, k, p)$;

    $nSize \leftarrow blockSize(N, n, j)$;

    $mInit \leftarrow startIndex(M, m, i)$;

    $kInit \leftarrow startIndex(K, k, p)$;

    $nInit \leftarrow startIndex(N, n, j)$;

    for $x \leftarrow mInit$ **to** $mSize$ **do**

        for $y \leftarrow nInit$ **to** $nSize$ **do**

            $sum \leftarrow \emptyset$;

            for $z \leftarrow kInit$ **to** $kSize$ **do**

                $sum \leftarrow sum + \alpha(A_{x,z} * B_{z,y})$;

            if $z = y$ **then**

                $C_{x,y} \leftarrow \beta * C_{x,y}$;

            $atomicAdd(C_{x,y}, sum)$;

Algorithm 3: $startIndex$

---

input : q, r, i

output: $Index$

begin

    Initialise:

    $sze \leftarrow \lceil \frac{q}{r} \rceil$;

    if $i = 1$ **then**

        $init \leftarrow 1$;

    else

        $init \leftarrow ((i - 1) * sze) + 1$;

    return $init$

3.2.2 Mapping Stage

After the splitting and allocation stage, the individual mappers compute their respective partial sums in parallel with no synchronisation nor communication. We are able to completely eliminate synchronisation because of the use of a structure called the *partial store* which keeps the individual partial sums from the mappers. The partial store is an $M \times N \times k$ structure with its atomic element denoted by $pSum_{\alpha,\beta,\gamma}$ where $1 \leq \alpha \leq M$, $1 \leq \beta \leq N$ and $1 \leq \gamma \leq k$. The computations in the individual mappers differ slightly from those in Algorithm 2. The $sum \leftarrow sum + \alpha(A_{x,z} * B_{z,y})$ instruction in Algorithm 2 is replaced with $pSum_{x,y,p} \leftarrow pSum_{x,y,p} + \alpha(A_{x,z} * B_{z,y})$. The illustration of how the partial sums $pSum_{\alpha,\beta,\gamma}$, are stored in the partial store, is given in Figure 4.

Algorithm 4: *blockSize*

---

input : q, r, i
output: *Size*
begin
   Initialise:
   $sze \leftarrow \lceil \frac{q}{r} \rceil$;

   if $i = 1$ then
      $\lfloor$ $blkSize \leftarrow sze$;

   else if $i = r \cap (q - \lfloor q/sze \rfloor * sze) \neq 0$ then
      $init \leftarrow (i - 1) * sze$;
      $blkSize \leftarrow init + (q - \lfloor q/sze \rfloor * sze)$;

   else
      $init \leftarrow (i - 1) * sze$;
      $blkSize \leftarrow init + sze$;

   return *blkSize*

3.2.3   Reduction Stage

We focus our discussions on only the reduction stage as it subsumes the merging stage in this peculiar application of the framework. In certain applications, especially in the MapReduce framework for distributed memory architectures, the merging stage provides support for fault tolerance of transient and permanent faults during the mapping and reduction stages.

The *Reduce* function waits for all the Map jobs to return. The number of processes required in the reduction is $m \times n$. Each process is responsible for the reduction of k blocks (See Figure 4). The algorithm for the allocation of blocks in the partial store is left out due to limitation of space. Each cell within a block in the *partial store* keeps the partial sum from the designated mapper as illustrated in Figure 4. The reduction algorithm (Algorithm 5), computes the total of the partial sums $pSum_{i,j,1}, pSum_{i,j,2}, ..., pSum_{i,j,k}$ and stores it in $C_{i,j}$.

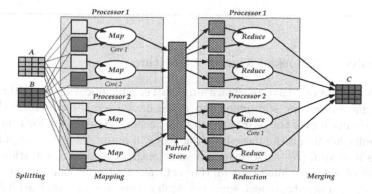

Fig. 3. *Stages of MapReduce Algorithm*

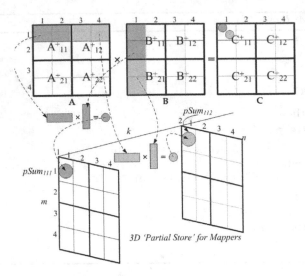

Fig. 4. *Map Function: A $4 \times 4 \times 2$ 'Partial Store' for matrix A and B using $M = 2$, $N = 2$ and $K = 2$*

Algorithm 5: Reduction

input : $i, p, j, M, K, N, m, k, n, \alpha, \beta$
output: $C_{i,j}^+$
begin
    Initialise:
    $mSize \leftarrow blockSize(M, m, i)$;
    $nSize \leftarrow blockSize(N, n, j)$;
    $mInit \leftarrow startIndex(M, m, i)$;
    $nInit \leftarrow startIndex(N, n, j)$;
    for $x \leftarrow mInit$ **to** $mSize$ **do**
        for $y \leftarrow nInit$ **to** $nSize$ **do**
            for $z \leftarrow 1$ **to** k **do**
                $C_{x,y} \leftarrow C_{x,y} + pSum_{x,y,z}$;

3.3 Analysis of Blocked Matrix Algorithm

It may seem quite odd that an algorithm (matrix multiplication algorithm) that can be expressed as one statement and three nested loops have received much research attention over the past three to four decades. The reason for this is that matrix multiplication is the basic building block in many scientific computations and since it is an $O(N^3)$ algorithm, these scientific codes or applications often spend a lot of computational time on the sections of the code that employ matrix multiplication. There have been some research efforts to minimise the $O(N^3)$ operations. For instance, the Strassen algorithm [14] achieves $O(N^{2.81})$ operations and the Coppersmith and Winograd's algorithm [15] achieves $O(N^{2.38})$. Unfortunately, these algorithms lack numerical stability as it achieves these reductions at the expense of additional additions and subtraction operations.

Consider the matrix multiplication operation $C \leftarrow AB$, where A, B and C are $M \times K$, $K \times N$ and $M \times N$ matrices. Let's suppose A, B and C are blocked using M, K and N as discussed in Section 3.1. We denote

$$t_s \quad as \quad \text{start up cost,}$$
$$\eta \quad as \quad \text{synchronisation cost,}$$
$$P \quad as \quad \text{number of processors}$$
$$\text{where } P \quad = \quad mkn$$

For simplicity, if we assume that $M = K = N = \mathbb{N}$, then the sequential time T_{seq} of the matrix multiplication algorithm is $O(\mathbb{N}^3)$. The parallel time T_{par} is the computation time for each block and the overhead time:

$$T_{par} = \frac{MKN}{P} + \tau \text{ , where } \tau = t_s + \eta$$

If $M = K = N = \mathbb{N}$ as stated earlier, then

$$T_{par} = \frac{\mathbb{N}^3}{P} + \tau \tag{3.3}$$

$$= O\left(\frac{\mathbb{N}^3}{P}\right) + \tau$$

There is no matrix block transfer overhead due to data locality. This cost is only incurred in distributed matrix multiplication algorithms. For the MapReduce version, the η is replaced by the wait time t_w (i.e. the waiting time for all mappers to return) for the Reduce function. Hence

$$T_{par} = O\left(\frac{\mathbb{N}^3}{P}\right) + \tau \tag{3.4}$$

$$\text{where } \tau = t_s + t_w$$

4   Experimental Environment/Setup

Experiments were conducted on two platforms. The first is a 64-bit Intel Quad-core processor with 12GB of RAM, running at 3.07GHz. The second is an Intel Xeon system with dual-socket quad-core hyper-threaded processors (a total of 16 cores), running at 3.02 GHz with 96GB main memory and running Scientific Linux 5.4.

4.1   Experiments Conducted

A number of experiments were conducted to compare the performance of our algorithms with existing ones. In the first set of experiments, we varied the sizes of the matrices A and B for constant number of processors or cores. The time taken to compute $C \leftarrow \alpha AB + \beta C$ for our algorithm was compared with the existing algorithms such as the LAPACK-BLAS, PLASMA, SRUMMA, and the Phoenix shared memory MapReduce library. The same experiments were conducted on the Intel Xeon system with 16 cores. The remaining sets of experiments were conducted to evaluate how our algorithms scale with varying cores and varying workloads. In this case, we first performed a weak scalability test, by keeping the sizes of both the matrices A and B constant at (5000×5000) and varying the number of processors or cores. The computation time of our two algorithms, in each case, were compared with the algorithms mentioned above. We then evaluated scalability over varying workloads and varying processors (cores). We call this strong scalability test. We finally computed the GFLOPS (Number of Floating point Operations Per Second), for these scalability tests and evaluated their performances. The last set of experiments were conducted to measure the speed up gained in each algorithm.

5   Experimental Results

Figure 5 shows the performance of our algorithms compared with existing ones for a constant number of processors or cores. The matrix sizes used in this experiment, are 2000×2000, 5000×5000, 6000×6000, 8000×8000 and 10000×10000 for both A and B, with the same blocking factor for all the algorithms. The graphs show the performances in time of all the algorithms. Our algorithm outperforms the PLASMA DGEMM which is a parallel implementation of the LAPACK-BLAS for multi-core architectures. The MapReduce version of our algorithms performs slightly slower than the blocked algorithm because of the wait time for all mappers to return and the cost incurred in allocating blocks of the *partial store* to the reducers. As the workload increases, there is a significant speedup in our algorithm in comparison with the other algorithms.

The results also show that simply using shared memory programming models such as OpenMP and Cilk to models such as OpenMP and Cilk to parallelise linear algebra routines linear algebra routines does not result in high peak performance. There is a need for fast and optimal parallel algorithms for such environments. Figure 8 shows the same results as discussed above except that we utilise more cores (i.e., 16 cores). The LAPACK-BLAS did not show any performance increase because it is insensitive to the multi-core architectures. This means that it only uses one core for its computation with some level of optimisation at the instruction level.

Figure 6 shows the computation time of the algorithms as the number of cores increases for the same size of matrices. This weak scalability test shows that the computation time for our algorithm decreases considerably as the number of cores increases. As $P = mkn$ increases, the block size decreases, thereby reducing the workload for each worker or processor.

Figure 9 shows a strong scalability test where we varied the number cores as well as the sizes of the matrices. This was to test whether the performance

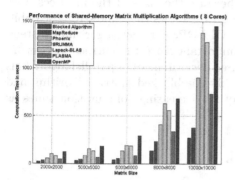

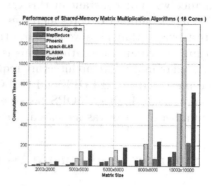

Fig. 5. Performance of Shared-Memory Matrix Multiplication Algorithm-8 Cores

Fig. 8. Performance of Shared-Memory Matrix Multiplication Algorithm-16 Cores

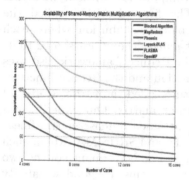

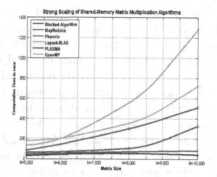

Fig. 6. Weak Scalability Test

Fig. 9. Strong Scalability Test

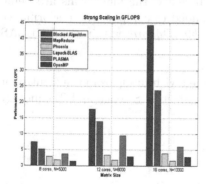

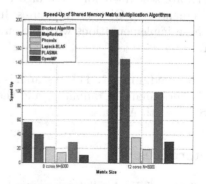

Fig. 7. Strong Scalability Test in GFLOPS

Fig. 10. Speed Ups of Algorithms

of each algorithm remained stable as the parameters are varied proportionally. Our algorithms still outperformed the other existing ones. LAPACK-BLAS performance was not constant in this case because the sizes of the matrices were varied as the number of cores increases. Figure 7 shows the same strong scalability test except that here we compute the GFLOPS for each algorithms instead of using the computation time. This is important since the current increase in the speed of multi-core architecture requires performances of parallel algorithms to be measured in MFLOPS and GFLOPS. The blocked matrix algorithm had an increasingly high GFLOPS because of its decreasing computation times as the number of cores was increased.

6   Summary and Future Work

This paper has presented two new dense matrix multiplication algorithms that can efficiently exploit shared-memory and multi-core architectures. These algorithms are based on blocked dense matrices where each block from the input matrices is assigned to a processor for computation without incurring communication cost with other processors. The first algorithm called the blocked matrix multiplication algorithm uses block distribution where each processor contributes to the block of the output matrix (i.e., C) assigned to it. The second algorithm which is based on the MapReduce framework also uses block allocation or distribution for both Map function and the Reduce function. All mappers keep their partial results in a structure called the *partial store* and the reducers sum the partial results to the output matrix. Our experimental results show that high peak performance can be attained if dense matrix linear algebra libraries such as LAPACK-BLAS, PLASMA and SRUMMA exploit such blocking schemes for shared-memory architectures. The performance of the two algorithms are stable across different multi-core platforms. Its good scalability makes it suitable for its integration in linear algebra libraries. A number future works are scheduled for these algorithms. Currently, the algorithms are being implemented on GPU architectures. It is intended to compare the performance of these implementations with the current *cublasDgemm* within the CUBLAS library.

Acknowledgement. This research is supported with funds from the Centre for High Performance Computing and the Department of Science and Technology (DST), South Africa.

References

1. Cannon, L.E.: A cellular computer to implement the kalman filter algorithm. PhD thesis, Montana State University (1969)
2. Choi, J., Dongarra, J., Walker, D.: Parallel universal matrix multiplication algorithms on distributed memory concurrent computers. Concurrency: Practice and Experience 6(7), 543–570 (1994)

3. van de Geijn, R.A., Watts, J.: Scalable universal matrix multiplication algorithm. Concurrency: Practice and Experience 9(4), 255–274 (1997)
4. Krishnan, M., Nieplocha, J.: Srumma: a matrix multiplication algorithm suitable for clusters and scalable shared memory systems. In: Proceedings of Parallel and Distributed Processing Symposium (2004)
5. Ranger, C., Raghuraman, R., Penmetsa, A., Bradski, G., Kozyrakis, C.: Evaluating mapreduce for multi-core and multiprocessor systems. In: Proc. of the 13th Int'l Symposium on High Performance Computer Architecture, pp. 13–24 (2007)
6. Yoo, R.M., Romano, A., Kozyrakis, C.: Phoenix rebirth: Scalable mapreduce on a large-scale shared-memory system. In: Proc. of the 2009 IEEE Int'l Symposium on Workload Characterization, pp. 198–207 (2009)
7. Dean, J., Ghemawat, J.: Mapreduce: Simplified data processing on large clusters. In: Proceedings of the 6th Symp. on Operating Systems Design and Implementation (2004)
8. Blackford, L., Choi, J., Cleary, A., DAzevedo, E., Demmel, J., Dhillon, I., Dongarra, J., Hammarling, S., Henry, G., Petitet, A., Stanley, K., Walker, D., Whaley, R.: Scalapack users guide. SIAM, Philadelphia (1997)
9. Anderson, E., Bai, Z., Bischof, C., Blackford, L., Demmel, J., Dongarra, J., Hammarling, S., Croz, J., Greenbaum, A., McKenney, A., Sorensen, D.: Lapack users guide. SIAM, Philadelphia (1992)
10. Jakub, K., Ltaief, H., Dongarra, J., Badia, R.: Scheduling dense linear algebra operations on multicore processors. Concurrency and Computation: Practice and Experience 22(1) (2010)
11. Bentz, J.L., Kendall, R.A.: Parallelization of General Matrix Multiply Routines Using OpenMP. In: Chapman, B.M. (ed.) WOMPAT 2004. LNCS, vol. 3349, pp. 1–11. Springer, Heidelberg (2005)
12. Hackenberg, D., Schöne, R., Nagel, W.E., Pflüger, S.: Optimizing OpenMP Parallelized DGEMM Calls on SGI Altix 3700. In: Nagel, W.E., Walter, W.V., Lehner, W. (eds.) Euro-Par 2006. LNCS, vol. 4128, pp. 145–154. Springer, Heidelberg (2006)
13. Alpatov, P., Baker, G., Edwards, C., Gunnels, J., Morrow, G., Overfelt, J., van de Geiju, R., Wu, J.: Plapack: Parallel linear algebra package. In: Proceedings of the SIAM Parallel Processing Conference (1997)
14. Strassen, V.: Guassian elimination is not optimal. Numerische Mathematick 14(3), 354–356 (1969)
15. Coppersmith, D., Winograd, S.: Matrix multiplication via arithmetic progressions. Journal of Symbolic Computing 9, 251–280 (1990)

Kernel Support for Fine-Grained Load Balancing in a Web Cluster Providing Streaming Service

Mei-Ling Chiang, Chen-Yu Yang, and Shin-Lu Lien

Department of Information Management
National Chi Nan University
Nantou, Puli, Taiwan R.O.C.
joanna@ncnu.edu.tw, shiriq@hotmail.com, lientuna@gmail.com

Abstract. In a server cluster supporting conventional streaming service, an on-going streaming connection between a client and a server cannot be migrated to another server. Therefore, if a film is too lengthy, it would occupy a server's resource for a long time. This may cause load imbalance among servers in a cluster providing streaming service. To solve this problem, we have proposed a new load-sharing mechanism which logically divides a film into several sections according to its film length and successive film sections of a film can be served in turn by different servers. By this way of sharing films' workload among streaming servers, a cluster thus can achieve more fine-grained load balancing among servers. To support this mechanism, a novel mechanism named RTSP Multiple Handoff is proposed to hand off an ongoing RTSP streaming connection among servers. The client would not notice the change of responding server. We have practically implemented these two mechanisms in the Linux kernel 2.6.18 on LVS-CAD cluster. The media player and the streaming server need not modify at all. Experimental results demonstrate that LVS-CAD with these mechanisms can achieve 107.52% better throughput and reduce 91.51% average response time compared with LVS cluster without using these mechanisms.

Keywords: Web Cluster; Multimedia Streaming; Content-aware Request Distribution.

1   Introduction

Nowadays, multimedia technology has been used in a variety of applications, such as long distance communication, online music store, and video-on-demand, etc. Because a single server cannot handle huge demands from explosively growing of clients, so server cluster has become an effective solution. A web cluster system has many merits such as flexibility, efficiency, and scalability. It consists of several web service providing servers and a load balancer that accepts and dispatches clients' requests to servers. To effectively utilize the system resource of the whole cluster, how to balance the loads among servers is very important.

For a web cluster providing streaming service, a conventional streaming service does not allow an ongoing streaming connection between a client and a server to be

Y. Xiang et al. (Eds.): ICA3PP 2012, Part I, LNCS 7439, pp. 458–472, 2012.

migrated to another server. A film would be served by the same server until the entire film is played to the end. If several streaming requests of lengthy or short films arrive at the same time, it will cause severe load imbalance among the streaming servers.

In this paper, to enable the sharing of the heavy streaming workload among servers, we propose a novel mechanism named RTSP Multiple Handoff that can hand off an ongoing streaming connection between a client and a streaming server to another streaming server as needed. The playback of the film on the client side is continuous and the client would not notice the change of responding server. Based on this handoff mechanism, we then propose a new load-sharing mechanism, in which a film can be logically partitioned into several sections and each successive film section can be served by different back-end server. Besides, it can dynamically determine how many sections a film should be divided according to its film length. Therefore, each film section will not be too lengthy, so serving the playback of a film section will not occupy a server's resource for a long time. In this way, because film sections of a film can be in turn served by different servers, the workload of a film can be effectively distributed to several servers. Thus, this mechanism can provide more fine-grained load balancing and improve the performance of the whole web cluster.

We have implemented these two mechanisms in the Linux kernel 2.6.18 on LVS-CAD [9] cluster. LVS-CAD cluster consists of a front-end server responsible for dispatching requests and multiple back-end servers for actually serving requests. In particular, the front-end server can analyze incoming packets and use layer-7 information to perform content-aware request dispatching at kernel level. For supporting RTSP Multiple Handoff mechanism, we have modified Linux kernel's source code for handing off an ongoing streaming connection between a client and a streaming server to another server. The media player and the streaming server are not modified at all. In fact, the handoff of a streaming connection is performed under the cooperation of the front-end server and the back-end server at the Linux kernel level. It is transparent to the client and the client will not notice the change of the responding server.

Experimental results demonstrate that with the proposed mechanisms, the throughput of LVS-CAD can outperform that of LVS [8] by 107.52%. The LVS-CAD cluster can reduce 91.51% of average response time as compared with the LVS.

2   Background Technology and Related Work

2.1   Quick Time Streaming Server (QTSS)

QTSS [2] uses streaming protocol suite including Real-time Streaming Protocol (RTSP) [12], Real-time Transport Protocol (RTP) [13, 14], and RTP Control Protocol (RTCP) to deliver video and audio streams in networks. When a client intends to watch a film on QTSS, the streaming connection has to be established first through RTSP methods based on TCP. After that, the video and audio streams will be transferred to the client by QTSS through RTP transmission based on UDP. Then, the decoder on the client will decode them according to the codec database. As the film is playing, the RTCP packets will be sent by the client and the server to each other periodically to monitor or adjust the transfer state, e.g. transfer rate, if it is too fast.

Figure 2 illustrates the packet flow of the streaming service. The OPTIONS method is used to negotiate acceptable RTSP methods between a client and the streaming server. The description of the film (RTSP/SDP) is delivered by the server as the reply of the DESCRIBE method to the client for setting up its media player. Subsequently, the client issues a SETUP request to establish a streaming connection with the streaming server. The server then will return a SETUP reply packet that contains a session key to recognize the streaming server. After the playing range in the PLAY request is designated by the client's media player, RTP streams are transferred by the server to the client immediately. Adjusted RTCP packets will be sent by two end points to adjust the transmission state periodically. When the film is played to the end, the client uses the TEARDOWN method to terminate the streaming connection.

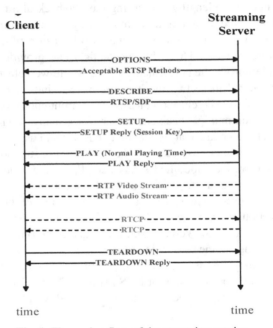

Fig. 1. The packet flow of the streaming service

2.2   LVS-CAD Web Cluster

Linux Virtual Server with Content-Aware Dispatching (LVS-CAD) [9] is a cluster developed for effectively sharing workload among a server group. LVS-CAD cluster includes a front-end server with layer-7 content-aware dispatching ability and several back-end servers. The front-end server and all back-end servers share a virtual IP address (VIP). Thus, clients will consider LVS-CAD as a single server. It uses direct routing mechanism [8] in packet routing, so back-end servers can return RTSP reply packets and RTP packets to clients directly, bypassing the front-end server.

The front-end server can analyze packets from client and use content of packets (i.e. layer-7 information such as URL) to dispatch requests to back-end server at the

IP layer of Linux kernel. Packet transmission is efficient since packet forwarding is done at the IP layer and response packets from back-end server are transmitted directly to the client, by passing the front-end server. Because content of packets is used in dispatching requests to back-end server, intelligent dispatching policy can be used. In particular, the scheduling of a back-end server to serve client's request is done on every request instead of every connection. Therefore, LVS-CAD can achieve more fine-grained load balancing among servers.

For dispatching a request to the most suitable back-end server, a mechanism must be developed to migrate an existing TCP connection from the original back-end server to the newly selected back-end server for handling the current incoming request. Therefore, LVS-CAD implements TCP rebuilding mechanism and Multiple TCP rebuilding mechanism on back-end servers for handing off an existing TCP connection between a client and a server to a different server. Besides, it applies fast three-way handshaking mechanism on the front-end server to enhance performance. It also supports web-based QoS to handle requests properly according to their priorities.

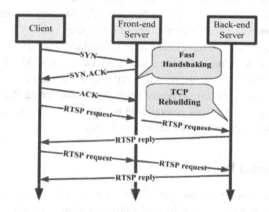

Fig. 2. Processing flow of RTSP Request on LVS-CAD

For a cluster such as LVS-CAD to provide streaming service, after a streaming connection is established, a film is conventionally served by the same streaming server until the entire film is played to the end. The flow of handling RTSP requests on LVS-CAD cluster is illustrated in Figure 2. The front-end server establishes a connection efficiently with the client by means of fast handshaking. Then the front-end server forwards the incoming RTSP request to the back-end server according to its designated scheduling algorithm. When receiving the RTSP request, the back-end server uses the TCP rebuilding mechanism to rebuild the existing TCP connection. After the TCP connection has been rebuilt, the back-end server can accept and serve this RTSP request. Finally, the back-end server returns the RTSP reply packet to the client directly. If a subsequent request which belongs to the same streaming connection comes in, it would be forwarded to the same back-end server. In this way, a film is served by the same server until the entire film is played to the end.

2.3   Request Dispatching Policies

In a server cluster, the request dispatching policy that the front-end server uses to select a back-end server for serving a client's request affects the performance of the whole cluster. Usually, content-aware dispatching policies perform better than content-blind policies. The typical examples are Locality-Aware Request Distribution with Replication (LARD/R)[11], Client-Aware Policy (CAP)[3], and Locality-Aware Request Distribution with Replication and Classification (LARD/RC) [5].

In LARD/R, one request can be served by a server set containing a set of servers. When a subsequent same request comes in, it will be dispatched to the least-loaded server in its server set. Since LARD/R does not distinguish types of requests, if a server serves too many CPU-bound or disk-bound requests, this may cause load imbalance and performance deterioration of the whole cluster.

CAP classifies requests into four categories that include Web publishing (i.e. static and lightly dynamic services), Web transaction (i.e. disk-bounded services), Web commerce, and Web multimedia. In CAP, each back-end server serves classified requests evenly since the front-end server dispatches requests using Round-Robin scheduling. Unfortunately, the proportion of CPU-bound to disk-bound requests would not be counterbalanced when either of them may occupy hardware resources of some back-end servers, so it may cause load imbalance, too.

LARD/RC combines the advantages of LARD/R and CAP. It classifies requests from clients into four types as defined in CAP and designates a single, or a set of most suitable servers to serve certain types of requests. Considering the difference of back-end servers, only the server that is available to serve the type of requests can be added into the request's server set, unlike LARD/R does.

2.4   Other Related Work

As far as we have surveyed, no works like us provide fine-grained load sharing for cluster-based streaming services by distributing a film's loading among servers. We propose the RTSP Multiple Handoff mechanism which allows different servers in turn to provide media data of successive film sections.

In the research of an up-to-date survey in web load balancing [6], the authors discuss basic architectures of web cluster systems and summarize the existent load balancing techniques. It also compares most of the existent content-blind and content-aware request dispatching policies.

There are some related researches of PC-based web clusters supporting QTSS streaming service. In the research of the PC cluster-based QTSS [7], the author has implemented a web cluster with content-blind request distribution for supporting QTSS. A RTSP streaming connection will be dispatched to the least-loading back-end server. The related research [4] has added fault-tolerant ability in PC cluster-based MP4 Video-on Demand server. The author proposes a backup mechanism for the front-end server that may fail while the web cluster is providing the streaming service.

Some researches address the issue of caching streaming media. New techniques are developed to use proxy caching for delivering streaming media. Several works use partial caching approaches [16,18] that divide media objects into smaller units so that only partial units are cached. Another research [4] discusses how storage strategies of films affect the performance of the whole web cluster. The author classifies films into three categories such as hot, middle, and cold types according to their click-through-rate. Hot-type films are stored in more back-end servers and cold-type films are stored in less back-end servers. Additionally, the author designs several formulas which consider the factor of film size in supporting different storage strategies. Because the click-through-rate will change dynamically in different time period, the storage strategy of the film copies has to be adjusted in an appropriate time interval.

3   Supporting Fine-Grained Load Sharing in a Web Cluster

Conventionally, a film is served by the same streaming server until the entire film is played to the end. That is, the streaming server for an on-going streaming connection cannot be changed while the film is playing. Therefore, load imbalance among servers in a cluster would occur if several streaming requests arrive at the same time.

In this paper, we propose a fine-grained mechanism to share the streaming load among servers and propose the RTSP Multiple Handoff mechanism for handing off an ongoing RTSP streaming connection among servers. Basically, a film can be logically divided into several film sections and film sections can be in turn served by different streaming servers. Besides, it provides the flexibility in setting the thresholds for determining how many sections a film would be logically divided. If the playing time of a film is longer, the film would be logically divided into more sections. For example, if the normal playing time of a film is more than 240 seconds, the film will be logically divided into three sections, and each film section can be served separately by different back-end server. If the normal playing time is between 120 and 240 seconds, the film is divided into two sections. So, two back-end servers will separately serve the requests for these two film sections. If the length of a film is less than 120 seconds, it will not be divided. These thresholds can be adjusted dynamically to divide a film into more sections.

3.1   System Overview

Our RTSP Multiple Handoff mechanism is implemented on the LVS-CAD cluster. The front-end server forwards incoming RTSP requests to back-end servers that have installed QTSS streaming server. Even when an on-going streaming connection is being migrated to another back-end server, clients will not feel any difference.

Figure 3 depicts how RTSP Multiple Handoff mechanism works using an example of a film that is divided into three sections and served by three back-end servers. When a client intends to watch a film, it will first establish a streaming connection with the streaming server by sending a series of the RTSP requests including the OPTION, DESCRIBE, SETUP, and PLAY packets to the front-end server. When the first back-end server sends the DESCRIBE reply packet to the client, it will also send the *npt* notification packet indicating the normal playing time (*npt*) of the film to the front-end server. The front-end server will record the normal playing time and store the following SETUP 3, SETUP 4, and PLAY request packets in its maintaining RTSP hash table. These information will be used later in migrating this streaming connection. A film may be logically divided into two or more sections, determined by its normal playing time. Since the playing range of a film is indicated by the *npt* field, the *npt* field in the RTSP PLAY request will be modified with the divided *npt* length of the film. While the RTSP SETUP requests and the modified RTSP PLAY request for the first film section have been forwarded to a selected back-end server, the back-end server will calculate and store the expected end sequence number of RTP packets of this connection in its maintaining RTP hash table. The streaming server on the back-end server then starts to transmit the media data of the first film section by sending RTP packets to the client for playing. When the RTP sequence number in an outgoing RTP packet approaches the stored expected end RTP sequence number, the back-end server will send a *play_over* notification packet to inform the front-end server to hand off this streaming connection to the selected new back-end server to continue serving this streaming connection.

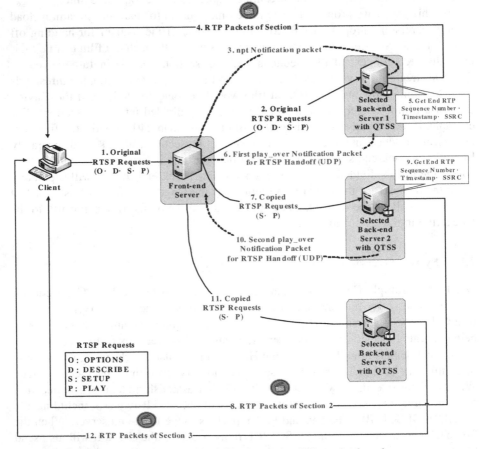

Fig. 3. An example of serving a film in turn by different back-end servers

After receiving the *play_over* notification packet, the front-end server will start to hand off the streaming connection. The front-end server will select a new back-end server and then forward the previously stored RTSP packets to the new back-end server for playing the second film section. Only SETUP 3, SETUP 4, and PLAY requests need to be sent to the new back-end server. In QTSS architecture, each streaming connection has a unique session key number for identification. In this way, the streaming server of the new back-end server will generate a new session key for this migrated connection. Therefore, when receiving the stored RTSP packets, the new back-end server must modify these RTSP packets with the new session key for this streaming connection. The new back-end server also must drop the reply packets of these RTSP packets; otherwise, if the client has received the extra RTSP reply packets, the streaming connection will be tore down immediately.

Figure 4 shows the processing of handing off an ongoing streaming connection to a new back-end server. The new back-end server maintains a RTP hash table just like the first back-end server does. The front-end server will send the end RTP sequence number, timestamp value, and the *ssrc* identifier of the previous film section to the new back-end server. The back-end server will store these values in the entry of the RTP hash table for this streaming connection. The RTP timestamp value determines the appropriate time interval for the RTP packets to be played back. The RTP *ssrc* identifier represents the source streaming server of a RTP packet. When the streaming connection has been migrated to the new back-end server, both two values will be initialized with the new values by the streaming server on the new back-end server.

In order to let the client be unaware of the change of the server responsible for serving the film, we have modified the RTP sequence number, timestamp value, and *ssrc* identifier in the outgoing RTP packets of the new back-end server. As a consequence, the sequence numbers of these RTP packets can be continued to the sequence numbers of the RTP packets in the previous film section.

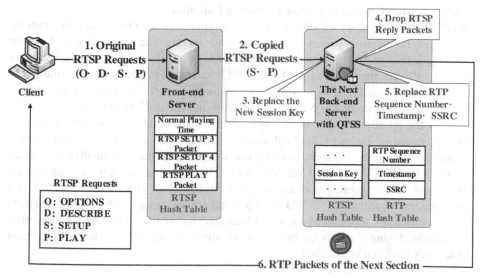

Fig. 4. Handing off an ongoing streaming connection to a new back-end server

3.2   Front-End Server Implementation

In RTSP Multiple Handoff mechanism, the front-end server is responsible for storing and forwarding RTSP request packets. These packets would be used in migrating the current streaming connection. The RTSP hash table is implemented for storing the normal playing time and RTSP request packets. The Linux kernel function for handling received IP packets (i.e. *ip_rcv()*) is modified to additionally handle the received notification packets from back-end servers for migrating the streaming connection.

3.2.1   Maintaining the RTSP Hash Table

To rebuild an existent streaming connection with the client in another back-end server, only RTSP SETUP and PLAY methods are essentially required. For the later processing of migrating an ongoing streaming connection, when receiving the RTSP DESCRIBE packet, the front-end server would establish a RTSP hash table entry by using the client's source IP address and port number as its hash key. This entry would store the normal playing time of the film and store the following SETUP and PLAY packets. The normal playing time is contained in the RTSP DESCRIBE reply packet. When the RTSP DESCRIBE reply packet is sent from the first back-end server, the first back-end server will send an *npt* notification packet to inform the front-end server. If the film has to be divided, the *npt* field in the RTSP PLAY packet must be modified. As the end of transmitting the RTP packets of the first film section, the back-end server will send a *play_over* notification packet to notify the front-end server to solicit RTSP Handoff. The *play_over* notification packet includes the end RTP sequence number, RTP timestamp value, and *ssrc* identifier information of the streaming connection for the previous film section. The front-end server will store these information in the RTSP hash table entry for this streaming connection.

3.2.2   Modification of Packet Receiving Function

In LVS-CAD cluster, a back-end server can communicate with the front-end server by sending a notification packet to the front-end server. The Linux kernel function *ip_rcv()* is responsible for processing all incoming packets at IP layer. The back-end server will send *npt* length of the film or RTP values of previous film section packaged in a notification packet to notify the front-end server. The front-end server then can use these information to perform RTSP Multiple Handoff mechanism.

After the RTSP hash table entry has been established and the new session key has been recorded in the entry, the back-end server will send a *session_key* notification packet to inform the front-end server. The front-end server will modify the stored copied RTSP SETUP 4 packet with the end RTP sequence number, the end timestamp value, and the *ssrc* identifier of the previous film section. The front-end server then forwards this modified RTSP SETUP 4 and the stored copied PLAY request packets with modified *npt* to the newly selected back-end server for rebuilding the streaming connection. Figure 5 shows the processing of notification packets when a RTSP hash table entry has been established.

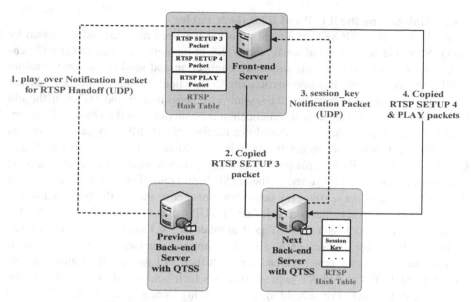

Fig. 5. Processing the *session_key* notification packet

3.2.3 Modification of LARD/RC Request Dispatching Policy

For LVS-CAD cluster to efficiently provide multiple types of services, the front-end server uses the content-aware LARD/RC [5] as its request dispatching policy. In the implementation, we modify LARD/RC policy for supporting streaming service. We add media file types into the supported file types of LARD/RC. While handing off the ongoing streaming connection is executed, LARD/RC will choose the least-loaded back-end server in the server set to be the next back-end server to provide the streaming service of the next film section. If all back-end servers in the server set are overloaded, LARD/RC will add another least-loaded server from the whole servers into the server set of this request. The timer will monitor server connection status in the designate time interval. LARD/RC will remove a back-end server from the server set if it is of maximum load at that time.

3.3 Back-End Server Implementation

In LVS-CAD, the back-end server can transmit RTSP reply packets and RTP streams to the clients directly. It maintains the RTSP hash table for retaining the new session key number from the new back-end server. This is because when it receives the copied RTSP SETUP 4 and PLAY packets from the front-end server, it has to modify them by replacing the old session key with the new session key. When a streaming connection has been migrated to a new back-end server, the RTP sequence number, timestamp, and the *ssrc* identifier of the outgoing RTP packets from new back-end server will also be replaced with these RTP values of previous film section. As a consequence, the next film section can be continuous with previous one.

3.3.1 Maintaining the RTSP and RTP Hash Tables

When the copied RTSP SETUP 3 request packet has been received and processed by the QTSS of the new back-end server, the QTSS of the new back-end server will generate a new session key for this streaming connection and send out a corresponding RTSP reply packet with this new session key to the client. However, this new session key would be different from the old session key generated by the QTSS of the old back-end server. Besides, since the client should be unaware of the change of responsible back-end server, the client should not receive this RTSP reply packet. For this handling, we modify the packet transmission function *ip_finish_output()* in Linux kernel to handle this RTSP reply packet. This reply packet would be discarded and the new section key would be stored in the RTSP hash table. The new back-end server then will then send the *session_key* notification packet to inform the front-end server that it is ready to receive the copied RTSP SETUP 4 and PLAY packets. We use the client's source IP address and RTSP port number as the hash key to insert an entry into RTSP hash table. Subsequently, after the front-end receives the *session_key* notification packet from the new back-end server, it then will forward the following copied RTSP SETUP 4 and PLAY request packets which hold the old session key to the new back-end server. For rebuilding the streaming connection, the new back-end server modifies the received copied RTSP SETUP 4 and PLAY packets for replacing the old session key with new one in the kernel. The QTSS in the new back-end server then will consider them as legal and start to provide the media data of the subsequent film section to the client by sending RTP packets.

3.3.2 Modification of Packet Transmission Function

Each QTSS method uses request-reply pair packets. That is, when the RTSP request packet is processed by the QTSS, the QTSS will respond with the RTSP reply packet to the client. After the streaming connection has been established, the RTP streams could be transmitted by the QTSS to the client. Therefore, we modify the Linux kernel function *ip_finish_output()* which handles each outgoing packet to fetch the RTSP values including session key and store them in an entry of the RTSP hash table in the back-end server. Furthermore, the RTP values of the previous film section sent by the front-end server will be stored in the RTP hash table entry of the back-end server. This modified *ip_finish_output()* function will modify each outgoing RTP packet sent from new back-end server by replacing RTP values with the stored RTP values in the RTP hash table to make these RTP packets continuous with the previous film section.

4   Performance Evaluation

4.1 Experimental Platform and Benchmark Tool

The purpose of our experiments is to demonstrate that LVS-CAD cluster using the proposed mechanisms can achieve better performance by effective load sharing when it provides HTTP and streaming services at the same time. We use ten PCs running as the clients to request HTTP and streaming services to LVS-CAD simultaneously. The

LVS-CAD cluster we have constructed uses a front-end server and eight back-end servers that have installed QTSS streaming server. Two simulator servers run as the database for supporting the server pages of SPECWeb2005 [15]. All servers are connected with 1 GB Ethernet and linked with ZyXEL GS-1124 switch. Table 1 shows our experimental platform.

Table 1. Hardware and software equipments in our experimental platform

	Front-end server	Back-end servers	Simulators	Clients
CPU	Intel P4 3.4GHz	Intel P4 3.4GHz	Intel P4 3.4GHz	Intel P4 2.4GHz
Memory	DDR 1GB	DDR 384 MB	DDR 1GB	DDR 256 MB
NIC (Mbps)	Intel Pro 100/1000	Intel Pro 100/1000	D-Link DGE-530T	Realtek RTL8139 / Intel Pro 100/1000 / D-Link DGE-530T
OS	Fedora core 6	Fedora core 6	Fedora core 6	Windows XP SP2
Kernel	Linux 2.6.18.1	Linux 2.6.18.1	Linux 2.6.18.1	-
IPVS Module	1.21	-	-	-
Web Server	Memcached 1.2.3-7	Apache 2.2.3	Apache 2.2.3	-
Streaming Server	-	QTSS 5.5.5	-	-
Media Player	-	-	-	VLC media player 1.1.0
Benchmark	-	-	SPECweb2005	SPECweb2005
Number of nodes	1	8	2	10

We use SPECweb2005 [15] as benchmark tool and it is composed of web servers, simulators, and web clients. The web servers listen to the HTTP port (port 80). In our experiments, we use LVS-CAD web cluster instead of a single web server as our platform. In addition, we install the Memcached [10] in the front-end server as a cache server and use two simulator servers as the application servers, such as database.

When the benchmark is running, web clients send a huge amount of requests to the HTTP port of LVS-CAD web cluster until the benchmark runs out of all of its requests. A master of the clients named prime client controls the other slave clients. The prime client will gather benchmark statistics into a report. We choose the E-commerce workload to measure the performance of our web cluster because it is most similar to the scenario of a business web site. Besides sending HTTP requests to LVS-CAD, the clients also run VLC media player [17] to watch films by sending RTSP request packets to LVS-CAD. All films are encoded by any-video-converter [1].

4.2   Experimental Results

The proposed mechanisms are implemented in LVS-CAD cluster with the content-aware LARD/RC request dispatching policy. Its performance is compared with LVS cluster which does not support any handoff mechanism. Because LVS can use only content-blind request dispatching policy, so it is either configured with Weighted

Least Connection (WLC) [8] or Weighted Round-Robin (WRR) [8] request dispatching policies to select a back-end server for serving requests in a connection.

To prove the performance improvement of the proposed mechanisms, LVS-CAD is configured with three different settings. The first one uses RTSP Multiple Handoff mechanism, so a film would be logically divided into several sections according to its film length. In the second one, all films are logically divided into two sections regardless of its film length. It would be named as RTSP Handoff mechanism. The last one does not use connection handoff and all films are not divided.

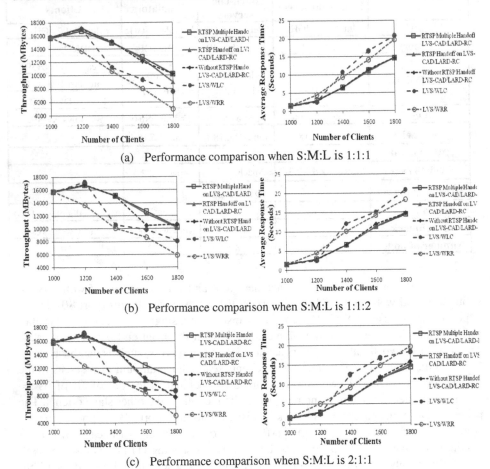

(a)   Performance comparison when S:M:L is 1:1:1

(b)   Performance comparison when S:M:L is 1:1:2

(c)   Performance comparison when S:M:L is 2:1:1

Fig. 6. Performance comparison of LVS and LVS-CAD under different configurations and various proportions of films

In each experiment, the runtime of SPECweb2005 is about 28 minutes. We keep the clients sending streaming requests to LVS-CAD for watching films to generate streaming workload continuously during the running period of the experiments. We test various scenarios for different proportion of short, medium, and long films. In the following experiments, "S" represents short films, "M" represents medium films, and

"L" represents long films. The bit rate is 2400K and the video resolution is 1280*720 (720p) for all films. We evaluate the throughput and average response time when the proportions of S, M, and L films are 1:1:1, 1:1:2, and 2:1:1. When the clients totally watch 10 short, 10 medium, and 10 long films in the experiment, S:M:L is 1:1:1. When the clients totally watch 8 short, 8 medium, and 16 long films, S:M:L is 1:1:2. When the clients totally watch 16 short, 8 medium, and 8 long films, S:M:L is 2:1:1.

Figure 6 shows the performance comparison of LVS and LVS-CAD under different configurations and various proportions of films. We use 3-minute films as the short films. The X-axis denotes the number of clients sending requests simultaneously in the experimental phase. The Y-axis denotes the total amount of web files transferred in Mbytes. Table 2 summarizes all evaluation results.

These results all demonstrate that LVS-CAD web cluster with RTSP Multiple Handoff performs best since it uses a more fine-grained way to effectively distribute streaming load among servers in cluster. In throughput comparison, it outperforms LVS-CAD using RTSP Handoff by at most 24.43% and outperforms LVS-CAD without using RTSP connection handoff by at most 36.34%. It outperforms LVS with no connection handoff by at most 107.52%. In the comparison of average response time, it outperforms LVS by at most 91.51%.

Table 2. Performance comparison of LVS-CAD with RTSP multiple handoff mechanism

(a)   Throughput comparison

Speedup of LVS-CAD using RTSP Multiple Handoff over other platforms	LVS-CAD		LVS	
	Without RTSP Handoff	With RTSP Handoff	Without RTSP Handoff	
Dispatching Policy	LARD/RC	LARD/RC	WLC	WRR
S:M:L 1:1:1	+ 5.53%	+ 13.28%	+ 36.34%	+ 106.32%
S:M:L 1:1:2	+ 20.97%	+ 2.74%	+ 46.62%	+ 74.03%
S:M:L 2:1:1	+ 36.34%	+ 24.43%	+ 46.21%	+ 107.52%

(b)   Average response time comparison

Speedup of LVS-CAD using RTSP Multiple Handoff over other platforms	LVS-CAD		LVS	
	Without RTSP Handoff	With RTSP Handoff	Without RTSP Handoff	
Dispatching Policy	LARD/RC	LARD/RC	WLC	WRR
S:M:L 1:1:1	+ 1.45%	+ 1.04%	+ 63.53%	+ 52.05%
S:M:L 1:1:2	+ 6.06%	+ 2.46%	+ 85.05%	+ 58.44%
S:M:L 2:1:1	+ 9.19%	+ 4.59%	+ 91.51%	+ 81.14%

5   Conclusions

We have proposed the RTSP Multiple Handoff mechanism and implemented it in the Linux kernel of LVS-CAD web cluster. This mechanism provides the flexibility that a film can be logically divided into several film sections according to its normal playing time and successive film sections of a film can be separately served in turn by different back-end servers. An existing ongoing streaming connection can be dynamically migrated to different streaming server and client will not notice the change of server. It achieves a more fine-grained way of load sharing among servers. Experimental results demonstrate that LVS-CAD cluster using RTSP Multiple Handoff mechanism can achieve 36.34-107.52% better throughput and reduce 52.05-91.51% average response time compared with LVS cluster without using RTSP Multiple Handoff.

References

1. Any-Video-Converter (June 2011), http://www.any-video-converter.com/
2. Apple Computer Inc., Apple - QuickTime - QuickTime Streaming Server (2003), http://www.apple.com/quicktime/products/qtss/
3. Casalicchio, E., Colajanni, M.: A Client-Aware Dispatching Algorithm for Web Clusters Providing Multiple Services. In: Proc. of 10th Int'l World Wide Web Conf., Hong Kong, May 1-5, pp. 535–544 (2001)
4. Chen, P.J.: Design and Implement of a PC-Cluster based Fault -Tolerant MP4 Video-on-Demand Server, Master Thesis, Institute of Computer Science and Information Engineering, National Cheng Kung University, Taiwan (2004)
5. Chiang, M.L., Wu, C.H., Liao, Y.J., Chen, Y.F.: New Content-aware Request Distribution Policies in Web Clusters Providing Multiple Services. In: The 24th Annual ACM Symposium on Applied Computing, Honolulu, Hawaii, USA, March 8-12 (2009)
6. Gilly, K., Juiz, C., Puigjaner, R.: An Up-to-date Survey in Web Load Balancing. In: World Wide Web, pp. 105–131 (2011)
7. Lin, W.Y.: Design and Implementation of a PC Cluster-Based QuickTime Streaming Server, Master Thesis, Institute of Computer Science and Information Engineering, National Cheng Kung University, Taiwan (2003)
8. Linux Virtual Server Website (Novemeber 2008), http://www.linuxvirtualserver.org/
9. Liu, H.H., Chiang, M.L., Wu, M.C.: Efficient Support for Content-Aware Request Distribution and Persistent Connection in Web Clusters. Software Practice & Experience 37(11), 1215–1241 (2007)
10. Memcached (March 2008), http://www.danga.com/memcached
11. Pail, V.S., Aront, M., Bangat, G., Svendsent, M., Druschelt, P., Zwaenepoelt, W., Nahumq, E.: Locality-Aware Request Distribution in Cluster-based Network Servers. In: 8th International Conference on Architectural Support for Programming Languages and Operating Systems (October 1998)
12. Schulzrinne, H., Rao, A., Lanphier, R.: Real Time Streaming Protocol (RTSP), RFC2326 (April 1998)
13. Schulzrinne, H., Casner, S., Frederick, R., Jacobson, V.: RTP: A Transport Protocol for Real-Time Applications, RFC1889 (January 1996)
14. Schukzrinne, H., Casner, S., Frederick, R., Jacobson, V.: RTP: A Transport Protocol for Real-Time Applications, RFC3550-RTP (July 2003)
15. SPECweb2005 (May 2008), http://www.spec.org/web2005
16. Tu, W., Steinbach, E., Muhammad, M., Li, X.: Proxy Caching for Video-on-Demand Using Flexible Starting Point Selection. IEEE Transactions on Multimedia 11(4), 716–729 (2009)
17. VLC (June 2011), http://www.videolan.org/vlc/
18. Wang, J.Z., Yu, P.S.: Fragmental Proxy Caching for Streaming Multimedia Objects. IEEE Transactions on Multimedia 9(1), 147–156 (2007)

Overcoming the Scalability Limitations of Parallel Star Schema Data Warehouses

João Pedro Costa[1], José Cecílio[2], Pedro Martins[2], and Pedro Furtado[2]

[1] ISEC-Institute Polytechnic of Coimbra
[2] University of Coimbra
jcosta@isec.pt, {jcecilio,pmom,pnf}@dei.uc.pt

Abstract. Most Data Warehouses (DW) are stored in Relational Database Management Systems (RDBMS) using a star-schema model. While this model yields a trade-off between performance and storage requirements, huge data warehouses experiment performance problems. Although parallel shared-nothing architectures improve on this matter by a divide-and-conquer approach, issues related to parallelizing join operations cause limitations on that amount of improvement, since they have implications concerning placement, the need to replicate data and/or on-the-fly repartitioning. In this paper, we show how these limitations can be overcome by replacing the star schema by a universal relation approach for more efficient and scalable parallelization. We evaluate the proposed approach using TPC-H benchmark, to both demonstrate that it provides highly predictable response times and almost optimal speedup.

1   Introduction

The star schema model has been used as the de facto model for storing Data Warehouses (DW) in Relational Database Management Systems (RDBMS). In this model, business performance metrics (facts) are stored in a central table (the fact table) and all relevant business perspective attributes (dimension data) are organized into a set of surrounding tables (dimensions). A fact table also stores a set of foreign keys that reference the surrounding dimensions, and usually contains a large number of tuples. It is highly normalized in order to reduce data redundancy and the fact table's size, since it represents a large proportion of the overall star schema size. On the other hand, dimension tables, which are usually significantly smaller in size but not in width, are stored as denormalized relations for performance purposes. The potential gain in storage space that could be achieved by normalizing dimensions does not pay off the overhead in query execution performance, requiring more complex query execution plans, extra memory and processing requirements for processing the additional joins.

Since DWs store historical business data, they are continuously growing in size, particularly the central fact tables that store data measures being produced by operational systems, stressing the limits of RDBMS, resulting in reduced query execution times. Parallel architectures are used handle such increasing data volume

Y. Xiang et al. (Eds.): ICA3PP 2012, Part I, LNCS 7439, pp. 473–486, 2012.
© Springer-Verlag Berlin Heidelberg 2012

and provide improved performance, by dividing data and processing among nodes, usually following a shared-nothing organization. Fact tables are partitioned among nodes and the surrounding dimensions are replicated so that each node can independently compute its partial results. However, parallel system scalability is constrained, not only by the network costs from exchanging temporary results between nodes, but also by the star schema model. As only the fact table is partitioned among nodes and dimensions are replicated, the fact table partition allocated to a node may be smaller than some larger dimensions. Therefore, adding more nodes to the parallel architecture will result in limited performance improvement, and thus resulting in sub-linear speedup.

In our work, we focus on the scalability limitations of the star schema model when deployed in large parallel shared-nothing architectures. We use a denormalized model approach to overcome such limitations and provide scalable and speedup capabilities.

In this paper, we discuss the scalability limitations of shared nothing-parallel architectures in processing large star schema DWs. We show that the assumption that dimensions are small and can safely be replicated among nodes without performance drawbacks isn´t correct, particularly when in the presence of large dimensions that need to be joined with the fact partitions, whose size may became relatively smaller than dimension as the number of nodes increases. Extending node partitioning to dimension tables changes the way query processing is done, and requires the usage of more complex parallel network joins and that large data volumes be exchanged between nodes. Consequently, the scalability is constrained by the network capacity and the volume of exchanged data. We show how these limitations can be overcome by replacing the star schema by a denormalized model approach for more efficient and scalable parallelization. We evaluate the proposed approach using TPC-H benchmark, to both demonstrate that it provides highly predictable response times and almost optimal speedup.

The paper is organized as follows: Section 2 discusses scalability issues of the star schema model; Section 3 shows how our approach that uses a denormalized schema can overcome the identified scalability limitations, and provide linear speedup. Section 4 presents a experimental evaluation using the TPC-H benchmark, and shows the superior capability of our approach in providing improved query performance and linear speedup. Section 5 discusses some related works and we present some conclusion remarks in Section 6.

2   Scalability Issues of the Star Schema Model

The star schema model offers a trade-off between storage size and performance in a single processing node. However, large DWs require parallel architectures to process such huge amounts of data with acceptable response times. DW star schemas usually are deployed in parallel architectures using a shared-nothing approach, which yields better performance and scalability than shared disk. In a shared-nothing organization, data is distributed among nodes so that they can compute partial results with their local data. Partial results computed locally by each node have to be send to the merger node. In a shared-nothing approach, while fact tables, of a star schema DW, are partitioned into smaller partitions and allocated to nodes, dimensions (regardless of their size) are replicated into each node, as illustrated in Figure 1.

Reducing the data volume of the fact tables into smaller and more manageable partitions allows the use of more inexpensive computer systems to host and process large, parallel data warehouses.

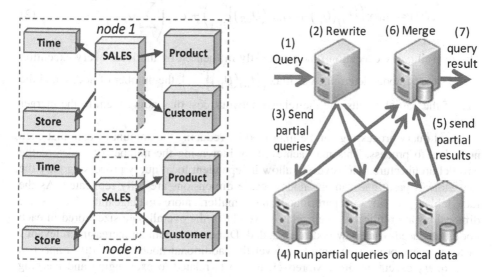

Fig. 1. Star-schema partitioning and placement   **Fig. 2.** Query processing in shared-nothing

This allocation allows each node to compute query partial results independently with its local data, as shown in figure 2. A query (1) received by a node (submitter node) is rewritten (2) and forwarded the processing nodes (3). Each processing node receives the rewritten query and executes it against the local data (4) before sending the partial results (5) to the merger node. The merger node, which may be the submitter node, waits for the intermediate results, and merges them (6) to compute the final query result, before sending it (7) to the user.

Definition: Consider that for a query Q, t is the query execution time, t_{rw} the time to rewrite and build the partial queries (2), t_{tpq} the time to transfer the partial queries to each node, t_n the local execution time on a node; t_{tpr} the time for a node to transfer its partial results to the merger node; t_m the time taken by the merger node to receive, merge partial results and compute the final result and t_s the time required to send the final results. The execution time t for a query Q is computed as

$$t(Q) = t_{rw}(Q) + \sum_{j=1}^{\eta} t_{tpq_j}(Q_p) + max\left(\left\{t_{n_j}(Q_p) + t_{tpr_j}(Q_{pR})\right\}_{j=1}^{\eta}\right)$$

$$+ t_{m_j}\left(\sum_{j=1}^{\eta} Q_{pR}\right) + t_s(Q_R) \tag{1}$$

In modern high speed networks, we may assume the query rewrite time (t_{rw}), the time required to send the partial queries to nodes (t_{tpq}) and the time spend to send the final query results back to the user (t_s) are neglectable, since represent a minimal fraction of the overall execution time. Therefore, t can be estimated as

$$t(Q) = max\left(\left\{t_{n_j}(Q_p) + t_{tpr_j}(Q_{pR})\right\}_{j=1}^{\eta}\right) + t_{m_j}\left(\sum_{j=1}^{\eta} Q_{pR}\right) \tag{2}$$

The overall query execution time t is mostly influenced by the local query execution of the slowest node, determined as $max\left(\left\{t_{n_j}(Q_p)\right\}_{j=1}^{\eta}\right)$, the number of nodes, and the size of the partial results and the related network cost of sending them to the merger node.

Local query processing can be improved by reducing the amount of data that each node has to process. This may achieved by increasing the number of nodes of the parallel architecture. However, to allow independent local query processing only the fact table is partitioned among nodes, while dimensions are fully replicated. As the fact tables are linearly partitioned into smaller, more manageable sizes, since dimensions are replicated, their relative weight in the overall data size stored in each node is reduced when new nodes are added. Dimensions gain an increasing relevancy in local query processing time to a level that additional nodes have little impact in local query execution time. Moreover, the costs related to exchanging and merging partial results increases with the number of nodes and gains an increasing weight in the overall query execution time t. Since network bandwidth is limited, this limits the scalability of the shared nothing architecture to process DW star schema.

Definition: *Considerer a parallel star-schema (P*) in a shared-nothing architectures, where f is the fact table and D is the set of dimension tables, with D={ D_i }$_{i=1,..,d}$, and d is the number of dimensions and η is the number of nodes. The storage size φ requirements of a node j, with j in {1,.., η} is computed as*

$$\varphi_j(P^*) = \varphi(D) + \frac{\varphi(f)}{\eta} \tag{3}$$

The storage requirement of each node is determined as the sum of the replicated dimensions and the size of the fragment of the fact table allocated to each node. Since local query performance is influenced by the amount of data to be processed, the dimension size is a performance bottleneck, particularly in large parallel infrastructures where the size of the fact table partition may be significantly smaller than some replicated dimensions.

Equi-partitioning may help in this matter, by partitioning both the fact table and some large dimension on a common attribute, usually the dimension primary key, and allocating into the same node a dimension partition' and the fact table' partition that contained related rows. However, since business data inherently does not follow a random distribution, and data is skewed, the used equi-partitioning may introduce another limitation to scalability, the data **equi-partitioning unbalancing**, with some nodes storing more data than others.

Definition: *In a parallel equi-partitioned star schema (P*Eq), where f is a fact table and D is the set of dimension tables, with D={ D_i }$_{i=1,...,d}$, and d is the number of dimensions and η is the number of nodes, D_E is an equi-partitioned dimension and D_{NE} the remaining dimensions, such that* $D_E \cup D_{NE} = D$. *The storage size φ requirements of a node j, with j in {1,.., η} is computed as*

$$\varphi_j(P^*Eq) = \varphi(D_{NE}) + \frac{\varphi(f)}{\eta} + \frac{\varphi(D_E)}{\eta} \tag{4}$$

With P^*E_q, the local query performance (t_n) of queries that join equi-partitioned dimensions (D_E) are processed faster since less data has to be read and joined. However, even with homogeneous nodes, while P* presents low variance in local query processing (t_n) to compute partial results for all submitted queries, P^*E_q exhibit higher variance due to the data equi-partitioning unbalancing.

A map-reduce-like approach is explored in [18][19] to overcome this limitation of load unbalance among nodes, by partitioning data into a large number of small data chunks, greater than the available nodes, with some being replicated for dependability or performance objectives. Chunks are processed as the nodes become available to process new data. However, this does not solve the increasing weight of dimension size in each node, and results in higher network costs since more partial results (one for each chunk) have to be sent to the merger node. Considering that k is the number of chunks, with k greater than the number of nodes, the query execution time t is computed as

$$t(Q) = max\left(\left\{t_{n_j}(Q_p) + t_{tpr_j}(Q_{pR})\right\}_{j=1}^{\kappa}\right) + t_{m_j}\left(\sum_{j=1}^{\kappa} Q_{pR}\right), \kappa \geq \eta \tag{5}$$

While queries over equi-partitioned dimensions witness a significant speedup, the remaining queries, which need to join non-equi-partitioned dimensions, are not enhanced, constraining the performance scalability. This is critical especially for large dimensions that cannot be equi-partitioned, like conforming dimensions (dimensions that used in multiple star schemas).

Alternately, to avoid replication of large non equi-partitioned dimensions and the related storage and processing costs, frequently these partitions are also partitioned and distributed among nodes, without being co-located according the fact table data. Consequently, queries that involves such dimensions, whose partial results were locally computed in each node, before being sent to the merger node, now have to be computed using parallel joins. Each node process partial results using local data, using replicated dimensions, and joins with the non-equi-partitioned dimensions through a parallel join. In a parallel join the local partial results are be partitioned among nodes in order to be joined with remained partitioned data. A performance evaluation of parallel joins is presented in [17]. Fig. 3 and 4 illustrates, respectively, the data storage allocation and query processing using parallel joins.

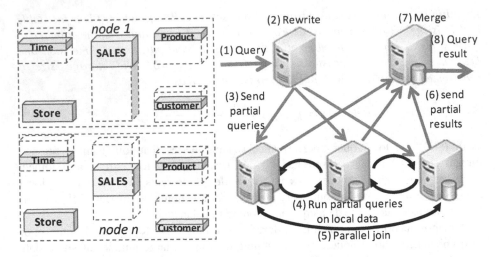

Fig. 3. Table partitioning and placement   **Fig. 4.** Query Processing using parallel joins

Query processing illustrated in Fig. 4 is similar to that in Fig.2, except the step 4. Each processing node receives the rewritten query and executes all the processing steps that can be locally processed exclusively with locally stored data (4a). For queries that have to join partitioned dimensions have to processed using parallel joins before sending the partial results (5) to the merger node. To minimize the data scalability limitation, by partitioning both fact and dimension tables, introduces another limitation – the **network scalability limitations**, raised from the network costs related to performing parallel joins. Scalability of shared-nothing architectures is thus constrained by those three correlated limitations: local data processing, node data unbalance, and in-network parallel joins.

Although, all the effort to devise improved parallel joins algorithms, this network scalability limitation introduced by parallel joins is not solved. In this paper, we advocate that scalability can only be attained by eliminating parallel joins, and changing the data organization in order to provide a true shared-nothing infrastructure where participating nodes can locally process partial results.

3   Overcoming the Scalability Limitations

In order to provide true scalability to parallel architectures parallel joins we have to eliminate network joins (network limitation) and change how data is locally stored and processed, without scalability limitations. To eliminate joins, at least the costly ones, we propose to apply denormalization to the fact and large dimension tables resulting into a single denormalized (wider) relation contained all related attributes (fact and dimension attributes). The star-schema, at the limit can be stored as a single fully denormalized relation containing all data.

A denormalized schema provides a less demanding and simpler model, which do not require joins, as data is already joined (denormalized) and physically stored as a single relation. A star schema model stored as a denormalized relation requires more storage requirements, since it includes data redundancy. However, since data is already joined together, several overheads of the star schema, such as primary and foreign keys and key related indexes are removed. As an example, the TPC-H benchmark these keys represent a 32% increase in the number of attributes and an overall 8% increase in storage size. [20] evaluated the impact of full denormalization of star schemas in both storage space and query performance on a single server. However, full (or partial) denormalization demands higher storage requirements (almost a 3× increase for TPC-H schema). [20][13] also demonstrated that schema denormalization provides predictable query execution times.

Although this model has more storage requirements, since all attributes of the star schema are physically stored into a single relation, query processing only involves reading this relation without the need to process costly joins, therefore it has lower memory and computational requirements and provides a high degree of predictability.

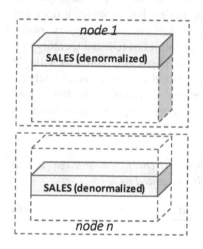

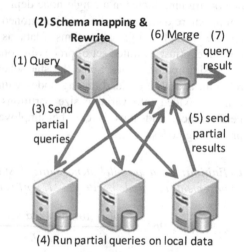

Fig. 5. *PDn** partitioning and placement   **Fig. 6.** *PDn** Query processing

Query processing over a denormalized relation distributed among nodes in a shared nothing fashion *(PDn*)*, illustrated in Fig. 6 is similar to that in Fig. 2. The main difference in query processing resides on step 2, which rewrites queries into a set of partial queries to be executed by local nodes. Besides rewriting, it also as to remove all join conditions and perform the necessary attribute mapping, translating all the existing references of the star schema model to the corresponding attributes in the denormalized relation. Additionally, some predicates have to be included to assure that aggregated results, particularly those related to dimension aggregates, do not include double-counting.

Optimal data distribution among nodes is a key issue in parallel, shared-nothing architectures especially when the nodes are not homogeneous. What amount of data should be allocated to each node to fully utilize the hardware infrastructure and deliver optimal execution time? A single relation provides more flexibility in determining how data should be distributed among nodes. For instance, round robin data allocation schema can be used to evenly distributed data in order to minimize query local query execution time variability.

As the local execution time to compute partial results t_{n_j} in each node, varies as a function of the amount of data that each node has to process, adding more nodes will proportionally decrease t_{n_j}. This is particularly relevant for tunning (balance) the amount of data that slower nodes, which constrains the overall query execution time (as expressed in equation 1), have process in order to compute its partial results. A single denormalized relation can be effectively distributed (partitioned) data among processing nodes, allowing a linear data distribution among nodes (equation 2) with a proportional boost in performance.

The additional storage requirements to hold the denormalized relation, which could be constraining factor in a single node deployment, is insignificant in a large parallel setup, where data can be linearly partitioned among nodes. Furthermore, it does not require complex join algorithms (data is already joined) and complex query optimizers (just a limited set of processing operations) and it has reduced memory and processing requirements. Since the star schema data is physically stored as a single relation, it can be divided among nodes with equally sized partitions. Alternately, it can be divided into variable size partitions and allocated according to the nodes' performance, and thus it can be employed in a large range of non-dedicated processing nodes.

Definition: *In a parallel denormalized star schema (PDn*), the storage size φ requirements of a node j, with j in {1,.., η} is linearly computed as*

$$\varphi_j(PDn^*) = \frac{\varphi(denormalized\ star\ schema)}{\eta}, j = \{1,..,\eta\} \tag{6}$$

Unlike the star-schema deployments on parallel architectures, the overall size of *PDn** remains constant, without data overhead increases when varying the number of processing nodes. Regarding storage requirements, *PDn** does not require additional storage space (no dimension replicas, no keys) as it can be fully horizontally partitioned. *PDn** can deliver predictable and almost invariant query response time. Since no joins are required, and query execution presents minimum memory requirements, the query execution time can be determined as a function of the employed access methods, the number and complexity of filtering conditions, the selected computations, the data volume and the underlying storage system.

4   Evaluation

We used the decision support benchmark TPC-H [6] deployed on a parallel architecture to evaluate the effectiveness of our approach in overcoming the scalability limitations. We built two evaluation setups using two distinct RDBMS systems: PostgresSQL 9.0 [7] or DbmsX, a well-known commercial RDBMS. The parallel infrastructure consisted in 30 processing nodes, each running a default Linux Server installation, interconnected with a gigabit switch. An additional node was used as the submitter, controller and merger node.

We created four types of schema: $P*$, the base TPC-H schema as defined in the benchmark, $P*Eq$ a equi-partitioned star schema, $P*Eq*P$ a equi-partitioned star schema with other partitioned dimensions, and $PDn*$ composed of a single relation. The former was populated with the TPC-H data generator tool (DBGEN) available at [6] and the latter with a modified version that generates the denormalized data as single flat file. We used a scale factor (SF) of 100.

We created and populated the data schema in each node. We created: $PDn*$ with 3, 10, 20 and 30 nodes, containing respectively $1/3^{rd}$, $1/10^{th}$, $1/30^{th}$ of the full denormalized data; and $P*Eq$ with 3, 10, 20 and 30 nodes, containing respectively $1/3^{rd}$, $1/10^{th}$, $1/20^{th}$ and $1/30^{th}$ of the data of tables ORDERS and LINEITEM equi-partitioned by O_ORDERKEY and fully replicating the remaining relations; and $P*Eq+P$ with 3, 10, 20 and 30 nodes, similar to $P*Eq$ and partitioned dimensions; and $P*$ with 3, 10, 20 and 30 nodes, containing respectively $1/3^{rd}$, $1/10^{th}$, $1/20^{th}$ and $1/30^{th}$ of LINEITEM and fully replicating the remaining relations. Fig. 8b) shows, the storage space allocated to each node for each schema with varying number of nodes.

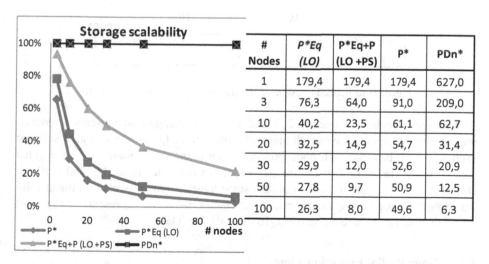

# Nodes	P*Eq (LO)	P*Eq+P (LO +PS)	P*	PDn*
1	179,4	179,4	179,4	627,0
3	76,3	64,0	91,0	209,0
10	40,2	23,5	61,1	62,7
20	32,5	14,9	54,7	31,4
30	29,9	12,0	52,6	20,9
50	27,8	9,7	50,9	12,5
100	26,3	8,0	49,6	6,3

Fig. 7. Storage scalability (a) data size in each node (in GB) (b)

While the total storage required by $PDn*$ in a 100 node setup is about 630GB, a linear storage increase without storage overheads, we observe that P*a increased to about 4900GB, $P*Eq$ increased to about 2600GB and $P*Eq+P$ increase to about 800GB.

4.1   Cost of Exchanging Partial Results

Query processing in a shared-nothing, parallel architecture as shown in equation 1 is influenced by the local partial query execution time (t_{nj}), and also the merge (t_m) and the exchange of the partial results (t_{tpr}) which are variable with the partial result size. The time required to rewrite (t_{rw}) and transfer of partial queries (t_{tpq}) are negligible. The network overhead to exchange partial results may be large and depends on the query and the number of nodes. Figure 8 depicts the time required to exchange the partial results (t_{tpr}) of queries Q1.. Q10, which need to be merged together by a merger node.

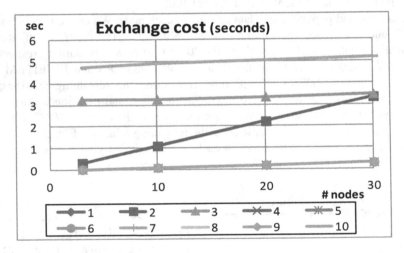

Fig. 8. Time needed to exchange partial results (t_{tpr}) for queries 1..10

With the exception of queries 2, 3 and 10, the exchange cost presents a reduced impact (below 1 sec) in the overall query execution time. Q2 presents an almost linear exchange cost, because each node produces almost the same amount of aggregated data that need to be sent to the merger node. On the other hand, Q3 and Q10 are almost invariant to the number of nodes, since aggregations groups are almost fully partitioned among nodes. In general, the exchange overhead represents at the most 8% of the local query execution (Q2,Q10) and 5% for (Q3).

4.2   Node Partial Execution Time

For schemas that produce locally query results, $P*$, $P*Eq$ and $PDn*$, we evaluated the average local partial execution time in each node. We omitted $P*$ results since $P*Eq$ equi-partitioning results are better than $P*$. Figure 9 depicts the results for a varying number of nodes, using postgreSQL (a) and DBmsX (b). In a 3-node setup, the average time is roughly equal, since each $P*Eq$ node has 1/3 of the fact data and the $\emptyset(\varphi)$ ratio (equation 2) is below 30% (figure 2).

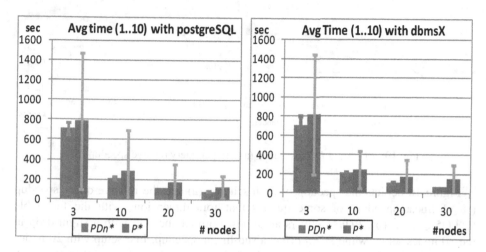

Fig. 9. Partial execution time in each node using a) PostgreSQL and b) DbmsX

From the figures 9 and 10, we observe that local execution time of $PDn*$ decreases almost linearly, as the data volume that each node has to process diminishes. Note that the depicted average results account the results of queries 1 to 10, including queries that do not process table LINEITEM. Increasing the number of nodes from 3 to 10, the node average response time of $PDn*$ decreases from 709s to 208s, while $P*Eq$ only decreases from 783s to 291s with PostgreSQL. We observe that DbmsX, presented a similar behavior, with $PDn*$ decreasing from 708s to 210s and $P*Eq$ decreasing from 820s to 245s.

Since $PDn*$ uses a simpler storage model, both RDBMS engines delivers almost the same query execution times (with variations smaller than 0.2%) while the same does not happens with $P*Eq$. This characteristic allows that more complex shared nothing architectures can be build using a set of heterogeneous database engines.

$PDn*$ delivers good performance results without using additional index structures and is unaffected by query selectivity. Globally we observe that the query execution of $PDn*$ time decreases linearly with the increase in the number of nodes, while the execution time in $P*Eq$ decreases at lower rates, due to the enormous volume of data stored in dimensions.

4.3   Speedup Analysis

$P*$ offers limited scalability since data is not fully partitioned amongst nodes, and dimensions are replicated or partially equi-partitioned, imposing limits on scalability.

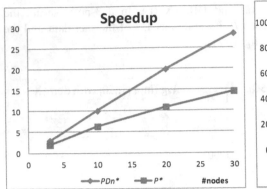 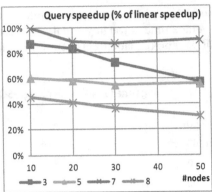

Fig. 10. *PDn** and *P*Eq* speedup (a) and per query relative speedup (b)

Figure 10 depicts the speedup of each schema (a) and the relative query speedup (% of linear speedup) of some queries that join dimensions with the fact table (Q3,Q5,Q7,Q8) (b). *PDn** delivers an almost optimal speedup with a slight drop in the 30 nodes setup, while *P*Eq* offers a sub-linear speedup. In a setup with 20 nodes we observe that the speedup delivered by *PDn** is two times greater than that with *P*Eq*. Figure 10-b) shows that all considered queries that join fact table with dimension tables return a sub-linear speedup. For instance, query 8 yields a maximum of 46% of the expected linear speedup with a 10 nodes setup, and drops with the increase on the number of nodes.

5   Related Work

In recent decades, both academia and industry have investigated different methods and algorithms for speeding-up the time required to process queries that join several relations. Research in join algorithms includes sort-merge, hash join, grace-hash join and hybrid-hash join [1][2][3][4], as well as access methods such as the Btree or Bitmap indexes [5]. Materialized views [6] use extra storage space to physically store aggregates concerning well-known and planned queries. Sampling [7] trades off precision for performance by employing the power offered by statistical methods to reduce the data volume that needs to be processed to compute an acceptable result.

Research on data partitioning and data allocation, includes [8][9] which exploit horizontal fragmentation and hash partitioning of relations and intermediate results to process parallel, multi-way join queries and increase parallelism; [10] exploits a workload-based data placement and join processing in parallel DW. A performance evaluation of parallel joins is presented in [17].Vertical partitioning and column-wise store engines [11] [12] proved to be effective in reducing the disk IO and thus boosting query performance. However, these works focus on improving query performance and minimize the cost of joining relations, not on providing predictable and invariant execution time.

Schema denormalization showed to be effective in providing predictable execution time[13][20]. [20] evaluated the impact of full denormalization of star schemas in both storage space and query performance on a single server. [13] provides consistent response times, by partitioning data by frequency to achieve good partitioning using fixed-length codes. Other works on denormalization [14], [15],[16] do not focus on the denormalization limitations of the star schema model, and they do not offer a clear insight into the query performance predictability and scalability over parallel shared-nothing architectures.

6   Conclusions

In this paper, we discussed the scalability limitations of the star schema model when deploying large DWs in parallel, shared-nothing architectures, and we proposed to merge the star schema relations in a single denormalized relation, in order to break the scalability limitations introduced by replicating large dimensions in parallel shared nothing deployments. Our approach (*PDn**), a parallel denormalized schema model does not have the limitations of the star schema model and delivers superior speed-up and scale-up capabilities. By storing data in denormalized fashion, it eliminates join processing costs, including the additional IO operations (random and sequential) when the available memory is insufficient to process in-memory joins, resulting in a simpler, RISC-like, predictable and time invariant model.

Using TPC-H benchmark and a commercial RDBMS and postgreSQL, we demonstrated that *PDn** delivers almost optimal speedup and scale-up performance without increasing the global data storage size. Since it provides almost linear speedup and predictable execution time, determined as a function of the data volume, it allows the fine-tuning of the amount of data that should be allocated to each node for top performance.

References

1. Pavlo, A., Paulson, E., Rasin, A., Abadi, D.J., DeWitt, D.J., Madden, S., Stonebraker, M.: A comparison of approaches to large-scale data analysis. In: Proc. of the 35th SIGMOD International Conference on Management of Data, pp. 165–178 (2009)
2. Patel, J.M., Carey, M.J., Vernon, M.K.: Accurate modeling of the hybrid hash join algorithm. In: ACM SIGMETRICS Performance Evaluation Review, NY, USA (1994)
3. DeWitt, D.J., Katz, R.H., Olken, F., Shapiro, L.D., Stonebraker, M.R., Wood, D.A.: Implementation techniques for main memory database systems. In: ACM SIGMOD Record, New York, NY, USA, pp. 1–8 (1984)
4. Harris, E.P., Ramamohanarao, K.: Join algorithm costs revisited. The VLDB Journal 5, 064–084 (1996)
5. Johnson, T.: Performance Measurements of Compressed Bitmap Indices. In: Proceedings of the 25th International Conference on Very Large Data Bases, pp. 278–289 (1999)
6. Zhou, J., Larson, P.-A., Goldstein, J., Ding, L.: Dynamic Materialized Views. In: Int. Conference on Data Engineering, Los Alamitos, CA, USA, pp. 526–535 (2007)

7. Costa, J.P., Furtado, P.: Time-Stratified Sampling for Approximate Answers to Aggregate Queries. In: International Conference on Database Systems for Advanced Applications (DASFAA 2003), Kyoto, Japan, p. 215 (2003)
8. Liu, C., Chen, H.: A Hash Partition Strategy for Distributed Query Processing. In: Apers, P.M.G., Bouzeghoub, M., Gardarin, G. (eds.) EDBT 1996. LNCS, vol. 1057, pp. 371–387. Springer, Heidelberg (1996)
9. Shasha, D., Wang, T.-L.: Optimizing equijoin queries in distributed databases where relations are hash partitioned. ACM Trans. Database Syst. 16(2), 279–308 (1991)
10. Furtado, P.: Workload-Based Placement and Join Processing in Node-Partitioned Data Warehouses. In: Kambayashi, Y., Mohania, M., Wöß, W. (eds.) DaWaK 2004. LNCS, vol. 3181, pp. 38–47. Springer, Heidelberg (2004)
11. Stonebraker, M., Abadi, D.J., Batkin, A., Chen, X., Cherniack, M., Ferreira, M., Lau, E., Lin, A., Madden, S., O'Neil, E., O'Neil, P., Rasin, A., Tran, N., Zdonik, S.: C-store: a column-oriented DBMS. In: Proceedings of the 31st International Conference on Very Large Data Bases, pp. 553–564 (2005)
12. Zhang, Y., Hu, W., Wang, S.: MOSS-DB: A Hardware-Aware OLAP Database. In: Chen, L., Tang, C., Yang, J., Gao, Y. (eds.) WAIM 2010. LNCS, vol. 6184, pp. 582–594. Springer, Heidelberg (2010)
13. Raman, V., Swart, G., Qiao, L., Reiss, F., Dialani, V., Kossmann, D., Narang, I., Sidle, R.: Constant-Time Query Processing. In: Proceedings of the 2008 IEEE 24th International Conference on Data Engineering, pp. 60–69 (2008)
14. Yma, P.: A Framework for Systematic Database Denormalization. Global Journal of Computer Science and Technology 9(4) (August 2009)
15. Sanders, G.L.: Denormalization Effects on Performance of RDBMS. In: Proceedings of the 34th Hawaii International Conference on System Sciences (2001)
16. Zaker, M., Phon-Amnuaisuk, S., Haw, S.-C.: Optimizing the data warehouse design by hierarchical denormalizing. In: Proc. 8th Conference on Applied Computer Scince (2008)
17. Schneider, D.A., Dewitt, D.J.: A Performance Evaluation of Four Parallel Join Algorithms in a Shared-Nothing Multiprocessor Environment, pp. 110–121 (1989)
18. Furtado, P.: Efficient, Chunk-Replicated Node Partitioned Data Warehouses. In: 2008 IEEE International Symposium on Parallel and Distributed Processing with Applications, Sydney, Australia, pp. 578–583 (2008)
19. Yang, C., Yen, C., Tan, C., Madden, S.: Osprey: Implementing MapReduce-Style Fault Tolerance in a Shared-Nothing Distributed Database. In: Proc. ICDE (2010)
20. Costa, J.P., Cecílio, J., Martins, P., Furtado, P.: ONE: A Predictable and Scalable DW Model. In: Cuzzocrea, A., Dayal, U. (eds.) DaWaK 2011. LNCS, vol. 6862, pp. 1–13. Springer, Heidelberg (2011)
21. PostgreSQL, http://www.postgresql.org/
22. TPC-H Benchmark, http://www.tpc.org/tpch/

Enhancing Service-Oriented Computing with Software Mobility

Hervé Paulino and Gilberto Camacho

CITI / Departamento de Informática
Faculdade de Ciências e Tecnologia, Universidade Nova de Lisboa
2829-516 Caparica, Portugal
herve@di.fct.unl.pt

Abstract. Service-oriented computing has emerged as a consensually accepted paradigm for the implementation and integration of distributed systems in heterogeneous environments. However, its basic request/response interaction model is not always adequate for communicating in both highly dynamic, and low bandwidth, networks. To overcome this limitation, we propose the seamless incorporation of software mobility with service-oriented computing to provide a powerful framework for service-oriented architectures to benefit from the advantages of the mobility paradigm. We instantiate the model as a middleware for the mobility of Java computations in Web service environments, and present some programming examples that illustrate the expressiveness of the proposed API. This middleware is currently being successfully used in the development of other service-oriented architectures, namely in the field of dynamic Web service architectures.

1 Introduction

Service-oriented computing (SOC) has emerged as a consensually accepted paradigm to abstract both software components and network resources. The composition of loosely-bound service-oriented components has been proved to be a good paradigm for the modelling of distributed applications, specially in heterogeneous environments, such as the ones targeted by mobile [8,21], pervasive [12], and grid computing [9,10]. However, the remote request/reply interaction model used in service-oriented architectures is not always adequate for networks with low bandwidth and high error rates.

Mobile agent systems, such as [2,13,19] can be used to migrate computations within service-oriented architectures (SOA), enabling local interaction and thus eliminating the need to maintain costly remote sessions. These systems, however, rely in the explicit notion of network node abstraction to express mobility, which burdens the SOA programmer with the management of both service and host identifiers. Moreover, common mobile agent development APIs require programs to specify the location of the resources, be it at development- or run-time, which is too restrictive for the requirements of dynamic environments where the execution context, namely the composition of the network is often not known in

Y. Xiang et al. (Eds.): ICA3PP 2012, Part I, LNCS 7439, pp. 487–501, 2012.

advance [17]. To overcome these limitations, the programmer is usually forced to deploy registries/directories of the available resources.

To tackle this problem we propose the seamless combination of the SOC and software mobility paradigms, providing a framework to easily incorporate mobility in service-oriented distributed applications. The seamless adjective emphasizes the fact that the use of mobility is orthogonal to the remainder steps of SOC's *find-bind-execute* paradigm, and that mobility is expressed in terms of service identifiers rather than host identifiers. This delegates the discovery of the location of the destination node(s) to the service discovery mechanism, removing it from the programmer's responsibilities.

The advantages of software mobility have been overshadowed by the security concerns it brings [3, 24] and the lack of robust infrastructural support [24]. Nonetheless, it is our opinion that the paradigm can be very useful in many of the environments where SOC plays an important role, namely in middlewares, where the code to migrate can be either known or controlled.

To this extent, this paper presents a middleware that instantiates the service-oriented mobility concept, initially formalized in [18], in Web environments. We rely solely on Web technologies to provide a interoperable framework that permits service-oriented platforms to benefit from the advantages intrinsic to the software mobility paradigm, such as reduced use of network bandwidth, disconnected execution, and low latency interaction [14]. In order to better illustrate the usefulness of the concept consider the following example:

- A service-oriented middleware that provides the means to extract information from data-streams (for instance a sensor network virtualised as a Web service), and emit notifications based on the computed results. Mobility can be used to move the computation towards (or closer) to the data source to, with that, reduce the amount of network traffic. Furthermore, assuming that the interface of the middleware supplies only the means to compose operations over streams, the code to migrate does not raise any security concerns, since is a sequence of such operations, and thus completely under the middleware's control.

The remainder of this paper is structured as follows: the next section describes the service-oriented approach to software mobility; Section 3 presents the developed middleware; Section 4 showcases some programming examples and how the platform has been evaluated. Section 5 compares our approach to existing work in the field and, finally; Section 6 presents our conclusions.

2   Service-Oriented Mobility

Service-oriented mobility enhances SOC by combining it with software mobility, making process locality transparent to the programmer by modelling mobility in terms of services: *migrate to a provider of service s_1 and execute process P_1* rather than the usual *migrate to node h_1 and execute process P_1*. The discovery of the location of the destination node(s) is relegated to a service discovery mechanism managed by a middleware layer (Figure 1).

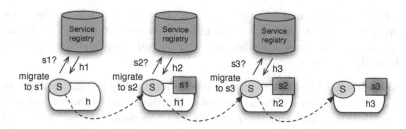

Fig. 1. Service-oriented software mobility

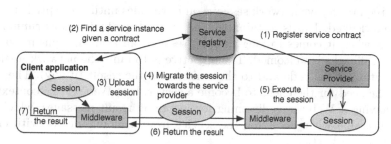

Fig. 2. Service-oriented session uploading

Our intention is not to replace the usual interaction models used in SOC, but rather to enrich the existing offer and, to that extent, provide a new alternative that can be used when appropriate. We have incorporated mobility in such a way that it is completely orthogonal to the remainder steps of the *find-bind-execute* paradigm used in SOC. Figure 2 illustrates how we have incorporated it as a new optional step between the *binding* and *execution* stages, enabling the *find-bind-migrate-execute* variant.

The will of the provider to receive incoming sessions can be verified at runtime, allowing for the selection of the mobility paradigm on-the-fly. Moreover, this will can be taken into consideration when negotiating service-level agreements (SLA).

2.1 Session Migration

Central to our model is the notion of session, which delimits the code to be migrated to the target host and interact with the target service provider.

The process of migrating such sessions requires a software layer placed between the client application and the service provider. As illustrated in Figure 2, this software layer must be present at both endpoints of the interaction. On the client side it is responsible for: a) building the session's closure; b) marshalling it; c) constructing the request message; d) establishing the connection to the target host, and; e) sending the message that comprises the session.

On the service provider side, its responsibilities include: a) receiving the session message; b) unmarshaling its contents; c) loading the session and its code dependencies (if any); d) launching the session's execution; e) collecting the result (if any); f) marshalling it, and g) sending it back to the client or propagating it to a new host (more on this on Subsection 2.3). The loading of code dependencies is necessary when not all the code required by the session is available at the provider side.

Asynchronous Upload: The synchronous request-reply communication mechanism maps straightforwardly into the uploading of sessions - the request uploads the session to the server, and the reply returns the result to the client application. However, although there is no communication while the session is being executed, the request-reply communication is connection-oriented and consequently requires active network sessions on both sides until the reply is received and acknowledged. This is sustainable, and even adequate, for short running sessions, but when it comes to long running sessions an asynchronous mechanism based on callbacks is welcomed. The objective is to limit the network session to the migration of the code and to the emission of the result (if any). The drawback is the need for the client to become a server. In a Web service context this means having a Web server listening for incoming result messages, which may not be desirable when accessing the service from a mobile device with energy consumption restrictions.

Nested Sessions: Service usage is not always disjoint, a session may interact with services other than the one to which it was uploaded to. The use of mobility in this context requires the migration of a session within a session, borrowing the concept of nesting long used in transactions.

2.2   Parallel Upload

The parallel upload consists on migrating one session to a set of hosts simultaneously, following a fork/join pattern. The client acts as the master that spawns as many sessions as available providers and waits for the lists of computed results, one per provider (if the session returns a result).

This feature can be useful if there are no data or causal dependencies between multiple executions of a session, allowing it to be uploaded simultaneously to all the target providers, thus enabling parallelism. Application examples include: performing management tasks, such as the installation of a piece of software in a set of hosts; collecting information, such as the patient record collection system of [16], and, performing computation over distinct sets of data, such as a runtime system for a map/reduce framework [5].

2.3   Workflows

Workflows of Web services, such a BPEL [15], play a important role in the construction of business processes in SOC. In this section we will describe the foundations on how to support workflows of sessions that may migrate to one or more service providers.

We want the model to remain session-centric, in other words, for a workflow to be built through session composition. Furthermore, for the sake of code

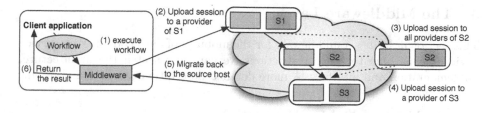

Fig. 3. An example of a workflow of sessions

reusability, we want the participation of a session in a workflow to be orthogonal to its implementation. We do not want to impose any special requirements on a session in order for it to be suitable for workflow integration. Given this, our requirements for building workflows through session composition are: 1. to allow a session to visit one or more instances of a service sequentially; 2. to allow a session to visit more than one instance of a service in parallel, i.e. to incorporate the parallel uploading of sessions in the construction of workflows; 3. to chain instances of items 1 and 2, and; 4. to pass the result computed by a session to another, procedure that we will refer to as *bridging*.

Figure 3 illustrates an example where sessions (a, b and c) travel to three services (S1, S2, and S3, respectively), being that, in the specific case of session b it travels to all the providers of service S2 in parallel.

From the mobility perspective, to have a session travelling a set of service providers relates closely to the concept of itinerary [13] widely used in mobile agent systems. A paradigm that does not fit in request-reply communication mechanisms discussed so far. Mobile agent applications typically travel along a set of network nodes, only having contact with their source host in two occasions: before being dispatched to the network and once the work is done. In fact, two of the premises of the mobile agent paradigm are: a) to eliminate network sessions, enabling disconnected execution (the source does not have to be connected to the network in order for the agent to execute), and, b) autonomy - the agent must be able to make choices without the user's intervention.

Our goal, however, is not to implement a new mobile agent system, but rather to enable session composition to provide the means for sessions to interact with a set of providers sequentially or in parallel. For that purpose we need to attend two essential aspects: **How to pass the result from a session to another in the workflow?** A session in a workflow may return a result that must be handed out to another session placed in a later stage. To define this relationship between sessions we introduce the *bridge* concept: two sessions are said to be bridged if the result of the execution of one is passed to the other. Listing 2 of Subsection 3.2 illustrates the construction of a workflow. **How to store results that do not have to be passed along?** For instance, when travelling a set of hosts gathering information - as the session travels, the data it collects must be stored for later retrieval by the client application. For this purpose we define the *data-repository* concept: a repository of all the results computed by sessions.

3   The Middleware Layer

This section describes a middleware for the mobility of Java code in Web service environments. Due to space restrictions we can only sketch the architecture, implementation and interface. A more detailed description can be found in [4].

3.1   Architecture and Implementation

The middleware is implemented as a software layer distributed among all the machines willing to upload and/or receive sessions and workflows. From the middleware's point of view, the itinerary is the basic mobility unit. Workflows are directly mapped into itineraries and the upload of a single session is implemented as an itinerary containing that one session.

An itinerary is thus composed by one or more sessions and is globally identifiable within the system. A session, in turn, has an itinerary-wide unique identifier, and comprises its closure (data and code) and its migration pattern: *sequential* or *parallel*. Sessions standing at the source end of a bridging operation also store the identifier of their counterpart. As is usual in Java, we are in presence of a weak mobility model, only the session's code and data state are migrated, not its execution state.

The middleware is responsible for managing the life of these itineraries, from the moment they are submitted, until they have completed their trip, and their results have been handed out to the invoking threads. Its general architecture is depicted in Figure 4.

Itinerary Upload: The middleware supports both the synchronous and asynchronous upload of itineraries. The process mostly transposes the steps enumerated in Section 2.1 to the context of the mobility of Java code in Web service environments. To these we add the need to associate the itinerary to the submitted asynchronous invocation. This is required to map received results to the rightful threads in asynchronous uploads.

Of the several modules that compose the client side of the middleware, the Itinerary Creator constructs the itinerary to store the submitted session or workflow; the Closure Builder collects the itinerary's closure, and; the Result Manager associates it to the submitted asynchronous invocation. The latter is also responsible for handing received results to the client application.

We are targeting Web service environments, hence communication within the middleware adheres to the Web service standards. This requires the existence of a Web service to handle the reception of both itineraries and results computed by

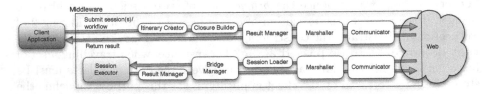

Fig. 4. General overview of the architecture

itineraries uploaded asynchronously. The conversion of the itinerary into an array of bytes, suitable for Web service communication, and the construction and emission/reception of the actual SOAP message are performed, respectively, by the Marshaller and Communicator modules, present on both ends of the communication.

Session Loading and Execution: On the server side, the reception of a new request causes the itinerary to be unmarshalled, and the next session in line to be selected for execution. The Session Loader loads all the code required by the session into a dedicated Java class loader. Each session has, thus, its own sandbox, which can be garbage collected as the session completes its execution.

The Bridge Manager verifies if a bridge with a previous session was established. If such is the case, the previously stored result is retrieved from the data-repository and made available to the current session through the invocation of method **void** handleBridge(R result) from interface Bridge<R>. This interface must be implemented by every session standing on the receiving end of a bridge.

The Session Executor executes the session by placing it in a queue that is consumed by a pool of threads. The pool's policy is parametrizable, allowing for configurable bounded and unbounded behaviours. Once the execution of the session terminates, the computed result is stored in the data-repository to be retrieved by the client application or for future bridging. Note that each result is labelled with information regarding to which session it relates to, and in which host it was computed on.

By default, the data-repository is piggybacked on the itinerary but the middleware provides the means for the programmer to opt for a remote repository, in the form of a Web service. This Web service is available in the middleware's distribution, but its up to the user to deploy it.

3.2 The API

The interface provided by the middleware to client applications assumes the form of a Java API that instantiates the concepts described in Section 2, namely the upload of sessions and workflows.

Session Creation and Uploading: Class Session<S, R> factorizes the functionalities required to migrate a session: S denotes the type of the service provider and R the type of the session's result. Listing 1 showcases a trimmed version of the classes' interface. The code to migrate is defined by providing a concrete implementation of abstract method R run(). The uploading (method upload()) receives as argument an object compliant with interface ServiceProvider, which abstracts the location to where a session can be migrated to. The invocation of upload() may throw an exception when the host running the target service provider does not support service-oriented mobility, in other words, is not running the middleware. To enable remote interaction, the API features method execute(), which runs the session asynchronously in the client machine. The management of whether the session is to be uploaded or locally executed can be delegated to the middleware - method uploadWP() instructs the middleware to upload the session whenever possible, and execute it locally otherwise.

```
abstract class Session <S,R> {
  abstract R run();
  Future<Result<R>> uploadWP(ServiceProvider<S> sp) {...}
  Future<Result<R>> upload(ServiceProvider<S> sp)
    throws UploadNotSupportedException { ... }
  Future<Result<R>> execute(ServiceProvider<S> sp) {...}
  Future<List<Result<R>>> uploadAllWP(
    List<ServiceProvider<S>> spList) { ... }
  Result<R> synchUploadWP(ServiceProvider<S> sp) {...}
  ...
  S getServiceProvider();
}
```

Listing 1. The interface of class Session

The parallel upload/execution of sessions is performed through methods upload-All(), executeAll(), and uploadAllWP(). All these receive a list of providers and return a list of results of type R. Moreover, there are synchronous variants of each of the previously presented methods, eg synchUploadWP(). Finally, method getService-Provider() returns the provider to which the session is bound (was uploaded) to.

The ServiceProvider interface allows for distinct methods for locating the target host. Currently two are provided: one that locates a service through its URL (much like in the usual mobility systems, where the location of the resource must be provided to the API) and, a second that retrieves from a directory a set (or all) services that respect a given description. Class Result represents a result computed by a session. It features methods to retrieve the actual result (getResult()) and the information regarding where it was computed on (getInfo()).

In [6], the authors distinguish between different kinds of resources: free transferable, fixed transferable, and non transferable; and different kinds of bindings to resources: by identifier, by value, or by type. In our work, the state of a session must be composed of *serializable* objects, otherwise an exception is raised. The default implementation provided by Java handles the copying of the resource, for now the construction of network references (to, for instance, non-transferable resources, such as a printer) must be handled by the programmer.

```
class Workflow {
  <S,R> void add(Session<S,R> s, ServiceProvider<S> sp);
  <S,R> void addAll(Session<S,R> s, ServiceProvider<S> sp);
  <S,R> void addAll(Session<S,R> s, List<ServiceProvider<S>> spList);
  void bridge(Session<S,R> source, Bridge<R> destination})
  Future<Result<?>> uploadWP() {...}
  ...
}
```

Listing 2. The interface of class Workflow

Workflows: The workflow concept is also instantiated as a Java class, Workflow, that features methods to add sessions in sequence (add()) and in parallel (addAll()). Sessions that stand on the receiving side of a bridge must implement interface Bridge<R> that specifies method **void** handleBridge(R result) mentioned in Subsection 3.1. The actual bridging is performed by method bridge() from the Workflow class. The method guarantees the sessions' type compliance by design - the type of the result to be propagated (R) is guaranteed to be compliant with the one expected by the receiving session. This is an important feature in the mobility context, where the resilience of the applications is crucial to avoid computational crashes during their trip.

Until this point, a session was a computational unit that produced a single result, computed by its run() method. This approach has the advantage of not imposing any special requirements on a session, in order for it to be suitable for composition. Nonetheless, sessions specially developed to be used as workflow stages may find this imposition to restrictive. With this in mind, the API extends the use of the data-repository concept to provide a tool that allows a session to produce several results, of distinct types, that can be later retrieved by the client application or by other sessions. These user-available data-repositories are maps from string identifiers to items of a given type. The middleware features methods to create new data-repositories (both local or remote), and to store and retrieve items from a repository. Thus, a session may be bound to multiple data-managers, which may hold values of different types, and may be either local to the itinerary or a remote service available on the network.

4   Evaluation

We begin this section by presenting a set of simple programming examples that showcase the usefulness and expressiveness of the proposed model. Next, we overview a performance evaluation that was conducted to asses the middleware's effective implementation.

4.1   Programming Examples

We have identified three main interaction patterns that take advantage of service-oriented mobility: 1. multiple message interaction with a service; 2. one or more interactions with a set of services of the same kind; 3. a workflow of interactions with several services. We illustrate the use of proposed middleware in the first and third categories with two small application scenarios.

Scenario 1: Consider a middleware that presents wireless sensor networks (WSNs) as Web services, such as the one proposed in [20]. Service-oriented mobility can be used to: a) enable the remote installation of filters, by processing the result of the performed queries at the source (the server side), thus decreasing network traffic, and; b) provide a stream-data like interaction model on top of a stateless service, by sending the processed items to a parametrizable URI (following, for example, a RESTful approach).

To accomplish such task, the client defines a filter by extending some pre-defined Java class, and uploads the session that will install it at the server side. The session, in turn, establishes the connection with the client, posts the queries to the service provider and handles the result to be processed by the filter. Listing 3 sketches this implementation, the fields of both classes are managed through omitted *getter* and *setter* methods.

```
class MyFilter extends Filter<Float> {
  private Stats stats = new Stats();
  private DataOutputStream out;
  private int counter = 0;  private int period = 10;

  void process(Float value) {
    stats.compute(value);
    if (counter++%period == 0) out.write(stats.read());
}}

class WSNSession<T> extends Session<TemperatureWsn> {
  private String query;
  private Filter<T> filter;
  private URL clientURL;

  void run() {
    HttpURLConnection client = new HttpURLConnection(clientURL);
    client.connect();
    filter.setOutputStream(new DataOutputStream(client.getOutputStream()));
    while (true)
      filter.process(getServiceProvider().query(query));
}}
```

Listing 3. The WSN example

Scenario 2: This scenario illustrates the usefulness of proposed workflow model. The example targets the lifecycle of a document, from proofreading, to layout definition and printing. We model it as a workflow of three bridged sessions, one for each chore (as depicted in Listing 4). We assume that the service provides are known beforehand, since, in this particular example, it is not usual to delegate this responsibility in some automatic search engine.

```
Workflow wf = new Workflow();
ProofReadingSession prs = new ProofReadingSession();
prs.setDocument(someDocument);
wf.add(prs, new ServiceProviderURL<ProofReadingService>(aURL);
DocLayoutSession dls = new DocLayoutSession("scientificArticle");
wf.add(dls, new ServiceProviderURL<DocLayoutService>(bURL);
PrintingSession ps= new PrintingSession(bookBindingDetails, deliveryAddr)
    ;
wf.add(ps, new ServiceProviderURL<PrintingService>(cURL);
wf.bridge(prs, dls);
wf.bridge(dls, ps);
Result<Bill> bill = wf.uploadWP();
```

Listing 4. Workflow creation example

The first session receives the given document (in some predefined format) and submits it to an automatic proofreading service (we opt for an automatic service for the sake of focus' and simplicity, the use of non-automatic services would require the session to wait for a notification, received via email or XMMP, and proceed from there). The second, picks up the document produced in the previous stage and submits it to a document layout service, which will format it according to the selected template. Finally, session three submits the PDF document (produced by the previous stage) to a printing service, specifying the book binding details and the delivery address, and returns the bill.

Note that the UploadNotSupportedException exception is automatically handled by the middleware. Whenever a stage of the workflow cannot migrate to a provider of the target service, the session is executed locally instead of migrated.

```
public class DocLayoutSession extends Session<DocLayoutService , PDFFile>
    implements Bridge<Doc> {
  private Doc doc;
  private String format;

  public DocLayoutSession(String format) { this.format = format; }
  public PDFFile run() {
    if (format.equals("scientificArticle"))
      return getServiceProvider().scientificArticle(doc);
    ...
  }
  public void handleBridge(Doc d) { doc = d; }
}
```

Listing 5. A workflow session (DocLayoutSession)

The sessions are similar in nature, therefore we only list the code for the second stage (Listing 5). The middleware guarantees that the bridge is established before the session's execution. Therefore, method run() may safely consult variable doc to retrieve the result produced by the previous stage and, from that point on, interact with the target service provider. The result is a PDF file formatted according to the providers' template for scientific articles.

4.2   Performance Evaluation

Throughout the years several comparative studies between software mobility and the client/server paradigm have been published [7, 23]. The conclusions are, in general, that mobility saves network bandwidth at the expense of increased server computation and, that it behaves better when the low-bandwidth situations.

We wanted to asses if our approach to mobility retains these properties, so it will be clear when it is advantageous to use it in the context of service-oriented Web applications. For this purpose, we performed a comparative analysis of the implemented middleware against the usual SOAP based client-server interaction paradigm used in service-oriented computing.

The values were measured on laptop computers with a Intel Core 2 Duo processor and 1GB memory running Windows 7 and the Apache Axis2 Web service engine. To better understand the impact of the network in this analysis, our study contemplates two networks with distinct bandwidths: 1Mbps and 100Mbps. The original study covered sessions with different sizes [4], however, in this presentation we set this parameter to a little over 30KBytes.

The first two graphs (Figures 5 (a) and (b)) plot the overhead of migrating a session relatively to remote interaction. The first addresses the migration of a session that performs a single request with variable processing times. We can observe that, as would be expected, the migration overhead becomes negligible as the size of the data to be exchanged in the interaction, or the request processing time, increases. We can also observe that the network's impact on the results is inversely proportional to its bandwidth. The second graph addresses a session that performs multiple interactions with a provider. Theoretically, as the number of interactions increase, there is a point where the overhead of migrating the session will weight less than the amount of data exchanged in the interactions. For this particular case (30KBytes), 15 interactions is that turning point.

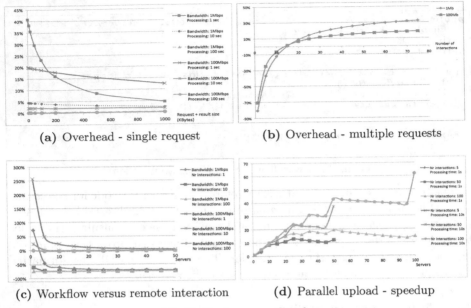

(a) Overhead - single request   (b) Overhead - multiple requests

(c) Workflow versus remote interaction   (d) Parallel upload - speedup

Fig. 5. Performance Graphs

The next analysis compares the use of a workflow to interact sequentially with a set of providers, in opposition to the sequential use of remote interactions. The graph plotted on Figure 5 (c) presents the overhead of opting for the workflow approach, varying the number of interactions with the provider, and the number of visited service providers (servers). Once more, mobility performs better when the network's bandwidth has real impact on the results.

Finally, we present a speedup analysis for the parallel upload of sessions. The evaluated session code performs a loop of N interactions with the target service, being N a parameter. We vary the total number of interactions performed by the set of sessions (5, 50, and 100), and the processing time of each interaction (1 and 10 seconds). For instance, configuration (number of interactions: 50, number of servers: 3) refers to three instances of the session: two with the N parameter set to 17, and one with N set to 16. The graph of Figure 5 (d) plots the results for the 100Mbps network. Given that parallel execution of sessions only compensates when the amount of work is significant, the speed of the network is almost negligible. The performance is bounded by the providers that receive the session with the larger number of interactions. For instance, when splitting 100 interactions by 45 sessions, at least one will perform 3 interactions, while when splitting by 50, all sessions perform only 2. This work distribution results in a performance deterioration when the increase of servers is not followed by a decrease in the maximum number of interactions performed by a single session, and in a significant gain when it is.

5   Related Work

This approach is the first to address the service-oriented software mobility problematic. Nonetheless, other proposals have addressed the combination of services and software mobility.

Mob [19] was the first language to combine services and mobile agents. It is a mobile agent scripting language where agents implement and require services, thus providing agent anonymity in inter-agent communication. There is no notion of session uploading, agents access services provided by other agents through remote method invocation. Mobility in Mob is strong, since the whole computation (the agent) that has the ability to move. However, this mobility is modelled in terms of network nodes not services.

WSMI [1] is an infrastructure that builds on the Web services standards to achieve interoperability between mobile agent systems, a major concern in the mobile agent field. Standardization is obtained by exporting mobile agent functions as a Web service interfaces.

In [22], Peters integrates mobile agents and services paradigms in the context of the SeMoA mobile agent system. Mobile agents and services can interact with each other, i.e. similarly to Mob, mobile agents can provide or require Web services, which in turn may be offered by other mobile agents. A specialized Web service engine translates Web service standard requests into SeMoA requests, enabling communication.

Ishikawa et al. [11] resort to the mobile agent technology to provide Web service integration in pervasive environments. The integration per se is specified in a BPEL process, the role of the agents is to migrate services providers between hosts, with the goal of reducing network traffic and the load on the users' mobile devices (assuming that these implement Web services). Agent behaviour is defined by a set of dedicated rules that separate the logic from behaviour. These contain a *local* keyword that allows the migration to be performed towards the first service invoked in a list of to be executed activities. This approach is the one that relates closer to ours, in the sense that migration can be performed towards a service provider disregarding its location. However, there are major differences in both approaches, Ishikawa focuses on inter service interaction, it assumes that some services can migrate between hosts (there is no discussion about the restrictions to this migration process - for instance, a service with a persistent store cannot migrate). The work presented in this paper is of a more fundamental nature, it provides the means to choose between remote and local interaction according to the environmental conditions. Thus, it could be used to implement the work of Ishikawa.

6   Conclusions

In this paper we introduced a middleware for service-oriented software mobility that seamless combines the software mobility and service-oriented computing paradigms. It is our opinion that this combination enhances SOC and provides an intuitive framework for the implementation of distributed applications. This is even more so true when applied to today's highly dynamic and volatile networks. The use of services to model client-server relationships provides the means for dynamic service discovery and binding. No longer the failure of a component as by itself a disruptive action on the system.

Our proposal is substantiated with the implementation of a prototype for the mobility of Java code in Web service environments. The prototype is fully functional and has been evaluated from different perspectives. The obtained results and our experience in its use to develop other service-oriented architectures allows us to conclude that the proposed model can be integrated in the development process of Java Web service applications with no significant burden. Essential to these results are the fact that: a) mobility has been incorporated as new optional step between the *binding* and *execution* stages of the usual *find-bind-execute* paradigm of service-oriented computing. Thus, no impositions are made on the interaction model. The actual use of mobility is dependent on the will of the provider to receive incoming code and on the evaluation of the benefits that the client will harvest (which is design and performance dependent). b) the API is simple, focusing on the essentials to provide a powerful support for software mobility in the context of Java Web services. The API provides the sequential and parallel upload of sessions, and the definition of workflows of sessions, laying the foundations for future incorporation in workflows of Web services, such as BPEL.

Regarding future work, our efforts will go to the application of service-oriented mobility in real-life applications, namely in the health-care field.

Acknowledgement. This work was partially funded by FCT MCTES under project MACAW-PTDC/EIA-EIA/115730/2009 and PEst-OE/EEI/UI0527/ 2011- Centro de Informática e Tecnologias da Informação (CITI/FCT/UNL) - 2011-2012.

References

1. Bellavista, P., Corradi, A., Monti, S.: Integrating web services and mobile agent systems. In: Proceedings of the First International Workshop on Services and Infrastructure for the Ubiquitous and Mobile Internet (SIUMI) (ICDCSW 2005), vol. 03, pp. 283–290. IEEE Computer Society (2005)
2. Bellifemine, F., Poggi, A., Rimassa, G.: Developing multi-agent systems with a fipa-compliant agent framework. Softw., Pract. Exper. 31(2), 103–128 (2001)
3. Brooks, R.R.: Mobile code paradigms and security issues. IEEE Internet Computing 8(3), 54–59 (2004)
4. Camacho, G.: Service-oriented Mobility of Java Code in Web Service Architectures. Master's thesis, Faculdade de Ciências e Tecnologia, Universidade Nova de Lisboa (2010)
5. Dean, J., Ghemawat, S.: Mapreduce: simplified data processing on large clusters. Commun. ACM 51(1), 107–113 (2008)
6. Fuggetta, A., Picco, G.P., Vigna, G.: Understanding Code Mobility. IEEE Transactions on Software Engineering 24(5), 342–361 (1998)

7. Gray, R.S., Kotz, D., Peterson, R.A., Barton, J., Chacón, D., Gerken, P., Hofmann, M.O., Bradshaw, J.M., Breedy, M.R., Jeffers, R., Suri, N.: Mobile-Agent versus Client/Server Performance: Scalability in an Information-Retrieval Task. In: Picco, G.P. (ed.) MA 2001. LNCS, vol. 2240, pp. 229–243. Springer, Heidelberg (2001)
8. Gu, T., Pung, H.K., Zhang, D.Q.: A service-oriented middleware for building context-aware services. J. Netw. Comput. Appl. 28, 1–18 (2005)
9. GuiLing, W., YuShun, L., ShengWen, Y., ChunYu, M., Jun, X., MeiLin, S.: Service-oriented grid architecture and middleware technologies for collaborative e-learning. Scc 2, 67–74 (2005)
10. Harrison, A., Taylor, I.: Service-oriented middleware for hybrid environments. In: Proceedings of the 1st International Workshop on Advanced Data Processing in Ubiquitous Computing (ADPUC 2006), p. 2. ACM Press (2006)
11. Ishikawa, F., Yoshioka, N., Honiden, S.: Mobile agent system for web service integration in pervasive network. Systems and Computers in Japan 36(11), 34–48 (2005)
12. Kalasapur, S., Kumar, M., Shirazi, B.: Evaluating service oriented architectures (SOA) in pervasive computing. In: 4th IEEE International Conference on Pervasive Computing and Communications (PerCom 2006), pp. 276–285. IEEE Computer Society (2006)
13. Lange, D.: Programming Mobile Agents in Java. In: Masuda, T., Tsukamoto, M., Masunaga, Y. (eds.) WWCA 1997. LNCS, vol. 1274, pp. 253–266. Springer, Heidelberg (1997)
14. Lange, D.B., Oshima, M.: Seven good reasons for mobile agents. Commun. ACM 42(3), 88–89 (1999)
15. Louridas, P.: Orchestrating Web Services with BPEL. IEEE Software 25, 85–87 (2008)
16. Marques, P., Robles, S., Cucurull, J., Correia, R., Navarro, G., Marti, R.: Secure integration of distributed medical data using mobile agents. IEEE Intelligent Systems 21(6), 47–54 (2006)
17. Mascolo, C., Capra, L., Emmerich, W.: Mobile computing middleware, pp. 20–58. Springer-Verlag New York, Inc. (2002)
18. Paulino, H.: An Abstract Machine for Service-oriented Mobility. Chapman & Hall/CRC Computational Science, vol. 2, pp. 199–233. CRC Press, William Gardner and Michael Alexander edn. (December 2008)
19. Paulino, H., Lopes, L.: A programming language and a run-time system for service-oriented computing with mobile agents. Software: Practice and Experience 38(7), 705–734 (2008)
20. Paulino, H., Santos, J.R.: A Middleware Framework for the Web Integration of Sensor Networks. In: Par, G., Morrow, P. (eds.) S-CUBE 2010. LNICST, vol. 57, pp. 75–90. Springer, Heidelberg (2011)
21. Paulino, H., Tavares, C.: SeDeUse: A Model for Service-Oriented Computing in Dynamic Environments. In: Bonnin, J.-M., Giannelli, C., Magedanz, T. (eds.) Mobilware 2009. LNICST, vol. 7, pp. 157–170. Springer, Heidelberg (2009)
22. Peters, J.: Integration of mobile agents and web services. In: Proceedings of The First European Young Researchers Workshop on Service Oriented Computing. , pp. 53–58 (2005)
23. Trillo, R., Ilarri, S., Mena, E.: Comparison and performance evaluation of mobile agent platforms. In: Proceedings of the Third International Conference on Autonomic and Autonomous Systems, p. 41. IEEE Computer Society (2007)
24. Vigna, G.: Mobile agents: Ten reasons for failure. In: 5th IEEE International Conference on Mobile Data Management (MDM 2004), pp. 298–299. IEEE Computer Society (2004)

An Insightful Program Performance Tuning Chain for GPU Computing

Haipeng Jia[1,2], Yunquan Zhang[1,3], Guoping Long[1], and Shengen Yan[1,3,4]

[1] Lab. of Parallel Software and Computational Science, Institute of Software,
Chinese Academy of Sciences
[2] College of Information Science and Engineering, The Ocean University of China
[3] State Key Laboratory of Computing Science, the Chinese Academy of Sciences
[4] Graduate University of Chinese Academy of Sciences
jiahaipeng95@gmail.com, zyq@mail.rdcps.ac.cn, guoping@iscas.ac.cn

Abstract. It is challenging to optimize GPU kernels because this progress requires deep technical knowledge of the underlying hardware. Modern GPU architectures are becoming more and more diversified, which further exacerbates the already difficult problem of performance optimization. This paper presents an insightful performance tuning chain for GPUs. The goal is to help non-expert programmers with limited knowledge of GPU architectures implement high performance GPU kernels directly. We achieve it by providing performance information to identify GPU program performance bottlenecks and decide which optimization methods should be adopted, so as to facilitate the best match between algorithm features and underlying hardware characteristics. To demonstrate the usage of tuning chain, we optimize three representative GPU kernels with different compute intensity: Matrix Transpose, Laplace Transform and Integral on both NVIDIA and AMD GPUs. Experimental results demonstrate that under the guidance of our tuning chain, performance of those kernels achieves 7.8~42.4 times speedup compared to their naïve implementations on both NVIDIA and AMD GPU platforms.

Keywords: Tuning Chains, Compute Intensity, Memory-bound Kernels, Computation-bound Kernels.

1 Introduction

As commodity computing accelerators, GPUs have been attracting the attention of more and more application developers because of their increasing computing power and programmability. However, we won't get the required performance without careful optimizations because the performance program has shifted from hardware designers to application developers. Unfortunately, it is challenging to tune program for GPUs because this progress requires deep technical knowledge of the underlying hardware. Furthermore, modern GPU architectures are becoming more and more diversified, which further exacerbates the already difficult problem of performance optimization. For programmers, it will be helpful to have a structured and insightful Optimization Chain that guides performance

Y. Xiang et al. (Eds.): ICA3PP 2012, Part I, LNCS 7439, pp. 502–516, 2012.

optimizations on GPUs. Most importantly, it needs to be understandable by most programmers.

This paper addresses this problem by proposing an insightful performance tuning chain for GPUs. The goal of this performance tuning chain is to help non-expert programmers with limited knowledge of GPU architectures implement high performance GPU kernels directly. We achieve it by providing performance information to identify GPU program performance bottlenecks and decide which optimization methods should be adopted, so as to facilitate the best match between algorithm features and underlying hardware characteristics. The proposed performance tuning chain has two functionalities. Firstly, it provides valuable insights on primary factors that affect the performance. Secondly, it identifies performance bottlenecks and decides which optimization methods should be adopted and the applied order of these selected optimization methods.

In this work, we define the compute intensity of specific hardware and algorithm respectively. We identify the algorithm is memory-bound or computation-bound by comparing these two features. We also model the main performance factors, define the optimization space, and build our performance tuning chain. One of the challenges in building the tuning chain is the discontinuous optimization space due to resource restrictions and the specific thread models of GPUs. We address it by introducing tradeoff chain which can provide insights for the performance improvement. Finally, we demonstrate the usage of tuning chain through optimizing three representative programs with different compute intensity (Matrix Transpose, Laplace Transform, and Integral) on both NVIDIA and AMD GPUs. Experimental results demonstrate that under the guidance of the tuning chain, performance of those kernels achieves 7.8~42.4 times speedup compared to their naïve implementations on both NVIDIA and AMD GPU platforms.

In summary, our key contributions are as follows: Firstly, we build an insightful performance tuning chain for both NVIDIA and AMD GPUs to guide GPU kernel optimization. Secondly, we demonstrate how performance tuning chain to help programmers do performance optimizations of GPU kernels. Thirdly, to the best of our knowledge, this is the first tuning chain that analyzes the differences between AMD and NVIDIA GPUs in their architecture characteristic and optimization strategies.

The remainder of this paper is organized as follows. We provide an overview of OpenCL programing model, GPU architecture and the classfication of GPU kernel in section2. Section 3 presents how to build tuning chain for different hardware architecture. Section 4 presents the performance evaluation and analysis in details. After discussing related work in section 5, we conclude this paper in section 6.

2   Background

2.1   OpenCL and GPU Architecture

OpenCL (Open Computing Language) is an open industry standard for general purpose parallel programming across CPUs, GPUs and other processors, giving

software developers portable and efficient access to the power of these heterogeneous processing platforms [17]. OpenCL allow users to create a great number of
threads which are much lighter than threads in traditional operating system to
compose an N-dimensional index space to run on GPUs. Those threads are then
grouped into work-groups which provide a more coarse-grained decomposition of
the index space. OpenCL also defines its hierarchical memory model which contains two memory spaces according to memory location, called on-chip memory
and off-chip memory. On-chip memory includes cache, local memory and register
files, and belongs to a single multiprocessor block. Off-chip memory is comprised
of texture, constant and global memory, and is much bigger and shared by all
threads, but may incur hundreds of cycles of latency for each memory access.

Although the architectures of the mainstream GPUs are very different, from
the highest level, all GPUs on the market at presents share certain architectural
similarities. Modern GPUs are all stream processors and throughput-orient devices that made up of hundreds of processing cores. All GPUs are made up of one
or more compute units, termed streaming multiple processors (SMs) for NVIDIA
GPU and SIMD cores for AMD GPU. A compute unit can be further broken
down into one or more processing cores, termed streaming processors (SPs) for
NVIDIA GPU and stream processing units for AMD GPU. All processing cores
in the same compute unit can communicate with each other through an on-
chip user-managed memory, termed shared memory for NVIDIA GPU and local
memory for AMD GPU. Beyond processor itself, GPUs also share a common hierarchical memory model as pre-described. Both NVIDIA GPU and AMD GPU
use SPMD (Single Program Multiple Data) programming model. During execution, threads in a work-group are grouped into smaller groups, termed warp for
NVIDIA GPUs contains 32 threads and wavefront for AMD GPU contains 64
threads, which are the multi-threading scheduling unit and execute in lockstep
in a SIMD fashion. All GPUs have a zero overhead scheduling strategy which
enables warps (wavefronts) execute interleaved to tolerate intra-warp stall.

The main architectural differences between NVIDIA GPU and AMD GPU are
the design of processing core and register files, which are scalar architecture for
NVIDIA GPU, and vector architecture for AMD GPU. This difference will lead
to difference in program optimization which will be discussed later. In this paper,
although we focus on the NVIDIA Tesla C2050 and AMD Radeon HD5850 GPU,
we believe that our performance modeling methodology is also applicable to any
GPU architecture. However, certain adaptations may be required.

2.2   Memory-Bound Kernel and Computation-Bound Kernel

According to the comparison of memory access time and computation time, GPU
kernels can be divided into two categories, memory-bound and computation-
bound kernels. However, we have no way to know the value of these two times
exactly. Especially we want to know the type of the kernel before we write and
run it. For this, we introduce the definition of compute intensity. In this paper,
compute intensity defines the number of single-precision floating-point calculations performed per byte of off-chip memory traffic. We define the compute

intensity of algorithm and special hardware respectively, and define the algorithm is memory-bound or computation-bound by comparing these two features.

Compute intensity of algorithm equals the total amount of computation divides the total amount of data required to transfer from off-chip memory. Compute intensity of special hardware equals the throughput of arithmetic instruction divides the throughput of memory access instruction. For simplicity, this value can also equal the peak performance of specific hardware divides the peak bandwidth. We take NVIDIA C2050 GPU as an example, with the peak performance of 1.03TFlops and peak memory bandwidth of 144GB/s, We can calculate the compute intensity of NVIDIA C2050 GPU is 7.2. If the Compute Intensity of a kernel is smaller than 7.2, we can see that this kernel is a memory-bound kernel for NVIDIA C2050, otherwise, it's a computation-bound kernel. Note that, kernel is memory-bound or computation-bound depends on the specific hardware architecture. For example, if the compute intensity of GPU A is 15 and a kernel with compute intensity of 12, we can see that this kernel is a computation-bound kernel for NVIDIA C2050 GPU, however, it is a memory-bound kernel for GPU A.

3   Performance Tuning Chain

When optimizing a GPU kernel, developers usually begin with a mental model of the target GPU hardware platform and write a naïve version. This version will be tested and iteratively optimized until the expected performance is achieved. This progress is difficult and consuming, especially when developers have limited knowledge of the GPU architecture. Performance tuning chain addresses this problem through providing valuable insights on primary factors that affect the performance. And then identifies performance bottlenecks and decides which optimization methods should be adopted and the applied order of these selected optimization methods.

Tuning chain is consisted of some important optimization methods. And these optimization methods are organized in order according to their performance impacts. First-order methods are addressed first, then the second-order, and so on. In this paper, performance tuning chain is divided into two types: threshold chain and tradeoff chain.

3.1   Threshold Chain

The off-chip memory bandwidth is often the constraining resource in kernel performance. Improving the utilization of the off-chip memory bandwidth is very helpful for achieving expected performance, especially for the memory-bound kernels. There are several optimization methods to improve it. These optimization methods constitute an tuning chain called threshold chain which means that performance aspects must be satisfied or mitigated in order to achieve good performance.

$$U_{BW} = \frac{\#MC\_used}{\#MC\_number} \times \frac{\#data\_MT\_validate}{\#data\_MT\_count} \tag{1}$$

Equation 1 shows how to calculate the utilization of the off-chip memory bandwidth. The first factor is the utilization of the memory channels. #MC_number represents the total number of memory channels. #MC_used represents the number of used memory channels by concurrent global memory accesses caused by all active wavefronts or warps. The second factor in equation 1 is the validate data ratio of one memory transaction. And #data_MT_count represents the count of the total data that one memory access request transfers. #data_MT_validate represents the count of the validate data. According to equation 1, improving the utilization of off-chip memory bandwidth, we must improve the utilization of the memory channels and the validate ratio of the data that one memory access request transfers. According to this, we define the optimization space:

Eliminate Channel Conflict (ECC), just as local memory (share memory in CUDA) is divided into multiple banks, global memory is divided into multiple partitions of 256-byte width on both AMD and NVIDIA GPUs. Global memory channel conflict is similar to local memory bank conflict, but experienced at a macro-level where concurrent global memory accesses by all active warps occur at a subset of channels, causing requests to queue up at some channels while other channels go unused. Channel conflict usually happens when a kernel use large memory stride access patterns. To eliminate channel conflict ensure that adjacent work-items read or write adjacent memory address is the best method.

Reduce Memory Transactions (RMT), a global memory access request is coalesced into as few memory transactions as possible, reduce memory transactions is an important optimization method for memory-bound kernels. Vector, continuous and alignment memory access are common optimization methods for GPUs.

Using FastPath (UFP), this method is only valid for AMD GPU specially. AMD Radeon HD 5000 series GPU have two, independent memory paths: FastPath and CompletePath. There is large difference in performance between them. Ensure that the data size that a thread access larger than 32bit or none atomics operations used when writing memory to make this kernel use FastPath rather than CompletePath. In general, this can improve the utilization of the peak bandwidth significantly.

According to the optimization space, we conclude that the most optimization methods for improving the utilization of off-chip memory bandwidth are continuous (adjacent work-items access adjacent memory address), vector and alignment memory access. Section 4.1.1 shows the impact of these three optimization methods on the utilization of memory bandwidth. We can conclude from experiment results that, for both NVIDIA GPU and AMD GPU, the most important optimization method is continuous access. However, the second important optimization methods are different. For NVIDIA GPUs, this method is alignment. However, for AMD GPUs, this method is vector memory access. Finally, these three optimization methods constitute the threshold tuning chain.

3.2   Tradeoff Chain

Make full use of the GPU compute resource is also very important for improving the performance of GPU kernels, especially for the computation-bound kernels.

There are also several optimization methods to improve it. These optimization methods constitute an performance tuning chain. However, because of the discontinuous of optimization space due to the resource restriction, it is not clear that one should maximize or minimize a particular performance aspect for an application on a given architecture. So this tuning optimization chain is called Tradeoff chain which only provides insights for the performance improvement but not accurately. This is very different from the threshold chain.

Equation 2 shows how to evaluate the computation performance of GPU kernels:

$$P_{comp} = \frac{\#total\_wavefronts}{\#active\_CUs} \times P_{wavefront} \times ava\_inst\_lat + T_{sync} \tag{2}$$

$$P_{wavefront} = \frac{\#threads\_per\_wavefront}{\#SIMD_{width} \times TLP} \times \frac{\#inst\_per\_thread}{\#pu\_per\_pe \times ILP} \tag{3}$$

The first factor of the equation 2 is the number of wavefront (warp) per compute unit. The first factor of equation 3 represents the performance assessment method of a hardware thread (wavefront or warp). #SIMDwidth represents the number of process elements (Stream cores for AMD GPU and CUDA cores for NVIIDA GPU) perf compute unit. TLP represents thread-level parallelism in one wavefront (warp). The second factor of equation3 represents the performance assessment method of a thread (work-item). #pu_per_pe represents the number of process unit per process element. ILP represents the instruction-level parallelism in one thread. ava_inst_lat represents the average latency of instruction. Tsync represents the latency of synchronous operations. According to equation 2, we also define optimization space for making full use of computation resources.

Developing Thread-level Parallelism (TLP), GPU is a throughput-orient device, and latency hiding depends on the number of wavefronts or warps per compute unit. Exploiting thread-level parallelism, providing enough threads for each compute unit, is the basic optimization method for GPUs.

Developing Instruction-level Parallelism (ILP), ensure the availability of independent instructions within a thread. This is usually achieved by loop unrolling and reordering the code to place the memory access or compute operations in adjacent code lines. This optimization is especially important for AMD GPU because of its vector architecture. Furthermore, make full use of instruction-level parallelism can achieve higher performance with lower occupancy, so that each thread can use more registers, which has the lowest access latency.

Reducing Dynamic Instruction Count per Thread (RDIS), the purpose of this optimize method is to increase the efficiency of the instruction stream. There are four main optimize methods for this: minimizing divergent threads within a wavefront or warp by using predication rather than control-flow; eliminating common subexpression by removing repeated calculations; loop-invariant code motion by moving the expression within a loop which result would not change during the loop's execution to a point outside the loop; loop unrolling. However, those optimizations must be balanced against increased resource usage, such as register files, which will limits the number of threads that can be executed simultaneously, and may be low performance significantly.

Instruction Selection Optimizations (INS), both NVIDIA GPUs and AMD GPUs have many different instructions with different throughput because of the differences in the number of functional units and the intrinsic characteristics of instruction self. For example, 24-bit integer MULs and MADs have five times throughput than 32-bit integer multiplies on AMD GPU. So, selecting the instructions with lower latency and higher throughput as much as possible is a very desirable method for instruction-bound kernels.

According to the optimization space, for making full use of GPU compute resource, there is no difference between NVIDIA GPU and AMD GPU in optimization method selected. That is developing TLP and ILP is the first important optimization method. And then are the RDIS and INS. However, developing ILP is more important for AMD GPUs than NVIDIA GPUs, because of the vector architecture of AMD GPUs. Section 4.1.2 discusses this result through a micro-benchmark. Finally, these optimization methods constitute the tradeoff tuning chain.

3.3   Data Locality

Another important method to improve the performance of a GPU kernel is to increase its compute intensity. This method can reduce the dependence of the off-chip memory bandwidth and improve the data reuse rate, so as to improve the performance. This can achieve by using on-chip memory, such as cache for read-only data, or local memory (share memory for NVIDIA GPU), to increase data reuse and reduce the times of access off-chip memory. Not that, when using local memory, we should avoid bank conflict which will decrease performance dramatically. We can alleviate or eliminate bank conflict easily through padding or other techniques. Like the performance of memory access and computing in-core to constrain performance through the creation of performance tuning chain, compute intensity is also constrain performance like a wall, we called compute intensity wall. We cannot achieve higher performance without improving the algorithm's compute intensity, especially for the memory-bound kernels. So when you use tuning chains to guide your optimization and the performance does not achieve your expectations, the first optimize method you can think is increasing the compute intensity through data locality.

3.4   Insightful Performance Tuning Chains

As discussed above, we can see that there are three main strategies to improve GPU kernel performance: improving the utilization of off-chip memory bandwidth, making full use of computation resources, and data locality. We also define three optimization metrics: threshold chain, tradeoff chain and compute intensity wall. This section, we use Roofline model[11] to organize these three metrics, so as to make them insightful. Figure 1 shows the performance tuning chain on NVIDIA C2050 GPU and AMD HD5850 GPU using Roofline model.

Using tuning chain to guide your optimization, there are four rules should always in your mind. Firstly, the compute intensity of a kernel determines the optimization region, and thus which optimization method needs to try. As shown in figure 1, the vertical red dash line represents a kernel with the related compute

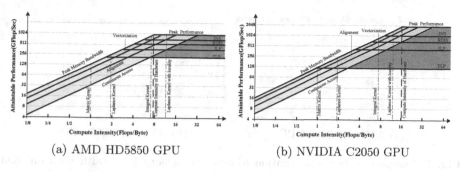

(a) AMD HD5850 GPU   (b) NVIDIA C2050 GPU

Fig. 1. Insightful Performance Tuning Chains using Roofline Model

intensity. If the dash line falls in the green area, suggesting the optimization work should only focus on the memory bandwidth optimizations. If the dash line falls in the blue area, suggesting the optimization work should only focus on the computation optimizations. If the dash line falls in the yellow area, should try both types of optimizations. Secondly, the node of tuning chain suggests the corresponding method that programmer should perform. Thirdly, the order of the nodes of tuniing chain suggests the optimization order. This is because we rank them from bottom to top according to their performance impacts on specific GPU architecture. For most kernels, only using the first two or three methods can achieve a relative high performance. Finally, the ridge point marks the minimum compute intensity required to achieve peak performance.

4 Evaluation

We divide the performance evaluation into two parts. The first part, we evaluate the performance impact of some important optimization methods on specific GPU architecture through three micro-benchmarks. The second part we demonstrate the usage of tuning chains through three typical applications. We run our programs on both NVIDIA C2050 GPU and AMD HD5850 GPU. Table 1 shows the configurations of the GPUs we employed in our experiments in detail.

Table 1. Configuration of the GPUs in our experiments

GPU	Clock Rate	PE	CU	Peak performance	Memory	Peak BW	Regisgers/CU	LDS/CU
AMD HD5850	0.725GHZ	288	18	2090GFlops	1.0GB	128GB/s	16K	32K
NVIDIA C2050	1.15GHZ	448	14	1030GFlops	3.0GB	144GB/s	16K	48K

4.1 Micro-benchmarks

Optimization of Global Memory Access. As we discussed in section 3.1, the most optimization methods to improve the utilization of off-chip memory bandwidth are vector, continuous and alignment memory access. This section we will discuss the different performance impacts of these three methods on different GPU platforms. For this, we design a copy micro-benchmark, performing read data from input array and then write them to the output array.

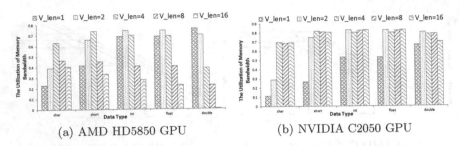

(a) AMD HD5850 GPU   (b) NVIDIA C2050 GPU

Fig. 2. Comparison of the utilization of off-chip memory bandwidth with different vector lengths

Figure 2 shows the differences in the utilization of off-chip memory bandwidth using different vector length among various data types between NVIDIA C2050 GPU and AMD HD5850 GPU. For NVIDIA C2050 GPU, we can see that there is very significant impact on performance when the length of vector varies. The vector types which achieve peak performance are char4, short4, int2, float2 and double. There are three reasons for this. Firstly, for NVIDIA GPU, if the data is alignment naturally, any access to global memory will be complied into a single global memory instruction if and only if the size of the data type is 1, 2, 4, 8 or 16 bytes. So the vector data types which size larger than 16 such as doule8 has very low performance. Secondly, for Fermi architecture, the access to global memory is cached and cache line is 128 bytes and maps to a 128-byte aligned segment in device memory. So the unit of one memory transaction is 128 bytes. If the size of the words accessed by a warp is little than 128 bytes, there are other words that don't need will be transfered, leading to the decreasing of the utilization of off-chip memory bandwidth. Thirdly, if the size of the words accessed by each thread is more than 4 bytes, a memory request by a warp is first split into separate 128-byte memory requests that are issued independently. So there is no much performance difference between float, float2, and float4.

For AMD HD5850 GPU, as figure 2B shows, there is also significant performance difference when using different vector length, especially char, char2 and short. The reason is that, there are two independent memory paths between the compute units and off-chip memory, called FastPath and CompletePath. And the difference in performance is significant when write memory. When a kernel has atomics operations and sub 32 bit data transfers, the kernel will use the CompletePath which will lead to very low performance. So when the data type that a thread accessed is char, char2 or short, will lead to decrease the utilization of off-chip memory bandwidth. We also can see that when the data type is int or float, there is also poor performance. This is because the internal memory path supports 128-bit transfers, which allows for greater bandwidth when transferring data in vectorization format.

We also show the utilization of off-chip memory bandwidth with different strides and offsets in Figure 3. We can see that, for both NVIDIA Tesla C2050 GPU and AMD HD5850 GPU, with the memory stride increasing, the performance degrading greatly. There are two reasons for this. Firstly, large memory

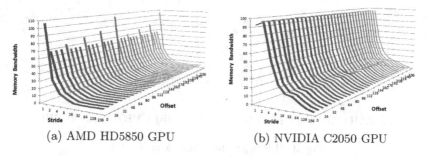

(a) AMD HD5850 GPU   (b) NVIDIA C2050 GPU

Fig. 3. Comparison of the utilization of off-chip memory bandwidth with various strides and offsets

stride can lead to channel conflict and bank conflict, which can decrease performance significantly. Secondly, a global memory access request from one wavefront or warp is coalesced into a few memory transactions, larger memory stride will lead to more memory transactions which will lead to performance decreasing. We also can see that, for NVIDIA Tesla C2050 GPU, offset can result in low performance when the offset is not a multiple of 128. This is because, on Fermi architecture, the access to global memory is cached and a cache line is 128 bytes, so the memory access requires 128bit alignment. However, for AMD HD5850 GPU, the performance gain by adjusting alignment is small, so generally this is not an important consideration for AMD GPUs.

Above all, we can see that, for both NVIDIA GPU and AMD GPU, the most important optimization method is to ensure that adjacent threads accesses adjacent address. However, the second important optimization methods for them are different. For NVIDIA GPU, this method is alignment, however, for AMD GPU, this is vector memory access.

ILP. In general, we develop TLP(Thread-Level Parallelism) to improve the utilization of the computation resources. Traditional GPU programming wisdom also suggests us always providing a large number of threads to increase occupancy which is the only way to improve latency hiding. However, we found that develop ILP (Instruction-level Parallelism) can also improve latency hiding. For this, we develop an ILP micro-benchmark. We only run one work-group (only use one compute unit), vary block size and ILP to test the impact of ILP on performance. Figure 4 shows the experiment results.

Figure 4A show the performance results of ILP micro-benchmark on NVIIDA C2050 GPU. We vary the ILP from 1 to 4. We found that, with the ILP increasing, the number of threads that need to achieve peak performance is decreasing. When ILP equals 1, the needed warps are 18, however, when ILP equals 4, the needed warps are only 5. This means that we can achieve peak performance by using fewer threads. That is, each thread can use more registers and local memory which have higher memory bandwidth than off-chip memory bandwidth. We also can see that increasing ILP and TLP can lead to performance improvement

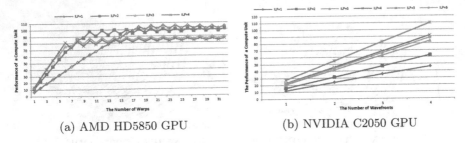

(a) AMD HD5850 GPU   (b) NVIDIA C2050 GPU

Fig. 4. ILP micro-benchmark on GPUs

up to some point. However, after that point, there is no performance improvement by merely increasing ILP and TLP.

Figure 4B shows the performance results of ILP micro-benchmark on AMD HD 5850 GPU. Different from NVIDIA C2050 GPU, we can only issue 4 wavefronts (256 threads) at most because one work-group can contain 4 wavefronts at most. Fortunately, this situation do not affect our observation of the performance impact of ILP. We can see that, when the number of wavefronts fixed, with the ILP increasing, the performance improving significantly. This is because AMD GPU adopts vector architecture. That is, each stream core contains five process elements, and can execute five independent instructions at one time. So when ILP equals five, ILP kernel achieves peak performance. When ILP is larger than five, six as an example, the performance will decrease. Above all, for AMD GPU, developing ILP is very important for improving performance.

So, we can see that, increasing occupancy is not the only way to improve latency hiding. Developing ILP can also improve performance with fewer threads. We also can see that developing ILP is more import for AMD GPU than NVIDIA GPU, because of the vector architecture of AMD GPU.

4.2 Case Studies

In this section, we will optimize three typical applications to demonstrate the usage of performance tuning chain. The red vertical line in figure 1 shows optimization regions of these three kernels in insightful performance tuning chain.

Matrix Transpose. In this section, we optimize the transpose algorithm of a matrix of char. The transpose operation of each element performs two address calculations, and each address calculation performs 4 floating-point operations, so the compute intensity of matrix transpose is 2*4/8=1 when we use char4 instead of char. According to tuning chain, our optimization work should only focus on the off-chip memory bandwidth optimizations.

Note that, in order to test the performance impact of alignment, we offset four bytes when we upload the matrix to GPU memory. According to tuning chain, our optimization work should perform in four steps. Firstly, we use char4 instead of char to make sure this kernel use FastPath for AMD GPU. Secondly, we use local memory to re-map the threads to tile elements to avoid uncoalesced memory

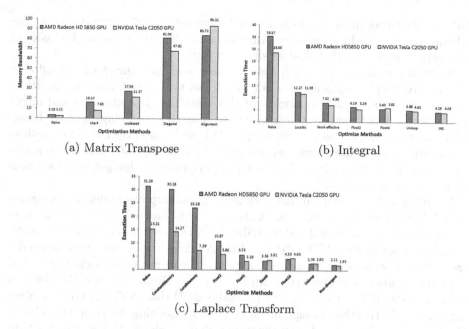

(a) Matrix Transpose   (b) Integral

(c) Laplace Transform

Fig. 5. Performance changes when satisfies optimizations one by one

writes. Thirdly, we use Diagonal block reordering technique [18] to eliminate off-chip memory channel conflict. Finally, we set offset equals 0. Figure 5a shows the performance changes when we optimize this kernel step by step.

From Figure 5a, we can see that the bottleneck of transpose kernel is off-chip memory channel conflict. Adopting diagonal technique can improve performance greatly for both AMD HD 5850 GPU and NVIDIA C2050 GPU. Vector memory access can improve performance better for AMD HD 5850 GPU than NVIDIA C2050 GPU. The same as our tuning chain suggests, alignment has an important influence on performance for NVIDIA GPU. However, this influence is smaller for AMD GPU. Under the tuning chain guidance, the performance improved by 26.1 and 42.4 times on AMD GPU and NVIDIA GPU respectively.

Laplace Transform and Integral Algorithm. Laplace transform algorithm is a widely used integral transform. This transformation is essentially bijection for the majority of practical uses. The matrix Laplace transform calculates the Laplace value of the source matrix by adding up the second x and y derivatives calculated using Laplacian.

The calculation of each element needs another 9 operators from source matrix around it and needs to perform 8 additions and 9 multiplications according Laplacian. In additional, it requires 9 iterations and 10 address calculations and each calculation performs four floating-point add and multiply operations. So the compute intensity of Laplace transform is 67/36=1.8. However, with this compute intensity, we can't obtain satisfied performance, and the nature of this algorithm also requires using local memory for data reusing. If the work-group is

16*16, calculating these 256 elements need to transfer17*17 = 289 elements from off-chip memory to local memory. After data locality, the compute intensity of this kernel reaches to 12.6. Just as shown in figure 1.

As tuning chain suggests, our optimization work not only focus on off-chip memory bandwidth optimization but also focus on computation optimization. Because the memory access pattern of this algorithm is continuous and alignment. So the most optimization method for improving off-chip memory bandwidth is vector memory access. Developing ILP is the most optimization method for improving the computation performance. Additional, RDIS and INS can also improve performance. Figure5b shows the performance changes when satisfies optimization methods on by one.

From figure 5b, we can see that data locality can improve performance significantly. Developing ILP, using float4 instead of float, is an important optimization method for both AMD GPU and NVIDIA GPU. However, when the vector length exceeds a value, 8 for AMD GPU and 4 for NVIDIA GPU, the performance decreased. This is because vectorization makes thread use more register files and limit the number of threads that can be executed simultaneously. We also can see that, using ILP is more efficient for AMD GPU than NVIDIA GPU. Reducing dynamic instruction through unlooping and minimizing divergent threads can also improve performance. Under the tuning chain guidance, the performance improved by 14.1 and 7.8 times on AMDGPU and NVIDIA GPU respectively.

Integral algorithm is an image algorithm, and usually used in the field of rapid feature evaluation, such as faceDection. The essence of this algorithm is implementing twice scan algorithm in turn on matrix rows and columns respectively. In finally implementation, we use the work-efficient scan algorithm that is explicated in[19], meanwhile, treating the rows and the columns of the target matrix as independent input array for the scan algorithm. Firstly, scan the rows of the matrix, and write the results to the output matrix in the order of column. Then use the same scanning kernel to compute the integral matrix. According to our algorithm, the compute intensity of this kernel is 7.2 after using locality, as we have to execute so many memory address calculation and iterations.

Just as the Laplace transform algorithm we discussed above, the optimization of integral kernel is also focus on both the off-chip memory bandwidth optimization and computation optimization. Figure 5c shows the performance changes when satisfies optimization methods on by one. Because the similarity in the optimization works between integral algorithm and Laplace transform, we don't describe the optimization progress in details in this paper.

5   Related Work

Enormous works have been investing on the performance analysis and optimization of GPU programs. Some performance analysis model has been proposed by prior works. Ryoo et al. [5] used Pareto-optimal curves to narrow the optimization space of GPU programs and introduce efficiency and utilization as single number metrics. N. K. Govindaraju [10] presented a memory model to analyze and improve the performance of nested loops on GPUs. S. Hong [6] presents a simple performance analytical model to capture a rough estimate of the cost of memory operations by considering the number of running threads and memory bandwidth. Baghsorkhi [2] introduced an abstract interpretation of a GPU kernel to identify performance bottlenecks and used work flow graph to predict execution time. Kothapalli [4] presented a performance prediction model to analyze pseudo code for a GPU kernel to obtain a performance estimate. However, because of the complexity of the underlying hardware architecture, it is difficult to predict performance accurately.

Certainly, these performance analysis models are powerful tools for optimizing. However, for a given kernel, they do not provide any insight into how to identify performance bottleneck and decides which optimization methods should be used. Compared to them, our work can guide programmers to write high performance program directly, rather than write a naive version first and then tune it again and again. There are also similar works to us: Yao Zhang[1] provided a quantitative way to analyzes GPU program performance, however, they didn't provide an easy-to-understand model; Samuel Williams[12] provided an insightful visual performance model, however, their works only for multi-core CPUs.

6 Conclusion

In this paper, we have proposed an insightful performance tuning chain for both NVIDIA and AMD GPUs to help non-expert programmers with limited knowledge of GPU architectures implement high performance GPU kernels directly. With the help of performance tuning chain, programmers can easily identify performance bottleneck and decides which optimization method should be used. Furthermore, from this tuning chain, we can see the differences in optimization strategies between NVIDIA and AMD GPUs because of their hardware architecture differences. Furthermore, we believe that our performance tuning chain has captured all the primary performance factors of GPU. Although this tuning chain is not accurate, we also believe that as long as the tuning chain can deliver on insight, it needs not to be perfect. Finally, we also demonstrate the usage of this tuning chain through three typical kernels with different compute intensity. Experiment results show that, with the help of this tuning chain, we can achieve high performance easily.

Acknowledgements. We would like to thank reviewers for their helpful comments to our work. This work is supported by the National High-tech R&D Program of China (No. 2012AA 010902, No. 2012AA010903), the National Natural Science Foundation of China (No. 61133005, No.61100066) and ISCAS-AMD Fusion Software Center. Dr. Guoping Long is supported by National Natural Science Foundation of China (Grant No. 61100072).

References

1. Zhang, Y., Owens, J.D.: A quantitative performance analysis model for GPU architectures. In: High Performance Computer Architecture, pp. 382–393 (February 2011)

2. Baghsorkhi, S., Delahaye, M., Patel, S.J., Gropp, W.D., Hwu, W.-M.W.: An Adaptive Performance Modeling Tool for GPU Architectures. In: Principles and Practice of Parallel Programming, pp. 105–114 (January 2010)
3. Daga, M., Scogland, T.R.W., Feng, W.-C.: Architecture-Aware Optimization on a 1600-core Graphics Processor. Technical Report TR-11-08. Computer Science, Virginia Tech.
4. Kothapalli, K., Mukherjee, R., Rehman, M.S., Patidar, S., Narayanan, P.J., Srinathan, K.: A performance prediction model for the CUDA GPGPU platform. In: International Conference on High Performance Computing, pp. 463–472 (2009)
5. Ryoo, S., Rodrigues, C.I., Stone, S.S., Baghsorkhi, S.S., Ueng, S., Stratton, J.A.: Program Optimization Space Pruning for a Multithreaded GPU. In: International Symposium on Code Generation and Optimization, pp. 195–204 (April 2008)
6. Hong, S., Kim, H.: An analytical model for a gpu architecture with memory-level and thread-level parallelism awareness. In: International Conference on Computer Architecture, pp. 152–163 (2009)
7. Jang, B., Do, S., Pien, H.: Architecture-Aware Optimization Targeting Multithreaded Stream Computing. In: Second Workshop on General-Purpose on Graphics Processing Units (2009)
8. Meng, J., Morozov, V.A., Kumaran, K., Vishwanath, V., Uram, T.D.: GROPHECY: GPU Performance Projection from CPU Code Skeletons. In: Conference on High Performance Computing (2011)
9. Bauer, M., Cook, H., Khailany, B.: CudaDMA: optimizing GPU memory bandwidth via warp specialization. In: Conference on High Performance Computing, Supercomputing (2011)
10. Govindaraju, N.K., Larsen, S., Gray, J., Manocha, D.: A Memory Model for Scientific Algorithms on Graphics Processors. In: ACM/IEEE Conference on Supercomputing (November 2006)
11. Williams, S., Waterman, A., Patterson, D.: Roofline: An Insightful Visual Performance Model for Multicore Architectures. Communications of the ACM, 65–76 (2009)
12. Lazowska, E.D., Zahorjan, J., Graham, G.S., Sevcik, K.C.: Quantitative System Performance: Computer System Analysis using Queueing Network Models. Prentice-Hall. Inc., Upper Saddle River (1984)
13. Fatahalian, K., Sugerman, J., Hanrahan, P.: Understanding the Efficiency of GPU Algorithms for Matrix-matrix Multiplication. In: Conference on Graphics Hardware, pp. 133–137 (August 2004)
14. Taylor, R., Li, X.: A Micro-benchmark Suite for AMD GPUs. In: International Conference on Parallel Processing Workshops, pp. 387–396 (2010)
15. Liu, W., Muller-Wittig, W., Schmidt, B.: Performance Predictions for General-Purpose Computation on GPUs. In: International Conference on Parallel Processing, pp. 50–57 (September 2007)
16. Sim, J., Dasgupta, A., Kim, H.: A performance analysis framework for identifying potential benefits in GPGPU applications. In: Proceeding of the 17th ACM SIGPLAN Symposium on Principles and Practice of Parallel Programming, New York (2012)
17. The OpenCL Specification, http://www.khronos.org/opencl/
18. Optimizing Matrix Transpose in CUDA, http://www.cs.colostate.edu/~cs675/MatrixTranspose.pdf
19. Parallel Prefix Sum(scan) with CUDA, http://developer.download.nvidia.com/compute/cuda/1_1/Website/projects/scan/doc/scan.pdf

Multi-core Fixed Priority DVS Scheduling

Liu Yang, Man Lin, and Laurence T. Yang

Department of Mathematics, Statistics and Computer Science
St. Francis Xavier University

Abstract. In this paper, we study offline and online DVS algorithms
for Fixed Priority tasks scheduled on multi-core systems. The offline
multi-core algorithm (MC-SSS) slows down tasks with a static slowdown
speed based on multi-core fixed priority schedulability analysis. And the
on-line algorithm (MC-ccFPP) combines load balancing algorithm and
cycle conservative slack analysis to slow down tasks. Experimental results for random tasks set are shown and the analysis of the experimental results is provided. Performance analysis studies the energy saving
for the offline multi-core algorithm (MC-SSS) and the online multi-core
algorithm (MC-ccFPP) for a variety of task sets with different CPU utilization, different number of tasks and different number of cores.

1 Introduction

Energy consumption is a critical design factor of embedded systems. Today's
embedded systems are becoming more and more complex and the computation
requirement puts pressure on the energy consumption of single core CPU. Multi-
core CPUs are therefore used more and more in embedded systems to achieve
energy efficiency.

Dynamic Voltage Scaling (DVS) is a software controlled technique to reduce
energy consumption. DVS is based on the fact that the consumption of energy
in CMOS is approximately quadratically dependent on the processor's supplying
voltage [14]. A DVS scheduling algorithm schedules the tasks in a system while
at the same time determines when and how much slowdown is assigned to the
tasks.

Based on scheduling policy, there are essentially two categories of multi-core
real-time scheduling methods: *fixed priority* (FP) multicore scheduling and *earliest deadline first* (EDF) multi-core scheduling. Based on whether a task is
able to migrate among the cores, the multi-core scheduling methods are classified into global multi-core scheduling and partitioned multi-core scheduling
methods. K. Lakshmanan et. al. have studied the partitioned fixed-priority preemptive scheduling for multicore platform [12]. Andersson and Josson also give
a discussion about partitioned and global methods for fixed priority preemptive
scheduling [1].

Multi-core power aware scheduling has started to gain attention recent years.
Fisher et. al. have proposed a thermal-aware global real-time scheduling on multicore system [5]. Guan et. al. have proposed a cache-aware scheduling and analysis for multicore system in 2009 [6]. A load balancing DVS algorithm on a soft

Y. Xiang et al. (Eds.): ICA3PP 2012, Part I, LNCS 7439, pp. 517–530, 2012.

real-time system has been developed [4] . Huang [7] developed a EDF DVS multi-core scheduling algorithm which is a dynamic priority scheduling. Recently, fixed priority DVS for multi-core systems has gained some attension. Qu has studied a multi-voltage algorithm for non-periodic tasks on multi-core system [16] with the focus on non-periodic tasks. In this paper, we will mainly focus on fixed priority DVS scheduling on multi-core systems for periodic tasks.

The key of DVS scheduling algorithm is to find the time slices that are idle, known as *slack time*. Slack time can be used to "slowdown" the processor in order to save energy. Slack time can be either found statically (off-line) or on-line. Therefore, we can determine the "slowdown" either on-line or off-line.

A common Off-line DVS technique is to slow down all the tasks to the same speed. The goal of the offline DVS method is to determine the minimum *Static Slowdown Speed* (SSS), such that the maximum energy saving can be achieved while guaranteeing the schedulability. Jejurikar and Gupta [8] used this technique to find SSS under non-preemptive task system based on the *Earliest Deadline First* (EDF) scheduling policy. We will explore this method in the context of multi-core system under fixed-priority scheduling policy.

Many online DVS algorithms have been proposed for single processor. Some examples are: [15] [2] [11] [10] and [18]. Each algorithm has its own assumptions. For example, *ccRM* method in [15] is a simple cycle conservative algorithm. *lp-WDA* algorithm developed by Kim et al. works for *Fixed Priority Preemptive* (FPP) scheduling policy. Other algorithms like [2] [10] use *Earliest Deadline First* policy which is not our focus. Fixed priority with preemption threshold scheduling policy have been proposed to save energy [18] and to reduce the number of preemptions [17]. Our online DVS for multi-core fixed-priority algorithms will combine cycle conservative slack analysis and load balancing algorithm.

The paper is organized as follows. First, the real-time models and some basic concepts will be described in Section 2. In Section 3, we will investigate scheduling feasibility analysis for fixed priority scheduling policy for multi-core systems, and then use the analysis method to find static slowdown speed. In Section 4, on-line DVS methods will be described. In the final Section, experiment results and evaluation analysis will be shown.

2   Models and Preliminaries

2.1   Real-Time Model

A real-time system usually has a set of periodic tasks. We name the tasks as τ_1, $\tau_2, \ldots \tau_N$. The *number of tasks* in a task set is denoted as N. Each task has a number of attributes. Each task has a *Period*, denoted as P_i. Each task has to finish before its *deadline* D_i. Each task has a *Computation Time* C_i. We have to consider this C_i as *Worst Case Execution Time* (WCET). Each task has a *priority* denoted as π_i. It can take value from 1 to N, all tasks have different priorities. A bigger π_i indicate a higher priority.

For each task, deadline is assumed to be equal to its corresponding period. We assume there is no context switch cost in both time and energy consumption.

Table 1. A Task Set Example

Tasks τ_i	Comp. Time C_i	Deadline/ Peroid D_i/P_i	Priority π_i
τ_1	1	8	3
τ_2	3	12	2
τ_3	5	22	1

The kernel scheduler kernel is based on two priority queues and one stack. One queue is called *ready queue*, it contains all the ready tasks. This priority queue sorts the task set according to tasks' priority. The tasks are released periodically. We assume that the kernel is aware of the period of each task and contains a priority queue called *IncomingQueue* to store the incoming tasks. The incoming-task queue sorts the tasks according to tasks' release time. Whenever a task finishes execution, its next instance will be put into the incoming-task queue. At each time unit, all the tasks in the incoming-task queue with realease time equal to the current time unit will be moved from the incoming-task queue to the ready queue. The *preemption stack* hosts preempted tasks. Once a running task τ_a is preempted by a higher priority task τ_b, τ_a will be push onto the stack. After τ_b finishes execution, τ_a can be resumed. Note that τ_a may have to yield to another higher priority task from ready queue. If τ_a has a higher priority than the head task in the ready queue, τ_a will be poped from the preemption stack and resume its execution.

2.2 Power Model

The total power consumption [14] of a CMOS-based processor consists of three parts. The first part is the dynamic power consumption $P_{dynamic}$. The second part is the static power consumption $P_{leakage}$. The last part is the inherent power cost in keeping the processor on, denoted as $P_{inherent}$.

$$P_{total} = P_{dynamic} + P_{leakage} + P_{inherent}.$$

Dynamic power consumption $P_{dynamic}$ is power consumed during circuit charging and discharging. The dynamic power consumption $P_{dynamic}$ can be written as:

$$P_{dynamic} = C_e \times V_{dd}^2 \times f,$$

where C_e is the switching capacity, V_{dd} is the supply voltage and f is the clock frequency.

$$f = \frac{(V_{dd} - V_{th})^\epsilon}{L_d \times K_6},$$

$$V_{th} = V_{th1} - K_1 \times V_{dd} - K_2 \times V_{bs},$$

Where V_{th} is the threshold voltage, which is a function of the body bias voltage V_{bs}. V_{th1}, ϵ, K_1, K_2 and K_6 are constants depending on the processor manufacture technology.

Static power consumption $P_{leakage}$ is produced by the leakage current which flows even when no task is being executed. For technology 65nm to 22nm, static power is dominant in the power consumption [9]. That is why in recent years, most researchers add static power to their power model. $P_{leakage}$ can be written as:

$$P_{leakage} = L_g \times (V_{dd} \times I_{subn} + |V_{bs}| \times I_{jun}).$$

The subthreshold leakage current I_{subn} can be writen as constant K_3, K_4, body bias voltage V_{bs}:

$$I_{subn} = K_3 \times e^{K_4 V_{dd}} \times e^{K_4 V_{bs}}.$$

The inherent power is the power to keep the processor on. Unlike the previous two kinds of power, the inherent power is not related to the supply voltage of the processor. The inherent power $P_{inherent}$ is fixed once the processor model is fixed. The constants for the power model can be found in [14].

3   Off-Line Multicore DVS Scheduling: MC-SSS

3.1   MC-SSS Algorithm

We now discuss multicore fixed priority DVS algorithm. We assume the voltage level of CPU can be continuously changed. The speed of a processor can be scaled down by a factor s $(0 < s < 1)$ and if there exist slacks.

The schedulablity analysis of multicore system is much more complex compared to single core's. Fortunately, Baker has already performed the multiprocessor fixed priority schedulability analysis [3]. We will employ this method to develop an off-line multicore DVS algorithm.

Corollary 14 (Utilization test). A set of sporadic tasks, all with deadline equal to period and utilization less than or equal to one, is guaranteed to be schedulable on m processors using preemptive rate monotonic scheduling if $\sum_{i=1}^{N} C_i/P_i \leq m/2(1 - u_{max}) + u_{min}$, where $u_{max} = max\{C_i/P_i | i = 1, \ldots, N\}$ and $u_{min} = min\{C_i/P_i | i = 1, \ldots, N\}$ [3].

The above utilization test is designed for a special case of fixed priority scheduling called *Rate Monotonic* (RM) [13] scheduling. RM assigns each task's priority based on the period (rate) of the tasks. In other words, RM assigns a higher priority to a task with smaller period. Using the utilization test, we can derive a function to determine whether the given task set is schedulable or not under m cores/processors. We name the function *RMmCoreSchedulable(TS, S)*, where TS is the a task set and S is the speed used to run the tasks in task set TS. In the *RMmCoreSchedulable(TS, S)* function, the calculation of the utilization depends on the utilization of the tasks, which in term depends on the slowdown speed of the system.

Our goal is to find the minimum slowdown speed (SSS). For a given task set TS, given two speeds S_1 and S_2, where $S_1 \leq S_2$, if $RMmCoreSchedulable(TS, S_1)$ holds, then $RMmCoreSchedulable(TS, S_2)$ holds. Thus, a binary search method can be used to find the minimum static slowdown speed (SSS) for multicore system. The binary search method (MC-SSS) is shown in Algorithm 2. Due to the fact that Algorithm 2 is a binary search algorithm, the complexity of a binary search algorithm is O(log n) where n is the number of scaling steps. We consider continuous voltage scheduling here. The precision of the floating point value will determine the number of scaling steps. Furthermore, the function $RMmCoreSchedulable()$ has a complexity of O(N), where N is the number of tasks per task set. The complexity of Algorithm 2 (MC-SSS) is thus $O(N \cdot logn)$.

Given a task set TS, the function is $RMmCoreSchedulable()$ is defined in algorithm 1. Note that $TS[i].C$ and $TS[i].P$ represent task i's computation time and period, respectively.

Algorithm 1. Function RMmCoreSchedulable(TS, S)

1: let m = getNumOfCores(),
2: let U represent Utilization
3: U = Sum $(TS[i].C/TS[i].P)$
4: return false if $U/S > m$
5: u_{max} = Max$(TS[i].C/TS[i].P/S)$
6: u_{min} = Min$(TS[i].C/TS[i].P/S)$
7: return true if $U/S <= m * (1 - u_{max}/S)/2 + u_{min}/S)$
8: **else** return false

Algorithm 2. Finding Multicore SSS algorithm (MC-SSS)

1: Let $S_{low} = S_{min}$ and $S_{up} = S_{max}$
2: **while** $S_{up} - S_{low} > 0$ **do**
3:     Let $S = (S_{low} + S_{up})/2$
4:     **if** RMmCoreSchedulable(TS, S) == True **then**
5:         $S_{up} = S$
6:     **else**
7:         $S_{low} = S$
8:     **end if**
9: **end while**
10: **return** S_{up}

Now, given a task set, with the algorithm MC-SSS, we can calculate the static slowdown speed for m cores. But we still need a scheduling algorithm to schedule the tasks to the cores. We adopt global scheduling algorithm instead of the partitioned one. Recall that the scheduler maintains two queues and one stack.

As Algorithm 3 shows, at the initial state, we assume that all the cores are empty and all the tasks have been loaded into *ReadyQueue*. Each core has a variable $load_i$ to keep track of the current workload. This variable $load_i$ is updated whenever a new task releases. Whenever a task τ_i is scheduled for execution, the first attempt of the scheduler is to put it on an idle core if an idle core exists. If there are more than one idle cores, the least loaded core will be selected to run the task. If all the cores are busy, task τ_i will preempt the running task that are running on the least loaded core.

Algorithm 3. Multicore Load Balancing Algorithm

1: **Initial:** All the cores are idle and all the tasks are in the *ReadyQueue*
2: Set the speed to SSS
3: **if** A task τ_i is scheduled for **EXECUTION then**
4:    **if** there is(are) idle core(cores) **then**
5:        Put τ_i to run on the least loaded idle core
6:    **else**
7:        **if** there exist running tasks with lower priority than τ_i **then**
8:            τ_i will preempt the task τ_j which runs on the least loaded core
9:        **end if**
10:    **end if**
11: **end if**
12: **if** A task τ_i is **COMPLETED then**
13:    Move τ_i to *IncomingQueue*
14: **end if**
15: **if** A task τ_i is **PREEMPTED then**
16:    Move τ_i to *PreemptionStack*
17: **end if**
18: **if** A task τ_i is **Re-ACTIVATED then**
19:    Move to τ_i to *ReadyQueue*
20: **end if**

3.2   Off-Line Multicore DVS (MC-SSS) Examples

Two examples will be studied in this section. One example illustrating the case when the multicore scheduling algorithm is applied without any power-saving method. The other example shows the multicore scheduling algorithm with MC-SSS method. Assuming a two-core processor is provided, Figure 1 shows the scheduling from time $t = 0$ to time $t = 25$ for the task set which is shown in Table 1.

The fixed priority preemptive scheduling policy is used in this example. As Figure 1 shows, the detailed schedules for two cores are shown separately. The upper part of the scheduling is for core 0, and the lower part of scheduling is for core 1. At time $t = 0$, all three tasks in the task set are ready and placed in the *ReadyQueue*. Task τ_1 and τ_2 have higher priorities, so they are selected to run. After task τ_1 finishes at $t = 1$, τ_1 will be placed into *IncomingQueue*. Then task τ_3 is selected for execution. At time $t = 8$, τ_1 will be reactivated again, since the period of τ_1 is 8. Task τ_1 will be popped from *IncomingQueue*, and will be pushed it into *ReadyQueue* and scheduled for execution. At time $t = 8$, core 0's workload is heavier than core 1's, we will schedule τ_1 to run on the least loaded core, which is core 1.

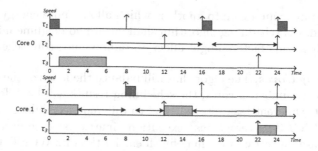

Fig. 1. Two-Core Fixed Priority Preemptive without Power Saving Method (a)

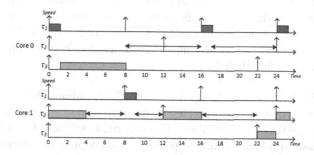

Fig. 2. Two-Core Fixed Priority Preemptive with MC-SSS Method (a)

Figure 2 shows the scheduling of a two core processor with MC-SSS method for fixed priority preemptive scheduling. In this case, 39.27% of the energy is saved. In order to find the static slowdown speed, we will use Algorithm 2. Based on Baker's Corollary schedulability test is satisfied with full speed, that is S=1. The detailed computation is as follows. Utilization (U) is the sum of Computation Time (C_i) over the Period (P_i). That is $U = C_1/P_1 + C_2/P_2 + C_3/P_3 \approx 0.602$. The $u_{max} = C_2/P_2 = 0.25$ and $u_{min} = C_1/P_1 = 0.125$. So $m/2(1 - u_{max}) + u_{min} = 2/2(1 - 0.25) + 0.125 = 0.875$, which is larger than its utilization. Thus the task set is schedulable. Using Algorithm 2, we can derive the static slowdown speed for a two core processor as 0.73. In Figure 2, every task's speed is slowdown to 73%. The energy consumption is only 58.8% compare to the energy consumption in Figure 1.

4   Online Multicore DVS Scheduling: MC-ccFPP

4.1   MC-ccFPP algorithm

For off-line scheduling, the speed is pre-calculated before task execution. Once the slowdown speed is calculated with off-line method, all the cores will run at the same speed. An online DVS method can change the voltage while the task set is executing, consequently further energy can be saved online. In this study, the global task migration model is adopted. In global task migration model, tasks can migrate from a core to another, which allows more energy saving. On the other hand, the scheduling algorithm shall ensure no deadline misses for the system. The following factors might affect an online multi-core scheduling.

1. **Number of Cores**. The algorithm will balance the loads of the cores. With the different number of cores, the scheduling results will be different.
2. **Task Set**. Different task sets will lead to different scheduling results.
3. **ACET/WCET**. Average case execution time/worst case execution time. In most cases, a certain task may finish earlier than its WCET, thus leaving some slack time for later use. The ACET (Average Case Execution Time) is the time we assume that will actually cost for the task. Previously, we assume ACET = WCET. In most cases ACET is smaller than WCET. This type of slack produced online is *dynamic slack time*. An instance's ACET is not known until it finishes execution. The larger ACET/WCET ratio is, the more dynamic slack is produced, the more slowdown can be achieved by dynamic DVS scheduling.

Since it is difficult to predict future task arrival, an online DVS algorithm must get as much information as possible in order to slowdown the processor and not to violate the timing constraints. The algorithm will use the information to determine **when** and **how much** to perform a slowdown on a certain task. The time point to make decision on the slowdown is called *scheduling point*. This is usually at the beginning of a newly released task.

How much slowdown speed for one instance at each scheduling point depends on how much slack time found using the online DVS algorithm. By looking at left figure in Fig. 3, we know that for core 0, there is no task running from time t=6 to t=16 and from time t=17 to t = 24. For core 1, the following time slots are empty $[3-8]$, $[9-12]$ and $[15-22]$. The goal of an online DVS algorithm is to find as much slack time as possible before a certain task executes. The best case is to use up all empty slots.

On the other hand, slack time has to be used properly. Overuse slack time might lead to deadline misses. One example is that in left figure in Fig. 3 for core 0. As the analysis shows, there are two empty time slots in the given time range. The total empty time that can be used to slowdown is 17 time units. At time t=0, task τ_1 is scheduled to run, but we cannot use all 17 time units to slowdown task τ_1. If we do so, task τ_1 will miss its deadline at time $t = 8$.

From this example, we know that an online algorithm needs to determine how much and when to slowdown tasks without making tasks missing their deadlines. Multicore Cycle-conserving FPP Scheduling (MC-ccFPP) is our proposed online DVS algorithm for multicore systems. Similar to single core cycle conservative DVS [15], MC-ccFPP slows down every task instance in its cycle on a core by the same amount.

As Algorithm 4 shows, the MC-ccFPP algorithm is the same as the ccFPP algorithm [17] except the part when a task T_i is at its scheduling point. Instead of just setting one frequency for a single core algorithm, we need to set a $frequency_m$ at a scheduling point for a certain core m. The basic idea of the algorithm is follows. A variable named C_left_i is defined to store the remaining workload need to be executed for a task τ_i. This variable is updated when the condition changes. These changes includes the state change from running to ready, from ready to blocking, from running to blocking and blocking to active. In all the cases of Algorithm 4 will take one step to finish except when task is schedule for execution.

Algorithm 4. Multicore Cycle-conserving FPP Scheduling (MC-ccFPP)

1: upon task_active(T_i) {When task T_i is put into **ReadyQueue**}
2:    set $C\_left_i = C_i$;
3: upon task_completion(T_i) {When task T_i is put into **IncomingQueue**}
4:    set $C\_left_i = 0$;
5: task_preemption(T_i) {When task T_i is put into **PreemptionStack**}
6:    set $C\_left_i \mathrel{-}= C\_done_i$;
7: upon task_execution(T_i) {When task T_i is running}
8:    decrement C_left_i at each tick;
9: upon task_schedule_for_execution(T_i) at core m {When task T_i is at its scheduling point}
10:    set C_m = 0;
11:    **for all** task τ_j in **readyQueue** scheduled at core m **do**
12:       $C_m \mathrel{+}= C_j$;
13:    set $C_d = $ time_until_next_deadline();
14:    $frequency_m = (C\_left_i + C_m)\ /\ C_d$;

At a scheduling point, load balancing Algorithm 3 will assign a core m to task τ_i. The MC-ccFPP algorithm needs to find the estimated workload c_m from the current scheduling point to next deadline for core m. Once workload c_m is found, the frequency for core m can be found by $frequency_m = (C\_left_i + \text{C\_m})\ /\ C_d$.

4.2   Online Multicore DVS (MC-ccFPP) Examples

The figure on the left of Fig. 3 represents the same content as Figure 1, but from a speed perspective. The figure on the right of Fig. 3 shows the result of applying the MC-ccFPP method. About 61% of energy is saved with this online DVS algorithm. The MC-ccFPP is better than the MC-SSS algorithm in this case. The energy saving of MC-SSS is about 39.27%.

In this two-core example, at time $t = 0$, all three tasks are ready for execution, so all of them are in the **readyQueue**. Task τ_1 and Task τ_2 will run on Core 0 and Core 1 separately. The earliest deadline amount task τ_1, task τ_2 and task τ_3 is $t = 8$. If we plan to schedule τ_1 on Core 0 and τ_2 on Core 1, the workload for Core 0 is 1 and the workload for Core 1 is 3. According to the load balancing algorithm, the next task τ_3 will be scheduled on a less loaded core, which is Core 0 in this case. The total estimate workload for Core 0 will be $C_1 + C_3 = 1 + 5 = 6$. The total estimate workload for Core 0 will be $C_2 = 3$. In this cycle [0-8], the speed for Core 0 can be calculated as $frequency_0 = 6/8 = 0.75$. The speed for Core 1 can be calculated as $frequency_1 = 3/8 = 0.375$.

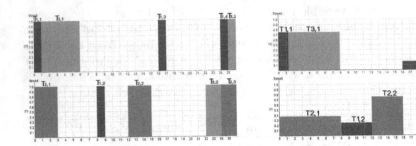

Fig. 3. Two-Core Online Multicore Fixed Priority Scheduling, Left (No DVS), Right (MC-ccFPP)

At time $t = 8$, task τ_1 is active again. According to the load balancing algorithm, τ_1 will be dispatched at a lower loaded core, which is Core 1 in this case. At time $t = 8$, the next deadline for task τ_1 is 16. The next deadline for task τ_2 is 12 and the next deadline for task τ_3 is 22. Since 12 is the earliest deadline, the next cycle is from time $t = 8$ to $t = 12$. In this cycle, task τ_2 and task τ_3 are both in the **IncomingQueue**. There is no further workload assigned to Core 1 except τ_1 itself. So the speed for Core 1 can be calculated as $frequency_1 = 1/4 = 0.25$. On the other hand, Core 0 will in an idle state due to that fact that no ready task exists.

5   Evaluation

5.1   Experiment Setting

Each test suite of the system is tested 100 times. A test suite has the following parameters: the number of tasks per task set (from 5 to 20 with an increasing step of 5), different utilization range (from 0.2 to 0.9 with an increasing step of 0.1) and different number of cores per processor tested. The details are shown in Table 2.

Table 2. Parameters of Generated Task Sets

Number of Cores	$2, 4, 8, 16$
Number of Tasks	$5, 10, 15, 20$
Utilization	$0.2 - 0.8$
Deadline/Period	$3 - 350$
Computation Time(WCET)	$1 - 5$

5.2   Energy vs. Utilization with Fixed Number of Cores

Next we show the experimental result for the relation between energy consumption and utilization. In the experiments we vary the number of tasks per task set, the algorithm used and the number of cores. In Fig. 4, the x-axis is the average utilization of the given task sets, y-axis is the normalized energy consumption. Figures in Fig. 4 plot energy versus utilization for differing number of cores. We can draw the following conclusions from these figures:

Increasing the number of cores results in more energy saving for both the MC-ccFPP algorithm and the MC-SSS algorithm. The least energy saving for a 2-core system ranges from 0% to 80%. The least energy saving for a 16 core system ranges from 50% to 90%.

When the Number of Cores m is Small

1. When the number of cores m is small, e.g, $m = 2$ shown in upper left in Fig. 4, the MC-ccFPP algorithm saves more energy than MC-SSS algorithm. The maximum energy saving can range from 50% to 80%.
2. When the utilization is small, e.g. $U = 0.2$, both MC-ccFPP and MC-SSS have the same amount of energy saving. With larger utilization, e.g. $U = 0.9$, MC-ccFPP algorithm will have better performance than MC-SSS algorithm.
3. For MC-ccFPP algorithm, the number of tasks per task set does not affect the amount of energy saving. But MC-SSS algorithm performs better with the larger number of tasks. For example, in Fig. 4, MC-SSS with 20 tasks can save more energy than a 5-task task set.

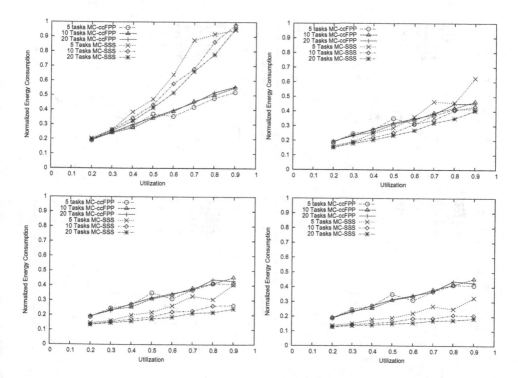

Fig. 4. Energy VS. Utilization with Different Number of Tasks, Upper Left (2 coress), Upper Right (4 cores), Lower Left (8 coress), Lower Right (16 cores)

When the Number of Cores m Becomes Larger

1. When the number of cores m becomes larger, e.g. $m = 4, m = 8$ and $m = 16$ shown in Fig. 4. The MC-SSS algorithm saves more energy comparing to the MC-ccFPP algorithm. The maximum energy saving can range from 80% to 90%.
2. Whether utilization is small or large, the MC-SSS algorithm always has more energy saving than MC-ccFPP algorithm. With the increasing of utilization, there will be a decrease of energy saved for both algorithms.
3. MC-SSS algorithm performs better with larger task set, e.g, a 20-task task set.

5.3   Energy vs. Utilization with Fixed Number of Tasks

Figures in Fig. 5 plot energy versus utilization with different number of cores in the processor. These figures show the following trend:

– For a 2-core system, MC-ccFPP will have more energy saving than the MC-SSS algorithm. For a 4-core or 16-core system, MC-SSS will have the better performance.

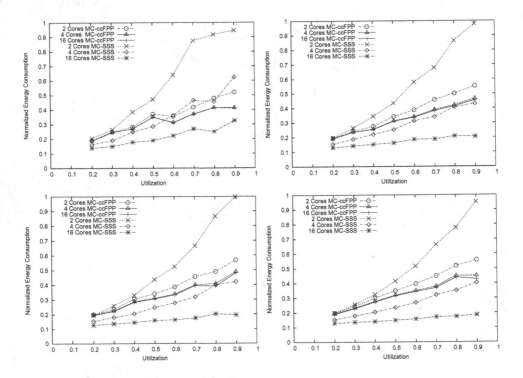

Fig. 5. Energy VS. Utilization with Different Number of Cores, Upper Left (5 tasks), Upper Right (10 tasks), Lower Left (15 tasks), Lower Right (20 tasks)

- The most energy saving is reached by a 16-core processor with MC-SSS algorithm. There will be 90% energy saving when utilization is $U = 0.1$. The least energy saving is reached by 2-core processor also with the MC-SSS algorithm. Almost no energy saving when utilization $U = 0.9$.

6   Conclusions and Contributions

In this paper, two DVS algorithms with load balancing technique on fixed priority multi-core platform have been described. One DVS algorithm (MC-SSS) is an off-line algorithm based on multi-core schedulability analysis. Another DVS algorithm (MC-ccFPP) is an online algorithm based on cycle conservative analysis. The load balancing technique uses greedy approach to balance the workload among different cores in a multi-core system. The MC-SSS algorithm is designed to collect static slack time. The online algorithm MC-ccFPP is designed to collect both dynamic slack and static slack time.

Performance analysis on the energy saving have been performed for the MC-SSS and MC-ccFPP for a variety of task sets with different CPU utilization, different number of tasks and different number of cores.

Acknowledgment. This work was supported by NSERC and NSERC RCD grant.

References

1. Andersson, B., Josson, J.: Fixed-priority preemptive multiprocessor scheduling: To partition or not to partition. In: Proceedings of International Conference on Real-Time Computing Systems and Applications, pp. 337–346 (2000)
2. Aydin, H., Melhem, R., Mosse, D., Mejia-Alvarez, P.: Dynamic and aggressive scheduling techniques for power-aware real-time systems. In: Proceedings of IEEE Real-Time Systems Symposium, London, UK, pp. 95–105 (December 2001)
3. Baker, T.P.: An analysis of fixed-priority schedulability on a multiprocessor. Real-Time Systems 32(1-2), 49–71 (2006)
4. Bautista, D., Sahuquillo, J., Hassan, H., Petit, S., Duato, J.: A simple power-aware scheduling for multicore systems when running real-time applications. In: Proceedings of IEEE International Parallel and Distributed Processing Symposium, pp. 1–7 (2008)
5. Fisher, N., Chen, J., Wang, S., Thiele, L.: Thermal-aware global real-time scheduling on multicore systems. In: Proceedings of IEEE Real-Time and Embedded Technology and Applications Symposium, pp. 131–140 (2009)
6. Guan, N., Stigge, M., Yi, W., Yu, G.: Cache-aware scheduling and analysis for multicores. In: Proceedings of International Conference on Embedded Software, pp. 245–254 (2009)
7. Huang, X., Li, K., Li, R.: A Energy Efficient Scheduling Base on Dynamic Voltage and Frequency Scaling for Multi-core Embedded Real-Time System. In: Hua, A., Chang, S.-L. (eds.) ICA3PP 2009. LNCS, vol. 5574, pp. 137–145. Springer, Heidelberg (2009)

8. Jejurikar, R., Gupta, R.K.: Energy aware non-preemptive scheduling for hard real-time systems. In: Proceedings of Euromicro Conference on Real-Time Systems, Palma de Mallorca, Spain, pp. 21–30 (July 2005)

9. Kim, N.S., Austin, T., Hu, J.S., Jane, M.: Leakage current: Moore's law meets static power. In: Proceedings of International Technology Roadmap for Semiconductors (2003)

10. Kim, W., Kim, J., Min, S.L.: A dynamic voltage scaling algorithm for dynamic-priority hard real-time systems using slack time analysis. In: Proceedings of Design, Automation and Test in Europe, pp. 788–794 (March 2002)

11. Kim, W., Kim, J., Min, S.L.: Dynamic voltage scaling algorithm for fixed-priority real-time systems using work-demand analysis. In: Proceedings of the 2003 International Symposium on Low Power Electronics and Design, pp. 396–401. ACM, New York (2003)

12. Lakshmanan, K., Rajkumar, R., Lehoczky, J.: Partitioned fixed-priority preemptive scheduling for multi-core processors. In: Proceedings of Euromicro Conference on Real-Time Systems, pp. 239–248 (2009)

13. Liu, C.L., Layland, J.: Scheduling algorithms for multiprogramming in a hard real-time environment. Journal of the ACM 20(1), 46–61 (1973)

14. Martin, S.M., Flautner, K., Mudge, T., Blaauw, D.: Combined dynamic voltage scaling and adaptive body biasing for lower power microprocessors under dynamic workloads. In: ICCAD 2002: Proceedings of the 2002 IEEE/ACM International Conference on Computer-Aided Design, pp. 721–725. ACM, New York (2002)

15. Pillai, P., Shin, K.G.: Real-time dynamic voltage scaling for low-power embedded operating systems. In: Proceedings of the 18th ACM Symposium on Operating Systems Principles, pp. 89–102. ACM Press (2001)

16. Qu, G.: Power management of multicore multiple voltage embedded systems by task scheduling. In: Proceedings of Parallel Processing Workshops, ICPPW 2007, pp. 34–40 (2007)

17. Yang, L., Lin, M., Yang, L.T.: Integrating preemption threshold to fixed priority DVS scheduling algorithms. In: Proceedings of The 15th IEEE International Conference on Embedded and Real-Time Computing Systems and Applications, pp. 165–171 (2009)

18. Yang, L., Lin, M.: On-line and off-line DVS for fixed priority with preemption threshold scheduling. In: Proceedings of The 6th International Conference on Embedded Software and Systems, pp. 273–280 (2009)

Comparing Checkpoint and Rollback Recovery Schemes in a Cluster System

Noriaki Bessho and Tadashi Dohi

Department of Information Engineering, Graduate School of Engineering
Hiroshima University, 1–4–1 Kagamiyama, Higashi-Hiroshima, 739–8527 Japan

Abstract. Cluster systems play a central role to realize high performance computing with relatively low cost, and at the same time are necessary the fault-tolerance features for the practical use. In this paper we develop stochastic models to evaluate the expected total recovery overhead for a cluster computing system with three well-known checkpoint and rollback recovery schemes; checkpoint mirroring, central file server checkpointing and skewed checkpointing, where the fault latency time after a system failure is given by a random variable. In general, since the multi-node failure as well as single-node failure may occur in the cluster system, it is not so easy to obtain the closed form of expected total recovery overhead. Based on a simple failure model, we do this by listing up all the possible combinations of probabilistic events caused by the multi-node failure. Further we compare the respective expected total recovery overhead with different checkpoint and rollback recovery schemes, and evaluate quantitatively the effectiveness of these schemes.

Keywords: Cluster computing, multi-node failure, rollback recovery, expected total recovery overhead, checkpoint mirroring, central file server checkpointing, skewed checkpointing, stochastic modeling.

1 Introduction

Cluster systems play a central role to realize high performance computing with relatively low cost, and at the same time are necessary the fault-tolerance features based on the multi-node redundancy and distributed computing. Cherckpointing and rollback/rollforward recovery are the commonly used environment diversity techniques to reduce effectively the recovery overhead after a system failure [15]. It is common to place checkpoints (CPs) to save the process information even in cluster systems to improve the fault-tolerance with low cost. The distributed computing property in cluster systems is based on a collection of autonomous nodes linked by a network and equipped with a software that makes it appear to its users as a single coherent computer system. It shares resources among geographically separate users, improves performance and speed, and provides the heterogeneous system architecture. Bhargava and Lian [1], Tong et al. [21], Cristian and Tukey [3], Wang and Fuchs [25] develop several kinds of checkpoint/rollback recovery (RB) scheme for distributed systems. Apart from the distributed computing property,

Y. Xiang et al. (Eds.): ICA3PP 2012, Part I, LNCS 7439, pp. 531–545, 2012.

since computer clusters are the reference architectures today for high-performance computing, a number of authors investigate the CP/RB mechanisms for cluster systems theoretically and empirically [19],[20].

Since cluster systems are usually deployed to improve performance and availability over that of a single computer, it is well known that there is a tradeoff relation between the recovery overhead and the operation overhead by checkpointing itself. That is, if CPs are frequently taken, a larger overhead by checkpointing itself will be incurred. Conversely, if CPs are seldom placed, a larger RB overhead after a system failure will be required. Hence, it is important to determine the *optimal* CP interval taking account of the trade-off between two kinds of overhead factors above [4],[5],[16]. Gelenbe at al. [6] consider an availability model for a distributed computer with failures. Gelenbe and Chabridon [7] also model the execution of distributed programs and give both analytical and simulation results on the average total execution time. Wong and Franklin [26] consider a simple Markov model to take place synchronous checkpointing in a distributed system with and without load redistribution. In the work by Klonowska et al. [9], the best possible RB schemes for any number of crashed node computers are considered under the assumption that the load on them is redistributed to other node computers in a distributed system.

Recently, considerable attentions are paid for the optimal CP/RB models in cluster computing. Cluster system is used mainly on a large-scale technology calculation widely, because it can build high efficiency computation environment at low cost. For the cluster system a high-reliability technology corresponding to the node failure to constitute a system is necessary. Furthermore, it is desirable that a high-reliability technology can support single node failure and multi-node failure. In particular, when a disorder occurred in file systems, so far various data recovery technology has been suggested because quick data recovery is necessary. Jones et al. [8], Liu et al. [10],[11],[12], Naksinehaboon et al. [13] develop several models to determine the optimal or sub-optimal CP interval. Bouguerra et al. [2] also give an analytical model with coordinated CP/RB for a large scale cluster system. It is worth mentioning that the above works are based on the direct application of the similar analytical techniques to the CP placement for coherent computer systems [4],[5],[16]. However, the above works did not consider the possibility of occurrence of *multi-node failure*.

In the typical cluster systems with multiple nodes, it is common to observe the multi-node failure caused by only one fault on the program. Plank [17] consider the checkpoint mirroring (MIR) and central file server checkpointing (CFS), and investigate the impact on the performance and functionality of coordinated checkpointing schemes. The former denotes the checkpointing by each processor node to its local disk, the latter is the one done by all processor nodes to a stable central file system. Through an experiment with network of workstations, Plank [17] explored several CP/RB schemes. A simple Markov chain model for the checkpoint placement in a cluster system is proposed by Vaidya [22], [24], where he combines MIR and CFS and develops the so-called two-level recovery schemes. The resulting Markov model is based on a continuous-time Markov chain (CTMC) and is rather simple. Plank and Thomason [18] also develop a birth-death type CTMC model to determine the checkpoint interval and processor allocation simultaneously in a cluster system.

Nakamura *et al.* [14] present an interesting checkpointing scheme called the skewed checkpointing (SC) whose idea is to change sequentially the nodes on which the CP data are saved. This enables us to reduce the system overhead and to handle multi-node failures in principle, without using redundant CPs. They show through an experiment that SC is quite useful CP placement method for cluster systems with multi-node failures. However, it should be noted that their formulation of the expected total recovery overhead is based on the sum of expected overhead occurred in each node, and is not taken the combination of recovery points into consideration. In other words, since the formation by Nakamura *et al.* [14] should be regarded as an approximation, the dependability evaluation with MIR, CFS and SC should be re-examined with well-established stochastic models.

In this paper we consider a somewhat different model to evaluate the expected total recovery overhead in a cluster system from [14],[18],[22],[24]. Suppose that a task operation on a cluster system starts at time 0 and that a system failure occurs. Following Vaidaya [23], it is assumed that the failure is caused by a latency fault such as an error data inserted at an arbitrary time. Once the system failure occurs, it is needed to identify the place of the latency fault in a backward manner and to find a suitable recovery point. Since the latency fault is randomly inserted before the system failure point, it is common to assume that the fault latency time from the insertion point to the system failure point is a non-negative random variable. In the CP/RB scheme for a cluster system with multi-node failure, the recovery point strongly depends on the fault latency time, because the domino effect may occur and the recovery point may be the initial time of a task operation. We develop a discrete-time stochastic model based on the Bernoulli probability and the uniform distribution, to evaluate the expected total recovery overhead after a system failure occurs. Based on this simple failure model, we derive the expected total recovery overhead under three CP/RB schemes; MIR, CFS and SC, by listing up all the possible combinations of probabilistic events caused by the multi-node failure, and compare them quantitatively.

2 Basic CP/RB Schemes

2.1 Checkpoint Mirroring

First we introduce k-MMIR (k-Mirror Checkpoint Mirroring) proposed by Plank [17]. Suppose that each node of a cluster system generates a checkpoint (CP) and saves the data in its local disk. In k-MMIR, these data mirrored at each CP are transmitted to k different nodes and are backed up. Since each CP data is replicated on k nodes, it is known that k-MMIR can tolerate k-multiple nodes failure. Figure 1 depicts the configuration of k-MMIR for a cluster system with N nodes, where one CP data on node P_1 is saved on $(k+1)$ nodes $P_1 \sim P_{k+1}$. In a fashion similar to P_1, the checkpointed data at each node P_i ($i = 1, \ldots, N$) is saved periodically in nodes $P_{(i+1) \bmod N}, \cdots, P_{(i+k) \bmod N}$. In the next CP, these

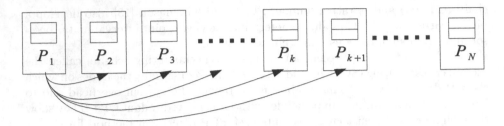

Fig. 1. Configuration of k-MMIR

data are replaced by new CP data, and the same cycle repeats again and again. In this k-MMIR scheme, once a system failure occurs, the recovery cost strongly depends on the number of failed nodes. If the number of failed nodes is less than or equal to k, then the RB is possible at the latest CP, otherwise, the recovery point may be the starting point of task processing in the worst case. In this way, if k is larger, then the cluster system with k-MMIR is more fault-tolerant. On the other hand, when k increases, the total CP overhead in the whole system also increases, because the CP cost is defined as the sum of the back-up cost at each node. These tradeoff relation motivates us to determine the optimal CP interval to reduce the total system overhead. The simplest example with $k = 1$ is 1-MMIR, which can tolerate only single node failure. In this case the CP overhead is smallest for saving the data on only one node.

2.2 Central File Server Checkpointing

Another feature of k-MMIR is the low-cost fault tolerance, because it does not assume a reliable central file server (CFS). In CFS checkpointing [17], it is assumed that there exists a completely reliable CFS and that the data at each node is saved on it. In Fig. 2, the process on each node P_i $(i = 1, \ldots, N)$ is periodically saved at CFS, and the data is rewritten in the next CP instant. In this case, the recovery

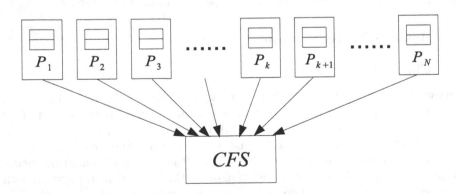

Fig. 2. Configuration of CFS

from system failure does not depend on the number of nodes, so that CFS enables to recover the whole system on the latest CP. In this sense, CFS is an ideal recovery scheme for multiple nodes failure. On the other hand, it is evident that the CP overhead in CFS is extremely expensive since the access to CFS is heavily concentrated. More precisely, the large amount of data have to be transmitted from all the nodes to CFS at each CP, and from CFS to all the nodes at the recovery just after a system failure. This means that both CP overhead and recovery overhead increase remarkably as the number of nodes increases.

2.3   Skewed Checkpointing

Nakamura *et al.* [14] propose an interesting checkpointing scheme called the skewed checkpointing (SC) whose idea is to change sequentially the nodes on which the CP data are saved. Suppose that there are N nodes, $P_1 \sim P_N$, in a cluster system. As mentioned above, 1-MMIR saves the CP data on i-th node P_i $(i = 1, \ldots, N)$ on $P_{(i+1) \bmod N}$. On the other hand, the skewed CP (SC) changes the node on which each CP data is saved in every CP placement. The significant problem is to determine the distance between each individual node and its backup node. Nakamura *et al.* [14] define the *skew distance* which is equivalent to the distance to the 2^{n-1} $(n = 1, \ldots, m)$-th node from the right and propose to take place 1-MMIR with different backup nodes, where n is the execution time of SCs, $m = \lfloor \log_2 N \rfloor$ is said the number of *cycles* and means the number of CPs at which the back up node returns to the initial point. In other words, the PC data on the node P_i is saved on its own local disk and $P_{(i+2^{n-1}) \bmod N}$ at the same time. Figure 3 is the configuration of SC with $N = 8$, where the CP data is saved on the right node in the first step, and is taken to 2^{n-1}-th distance in the n-th step. When $N = 8$, it is obvious to see $m = 3$, so that the node at $(m + 1)$-st CP is same as the first node.

Next, we describe the recovery operations in SC. Once a system failure occurs, the RB is taken place at the latest CP before the recovery point. In 1-MMIR, it is evident that the RB on the latest CP is possible for a single-node failure. On the other hand, if a multi-node failure occurs, then the information on only the latest CP may be inconsistent and may not be able to be the suitable recovery point [17]. Even in SC, it is shown that the recovery from a single-node failure is possible on the latest CP, but the number of failed nodes depends on the value of cycle, m, before the occurrence of a multi-node failure. In other words, the available CP is determined by the combination of failed nodes experienced. Suppose that a multi-node failure occurs after n-th CP and j $(= 2, \ldots, N)$ nodes fail. It is said that the n-th CP is *available*, if a pair of nodes to copy and save in each cycle are not included in the failed nodes. In the first cycle, if $n \geq j$, then the latest available CP from n-th to $(n - j)$-th ones can be the recovery point. In the second cycle, if $m \geq j$, then the latest available CP from n-th to $(n - j)$-th ones can be the recovery point. By taking account of combination of failed nodes, the CP as the recovery point has to be identified. It is said that the n-th CP is *available*, if both sender and receiver in n-th CP are not included in the failed nodes.

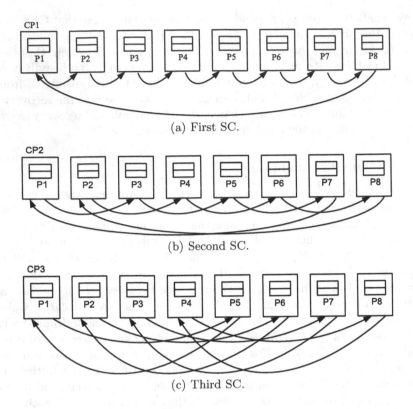

(a) First SC.

(b) Second SC.

(c) Third SC.

Fig. 3. Configuration of SC ($N = 8$)

When the recovery point is located just after the latest available CP, the roll-forward recovery (RF) is taken place from each failed node. Figure 3 illustrates an example of a RB operation when a multi-node failure occurs just after the second CP in the second cycle. In this case, if the latest CP data is available for multi-node failures on P_1 and P_2, it is possible to return back to CP_2 for the RB. However if multi-node failures occur on P_1 and P_3, the latest information on P_1 is saved on P_3, hence CP_2 but not CP_1 can be the recovery point. In the case where the recovery point is located in the time point after the latest available CP, each node can be taken place the RF on the recovery point.

3   Analysis

3.1   Failure Model Description

We develop a stochastic model with three kinds of CP/RB schemes in this section. Suppose that a cluster system with N nodes operates on a discrete time $n = 0, \tau, 2\tau, 3\tau, \cdots$ with the minimum time unit τ and is checked point at time instant $n\tau$ ($n = 1, 2, \cdots$) periodically. Suppose that a system failure occurs at time n_0 $(= \tau, 2\tau, \cdots)$, and that i CPs are experienced before that time, where the elapsed time from the latest CP to the failure point is given by $a \cdot \tau$, where a is an integer value. Then we have $n_0 = (a + i \cdot n)\tau$. In the cluster system, N nodes are mutually independent and identical, and their failure probability is given by the Bernoulli probability p $(0 < p < 1)$. Then the probability that w node failures occur is given by the binomial distribution; $f_w = \binom{N}{w} p^w (1 - p)^{N-w}$. Looking back from the failure point n_0, the fault latency time T is also randomly distributed having the probability mass function (p.m.f.) $g(j)$ with integer-valued support $j \in [0, n_0]$, where $\sum_{j=0}^{n_0} g(j) = 1$. In this case, it can be seen that the recovery point is located before the fault latency time (see Fig.4).

We consider the recovery scheme with two simple cases; the case where a system failure occurs after the latest CP in Fig. 4 (a), and the case where a system failure occurs between the latest and the second latest CPs in Fig. 4 (b). In the former case, since no CP is placed during the fault latency period, all CPs are available and the recovery point can be the latest CP, which depends on the combination of failed nodes. After completing the RB operation on the latest CP, the RF operation takes place to the recovery point. In the latter case, the latest CP is placed during the latency time period and cannot be the recovery point. Hence, the RB operation takes place to the available CP just before the latest CP, and the RF operation also does to the recovery point.

3.2 k-MMIR

The expected total recovery overhead in this paper is defined as the conditional expectation of time length to recover the system, given the system failure point n_0, where it consists of the identification time of a latent fault and the RB time. More specifically, if the fault latency time measured from the system failure point is given by the integer-valued random variable T, then the identification time is proportional to T and is given by αT, where α (> 0) is a positive constant (integer). Once the occurrence time of the latent fault can be identified, then the RB time is proportional to an integer-valued constant β (> 0). Noting that the most recent data is saved on each CP, we can consider two cases on fault latency time; (i) $T \leq a \cdot \tau$ and (ii) $a \cdot \tau < T$. In (i), when the number of failed nodes is less than or equal to k, the recovery point becomes the i-th CP, where the time overhead for RB is proportional to the time interval $a - T$ and is given by $\beta(a - T)$, where β is also an intere value.

Since the probability that the number of failed nodes is k is given by $\sum_{w=1}^{k} f_w$, we have the expected total recovery overhead in this case by $(\sum_{w=1}^{k} f_w) \sum_{j=1}^{a} [\alpha(j) + \beta(a - j)] \tau g(j) / (1 - f_0)$, using the conditional p.m.f. of the random variable T, $g(j)/(1 - f_0)$. On the other hand, if the number of failed nodes is strictly greater than k, then the i-th CP is not the recovery point, so that the RB procedure goes back to the initial point of a task. In this case, since the expected total rollback recovery time is given by $\beta((a + i \cdot n) - T)$ and the probability that the failed nodes is greater than k is $1 - (\sum_{w=1}^{k} f_w + f_0)$, we

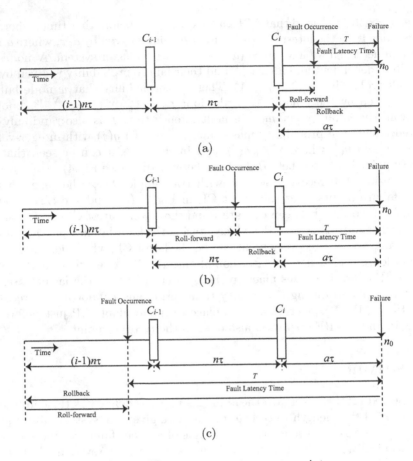

Fig. 4. Three patterns on recovery point

have the expected total recovery overhead by $(1 - (\sum_{w=1}^{k} f_w + f_0)) \sum_{j=1}^{a} [\alpha(j) + \beta((a + i \cdot n) - j)]\tau g(j)/(1 - f_0)$. In (ii), it is evident that there does not exist an available CP, so the recovery point becomes the initial point of a task if a fault is inserted. Then, since the RB time is given by $\beta((a + i \cdot n) - T)$, we have the expected value $(1 - f_0) \sum_{j=a+1}^{a+i \cdot n} [\alpha \cdot j + \beta((a + i \cdot n) - j)]\tau g(j)/(1 - f_0)$.

Finally, the expected total recovery overhead in k-MMIR, provided that a system failure occurs at time n_0, is given by

$$
R_{MIR}(n, i) = \Big\{ \sum_{w=1}^{k} f_w \sum_{j=1}^{a} [\alpha j + \beta(a - j)]g(j)
$$

$$
+ \Big[1 - \big(\sum_{w=1}^{k} f_w + f_0\big)\Big] \sum_{j=1}^{a} [\alpha j + \beta((a + i \cdot n) - j)]g(j)
$$

$$
+ (1 - f_0) \sum_{j=a+1}^{a+i \cdot n} [\alpha j + \beta((a + i \cdot n) - T)]g(j) \Big\} \tau/(1 - f_0). \quad (1)
$$

3.3   CFS

In a fashion similar to k-MMIR, we consider two cases in CFS; (i) $T \le a \cdot \tau$ and (ii) $a \cdot \tau < T$. In (i), if the number of failed nodes is greater than or equal to one, then it is possible to rollback to the i-th CP. This is a different point from k-MMIR, because the feasibility to RB at the i-th CP does not depend on the number of failed nodes. In this case, the expected recovery time is given by $(1-f_0)\sum_{j=1}^{a}[\alpha j + \beta(a-j)]\tau g(j)/(1-f_0)$. The similar discussion is applied to the case (ii) and enables to obtain the expected total recovery overhead by $(1-f_0)\sum_{j=a+1}^{a+i\cdot n}[\alpha j + \beta((a+i\cdot n)-j)]\tau g(j)/(1-f_0)$. Finally, we get the expected total recovery overhead in CFS, provided that a system failure occurs at time n_0, by

$$R_{CFS}(n,i) = \left\{ (1-f_0)\sum_{j=1}^{a}[\alpha j + \beta(a-j)]g(j) \right.$$

$$\left. +(1-f_0)\sum_{j=a+1}^{a+i\cdot n}[\alpha j + \beta((a+i\cdot n)-j)]g(j) \right\}\tau/(1-f_0). \quad (2)$$

3.4   SC

Next, we consider SC. Since the cycle, say, the number of saved CPs, is $m = \lfloor \log_2 N \rfloor$, we can consider three cases in terms of the occurrence time of a latent fault T; (i) $bT \le a\tau$, (ii) $a\tau < T \le (a+n)\tau, \cdots, (a+(m-2)n)\tau < T \le (a+(m-1)n)\tau$, (iii) $(a+(m-1)n)\tau < T$. More specifically, in the case of $N = 4$, we just consider three cases; (i) $T \le a\tau$, (ii) $a\tau < T \le (a+n)\tau$, (iii) $(a+n)\tau < T$. In SC, since the recovery points may be different in accordance with the combination of failed nodes, it is necessary to consider the combination of failed nodes. This is a quite different point from k-MMIR which depends on only the number of failed nodes in a cluster system. In (i) $T \le a\tau$ (hereafter we consider only $N = 4$), if the number of failed nodes is less than or equal to 2 and if the i-th CP is available, then the RB procedure goes back to the i-th CP and its probability is given by $f_1 + (2/3)f_2$. Then, we have the expected recovery overhead by $(f_1 + (2/3)f_2)\sum_{j=1}^{a}[\alpha j + \beta(a-j)]\tau g(j)/(1-f_0)$. If the number of failed nodes is less than or equal to 2 but if the i-th CP is not available, then the system can rollback to the $(i-1)$-st CP, where the expected recovery overhead is given by $(1/3)f_2\sum_{j=1}^{a}[\alpha j + \beta((a+n)-j)]\tau g(j)/(1-f_0)$ with the probability $(1/3)f_2$. While $T \le a\tau$ and the number of failed nodes is strictly greater than 2, then all the CPs are not available and the system has to be rollbacked to the initial point of a task. In this case, the probability that the number of failed nodes is strictly greater than 2 becomes $1 - (f_0 + f_1 + f_2)$, so that the expected recovery overhead is given by $(1-(f_0+f_1+f_2))\sum_{j=1}^{a}[\alpha j + \beta((a+i\cdot n)-j)]\tau g(j)/(1-f_0)$.

In (ii) $a\tau < T \le (a+n)\tau$, the i-th CP is not available and the number of failed nodes is less than or equal to 2. Then it is possible to rollback to the $(i-1)$-st CP. Since the probability that the number of failed nodes is less than or equal to 2 is $f_1 + f_2$, the expected recovery overhead is given by $(f_1 + f_2)\sum_{j=a+1}^{a+n}[\alpha j + \beta((a+n)-j)]\tau g(j)/(1-f_0)$. On the other hand, if the number of failed nodes is strictly greater than 2, then all the CPs are not available and the recovery point becomes the initial point of a task. Then, we have the expected recovery overhead by $(1 - (f_0 + f_1 + f_2)) \sum_{j=a+1}^{a+n} [\alpha j + \beta((a + i \cdot n) - j)] \tau g(j)/(1 - f_0)$. In (iii) $(a + n)\tau < T$, there does not exist available CP, so that the recovery point is the starting point of the task, where the time length of RB is given by $(a + i \cdot n) - T$ and its associated cost is $\beta((a + i \cdot n) - T)$. Since the probability that a system failure occurs is $1 - f_0$, the expected recovery overhead in this case is given by $(1 - f_0) \sum_{j=a+n+1}^{a+in} [\alpha j + \beta((a + in) - j)] \tau g(j)/(1 - f_0)$. Finally, by taking the sum of all expected recovery overhead values in the case of $N = 4$, we have the expected total recovery overhead in SC:

$$
\begin{aligned}
R_{SC}(n, i) = \Big\{ &(f_1 + (2/3)f_2) \sum_{j=1}^{a} [\alpha j + \beta(a - j)] g(j) \\
&+ (1/3) f_2 \sum_{j=1}^{a} [\alpha j + \beta((a + n) - j)] g(j) \\
&+ (1 - (f_0 + f_1 + f_2)) \sum_{j=1}^{a} [\alpha j + \beta((a + i \cdot n) - j)] g(j) \\
&+ (f_1 + f_2) \sum_{j=a+1}^{a+n} [\alpha j + \beta((a + n) - j)] g(j) \\
&+ (1 - (f_0 + f_1 + f_2)) \sum_{j=a+1}^{a+n} [\alpha j + \beta((a + i \cdot n) - j)] g(j) \\
&+ (1 - f_0) \sum_{j=a+n+1}^{a+i \cdot n} [\alpha j + \beta((a + i \cdot n) - j)] g(j) \Big\} \tau/(1 - f_0). \quad (3)
\end{aligned}
$$

Similar to the case with $N = 4$, we obtain in the case of $N = 16$ as

$$
\begin{aligned}
R_{SC}(n, i) = \Big\{ &(f_1 + (14/15)f_2 + (3/7)f_3 + (10/39)f_4) \sum_{j=1}^{a} [\alpha j + \beta(a - j)] g(j) \\
&+ ((1/15)f_2 + (17/42)f_3 + (8/39)f_4) \sum_{j=1}^{a} [\alpha j + \beta((a + n) - j)] g(j) \\
&+ ((1/6)f_3 + (11/39)f_4) \sum_{j=1}^{a} [\alpha j + \beta((a + 2n) - j)] g(j) \\
&+ (10/39) f_4 \sum_{j=1}^{a} [\alpha j + \beta((a + 3n) - j)] g(j) \\
&+ (1 - (f_0 + f_1 + f_2 + f_3 + f_4)) \sum_{j=1}^{a} [\alpha j + \beta((a + i \cdot n) - j)] g(j) \\
&+ (f_1 + f_2 + (5/6)f_3 + (6/13)f_4) \sum_{j=a+1}^{a+n} [\alpha j + \beta((a + n) - j)] g(j)
\end{aligned}
$$

$$+((1/6)f_3 + (11/39)f_4) \sum_{j=a+1}^{a+n} [\alpha j + \beta((a+2n) - j)]g(j)$$

$$+(10/39)f_4 \sum_{j=a+1}^{a+n} [\alpha j + \beta((a+3n) - j)]g(j)$$

$$+(1 - (f_0 + f_1 + f_2 + f_3 + f_4)) \sum_{j=a+1}^{a+n} [\alpha j + \beta((a+i\cdot n) - j)]g(j)$$

$$+(f_1 + f_2 + f_3 + (29/39)f_4) \sum_{j=a+n+1}^{a+2n} [\alpha j + \beta((a+2n) - j)]g(j)$$

$$+(10/39)f_4 \sum_{j=a+n+1}^{a+2n} [\alpha j + \beta((a+3n) - j)]g(j)$$

$$+(1 - (f_0 + f_1 + f_2 + f_3 + f_4)) \sum_{j=a+n+1}^{a+2n} [\alpha j + \beta((a+i\cdot n) - j)]g(j)$$

$$+(f_1 + f_2 + f_3 + f_4) \sum_{j=a+2n+1}^{a+3n} [\alpha j + \beta((a+3n) - j)]g(j)$$

$$+(1 - (f_0 + f_1 + f_2 + f_3 + f_4)) \sum_{j=a+2n+1}^{a+3n} [\alpha j + \beta((a+i\cdot n) - j)]g(j)$$

$$+(1 - f_0) \sum_{j=a+3n+1}^{a+i\cdot n} [\alpha j + \beta((a+i\cdot n) - j)]g(j) \Big\} \tau/(1 - f_0). \tag{4}$$

4   Numerical Illustrations

Here we derive the optimal CP policy (n^*, i^*) which consists of the optimal CP interval and the number of CPs, by minimizing the expected total recovery overhead $R(n, i)$. Suppose that the fault latency time obeys the discrete uniform distribution having the p.m.f. $g(j) = 1/n_0 = 1/(a + i \cdot n)$. The other model parameters are given by $n_0 = 10,000$, $20,000$, $30,000$, $\alpha = 1$, 10, 100, $\beta = 1$, $\tau = 1$, $p = 0.001$, $N = 4$, 8, 16. As the general trend, it can be observed that since the resulting optimal CP interval is longer as the failure time becomes longer, the number of CPs tends to decrease according to the kind of CP/RB schemes. This tendency becomes remarkable as the number of nodes in a cluster system increases. Furthermore, it can be shown that the expected total recovery overhead is reduced as the number of nodes increases or the node failure probability decreases. This observation satisfies our intuition.

Tables 1–3 present the dependence of the failure time n_0 and the parameter α on the optimal CP policies (n^*, i^*) in three CP/RB schemes. Surprisingly, it can be seen that k-MMIR does not depend on the value of k in this parameter setting and provides the almost same performance as CFP, though the resulting CP policies are different. This is due to the assumption that the fault latency time is uniformly distributed. Comparing SC with k-MMIR and CFS, it can be shown that CS can give the lower expected total recovery overhead for all cases. This result suggests that SC is superior to the other two CP/RB schemes in terms of effective recovery operation. In general, since the CP overhead in real cluster systems is relatively small, the recovery overhead occupies the large amount of the system overhead. In such a situation, it can be concluded quantitatively that SC is better than k-MMIR and CFS.

Table 1. Optimal CP policy and its associated expected total recovery overhead with varying failure time via k-MMIR ($N = 16$, $p = 0.0001$)

k	n_0	α	(n^*, i^*)	$R_{MIR}(n^*, i^*)$	k	n_0	α	(n^*, i^*)	$R_{MIR}(n^*, i^*)$
		1	(250,39)	9756			1	(250,39)	9756
	10000	10	(286,34)	54727		10000	10	(286,34)	54727
		100	(477,20)	504596			100	(477,20)	504596
		1	(488,40)	19525			1	(488,40)	19525
1	20000	10	(572,34)	109450	5	20000	10	(572,34)	109450
		100	(910,21)	1009180			100	(910,21)	1009180
		1	(469,63)	29539			1	(469,63)	29539
	30000	10	(682,43)	164339		30000	10	(682,43)	164339
		100	(1072,27)	1514020			100	(1072,27)	1514020
		1	(250,39)	9756			1	(250,39)	9756
	10000	10	(286,34)	54727		10000	10	(286,34)	54727
		100	(477,20)	504596			100	(477,20)	504596
		1	(488,40)	19525			1	(488,40)	19525
2	20000	10	(572,34)	109450	6	20000	10	(572,34)	109450
		100	(910,21)	1009180			100	(910,21)	1009180
		1	(469,63)	29539			1	(469,63)	29539
	30000	10	(682,43)	164339		30000	10	(682,43)	164339
		100	(1072,27)	1514020			100	(1072,27)	1514020
		1	(250,39)	9756			1	(250,39)	9756
	10000	10	(286,34)	54727		10000	10	(286,34)	54727
		100	(477,20)	504596			100	(477,20)	504596
		1	(488,40)	19525			1	(488,40)	19525
3	20000	10	(572,34)	109450	7	20000	10	(572,34)	109450
		100	(910,21)	1009180			100	(910,21)	1009180
		1	(469,63)	29539			1	(469,63)	29539
	30000	10	(682,43)	164339		30000	10	(682,43)	164339
		100	(1072,27)	1514020			100	(1072,27)	1514020
		1	(250,39)	9756			1	(250,39)	9756
	10000	10	(286,34)	54727		10000	10	(286,34)	54727
		100	(477,20)	504596			100	(477,20)	504596
		1	(488,40)	19525			1	(488,40)	19525
4	20000	10	(572,34)	109450	8	20000	10	(572,34)	109450
		100	(910,21)	1009180			100	(910,21)	1009180
		1	(469,63)	29539			1	(469,63)	29539
	30000	10	(682,43)	164339		30000	10	(682,43)	164339
		100	(1072,27)	1514020			100	(1072,27)	1514020

Table 2. Optimal CP policy and its associated expected total recovery overhead with varying failure time ($N = 16$, $p = 0.0001$)

<table>
<tr><td colspan="4" align="center">(i) CFS.</td><td colspan="4" align="center">(ii) SC.</td></tr>
<tr><td>n_0</td><td>α</td><td>(n^*, i^*)</td><td>$R_{CFS}(n^*, i^*)$</td><td>n_0</td><td>α</td><td>(n^*, i^*)</td><td>$R_{SC}(n^*, i^*)$</td></tr>
<tr><td rowspan="3">10000</td><td>1</td><td>(250,39)</td><td>9756</td><td rowspan="3">10000</td><td>1</td><td>(477,20)</td><td>8322</td></tr>
<tr><td>10</td><td>(286,34)</td><td>54727</td><td>10</td><td>(1000,9)</td><td>52004</td></tr>
<tr><td>100</td><td>(477,20)</td><td>504596</td><td>100</td><td>(1429,6)</td><td>501376</td></tr>
<tr><td rowspan="3">20000</td><td>1</td><td>(488,40)</td><td>19524</td><td rowspan="3">20000</td><td>1</td><td>(1053,18)</td><td>16343</td></tr>
<tr><td>10</td><td>(572,34)</td><td>109449</td><td>10</td><td>(1429,13)</td><td>105310</td></tr>
<tr><td>100</td><td>(910,21)</td><td>1009180</td><td>100</td><td>(1539,12)</td><td>1005080</td></tr>
<tr><td rowspan="3">30000</td><td>1</td><td>(469,63)</td><td>29539</td><td rowspan="3">30000</td><td>1</td><td>(1250,23)</td><td>25521</td></tr>
<tr><td>10</td><td>(682,43)</td><td>164338</td><td>10</td><td>(1579,18)</td><td>159519</td></tr>
<tr><td>100</td><td>(1072,27)</td><td>1514020</td><td>100</td><td>(2308,12)</td><td>1507590</td></tr>
</table>

5   Conclusions

In this paper we have developed the performance models with three checkpoint and rollback recovery schemes; checkpoint mirroring, central file server checkpointing and skewed checkpointing, and compared them in terms of the expected total recovery overhead. Based on the quantitative comparison of these models, it has been concluded that the skewed checkpointing was superior to the other checkpoint and rollback recovery schemes. This conclusion is exactly same as [14], although they have derived it from the different model assumptions. We have considered a special situation where the failure time was given, but the fault latency time was uniformly distributed. In the future, we will carry out under different model assumptions on the fault latency time distribution and will analyze a different model with a forward manner, such that the failure time is given by a random variable but the recovery point is given in accordance with the combination of failed nodes.

References

1. Bhargava, B., Lian, S.-R.: Independent checkpointing and concurrent rollback for recovery in distributed systems – an optimistic approach. In: Proceedings of the 7th IEEE Symposium on Reliable Distributed Systems (SRDS 1988), pp. 3–12. IEEE CPS (1988)
2. Bouguerra, M.-S., Gautier, T., Trystram, D., Vincent, J.-M.: A Flexible Checkpoint/Restart Model in Distributed Systems. In: Wyrzykowski, R., Dongarra, J., Karczewski, K., Wasniewski, J. (eds.) PPAM 2009. LNCS, vol. 6067, pp. 206–215. Springer, Heidelberg (2010)
3. Cristian, F., Tukey, J.W.: A timestamp-based checkpointinmg protocol for long-lived distributed computations. In: Proceedings of the 10th IEEE Symposium on Reliable Distributed Systems (SRDS 1991), pp. 2–10. IEEE CPS (1991)
4. Gelenbe, E., Derochette, D.: Performance of rollback recovery systems under intermittent failures. Communications in the ACM 21(6), 493–499 (1978)

5. Gelenbe, E.: On the optimum checkpoint interval. Journal of the ACM 26(2), 259–270 (1979)
6. Gelenbe, E., Finkel, D., Tripathi, S.K.: Availability of a distributed computer system with failures. Acta Informatica 23, 643–655 (1986)
7. Gelenbe, E., Chabridon, S.: Dependable execution of distributed programs. Simulation Practice and Theory 3, 1–16 (1995)
8. Jones, W.M., Daly, J.T., DeBardeleben, N.: Impact of sub-optimal checkpoint intervals on application efficiency in computational clusters. In: Proceedings of the 19th ACM International Symposium on High Performance Distributed Computing (HPDC 2010), pp. 276–279. ACM (2010)
9. Klonowska, K., Lennerstad, H., Lundberg, L., Svahnberg, C.: Optimal recovery schemes in fault tolerant distributed computing. Acta Informatica 41(6), 341–365 (2005)
10. Liu, Y., Leangsuksun, C.B., Hertong, S., Scott, S.L.: Reliability-aware checkpoint/restart scheme: a performability trade-off. In: Proceedings of IEEE International Cluster Computing (CLUSTER 2005), pp. 1–8. IEEE CPS (2005)
11. Liu, Y., Nassar, R., Leangsuksun, C., Naksinehaboon, N., Paun, M., Scott, S.L.: A reliability-aware approach for an optimal checkpoint/restart model in HPC environments. In: Proceedings of IEEE International Conference on Cluster Computing (CLUSTER 2007), pp. 452–457. IEEE CPS (2007)
12. Liu, Y., Nassar, R., Leangsuksun, C., Naksinehaboon, N., Paun, M., Scott, S.L.: An optimal checkpoint/restart model for a large scale high performance computing system. In: Proceedings of IEEE International Symposium on Parallel and Distributed Processing (IPDPS 2008), pp. 1–9. IEEE CPS (2008)
13. Naksinehaboon, N., Liu, Y., Leangsuksun, C., Nassar, R., Paun, M., Scott, S.L.: Reliability-aware approach: an incremental checkpoint/restart model in HPC environments. In: Proceedings of 8th IEEE International Symposium on Cluster Computing and the Grid (CCGRID 2008), pp. 783–788. IEEE CPS (2008)
14. Nakamura, H., Hayashida, T., Kondo, M., Tajima, Y., Imai, M., Nanya, T.: Skewed checkpointing for tolerating multi-node failures. In: Proceedings of 23rd IEEE International Symposium on Reliable Distributed Systems (SRDS 2004), pp. 116–125. IEEE CPS (2004)
15. Nicola, V.F.: Checkpointing and modeling of program execution time. In: Lyu, M. (ed.) Software Fault Tolerance, pp. 167–188. John Wiley & Sons, New York (1995)
16. Ozaki, T., Dohi, T., Kaio, N.: Numerical computation algorithms for sequential checkpoint placement. Performance Evaluation 66, 311–326 (2009)
17. Plank, J.S.: Improving the performance of coordinated checkpoints on networks of workstations using RAID techniques. In: Proceedings of 15th IEEE International Symposium on Reliable Distributed Systems (SRDS 1996), pp. 76–85. IEEE CPS (1996)
18. Plank, J.S., Thomason, M.G.: Processor allocation and checkpoint interval selection in cluster computing systems. Journal of Parallel and Distributed Computing 61(11), 1570–1590 (2001)
19. Riteau, P., Lebre, A., Morin, C.: Handling persistent states in process checkpoint/restart mechanisms for HPC systems. In: Proceedings of the 9th IEEE/ACM International Symposium on Cluster Computing and the Grid (CCGRID 2009), pp. 404–411. IEEE CPS (2009)
20. Tikotekar, A., Vallee, G., Naughton, T., Scott, S.L., Leangsuksun, C.: Evaluation of fault-tolerant policies using simulation. In: Proceedings of 2007 IEEE International Conference on Cluster Computing (CLUSTER 2007), pp. 303–311. IEEE CPS (2007)

21. Tong, Z., Kain, R.Y., Tsai, W.T.: A low overfead checkpointing and rollback recovery scheme for distributed recovery. In: Proceedings of the 8th IEEE Symposium on Reliable Distributed Systems (SRDS 1989), pp. 12–20. IEEE CPS (1989)
22. Vaidya, N.H.: A case for two-level distributed recovery schemes. In: Proceedings ACM SIGMETRICS Conference on Measurement and Modeling of Computer Systems (SIGMETRICS 1995), pp. 64–73. ACM (1995)
23. Vaidya, N.H.: Impact of checkpoint latency on overhead ratio of a checkpointing scheme. IEEE Transactions on Computers 46(8), 942–947 (1997)
24. Vaidya, N.H.: A case for two-level recovery schemes. IEEE Transactions on Computers 47, 656–666 (1998)
25. Wang, Y.-M., Fuchs, W.K.: Optimistic message logging for independent checkpointing in message-passing systems. In: Proceedings of the 10th IEEE Symposium on Reliable Distributed Systems (SRDS 1992), pp. 147–154. IEEE CPS (1992)
26. Wong, K.F., Franklin, M.: Checkpointing in distributed systems. Journal of Parallel and Distributed Systems 35(1), 67–75 (1996)

Causal Order Multicast Protocol Using Minimal Message History Information

Chayoung Kim and Jinho Ahn[*]

Dept. of Computer Science, College of Natural Science, Kyonggi University
Suwon, Gyeonggi-do 443-760, Republic of Korea
{kimcha0,jhahn}@kgu.ac.kr

Abstract. Many applications of cloud-based P/S systems require communication services providing reliable message delivery and high scalability with flexible consistency simultaneously. Gossip communication is becoming one of the promising solutions for addressing P/S scalability problems in providing information propagation functionality by exploiting a mixture of diverse consistency options in the cloud-based P/S. In particular, despite the importance of both guaranteeing message delivery order required and supporting managing performance in cloud-based P/S systems, there exist little research works on development of gossip-style dissemination protocols to satisfy all these requirements. In this paper, we present a causal message order protocol with the information of only the predecessors immediately before the messages to subscribers from their chosen brokers. In the protocol, brokers might guarantee consistently causally ordered message delivery among themselves by aggregating the information of all ancestors before the messages. On the other hand, only the information of the predecessors immediately before the messages piggybacked on each multicast message is transmitted from brokers to subscribers through gossip-style disseminations. Its feature might be highly scalable and suitable for the area of the applications requiring only the minimum causal information of message delivery with flexible consistency.

Keywords: Cloud-based Publish/Subscribe, group communication, reliability, scalability, causal message delivery ordering.

1 Introduction

There has been increasing emphasis in managing end-to-end message delivery performance, as distributed computing applications that involve event-based response to real world sensing become more common [9], [17], [21]. In this messaging system, there are two common paradigms, queuing and publish/subscribe (P/S) [6], [9]. Message queuing [6] is used to connect loosely coupled components, providing buffering between pairs of hosts over point-to-point. P/S messaging follows many-to-many communication patterns, allowing a decoupling between senders and receivers to interact with publishers and subscribers. P/S messaging is flexible and able to manage

---

[*] Corresponding author.

Y. Xiang et al. (Eds.): ICA3PP 2012, Part I, LNCS 7439, pp. 546–559, 2012.

achievable performance by exploiting the decoupled nature of P/S and the performance management benefits of overlay networking [9]. Recently, there are two trends in P/S paradigm, the ever increasing number of sense-and-respond applications based on a number of physical or logical sensors and the emergence of cloud computing [13]. Cloud computing offers the compute infrastructure, platform, and applications as services to one or more tenant organizations [2], [3], [13]. There has been a large body of academic research to provide P/S functionality in a completely decentralized peer-to-peer(P2P) environment using gossip-style disseminations as communication protocols between peers [7], [11]. These systems [7], [11] target the adverse conditions in P2P such as unreliable links and high node churn rates due to frequent peers leave/join. In this paper, the proposed protocol is appropriate for a cloud-based P/S services provisioned from brokers, where the network connections are much more reliable, the node memberships are much more stable and users according to their interests subscribe to their chosen brokers. In our protocol, P/S systems use dedicated and interconnected brokers to process events between users based on gossiping, i.e., P/S systems in the same manner as Patrick et. al. [11] shows. Recently, gossip protocols seem more appealing in many P/S systems because they are more scalable than traditional reliable broadcast [5] and network-level protocols deriving from IP Multicast [7].

A number of cloud providers have offered a series of cloud-based services such as queuing [6], storage and database services [2], [3]. BlueDove [13] uses the same one-hop lookup like in Cassandra [12], but it provides a P/S service instead of a storage service. In cloud-based P/S services, managing latency, per some latency requirement, and providing reliable message delivery is still a challenge [9]. Many applications of cloud-based P/S systems require communication services providing reliable message delivery and high scalability with flexible consistency, simultaneously. Recently, there are many cloud applications and products to offer strong consistency guarantees. Isis^2 system [3] supports virtually synchronous process groups [5], includes reliable multicasts with various ordering options, and constructs diverse replication solutions with order-based consistency in cloud-based services. In process groups of Isis^2, the system would load-balance the reads and route updates, issuing the needed multicasts ordering. But, Isis^2 system [3] only considered full-fledged atomic ordering and FIFO ordering, not causal ordering. Causal ordering is more useful than strong atomic ordering [5] for many distributed applications in which a large number of processes request collaboratively and interactively.

Causal ordering protocols ensure that message m_1 is delivered before m_2, if the logical timestamp of m_1 happened before m_2. Causal ordering protocols have turned out to be adequate for distributed virtual applications having a variety of collaboration features, such as chat windows, p2p video, replication and coordination in which users could see and talk to each other and post and use contents like in the massively-multiplayer online games [8] and especially, cloud services in those applications are faster and more scalable by a series of asynchronous steps that each use local data replicas and are designed to tolerate unplanned failures in the way that consistency is substantially weakened [3].

In cloud-based P/S, if causal ordering protocol is performed by the all brokers on global member views, it are likely to be highly overloaded on each group member and not scalable because it often relies on the assumption that every member knows about each other [4]. In order to address this problem, promising gossip protocols should have all the required features by achieving a high degree of reliability and strong message delivery ordering guarantees offered by deterministic approaches, even if every participating member has a local view about the group [7]. Also, Isis^2 system [3] build protocols that replicate data optimistically and later heal any problems that arise, perhaps using gossiping [4]. The existing protocol [15] presents that each member manages the causal ordering information of the sent and received messages based on the context graph in terms of which the semantics of send and receive are defined instead of the whole set of vectors of the all group members [5]. In gossip protocols, every member periodically gossips about the messages to a randomly chosen subset of others, called gossip targets among its local view. A member which has received the messages will be termed infected and the number of gossip rounds it takes to infect all members depends on the number of members in the participating group. In the protocol [15], there might be messages sent by some brokers outside of the each member's local view and they are available for the other brokers to receive by gossip-style disseminations.

In this paper, we present a broker-based causal order multicast protocol that the brokers aggregate the information of interesting topics and periodically gossip about the multicast messages based on each local view of gossiping, guaranteeing causally ordered delivery of the messages. And the broker transmits the messages including the information of only the predecessors immediately before them to subscribers by gossip-style disseminations instead of the information of all ancestors before them. Its features might result in its very low cost communication overhead between brokers and subscribers because the information of the predecessors immediately before the messages is in the structure of one-dimensional vector instead of two-dimensional graph [15]. In the proposed protocol, aggregation and reduction of causal ordering information is dedicated to brokers in order to relief application subscribers. Its features might be highly scalable and suitable for the area of the applications requiring only the minimum causal information of message delivery with flexible consistency.

2   The Proposed Protocol

2.1   Basic Idea

In P/S systems of our proposed protocol, the brokers are selected from common sensors, as publishers to send topics to their subscribers and subscribers receive messages matching their interests published at brokers through their chosen brokers. The mapping of subscribers and brokers is entirely driven by the application matching their interest topics. Recently, much research has been devoted to designing broker selection methods that best suits application needs [1], [17], [21]. Common sensors can update information periodically to some of their brokers through gossip-style disseminations [10], [16]. The brokers might aggregate the reporting information based on the application subscribers' needs, while guaranteeing the causally ordered delivery of messages. The subscribers receive the aggregated information from their chosen brokers by gossip-style disseminations. In the protocol, each broker manages the notation of causal relationship among the event messages based on the context graph [15] in terms of which the semantics of send and receive are defined. Although each broker is based on its local view of gossiping, if a message is included the context graph, and as a consequence, it is available for the other brokers to receive. If a broker receives the context graph, it knows what it should have received.

Every broker generates a multicast message and puts its ID, the sequence number and the group lists of all groups that it participates on the multicast message. The broker attaches the multicast message to the leaf nodes referred as the predecessors immediately before it in its context graph for causal message ordering. And the broker sends the multicast message including its context graph to other brokers participating in all multicast groups. When a broker receives the multicast message, then it compares its context graph with the context graph piggybacked on it, in which all ancestors before it are summarized. If the receiver has already received all messages preceding the multicast message, it delivers the multicast message to the application layer. On the other hand, the broker disseminates the multicast message including the information of only the predecessors immediately before it to subscribers instead of its context graph summarizing all ancestors before it. The subscribers compare its context graph with the information of the predecessors immediately before it. If the subscribers had already received the immediate predecessors, they deliver the multicast message. In the proposed protocol, as [15] protocol shows, brokers might send and receive the information of causally ordered delivery about which they have received or sent what all ancestors before the messages. On the other hand, only the information of the predecessors immediately before the corresponding messages piggybacked on each multicast message is transmitted from brokers to subscribers. Its features might result in its very low cost communication overhead in between brokers and subscribers.

2.2   Algorithm Description

In figure 1, each broker represents two-dimensional grids of interests in which users might be related as publishers and subscribers. Broker A, B, and C are in group G_1 and A, B, and D are in group G_2. There are three local views, {D, A}, {A, B}, and {B, C}. If A wants to send its message m_1 to all members in G_1 and G_2, then A selects B in its local view and sends m_1 to B, which is an overlapping member in G_1 and G_2. After receiving m_1, B selects C in its local view and sends it to C. Then, B selects D in its local view and sends it to D. So, the generated message by A is disseminated to G_1 and G_2. All brokers of the proposed protocol do not have all group members participating in interesting groups in their views, but they could send their messages to all group members participating in interesting groups by gossiping based on overlapping local views.

Figure 2 shows how brokers send events among themselves in grids in Figure 1. In Figure 2, broker A in G_1 sends a message to G_1 and broker D in G_2 sends a message to G_2. In the grids, some of brokers participating in G_1 and some of them are in both G_1 and G_2 according to application needs. Each broker receives messages sent to it, delays them if necessary, and then delivers them in an order consistent with causality. A vector [5] or a context graph [15] piggybacked on each message is dealing with the notation of maintaining the causal relationship that holds among "message send" events with the corresponding "message receive" events.

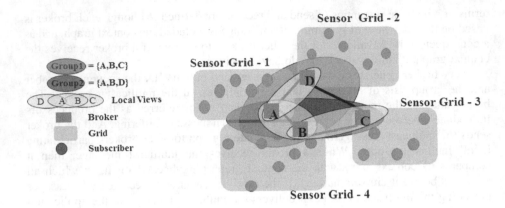

Fig. 1. A Wireless Sensor Network

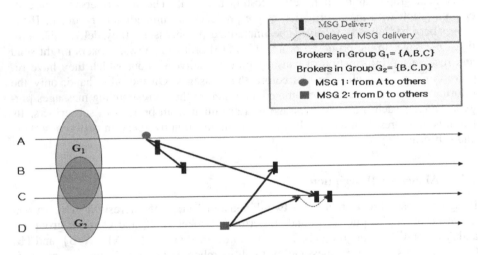

Fig. 2. Messages among Brokers

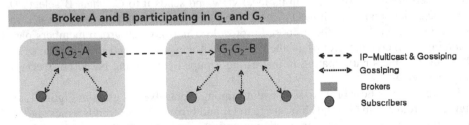

Fig. 3. Gossip-style disseminations between brokers and subscribers

Figure 3 shows how brokers and subscribers perform their communications. In figure 3, brokers use IP-Multicast and gossip-style disseminations between themselves. Information aggregated by brokers is transmitted from brokers to subscribers through gossip-style disseminations. In the grids of interest, the subscribers send subscriptions to brokers associated with matching their topics. So, the subscribers becoming a joiner of A receive all of the multicast messages of G_1 and G_2. In other words, If end users to receive messages from G_1 and G_2, they might subscribe to brokers participating in G_1 and G_2.

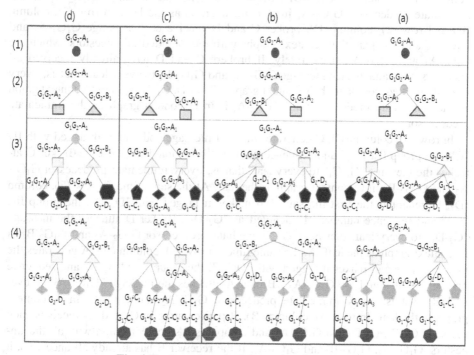

Fig. 4. Each context graph in overlapping groups

These examples from row (1), column (d) to row (4), column (a) of figure 4 show how in detail each broker = {A, B, C, D} participating in G_1 = {A, B, C} and G_2 = {A, B, D} generates a multicast message, puts ID, the sequence number and the group lists on it, and attaches it to the leaf nodes of the context graph. Column (D) is the context graph of broker D, column (C) is the one of broker C, column (B) is the one of broker B and column (A) is the one of broker A. In figure 4, "G_1" is the name of group G_1 and "A_1" is the message generated by A at first. When A participating in G_1 receives a multicast message, A verifies that all messages preceding it have been already received by comparing its context graph with all the ancestors before it.

In row (1), column (A), when A in G_1 and G_2 generates the first multicast message and makes it tagged with ID "A", the group lists "G_1G_2" and sequence number "1" denoted as " G_1G_2-A_1". Broker A makes A' context graph with G_1G_2-A_1 as the root and sends the message G_1G_2-A_1 to other brokers participating in G_1 and G_2. In row (1), column (B), row (1), column (C) and row (1), column (D), broker B, C, and D receive message G_1G_2-A_1 and make their context graph with G_1G_2-A_1 as the root.

In row (2), column (A), A generates the second message and makes it tagged with ID "A", the group lists "G_1G_2" and sequence number "2" denoted as "G_1G_2-A_2". Broker A attaches the message "G_1G_2-A_2" to the immediate predecessor G_1G_2-A_1 in A' context graph as the leaf. At the same time, in row (2), column (B), B generates the first message and makes it tagged with ID "B", the group lists "G_1G_2" and sequence number "1" denoted as "G_1G_2-B_1". Broker B attaches the message "G_1G_2-B_1" to the immediate predecessor G_1G_2-A_1 in B' context graph as the leaf. In row (2), column (C) and row (2), column (D), broker C and D receive each message G_1G_2-A_2 and G_1G_2-B_1 and compare their context graphs with the included all ancestors, which are G_1G_2-A_1 and G_1G_2-A_1, respectively. If brokers C and D have already received all ancestors, they attach each message G_1G_2-A_2 and G_1G_2-B_1 to every leaf, that is, every immediate predecessor in their context graphs. That is, G_1G_2-A_1 is in C' context graph as the immediate predecessor and G_1G_2-A_1 is in D' context graph as the immediate predecessor.

In row (3), column (C), C generates the first message and makes it tagged with ID "C", the group list "G_1" and sequence number "1" denoted as "G_1-C_1". Broker C attaches the message "G_1-C_1" to every leaf, that is, every immediate predecessor G_1G_2-A_2 and G_1G_2-B_1 in C' context graph as the leaf. At the same time, in row (3), column (D), D generates the first message and makes it tagged with ID "D", the group list "G2" and sequence number "1" denoted as "G_2-D_1". Broker D attaches the message "G_2-D_1" to every leaf, that is, every immediate predecessor G_1G_2-A_2 and G_1G_2-B_1 in D' context graph as the leaf. At the same time, in row (3), column (A), A generates the third message and makes it tagged with ID "A", the group lists "G_1G_2" and sequence number "3" denoted as "G_1G_2-A_3". Broker A attaches the message "G_1G_2-A_3" to every leaf, that is, every immediate predecessor G_1G_2-A_2 and G_1G_2-B_1 in A' context graph as the leaf. In row (3), column (B), B participating in G_1 and G_2 receives each message G_1-C_1, G_2-D_1 and G_1G_2-A_3 and compares B's context graph with all the ancestors, G_1G_2-A_2, G_1G_2-B_1 and G_1G_2-A_1. If the receiver B has already all ancestors, it attaches each message G_1G_2-A_3, G_1-C_1 and G_2-D_1 to every leaf, that is, every immediate predecessor G_1G_2-A_2 and G_1G_2-B_1 of B' context graph.

Therefore, as this example from row (1), column (d) to row (4), column (a) of figure 4 shows, (G_1G_2-A_1, G_1G_2-A_2, G_1G_2-B_1, G_1-C_1, G_2-D_1, G_1G_2-A_3), (G_1G_2-A_1, G_1G_2-B_1, G_1G_2-A_2, G_1G_2-A_3, G_1-C_1, G_2-D_1), and (G_1G_2-A_1, G_1G_2-A_2, G_1G_2-B_1, G_2-D_1, G_1G_2-A_3, G_1-C_1) are all valid causal orderings for each broker, where different participants might see a different ordering.

The summary of immediate predecessor messages at each step in Figure 4.		
Each step (each row in Figure 4)	The immediate predecessor messages	Generated messages
(1)	Nothing	G_1G_2-A_1(The Root)
(2)	[G_1G_2-A_1]	G_1G_2.A_2 and G_1G_2.B_1
(3)	[G_1G_2-A_2 , G_1G_2-B_1]	G_1G_2.A_3, G_1.C_1 and G_1.D_1
(4)	[G_1G_2-A_3 , G_1-C_1]	G_1-C_2

Fig. 5. The information of predecessors immediately before the corresponding message

Figure 5 shows the summary of the information of only the predecessors immediately before the corresponding messages with which brokers send the multicast messages piggybacked to subscribers. The immediate predecessors of the leaves are parent nodes in the context graph. Brokers disseminate the multicast messages including the information of only the predecessors immediately before the corresponding messages to subscribers for guaranteeing causally ordered delivery instead of the information of all ancestors. Figure 5(2) shows the information of the predecessors immediately before $[G_1G_2\text{-}A_1]$ with which brokers send $G_1G_2\text{-}A_2$ and $G_1G_2\text{-}B_1$ piggybacked. Figure 5(3) shows the information of the predecessors immediately before $[G_1G_2\text{-}A_2, G_1G_2\text{-}B_1]$ with which brokers send $G_1G_2\text{-}A_3$, $G_1\text{-}C_1$ and $G_1\text{-}D_1$ piggybacked. Figure 5(4) shows the information of the predecessors immediately before $[G_1G_2\text{-}A_3, G1\text{-}C_1]$ with which brokers send $G_1\text{-}C_2$ piggybacked. The least information of causally ordered delivery, that is the predecessors immediately before the corresponding multicast messages, is transmitted from brokers to subscribers for very low cost communication overhead.

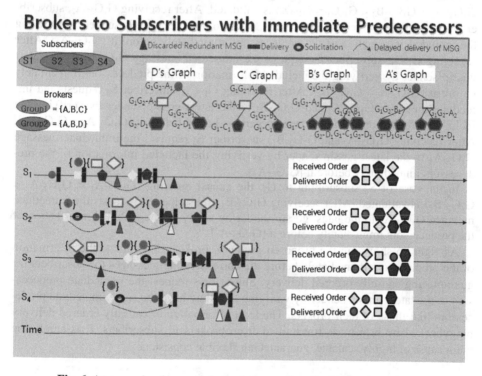

Fig. 6. An example of immediate predecessors from Brokers to Subscribers

Figure 6 shows how in detail broker groups $G_1=\{A,B,C\}$ and $G_2=\{A,B,D\}$ gossip about the multicast messages including the information of the predecessors immediately before the corresponding messages to subscribers=$\{S_1,S_2,S_3,S_4\}$. In the example of Figure 6, there are the context graph of D participating in G_2, the one of C participating in G_1 and the one of B and the one of A participating in G_1 and G_2, respectively. Subscriber S_1 subscribes to C in G_1, S_2 and S_3 subscribe to A or B in both G_1 and G_2, and S_4 subscribe to D in G_2. In figure 6, let m < m' denote the process that sent or received m' had either sent m or already received m. So, they are represented in different colors in figure 6. And let m = m' denote two messages m and m' that are independent of each other are said to have been sent at the same logical time and represented in the same color. Each broker makes causal ordering information in what order is G_1G_2-A_1 (red, circle) -> G_1G_2-A_2 (yellow, rectangle) = G_1G_2-B_1 (yellow, diamond) -> G_1-C_1 (blue, pentagon) = G_1-D_1 (blue, hexagon).

In the case of S_1 subscribing to G_1, the causal ordering (G_1G_2-A_1< G_1G_2-A_2 = G_1G_2-B_1 < G_1-C_1 = G_1-D_1) is validated. On receiving the message G_1G_2-A_2, subscriber S_1 verifies the information of the predecessors immediately before [G_1G_2-A_1]. After receiving the message G_1-C_1, subscriber S_1 requests the immediate message G_1G_2-B_1 to the latest gossip sender by verifying the included information of the predecessors immediately before it [G_1G_2-A_2= G_1G_2-B_1] because it knows that the predecessors G_1G_2-B_1 is not received.

In the case of S_2 and S_3 subscribing to G_1 and G_2, the causal ordering (G_1G_2-A_1 < G_1G_2-A_2 = G_1G_2-B_1 < G_1-C_1 = G_1-D_1) is validated. After receiving G_1G_2-A_2, subscriber S_2 requests the immediate message G_1G_2-A_1 to the latest gossip sender by verifying the included information of the predecessors immediately before it [G_1G_2-A_1]. After receiving G_1-D_1, subscriber S_2 requests the immediate message G_1G_2-B_1 to the latest gossip sender by verifying the included information of the predecessors immediately before it [G_1G_2-A_2= G_1G_2-B_1]. After receiving G_1-C_1, subscriber S_3 requests the immediate messages G_1G_2-A_2 and G_1G_2-B_1 to the latest gossip sender by verifying the included information of the predecessors immediately before it [G_1G_2-A_2 = G_1G_2-B_1]. After receiving G_1G_2-A_2 and G_1G_2-B_1, subscriber S_3 requests the immediate message G_1G_2-A_1 to the latest gossip sender by verifying the included information of the predecessors immediately before it [G_1G_2-A_1].

In the case of S_4 subscribing to G_2, the causal ordering (G_1G_2-A_1 < G_1G_2-A_2 = G_1G_2-B_1) is validated. After receiving G_1G_2-B_1, subscriber S_4 requests the immediate message G_1G_2-A_1 to the latest gossip sender by verifying the included information of the predecessors immediately before it [G_1G_2-A_1].

As figure 6 shows, in the proposed protocol, brokers disseminate the information of the predecessors immediately before the corresponding messages to subscribers for guaranteeing causally ordered delivery. Subscribers request the immediate predecessors to the latest gossip sender by verifying that they have the same immediate predecessors like those of their brokers. The least information of causally ordered delivery piggybacked by brokers is transmitted from brokers to subscribers. It is surely the main cause of highly scalable, guaranteeing flexible consistency.

2.3   Proof of the Protocol

Define:
Let p_i denote a participant process, G_a be a group of processes. Let M denote the set of messages processes exchange with each other, < (read "precedes") be a transitive relation on M and m_j be a member of M. Let E be a set of edges whose element is (m_j, m_k) and $G_a = (M_a, E_a)$ denote the directed acyclic graph representation of <.

Rule 1: Every new message piggybacking overlapping group lists is attached to all the leaves in G_a.

Rule 2: If G_1G_2-m' < G_1G_2-m, G_1G_2-m' transmitted causally before G_1G_2-m will be delivered at p_j before G_1G_2-m is delivered.

1. Causality is never violated (Safety).

Proof: Consider the actions of a process p_j, that is involved in both overlapping groups G_1 and G_2 and receives two messages G_1G_2-m_1 and G_1G_2-m_2 such that G_1G_2-m_1 < G_1G_2-m_2.

Basic Idea:

A message m_i is not delivered but buffered until its immediate predecessors are delivered.

Case 1: G_1G_2-m_1 and G_1G_2-m_2 are both transmitted by the same process p_j.
This case is trivial.

Under Rules 1 and 2 in the protocol, G_1G_2-m_2 can only be delivered after G_1G_2-m_1 has been delivered.

Case 2: G_1G_2-m_1 and G_1G_2-m_2 are transmitted by two distinct processes p_i and p_i'. By induction on the messages received by p_j, we will prove that G_1G_2-m_2 cannot be delivered before G_1G_2-m_1. Assume that G_1G_2-m_1 has not been delivered and p_j has received k messages.

Since G_1G_2-m_1 < G_1G_2-m_2, we have an immediate predecessor of G_1G_2-m_2, G_1G_2-m_1 -

------------------   Relation (1)

Base step:

The first message delivered by p_j cannot be G_1G_2-m_2. Recall that if no messages have been delivered to p_j, there are no paths and predecessors in the graph of p_j, G_{pj}. By the Rule 1, G_1G_2-m_2 cannot be attached to G_{pj}. So, G_1G_2-m_2 cannot be delivered by p_j.

Inductive step:

Suppose p_j has received k messages, none of which is a message G_1G_2-m such that G_1G_2-m_1 < G_1G_2-m.

If G_1G_2-m_1 has not yet been delivered, then there are no paths comprising of one-length edge, (G_1G_2-m_1's predecessor, G_1G_2-m_1) in G_{pj}.   -------------------- Relation   (2)

Because of Rule 1, if a new node is a leaf, there cannot also be any path comprising of one-length edge through another node to the new node. So obviously, a path from G_1G_2-m_1's predecessor to G_1G_2-m_1 comprises of one-length edge. Therefore, we can see the case that the existence of a path comprising of longer than one-length edge from G_1G_2-m_1's predecessor to G_1G_2-m_2 implies that there cannot exist any path comprising of one-length edge from G_1G_2-m_1's predecessor to G_1G_2-m_2 in the process made by merging G_1G_2-m_1's predecessor with G_1G_2-m_2 in G_{pj}. From Relations (1) and (2), it follows that there is no immediate predecessor of G_1G_2-m_2 in G_{pj}. By application of the rules of our protocol, the $k+1$st message delivered by p_j cannot be G_1G_2-m_2.

2. Every message in overlapping groups is indeed delivered (liveness).

Proof:

Suppose there exists a multicast message G_1G_2-m sent by process p_i in overlapping groups G_1 and G_2 that can never be delivered to process p_j. The rules of the protocol imply that the number of immediate predecessors happened before G_1G_2-m in G_{pj} is smaller than the number of immediate predecessors piggybacked on G_1G_2-m. The number of messages that must be delivered to p_j before G_1G_2-m is finite. Communication links are fair-lossy, but correct processes can construct reliable communication links on top of fair-lossy links by periodically retransmitting messages. So, in the absence of failures and after some finite time, all these messages will have arrived at p_j. If every such message had been delivered, then we would have known that the number of immediate predecessors happened before G_1G_2-m in G_{pj} is bigger than the number of immediate predecessors piggybacked on G_1G_2-m and G_1G_2-m could be delivered; contradiction.

So, there exists at least another message G_1G_2-m' which will not be delivered to p_i and should be before G_1G_2-m. If G_1G_2-m' is in waiting buffer, then the number of immediate predecessors piggybacked on G_1G_2-m' is smaller than that of immediate predecessors piggybacked on G_1G_2-m. We can thus apply the same reasoning to G_1G_2-m' as to G_1G_2-m, which completes the proof by finite decreasing induction.

3   Related Works

There have been a large number of academic researches on P/S systems, classified into topic-based, attribute-based, and content-based depending on the matching model. In many P/S systems designed for enterprise environments, subscribers establish affinity with brokers and connect to their chosen brokers. A subscriber sends subscriptions and receives the messages matching their interests published at its chosen broker. Content-based P/S networks scale to large numbers of publishers and subscribers by having brokers summarize subscriptions from subscribers and downstream brokers based on coverage relationships ("subsumption") between subscriptions. In some P/S systems like completely decentralized P2P without dedicated brokers, structured overlay techniques like DHT (CAN [18], PASTRY [19], CHORD [20]) for distributing subscriptions and messages in dynamics such as node churns and unreliable links are usually used. Pastry [9] uses routing based on address prefixes built over distributed index trees, Chord [20] forwards messages based on numerical differences with their destinations and CAN [18] routes messages in a d-dimensional space. In comparison, there is much less dynamics in a cloud-based P/S. In this cloud-based P/S, BlueDove [13] can use much simpler techniques such as one-hop lookup for scalable organization of dedicated brokers. A large number of cloud providers have offered a series of cloud-based services such as queuing, storage and database services. The most relevant one to BlueDove is the Amazon Simple Notification Service (Amazon SNS) [22] that provides topic based P/S. Cassandra [12] is a highly scalable and elastic storage system for cloud applications. And there are researches in the area of sensor network communications based on the P/S to approach the problem of querying sensors from mobile nodes [10], [16]. Isis^2 system [3] explores a new consistency model for data replication in first-tier cloud services. The model combines agreement on update ordering with a form of durability that they call amnesia freedom. Their experiments confirm that this approach scales and performs surprisingly well. But, in this system, there are satisfied full-fledged atomic delivery ordering and FIFO delivery ordering, not causal delivery ordering. SENSTRACT [16] is mapping from queries to topics and the corresponding underlying sensor network structure. SENSTRACT [16] is a tree-based P/S system structured by service providers as roots, representing one of the data-centric routing protocols for data dissemination of sensor networks.

Recently, there is a multicast platform based on a gossip technique, Quicksilver Multicast Platform [14]. Quicksilver [14] provides the scalable and extensible communication infrastructure needed to make objects "live" and "distributed". Each object has object-specific logic implementing some abstraction, such as gossip-based overlay network. The key point of [8] involves the embedding of Quicksilver's live objects into Windows. Birman et al. [4] proposes bimodal multicast thanks to its two phases: a "classic" best-effort multicast such as IP multicast is used for the first through dissemination of messages. The second phase assures reliability with a certain probability by using gossip-based retransmissions. But Lpbcast [7] proposes gossip-style broadcast mechanisms based on a local view instead of a global view. Lpbcast [7] is a completely decentralized protocol because of requiring no dedicated brokers for membership management.

To ensure causal message ordering in [15], an inter-process communication mechanism, called Psync, encodes partial ordering with each message. But this approach is not based on P/S systems. Early work like in [5] mostly focuses on stronger notions of agreement and also membership than the proposed protocols discussed in this paper. Because each process manages a vector of integers per group and timestamps messages with the whole set of vectors of all the sending processes, every process knows every other processes in participating all groups. So, this protocol is correct but very expensive.

4   Conclusions

In this paper, we present a broker-based causal order multicast protocol in cloud-based P/S models provisioned from brokers, where the network connections are much more reliable and stable. In our proposed protocol, the brokers are selected from common sensors, as publishers to send topics to their subscribers and subscribers send subscriptions and receive messages matching their interests published at brokers through their chosen brokers. In this protocol, each broker periodically gossips about the multicast message based on its local view, guaranteeing causally ordered message delivery by aggregating the information of all ancestors in the structure of context graph piggybacked on the multicast message. On the other hand, each broker transmits the multicast message including the information of only the predecessors immediately before the corresponding multicast messages to subscribers by gossip-style disseminations rather than the information of all ancestors. Its features might result in its very low cost communication overhead between brokers and subscribers because the information of the predecessors immediately before the corresponding multicast messages for causality is in the structure of one-dimensional list. Therefore, these features of the protocol might be significantly scalable in the cloud-based P/S applications requiring only the minimum causal information of message delivery with flexible consistency.

References

1. Akyildiz, I., Su, W., Sankarasubramaniam, Y., Cayirci, E.: A survey on Sensor Networks. IEEE Communications Magazine 40, 102–114 (2002)
2. Birman, K.P., Ganesh, L., Renesse, R.V.: Running Smart Grid Control Software on Cloud Computing Architectures. In: Workshop on Computational Needs for the Next Generation Electric Grid, Cornell
3. Birman, K.P., Huang, Q., Freedman, D.: Overcoming CAP with Consistent Soft-State Replication. IEEE Internet Computing 12, 50–58 (2012)
4. Birman, K., Hayden, M., Ozkasap, O., Xiao, Z., Budiu, M., Minsky, Y.: Bimodal Multicast. ACM Transactions on Computer Systems 17, 41–88 (1999)
5. Birman, K., Schiper, A., Stephenson, P.: Lightweight Causal and Atomic Group Multicast. ACM Transactions on Computer Systems 9, 272–314 (1991)
6. Chen, H., Ye, F., Kim, M., Lei, H.: A Scalable Cloud-based Queuing Service with Improved Consistency Levels. In: 30th IEEE International Symposium On Reliable Distributed Systems, pp. 229–234. IEEE Press, Madrid (2011)
7. Eugster, P., Guerraoui, R., Handurukande, S., Kouznetsov, P., Kermarrec, A.-M.: Lightweight probabilistic broadcast. ACM Transactions on Computer Systems 21, 341–374 (2003)
8. Freedman, D., Birman, K., Ostrowski, K., Linderman, M., Hillman, R., Frantz, A.: Enabling Tactical Edge Mashups with Live Objects. In: 15th International Command and Control Research and Technology Symposium (ICCRTS 2010), Santa Monica (2010)
9. Guo, S., Karenos, K., Kim, M., Lei, H., Reason, J.M.: Delay-Cognizant Reliable Delivery for Publish/Subscribe Overlay Networks. In: 31st IEEE International Conference on Distributed Computing Systems, pp. 403–412. IEEE Press, Minneapolis (2011)
10. Intanagonwiwat, C., Govindan, R., Estrin, D.: Directed diffusion: A scalable and robust communication paradigm for sensor networks. In: 6th Annual International Conference on Mobile Computing and Networking (MobiCOM 2000), pp. 56–67. ACM, Boston (2000)
11. Jayaram, K.R., Eugster, P.: Split and Subsume: Subscription Normalization for Effective Content-based Messaging. In: 31st IEEE International Conference on Distributed Computing Systems, pp. 824–835. IEEE Press, Minneapolis (2011)
12. Lakshman, A., Malik, P.: Cassandra - a decentralized structured storage system. In: ACM LADIS 2009 (2009)
13. Li, M., Ye, F., Kim, M., Chen, H., Lei, H.: BlueDove: A scalable and elastic publish/subscribe service. In: IEEE International Parallel & Distributed Processing Symposium, pp. 1254–1265. IEEE Press, Anchorage (2011)
14. Ostrowski, K., Birman, K., Dolev, D.: QuickSilver Scalable Multicast. In: 7th IEEE International Symposium on Network Computing and Applications (IEEE NCA 2008), pp. 9–18. IEEE Press, Cambridge (2008)
15. Peterson, L., Buchholzand, N., Schlichting, R.: Preserving and using context information interprocess communication. ACM Transaction Computer Systems 7, 217–246 (1989)

16. Pleisch, S., Birman, K.: SENSTRAC: Scalable Querying of SENSor Networks from Mobile Platforms Using TRACking-Style Queries. International Journal of Sensor Networks 3, 266–280 (2008)
17. Pottie, G., Kaiser, W.: Wireless Integrated Network Sensors. Communications of the ACM 43, 51–58 (2000)
18. Ratnasamy, S., Francis, P., Handley, M., Karp, R., Shenker, S.: A scalable content addressable network. In: ACM SIGCOMM 2001 (2001)
19. Rowstron, A., Druschel, P.: Pastry: Scalable, Decentralized Object Location, and Routing for Large-Scale Peer-to-Peer Systems. In: Guerraoui, R. (ed.) Middleware 2001. LNCS, vol. 2218, pp. 329–350. Springer, Heidelberg (2001)
20. Stoica, I., Morris, R., Karger, D., Kaashoek, M.F., Balakrishnan, H.: Chord: A scalable peer-to-peer lookup service for internet applications. In: ACM SIGCOMM 2001 (2001)
21. Yick, J., Mukherjee, B., Ghosal, D.: Wireless sensor network survey. Computer Networks 52, 2292–2330 (2008)
22. Amazon simple notification service, http://aws.amazon.com/sns/

Author Index